BEHAVIOR THERAPY
Appraisal and Status

McGRAW-HILL SERIES IN PSYCHOLOGY

Consulting Editors
NORMAN GARMEZY
RICHARD L. SOLOMON
LYLE V. JONES
HAROLD W. STEVENSON

Adams *Human Memory*
Beach, Hebb, Morgan, and Nissen *The Neuropsychology of Lashley*
Von Békésy *Experiments in Hearing*
Berkowitz *Aggression: A Social Psychological Analysis*
Berlyne *Conflict, Arousal, and Curiosity*
Blum *Psychoanalytic Theories of Personality*
Brown *The Motivation of Behavior*
Brown and Ghiselli *Scientific Method of Psychology*
Butcher *MMPI: Research Developments and Clinical Applications*
Cofer *Verbal Learning and Verbal Behavior*
Cofer and Musgrave *Verbal Behavior and Learning: Problems and Processes*
Crafts, Schneirla, Robinson, and Gilbert *Recent Experiments in Psychology*
Crites *Vocational Psychology*
Davitz *The Communication of Emotional Meaning*
Deese and Hulse *The Psychology of Learning*
Dollard and Miller *Personality and Psychotherapy*
Edgington *Statistical Inference: The Distribution-free Approach*
Ellis *Handbook of Mental Deficiency*
Epstein *Varieties of Perceptual Learning*
Ferguson *Statistical Analysis in Psychology and Education*
Forgus *Perception: The Basic Process in Cognitive Development*
Franks *Behavior Therapy: Appraisal and Status*
Ghiselli *Theory of Psychological Measurement*
Ghiselli and Brown *Personnel and Industrial Psychology*
Gilmer *Industrial Psychology*
Gray *Psychology Applied to Human Affairs*
Guilford *Fundamental Statistics in Psychology and Education*
Guilford *The Nature of Human Intelligence*
Guilford *Personality*
Guilford *Psychometric Methods*
Guion *Personnel Testing*

CYRIL M. FRANKS, *Editor*

Psychology Service and Research Center
New Jersey Neuropsychiatric Institute, Princeton

BEHAVIOR THERAPY
Appraisal and Status

McGRAW-HILL BOOK COMPANY

New York   St. Louis   San Francisco   London
Sydney   Toronto   Mexico   Panama

BEHAVIOR THERAPY: Appraisal and Status

Library of Congress Catalog Card Number 70–78956
21903

1 2 3 4 5 6 7 8 9 0   MAMM   7 6 5 4 3 2 1 0 6 9

TO VIOLET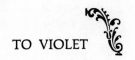

FOREWORD

Behavior therapy (or conditioning therapy)—the set of therapeutic methods based on experimentally established principles of learning—is essentially applied basic research. It derives mainly from experimental psychology, but also owes something to physiology and pharmacology. It is consistent with the general body of modern medicine in seeking to reverse or control disease through knowledge of the mechanisms upon which disease depends. Medicine long ago substituted this philosophy for its traditional empiricism. The field of psychological medicine alone lagged behind. Only in the past few years, with the rise of behavior therapy, has it begun to come into line.

Behavior therapy was conceived in 1920 out of Watson and Rayner's celebrated experiment on Little Albert. Having conditioned Albert to react with fear to a white rat and, by generalization, to other furry objects, they suggested that the conditioning might be overcome in four possible ways—by experimental extinction, by "constructive" activities around the feared object, by "reconditioning" through feeding the child candy in the presence of the feared object, or by procuring competition with fear by stimulating erogenous zones in the presence of the feared object. The last three of these suggestions are all on the counterconditioning model, which, as most readers of this book will recognize, has come to have a preeminent place in behavior therapy of neuroses. Unfortunately, Albert left the hospital before they could try out any of their suggestions. But what is more important is that the first unequivocal demonstration that neurotic fear could be learned had led to the logical deduction that a learning procedure ought to be effective for removing the fear.

Not long afterwards, one of Watson and Rayner's suggested treatments was put to trial by Mary Cover Jones (1924), who gave a detailed illustration of it in her classic account of the case of Peter. This child had a severe fear of a white rat, and the fear "extended to a rabbit, a fur coat, a feather, cotton-wool, etc., but not to wooden blocks and similar toys." The fear was overcome by systematically bringing a rabbit closer to Peter while he was eating food that he liked. It is interesting to note that the therapeutic program suffered a temporary setback after a large dog had jumped at Peter while he was entering a taxi. It is this kind of event that, in modern behavior therapy practice, has been found to be the one and only reason for "relapse." With Mary Cover Jones' successful implementation of Watson & Rayner's theoretical expectation, *behavior therapy was born.*

But for a quarter of a century the birth was hardly noticed. Nobody wanted to have anything to do with it. The psychoanalytic *Zeitgeist* had persuaded almost everybody that simple learning principles could have no relevance to the "deep" problems of psychopathology. Dunlap's (1932) introduction of the extinction mechanism into clinical practice, and Guthrie's (1935) attempt to systematize the use of learning principles produced little response. Only rarely was there a report of the practical application of a principle. A shining example was Max's (1935) account of aversion therapy of a homosexual fetish. The publication of Salter's *Conditioned Reflex Therapy* (1950) aroused some popular interest in the idea of applying conditioning methods to abnormal behavior; but the book had little impact among psychologists, because the main clinical method described had no apparent relation to experimentally established principles. Shoben's (1949) paper on psychotherapy as a problem of learning seriously suggested a major role for conditioning principles in therapy, but made them subsidiary to a psychoanalytic model.

A springboard for an access of interest in behavior therapy was my article, "Experimental Neurosis as Learned Behavior" (1952a), a fairly comprehensive summary of experiments I had carried out in 1947–1948 which demonstrated that both the production and the elimination of neuroses in cats were functions of principles of learning. The same principles (and later some others) were subsequently applied to human neuroses in a variety of ways (Wolpe, 1954, 1958; Eysenck, 1960, 1966). In the next few years, operant conditioning principles were introduced into the therapeutic field, and they have since come to be increasingly widely applied (Ullmann & Krasner, 1965; Franks, 1964).

The publication of rapidly increasing numbers of books and research papers and the appearance of a journal devoted to behavior therapy testify to vigorous activity and a growing interest. But behavior therapy is a long way from achieving the primacy that the rest of the field of medicine gives to treatments based on experimentally established principles. It is still not generally practiced and taught. Its acceptance, though rapidly growing, is still relatively small. Speculative "systems" such as psychoanalysis and nondirective therapy still predominate and even proliferate, as evidenced, for example, by self-disclosure therapy (Jourard, 1964) and reality therapy (Glasser, 1965). The value of the methods these generate is as purely empirical a question as if they had been picked out of a hat. The probabilities are against them; and there is no reason to believe that any of them has struck it lucky.

Nevertheless, every now and then, a procedure that has not been suggested by any basic principle does turn out to be effective. For the behaviorist such an empirical discovery is another kind of starting point for new research directed primarily toward elucidating the mechanisms. This is a fascinating endeavor, not only because it helps to build our picture of the universe, but also because it has the practical result of shaping procedures into more efficient and economical forms, partly by weeding out nonessentials.

An example of current interest is the carbon dioxide treatment for "free-floating" (pervasive) anxiety. Clinically, it has repeatedly been shown that, as a rule, a small number of single, full-capacity inhalations of a mixture of carbon dioxide and oxygen rapidly diminished pervasive anxiety (Wolpe, 1958). This was a lucky find, not suggested by any experimentally established principle. LaVerne (1951) first suggested this method as a general treatment for neurosis; later, while experimenting with it, I noticed its remarkable effect on pervasive anxiety, which I described for the first time in 1954. The exciting question is how carbon dioxide therapy works. The action is not that of a drug, because the state of calm may last for hours, days, or weeks—long after the blood level of carbon dioxide has receded to normal; and it is clear that the gas cannot produce a lasting tissue change (Gellhorn, 1967). Almost certainly, then, it is a matter of learning. The first requirement is to determine what elements in the procedure are really necessary for the production of its effects. Does the sensory drama of the treatment act as a source of suggestion? Do the effects occur because the excitation caused by the gas acts as a counter-conditioner of anxiety, or for some other reason? Some explorations were started by Slater & Leavy (1966). They found that the effects are not due either to the fact of inhaling *some* gas or to deep respiratory movements such as carbon dioxide causes. Weinreb (1966) obtained some data contradicting the suggestion that the effects may be attributed to an especially strong kind of suggestion associated with a powerful sensory experience. He found that strong inhalations of aromatic spirits of ammonia do not have a significant anxiety-reducing effect. We are about to conduct further experiments here on this point, utilizing amyl nitrite inhalations, or strong electric shocks to a limb. Increasingly, it begins to look as though carbon dioxide produces change because its excitatory effects are reciprocally inhibitory of the anxiety responses evoked by such pervasive stimuli as space, time, and bodily feelings. Substantiation of this suspicion might lead to applications in the deconditioning of specific neurotic anxiety and perhaps other unadaptive habits. And then, of course, we should want to know more about the intimate mechanisms of this excitatory response.

The foregoing illustrates that, no matter what the starting point of an inquiry may be—whether the testing of a principle or the investigation of a casual observation—the central interest of the behaviorist is always in lawful relations, because this knowledge alone can give him controlling power in the sector of nature with which he is concerned. Stressing the primacy of lawful relations has just now become particularly important, because, to many outsiders, behavior therapy has acquired the semblance of a hodgepodge of symptom-directed "activity" therapies. An important factor in creating this impression is that recently a motley assortment of people in the clinical field have been "incorporating" behavior therapy techniques into their practices. Most of these people lack the appropriate theoretical background, and some do not even understand the elementary fundamentals of behavior therapy. Yet, they quite often represent themselves as "behavior therapists," make learned pronouncements about behavior therapy, and even engage in "teaching" it to others. An outsider could excusably conclude from all this that behavior therapy is a collection of techniques that can be added to almost anybody's armamentarium. But what this activity amounts to is a new eclecticism, which differs from earlier ones only in including behavior therapy techniques.

The social attitude behind an eclectic position is, of course, very often a benevolent one. This is manifestly true of such a therapist as Glick (1967), a psychoanalyst who, finding that a number of his patients were failing to respond satisfactorily to his accustomed techniques, acquainted himself with some methods of behavior therapy and applied them to the patients with considerable success. The intellectual orientation of the eclectic is, however, inevitably barren. Whether he is "atheoretical" or endeavors to squeeze "foreign" ideas into his previous theoretical system, he has no consistent rules to guide either his thoughts or his actions. Eclectics who have started from a behavoristic position (e.g., Lazarus, 1967a) are in this respect no better off than the others. But, in my opinion, their very existence fosters the misconceptions about behavior therapy to which I have referred.

At the present juncture, nothing can be more salutary or timely than a book like this one. There are many reports in the literature of experimental findings, and there are numerous texts on behavior therapy per se, but, to the best of my knowledge, the present volume is unique in its attempt to present, survey, and appraise the vast canvas of behavior therapy in all its phases and facets. The distinguished author, Dr. Franks, is a colleague whom I have known closely for many years, and I can think of very few individuals better qualified to accomplish this onerous and important task. He has assembled and skillfully integrated into one volume a unique collection of new and highly significant contributions, adding to them his own comprehensive and penetrating overview of the whole field.

The work that this text reports and the points of view that it represents are in the mainstream of the developments that have made behavior therapy what it is today. Those who are attuned to the message of the volume will gain from it keen satisfaction while substantially advancing their understanding of the field and its problems. We can also hope that at least some of those individuals who wander confusedly in a phenomenological and mentalistic world devoid of determinable laws will likewise profit from this book and will be guided by it into the path of science.

JOSEPH WOLPE, M.D.

Professor of Psychiatry
Temple University School of Medicine
and Eastern Pennsylvania Psychiatric Institute

PREFACE

The behavior therapy literature is growing at an astonishing—one might almost say alarming—rate. But, despite the apparently unending flow of words, there is no one volume devoted exclusively to the task of appraising the whole field. This task, then, is the primary purpose of the present volume. We leave it to the reader to judge to what extent we have succeeded.

The need for a comprehensive appraisal became apparent during the many invigorating sessions which gave birth to the Association for Advancement of the Behavioral Therapies (now known as the Association for Advancement of Behavior Therapy). Among the numerous professional colleagues and friends who helped in this formative process, it is a special pleasure to acknowledge the influences of Dr. Edward Dengrove, Dr. Robert Fried, Dr. Martin Gittelman, Dr. Richard Rubin, and Andrew Salter. Debate with my unswervingly psychodynamic—but open-minded—friend, Dr. Leonard Blank, provided the necessary counterbalance and recognition that some systematic appraisal of the field of behavior therapy was much needed. My viewpoint was further broadened, and yet sharpened, by a still on-going series of lively but amiable dialogues with Dr. Arnold Lazarus about such matters as "technical eclecticism" and the concept of behavior therapy as a science. Despite—or, perhaps, because of—our theoretical differences, Dr. Lazarus has contributed significantly to the development of this volume even though he is not directly represented among the formal list of authors.

If my thinking is less doctrinaire than it was a decade ago, this is also due in no small measure to the efforts of Dr. Dorothy C. Susskind. By unfailing example and encouragement, she showed how it was possible to be an objective scientist and a responsive clinician at one and the same time. But, most of all, gratitude is extended to my dear wife, Dr. Violet Franks, truly a lady for all seasons, who never ceases to amaze me with her ability to integrate the difficult roles of life partner and professional critic, to the mutual enhancement of both.

My gratitude also goes to Mrs. Jane Carpenter for her willingness to perform with patience and a smile the many tedious secretarial tasks associated with the production of this volume; to my colleagues in the Psychology Service and Research Center for their interest and support; to Dr. Helena Temmer and Mrs. Elizabeth Travers for their editorial assistance with the first chapter; to Dr. Henry P. David for his encouragement over the years; to Walter Maytham and David Dunham of McGraw-Hill for their forebearance and superego activities (if I may be forgiven this bit of heresy); to Dr. Russell N. Carrier, Dr. Robert S. Garber, and psychiatric colleagues at the Carrier Clinic, Belle Meade, New Jersey, for many stimulating discussions; and to Dr. Michael Mendelson, medical director and chief executive officer of the New Jersey Neuro-Psychiatric Institute, who, with other members of the professional staff, provided both encouragement and a milieu conducive to research and other creative endeavors. Last, but certainly not least, it is with profound pleasure that I take this opportunity of thanking Dr. Joseph Wolpe for his thought provoking Foreword. For a variety of reasons, this volume would have been incomplete without Dr. Wolpe's timely words and constant reinforcement.

The indexing of a book such as this is a formidable task, and it could not have been accomplished so readily without the timely assistance of Mr. and Mrs. Stephen C. Lower, who assumed a large share of the responsibility for the Subject Index at short notice.

We are also grateful to the following distinguished authors whose writings or other materials have been reproduced: A. A. Lazarus, J. Wolpe, M. Katahn, J. H. Koplin, W. Sargant, G. C. Davison, T. Ayllon, E. Haughton, N. H. Azrin, W. C. Holz, R. L. Solomon, G. Razran, K. Salzinger, W. Schofield, I. Stevenson, H. Narrol, A. Weinberg, L. Krasner, L. P. Ullmann, M. P. Feldman, M. J. MacCulloch, K. Heller, R. D. Cartwright, A. Bandura, I. Gregory, H. Toch, W. B. Cameron, B. Glass, I. Chein, D. H. Ford, H. Urban, C. B. Truax, F. Wertham, S. Rachman, H. J. Eysenck, B. F. Skinner, J. Greenspoon, I. M. Marks, M. G. Gelder, H. Spiegel, N. Shainess, H. Kalish, and A. W. Staats.

The sources of these citations are as follows, and again we extend our gratitude: Psychological Reports; the Association for Advancement of Behavior Therapy; the American Psychological Association; Penguin Books; the Journal of the Experimental Analysis of Behavior; Appleton-Century-Crofts; the Journal Press; Prentice-Hall, Inc.; the American Medical Association; McGraw-Hill Book Company; Holt, Rinehart and Winston; Pergamon Press; W. B. Saunders; Bobbs-Merrill; Random House; University of North Carolina Press; Society for the Study of Psychological Social Issues; International Science Press; Basic Books; and the Royal Medico-Psychological Association.

At this late stage I still have some misgivings over the title, which was originally in the plural form—*The Behavior Therapies.* I am still not *certain* whether the use of the singular is justified since it assumes a unified body of knowledge and an underlying conceptual harmony which may be more in the nature of wishful thinking than an obtained objective at this time.

A long book merits a short preface, and every behavior therapist knows the value of modeling behavior. If this book is long, I hope it is also comprehensive. This could hardly have come about without the splendid cooperation of my fellow contributors. My gratitude therefore goes out to my co-authors. Without them, this book in its present form would have been literally impossible. I realize, also, that certain areas of behavior therapy have been either excluded or dismissed in what some may think a rather cavalier fashion, and that the first chapter is heavily biased in favor of the Pavlovian tradition. The responsibility for these decisions is entirely mine.

Despite the above limitations, the hope of all concerned with the production of this volume is that it will contribute significantly to the coming of age of behavior therapy and to the assumption of the perspective, if not of adulthood, then at least of late adolescence.

Cyril M. Franks

CONTENTS

LIST OF CONTRIBUTORS

Donald M. Baer
Department of Human Development and Family Life
University of Kansas

Earl C. Brown
Department of Psychology
Georgia State College

Alexander M. Buchwald
Deparment of Psychology
Indiana University

Joseph R. Cautela
Department of Psychology
Boston College

Sanford I. Cohen
Department of Psychiatry and Biobehavioral Sciences
Louisiana State University Medical Center

Gerald C. Davison
Department of Psychology
State University of New York at Stony Brook

Cyril M. Franks
Psychology Service and Research Center
New Jersey Neuropsychiatric Institute, Princeton

Kenneth Heller
Psychological Clinic
Indiana University

Frederick H. Kanfer
Department of Psychology
University of Cincinnati

Leonard Krasner
Department of Psychology
State University of New York at Stony Brook

Luciano L'Abate
Department of Psychology
Georgia State College

Peter J. Lang
Department of Psychology
University of Wisconsin

G. Alan Marlatt
Department of Psychology
University of Wisconsin

Gerald R. Patterson
Oregon Research Institute
Eugene, Oregon

Gordon L. Paul
University of Illinois

Jeanne S. Phillips
Department of Psychology
University of Massachusetts

Stanley Rachman
University of London Institute of Psychiatry
London, England

Kurt Salzinger
Biometrics Research
New York State Department of Mental Hygiene
New York, New York

George Saslow
Department of Psychiatry
University of Oregon Medical School

James A. Sherman
Department of Human Development and Family Life
University of Kansas

John R. Teasdale
University of London Institute of Psychiatry
London, England

Leonard P. Ullmann
Department of Psychology
University of Illinois

Joseph Wolpe
Temple University School of Medicine and
Eastern Pennsylvania Psychiatric Institute

Richard D. Young
Psychological Clinic
Indiana University

BEHAVIOR THERAPY
Appraisal and Status

Behavior Therapy and Its Pavlovian Origins:
Review and Perspectives

CYRIL M. FRANKS

New Jersey Neuropsychiatric Institute
Princeton, New Jersey

Introduction

Although virtually all psychologists accept the premise that human behavior is orderly, sharp differences arise with respect to the meaning of this vague premise and its implications for therapeutic change. Even among those who style themselves behavior therapists there is disagreement, and establishing a definition of behavior therapy which is acceptable to all is a far from simple task. *Behavior therapy*, a term independently coined by Lazarus (1958) and by Eysenck (1959), is presumably concerned with human behavior and learned changes in behavior. Any response made by a person, whether it be a motor movement or a verbal statement, is behavior. As we are unable, by the very nature of things, to share directly in the personal experiences of another, all that we can observe is a person's description of his feelings or perceptions by word or gesture (Maher, 1967, p. 5). Responses alone are the data available to the student of human behavior, and all else is a matter of inference and construct.

Learning is defined provisionally by Hilgard as "the process by which an activity originates or is changed through reacting to an encountered situa-

1

tion, provided that the characteristics of the change in activity cannot be explained on the basis of native response tendencies, maturation or temporary states of the organism (e.g., fatigue, drugs, etc.)" (Hilgard, 1956, p. 3). Theories of learning tend to fall into one of two major categories: stimulus-response (SR) theories such as those of Pavlov, Skinner, Guthrie, and Hull; and cognitive or field theories such as those of Tolman, Lewin, the gestalt psychologists, and even Freud.

If behavior is defined in terms of response, then behavior therapy becomes a matter of response modification involving the application of some SR type of learning theory. More explicitly, behavior therapy may then be defined as the beneficial modification of behavior in accordance with experimentally validated principles based upon SR concepts of learning and the biophysical properties of the organism.

This definition carries with it a number of important corollaries. First, and perhaps foremost, not all "behavior therapists" limit themselves to a conventional SR model of learning. We shall return to this matter later in this chapter.

Second, although there is a bewildering conglomeration of techniques, the definition employed above refers to "behavior therapy" in the singular. Wilson & Evans (1967) may be justified in taking the Association for Advancement of the Behavioral Therapies[1] to task for its use of the plural form. If all forms of behavior therapy are predicated upon the common, explicit, systematic, and a priori usage of learning principles to achieve well-defined and predetermined goals, then it is incorrect to speak of "behavior therapies." The term *behavior therapies*, it is argued, implies little more than a grab bag of behaviorally oriented therapeutic techniques.

Third, for most behavior therapists, the preferred sequence of events is from experimental observation to clinical practice. This may be contrasted with the approach of traditional psychotherapists, in which the sequence is often reversed.

Fourth, no one SR theory of learning is stipulated. While the majority of investigators prefer systems derived directly from the notions of Hull, Skinner, and Pavlov, the principles of other learning theorists are also being utilized (e.g., Patterson, 1965, uses concepts stemming from the writings of Guthrie).

Fifth, while psychologists engaged in behavior modification make use of diverse and often elaborate theories to describe their operations, the number of basic concepts is surprisingly small. However, these basic concepts (such as the seemingly paradoxical notion that behavior is a function of its consequences) are firmly established and common to most theories of learning. This remains true despite the fact that these theories of learning are often in con-

---

[1] In the fall of 1968 the members of this Association voted to change the name to the *Association for Advancement of Behavior Therapy*.

flict with each other with respect to detail and have not been established as "valid" in the scientific sense of the term. For this reason, it is probably better, at this stage, to regard behavior therapy as based upon specific principles of learning rather than upon inclusive theories.

Sixth, the fact that only a few concepts are presently employed does not necessarily preclude the eventual introduction of additional concepts as needed. For example, it is possible that cognitive and perceptual processes, viewed strictly as constructs which can be accounted for in terms of behavior and the properties of matter, may need to become part of the SR theorist's conceptual model.

Seventh, abnormal behavior is not regarded solely as a matter of faulty learning: genetic and biochemical factors may also need to be taken into consideration.

Eighth, even in the medical setting the principles employed in behavior modification are predominantly those of experimental psychology. This may be contrasted with the practices of traditional psychotherapy, in which the medical model is tacitly, and often explicitly, followed.

A striking illustration of the differences between behavior therapy and traditional psychotherapy is exemplified by the respective treatments of the issue of symptom substitution. Whereas, in behavior modification, it can be good practice to treat the maladaptive behavior directly, in the psychodynamic (medical) model the overt maladaptive responses are usually assumed to be symptomatic of some underlying problem and therefore to need treatment by "getting at the underlying cause" (e.g., Spiegel, 1967). However, it does not follow that there is inevitably no place in the world of the behavior therapist for the notion of symptom substitution. While there is no reason to accept the dogma that conditioning therapy inevitably leads to symptom substitution, the opposing point of view, as developed by Yates (1958) in his outright dismissal of symptom substitution as a psychoanalytic myth and by Ullmann & Krasner (1965, p. 15) in their insistence that "there is no place in a psychological model for the concept of a symptom," would appear to be neither substantiated nor necessary. As Goldiamond, Dyrud, & Miller (1965) point out, when the dermatologist states that the skin rash is symptomatic of a blood disturbance, what he means behaviorally is that the primary treatment is to be focused not on the presenting symptom but on something else, namely the blood disturbance. Similarly, to refer to symptomatic behavior implies that we may be treating some other behavior (either with or without treating the presenting symptom) rather than restricting our attentions to the presenting behavior. In all probability, once the behavioral deficits are overcome, the maladaptive symptomatic behavior will decrease.

The occurrence of maladaptive behavior following treatment is not necessarily inconsistent with the behavioral model. For example, if one maladaptive behavior is successfully extinguished, a child may resort to another to gain his ends, and then to another—all part of that individual's hierarchical repertoire of maladaptive behavior. An examination of the circumstances under which symptom substitution occurs is thus likely to be more profitable than an engagement in partisan polemics (see Lazarus, 1965; Cahoon, 1968). Both the Pavlovian model and the model of social learning theory (e.g., Bandura & Walters, 1963) make explicit the notion that, under certain circumstances, the elimination of one rewarding but deviant pattern may cause another deviant set of responses to achieve prominence. According to Pavlovian theory, neurotic behavior (i.e., symptoms) represents the external manifestation of pathological occurrences within the central nervous system (CNS). Therefore, treating the symptom alone without also attempting to remedy the central pathology could result in symptom substitution (see Franks 1966b; McConaghy, 1964).

The behavioral and psychodynamic schools of therapy differ radically in more ways than their approach to the issue of symptom substitution. In 1959 Eysenck listed what he believed to be the more important differences between the two. From the superior vantage point of 1969 his tabulation may seem naïve; nevertheless, though it may do less than justice to psychodynamic theory, this pioneering affirmation—with all its bias and oversimplification—clearly sets forth the foundations of the behavior therapy position. For this reason, it is reproduced here (Table 1). In the past decade, it is not so much the foundations of behavior therapy which have changed as the perspectives. To appreciate the significance of these developments, it is necessary to take a detailed look at their historical antecedents.

Historical Overview

Even if the terminology is different, techniques of behavior modification are as old as the proverbial hills, and history, folklore, and legend are replete with colorful illustrations of the process at work. For example, the Chinese dynastic histories yield a delightful little vignette about an emperor's son who systematically harnessed the principles of operant conditioning to bring about the assassination of his father by the royal cavalry (see Kreuger, 1961). If this fails to meet the basic requirements of a therapeutic regimen, the same can hardly be said of the efforts of Pliny the Elder to eradicate "alcoholism . . . but not the man." The ingenious methods listed by Pliny in his *Historiae Naturalis* for the creation of an aversion to alcohol ranged from physical or social punishment to the placing of putrid spiders in the bottom of the unfortunate victim's glass (Franks, 1963b). In seventeenth-century Turkey, smokers were dragged through the streets of Constantinople with their pipes pierced through their noses (Van Proosdij, 1960). In the early 1800s Johan Christian Reil treated stuporous depressed patients by infesting them with scabies, a procedure which effectively induced the motor reinforcement of scratching (Zilboorg & Henry,

Table 1   *Tabulation of the More Important Differences between Freudian Psychotherapy and Behavior Therapy*

Freudian psychotherapy	Behavior therapy
1. Based on inconsistent theory never properly formulated in postulate form.	1. Based on consistent, properly formulated theory leading to testable deductions.
2. Derived from clinical observations made without necessary control, observation, or experiments.	2. Derived from experimental studies specifically designed to test basic theory and deductions made therefrom.
3. Considers symptoms the visible upshot of unconscious causes ("complexes").	3. Considers symptoms unadaptive CRs.
4. Regards symptoms as evidence of repression.	4. Regards symptoms as evidence of faulty learning.
5. Believes that symptomatology is determined by defense mechanism.	5. Believes that symptomatology is determined by individual differences in conditionability and autonomic lability, as well as accidental environmental circumstances.
6. All treatment of neurotic disorders must be historically based.	6. All treatment of neurotic disorders is concerned with habits existing at present; historical development is largely irrelevant.
7. Cures are achieved by handling the underlying (unconscious) dynamics, not by treating the symptom itself.	7. Cures are achieved by treating the symptom itself, i.e., by extinguishing unadaptive CRs and establishing desirable CRs.
8. Interpretation of symptoms, dreams, acts, etc., is an important element of treatment.	8. Interpretation, even if not completely subjective and erroneous, is irrelevant.
9. Symptomatic treatment leads to the elaboration of new symptoms.	9. Symptomatic treatment leads to permanent recovery, provided autonomic as well as skeletal surplus CRs are extinguished.
10. Transference relations are essential for cures of neurotic disorders.	10. Personal relations are not essential for cures of neurotic disorder, although they may be useful in certain circumstances.

SOURCE: H. J. Eysenck. Learning theory and behavior therapy. *Journal of Mental Science*, 1959, **105**, p. 67.

1941). In 1845 a case was presented at the Royal Academy of Medicine in Paris in which an obsessional patient was successfully treated by a procedure that comes remarkably close to "reciprocal inhibition" (Stewart, 1961). The "moral orthopedics" of the nineteenth-century Swiss psychiatrist, DuBois, also closely resemble "reciprocal inhibition" (see Bromberg, 1959), and in 1891, the nurse Annie Payson Call employed relaxation and "mind training" to relieve tension (see Wolberg, 1954).

While such examples provide interesting illustrations of the principles of conditioning as part of the general stream of development, it is of greater relevance to consider those events and individuals which appear to be more directly the precursors of behavior therapy as we know it today. The concept of the classical conditional reflex did not begin with Pavlov. Throughout the preceding decades many a distinguished philosopher and scientist, influenced, no doubt, by the associationist traditions of British empiricism and the doctrines of French materialism, had observed and sought to explain, after the fact, many of the essential phenomena of the conditional reflex. Thus James Ward, in an 1878 discussion of ideation in the *Encyclopaedia Britannica,* pointed out that "the dog's mouth waters at the *sight* of food, but the gourmand's mouth will also water at the *thought* of it." As part of his lecture series in Paris (ca. 1855), Claude Bernard described the phenomenon of salivary conditioning in the horse (Rosenzweig, 1959). And Raehlmann, a German ophthalmologist, in 1890 proposed behaviorist axioms and in 1902 reported an experiment involving conditional discrimination in an infant (Wesley, 1968).

Pavlov introduced what would now be termed *program research* into the experimental study of conditioning. Whereas most earlier investigators confined their endeavors to the demonstration of already-established conditional responses, it was Pavlov who initiated a program of systematic study into the formation and extinction of deliberately induced new conditional reflexes. Of the many influences upon Pavlov, that of Sechenov was undoubtedly the most significant. Sechenov, the father of Russian physiology and the discoverer of the phenomenon of central inhibition, was a remarkable man in many ways, a man in the center of the Russian scientific and intellectual life, debate, and furor of his times. Dostoyevsky and others deplored his materialism, Turgenev attended his lectures, Tolstoy referred to his writings in *Anna Karenina,* and scientists in general endorsed his point of view (see Razran, 1965).[2]

As with Pavlov and the classical conditional reflex, Sechenov, by his practical investigations of the phenomenon of central inhibition, was the first to replace philosophical deliberation and incidental observation with rigorous experimentation. Closely related to Sechenov's work—and also much neglected by behavior therapists—is the work of Sherrington. Prior to Sherrington's demonstration that inhibition is an active process, it was generally believed that inhibition was merely an absence of excitation (see Sherrington, 1906; Diamond, Balvin, & Diamond, 1963).

Acclaim rightly belongs to Pavlov, but he was not the only Russian

[2] For further biographical notes about Sechenov and his era see: Diamond, Balvin, & Diamond, 1963; Koshtoyants, 1964; R. I. Watson, 1963; Wells, 1956. Also available now in English, thanks to the American Institute of Biological Sciences and the American Psychological Association, is a 1965 edition of Sechenov's delightfully written *Autobiographical Notes,* completed about a year before his death in 1905.

scientist of his day dedicated to objectivity and the method and study of the reflex. Whereas Pavlov delayed presentation of what he called a "full and systematized exposition" of his researches until 1924, and major translations of his reports did not appear until after this date, the "reflexology" of his rival, Bekhterev, had been translated into French and German as early as 1913 (see Diamond, Balvin, & Diamond, 1963; Kaplan, 1966). Thus, though Pavlov is now a dominant world figure of his era, this was certainly not true in the first quarter of this century when his work remained virtually unknown outside Russia.[3]

The Contribution of Pavlov

Pavlov distrusted absolutism in any form, and it was no accident that he employed the term "conditional" in his writings rather than "conditioned." His intent was to convey the essentially temporary nature of the connections thus formed, connections which lacked the certainty and regularity of innate or "unconditional" reflexes. For Pavlov, as for Sechenov, the conditional reflex was a creative, emergent activity of the organism, not a stereotyped and unchanging process (see Makarov, 1966).

In Pavlov's first book to be translated into English the terminology was correct; it was in later translations, possibly from the German, that the misleading term "conditioned" was introduced. Gantt deliberately maintained this inaccuracy in the interests of "conformity against accuracy"—a decision which he claims to have regretted ever since (Gantt, 1966). Whatever the origins of this error and the reason for its perpetuation, the impact upon American psychology and psychiatry has been profound. For example, in a lecture at the Philips Clinic in 1966, Jules Masserman, presumably with intent to take Pavlov to task for implying that the conditional reflex connoted some form of fixed, unvarying action, is reported to have stated categorically, "I have never seen a conditioned reflex, though others may have." These words would probably never have been uttered had the correct translation been in vogue (Gantt, 1966).

Perhaps because of this error, it is commonly assumed that Pavlov had a limited approach to behavior in which the sum total of psychological phenomena, and even of physiological functioning, is no more than the classical conditional reflex. Nothing could be further from the truth. Pavlov stressed continually that the classical conditional reflex was governed by the same processes and principles that control other phenomena, such as "trial-and-

---

[3] Bekhterev's major book was published in English in 1932. The standard translations of Pavlov's books are as follows: Pavlov, 1927, 1928, 1941, 1960. Apart from Pavlov's autobiography (Pavlov, 1955), the following biographical material is available in English: Asratyan, 1953; Babkin, 1949; Frolov, 1937; Gantt, 1962.

error" learning, and that his fundamental concern was not with conditioning per se but with the course of higher nervous activity and the properties of the two central processes of excitation and inhibition (see Bridger, 1958).[4] Instead of reducing behavior to simple stimulus-response (SR) sequences, Pavlov viewed behavior as the result of complex interactions within the central nervous system, involving irradiation and concentration of excitatory and inhibitory processes and including both positive and negative induction effects (see Minz, 1964; Franks, 1964).

Working primarily with dogs, Pavlov found that so-called experimental neuroses could be established in a variety of ways, all of which involved some form of collision or excessive activity of two central processes: inhibition and excitation. Eventually, five principal means of achieving a "breakdown" (persistent maladaptive behavior) were noted: (1) the use of intense stimuli (first observed during the Leningrad floods of 1924), (2) increasing the delay between the presentation of the signal and the food, (3) inducing increasingly difficult tasks of conditional discrimination, (4) continually alternating positive and negative stimuli in a conditioning task, and (5) physical stress.

But not all the dogs responded in similar fashion to seemingly similar stimuli, which led Pavlov to classify his animals according to their reactivity and so to develop his well-known theory of types (see Wortis, 1962; Lynn, 1966a; MacMillan, 1963; Franks, 1964). Drawing parallels with the fourfold Hippocratic classification of temperament, Pavlov attempted to account for human neuroses and psychoses in terms of his animal typology, at first based exclusively upon differences in balance between his two central processes but later extended to include the concepts of strength and motility. Gradually, Pavlov became aware of the fundamental difference between man and animals, namely that man's cerebral cortex has within it the unique gift of language and speech, a second signal system in which words stand for the sights and sounds of the first signal system.[5] The study of this second signal system resulted in the introduction by Pavlov of an additional and specifically human typology. In the artistic type the first signal system predominates over the second; in the thinking type the second predominates over the first; and in the intermediate type the systems are balanced.

Psychiatric disease processes were described by Pavlov in terms of disruption of the normal processes of excitation and inhibition, treatment being

---

[4] If, with Brozek (1966), we examine the appropriate indexes to Soviet professional literature, no separate entry will be found under the rubric *conditioning*. This is because conditioning is no more than a technique—if perhaps the key one—for the study of the "physiology of higher nervous activity" (to use accredited Pavlovian terminology).

[5] This second signal system can be highly telegramatic and one word can convey many meanings or be a kind of shorthand for a complex ideational sequence, the phrase "behavior therapist"—if spoken aloud—providing a striking example: there is both diversity and complexity of meaning to the words "behavior therapist."

aimed at the direct modification of this disruption. Thus, sleep therapy—regarded by Pavlov as akin to hypnosis (see Das, 1958)—is still used by Pavlovians to protect the organism from stress. Another important assumption of Pavlov pertains to the concept of protective inhibition. Protective inhibition is a process of inhibition brought about by excessive or prolonged stimulation, and its presumed function is to protect the nervous system from biological overstrain. Pavlov assumed that dogs and individuals with weak nervous systems generate protective inhibition much more readily than those with strong nervous systems. Thus, to a Pavlovian, schizophrenia is seen, in one respect, as a state of intense protective inhibition, which, in turn, strengthens the cortical cells and provides them with an opportunity to recover from their exhausted state (see Lynn, 1963).

While nothing but the highest commendation can be given to a man who embarks upon a new phase of activity at the age of eighty, it must also be noted that, whereas Pavlov's animal data and subsequent theories were firmly rooted in the methodology of the laboratory, his later observations about humans were little more than speculation. Ironically enough, Pavlov fell into the very error, making premature analogies between the laboratory and the clinic, that he cautioned others to avoid. He was, perhaps unwittingly, influenced to make this error by an inclination to accept too readily, and too literally, the formulations, labels, and theories about psychiatric disorders given to him by the psychiatrists.

Some other comments of a general nature are also in order. Thus, Pavlov assumed that the breakdowns in his dogs were simplified versions of breakdowns in man. This highly questionable assumption is a matter of more than academic interest to behavior therapists. For example, the interpretation and extension of Masserman's well-known studies with cats is a cornerstone in Wolpe's model of behavior therapy. If one applies Hebb's (1947) six criteria for "neuroses" to either Pavlov's dogs or Masserman's cats, considerable doubt arises (for discussion of this point, see Broadhurst, 1960; Lynn, 1966a). Thus, while many prominent Western psychiatrists think Pavlov's findings have close relevance for the study of human behavior, others are less certain. In any case, 24 basic types can be deduced from Pavlov's system, and although Pavlov cautioned against the assumption that there were only 4 types, the possibility that there are more than 4 has been largely neglected ever since (see Mac-Millan, 1963; Teplov and Nebylitzyn, 1963).

The notion that the cortex is essential to conditioning is no longer tenable. And Loucks (1933) failed to find evidence in support of Pavlov's supposition that excitation and inhibition irradiate and concentrate in a wave-like manner as they move across the cortex. Thus, while there is neurological evidence in support of certain Pavlovian concepts (e.g., the work of Ratliff, Hartline, & Miller, 1963, provides some neural support for the contention that excitation and inhibition can induce one another), much of Pavlov's theory is best regarded as quasi-neurological and as overstepping its empirical foundations (see Konorski, 1948). Hence, any leap from such speculation to statements about neuroses and psychoses must be regarded with special caution[6] (see Hilgard & Bower, 1966, p. 61).

In summing up Pavlov's contribution, it has to be said that he failed to achieve his major aims of explaining the physiological activity of the cerebral cortex and of accounting for behavior in objective, physiological terms. Therefore, until there is direct physiological demonstration of the alleged neural events, it is essential to recognize many Pavlovian concepts for what they are —working inferences drawn from behavioral facts observed in experiments (see Kimble, 1967, for a more extended discussion of this topic). Perhaps the most encouraging post-Pavlovian developments within the Soviet Union pertain to the increasing emphasis upon the separation of fact and interpretation, and it is to these that we turn next.

Post-Pavlovian Developments within the U.S.S.R.

The majority of projects carried out in the U.S.S.R. still follow the traditional Pavlovian methodology. Such studies are usually based upon too few subjects for meaningful generalizations to be made; too few details are reported, and anything but the most rudimentary quantification is scrupulously avoided. By contrast, Western studies in the same area tend to be theoretically overdetermined. To be considered scientifically respectable, they have to be based upon some explicit rationale designed to test some specific hypothesis, and if the experiment can decide between two incompatible theories or predictions, so much the better. But, in so doing, the individual deviant datum either becomes rejected or immersed in the pool of numbers and averaged into the bottomless well of obscurity. The typical Pavlovian experiment is of an extended nature, taking up many sessions and many hours for each of a small number of subjects. The typical American conditioning experiment is carried out with many subjects—usually college sophomores—each of whom devotes, at most, one hour for a one-session study designed to explore only two conditioning phenomena: acquisition and extinction.

The work of the late B. M. Teplov and his associates, in particular

---

[6] But, in Pavlov's defense, it should be noted that he was always open to correction and ready to change his conclusions in the face of fresh evidence. Pavlov's belief in the inheritance of acquired conditional reflexes is a case in point. In 1923 Pavlov read a paper in which, on the basis of data obtained by one of his students, he concluded that conditional reflexes could be inherited (actually the data indicated that successive generations required fewer and fewer trials to form a conditional reflex). But replication failed to confirm this experiment, and in 1926 Pavlov told Gantt that he regarded these earlier conclusions about the inheritance of conditional reflexes as one of the biggest errors of his scientific career (see Brozek, 1964, p. 520).

V. D. Nebylitzyn, represents a striking evolution of Pavlovian tradition and is of significance on several accounts. First, while recognizing the genius of Pavlov, they explicitly regard his concepts as plausible hypotheses worthy of systematic investigation rather than as cut-and-dried *faits accomplis;* second, while recognizing the need for the detailed study of the individual case, they recognize also the need to employ sophisticated methods of experimental inquiry and statistical analysis; third, they recognize the need for a firm psychophysiological or biological basis to their concepts and so include appropriate tests in their battery; fourth, while working within a physiological framework, they are careful to make explicit the importance of the environment and the fact that man is a social animal who acts on the environment as well as having the environment act on him.

Their methodological starting point is the partly hypothetical neurophysiological level of the mechanisms of brain functioning. Laboratory procedures, especially conditioning, are used to delineate individual differences in the manner in which people vary at this "central" level. Only then are correlations sought between individual differences at this central level and differences in behavior and personality functioning. Although the work is done with groups, the focus is also upon the datum which apparently refutes the rule. Correlations which, despite their statistical significance, account for a trivial proportion of the variance are regarded as meaningful and of interest, but far from sufficient in themselves (see Franks, 1964, 1967a; Gray, 1964, 1967; Lynn, 1966a, 1966b; Teplov, 1961; Teplov & Nebylitzyn, 1963). With three noticeable exceptions (stemming from the laboratories of Eysenck and Gray in England, and Mangan and his students in Australia), investigators outside the Soviet Union have paid surprisingly little attention to this line of endeavor.

Soviet investigations into higher nervous activity are renowned for their variety, and from the point of view of the traditional Western experimental psychologist, some of their work on *interoceptive conditioning* carries them into very unusual parts of the human organism. Interoceptive conditioning may best be defined as classical conditioning in which either the conditional stimulus or the unconditional stimulus or both are delivered directly to the mucosa of some specific viscus. (Bykov's investigations in this area are readily available in English, 1957, and penetrating commentaries on this and similar studies—some not as yet translated—are provided by Razran, 1961, 1965.)

Unlike the contrived and more inconsequential responses of the typical laboratory experiment, such as the conditional eyeblink, the reactions brought about as a result of interoceptive conditioning are likely to be of direct relevance to the practicing clinician. Such reactions are easily induced, frequently encountered in the "natural" setting, and of a largely "unconscious" nature. If Freud's therapeutic goal was to make conscious that which was previously unconscious, Bykov's investigations would seem to be progressing along a similar road—at least in that they are attempting to bring relationships between hidden elements into view. Whether, as Razran seems to think, such investigations could eventually lead to a physiological justification for certain Freudian constructs is debatable. But, certainly, these developments hold promise of a conditional response explanation of unconscious visceromotor accompaniments of anxiety and other conditional emotional reactions. Thus, argues Razran (1961), not only, for example, may the unconscious visceromotor accompaniments to conscious feelings of anxiety become conditional stimuli for the production of, say, constipation, but unconscious rectal distensions, or sensations of constipation, may equally be conditioned to bring about anxiety, gout, asthma, hypertension, or any other functional disturbance.

Semantic conditioning, or *conditioning to meaning,* arose out of Pavlov's concept of the second-signal system and the early work of Krasnogorsky and Ivanov-Smolensky. In one experiment (Ivanov-Smolensky, 1927) a child was instructed to press a rubber bulb whenever a given signal appeared. A second signal was then associated with this "unconditional stimulus," so that eventually a conditional bulb-pressing response was established to this new signal. Luria, who is primarily interested in the development of voluntary control in the child through the use of language, has adapted this basic experiment to the study of the second signal system as a modifier of behavior. It might be noted that, whereas Western scientists such as Hilgard and Bower (1966) concern themselves with the classical or instrumental nature of such paradigms, for Soviet investigators the question of *how* learning is controlled is of more significance than any discussion of the purity of the paradigm (e.g., Asratyan, 1967; Beritoff, 1965; Luria, 1961; Platonov, 1955). This line of endeavor should not be equated with Western *verbal conditioning,* in which attempts are made to modify the words that a subject—or patient—uses by reinforcing certain of his utterances and extinguishing others (e.g., Krasner, 1958).

A third area of post-Pavlovian development within the Soviet Union pertains to the *orienting* or *orientation reflex*—the "what is it" reflex or "reflex of curiosity," to use Pavlov's early terminology, the tendency of the organism to orient toward (pay attention to) any novel stimulus regardless of its origins (see Hilgard & Bower, 1966, pp. 68ff; Lynn, 1966a, 1966b; Voronin, Leontiev, Luria, Sokolov, & Vinogradova, 1965). The adaptive significance of the orientation response is twofold: first, it prepares the organism for emergency reaction; second, through habituation, it avoids waste of energy in pointless resistance to meaningless distractions. The very persistence of an orienting response indicates that—at least to that person—the instigating stimulus is one which requires that a reaction be made to it. Thus, what was originally just a source of trouble in Pavlov's laboratory (necessitating the construction of soundproof rooms) later became of interest in its own right and led to meaningful study.

In terms of daily practice, the therapeutic programs of Soviet institutions might be expected to reflect these developments and manifest a characteristically Pavlovian and dialectic flavor in which the emphasis is upon the larger social environment of the group rather than upon the psychological life of the individual. To a large extent this is so, and yet—while the term behavior therapy remains foreign to Soviet investigators—it is surprising to what extent recent mental health developments in Russia also mirror the multidisciplined behavioral approaches of the West.

This typically Soviet integration of pedagogic, public health, and medical approaches is well exemplified by the technique of "rational therapy," as practiced at the Bekhterev Institute in Leningrad. The first phase of the therapeutic regimen is twofold: medical—pharmacology, hypnosis, sleep therapy, and the like are instituted in accordance with Pavlov's notion of protective inhibition for the fatigued cortical cells; social—an environmental situation is established that is acceptable for the stages to follow. In the second phase, "clarification," the patient is helped to understand the purpose and consequences of his maladaptive behavior (symptoms) in terms of his specific problems and his total life situation. In the third phase, learning principles are systematically applied to the active "reconstruction" of new patterns of behavior. In the final or "training" phase, the patient learns to perfect and maintain these newly acquired habits within the real-life situation, and to become increasingly independent of the therapist (see Kiev, 1968, pp. 16ff.; Winn, 1961).

Psychotherapy is thus viewed as a complex process of modifying the essentially plastic central nervous system, of extinguishing pathologically conditioned connections, and of forming healthy new ones in which both the processes of excitation and inhibition and the two signal systems are in harmony with each other. To achieve this end, a wide range of behavioral and physiological techniques is employed, ranging from medication, sleep, and hypnosis to work therapy and restructuring of the patient's life in his socioeconomic setting. It is hardly necessary to belabor the similarities between these notions and the broad-spectrum developments which are taking place in the West.

Conditioning outside the Soviet Union: The Present Behavioral Scene

The numerous attempts to relate Pavlovian excitation and inhibition to learning theory and personality variables are too well known to need detailed description here, except perhaps to point out that the road is hazardous and still largely uncharted (see Franks, 1963a). Of the many Western investigators who employ the Pavlovian framework in a clinical setting, the names of Alexander (1958), Astrup (1962, 1965), Ban (1964), and Salter (1949) come readily to mind. But the pioneer is undoubtedly Horsely Gantt, one of the few remaining pupils of Pavlov still active in the field. Apart from his unique position as the founder of the Pavlovian Laboratory at the Johns Hopkins School of Medicine, the Pavlovian Society of North America, and the journal *Conditional Reflex,*

Gantt's clinical contribution stems from his attempts to tease out the relative roles of central versus peripheral structures and from his demonstration of differential rates of extinction among the various body systems (see Franks, 1964; Gantt, 1958).

If it is true that the Pavlovian tradition as a philosophic system has had little direct impact upon American psychology, this can hardly be said of Pavlovian technology and theory. Even while painstaking neurophysiological research continues, for the most part, to refute the quasi-neurological notions of Pavlov, techniques of classical conditioning remain in vogue. The trend, if there is any trend, seems to be away from elaborate deductive-postulate systematization such as that of Hull, and away from the atheoretical operationalism of Skinner, towards an experimentally geared interactionism in which behavioral and neurophysiological data are meaningfully coordinated—in other words, back to the goals of Pavlov, but with the added advantages of modern techniques, equipment, and neurophysiological knowledge.

If the present scene is behavioral, it is certainly not identical with the familiar Watsonian behaviorism of 1913, with its uncompromising rejection of mental states and its insistence upon an extreme reductionism in which the psychological event is dissolved into neural, muscular, and glandular acts. As Kantor (1968) points out, Watsonian behaviorism is but one stage in the long evolution of psychological behaviorism. Contemporary behaviorism, or *functional behaviorism*, to employ Keehn's (1964) term, stresses the role that "awareness" plays in the functional control of behavior, whereby behavior evoked by private, conscious experiences can be brought under public control.

Ever since Skinner distinguished between respondent and operant learning in 1935, operant conditioning seems to have captured the imagination of researcher and clinician alike. We hope that the Pavlovian emphasis of the present survey will serve to remind the reader of the contributions to behavior therapy made by classical conditioning and the Pavlovian tradition. While the theoretical differences between classical and operant conditioning (which the Russians term *instrumental conditioning* and Thorndike terms *learning by trial and error*) are blurred, possibly artificial, and regarded by the Russians as unimportant (see Asratyan, 1967; Gantt, 1967), in practice the distinction is of major significance. Whereas Pavlovian conditioning is essentially an example of Aristotelian association by contiguity, and the food in the famous bell-and-salivation situation is primarily a stimulus for salivation, in the operant model the food functions as a reinforcer. Out of this disarmingly simple innovation arose the whole school of operant psychology and its vast range of ingenious applications.

Skinner and his followers claim to be atheoretical and to operate within an empirical tradition which involves neither the mentalism underlying the use of intervening variables nor the neurologizing associated with the use of hypothetical constructs. To the extent that this is true, these researchers differ from those broad-spectrum behavior therapists whose concepts are so broad that they seem, at times, to embrace phenomenology; from the Pavlovians, who engage in direct neurological conjecture; and from the Hullians, Wolpians, Eysenckians, and others who make extensive use of molar constructs of a quasi-neurological nature.

Behavior Therapy and Clinical Psychology

It is no longer necessary to convince even the most doggedly psychodynamic clinical psychologist that much of human behavior is learned. Most clinicians pay some lip service to the language of learning theory—hence the promiscuous use of terms such as "reinforcement" and "generalization"—but without any real understanding of what is involved. In a sense, however, this is no worse than the dogma of those who believe that the "new" clinical psychology —as represented by their interpretation of behavior therapy—is the ultimate in psychological development and that a potentially universal panacea has been discovered. To understand this situation, it is necessary to take a brief, and perhaps speculative, look at the development of clinical psychology over the past three or four decades.

Clinical psychology as a profession mushroomed into the daylight of the mental health world in the years immediately following World War II. At this time there was both a need for mental health workers of any description and a tremendous gap between supply and demand. Psychiatrists graciously, or sometimes not so graciously, admitted clinical psychologists into the hallowed precincts of therapy and sanctioned functions other than testing. It would also appear that, through circumstances that were not altogether his fault, the clinical psychologist found himself maneuvered into a position of omnipotence in which he was forced to answer all sorts of implicitly profound diagnostic questions—questions that actually, even in the present state of knowledge, remain unanswered. The clinical psychologist was expected to provide authoritative answers to intrinsically unanswerable questions, and he tended to accept this role uncritically, deemphasizing the need for appraisal. Only gradually did he begin to question not merely his techniques and tools, but also his roles and his philosophy. In the questioning, it perhaps became apparent to some that, if the future for emotionally disturbed patients was brighter in the fifties than it had been half a century earlier, the improvement was primarily due to advances in four general areas: (1) psychopharmacology and biochemistry; (2) electroconvulsive therapy and other physical procedures; (3) psychotherapy; and (4) finally, that vast area pertaining to a slowly emerging sense of informed public responsibility for the mentally ill. Perhaps equally apparent, however, were the facts that, although the psychologist made a worthy contribution as a team member, his role vis-à-vis the first two of these areas was, of necessity, secondary, and that his contribution to the fourth area followed from his role as a concerned citizen rather than as a professional specialist. The third area, psychotherapy, while a legitimate area of inquiry for the psychologist, could hardly be claimed as his special domain. Thus, in none of these areas was the psychologist making a unique contribution by virtue of his profession alone.

As an initial "solution," there was a tendency to assume that, while the psychodynamics of Freud represented some kind of fundamental psychiatric verity, it was both feasible and desirable to translate these truths into terminology more acceptable to the experimental psychologist than the language of psychoanalysis (e.g., Dollard & Miller, 1950; Mowrer, 1950; Shoben, 1949). Gradually, as Ullmann & Krasner (1965) ably document, such dictionary-construction tactics and their underlying assumptions were abandoned in favor of an approach which was consistently behavioral at all levels. The data and methodology of the laboratory were adapted and extended to the clinical situation and the natural setting, and the need for psychodynamic assumptions was regarded as totally unnecessary.

Curiously, despite the existence of a detailed knowledge of the principles of classical and operant conditioning for over half a century, it is only during the present decade that psychologists have begun to apply these principles earnestly and systematically. It took over forty years for the clinical community to follow paths laid down by pioneers such as Jones (1924) and Watson & Rayner (1920). There are two probable reasons for this hiatus: first, the rise of the more spectacular schools of psychoanalysis, and second, the absence of clinical psychology as we know it today, with the result that these early efforts to apply learning-theory principles remained largely within the academic setting and failed to reach the practitioners (see Kushner, 1968).

The more enthusiastic—"more extreme" would be a less charitable description—behavior therapists became convinced that here, at last, the psychologist could make a unique contribution and assume a role of direct leadership. Behavioral planning, it was believed, could solve all emotional ills if only the diligent and rigorous application of laboratory-derived principles of learning theory were applied to the natural situation. In his eagerness to "go it alone," this new breed of psychologist vehemently rejected the medical model with its terminology and its implications. Along with the word "clinical" and its connotation of "bedside," terms such as "patient," "diagnosis," "therapy," "symptom," "cure," and "psychopathology" were viewed with anathema. In this new world that certain behavior therapists were trying to mold, there was no place for any model other than that of the conventional SR theorist. Thus, concepts such as "consciousness," "perception," and "cognition" were summarily dismissed as being unnecessary, unscientific, and mentalistic.

At first, these enthusiastic behavior therapists were also rather naïve, focusing upon the presenting symptom and its elimination by either operant or classical conditioning procedures. Within the space of less than one decade, this approach gave way to the "total behavioral approach" and the advent of the behavioral clinician (see Franks, 1966a, 1967b). The realizations arose that treating the presenting complaint by one or two stereotyped conditioning procedures is usually not sufficient, and that applying a variety of behavioral techniques to the overall behavioral management of the patient is often necessary.

In making the point that behavior therapy evolved from a naïve "simplicity" to the stage of total behavioral management, it is important to emphasize that the behavior therapist and the conventional psychotherapist usually place two quite different meanings on the epithet "simplistic." To the total behavioral therapist, the early SR-directed behavioral clinician of less than a decade ago is simplistic because, in essence, he focuses upon the presenting symptom and ignores the rest of the person. To the psychodynamic therapist, both early and contemporary behavior therapists are simplistic because of their "naïve" insistence upon taking behavior at face value rather than as symbolic of some unconscious inner world.

Even while the behavioral critics of "simplicity" advocated, and indeed practiced, a more total behavioral management, they still resolutely insisted that problems of consciousness and the like either did not exist or were beyond the realm of science. An alternative strategy, which is now being voiced by the avant-garde in our midst, is to embark upon an increasingly sophisticated experimental analysis of the variables that control behavior rather than to attribute such unaccounted-for variance to concepts beyond behavioral science, such as consciousness. In so doing, however, it is important that we avoid substituting learning-theory pseudoexplanation for psychoanalytic pseudoexplanation. Attribution of unaccounted-for variance in behavior to neatly labeled concepts such as "awareness" and "consciousness" is a prime example of what Wiest (1967) so aptly terms *pseudoexplanation by mere naming*, which creates a false sense that one is actually explaining something. As Wiest reminds us, Tolman's insistence that intervening variables must eventually be defined in terms of relations between observables is still good advice. For example, in the field of perception—long ignored by the more blinkered of SR behavior therapists—complex perceptual phenomena have been successfully integrated into the learning-theory framework (e.g., Goldiamond, 1962; Postman, 1963; Sokolov, 1963).

In their dismissal of Western associationism as "vulgar materialism," Soviet psychologists seem to have arrived at a similar position—if from different premises. While adopting a position of consistent monism which regards matter as primary, they give consciousness a valued role as a real and important property of organized matter (see Brozek, 1966; Gray, 1966; Winn, 1961). Without going into the intricacies of dialectic materialism and the doctrine of reflection (the belief that psychological processes are the reflections of objective reality), it must be stressed that, for most Soviet psychologists, the process of mediation between the external world and the self is an active and dynamic one in which there is little place for the simplistic concepts of mechanistic behaviorism. Thus, consciousness is defined by one Pavlovian therapist as that property of the brain of "reflecting the objective world, acting through the sense organs in the brain of man" (Antonov, 1958). Along with other processes (such as cognition, memory, and emotion), consciousness in the full meaning of the word is regarded as unique to man because man alone possesses the second signal system. It is unfortunate that some American psychologists still seem to adhere tenaciously to the erroneous belief that the Pavlovian tradition encompasses a view of man as a kind of dehumanized atomistic mechanism (e.g., Stafford & Combs, 1967).

A related development which requires documenting is the emergence of what Lazarus (1967a) terms *broad-spectrum behavior therapy* and the doctrine of *technical eclecticism*. Bemoaning the fact that there is "an increasing number of behavior therapists who employ systematic desensitization almost exclusively" (Lazarus & Serber, 1968), Lazarus makes a plea for a broad-spectrum approach to behavior therapy involving an atheoretical eclecticism in the use of techniques.

To quote Lazarus (1967a, pp. 415 ff.):

> Can a practicing psychotherapist afford to ignore any effective technique, regardless of its theoretical origins? Obviously a technique derived from a source or system which is at variance with one's own theoretical beliefs may nevertheless possess healing properties—not necessarily for reasons which attach to the theories of its originator ... it is not necessary to accept or reconcile divergent theoretical systems in order to utilize their techniques ... to read through the vast mass of literature on psychotherapy, *in search of techniques*, can be clinically enriching and therapeutically rewarding. However, this should not presuppose a random melange of techniques taken eclectically out of the air. While the basic point of this paper is a plea for psychotherapists to try several effective techniques (even those not necessarily prompted by the logic of their own theories), it is nevertheless assumed that any selected maneuver will at least have the benefit of empirical support. Complete unity between a systematic theory of personality and an effective method of treatment derived therefrom remains a cherished ideal. Meanwhile, it is well for the practicing psychotherapist to be content in the role of a technician rather than that of a scientist and to observe that those who impugn technical proficiency are often able to explain everything but to accomplish almost nothing.

Thus, for Lazarus, a broad-spectrum behavior therapist is a kind of technically eclectic psychologist who, in addition to his repertoire of the more usual psychotherapeutic procedures such as support, guidance, insight, catharsis, and interpretation (not psychoanalytic), is also aware of operant principles and trained to employ behavioral techniques such as desensitization, assertive training, aversive conditioning, and the like. It might be noted that this definition is couched more in terms of what the nonbehavior therapist omits than in terms of any set of positive principles espoused by the behavior therapist per se. It might also be noted that the major difference between "broad-spectrum behavior therapy," as conceived by Lazarus, and "broad-spectrum therapy," the term the general psychiatrist would probably use, seems to be that the former is confined to so-called psychological treatment methods whereas the latter encompasses literally any process that the therapist considers to be therapeutic, including physical methods of treatment such as drugs, surgery, and electroconvulsive therapy. Broad-spectrum behavior therapy can thus be practiced by any mental health worker, whereas broad-spectrum therapy must, by definition, be confined to the physician.

When Lazarus accuses certain behavior therapists of being simplistic, he seems to imply that, if they should not probe the psychoanalytic depths, then at least they should do more than confine themselves to demonstrable SR relationships, no matter how complex. But to every thesis there is an antithesis, and in this case, the antithesis is presented clearly and forcefully by Wolpe, who argues, in effect, that the distinctive concepts of behavior therapy will vanish into mediocrity if Lazarus's principles are pursued to their logical extreme. In Wolpe's (1968, pp. 1ff.) own words, there is:

> ... a tendency to lose sight of the distinctive character of behavior therapy as a development within a scientific discipline ... we are sometimes accused of being chauvinistically aggressive. We are also chastised for intolerance because we do not agree that the best parts of all systems could be amalgamated into a "supertherapy." It is an eclectic illusion that every mode of psychotherapy must contain something uniquely valuable. While all therapies probably obtain some cures, the likelihood is that most of these are due to nonspecific and usually inadvertent emotional reactions of the patient to the therapist. It is, of course, possible that here and there a maneuver specific to one of the "schools" of psychotherapy has special effects, but in every instance this would need to be demonstrated before it could be accepted. So far, demonstrations have rarely been forthcoming.
>
> The increasing variety of people who carry out behavior therapy techniques has led to much confusion about what constitutes a behavior therapist. There is a widespread idea that a behavior therapist is anybody who uses behavior therapy techniques. The use of a technique can be quite a mechanical matter, requiring no particular intellectual orientation. What distinguishes the behavior therapist is that, while moved to help his patients by feelings of warmth and compassion, he thinks of each of them as an intricate system of neurophysiological and related mechanisms, and of their inappropriate or inadequate habits in terms of the stimulus-response relationships that these mechanisms subserve. He perceives therapy as the process of changing these

relationships, and bases his strategy exclusively upon his knowledge of experimentally established principles of learning against a background of physiology. He operates in this way whether the stimulus is exogenous or endogenous, simple or complex, a bodily sensation or a mental image; and whether the response is motor, autonomic or imaginal, or any combination of these. In short, a behavior therapist is a *behaviorist* who does behavior therapy.

Historically, the short-term progression over the present decade seems to be away from an emphasis by the behavior therapist upon the rather doctrinaire and simplistic thinking of the early sixties and toward the broad-spectrum behavioral management of more recent years, if not toward the more extreme "liberalism" of writers such as Lazarus. Whether these developments imply a *rapprochement* between behavior therapy and the body general of clinical psychology remains to be seen. Whether such a *rapprochement* is desirable from the point of view of the majority of behavior therapists must also remain an open question.

Behavior Therapy and Cultural Differences

It is perhaps inevitable that such situations as the Wolpe-Lazarus dichotomy must emerge. Their existence reflects differences between individuals as well as between theories and philosophies. But, while the differences between Wolpe and Lazarus cannot with justification be attributed to the effects of vastly different cultural traditions, neither theories nor individuals can be meaningfully divorced from the cultures from which they emerge. It is therefore necessary to take into consideration the *Weltanschauung*, the political, social, and philosophical premises of a society, in any appraisal of the behavior therapy scene within that setting.

When one thinks of cultural and other differences with respect to behavior modification the usual tendency is to think in terms of transfer from one culture to another and the concomitant new factors which might have to be taken into consideration. For example, the concept and nature of tokens in the setting up of a so-called token economy will depend very much on the group with which one is dealing. Not only will the behaviors to be rewarded and the nature of the rewards change from culture to culture, and within cultures from one subgroup to another, but even the very notion of reward itself is culturally determined. It is quite conceivable that, in some societies, competitiveness, aggressive individualism, and the profit motive would be viewed as personally and socially undesirable.

No one would refute the need to take into account cultural differences in planning and establishing any program of behavior therapy in a new setting, and no one would gainsay the need for research in these contexts.

A matter of perhaps equal importance, if less obvious relevance, is the need to consider the impact of cultural and allied differences upon the behavior therapist. Regardless of any obvious similarities or differences in training, different societies, and even different subcultures within societies, are likely to influence behavior therapists within the societies differentially. Hence there are implicit philosophical and attitudinal differences, and the explicit choice of technique varies in accordance with the society wherein the therapist has his practice. A truly theory-free and culture-free eclecticism would seem to be impossible.

Perry London (1964) has made the valid point that, regardless of the appealing and plausible nature of a theory, it is techniques that are actually used on people, and not theories. But this is only part of the truth since, while any technique can usually be integrated at will into a variety of theoretical systems or into none, effective appraisal and development of techniques is more likely to come about within some planned theoretical framework than outside it. At least, this is the viewpoint of the behavioral scientist and of the majority of individuals who have contributed the most to behavior therapy as we know it today.

In the best of all possible worlds, it would seem to be highly desirable for the therapist to aspire to be a scientist even if this goal were difficult to realize. To function as a scientist, it is necessary to espouse some theoretical framework. For reasons too obvious to detail here, this is especially true of the behavioral therapist whose very strength lies in the methodology of the scientist, the emphasis upon operational clarity, the establishment of testable predictions generated from some theory of learning, and the eventual delineation of lawful relations between behavior and the variables which control it. Even in this less than the best of all possible worlds, the belief that it is possible somehow to escape the impact of either the prevailing cultural *Zeitgeist* or the philosophical and historical backgrounds within which a technique arose would appear to be erroneous. How the behavior therapist practices (including his choice of technique, his approach to the problems of general strategy, and his specific relationships with his patient) thus depends both upon his explicit theoretical orientation and upon his implicit philosophical and cultural milieu. Cultural differences play a modulating role in determining both his present position and the directions he will eventually take. Behavior modifiers may be able to modify the impact of their cultural milieu, but they cannot escape from it.

Behavior Therapy: Present Status and Future Developments

As previously mentioned, the technology of behavior modification seems to rest upon surprisingly few fundamental principles. Virtually all techniques known today are predicated upon the axiom that behavior is a function of its consequences plus one or two rules of associative learning (see Franks & Susskind, 1968). Because the more practical parameters are of greater interest, the tendency is for the clinical investigator to ignore questions pertaining to basic issues. For example, it is customary to refer to patients as good or bad "conditioners" despite the fact that no general factor of conditionability has been shown to exist in either the laboratory or the clinic.[7] Equally questionable are the implicit assumptions about the consistency and nature of acquisition and extinction conditioning patterns within the therapeutic situation. Can it be assumed, on the basis of a concomitance that is sometimes observed between certain measures of acquisition and extinction in the laboratory, that there must inevitably be a high positive relationship between the rapidity and strength with which new responses are acquired during behavior therapy and the resistance to therapeutic extinction of possibly quite different responses which are already in existence? Similar issues arise with respect to the generalization of conditional responses during therapy. If the basic parameters of laboratory conditioning are still in dispute (e.g., Eysenck, 1962, 1965c; Franks, 1963a; Lovibond, 1964; Ross & Hartman, 1965), it is hardly surprising that the relationships between conditioning in the laboratory and conditioning in the clinical situation remain unclear. Unfortunately, many clinical investigators proceed as if the relationships were clear.

Behavioral modification needs the backing of a well-developed technology of behavioral assessment; so far, such a technology is lacking. Several individuals have developed assessment procedures based upon conditioning, but their usefulness is limited by failure to consider such basic issues as those outlined above, and also by the complexities of the procedures involved, often requiring sophisticated apparatus and a skilled technician. For example, Gantt (1950) has developed a hierarchical test battery of adaptive conditional response function, involving the ability to form and generalize differential as well as simple conditional responses in a variety of classical and instrumental conditioning situations arranged in order from the least serious (disturbance of the latency period and speed of formation of the conditional response) to the most serious (lack of retention of the old conditional response and the failure to form certain unconditional responses—the latter found only in patients with severe neurological impairment). Another investigator, Alexander (1962), has developed a galvanic skin response (GSR) conditioning technique for making the often-difficult differential diagnosis between physical and psychogenic pain states. Ban & Levy (1961) have developed a diagnostic eyeblink

---

[7] It might be noted that a similar situation occurs with respect to the concept of inhibition, a term in wide use even though the existence of a general factor of inhibition is quite equivocal. The addition of various qualifying adjectives, such as "reciprocal," "internal," "conditioned," "basal," and "reactive," serves merely to confound the confusion (see Franks, 1967c).

conditioning technique which, they claim, provides "measurable evidence of change in patients exposed to any treatment regime," and Morgenstern, Pearce, & Rees (1965) have attempted to predict the outcome of behavior therapy by means of psychological tests. But few individuals have managed to integrate these procedures into a research framework which includes data obtained from both the clinic and the real-life situation.

As behavior therapy grows up and acquires a broader perspective, so the exhortative thunder of some of the earlier writers in the field is being replaced by objective appraisal and sober consideration of data, techniques, and goals. As Hunt & Dyrud (1968) suggest, the future of behavior therapy may depend in part upon the success with which it can avoid becoming entrapped in simplistic analysis. Again, it must be stressed that by "simplistic" we do not wish to imply any need to return to phenomenology or psychodynamic speculation, nor do we wish to suggest that, to achieve maximum effectiveness, behavioral and psychodynamic approaches should sometimes be combined (e.g., Leventhal, 1968; Marks & Gelder, 1968). As far as we are concerned, such a dilution would represent a watering down and a regressive step in the evolution of behavior therapy. All that is suggested is that it may be necessary to broaden our behavioral horizons to include within their purview the controlling contingencies that are at present subsumed under such phenomenological and mentalistic rubrics as "awareness," "consciousness," and "cognition."

Much basic and applied research needs to be undertaken if the behavior therapist is to meet the objections of his many critics, both temperate and otherwise. Investigations of individual "failures" are essential (e.g., Feldman, 1966; Moss & Edwards, 1964), and every attempt must be made to account for "successes" in terms of alternative models. When competent critics such as Weitzman (1967) conclude that the efficacy of desensitization may be just as readily explained according to Freudian ideas as according to Hullian principles, it is necessary to treat such contentions with respect. In the words of Popper (1962), "if you are interested in the problem which I tried to solve by my tentative assertion, you may help me by criticizing it as severely as you can, and if you can design some experimental test which you think might refute my assertion, I shall gladly, to the best of my powers, help you to refute it."

Many individuals have attempted to criticize behavior therapy, and many a dialogue of rebuttal and counterrebuttal has ensued (e.g., Breger & McGaugh, 1965, 1966; Rachman & Eysenck, 1965; Wiest, 1967; Weitzman, 1967). While some psychologists present cogent and well-formulated arguments, others— such as Breger & McGaugh—permit subjective overtones to interfere with their critical faculties. One may indeed sympathize with Rachman & Eysenck (1966) when they accuse Breger & McGaugh of presenting "doubtful assertions . . . as if they were self evident truths."

If some curious psychometrician were to attempt a factorial analysis of these multifarious attacks, he would probably be able to identify at least four oblique factors: first, the many who object both pragmatically and philosophically to the "dehumanization" of the individual and all that this implies; second, those who think that behavior therapy is simplistic in that it ignores or denies the existence of "deep" unconscious mechanisms (e.g., Freeman, 1968); third, those who insist that learning-theory explanations are insufficient to account for the complexities of psychotherapy (e.g., Breger & McGaugh, 1965); and fourth, those who sympathize with the behavioral approach but criticize many aspects of the current work in terms of its scientific and methodological limitations and other deficiencies (e.g., Beech, 1963; Gelder, 1968; Lovibond, 1966; Meyer & Crisp, 1966; Peterson & London, 1964).

Detailed presentation and discussion of these issues are readily available elsewhere. The charge of "dehumanization" is expressed in many forms: "denial of free will" (e.g., Oerton, 1965; Rogers, 1961); "against God and for the robotisation of a free people" (e.g., May, 1962; Chein, 1962); "inhumane" (e.g., Lucero, Vail, & Scherber, 1968); and "impersonal" (e.g., Murray, 1963). For interesting and, to our way of thinking, effective responses to these and other accusations, the reader is referred to commentaries by Goldiamond (1965), Kanfer (1965), Krasner (1962, 1966), Lomont (1964), Miron (1968), Ulrich (1967), and Wiest (1967). To those few who still avow that the key to man's psychological world lies in the psychodynamics of Freud and that, at best, the successes of behavior therapy can be only superficial, there are many telling—and sometimes less telling—rejoinders (e.g., Eysenck & Rachman, 1965; Ullmann & Krasner, 1965). But polemics from either side tend to obscure rather than to clarify issues, since the protagonists all too often begin with divergent goals, different criteria, and incompatible terms of reference, and thus inevitably fail to communicate.

As for the third and fourth hypothetical factors—not to mention the second—we are well content to let future investigations resolve the merits and demerits of the respective paradigms. In this respect we concur with Katahn & Koplin (1968, p. 148) in their conclusions that:

> ... argument will in no way decide which approach will be more fruitful, and arguments based upon premises irrelevant to opposing theoretical frameworks will not convince antagonists that they are somehow "wrong." Since certain of the goals of each group are nonoverlapping, it seems only reasonable to encourage competent and creative psychologists to pursue their own preferred approach. Intensive work within each paradigm will ... eventually lead to the dominance of one paradigm over the other as the more productive conceptualization.

As in spheres of man's endeavor beyond psychology, we hope that the spirit as well as the letter of the above advice will be taken. If behavior modifiers cannot learn to modify their behavior, then who can? It is in the firm belief that behavior modification is eminently amenable to appraisal, fact finding, and a continuous process of modification that the present volume is projected. All the evidence augurs well for the future of behavior therapy; the times are appropriate, diverse views are being presented by competent investigators in the field, and significant developments are beginning to emerge.

The "we are better than you" stage is being abandoned in favor of well-designed and precisely executed studies. Thus, in contrast with reviews of less than a half decade ago (e.g., Grossberg, 1964), it is now readily possible to detect a "small but growing number of carefully designed behavior-therapy case studies which meet most, if not all, of the suggested evaluation criteria and which convincingly demonstrate the power and efficiency of behavioristic treatment approaches" (Gelfand & Hartmann, 1968). Current literature no longer presents mainly anecdotal single-case studies which serve no apparent purpose other than the extension of a particular technique to a new disorder. As behavior therapy comes of age and an increasing number of academic departments and medical schools include it within their formal programs, behavior therapists themselves are developing an increasing sense of responsibility to their profession and to the community at large.

Particularly encouraging is the recent establishment of a behavior therapy teaching unit in which the treatment of patients rather than the study of "laboratory phobias" is the primary concern (Poser, 1967; Poser & Ashem, 1968). The emphasis in this unit is upon a diversity of techniques and a belief that equal participation by psychologists, psychiatrists, and other pertinent clinical and research personnel, working within the aegis of a multiorientated parent setting, can best serve the interests of behavior therapy. By the same token, there is a need for exploration not only of many kinds of therapy but also of many kinds of strategy and therapeutic models. Although Albee (1966) and Ullmann & Krasner (1965) have presented compelling arguments in favor of the abandonment of the medical model, the behavior therapist would also do well to ponder the perhaps even more compelling arguments presented by McKeachie (1967) in favor of multiple models, including the medical. If behavior therapists decide to abandon the medical model, then they have to contend with a number of practical and philosophical questions which cannot be overlooked with impunity. If the medical model is rejected in favor of a purely psychological one—learning-theory-oriented or otherwise—then what of the physiological bases of behavior? What of possible genetic and biochemical bases? Can a purely psychological model be meaningfully, or even fully effectively, applied if it is devoid of any extrapsychological links or anchors? Can the psychologist, behavioral or otherwise, "go it alone" in theory or in practice? The impact of such questions and their answers is crucial to the future directions which practice and training in behavior therapy might take.

Behavior therapy presents special problems in that it requires a combination of diverse skills and orientations—and perhaps personality traits—rarely found in any one individual: the detached attention to detail, design, and statistical control of the experimentalist; the sympathetic, concerned, and person-oriented, but not sentimental, attitudes that obtain in the better clinical settings; the awareness of constitutional, genetic, and physiological parameters that come from a full knowledge of the individual as a biological organism; the emphasis upon learning principles as effective modifiers of behavior. If formal training schools for behavior therapy are to be established, they will surely prosper best in an atmosphere which takes cognizance of all these variables. While we strongly disagree with Andrews (1966) in his disdain for what he terms "institutionalization" (e.g., the holding of one-sided symposia and the founding of specialized journals such as *Behaviour Research and Therapy*), we do recognize the need for continual dialogues among the various schools and for communication-expanding activities rather than a narrowing of horizons. As a first step, it is necessary to embark upon an intragroup appraisal, and this appraisal is the intent of the present volume. It would be particularly unfortunate, however, if such an activity—no matter how necessary—were regarded as somehow sufficient in and of itself.

PART ONE

Evaluation and Appraisal

1

Behavior Modification Research:
Design and Tactics

GORDON L. PAUL
University of Illinois, Urbana, Illinois

Following the definitions offered by Krasner & Ullmann (1965), *behavior influence* is taken to be a generic term encompassing the total field of psychological interest relating to the control, change, or modification of human behavior. As such, the psychology of behavior influence includes research on hypnosis, attitude change, "conditioning," drugs, social movements, education, instrumental learning, etc.—any study or practice concerned with the alteration of human behavior. *Behavior modification*, on the other hand, refers to a special subarea of behavior influence with a specific intent—the clinical goal of treatment. Behavior modification research is thus focused upon the techniques, principles, and processes directly relevant to the alteration of deviant or distressing clinical behavior. As such, behavior modification includes many treatment approaches which have gone under a variety of labels in the past: e.g., emotional reeducation, counseling, rehabilitation, retraining; numerous "therapies"—group, milieu, machine, activity, occupational, sleep; even more "psychotherapies"—psychoanalytic, client-centered, behavioral, rational, pastoral, etc.

Traditionally, the overwhelming majority of literature concerning behavior modification has gone under the rubric of "psychotherapy." Perhaps the most generally acceptable definition of psychotherapy follows the essentials proposed by Winder (1957) in which: (1) There is an interpersonal relationship of some duration between two or more people. (2) One of the participants (the therapist) has had special experience and/or training in the handling of human problems and relationships. (3) One or more of the participants (clients) have entered the relationship because of dissatisfaction with their emotional, behavioral, and/or interpersonal adjustment. (4) The methods used are psychological in nature. (5) The procedure of the therapist is based upon some formal theory regarding mental disorder in general and the specific disorder of the client in particular. (6) The aim of the process is the amelioration of the difficulties which cause the client to seek the help of the therapist. While this definition appears adequate for the majority of behavior modification practices in vogue from the late nineteenth century to the mid-1960s, it seems unduly restrictive for the potential range of procedures which have been, or might be, applied to the clinical alteration of behavior (Goldstein, Heller, & Sechrest, 1966). However, in a very real sense, the history of research on psychotherapy is a history of behavior modification research—a history from which future investigations can only profit.

The History of Behavior Modification Research

Bolgar (1965) points out that, "The case study method is the traditional approach of all clinical research. It is essentially exploratory in nature; it focuses on the individual, and it aims primarily at discovering and generating hypotheses." Not only is the case study method the traditional approach, but prior to 1920, it appeared to be the *only* approach in behavior modification "research." From the beginning of such a prescientific era, professional groups having social responsibility for behavior modification (i.e., physicians and clergymen) were forced to develop procedures and techniques of treatment on the basis of observations and inferences from individual clinical cases. Those hypotheses and procedures which could be communicated clearly or with exciting content tended to attract followers to their inventor, resulting in a variety of "schools" of behavior modification theory and practice. Unchecked by empirical data, proponents of each school decried the practices of one another, and the slowness with which other professionals saw the value of favored treatment methods (e.g., Jones, 1910).

While the case study method does have a place in behavior modification research, that place, as elaborated below, is not in the evaluation of treatment. Unfortunately, in the modern prescientific era, this limitation was not recognized. Based only upon case study data, assertions such as the following were common: "The results obtained by the treatment are unquestionably very gratifying. They surpass those obtained by simpler methods in two chief respects; namely, in permanance and in the prophylactic value they have for the future" (Brill, 1909). Even while prescientific schools were developing, the lack of an empirical foundation for specific treatment practices was recognized and verbalized, often in ungentle terms. Hoche, for example, in 1910 maintained that followers of particular schools of behavior modification did not constitute scientific schools but cults concerned with articles of faith rather than facts. He further elaborated the main features of the movement which characterized the cult: fanatic faith, intolerance toward unbelievers, "worship" of the "Master" and willingness to swallow the most "unreasonable" assumptions, fantastic overestimation of present and possible future attainments by the cult. Hoche further offered the suggestion that the spread of such a movement resulted from the general inefficiency of most therapeutic measures in existence at that time and from the general lack of "historic sense and philosophic schooling" among adherents (Patrick & Bassoe, 1910).

Perhaps as a result of criticisms such as Hoche's, combined with the practical necessities of justifying monetary expenditures, concern gradually began to shift towards "demonstrating the effects" of the behavior modification practices of given schools, institutions, or clinics. The period from roughly 1920 to the mid-1940s might, then, be called the demonstration era. During this period, detailed case reports by therapists of varied persuasion related numerable "successes." Additionally, reports of "percentage success" began to appear from specific hospitals, institutes, clinics, etc. (see Eysenck, 1952). Characteristic of "demonstration studies" of this era were the use of overall judgments of success by the involved participants as criteria; little concern with specific procedures of behavior modification beyond the mention of the general "school" affiliation; concern only with those persons treated, usually described by "diagnostic category"; practical rather than scientific impetus for gathering data; retrospective rather than prospective "design." The net result of demonstration studies on the theory and practice of behavior modification, if any, appears to have been the strengthening and inculcation of ongoing theories and procedures within various schools. "How-to-do-it" books, lectures, and apprenticeships within each school proceeded to flourish, each of which was sure of the ultimate "truth" of its own way of doing things.

Growing out of the demonstration era and the relatively "fixed" concepts of treatment which were established, concern began to be expressed about "appropriate" evaluation of behavior modification procedures. Although these concerns appear to have been limited to theoretical "school" lines (e.g., Glover, Fenichel, Strachey, Bergler, Nunberg, & Bibring, 1937; Knight, 1941), they seem to have forecast the beginnings of the scientific era which started to emerge in the late 1940s. At that time, as much a result of World War II as anything else, psychologists and psychiatrists whose training had exposed them both to scientific method and to the needs of behavior modification were beginning their productive years. Carl Rogers at the University of Chicago, William Snyder at Pennsylvania State, and J. McV. Hunt in New York stand out as pioneering and continuing influences in these early attempts to apply scientific method to behavior modification research.

By the early 1950s, the scientific era in behavior modification research had become a fact among methodologists, if not among practitioners and applied investigators. The lack of empirical knowledge concerning the procedures and effects of established practices of behavior modification was openly and forcefully brought to the attention of the scientific and professional world (e.g., Raimy, 1950; Eysenck, 1952). Problems of design and methodology in the evaluation of psychological treatment, even within the currently accepted models became quite explicit (e.g., Miller, 1951; Thorne, 1952). Considerable effort was directed to development and evaluation of necessary measurement techniques (Mowrer, 1953). Perhaps most important of all developments, behavior modification research was placed in proper perspective with other areas of behavior influence, such as education, and the classes of variables, minimal methodological requirements for evaluation, and suggested strategies for programatic investigation appeared in the literature (e.g., Edwards & Cronbach, 1952; Eysenck, 1952; Hunt, 1952; Meehl, 1955; Watson, 1952; Zubin, 1953).

The scientific era of the 1950s through the early 1960s witnessed phenomenal activity in behavior modification research. More sophisticated evaluation studies were attempted, and articles on methodology continued to appear. However, in retrospect, the sociological features of this productive period of research reveal the degree to which investigators were bound by the prior history and practices of behavior modification. Even though evaluation studies became more sophisticated, the majority remained essentially demonstration studies in the sense that evaluation was directed towards "natural ongoing psychotherapy." The practices of various "schools" of treatment appeared to have become so well established for their followers that "naturalistic observation" of the current practices seemed to become an end in itself. In their "epilogue" to the first American Psychological Association (APA) conference on research in psychotherapy, Parloff & Rubinstein (1959) summarize this period of the scientific era in the following way: "Basic problems in this field of research have remained essentially unchanged and unresolved. This may be due in large part to the fact that both the investigator and the therapist have managed to preserve their favorite concepts, assumptions, values and hypotheses by hermetically sealing them in layers of ambiguity."

The first APA conference (Rubinstein & Parloff, 1959) also revealed related sociological problems. Emotional commitments were strong, leading to more complexities and difficulties in evaluation research on behavior modification than in other research areas. "Status" concerns were found to be important obstacles to progress, in that evaluation studies were not only more difficult but were associated with "applied" rather than "basic" science, and in an area which was classically characterized by the "most superficial and unsophisticated research attempts." The realization that criteria of change varied with the theoretical frame of reference of the investigator came explicitly to the fore, resulting in conflicts between "schools" and in statements such as ". . . the investigator's selection of specific criteria [is] a premature and presumptuous value judgement." A related problem, seldom mentioned in polite society, is that few investigators can afford to devote to evaluation studies the disproportionate amount of time required, when their own evaluation is in terms of the "publish or perish" criterion of current academic settings.

With a few notable exceptions such as Jerome Frank's group at Phipps Clinic and Barbara Betz and John Whitehorn at Johns Hopkins Hospital, most large-scale, programatic researchers during this period reacted to the sociological and methodological difficulties of evaluative behavior modification research with what Zubin (1964) calls a "flight into process." Research effort was focused on the ongoing interaction between client and therapist in the "natural" process of treatment. Behavior modification research really became personality theory research within a behavior modification context. Intratreatment criteria predicted from the personality theory under investigation, rather than the clinical goal of external change, then rightly became the major interest. Within the relatively fixed notions of traditional approaches to behavior modification, such process investigations were considered necessary, first, in order to identify the "important" variables before evaluations could be meaningful (Hoch, 1964) and, second, because "good" theories of treatment and personality were expected to go hand in hand (Luborsky & Strupp, 1962).

While all the above difficulties surrounding the active behavior modification research of the 1950s resulted in little more substantial knowledge than in previous eras (Eysenck, 1961), the field as a whole profited. The few systematic attempts at evaluation resulted in a clearer statement of the necessities and means of controlling extraneous variables (Frank, 1966). The first APA conference (Rubinstein & Parloff, 1959) provided the opportunity for research workers to see the extent to which preconceived notions were directing research away from progress, and to identify the major areas where ambiguity existed. The focus of interest again returned to methodology, resulting in some clarification of the criterion problem in particular (Zax & Klein, 1960; Luborsky & Strupp, 1962), and in a sharpening of the variables which had to be considered in behavior modification research (Strupp & Luborsky, 1962). The second APA conference (Strupp & Luborsky, 1962) also revealed some "loosening" of traditional "school" fixations and of the mystique surrounding "psychotherapy," with broadening limits of tolerance for divergent approaches to the study and practice of behavior modification. Although the general state of behavior modification research in the early 1960s has been characterized as "chaotic" (Colby, 1964), it has resulted in the open communication of principles and methods of research to groups which had not been reached before (e.g., Hoch & Zubin, 1964; Lesse, 1964). The distinction between process and outcome has been clarified by Greenhouse (1964) in noting that the importance of "process" research for behavior modification is not a function of personality theory but a function of the relationship of process variables to outcome.

THE STATUS OF BEHAVIOR MODIFICATION RESEARCH: MID-1960s

Active scientific pursuit of knowledge concerning behavior modification has now passed its twentieth anniversary, and the minimal requirements of research design and controls have been present in the literature for over fifteen years. It thus becomes discouraging to see the status of behavior modification research in the mid-1960s correctly summarized as: "The present state of our knowledge is such that strong doubts can be expressed about virtually all psychological practices. Virtually none of them rest upon a firmly verified foundation of knowledge" (Bordin, 1966). Even though the early 1960s have seen increasing sophistication in the design and conduct of a few studies on behavior modification, the slight impact of behavior modification research is evident when Shlien (1966) points out that, "Continued subscription is based upon personal conviction, investment, and observation rather than upon general evidence." A careful reading of Eysenck's third review of the outcome literature and the numerous attendant discussion papers (Eysenck, 1966) forcefully emphasizes the truth of the statements of both Bordin and Shlien. Voices from the past are still heard with emotional polemics based upon belief and opinion. Inculcated with traditional views, some even suggest that behavior modification research cannot be accomplished (e.g., Hyman & Berger, 1966). Others point out that the continued promulgation of specific approaches to behavior modification in the absence of scientific evidence constitutes a kind of cult (Davidson, 1966); indeed, these charges are not unlike the ones leveled by Hoche over fifty-five years ago, and it is likely that they result from the existence of similar factors (Patrick & Bassoe, 1910).

However, behavior modification research in the mid-1960s stands on a new frontier with a much more solid foundation than current achievements suggest. Traditional "blinders" are more openly challenged, e.g., "It is high time that we cease molding patients to certain stock theories and techniques. To the contrary, theory and technique must reflect the truths and realities of today and tomorrow" (Lesse, 1966). Two important books have appeared which place behavior modification research in the mainstream of the psychology of behavior influence, not only conceptually but empirically (Goldstein et al., 1966; Krasner & Ullmann, 1965). Articles on research methods which are theoretically bound have been more clearly stated (see Hoch & Zubin, 1964; Gottschalk & Auerbach, 1966). In addition to the identification, clarification, and partial solution of research problems and obstacles to progress contributed by the two conferences of the APA (Rubinstein & Parloff, 1959; Strupp & Luborsky, 1962), two books of readings have appeared which reprint the classic papers on methodological principles and design for behavior modification research (Goldstein & Dean, 1966; Stollak, Guerney, & Rothberg, 1966). General considerations of the principles of research on clinical problems (Holt, 1965), and the specific concerns for necessary design and control operations in behavior modification research have been clearly stated (Campbell & Stanley, 1966; Frank, 1966; Goldstein et al., 1966; Paul, 1966). In addition, both the major errors and faults of previous behavior modification research and the justifiable conclusions to be included in future research have been summarized (Bergin, 1966; Farnsworth, 1966; Kiesler, 1966). In other words, the scientific era in behavior modification research to the mid-1960s has resulted in the identification and clarification of the methodological and sociological obstacles of the past, and has provided a firm methodological foundation on which future investigations may build. In fact, the number and nature of the books and articles that appeared in 1965 and 1966, as well as the present volume, suggest that the stage is set for a new era in behavior modification research, if it is not already under way—namely, the experimental era.

Scientific Research and Behavior Modification

It seems generally agreed (e.g., Strupp, 1960) that all scientific research consists of a special way of answering questions such that the knowledge obtained, and the *means* by which the knowledge was obtained, are public, demonstrable, reproducible, and communicable. The basic purpose of all psychological research has been succinctly stated by Underwood (1957) as the discovery of phenomena (i.e., behavioral events or changes), the variables which affect them, and the lawfulness of the effects—in other words, the establishment of cause-effect relationships. The essence of scientific research is, then, experimental method in which the effects of variables (phenomena) upon other variables (phenomena) are observed through manipulation and selection. Underwood further points out that sound and precise experimentation does not hinge on knowing all relevant variables in advance; in fact, it is precisely through the manipulation of variables whose influence upon a given phenomenon is unknown that relevant variables are likely to be identified. Research design provides the basic vehicle for obtaining such scientifically valid knowledge, and there is really only one principle of design: the experiment should be designed so that the effects of the independent variables can be evaluated unambiguously. However, in order to draw a conclusion about the influence of any given variable, it is necessary that the variable be systematically manipulated alone somewhere in the design (Underwood, 1957).

It is also clear that the scientific status of any given piece of research is not a function of the source of the questions to be answered or the hypotheses to be tested (Holt, 1965; Campbell & Stanley, 1966). While programmatic research which tests hypotheses derived from principles or results of previous research may advance knowledge more systematically, the evaluation of the method and design of a specific investigation is the same whether the questions asked arose from simple curiosity, practical necessity, systematic theory, or previous empirical findings. Distinctions such as "pure" and "applied" or "technological" and "basic" research refer to the source of questions to be answered or the use to be made of the knowledge obtained, but the methods used for the discovery of the phenomena and the establishment of cause-effect relationships are the same. Thus, as Holt (1965) states, "The experimental method is essentially reality testing refined and systematized. . . . It is largely a matter of focusing on answerable questions and of introducing enough controls so that it is possible to trust and understand the answers."

Especially when viewed as but one aspect of the psychology of behavior influence, it seems obvious that the principles and methods of behavior modification research are basically no different from any other experimental design problem. In fact, Goldstein et al. (1966) point out that the classification of a given investigation as behavior modification research often depends upon the stated intent of the investigator to relate the knowledge obtained to the clinical treatment situation. However, the same methodological considerations apply whether the research is related to behavior modification by intent of the investigator or whether the research takes place directly within the clinical context of behavior modification. The major differences are in the greater number and complexity of variables in the latter situation. Similarly, the justification for experimentation on the clinical alteration of behavior is the same as that recently stated for education, ". . . not as a panacea, but rather as the only route to cumulative progress" (Campbell & Stanley, 1966).

As with any scientific research, investigations of behavior modification must fit the design to the questions asked. Historically, behavior modification research has been dichotomized into "process" and "outcome" investigations, depending upon whether questions were asked about the "ultimate" change in clients' behavior after treatment termination (outcome) or about the way in which intratreatment phenomena transpired (process). On the one hand, the process-outcome dichotomy must be seen as a false one to be set aside, since the establishment of solid cause-effect relationships for outcome necessitates the specification of independent variables often considered under "process." On the other hand, "process" may refer to studies designed to answer questions related to determining mechanisms of change or related to testing competing explanatory hypotheses of how changes come about. While experimental operations and designs may focus on both sets of questions concurrently, it is possible and often desirable for behavior modification research to focus on outcome questions without including the necessary operations for identifying mechanisms of change. This distinction relates to problems which are common to all scientific research, but which seem to have been all too frequent in the history of behavior modification—specifically, research errors.

Underwood (1957) defines research errors as discrepancies between what is concluded and what can be concluded as a consequence of the experimental operations. Because behavior modification research is concerned with the use to be made of obtained knowledge in practical application, two major areas for research errors become important. Campbell & Stanley (1966) distinguish these areas in terms of the internal and external validity of experimental design. Internal validity refers to the degree to which plausible rival hypotheses have been ruled out in the design, particularly those resulting from extraneous variables whose effects might be confounded with the independent variables. Underwood terms internal research errors, in which stimulus variables from different classes (environmental, task, subject) are confounded, as "lethal errors" because there is no way that a scientifically meaningful conclusion can be reached from the experimental operations. Without internal validity, whether in behavior modification research or any other area of research, an experiment is uninterpretable. External validity refers to the generalizability of knowledge obtained in a given experiment to different populations of variables. Specifically because the knowledge obtained in behavior modification research is, by definition, eventually directed toward applied technological usage, research errors in the form of overgeneralizations are more dangerous than in many other areas of scientific research. Unlike internal validity, external validity may be established only by additional investigation. While such external errors are unlikely to be "lethal" in the same sense as internal errors, the past history of behavior modification is replete with external errors which may be the logical basis for the cultlike polemics often characteristic of the field.

Many of the sources of both internal and external errors in past behavior modification research have resulted from asking the wrong questions. Kiesler (1966) has summarized this evidence under what he calls "uniformity assumption myths." It boils down to the fact that nearly all domains of variables are considerably more heterogeneous than our descriptive shorthand labels suggest. Neither independent nor dependent variables are adequately considered and overgeneralization of inadequate data results, because such broad categories are included in questions such as: Does behavior therapy work for neurotics? Does client-centered therapy work for schizophrenics? Does bobe-mycin work for mental illness?

The Domains of Variables in Behavior Modification Research[1]

Before the "right" questions can be asked and appropriate research strategies applied in order to obtain answers, the important domains and classes of

[1] This section draws heavily upon G. L. Paul, The strategy of outcome research in psychotherapy. Psi Chi address presented at the meeting of the Midwestern Psychological Association, Chicago, May, 1966.

variables relevant to behavior modification research must be considered irrespective of theoretical predilections of therapists or investigators. By providing adequate description, measurement, or control operations to each relevant class of variables, both internal and external validity may be more readily identified, consequently allowing for more rapid accumulation of solid empirical knowledge.

Levinson (1962), Krasner (1962a, 1962c), and Kiesler (1966) have considered in detail the domains of variables of importance in psychotherapy research. While behavior modification is not restricted to features characteristic of psychotherapy, the classes of variables which have been identified are essentially identical, and the structure and terms associated with psychotherapy will be used for convenience of reference.

CLIENTS

The major essential ingredient in behavior modification research is the presence of one or more clients to be treated. Depending upon the particular context, clients may be called subjects, patients, students, inmates, and so forth. The client domain may be separated into three logical classes of variables to be considered in research and practice.

Distressing Behaviors. Clients will come to treatment in order to obtain "help" in changing some aspect of their behavior which they, or someone else, find distressing. This distressing behavior may be motoric, autonomic and emotional, or it may be cognitive and ideational. Both the number and the nature of distressing behaviors may vary within an individual client and across clients, and may change over a period of time. This class of variables, then, includes the full range of problems which the human organism may present for treatment, from impotence to tangential thought. While variables within this class may be treated as independent variables in behavior modification research, change in variables within the class must always be included as dependent variables.

Relatively Stable Personal-Social Characteristics. Clients will also vary on a broad range of characterisics such as sex, age, intelligence, socioeconomic background, extroversion, and anxiety. They may also vary on relatively stable characteristics directly related to treatment, such as motivation and expectancies. This class of variables includes the full range of individual differences for clients, excluding the distressing behaviors which bring them to treatment. As such, variables within this class may interact with variables from other domains and classes, and may be treated as independent variables, described and controlled, or may be treated as dependent variables.

Physical-Social Life Environment.   Clients will seldom spend all, or even a major part of, their time in the treatment context, and the environments in which they spend their lives will vary greatly. The nature of clients' life environment, including family, friends, work situation, and use of drugs, may present assets or liabilities for change in distressing behaviors. Additionally, variables in this class may set the time or place for the occurrence of distressing behaviors, and may therefore become directly related to treatment. This class of variables includes essentially all the intercurrent life experiences impinging upon the client outside of the treatment situation. Since, historically, variables within this class have caused problems of confounding, they usually present a problem of control. They might also be treated as independent variables by selection or manipulation and occasionally as dependent variables. However, it should be noted that, by definition, programs which are directed at behavior modification through manipulation of certain variables in the clients' environment remove those variables from this class and place them in one of the following classes.

THERAPISTS

The other essential ingredient in behavior modification research is the presence of one or more therapists to do the treating. It is within the therapist domain that most divergence from traditional practices may be found in the future. *Therapist* as used here refers to the "behavior modifier," which in the usual context means the single individual who conducts one-to-one or one-to-group treatment. However, *therapist* may also be used collectively to refer to a treatment staff of a hospital ward, or even to nonpersonal behavior modifiers such as computers, tape recorders, or vending machines. The essential feature defining this domain is that the therapist is the agent through which behavior modification is to occur. The therapist domain may also be separated into three logical classes of variables to be considered in research and practice.

Therapeutic Techniques.   Therapists use specific therapeutic techniques through which they attempt to alleviate or change the distressing behavior of the client. The therapeutic techniques may be discrete, specific actions or a complex series of actions and strategies. They may vary in number and nature, and they may change over specified periods of time in relation to other variables. This class of variables, then, includes the full range of procedures which might be used in an attempt to change clinical behavior from the automated disbursement of a gum ball to the standard conduct of classical psychoanalysis. While variables within this class may be treated as dependent variables in behavior modification research, they are nearly always treated as the independent variable of most pertinent interest.

Relatively Stable Personal-Social Characteristics. Therapists may also vary on a broad range of personal and social characteristics, including those on which clients may vary. Therapists may also vary on a number of characteristics related to treatment, such as experience, prestige, confidence, "conditions" established, and "school" of therapeutic theory. When the "therapist" is a mechanical device, physical characteristics may become even more important variables; and personal-social characteristics may become "variable" with the presence or absence of a person. When the "therapist" is a group of staff members, the characteristics of the group as well as individual members may also become important variables. This class of variables includes the full range of individual differences for therapists, excluding the therapeutic techniques designed to modify behavior. As such, variables within this class may be treated as independent variables, described and controlled, and occasionally treated as dependent variables.

Physical-Social Treatment Environment. The environments in which given therapists or treatments operate may also vary over broad ranges. The nature of the institutional setting, whether home, school, office, clinic, hospital, battle-field, or some other place, may also interact with other classes of variables. Characteristics such as public-private, fee–no-fee, and new-old may produce effects or may affect other variables. Within the usual range of practices, variables in this class may be relatively less important than those in other classes; however, they can be quite important and should definitely be described. They may also be treated as independent variables, controlled, and occasionally treated as dependent variables.

TIME

The third major domain in behavior modification research is time. Although time is typically treated as a task variable in experimental research, it is separated here for expository purposes because, in addition to task variation, certain events in time mark points of research focus. The important events in time for behavior modification research may be delineated in relation to client-therapist contact as the following: (1) initial client contact, (2) pretreatment, (3) treatment, initial structuring, (4) treatment, main application, (5) treatment, termination, (6) posttreatment, (7) follow-up. As a task variable, time may vary within and between each of the periods listed above; it may be treated as a set of independent or dependent variables, or it may be described and controlled. As points of research focus marked in time, the questions asked in behavior modification research will determine the importance of assessment within and between each of these periods, as well as the importance of variables within each domain or class for any given time period.

CRITERIA

Since, by definition, behavior modification research is concerned with the clinical goal of treatment, the criteria of treatment effectiveness become an important consideration. The definition of dependent variables at some level of quantification is a necessary part of any piece of scientific research. Additionally, specification or assessment of variables within each of the above classes, with acceptable reliability and validity, is no less important for behavior modification research than is the specification and assessment of outcome criteria; however, the degree of confusion surrounding the "criterion problem" in the past justifies its consideration as a separate "domain."

Historically, lack of agreement on criteria among clients, therapists, and investigators has been the rule (Parloff & Rubinstein, 1959). The appropriate time, place, and instrumental focus for assessment have varied so broadly that little agreement has occurred within a single investigation, let alone across investigations (Cartwright, Kirtner, & Fiske, 1963; Luborsky & Strupp, 1962; Zax & Klein, 1960). The major basis for this difficulty in the past appears to result from the different frames of reference utilized by persons in different roles for assessing change. Most criteria have been selected from some theoretical frame of reference without regard to the variability of clients and problems. Theoretically derived criteria may be unrelated or only partially related when the guiding theories differ. Similarly, criteria derived from theory seldom coincide with the clients' frame of reference since few clients enter treatment with a request to reduce their "self-ideal discrepancy," to increase their "conditionability," or to become a "genital personality." Nor are clients or society directly concerned with intratherapy changes per se, unless these changes are related to the clients' behavior and functioning outside the treatment setting.

It seems, then, that the major criteria of effectiveness for behavior modification must also be established outside theoretical boundaries. Logically and ethically, the practical aspects of behavior modification require that the criteria of effectiveness depend upon the purpose of treatment. Since the purpose of treatment—in fact, the basis for existence of the field—is to help with the problems for which help was asked, the real question of effectiveness is whether or not the distressing behaviors which brought the clients to treatment have changed in the desired direction without producing new problems (Astin, 1961; Battle, Imber, Hoehn-Saric, Stone, Nash, & Frank, 1966; Betz, 1962; Ewing, 1964; Ford, 1959; Hoppock, 1953; Rickard, 1965). Second, since the distressing behaviors were brought into treatment, the most important and meaningful test of effectiveness is the change in the clients' distressing behavior outside treatment (Luborsky & Strupp, 1962). The *minimum* requirement for any experiment on behavior modification, therefore, is that the dependent variables include change in the clients' distressing behaviors from pretreatment to posttreatment, assessed external to treatment proper. Specific questions may direct assessments to other time periods, or to additional dependent variables; however, the importance and relevance of any other variable or procedure for behavior modification research must be a function of its relationship to this change (see Goldstein & Dean, 1966; Goldstein et al., 1966; Greenhouse, 1964; Paul, 1966).

Traditionally, status at long-term follow-up has been considered the appropriate time period for evaluation of behavior modification procedures (Sargent, 1960). However, recent writers (Goldstein et al., 1966; May, Tuma, & Kraude, 1965; Stone, Frank, Nash, & Imber, 1961; Paul, 1968) have begun to question the "follow-up dogma" on the basis of the inherent methodological problems involving differential dropout of clients and instrument errors which prevent meaningful assessment. Additionally, these investigators point out that the longer the intervening time between posttreatment and follow-up assessments, the greater the influence of intercurrent life experiences in relation to the influence of therapeutic procedures. While the stability of treatment effects is an important question, the length of time between treatment termination and follow-up should be dictated on the basis of the likelihood of "relapse" as determined from pretreatment stability of the distressing behavior. Current evidence suggests that the best general tactic would be relatively short-term follow-ups in which total-sample assessment could be maintained. By assessing change at two or more follow-up periods, trends of "relapse," stability, or continued "improvement" could be determined. However, the follow-up question does not detract from the use of pre-post change in distressing behavior as the criterion for establishing cause-effect relationships—it merely adds further information.

Instruments.   Although the means of specifying or assessing variables in all the above classes is important, the instrumentation for assessing the nature and degree of distressing behavior and change is of prime concern, since no other factors are intelligible without adequate assessment of effectiveness. Loevinger (1965) points out that what the methodologists should contribute to assessment is ". . . not a bag of statistical tricks, but the habit of rigorous and precise thought and a sense of where to look for errors that bias the result." The major considerations of desirable measurement characteristics, sources of bias, and most promising approaches have been presented in the literature (see Campbell & Stanley, 1966; Cartwright, Kirtner, & Fiske, 1963; Cronbach, 1960; Eysenck, 1966; Farnsworth, 1966; Harris, 1963; Zax & Klein, 1960).

Lehmann (1964) points out that people represent not only "unstable systems" in the sense of undergoing changes in time, but "responsive systems" in relation to stimuli, and "transactional systems" in relation to each other. Because of these characteristics, subjective reports or ratings of change by involved participants (clients and therapists) have been notoriously biased. Similarly, obvious paper-and-pencil tests are open to deception, and external observers may be biased by knowledge of treatment, or may change in "calibration" over time. Intratherapy measures and subtle tests, such as projective techniques, must derive validity from their relationship to external behavior, and thus are inadequate at the present stage of development.

While methodologists generally agree that the least used but most desirable measures are objective behavioral criteria external to the treatment situation, progress has been slow in the development of such assessment instruments. Guidelines for specific criteria may, however, be obtained by considering the process which leads an individual to contact a therapist: He does something, under a set of circumstances, which disturbs someone sufficiently that action results—he enters treatment (Ullmann & Krasner, 1969). The "something" he does consists of the distressing behaviors which lead him to treatment. However, since the distressing behaviors occur under a "set of circumstances," it does not seem necessary to attempt measurement of change "in general" or under *all* circumstances. Rather, assessment can and should be more or less specific regarding time and situation. Such "work-sample" assessments for selected target behaviors then become more feasible and appear to be the most meaningful. Many distressing behaviors may be ideational or affective behaviors which show few external referents other than the client's own verbalizations. In these instances, questionnaires or paper-and-pencil tests can be desirable assessment instruments; however, it seems profitable to delineate specificity to time and situation for such instruments, as well as to include validity scales to determine the possibility of faking or bias. Other types of instruments which have been used include social action and performance effects, physiological measures, and behavioral frequencies.

Although the field sorely needs the development of standard assessment instruments of this type, current methodology is sufficient to provide a broad range of reliable, unbiased, external criterion-assessment techniques. However, at our current state of knowledge, there appears to be little question that multiple instruments are required in order to establish the validity of assessment within and between investigations. Additionally, due to the "reactive" and "transactional" nature of the subjects of behavior modification research, care must be taken to control for instrument errors. These would include the possible changes in "calibration" over time, and relevant knowledge of the experimental period or treatment condition, mentioned above, when using observers or raters. Instrument errors could also come about through unknown effects of repeated testing, unless appropriate controls are included. "Statistical" regression is a further possible instrument error which is always present in behavior modification research since the focus of interest is on deviant members of the population.

THE QUESTIONS TO BE ANSWERED

Delineating the domains and classes of variables, and specifying the criteria of effectiveness, as above, the ultimate questions to be answered in behavior modification research appear to be: What treatment, by whom, is most effective for this individual with that specific problem, under which set of circumstances, and how does it come about?

Posed in this manner, it seems obvious that no single study will ever be able to answer the ultimate question. Further, for meaningful knowledge to accumulate across studies, it will be necessary for every investigation to specify the aspect of the question for which answers are sought, and to describe, measure, or control in an adequate manner each of the classes of variables identified above.

Research Design and Possible Level of Product

Given the questions to be asked and the classes of variables involved, the means of obtaining answers or partial answers becomes a problem of design and tactics. In view of the complexity of the variables, and the past history of inappropriate design in behavior modification research, concern must be directed to the *possible* level of product which may be obtained through different levels of design. Several volumes are available on general experimental design and principles of research (e.g., Edwards, 1960; Holt, 1965; Sidman, 1960; Underwood, 1957); however, concern here is with those designs which are of most importance to behavior modification research, through either frequency or desirability of application.

The possible level of product of a design refers primarily to the internal validity of an investigation and, consequently, to uncontrolled sources of influence or confounding. Campbell & Stanley (1966), Frank (1966), Goldstein et al. (1966), and Paul (1966) have all recently considered various aspects of experimental design with direct relevance for behavior modification research, and the following discussion draws heavily on these sources.

In considering the possible level of product obtainable, it is assumed here that reliable and valid assessment of the clients' distressing behaviors has been obtained, even though the establishment of instrument validity may have to take place through multiple-method measures within the study. The "retrospective study" which appears from time to time in the literature may be largely discounted on this basis alone, since a search of clinical records to obtain description or "measurement" of variables nearly always precludes adequate, unbiased assessment due to the nature of the data source. Additionally, while the rationale of retrospective studies may be the same as that of planned prospective experiments, the inherent methodological problems are so nearly insurmountable that the field would likely profit by their absence (see Underwood, 1957).

INDIVIDUAL CASE STUDY

Though the individual case study, characterized by uncontrolled observation without measurement, was the traditional approach of the past (Bolgar, 1965), such studies have essentially no formal scientific value. The basis of scientific evidence always involves making at least one comparison. In the individual case study without measurement, these comparisons are between uncontrolled assumptions about all aspects of the client and therapist domains, and similarly uncontrolled assumptions about what would have happened in the absence of therapeutic intervention. Without measurement at some level, even the comparison of change remains an assumption which limits the level of product to the development of crude hypotheses.

By introducing assessment, at least at pretreatment and posttreatment, some basis of comparison is introduced into the individual case study. However, the establishment of cause-effect relationships is still precluded because of the absence of control over alternative sources of influence upon any observed change in the clients' distressing behavior. Many of these sources of influence compose "lethal errors" in the Underwood sense of confounding between classes of variables. The major source of interdomain confounding consists of the possibility of extratreatment events in the clients' physical-social life environment producing change in the distressing behaviors. Similarly, "spontaneous" fluctuations of biological or psychological processes within the client remain uncontrolled sources of influence. These fluctuations might occur in the distressing target behaviors themselves, or in relatively stable personal-social characteristics which interact with or otherwise influence the distressing behaviors. The longer the period of time between assessment periods, the more plausible do these errors become.

Intradomain confounding, though less lethal, similarly prevents the establishment of cause-effect relationships for specific treatment techniques in the individual case study with pre-post measurement. The major source of error in this respect is the possible confounding of the effects of the therapists' relatively stable personal-social characteristics with the effects of the therapeutic techniques assumed to produce change. A related source of error is the ubiquitous placebo effect. The placebo effect refers to the client's responsiveness to additional attention received and his resulting "faith" in the occurrence of change. This responsiveness and faith are inherent in any contact pertaining to behavior modification and are hence termed *nonspecific effects*. Nonspecific responsiveness constitutes a plausible source of influence in the individual case study in two ways: (1) unknown and uncontrolled effects of testing or assessment and (2) unknown and uncontrolled effects of merely "being treated." Since all potential instrument errors also remain uncontrolled in the pre-post case study, change in calibration over time and statistical regression are highly plausible bases for any assumed change in target behaviors, and bias from knowledge of treatment conditions is nearly impossible to rule out in this approach.

Additional limitations are placed on the pre-post case study by the fact that no direct comparisons are available for establishing definitions of domains, classes of variables, or the skill of the therapist within the study. The skill of the therapist can be assessed by careful description or rating procedures; however, the possibility of interactions between classes remains uncontrolled, and selection bias or differential client attrition appear to be inherent sources of possible error in any single-subject approach. The result of all of these uncontrolled sources of error is that the pre-post case study design cannot establish any cause-effect relationship in isolation but may, through the introduction of measurement, result in strengthened hypotheses.

There are two variations on the individual case study which introduce enough additional controls over the simple pre-post design that Campbell and Stanley refer to them as "quasi-experimental designs." These are the *time-series design* and the *equivalent time-samples design*. The time-series design is a form of "own-control," in which multiple assessment is made both before and after the treatment period—at a minimum, corresponding to initial contact, pretreatment, posttreatment, and follow-up, with equal time periods between assessments. To the extent that changes in the dependent variables occur only after the introduction of treatment, with stability of multiple-assessment periods before and after treatment, statistical regression and changes in instrument calibration over time become less plausible sources of error. Similarly, nonspecific reactions to testing per se become less plausible influences, although the possibility is introduced that multiple testing itself may influence the effectiveness of treatment procedures. Spontaneous fluctuations within the client also become less plausible to the extent that pretreatment and posttreatment time series are stable. Additionally, to the extent that the pretreatment time series extends over extremely long periods in which other treatments have been attempted repeatedly (i.e., chronic cases), the nonspecific placebo effect becomes less plausible, but cannot be ruled out. The carefully done time-series case study thus has several advantages over the pre-post case study; however, the lethal possibility of confounding by extratreatment life events remains, as do intradomain confounding of therapist characteristics and techniques, and client characteristics and target behaviors. Possible assessment error resulting from knowledge of treatment conditions still exists, as do the inherent errors of any single-subject approach. The additional control of the time-series design does result in further strengthening of hypotheses and in a level of product suggesting correlational conclusions but not cause-effect conclusions.

The equivalent time-samples design may be viewed as an extension of the time-series design with multiple applications of treatment. One form of the equivalent time-samples design entails the alternation of treatment and no-treatment periods with a minimum of two assessments between each treatment application—posttreatment and pretreatment. The second form is the A-B-A own-control design, in which the target behavior is repeatedly altered first in one direction and then in the other, contingent upon application of therapeutic techniques with concurrent measurement within the treatment period. If the time periods for treatment application are sufficiently short and are essentially random to rule out seasonal or cyclical variations in extratreatment environmental events, this design may render unlikely any rival explanation of change based upon the coincidence of environmental variables, as well as the sources of error controlled in the time-series design. However, in addition to the possibility of multiple testing influencing the effectiveness of treatment procedures, multiple-treatment application may also influence its effectiveness. Thus, while strong additional controls are introduced by this design, confounding within the client and therapist domains remains a problem, as do all the inherent difficulties of a single-subject approach. Within the limits imposed by the single-subject approach in isolation, the equivalent time-samples case study provides the strongest hypotheses of cause-effect relationships between domains which can be obtained with the product level of correlational conclusions.

NONFACTORIAL SINGLE-GROUP DESIGN

The nonfactorial single-group design may be thought of, essentially, as a combination of case studies. Consequently, all the above discussion concerning problems and designs in the case study approach apply to the single-group design, except for the fact that the number of replications is greater than one. The presence of replications, however, increases confidence in the reliability of a finding to the extent that the level of product may be increased a step for each variation of the design. Thus, all sources of error and confounding present in the pre-post case study are present for the single group of clients with assessment before and after treatment, except that the selection bias and pretreatment differential attrition are less likely. By including a number of clients or problems in the study, comparisons within this class of variables become possible, with the result that correlational conclusions may be reached within the client domain, and hypotheses concerning treatment effects may be further strengthened. However, due to the lethal errors still present in this design, no cause-effect relationships can be established as a product.

The time-series design over a group of clients or problems similarly shares the advantages, disadvantages, and potential experimental errors of the time-series case study, except for the addition of replications. Like the pre-post group design above, pretreatment selection biases and differential attrition are less likely, and to the extent that the time-series design shows reliable change across clients in the group, correlational conclusions may be reached with regard to the effects of treatment contact. However, confounding both within and between domains and classes of variables, and the other potential errors of the time-series case study, remain such that the level of product does not allow establishment of cause-effect relationships. Hypotheses may be strengthened, however, as individual studies move across classes of variables.

The equivalent time-samples group design, especially the A-B-A own-control type of design, shares the advantages of the above single-group designs. Further, when it is reliably demonstrated that behavioral changes across clients are temporally contingent upon the therapeutic procedures, especially when the time periods for these changes vary between clients, the influence of extraexperimental events becomes highly unlikely, and cause-effect relationships between gross domains may be established. As long as sufficient time-series assessments are included before and after the treatment period, most instrumental errors may be evaluated; however, possible bias from knowledge of treatment conditions remains, as do the possible biasing effects of multiple application of testing and treatment. Similarly, confounding within the therapist and client domains, as well as nonspecific placebo effects, remains uncontrolled, with the result that specific cause-effect relationships cannot be established for client or therapist characteristics or for specific therapeutic techniques. Correlational conclusions may be obtained for more specific variables, and these hypotheses may be strengthened as the equivalent time-samples design moves across different classes of variables in separate studies. It is important to note that a carefully executed equivalent time-samples design appears to be the only nonfactorial design which can establish any cause-effect relationship without the inclusion of control groups.

NONFACTORIAL GROUP DESIGN WITH UNTREATED CONTROLS

The nonfactorial design in which one group of clients receives treatment while an equivalent group does not, with both groups assessed before and after the treatment period, constitutes the classical "true experiment." This design maintains its status due to the fact that the inclusion of the equated untreated group so neatly controls for lethal errors when the experiment is properly constructed. Extraexperimental environmental events and fluctuations in biological or psychological processes over time which might effect target behaviors should be manifested equally in treatment and control groups when the time periods are concurrent. Similarly, any reactive effects of undergoing assessment, change in instrument calibration over time, or statistical regression should affect both groups equally. The latter characteristics point out an advantage of this design over the single-group time-samples design, which would allow identification of instrument errors, but would not allow adequate assessment of effects when such errors were present. The pre-post control-group design provides a base line for assessing change over and above such effects even when they are present. An additional advantage of the control-group design is that knowledge of treatment conditions may be ruled out as a source of bias by keeping assessors or scorers unaware of clients' status as members of the treatment or the control group. The major potential error inherent in the pre-post control-group design is differential attrition between the treatment and control groups which would destroy their equivalence. However, the design explicitly allows for the identification of differential attrition, and the probability of control-group attrition may be lowered by combining the time-series design with the current design in such a way that the "waiting period" for later treatment provides the untreated group for current investigation.

The level of product possible with the pre-post control-group design does allow the establishment of cause-effect relationships between domains which rule out lethal errors. However, specific cause-effect relationships cannot be established concerning therapist characteristics separate from treatment techniques, client characteristics separate from distressing behaviors, or specific therapeutic variables as distinct from nonspecific placebo effects, since confounding of variables within the therapist domain and interactions are not controlled. Nonspecific placebo effects can be partially controlled by combining the time-series or equivalent time-samples design with the control-group design, thus establishing a stable base line of nonresponsiveness to previous treatments. Another possible source of error in the pre-post control-group design is that pretesting may influence response to treatment. This source of error actually relates to external validity rather than internal validity, and seems to have been of more concern than necessary for behavior modification research, since nearly all treatment conditions should include a pretest in order to determine the appropriate class and level of behaviors to be modified and, someday, the appropriate technique. However, if there is serious concern about the influence of a pretest, Campbell and Stanley provide two modifications of the nonfactorial control-group design that make possible avoiding or assessing this effect. The first modification is the posttest-only design, in which clients are randomly assigned to treatment and control groups, but assessed only at the posttreatment period. The major problem with this design is that equivalence of the two groups is not established prior to the treatment period. While complete randomization may theoretically establish equivalence, the number of clients required to do so would normally be prohibitive for behavior modification research. In addition, the posttest-only design may not allow for identification of differential attrition between groups, and it provides less precise information on the production of changes. The second modification is the

Solomon Four-Group Design which combines the pre-post control-group design and the posttest-only design into a single study. The latter alternative appears more practical, and also more sensitive for behavior modification research when there is a serious question concerning a testing by treatment interaction.

An important point with regard to the level of product with any control-group design, is to be aware of what the "control group" controls for. The level of product and reduction of experimental error obtained through the pre-post control-group design is a function of the *equivalence* of the treatment and control groups on relevant factors. For behavior modification research, it appears that equivalence must be assured on at least the level and class of target behavior and client motivation to change, with other characteristics and classes of variables within the client and environmental domains assigned equivalence to the extent of randomization. To the extent that "control groups" systematically differ from treatment groups on any characteristic, the precision of control is lost. This is especially important with regard to "normal controls" who deviate both in motivation and level of target behavior, since these individuals would not be expected to change over time, to show statistical regression effects, or to be as responsive to environmental events. The normal control may provide interesting data concerning the degree of approximation or divergence from the "norm" before and after treatment, but cannot provide the necessary experimental controls.

All the preceding discussion with regard to the nonfactorial pre-post control-group design applies equally well to studies in which the second group constitutes another treatment group rather than an untreated control group; however, the level of product is lower. If differences were found between two treatment groups, cause-effect relationships could not be established, since in addition to intradomain confounding, two alternatives would exist: One group "got better," or one group "got worse." Without the no-treatment control group, these alternative hypotheses could not be distinguished. The results would be of even less value if no differences between treatment groups were obtained, since a third alternative—no change over base-rate improvement— would be possible. The necessity of including untreated control groups for establishing base-rate improvement for the client population under consideration is particularly important since the "two-thirds improvement without treatment," which has been perpetuated, is both without foundation (see Kiesler, 1966) and empirically incorrect in given populations (Paul, 1967). The addition of more than one treatment group to a nonfactorial pre-post control-group design might aid in clarification and might lead to the addition of more correlational conclusions concerning the effects of specific variables, just as would additional studies over different variables and classes. However, the level of cause-effect products would remain the same due to confounding within domains.

FACTORIAL GROUP DESIGN WITH UNTREATED
AND NONSPECIFIC-TREATMENT CONTROLS

It should be clear by this point that the only design which offers the possibility of establishing cause-effect relationships for even complex variables within classes in behavior modification research is the factorial group design. This is the case because the important classes of variables for behavior modification research are so closely intertwined that the only way a given variable can be "systematically manipulated alone somewhere in the design" is through the factorial representation of the variables of interest in combination with appropriate controls. Actually, there is no single factorial design for behavior modification research, but rather as many and as complex designs as are required by the number and nature of the questions asked. The basic model of the factorial design starts with the pre-post control-group design, and factors, "levels" of factors, and groups are added as required by the nature of the cause-effect relationships to be investigated. Therefore, all sources of error which are controlled in the design discussed above are also controlled in the factorial study with an untreated control group. Additional control groups and assessments may be added as necessitated by the questions asked of the design. The crucial feature for such "novel" control groups is that the specific or complex aspect of a given variable occur at one or more levels in treatment groups, that it not occur in the control group, and that all other features occur in both treatment and control groups.

Intradomain confounding in nonfactorial designs prevents the establishment of cause-effect relationships for specific treatments or sets of therapeutic techniques as distinct from the effects of therapist characteristics and nonspecific placebo effects of "undergoing treatment." Specific cause-effect relationships and interactions for each of these classes of variables may be evaluated in the factorial design by the inclusion of another equated group of clients to receive "pseudotreatment" or an "attention-placebo" procedure which includes all the nonspecific aspects of "treatment" except for the therapeutic techniques to be evaluated. A number of therapists or groups of therapists differing on relatively stable personal-social characteristics may then be factorially represented both in the "real-treatment" and "pseudotreatment" groups. Thus the overall (main) effects of levels or types of therapist characteristics, of attention-placebo conditions, and of the specific complex of therapeutic techniques may be evaluated, and interactions between these classes of variables may also be determined. Similarly, the interactions and differential effects of treatment variables may be separated for different types or levels of distressing target behavior and for different types or levels of relatively stable personal-social characteristics of clients by selecting independent variables and forming experimental and control groups to represent the classes of variables factorially.

While the factorial design provides the level of product to establish cause-effect relationships for all classes of variables, the design does not need to undertake such a task. An additional advantage of the factorial design lies in the fact that it can also control for the influence of classes of variables within domains in order to establish cause-effect relationships for specific sets of variables and parameters, unconfounded by variables which are not of direct interest in a given study. For example, if the question to be answered is concerned with determining cause-effect relationships for treatment techniques, but not for therapist characteristics per se, the latter class of variables may be controlled by making therapist characteristics as heterogeneous as possible within treatment groups, but equated across treatment and pseudotreatment groups. The same procedure may be followed for any class of variables to which a specific question is not directed; however, since all classes of variables described earlier may influence the results of behavior modification research, information is lost when any class is controlled rather than manipulated. Because controls are less than perfect, especially when dealing with the small samples necessitated in behavior modification research, assessment and description of classes of variables not treated as independent variables should be the rule. The latter procedure then may provide the basis for correlational analyses which can rule out the influence of extraneous factors, or provide hypotheses concerning potential parameters of classes of variables to be experimentally tested in future studies.

Since the factorial design with untreated and nonspecific controls does allow analytical cause-effect relationships to be derived for specific sets of variables, it may also be used to test hypotheses concerning the mechanisms of change—"how" change comes about. Because of the nature and complexity of the variables in the behavior modification context, such a factorial design appears to be the lowest-level design which may unambiguously provide the necessary analytical information for testing empirical or theoretical hypotheses about mechanisms of change in the real-life situation. It should be noted, however, that the complexity of a factorial design, whether directed towards applied technological or basic theoretical aspects of the ultimate question, does not relieve the necessity for the final criterion of knowledge to rest on replication of findings over different contexts, instruments, and investigations.

LABORATORY-BASED DESIGNS

The standard of scientific research and experimentation has always been the laboratory-based study in which cause-effect relationships may be established as a result of the precision of experimental isolation, manipulation, and control of relevant variables. As such, investigations conducted in the laboratory are not limited to a single design, but provide for designs which allow the highest level of possible product in terms of establishing analytical cause-effect relationships for specific, precisely defined variables. Because of the complexity of the classes of variables and because of ethical considerations, many aspects of the ultimate question to be answered by behavior modification research are impossible or unfeasible to undertake directly in the clinical context. Control of many potential research errors and extraneous variables may be obtained in the laboratory through isolation, in which classes of variables are controlled by their absence or exclusion. Other classes of variables may be controlled through greater precision of measurement and regulation of antecedent conditions. Further clarity may be achieved by experimentation on variables or classes of variables which are less complex, but analogous to those involved in the clinical context of behavior modification. The latter feature of laboratory-based behavior modification research has led to the use of *experimental analog* as a descriptive term for the general approach.

Nowhere is the relationship between behavior modification research and the broader psychology of behavior influence more clear than in the desirable intercourse between the experimental-analog approach and research approaches within the clinical context (see Goldstein et al., 1966; Krasner & Ullmann, 1965; Ullmann & Krasner, 1965). As indicated earlier, the scientific status of any given investigation is not a function of the source of hypotheses tested, or the use of the knowledge obtained. Thus, laboratory research in the area of behavior influence may contribute a substantial body of knowledge on techniques, principles, and processes of changing behavior without reference to clinical behavior modification. However, these studies become "experimental analogs" or "behavior modification research" to the extent that generality across classes of variables have implications for or relevance to the alteration of deviant or distressing clinical behavior.

Goldstein (1966) suggests three ways in which laboratory-based investigations may have implications for clinical behavior modification: selection, prediction, and explanation. Laboratory studies have implications for the selection of specific variables for investigation in the behavior modification context to the extent that they have been isolated as prominent factors in other contexts of behavior influence. The findings of nonclinical laboratory studies may provide the bases for predicting relationships in the clinical context, including the prediction that laboratory-derived techniques or principles may be effective in altering clinical behavior in specified ways. As such, the experimental analog may form a solid basis for development of hypotheses to be tested in the context of treatment regarding the influence of new therapeutic techniques, types of therapists, and treatment environments, or the response of different types of clients and target behaviors, as well as the relationship of parameters of variables in all classes and domains. The implications of laboratory studies for explanation in behavior modification refer to the interpretation of research findings. The data and materials presented by Goldstein et al. (1966) and Krasner & Ullmann (1965) make a strong case for laboratory-based findings as the best resource for knowledge on the principles and processes of behavior change, whether the phenomena are derived from established therapeutic practices via "simplification" (e.g., Bordin, 1965), or extended to new findings in the clinical context via "extrapolation" (e.g., Goldstein & Dean, 1966). In fact, the complexity of the variables involved and experimental designs needed to establish the specific cause-effect relationships required to determine probable mechanisms of change suggests that laboratory-based experiments may be the approach of choice in answering questions of "how" behavior modification comes about.

Thus, laboratory-based designs provide the highest level of possible product in behavior modification research—a powerful and economical means for determining specific cause-effect relationships. On the one hand, the generality of particular conclusions from experimental analogs to the real-life behavior modification context must be a function of the degree to which the variables studied in the laboratory share the essential characteristics of the variables in the clinical context. On the other hand, the relevance of findings from experimental analogs for research within the clinical context is a function of the degree to which a basis is provided for selection, prediction, and explanation. As with any test of generalized hypotheses, however, "hard" conclusions concerning the ultimate question for real-life behavior modification must be eventually obtained in the real-life situation.

Tactical Use of Different Levels of Research[2]

Since the ultimate question asked of behavior modification research can never be answered by a single study, and in such research an inverse relationship often exists between level of product and investment of time, money, and personnel, consideration must be given to the need, place, and value of different levels of design and approach. In addition to reliable, unbiased, multiple-measure assessment of change in the clients' distressing (target) behavior outside the treatment situation, it appears that the *minimum* requirement for any investigation in the area should include: (1) specification of the aspect of the ultimate question for which information is sought and (2) adequate definition or description of variables within each class and domain discussed earlier. If these requirements alone were fulfilled, the evaluation of individual studies and comparison of classes of variables and results from one investigation to another, or from research to applied situations, could be sufficiently clear that the cultlike developments of the past and present might be prevented. However, over and above these minimum requirements, continuing series of well-

[2] This section draws heavily upon G. L. Paul, The strategy of outcome research in psychotherapy. Psi Chi address presented at the meeting of the Midwestern Psychological Association, Chicago, May, 1966.

controlled, factorially designed experiments appear to be not only the most efficient way to obtain knowledge relevant to the ultimate question (Edwards & Cronbach, 1952), but probably the only way. Other approaches are needed, both before and after factorial designs with untreated and nonspecific-treatment controls; however, these other approaches must be utilized on the basis of the possible level of product in relation to the degree of knowledge already established with regard to the variables and phenomena concerned.

FACTORIAL DESIGNS

The complexity which could conceivably be introduced into a factorial study with untreated and nonspecific controls is readily apparent. For example, if only two levels or types of variables from each class were to be included, the experiment would have 256 separate cells, requiring 512 clients, 384 of whom would have to be seen in treatment contact by an unreasonable number of therapists. Therefore, even within the factorial study, tactical decisions must be made on the basis of current knowledge and the relative importance of the different domains and classes of variables. The aspect of the ultimate question in a given investigation determines which classes of variables will be treated as independent variables. Thereafter, the tactical decisions essentially boil down to questions of homogeneity within classes. On the basis of the knowledge existent in behavior modification in the mid-1960s, it seems that early studies should focus on establishing the basic phenomena—i.e., cause-effect relationships between treatment techniques and change in distressing behaviors. Once the phenomena are established, additional aspects of the ultimate question for given problem behaviors or treatment procedures may be directly attacked.

Even though change in clients' distressing behavior will aways be involved as a dependent variable, a tactical decision must be made on the selection of such target behaviors. Since the severity of distressing behavior is likely to vary even within a single class (e.g., alcoholism), and resistance to change will probably vary even more between classes (e.g., alcoholism versus insomnia), the current tactical choice appears to favor selection of clients on the same class of target behaviors, perhaps stratified according to severity as an additional variable. Even with client selection on a single type of target behavior, variation may be wide for both additional distressing behaviors and relatively stable personal-social characteristics of clients. While clients can be classified on the basis of these additional factors by treating the factors as independent variables, practical considerations suggest that this may not be the best strategy for early factorial studies (Frank, 1966; Paul, 1966). The same considerations seem to be the case for the physical-social environment of the clients. Rather, at an early stage of experimental research, greater clarity may be obtained by allowing a moderate level of heterogeneity on these classes of variables, with measurement of sufficient strength that correlational analyses with outcome can provide suggestive evidence of possible influencing parameters to sharpen hypotheses concerning independent variables in subsequent studies. Current evidence suggests that groups should be equated on expectancy and motivation for change, unless these characteristics are to be treated as independent variables (Goldstein, 1962; Battle et al., 1966). By allowing a moderate level of heterogeneity in other classes of variables within the client domain, equating groups at least by randomization, description may be made more adequate for comparison across studies, and generalization will not be as restricted as it would with maximum homogeneity in all classes.

The independent variable of most interest in the early factorial study is the treatment procedure or therapeutic technique proposed to be effective in altering the clients' distressing behavior. A tactical decision on homogeneity must also be made here. However, these decisions are complicated due to the fact that most current therapeutic procedures have become well established without a solid research base and, further, have reached the point of being an individual art which varies from one therapist to another. One tactical approach to dealing with the problem of such "old" techniques in the factorial design would be to allow complete flexibility among a group of therapists, with their preferred technique, across several clients with the same distressing behavior, to determine which therapists were reliably effective. After effectiveness was established, audio or video recordings could be examined to determine what the effective therapists did, or further laboratory studies could be conducted with effective therapists as subjects. The difficulty with this approach, even with the same therapists concurrently conducting nonspecific treatments, is that overlap in treatment technique is unknown, and ready comparison to other treatment techniques is not allowed. On the other hand, if each set of treatment techniques were homogeneous within groups across therapists, immediate knowledge of technique effectiveness would be available.

Thus, whether dealing with "old" or "new" treatment techniques, the tactical choice favors homogeneity of treatment technique across therapists. For evaluations of "old" treatments, it would be necessary to obtain a complete statement of technique and to ensure uniformity of relevant aspects through discussion of the essential features among therapists. For "new" treatments, complete elaboration to the extent of written manuals, demonstrations, and "practice" cases seems essential. With both old and new treatment techniques, constant monitoring of the conduct of treatment is needed to ensure appropriate application of techniques. In the absence of constant monitoring, replication of independent variables will not be possible, and evaluation of misapplied procedures tells little. One means of increasing the likelihood of homogeneity of treatment technique would be to provide a single, expert monitor-supervisor for each treatment technique to be evaluated.

Mention should also be made of a related aspect of the application of specific therapeutic techniques which has often been overlooked. This is the nonspecific skill of therapists in establishing a working relationship with clients, within which specific techniques are utilized. Even if the therapist should be a complex body of staff, or a nonhuman device, at some time early in the structuring stage of treatment, a working relationship must be established. Unless the techniques involved in establishing such a relationship are to be treated as independent variables, these nonspecific skills of clinical interaction should be consistent across treatment groups and should be present at a high level, otherwise, intraclass confounding may result (e.g., see Bergin, 1966; Kiesler, 1966). The two usual means of insuring such nonspecific skills are (1) selecting experienced individuals with a reputation for their ability in this regard and (2) training individuals until a common, high level of clinical skill exists prior to the conduct of any given treatment.

Because of the investment of time, money, and personnel required by the factorial study with untreated and nonspecific controls, it appears to be good strategy to obtain maximum usage from these controls by evaluating two or more treatment techniques in the same design. This could be accomplished by extending therapists across more than one therapeutic technique, in addition to the nonspecific treatment, or by introducing different therapists with different techniques into the design, overlapping the conduct of the nonspecific treatment. In either case, main effects may be evaluated for techniques and for therapists, as well as interactions. The tactical choice of treatments to be evaluated in comparative factorial studies should, it seems, also take into account the most promising treatment techniques, and the practicality involved for any given distressing behavior. Usually this choice will involve at least one "old" technique already in use, and one "new" technique which other sources suggest may be more effective. Additionally, if the therapeutic techniques are derived from competing theoretical formulations, a further contribution may be made to basic science, as well as to the ethical-technological aspects.

Therapist characteristics, like client characteristics, may vary widely even when homogeneous treatment techniques are used. The inclusion of a nonspecific treatment group in the factorial study, conducted by the same therapists, allows control for differing effects of variables within this class; however, specific variables within this class may also be treated as independent variables through selection or manipulation. Any study which might attempt to compare machine-conducted treatment with person-conducted treatment would necessitate inclusion of this class as independent variables. However, in other circumstances, the best strategy for early factorial studies, again, appears to be a moderate level of heterogeneity on therapist characteristics such that adequate description could be made for cross-study comparisons without undue restrictions on generalization. Similarly, measurement of therapist characteristics, even if these characteristics are not treated as independent variables, should be strong enough that correlational analyses with outcome can provide suggestive evidence to sharpen hypotheses of possible influencing parameters which may be treated as independent variables in subsequent investigations.

In practice, the physical-social treatment environment is likely to be constant for any given investigation. When this is the case, adequate description for cross-study comparison should be sufficient, and is likely to be the best strategy for early investigations. Should more than one facility be involved, however, it is important to control possible influences by conducting all treatments, controls, etc., across all facilities. Within normal limits, this class of variables appears least important as a source of influence, but these sources may be evaluated by having each therapist, or class of therapists, conduct each treatment with several clients in two or more differing facilities.

All aspects of the time domain may also be treated as independent variables, e.g., to determine the influence of the spacing or duration of sessions. However, the best strategy for early factorial studies, especially comparative studies, appears to be homogeneity within the time domain. A moderate degree of heterogeneity of timing in factorial studies might increase the generalizability of cause-effect relationships, but a conservative approach of first establishing the relationship under specified time conditions seems a better tactical approach at the present.

Of course, the more factors which can be feasibly included in the factorial design, the more information may be obtained regarding the generalizability of results. Once cause-effect relationships are established between specific treatment procedures and change in clients' distressing behaviors for specified classes of variables, continuing series of subsequent factorial studies may provide the most information within each investigation for extending knowledge across different classes of clients, therapists, distressing behaviors, and various other parameters. However, due to the complexity, expense, and difficulty of conducting such factorial studies, using lower levels of design or laboratory-based experiments often might be better tactical choices as intermediate steps between factorial studies, than would declaring a moratorium on research until the next factorial study could be undertaken.

LOWER LEVEL CAUSE-EFFECT DESIGNS

Nonfactorial group designs with untreated controls can establish cause-effect relationships in the same manner as factorial designs. However, since the nonfactorial design cannot separate within-class confounding, its utility must be considered in relationship to the available knowledge concerning the effectiveness and applicability of treatment techniques. Following a factorial study, the nonfactorial design may have immense value in extending treatment evaluation across classes, i.e., to different types of clients, problems, therapists, treatment settings, and variations in the time domain and other treatment parameters. The limiting factor with this usage is that, for the accumulation of knowledge to remain precise, new variation can be introduced into only one class of variables at a time. Selective "gambling," by introducing new variation in a number of classes at the same time, e.g., different types of therapists and clients, may have a considerable "payoff" if the previously obtained cause-effect relationship is again found. However, if the relationship is not obtained, neither the design nor previous research can provide information on which class of variables may have been responsible. The second strategic use of the nonfactorial design with untreated controls is prior to the factorial experiment. Here this design may serve the extremely necessary function of providing global validation of promising hypotheses concerning various classes of variables, especially treatment procedures. Since confounding is possible within classes of variables, from a scientific point of view, this usage serves only a mapping function. Practically, however, this mapping function has considerable value; only the promising therapists or treatment techniques need be included in later factorial studies, and only effective procedures need be continued in clinical practice. Additionally, therapists or techniques which cause clients to "get worse" can be immediately identified and redirected. What is most astounding about the past history of behavior modification research is the fact that so few investigations have even reached this level of methodology.

Since the single-group equivalent time-samples design allows the same level of product as the nonfactorial design with untreated controls, its tactical position is essentially the same. Due to the relative advantages of each type of design, discussed earlier, the equivalent time-samples design might best be applied to chronic institutionalized populations, and where strengthened hypotheses concerning specific variables are desired. In addition to strengthening hypotheses concerning specific variables before the factorial study, and establishing cause-effect relationships across domains, a large number of studies with this level of product may result in a stronger level of product over time than any single study in isolation. In other words, a number of such studies may cancel out the within-class confounding of each individual study to the extent that some assurance of specific cause-effect relationships may exist. To be certain, however, the factorial study should still be performed.

CASE STUDIES AND UNCONTROLLED SINGLE-GROUP DESIGNS

Since all other nonfactorial single-group designs and individual case studies cannot establish cause-effect relationships, the tactical use of these approaches must always be considered an intermediary step. The individual case study without measurement appears to be of use *only* in the earliest phase of the clinical development of techniques. Thus, crude hypotheses may be developed, or new procedures based upon principles or techniques developed in the laboratory may be tried out. The case study with measurement, including the time-series and equivalent time-samples design, constitutes the first step in validation by establishing correlational conclusions and communicating procedures to others. Before research designs with higher-level products are undertaken in the clinical context, the tactical use of the case study may serve to sharpen procedures and strengthen hypotheses concerning promising techniques and parameters. Following higher-level designs, case studies with measurement may serve as the initial step in broadening the limits of application of techniques across classes of variables, and developing hypotheses concerning the influence of different parameters of variables which might increase or limit treatment effectiveness. The hypotheses of a promising treatment technique and the parameters of influence and applicability can be strengthened as case studies with measurement accumulate across classes and domains of variables, through the uncontrolled single-group design; however, these approaches at best can serve a mapping function, and can never validate a specific technique, nor adequately test hypotheses concerning mechanisms of change.

LABORATORY ANALOGS

Since laboratory studies offer the highest-level product of cause-effect relationships between specific variables, the tactical placement of experimental analogs is important. The advantages of laboratory studies, and their potential contributions in terms of selection, prediction, and explanation were discussed earlier. The role of laboratory research in relation to other research approaches should be considered.

Following a factorial design in the clinical context, analytic laboratory research may be undertaken specifically to determine mechanisms of change, and to evaluate different parameters of influence within classes of variables, including the refinement of specific aspects of effective treatment procedures. Particularly when such research is undertaken on behaviors which are analogous to distressing clinical behavior, the complicating features of placebo effects may be removed; however, the related problems of experimenter bias (Rosenthal, 1963) and demand characteristics (Orne, 1962) must be taken into account. After analytic research under the more stringent and economical conditions of the laboratory has determined probable mechanisms of change, and narrowed effective parameters of influence, hypotheses derived from this research may then be returned to the clinical context for evaluation. Before embarking upon controlled research in the clinical context, laboratory-based designs may serve the major purposes of developing techniques of changing behavior and explanatory principles, and the determination of parameters of influence from which new therapeutic techniques may be derived. This is the approach strongly favored by Goldstein et al. (1966) and Krasner & Ullmann

(1965), since a stronger basis of empirical knowledge would underlie all classes of variables once new procedures were tested in the clinical context. Thus, many superfluous aspects of clinical procedure and theory could be avoided.

The ideal tactic for future behavior modification research would be (1) systematic development of treatment techniques in the laboratory, (2) trial and modification through case studies and single-group experiments, (3) evaluation in control-group studies, (4) comparative, factorially designed experiments. However, cumulative knowledge is slow in coming, and current practices are such that each investigator will be likely to continue with his preferred method of investigation, be it experimental analogs, clinical hypothesis formation, or controlled research. Since research training does not ensure ability or acquaintance with the range of problems and issues existent in the clinical situation, and clinical "savvy" does not ensure ability or acquaintance with the problems and issues of research, this state of affairs may not be an unfortunate one. Thus, as the field of behavior modification enters the experimental era, all levels and approaches to the ultimate question may be expected to continue. It is to be hoped, however, that each approach will be seen in perspective, in its relationships both to other approaches and to the actual level of product obtained, so that future generations may view the field as a composition of "artisans" or "scientists," whether research or applied, rather than as cultists bound by historical inheritance.

Chapter Summary

This chapter was concerned with the design of investigations, and with the procedural tactics needed, for accumulating knowledge in the area of behavior modification—that subarea of the psychology of behavior influence focused upon clinical treatment. After tracing the history of behavior modification research through the prescientific, demonstration, and scientific eras, the current status of research in the area was summarized. While the great majority of current practices still appears to be based upon the beliefs and opinions of individuals or "cults," it was suggested that the historical development of behavior modification research had resulted in the identification and clarification of both sociological and methodological obstacles of the past. The latter developments were seen as setting the stage for a new era in behavior modification research—the experimental era.

The characteristics and requirements of scientific research in general were then discussed, and the conclusion was that the principles and methods of behavior modification research appear to be no different than any other experimental design problem, except for the greater number and complexity of variables. The variables were presented in terms of the need for adequate descriptive, measurement, or control operations across domains and classes, including: the distressing behaviors, relatively stable personal-social characteristics, and physical-social life environments of clients; the therapeutic techniques, relatively stable personal-social characteristics, and physical-social treatment environments of therapists; and time, both as a variable and for marking points of research focus. After a discussion of the "criterion problem" and instrumentation for assessing treatment effectiveness, the ultimate question to be answered in behavior modification research was posed as: What treatment, by whom, is most effective for this individual, with that specific problem, under which set of circumstances, and how does it come about?

Since the ultimate question can never be answered in any single investigation, the possible levels of product (e.g., hypothesis formation, cause-effect evidence) obtainable with different research designs were detailed, with focus upon identification of inherent uncontrolled sources of error and confounding. The research designs considered from this frame of reference included: individual case studies and nonfactorial single-group designs, ranging from simple case reports through more sophisticated time-series and time-samples designs; nonfactorial designs with untreated controls; multiple-treatment designs; factorial group designs with untreated and nonspecific-treatment controls; and laboratory-based designs. Although factorial designs were shown to be capable by themselves of establishing cause-effect relationships between specific variables of importance in behavior modification research, an inverse relationship exists between the level of product and the necessary investment of time, money, and personnel. Therefore, the tactical need, place, and value of different levels of design were considered in terms of the level of product obtainable, the degree of knowledge already established, and the aspect of the ultimate question to be strategically approached. While "ideal" tactics for programmatic accumulation of knowledge have been suggested, as behavior modification research enters the experimental era, the placement of individual studies in perspective to others and to the actual level of product obtained promises to provide more firmly established knowledge than was ever possible before.

2

Outcome of Systematic Desensitization
I: Background, Procedures, and Uncontrolled
Reports of Individual Treatment

GORDON L. PAUL
University of Illinois, Urbana, Illinois

"Anxiety" and the "mechanisms of defense" have traditionally been considered the very core of the functional behavior disorders. In 1950, Hoch & Zubin (1950, p. v) aptly reflected the dominant thinking in the field by stating, "it is widely recognized that anxiety is the most pervasive psychological phenomenon of our time and that it is the chief symptom in the neuroses and in the functional psychoses." Since the Hoch & Zubin symposium, however, many theorists have argued convincingly that sociocultural factors, learning deficits, modeling, external reinforcement contingencies, and other events are often more important determinants of maladaptive behavior in given clinical cases. Further, they have argued that the concept of anxiety has been reified and endowed with so many extraneous and surplus meanings that it frequently poses a hindrance to communication (see Ullmann & Krasner, 1969). Nevertheless, few would question the experimental and clinical importance of the phenomena associated with anxiety or the large numbers of individuals seeking psychotherapeutic help on the basis of such phenomena.

An excellent summary of recent experimental and theoretical perspectives on anxiety may be found in Spielberger's (1966a) *Anxiety and Behavior*. Following Spielberger (1966b), research findings suggest that "anxiety" may best be thought of as a shorthand term for a complex pattern of response characterized by subjective feelings of apprehension and tension accompanied by or associated with physiological activation or arousal. Such a definition does not distinguish between anxiety and fear. It does, however, help clarify communication by distinguishing anxiety from eliciting stimulus conditions, and from escape or avoidance responses (defenses) which may result.

Historical Origin and Development

It was through such distinctions as the latter that Joseph Wolpe began the work which ultimately led to the development of systematic desensitization. In the mid-1940s, guided by the Hullian concept of "conditioned inhibition" (Hull, 1943), Wolpe undertook a series of animal studies which led him to the conclusion that the most satisfactory way of treating "conditioned" anxiety was through a gradual counterconditioning approach. Wolpe noted the similarity of these procedures to Jones's (1924b) treatment of a fearful child and, basing his psychological theorizing on Hull, offered neurophysiological speculations for the effectiveness of counterconditioning procedures by extrapolations from Sherrington's (1906) concept of "reciprocal inhibition."

On the basis of the above observations and theory, Wolpe formulated a counterconditioning hypothesis for eliminating maladaptive anxiety, which he termed the "reciprocal inhibition principle." According to this principle (Wolpe, 1958, p. 71), the ability of given stimuli to evoke anxiety will be permanently weakened (and hence, the anxiety alleviated), "[if] a response antagonistic to anxiety can be made to occur in the presence of anxiety-evoking stimuli so that it is accompanied by a complete or partial suppression of the anxiety responses." Wolpe then proceeded to delineate gross response patterns with humans which were both manipulable and incompatible with anxiety. This search led him to Jacobson's (1938) progressive relaxation training, since deep muscle relaxation appeared to produce both a reduction in physiological arousal and a pleasant affective tone.

Wolpe soon found that in vivo relaxation was often impractical because the anxiety-eliciting stimuli could not be controlled. He then began experimenting with phobic clients who were asked to confront anxiety-eliciting stimuli only by imagining their presence, concluding that the imaginal presentation of such stimuli was an effective substitute for concrete stimuli. Wolpe was quick to see the advantages of flexibility and control which were afforded, since social situations could be imagined as well as concrete objects. Further, not only could events of the past or future be presented to the client, but intensity could also be controlled. Thus, in the early 1950s Wolpe combined the procedures from his animal studies into a treatment package for human anxiety which he called "systematic desensitization." The incompatible response was deep muscle relaxation, and the counterconditioning procedure was followed by presenting anxiety-eliciting stimuli through imagery in a hierarchical order from least to most disturbing.

It should be noted that both "gradual-approach" methods and counterconditioning principles had previously been proposed by many writers for treating anxiety and phobic disorders, some of which involved the imaginal presentation of eliciting stimuli: Such terms as "deconditioning" (Burnham, 1924), "graded tasks" and "dosing anxiety" (Dollard & Miller, 1950), "reconditioning" and "hypnotic desensitization" (Wolberg, 1954), "paradoxical intention" (Frankl, 1960), and "autogenic training" (Schultz & Luthe, 1959) all refer to therapeutic procedures which share, in part, either principles or techniques with systematic desensitization therapy. In fact, systematic desensitization appears to provide a package which combines two of the three ways for producing "associative inhibition" which Guthrie proposed in 1935 and again in 1938 (Guthrie, 1962, pp. 60–61): "The first . . . consists in introducing the stimulus at such weak strengths that it will not cause the response and then gradually increasing the intensity of the stimulus, always taking care that it is below the 'threshold' of the response. . . . The second . . . consists in presenting the cues for the unwanted action . . . , but at the same time preventing the response by other controls of the situation, seeing to it that the response is inhibited." Thus, working independently of several predecessors, Wolpe arrived at essentially the same therapeutic principle of counterconditioning as the primary guide for treating anxiety. However, Wolpe's most unique and important contribution may lie in the careful clinical follow-through of stimulus analysis, means of presentation, and incompatible responses. The resulting systematic desensitization package, although similar to other procedures, constituted a true innovation and the first broadly applicable and operationalized specific treatment program for maladaptive anxiety.

Like the majority of his predecessors, Wolpe limited his initial explorations of systematic desensitization therapy to "simple" phobias, primarily because the distinctive feature of a classical phobia is the presence of ostensible stimulus antecedents of anxiety (Wolpe, 1952b). However, by the time of his second major clinical report of the treatment technique (Wolpe, 1954), systematic desensitization had come to be the major procedure for the direct treatment of anxiety in even the most complex cases (see Wolpe, 1964a). Through analysis of overt and covert eliciting stimuli, direct treatment of anxiety (hence, appropriateness of systematic desensitization) could be considered of fundamental clinical importance in a wide variety of cases: (1) when anxiety, of sufficient duration or intensity to cause extreme subjective distress, is elicited in the absence of objective danger or threat; (2) when the response pattern of anxiety becomes sufficiently specific to produce tissue change of the sort seen in so-called psychophysiological or psychosomatic disorders; (3) when the intensity of anxiety results in a breakdown of efficient performance of complex behavior; (4) when adaptive behavior in the client's repertoire is inhibited to avoid anxiety; (5) when maladaptive behaviors are learned and maintained to alleviate or avoid anxiety.

The Systematic Desensitization Package

As indicated above, many different gradual-approach or tolerance methods have been called "desensitization"; however, systematic desensitization therapy, as developed by Wolpe, refers to a specific set of operations to which the term must be limited if it is to remain meaningful. Thus, *systematic desensitization*, or simply *desensitization*, as used here is limited to a treatment package which systematically includes: (1) training in deep relaxation, (2) constuction of hierarchies of anxiety-eliciting stimuli, (3) desensitization proper—the graduated pairing, through imagery, of anxiety-eliciting stimuli with the relaxed state.

The standard conduct of desensitization is within a one-to-one therapeutic relationship which includes the nonspecific therapist's skills and aspects common to any clinical interaction. Thus, before systematic desensitization is undertaken, the usual clinical preliminaries are carried out: i.e., establishing rapport, assessment of the nature and basis of the client's problems, determination of assets and liabilities, and specification and explanation of treatment programs deemed appropriate. Attempts are typically made to alleviate any external sources of conflict, and to correct misperceptions or other maladaptive behaviors which result in realistic anxiety reactions, even when desensitization is considered appropriate. These therapeutic maneuvers are usually attempted before desensitization, and may form a part of assessment; however, when systematic desensitization is indicated, it is conducted as soon as possible, and may be in parallel with measures instituted in the external environment.

THE TECHNICAL OPERATIONS

While systematic desensitization therapy is defined by the three sets of operations indicated above, many variations in the operations and their parameters are possible. Nuances in procedure become important to the extent that they may or may not be pertinent to success.

Relaxation Training. The method of relaxation used is typically a much abbreviated version of Jacobson's (1938) progressive relaxation training. With this technique, the client is taught to relax by successively tensing and releasing gross muscle groups throughout the body on instruction from the therapist, frequently aided by suggestions of warmth, relaxation, and calmness. Attention is focused upon identification of localized tension and relaxation, and care is taken to limit competing stimuli and responses. The usual procedure during relaxation training is to devote about half of each therapy hour to the training procedure, and to have the client practice between sessions.

Within the abbreviated Jacobson procedure, several variations are possible: The sequence and combination of muscle groups may vary, as well as the number of muscle groups covered in a single training session. The time devoted to training may vary both within sessions and in total training time. Similarly, the timing of tension and release phases may vary, as well as the use of abrupt-release or gradual-release instructions. Considerable variation may be found in the extent to which suggestion is used, with formal training in "hypnotic induction" sometimes added. Some workers have also substituted audio-taped instructions for progressive relaxation training, rather than direct training by the therapist. Occasionally, therapists do not use the abbreviated Jacobson procedure at all, but attempt to induce relaxation entirely by hypnotic procedures or by autogenic training (Schultz & Luthe, 1959). These nuances in operational procedure for relaxation training become important to the extent that they may differ in the efficiency or effectiveness of inducing a sufficient degree of relaxation to inhibit anxiety, since success in desensitization proper presumes a deep and reliable state of relaxation.

Anxiety Hierarchies.   Anxiety hierarchies are graded lists of anxiety-eliciting stimuli, typically falling along the primary or secondary stimulus generalization gradient of the most intense stimulus complex operative in the client's current life environment. Ideally, the items (individual complex stimuli) in a hierarchy are constructed to form subjective equal intervals of just noticeable differences in the degree of anxiety elicited, running from the weakest noticeable response to the strongest. The construction of anxiety hierarchies typically begins at about the same time as relaxation training, during the first half of each session. The data from which the hierarchies are formed are drawn from detailed assessment interviews which focus upon the historical and current stimulus contingencies evoking anxiety, and the duration and degree of disturbance. Psychological tests or questionnaires may provide initial information, and clients are frequently asked to list all distressing thoughts, feelings, and situations as an extratherapeutic task. After the fundamental sources of maladaptive anxiety have been determined, the therapist and client set about arranging the stimuli within hierarchies, being careful to develop specific, detailed, concrete items of appropriate spacing. Depending upon the nature of the client's problems, multiple hierarchies may be formed. Additionally, a careful assessment is made of factors which may alter the intensity of reaction to any given stimulus, to allow the therapist greater control during desensitization proper. It is also understood that initial hierarchies are subject to alteration as new data may appear during treatment.

Hierarchies may be classified into two basic types—thematic and spatial-temporal. *Thematic hierarchies* are focused about some "cluster" of anxiety-eliciting stimulus configurations which indicate a common defined mediational feature or theme. Such themes may be based upon stimulus classes which are associated through spatial or temporal contiguity, through similarity of physical attributes, through function, or through internal responses, as well as through any other dimension of semantic or symbolic generalization or "meaning." Thematic hierarchies may be limited to a simple concrete theme, such as dogs, elevators, or storms, or they may be focused upon more complex or abstract themes, such as criticism, rejection, or death. The chief characteristic, in either case, is that the items of the hierarchy consist of discrete stimuli which differ qualitatively or quantitatively while incorporating increasing degrees of the defined feature.

Spatial-temporal hierarchies, on the other hand, are focused upon a target event which can be fixed in time and space, with items of the hierarchy consisting of points along the approach gradient to the target. The target would usually consist of the most anxiety-producing situation or event possible in the client's life, and might involve either single or multiple thematic features.

Combined hierarchies may also be formed. Within a thematic hierarchy, some items may constitute "subtargets" which are preceded by spatial-temporal stimulus items falling along the approach gradient of the subtarget, to be followed by a qualitatively different thematic item higher in the hierarchy. Similarly, stimulus features from several different themes may be added to items in a spatial-temporal hierarchy, to a graduated degree, prior to the final target item.

Like nuances in relaxation training, variations in the type of hierarchy and in the type and calibration of items become important to the extent that they may differ in their efficiency or effectiveness in alleviating various classes of distressing behavior. Because appropriate hierarchy construction, at the present time, relies more upon specific knowledge of the laws of learning and "clinical acumen" than upon operational criteria, considerable difficulty might be anticipated with "naïve" therapists, since treatment success also presumes the identification of fundamental (central) rather than irrelevant (peripheral) sources of anxiety.

Desensitization Proper.   Prior to desensitization proper, the client's imagery is evaluated to assure that the imaginal presentation of stimuli does elicit anxiety, that he imagines himself clearly in the anxiety-eliciting situations, and to determine any time lag involved in requests to start or stop images. If there is difficulty with any of these aspects of the image, desensitization proper does not begin until the difficulty is corrected by further training. Once imagery has been tested, hierarchies have been constructed, and deep relaxation has been reliably achieved, desensitization proper can begin.

The procedure for desensitization proper then continues as follows: A deep state of relaxation is induced (usually by a much briefer method than that used in initial training), and instructions are given to signal even the slightest degree of tension, discomfort, or anxiety. The lowest item in a hierarchy is then presented by verbal instructions from the therapist, after which the therapist pauses briefly to allow unimpeded imagination of the item. After the appropriate exposure time, the client is instructed to stop visualizing the scene and merely continue relaxing. When desensitization proper is unimpeded by elicited anxiety, each hierarchy item is repeated (at least two presentations) in the same manner, working up the hierarchy from weakest to strongest stimuli, with the therapist ensuring that higher items are not presented until each lower item can be imagined without disturbance. Should any given item result in disturbing reactions, the client is immediately instructed to stop visualizing the scene, and relaxation is again induced—often aided by instructions to visualize a neutral or pleasant scene. Following the occurrence of anxiety in response to a given item, the same item may be again presented in "diluted" form (either by shortening presentation time or by adding factors to the scene which are known to lower the intensity of response), or a lower item from the hierarchy may be reintroduced. Each session is concluded with a "successful" item presentation, and following sessions begin where previous sessions terminate, until all hierarchies have been completed. When multiple hierarchies are to be desensitized, progress through the hierarchies may be concurrent (items from different hierarchies presented during a single session) or sequential (one hierarchy completed before another is started). Combined sequential and concurrent coverage of hierarchies may also be involved in a single desensitization case; for example, a spatial-temporal hierarchy might be first desensitized alone, followed by concurrent desensitization of two or more thematic hierarchies.

Lazarus (1964c) has called attention to several possible parameter variations within desensitization proper. Both the duration of scenes (i.e., effective length of vivid stimulus presentation) and the interval between scenes may vary. Similarly, as in other types of therapy, the duration and spacing of sessions may vary during desensitization proper as well as during relaxation training and hierarchy construction. Besides the number of hierarchies drawn upon during a single session, the total number of stimulus presentations during a session may vary; however, once the timing parameters are established, the number of presentations may be a direct function of the client's response. While it is agreed that higher items should not be presented until lower items can be imagined without disturbance, variation may exist in the manner of handling items which elicit anxiety in excess of relaxation, and in the criteria of number and duration of item presentation before moving to the next, more disturbing item. These nuances of procedure, like those of relaxation training and hierarchy construction, become important to the extent that they may relate to the efficiency or effectiveness of treatment outcome. However, it should be noted that stimulus configurations which are either unclear or of too short duration during desensitization proper might lead not only to a failure of treatment but, at least theoretically, to serious setbacks later in treatment. Similarly, prolonged exposure to a very disturbing scene is believed capable of actually increasing the severity of anxiety (see Wolpe & Lazarus, 1966).

THE FOCUS ON OUTCOME

The ultimate question to be answered about behavior modification has been posed: "What treatment, by whom, is most effective for this individual with that specific problem, under which set of circumstances, and how does it come about?" (Paul, Chapter 1). Since systematic desensitization consists of a set of procedures and strategies which are hypothesized to be appropriate for specific problems in which the direct treatment of anxiety is considered of fundamental importance, the basic assessment of effectiveness or outcome is of particular significance. The assessment of outcome may be viewed as an evaluation of the cause-effect relationships between systematic desensitization as the independent variable (i.e., what treatment) and change in distressing target behaviors related to anxiety as dependent variables (i.e., that specific problem). Without establishing these basic phenomena, other aspects of the ultimate question with regard to systematic desensitization would have little meaning (see Paul, Chapter 1). Therefore, a critical review of all available papers[1] that report the application of systematic desensitization therapy is presented in this chapter and the following chapters, with major focus on outcome and the range of problems treated. Parameter variations within systematic desensitization will be reviewed to the extent that outcome may be affected. Of the other aspects of the ultimate question, therapist characteristics (i.e., by whom), client characteristics (i.e., this individual), life and treatment environments, as well as time dimensions (i.e., which set of circumstances) will be secondarily evaluated with regard to both range of application and possible influence on treatment outcome (see Paul, Chapter 3).

Even though systematic desensitization was developed from the counterconditioning hypothesis, assessment of outcome does not necessarily provide evidence concerning mechanisms of change (i.e., how change comes about). While failure of the procedure, when properly applied, does cast doubt on the underlying theory, success per se does not validate the theory. This aspect of

---

[1] Available papers include attempted coverage of all published works to January, 1967, and unpublished or "in-press" papers received by that date in response to over 300 requests sent by the author to universities, hospitals, and clinics in the United States, United Kingdom, New Zealand, Australia, Newfoundland, etc. Appreciation is expressed to Don R. Thomas for assistance in obtaining and collating references, and to Douglas Bernstein for assistance in surveying and abstracting articles.

the ultimate question requires a different focus and strategy, and relevant data may be found elsewhere (see Lang, Chapter 4). The major focus of this chapter and the next, then, will be on outcome, with the counterconditioning principle merely taken as a working hypothesis of the major effective mechanisms involved.

Review of the Literature—I

CASE REPORTS AND UNCONTROLLED GROUP STUDIES OF INDIVIDUAL SYSTEMATIC DESENSITIZATION

Joseph Wolpe. The work of Joseph Wolpe, the innovator of systematic desensitization therapy, holds a place of prominence as the first systematic report of the application of the treatment procedure. Wolpe (1952b, 1954, 1958) has presented the results of three consecutive series of outpatients, totaling 210, to whom he had applied techniques based upon reciprocal inhibition. Since Wolpe views systematic desensitization as merely one form of application of his basic therapeutic principle, he has presented only one detailed statistical report on the results of this procedure alone (Wolpe, 1961). In that report, summary data were presented on thirty-nine cases randomly selected from his files.

The evaluation of outcome used by Wolpe is a five-point rating scale based upon "symptomatic improvement, increased productiveness, improved adjustment and pleasure in sex, improved interpersonal relationships, and ability to handle ordinary psychological conflicts and reasonable reality stresses." Only those patients rated in the top two points of the scale are considered treatment successes, which means, for systematic desensitization, a requirement that anxiety and related maladaptive behaviors retain "not more than 20 per cent of its original strength" (see Wolpe, 1961). While several case outcomes have been validated by direct observation in the life situation and by unbiased reports of others, the only consistent basis for Wolpe's outcome ratings are the patient's self-reports of changed responses in the presence of previous anxiety-eliciting stimuli in the extratherapeutic environment. The Willoughby scale is routinely administered as part of assessment at the beginning of treatment, but only occasionally is it readministered at termination.

Since Wolpe assumes that systematic desensitization is appropriate only for neurotics, individuals whom he diagnoses as schizophrenics or psychopaths are not accepted for treatment. Wolpe's policy is to accept every presenting case diagnosed as neurotic for treatment. In reporting case results, misdiagnosed psychotics and psychopaths, as well as cases who have not had a "fair trial" of treatment are excluded. Stevenson has drawn attention to the problems that arise when data on the type and number of excluded cases are not available, since an additional 85 cases were so handled in the combined series of 210 reported (see Wolpe, 1964b). While it does seem valid to exclude cases who terminate after assessment but before treatment is under way, the nature and number of such cases would be desirable to estimate base rates, even though no information would be provided relative to specific treatment techniques. On the other hand, considering the notorious unreliability of psychiatric diagnosis, exclusion of cases on the basis of "misdiagnosis" is likely to introduce a positive selection bias into the cases reported. Fortunately, Wolpe's random sample of systematic desensitization cases was more explicit than his previous reports in regard to cases excluded. Thus, of the total folders sampled, 13 percent were considered eligible for systematic desensitization but were excluded because of termination before active treatment was started (two to six sessions), and approximately 4 percent were excluded on the basis of misdiagnosis.

From a thorough survey of all of Wolpe's available writings, it appears that systematic desensitization therapy has been applied to approximately 150 cases included in his three series and additional reports, covering about ten years of private practice. Of these, well over half (86 separate cases) were presented in enough detail in his four summary reports (Wolpe, 1952b, 1954, 1958, 1961) or illustrative papers (e.g., Wolpe, 1959, 1962; Wolpe & Lazarus, 1966) to identify relevant parameters and outcomes, for individual cases. The majority of these 86 cases came from his 1958 book, in which 61 desensitization cases could be identified, and from the 1961 paper reporting on 39 cases, of which 16 overlapped with other detailed reports. Of these 86 cases, one may be excluded from evaluation since the case was terminated early when Wolpe left South Africa (Wolpe, 1958, p. 213, 80). Data on the remaining 85 cases (40 females, 45 males) form the basis of this review, and should be representative of the 150 total cases treated by systematic desensitization.

The distressing behaviors treated cover a wide range of problems in which the major presenting features were high states of anxiety and inhibition of adaptive behavior, such as interpersonal and situational anxieties, claustrophobia, agoraphobia, and other numerous and complex phobias. Desensitization was also applied occasionally to reactive depression and "inferiority feelings," presumably when these problems were a result of failure to perform adaptive behavior inhibited by anxiety. Psychophysiological reactions, such as peptic ulcer and dermatitis, and maladaptive behaviors maintained by anxiety reduction, such as obsessions, exhibitionism, and kleptomania, were also treated by desensitization. The major presenting problems which might be characterized as a breakdown of efficient performance of complex behavior, treated by desensitization, are sexual (impotence and frigidity) and stuttering. It should be noted that cases described or selected on the basis of a common class of maladaptive response (e.g., obsessions, agoraphobia, impotence) may vary so widely in the class or classes of anxiety-eliciting stimuli that meaningful comparisons with other cases are difficult or impossible. Common classes of eliciting stimuli provide a more clear-cut comparative basis; however, few writers provide such information, and Wolpe does so only when presenting hierarchy themes.

The great majority of cases were white, middle-class South Africans, although a few more recent cases were treated in the United States. All were treated as private outpatients, about 73 percent by referral. Their age range was eleven to sixty-eight years with a median of thirty-three years. Since the focus of Wolpe's work was on the total treatment of private cases, rather than specific evaluation of the effects of systematic desensitization, the majority also were treated by other techniques deemed appropriate to the nature of additional problems—primarily by assertion training. Thus, while the total number of sessions for desensitization cases ranged from 8 to 263 (Mdn = 23), over a period of 1 to 75 months (Mdn = 7), the number of sessions devoted to desensitization proper ranged from 4 to 217 (Mdn = 13). The median difference of 10 sessions thus includes not only assessment, relaxation training, and hierarchy construction, but other therapeutic techniques as well. The number of individual hierarchies per patient was found to range between 1 and 36 (Mdn = 2), and the number of sessions devoted to desensitization per hierarchy ranged from 1.6 to 72.3 (Mdn = 8). These figures differ slightly from those presented by Wolpe (1961) because of the addition of more cases and because medians are reported, rather than means, in order to lessen the effect of a few extreme cases. As Wolpe (1964a) has reported for the third series in general, fewer sessions were expended on noncomplex cases, and more on complex ones.

Of the 85 cases surveyed, Wolpe rated 78 as treatment successes, as defined above. However, one case (Wolpe, 1958) rated as a treatment failure may be considered a desensitization success by Wolpe's criteria, and one case (Wolpe, 1958; also Wolpe, 1961) rated a treatment success was a desensitization failure. The resulting figure of 78 successes from 85 cases results in a positive outcome for approximately 92 percent of reported cases treated by systematic desensitization—slightly better than Wolpe's (1958) figures for all treatment techniques. Follow-up contacts were made on 21 cases for periods of 6 to 48 months without a single report of relapse or symptom substitution. Four of the seven rated failures were attributed to difficulties with imagery, and three terminated due to a felt lack of progress. There appear to be no reliable differences in type of distressing behavior, personal characteristics, or anything else which differentiate the failures from the successes. If it is assumed, however, that an additional 3 to 4 cases (4 percent) were excluded from those reported on the basis of "misdiagnosis," the "success rate" for all cases treated by systematic desensitization would be in the neighborhood of 88 percent.

Wolpe (e.g., 1958, 1964b) frequently reports the success rates of his work compared with those of other series from psychoanalytic workers. While such figures may offer interesting comparisons of the number of cases accepted and of the lengths of treatment, it should be clear that sound comparisons of outcome cannot be obtained due to the uncontrolled nature of selection, types of distressing behaviors, client and therapist characteristics, environmental influences, and outcome criteria in all such reports (Paul, Chapter 1). In Wolpe's work, for example, cause-effect relationships cannot be established, primarily because his characteristics as a therapist are completely confounded with the treatment techniques, and the outcome criteria are derived from involved participants, thus allowing bias in all respects. Wolpe has been attuned to some of these problems, and did present the only time-samples single-case study design in the systematic desensitization literature (Wolpe, 1962). In this study, the treatment procedures were modified by delaying history-taking and by massing treatment sessions at intervals of four to six weeks in order to exclude alternative explanations of success. Additionally, a medical student conducted nine sessions during desensitization proper, in an attempt to rule out suggestion and transference effects. As a result of these procedures, with the addition of external observation of progress, the conclusions can reach the correlational level but still fall short of establishing cause-effect relationships for systematic desensitization per se. Similarly, Wolpe (1958) presented available pre-post Willoughby scores of successful cases in his third series. Of these, twenty-eight were desensitization cases and all showed significant improvement as evaluated by .05-level two-sided cutoffs based upon Willoughby's (1934) norms. Unfortunately, no adequate norms are available for comparable clinical populations, and these data therefore must also remain suggestive.

In summary, Wolpe's reports of systematic desensitization therapy cannot be taken as sufficient evidence for the specific success of the procedure. However, his pioneering contribution cannot be underestimated in developing and describing the procedures and operations, carefully recording and observing the results of his own practice, exploring the possible range of application of the technique, and providing a catalytic base of hypotheses and correlational data concerning the effectiveness of systematic desensitization for later work.

Arnold Lazarus.   The work of Arnold Lazarus stands as one of the most carefully considered series of uncontrolled clinical reports in the literature, and certainly reflects the most prodigious application of systematic desensitization in clinical practice. Lazarus and Rachman (1957), both students of Wolpe, provided the first report of the successful use of desensitization by therapists other than Wolpe. Since that early paper, covering five cases, Lazarus has published case studies involving one to sixteen clients to illustrate the use of individual systematic desensitization with a 9½-year-old child (Lazarus, 1960), stutterers (Lazarus, 1964a), and frigid women (Lazarus, 1963a). Later case reports (Lazarus, 1964b, 1965b) have appeared with the purpose of demonstrating the need to identify primary rather than peripheral classes of anxiety-eliciting stimuli in desensitization, with illustrative problems including agoraphobia, social anxiety, claustrophobia, reactive depression, hyperventilation syndrome, generalized anxiety, abdominal spasms, and compulsions. Other case material has appeared to show the wide range of stimuli that might be involved in such singular problems as impotence (Lazarus, 1965a), and to illustrate the need to combine systematic desensitization with other treatment procedures for problems such as alcoholism (Lazarus, 1965c).

Lazarus (1963b) published one summary evaluation of the result of outpatients who had consulted him up to early 1963, totaling 408 patients, which included all but 7 of the cases involved in the above reports. He, like Wolpe, considers systematic desensitization to be only one form of application of a basic therapeutic principle, and as such, did not break down cases for this procedure alone. Additionally, the 1963 report was focused upon 126 "severe" cases, with only passing reference to the larger total, which also included cases that had terminated within one to six sessions, before application of treatment procedures had been undertaken. More recently (Wolpe & Lazarus, 1966) Lazarus has recomputed his results, excluding those cases, and he was kind enough to provide the reviewer with more detailed data and information regarding only those cases in which systematic desensitization was applied (Lazarus, 1967b). It should be noted that detailed data regarding specific number of sessions, duration, etc., were no longer available on 64 cases and were necessarily based upon estimates. However, these cases constitute less than 29 percent of the total, and do not differ significantly from those on which data were available.

The evaluation of outcome used by Lazarus is a five-point rating scale (from deteriorated to completely recovered) based upon complete freedom from symptoms, evidence of ability to enter into and maintain congenial interpersonal relationships, ability to gratify basic needs and strivings creatively and realistically, and ability to endure frustration and deprivation and to adjust to inimicable conditions. Lazarus's awareness of the problem of bias in such therapist ratings is worth noting. He attempted to guard against bias by obtaining external reports from referring physicians (70 percent) and from patients' families, friends, employers, workmates, etc., as well as by referring to the patients' own self-reports. He further attempted to correct his own possible bias, stating, "If a query, or the slightest doubt arose concerning the areas and extent of improvement, a patient was relegated to a lower category. . . . It is the writer's contention that only a rigorous and uncompromising attitude to therapeutic results can reveal whether specific methods employed are of any value." (1963b, p. 75). Only those cases rated in the top two categories are considered treatment successes.

The published reports cover a total of 220 cases to whom individual systematic desensitization had been applied. Of the total, 213 cases were included in the 1963 summary, and they include all patients over the age of fifteen who had consulted Lazarus and received more than one session of desensitization at the time of that report. All but four of the 220 were white South Africans, with the remainder from the United States. All cases were treated as private outpatients, ranging in age from 9½ to 70 years (Mdn = 35), with females accounting for 70 percent of the total. Like Wolpe, Lazarus was focused upon the total treatment of private cases rather than upon evaluation of systematic desensitization, so that almost all cases also received differential relaxation training, assertion training, and behavioral rehearsal, while several other subsidiary methods were used with some. Thus, while the total number of sessions ranged from 3 to over 200 (Mdn = 16) over a period of 1 week to 4 years (Mdn = 5.5 months), the number of sessions devoted to desensitization proper ranged from 2 to 200 (Mdn = 12). On the average, about four sessions were devoted totally to assessment, relaxation training, hierarchy construction, and other therapeutic techniques, with other therapeutic techniques continued concurrently with desensitization proper in most cases. The number of individual hierarchies per patient ranged from 1 to 6 (Mdn = 2), with the number of sessions of desensitization per hierarchy ranging from 2 to 50 (Mdn = 10). A co-therapist was present in 18 cases; however, Lazarus conducted desensitization alone in all but one of these.

The great majority of distressing behaviors treated were characterized by high states of anxiety and inhibition of adaptive behaviors, reported as interpersonal and social anxiety, generalized anxiety, and numerous phobias, including agoraphobia and claustrophobia. Several cases of "panic" and "pervasive anxiety" were also treated, with these problems differentiated from generalized anxiety on the basis of failure to identify eliciting stimuli. Reactive depression and "passivity" were also occasionally treated by desensitization when they appeared to result from the inhibition of adaptive behavior. Obsessive-compulsive responses and alcoholism were treated by desensitization when they appeared to be maintained by avoidance or alleviation of anxiety, as were hysterical paresis and disturbances of audition and vision. Psychophysiological or psychosomatic disorders included presenting problems such as migraine headaches, asthma, abdominal spasms, epigastric pain, and palpitations, while impotence, frigidity, and stuttering were the major problems which could be characterized as a breakdown of efficient performance of complex behavior. It was Lazarus's policy to administer a pretreatment assessment battery to all patients, including the Willoughby scale, a Sentence Completion Test, and Bernreuter's self-sufficiency scale. The Maudsley Personality Inventory (MPI) was added to the battery for about one-fourth of the cases, and all were rated by Lazarus on a five-point scale of intensity of suffering and incapacitation prior to treatment. The correlation of these severity ratings with MPI neuroticism and Willoughby scores was exceptionally high (r = .95 and .93, respectively), with 56 percent of treated cases rated as severely disturbed. The treated population as a whole were anxious introverts as indicated by a correlation of .85 between neuroticism and introversion on the MPI, with MPI neuroticism and Willoughby scores correlating .96.

Of the total 220 cases receiving more than one desensitization session, Lazarus rated 190 as treatment successes as defined above, resulting in a positive outcome for approximately 86 percent. However, Lazarus also followed Wolpe's practice of excluding cases in which desensitization had been applied to cases later diagnosed as psychotic. Three such cases were treated during the period covered by the published reports (Lazarus, 1967b), in addition to the 220. If these three cases are counted as therapeutic failures, the success rate becomes approximately 85 percent. Follow-up contacts were made over periods of 3 to 48 months (Mdn = 22) on 39 "successful" cases for which external reports were also available. On follow-up, 1 case of "relapse" occurred following an accident 8 months after treatment termination, and 2 cases of "temporary relapse" or additional problems which might tenuously be considered "symptom substitution" were reported to have occurred and again recovered. The majority of cases appeared not only to have maintained gains, but to have progressed further.

In attempting to identify differences between successful and unsuccessful cases, neither sex nor age differentiated the groups, nor did general complexity. However, cases of "panic" and "pervasive anxiety" received relatively lower percentages of success ratings than other problems, presumably the result of inability to construct adequate hierarchies. The only clear-cut distinguishing feature between successes and failures was that the failure group produced significantly higher scores on both Willoughby and MPI neuroticism scales, and received significantly higher intensity ratings prior to treatment. The failure group also had significantly lower pretreatment MPI extroversion scores; however, in view of the high correlation with neuroticism in the population, such a finding may be more an indicant of general severity of disability than a personality characteristic. Also, cases complaining of panic or pervasive anxiety are confounded with severity and length of disturbance, with the lowest percentage of success reported (41 percent) for 44 cases with a previous history of ten or more years of treatment by other therapists. The low success rate with stutterers reported in the summary article (Lazarus, 1963b) also appears to be a function of severity, as this type of distressing behavior was found to respond nearly as frequently as any other when all treated cases were considered. Thus, of the 30 rated failures, 26 were accounted for by those with ten or more years of previous treatment, and the remainder attributed to poor rapport and motivation.

Like the Wolpe reports, these cases reported by Lazarus cannot be taken as evidence of cause-effect relationships between systematic desensitization and change in distressing behavior, due to the possible confounding of therapist characteristics, other techniques, and environmental experiences as well as the lack of reliability and validity data for outcome criteria. However, as a result of

his care in reporting details of treatment, and his reliance upon external reports of "significant others" for outcome ratings, Lazarus's reports go far in
strengthening hypotheses concerning: the usefulness of systematic desensitization in the hands of a well-trained, experienced clinician; the necessary care
and skill in the application of the technique; the necessary nonspecific clinical
skills upon which the procedure should be applied; the range of problems for
which desensitization might be applicable; and client characteristics which
might interact with outcome.

Hain, Butcher, & Stevenson.   Hain, Butcher, & Stevenson (1966) have published the third major uncontrolled clinical series on systematic desensitization.
From among patients at the University of Virginia School of Medicine, 27 (14
male, 13 female) inpatients and outpatients, ranging in age from twenty-three
to sixty-seven years (Mdn = 37), were selected on the basis of presenting complaints of anxiety or related distressing behaviors which were "sufficiently
localized" that anxiety-eliciting stimulus situations could be easily identified.
All patients were diagnosed as psychoneurotics and judged of sufficient intelligence and motivation to participate in desensitization therapy. Of the problems
treated, only a few were reported on the basis of reponse classes, which included: impotence, paroxysmal tachycardia, ejaculatio praecox, headaches,
obsessions, shyness, anxiety attacks, and tension states. The majority of cases
were reported in terms of the stimulus classes identified as eliciting anxiety and
related distressing behavior, and these covered a wide range: hostility, criticism, sex, girls, public and social appearances, assertion, father, teachers, heart
attacks, being alone, social occasions, public speaking, people, travel, giving
injections, driving, church functions, elevators, being thought ill, and germs.
The duration of distress varied from 4 months to 50 years (Mdn = 8.6 years),
12 patients had previously undergone treatment, and all were rated as
markedly to severely disabled prior to systematic desensitization.

Therapy was conducted by Butcher (N = 20) and Stevenson (N = 7),
both of whom had considerable clinical experience. No data are presented concerning the specific operations used in systematic desensitization, beyond reference to Wolpe (1958, 1961), and this series appears to represent the first application by both therapists. However, the authors note that they had previously had the advantage of discussing technique with Wolpe and had observed
him employing it. Like the previous series, treatment procedures were not
limited solely to systematic desensitization; however, unlike the previous
series, the therapists considered themselves "avowed eclectics," rather than
"behavior therapists." The total number of treatment sessions ranged from
1 to 64 (Mdn = 16) one-hour sessions over periods of 1 day to 22 months
(Mdn = 5 months). Since no further data are provided, the number of sessions
devoted to assessment, relaxation training, hierarchy construction, and other
therapeutic procedures as well as desensitization remains unclear.

Assessment procedures consisted of therapist ratings before and after treatment on a 5-point (from absent to severe) Symptom Severity Scale related to the degree of interference in normal work and social activities. The bases for these ratings, like the Wolpe ratings above, were patient self-reports of extratherapeutic encounters with stressful stimuli. Similar ratings were also made on a Functional Status Scale concerning several occupational, social, and sexual spheres. "General improvement," as distinct from the specific improvement of the Symptom Severity Scale, was also rated at termination of treatment on a 4-point scale (from worse to marked improvement). In an attempt to reduce the effect of observer bias in such ratings, an independent rating of general improvement and pre-post symptom severity was obtained from Hain. However, the "independent" ratings were made from case summaries provided by the therapists, and the independent rater was aware of the time of rating and the occurrence of treatment. Additionally, no validity data are presented, and interrater reliability is reported only to the extent that ratings fell within one scale unit of each other in every case but one. In view of these factors, the outcome assessment of the present report may be considered no more or less reliable or valid than those reported by Wolpe and Lazarus.

For the entire group of patients, an average reduction of 2 scale units was obtained for specific symptom severity, and a mean general improvement rating of 2.5 (marked improvement) was given at treatment termination. Of the 27 patients treated, 21 were considered specific treatment successes (78 percent), while 19 also showed additional marked general improvement (70 percent). The authors reported no indication of symptom substitution; rather, general improvement in other areas appeared to be a function of improvement in specifically treated problems. Follow-up contacts were made with 14 "improved" cases over a period of 2 to 48 months (Mdn = 12). Of these, 3 cases were rated as showing additional improvement and 2 cases as showing relapse. No differences in number, frequency, or duration of treatment sessions, nor in severity or duration of disability, were found between cases rated successful and those considered failures. Although individual data are not presented for treatment failures, the authors suggest that the following were involved: difficulties in constructing central, stable, properly graded hierarchies; inadequate relaxation; difficulties with imagery; presence of realistic environmental stress; and premature termination for financial reasons. Unfortunately, the results of the two therapists were not compared, and therefore not even suggestive evidence is available on possible effects of therapist characteristics.

In summary, the report of Hain et al., taken alone, offers no more evidence of the specific efficacy of systematic desensitization therapy than the previously reviewed series of reports. Nor can detailed comparisons be made with other outcome reports because of the uncontrolled nature of all domains of variables. It does, however, strengthen hypotheses concerning the effectiveness of the technique and the range of problems which might be applicable for treatment, and it does provide suggestive data on results of experienced "eclectic" clinicians' attempts to apply the procedure without intensive training or supervision.

Lazovik & Lang.   Lazovik & Lang (1960) reported a pilot study of systematic desensitization which was unique in many respects. The study was an attempt to standardize the treatment technique and produce the phenomenon of systematic desensitization in the laboratory. From six students who agreed to participate in an experiment following an interview request, four snake-phobic subjects (three females, 1 male), twenty, twenty-three, forty-two, and fifty years of age, were selected on the basis of the severity of fear elicited by non-poisonous snakes. Additional screening procedures included administration of the Stanford Hypnotic Susceptibility Scale, the Minnesota Multiphasic Personality Inventory (MMPI), the Pittsburgh Revision of the MPI and a psychiatric interview—all focused toward exclusion of psychotic individuals. Assessment of treatment effectiveness was based upon pre-post tape-recorded interviews focused upon subjects' reports of response in the presence of snakes, and upon an actual in vivo avoidance test. The latter procedure consisted of requesting each subject (S) to enter a room which contained a live snake in a glass cage, 15 feet from the entrance. Each S was then encouraged to approach the snake as closely as possible, and to hold it if approached. The closest point of approach was then recorded by an experimental assistant who conducted all assessments, and was not involved in the administration of treatment.

Treatment, conducted by Lang or Lazovik, was standardized by following a mimeographed manual which limited interactions to those involved directly with systematic desensitization. Although both therapists were experienced clinicians, neither had apparently used desensitization before this study. A total of 13 sessions (15 for one S), lasting between 30 and 60 minutes, was held with each S, limited in time to seven weeks total duration. About 15 minutes of each of the first 3 sessions were devoted to hierarchy construction, and half of each of the first 5 sessions to relaxation training. Half of each of 3 sessions (sessions 4 to 6) was devoted to training in hypnotic induction, and the seventh session consisted of a readministration of the Stanford Scale. Beginning with the eighth session, desensitization proper proceeded for 6 sessions (8 sessions for one S) until the time limit was reached. Possibly due to the therapists' inexperience in hierarchy construction, sufficient problems arose with the grading and placement of items during desensitization proper that no S completed the entire hierarchy in the two-week period available.

In spite of difficulties with appropriate grading of hierarchies, three of the four Ss showed marked reduction both in self-report of fear in the presence of snakes and in their approach to the live snake in the avoidance test following systematic desensitization. The one S who did not show improvement revealed that she had never experienced reduction of anxiety with the imagined stimuli during desensitization proper, but had failed to communicate this to the therapist until the last session. Five months after treatment termination, a follow-up assessment, consisting of both interview and avoidance tests, on two Ss revealed both to have maintained their improvement.

While the lack of a no-treatment control group in this study prevents the establishment of cause-effect conclusions, the inclusion of external in vivo assessment leaves little question that therapeutic change did occur. Lazovik & Lang consider this an analog investigation on two counts: (1) while the phobic reactions of treated Ss were indeed severe, their nature was such that they were not significant life problems; (2) the therapists presented themselves as experimenters with an impartial attitude toward success, rather than as therapists attempting to help clients. However, this study provides the first report of suggestive evidence on systematic desensitization procedures applied alone with external assessment of effectiveness, extending the use of the procedure in a more standardized manner to two additional therapists and a new type of treatment environment.

Paul. Paul (1964) also reported two cases in detail in which external evidence was available and systematic desensitization was applied under more controlled conditions. The purpose of the report was to present suggested modifications and formalization of procedure directed toward increasing the efficiency of systematic desensitization therapy. The cases to illustrate the procedure were selected from an unpublished series of pilot clinical case studies by the author which were focused upon developing specific technique parameters, with one case drawn from a controlled pilot study reviewed later (Paul, Chapter 3). When these cases were treated, the therapist had considerable clinical experience, but his experience in desensitization was limited to a few (8 to 10) of these exploratory clinical studies. Both cases were students referred to a university clinic after failing to respond to treatment elsewhere. The first case was an eighteen-year-old female treated solely by desensitization for test anxiety of six years duration. Following a brief history and presentation of rationale during the first hour, hierarchy construction began. During the second hour, construction of a 10-item hierarchy was completed, relaxation was induced, and desensitization proper was begun. Desensitization was completed in two more hours, for a total of 4 sessions over a two-week period. In addition to the subjects, self-reports of feeling "just grand" during examinations after treatment, GSR recordings taken during desensitization proper revealed responses to hierarchy items prior to desensitization, followed by a lack of detectable response to the same items after desensitization. Additionally, overall college grades improved from C's and D's prior to treatment to A's and B's following treatment and remained at the higher level at a follow-up thirteen months after treatment termination.

The second case was a twenty-one-year-old male with a severe phobic reaction to army uniforms, persons in his ROTC drill section, the building in which ROTC was held, and essentially any stimuli related to ROTC or the army. Severe reactions characterized by violent spasms, vomiting, palpitations, and fainting were almost continuous due to required weekly attendance at ROTC. Five months prior to referral, the client had become nearly totally withdrawn and his grades had dropped from a B— average to a D— average, placing him on probation. Over a seven-week period, 1 diagnostic interview and 11 therapy sessions were held. Relaxation training, hierarchy construction, and hypnotic training were completed in 3 sessions, and a twenty-four-item spatial-temporal hierarchy was desensitized during 5 of the remaining 8 sessions. The other 3 sessions were devoted to discussing future plans and alternatives, interpersonal relationships, etc. Since the subject was required to attend ROTC every week, a session-by-session check was available by observing his attendance and the presence or absence of the customary anxiety reaction. These observations revealed a direct correspondence with items completed during desensitization and a corresponding failure to change following sessions where desensitization was not carried out. On termination of treatment, the client completed the remaining two months of required ROTC, reporting no anxiety, and his grades climbed to a B+ average. A ten-month follow-up revealed that the grades were maintained, and the client reported no further difficulties, even though he spent the summer on an army base.

Like the reports reviewed above, these case studies cannot be taken as evidence that systematic desensitization was responsible for the changes observed. They do, however, provide additional suggestive evidence through the controlled application of systematic desensitization to distressing behaviors which were significant life problems for the clients by yet another therapist in another treatment environment. Additionally, the nonreactive nature of the indicants of change (grades, GSR, attendance) lessens the possibility of bias arising from sole reliance on judgments from involved participants.

Other Case Studies.   Several therapists have reported on other case studies, and the major features of these studies, as well as those reviewed above, are summarized in Table 2–1. In addition to cases included in their other writings, both Rachman (1959) and Lang (1965a) present reports of original cases to illustrate the use of systematic desensitization. Rachman's report, one of the earliest in the literature, dealt with a schoolteacher who experienced anxiety and fainting associated with injections or attempted insertion of sanitary tampons, as well as pain during coitus. An 8-item hierarchy on the sanitary tampon theme was desensitized in 8 sessions, and a 9-item injection hierarchy in 14. Extratherapeutic practice was also employed. On follow-ups at six and twelve weeks, the client reported regular use of internal sanitary tampons, pleasurable coitus, and having received an injection without difficulty. Her Willoughby score

Table 2-1 Summary of Uncontrolled Case Reports and Group Studies of Individual Systematic Desensitization Therapy*

Author	Clients					Therapists		Assessment Procedure†	Treatment			Outcome†
	Problem treated	Characteristics				Characteristics			No. of sessions	Total duration	Follow-up	
		No.	Sex	Age	Other	No.	Other					
(1) Wolpe (1952b) (2) Wolpe (1954) (3) Wolpe (1958) (4) Wolpe (1961) (5) Wolpe (1962)	Mixed†	150*	M=53% F=47%	11–68 Mdn=33	"Neurotics"—all private outpatients	1	All Wolpe (Medical student on 1 case)	Observation and self-report; T-rating; Willoughby	8–263 Mdn=23	1–75 months Mdn=7	6–48 months (N=21)	+ (88–92%)
(6) Lazarus and Rachman (1957) (7) Lazarus (1960) (8) Lazarus (1963a) (9) Lazarus (1963b) (10) Lazarus (1964a) (11) Lazarus (1964b) (12) Lazarus (1965a) (13) Lazarus (1965b) (14) Lazarus (1965c)	Mixed†	220*	M=30% F=70%	9-1/2–70 Mdn=35	"Neurotic introverts"—all private outpatients	3	All Lazarus, except (6), 2 cases treated by Rachman; (8) 1 case with co-therapist	Pretreatment battery; T-rating; external reports	3–200+ Mdn=16	1 week to 4 years, Mdn=5.5 months	3–48 months (N=39)	+ (85–86%)
(15) Hain et al. (1966)	Mixed†	27	M=14 F=13	23–67 Mdn=37	"Neurotic" hospital inpatients and outpatients	2	"Avowed eclectics"	Self-report; T&O rating	1–64 Mdn=16	1 day to 22 months Mdn=5 months	2–48 months (N=14)	+ (78%)
(16) Lazovik and Lang (1960)	Snake phobia	4	M=1 F=3	20, 23, 42, 50	Student volunteers	(2)	"Experimenters"	Multiple; external avoidance test	13–15	7 weeks	5 months (N=2)	(75%)
(17) Paul (1964) Test anxiety		(1)	F	18	Student outpatients	1	"Eclectic"	GSR; grades	4	2 weeks	13 months	+
"Army" phobia		1	M	21		(1)	University clinic	Attendance	12	7 weeks	10 months	+
(18) Rachman (1959)	Injection phobia	1	F	24	Teacher outpatient	(1)	Hospital clinic	Willoughby self-report	22	3 months	3 months	+
(19) Lang (1965a)	Anorexia	1	F	23	Nurse outpatient	(1)	University clinic	Self-report; weight	70	11 months	12 months	+
(20) Hallsten (1965)	Anorexia; phobia	1	F	12	Inpatient	1	Hospital	Self-report; weight	12	9 weeks	5 months	+
(21) Kushner (1965)	Traumatic phobia	1	M	17	"Hot-rodder" outpatient	1	Clinic	Mother's report	6	2.5 weeks	3 months	+
(22) Ashem (1963)	Disaster phobia	1	M	27	Inpatient	1	Hospital	Wife's report	21	?	3 months	+

Table 2-1 *Summary of Uncontrolled Case Reports and Group Studies of Individual Systematic Desensitization Therapy (cont'd)*

Author	Problem treated	Clients Characteristics No.	Sex	Age	Other	Therapists Characteristics No.	Other	Assessment Procedure†	Treatment No. of sessions	Total duration	Follow-up	Outcome†
(23) Cautela (1965a)	Anxiety neurotic	1	M	33	Outpatient 2.5 years	1	"Originally dynamic"	Self-report	6	6 weeks	6 months	+
(24) Cautela (1965b)	Mixed†	3	M=1 F=2	23, 35, 45	Outpatients	(1)		Self-report	12–?	?	5 months (N=1)	+
(25) Bond and Hutchinson (1960)	Exhibitionism	1	M	25	"Sociopath"	2	Forensic clinic	Police, wife report	46	16 months	Contin.	+
(26) Gold and Neufeld (1965)	Homosexuality	1	M	16	Court referral	2?	Hospital	Self-report	10	4 weeks	12 months (7 sessions)	+
(27) Cowden and Ford (1962)	Interpersonal Anxiety	1	M	27	"Paranoid schizophrenic"	2?	Hospital	External reports	18	4 months		+
	Compulsion	1	M	42		(2?)			56	?		−
(28) Geer (1964)	Lice phobia	1	F	17	Psychotic MMPI	1	Univ. clinic	Test battery	16	16 weeks	3 months	+
(29) Meichenbaum (1966c)	Hysterical ptosis	1	M	43	"Hysteric"	1	Hospital	External reports	26	4.5 months	3 months	+
(30) Agras (1965)	Multiple phobias	6	?	?	?	1	Medical school	GSR during therapy	?–7	?		+
(31) Kraft and Al-Issa (1965a)	Traffic phobia	1	M	37	"Anxious extrovert"	1	Hospital clinic	Test battery	25	3 months	6 months (10 sessions)	+
(32) Kraft and Al-Issa (1965b)	Heat phobia	1	F	24	Inpatient	1?	Hospital	Avoidance test	41	2 months	12 months (Contin.)	+
(33) Brough et al. (1965)	Animal phobias	1	F	39	Inpatient	3?	Hospital	Husband's report	46	23 weeks	12 months	+
(34) Walton and Mather (1963)	Speech impediment	1	M	40	Anxious introvert	2?	Hospital clinic	Self-report	47	?	6 months	+
(35) Gray et al. (1965)	Vocal nodules	1	F	29	Outpatient	1?	Speech clinic	Laryngeal examination	15	3 weeks	10 weeks	+
(36) Beyme (1964)	Hyperesthesia	1	M	36	"Hysteric"	1	Private?	Saliva flow?	12	?	12 months	+
(37) Madsen and Ullmann (1967)	Frigidity	1	F	?	Student outpatient	2	(Husband also)	Husband's report	12	?	9 months	+
(38) Shafer and Jaffe (1965)	Kleptomania	1	F	59	Court referral	1?	"Medical hypnotist"	Self-report	12	3 months		−
	Driving phobia	1	M	37	Outpatient	(1?)		Self-report	24	6 months	18 months	+

Table 2-1 Summary of Uncontrolled Case Reports and Group Studies of Individual Systematic Desensitization Therapy (cont'd)

| Author | Problem treated | Clients — Characteristics | | | | Therapists | | Assessment Procedure† | Treatment | | | Outcome† |
		No.	Sex	Age	Other	No.	Characteristics — Other		No. of sessions	Total duration	Follow-up	
(39) Weinberg and Zazlove (1963)	Dog phobia	2	?	?	Extraverted student volunteer	2?	"Impersonal and inexperienced"	GSR during therapy	12, 16	8 weeks	?	?
	Bug phobia	1	?	?		(2)?			19	8 weeks?	?	?
(40) Meyer (1957)	Blackouts, fears	1	M	42	Inpatient	1	Hospital	GSR during therapy	?	?	?	—
(41) Meyer and Crisp (1966)	Phobias?	?	?	?	?	(1)+? ?		Ratings	?	?	?	—
(42) Schmidt et al. (1965)	?	?	?	?	?	? ?		Ratings	?	?	?	?
(43) Cooper (1963) (44) Marks and Gelder (1965) (45) Cooper et al. (1965)	Agoraphobia and "other phobias"; obsessives?	?, 13–16	? M=10% F=90%	? Mean: 28–34	"Neurotics"— inpatients and outpatients	?	Inexperienced; students, registrars, academic psychologists	Ratings from case records (retrospective)	? Mean: 27–56	? Mean: 4–6 months	1 year	? (67–76%) at follow-up
(46) Gelder and Marks (1966)	Agoraphobia, frigidity, interpersonal problems	10	M=2 F=8	Mean: 34.5	Severely incapacitated inpatients	?	Inexperienced registrars	T-, Pt-, A- ratings; test battery	? 3–141 Mean: 69	? 1–47 weeks Mean: 23	1 year	? 70%
(47) Gelder et al. (1964) (48) Gelder et al. (1967)	Agoraphobia. Social and "other" phobias	16	M=6 F=10	Mean: 30.8	Severely incapacitated outpatients	5	4 had no previous desensitization experience	T-, Pt-, A- ratings; test battery	? Mean: 36	Mean: 9 months	Mean: 16 months	+ (75%) at follow-up
(49) Ramsay et al. (1966)	"Phobias"	20	?	Freshmen	Students	3	Undergrads	Fear therm, avoidance test	2–4†	2 weeks	None	+
(50) Koenig and Masters (1965)	Smoking	14	M=9 F=5	19–25	Student volunteers	7	5 inexperienced grad students	Tally sheets, self-report	10	5–6 weeks	6 months	+?
(51) Pyke et al. (1966)	Smoking	22	?	?	Paid volunteers	3?	Inexperienced ?	Tally sheets, self-report	10	10 weeks	19 weeks	?

* Table classifications correspond as closely as feasible to the domains of variables presented in Paul (Chapter 1). A separate classification of environmental variables has not been included due to a consistent lack of data in published reports. Therefore, when environmental data are available, they are included as "other characteristics" of clients or therapists.
† See text for details.

dropped from 44 to 26. Lang (1965a) treated a nurse whose primary complaints were vomiting and loss of appetite resulting in a 20-pound weight loss, although pervasive anxiety, fear of travel, and severe anxiety in a number of situations were identified as contributing problems. After failure to produce counterconditioning by having the client eat candy, 60 sessions of desensitization to 7 different hierarchies, combined with assertion, resulted in her regaining the lost weight, purchasing a car, and reporting improvement in other areas.

Hallsten (1965) reports desensitization of a second case of anorexia in an inpatient adolescent. A fear of storms was treated in 2 sessions, followed by 9 sessions desensitizing a hierarchy on the theme of fear of gaining weight. External evidence of improvement was available in a weight increase from 57 to 77 pounds, normal for her height and age. Kushner (1965) describes the short-term treatment of a male adolescent "hot rodder" who suffered from anxiety in his car, insomnia, irritability, poor appetite, and inability to concentrate in studies, following an automobile accident. Following 5 sessions of desensitization on the traumatic theme over a two-week period, the client reported that all presenting problems were alleviated, and this was corroborated by his mother. The favorable report was repeated by phone in a three-month follow-up. Treatment of a sales administrator who had previously received two years of dynamic psychotherapy and six bouts of electroconvulsive therapy (ECT) is reported by Ashem (1963). In this case, fear of atomic attack reportedly led to avoidance of movies, radio, newspapers, etc., to complete avoidance of interpersonal contact, and to excessive drinking until hospitalization ensued. Three sessions were devoted to relaxation training and hierarchy construction, resulting in an 8-item hierarchy on radio and TV disaster reports, and a 14-item hierarchy on newspaper accounts of disaster. A 4-item "approach" series was also employed, but it should be noted that this "hierarchy" appears to be a series of direct suggestions, since no actual stimuli were imagined. After 19 sessions of desensitization proper, the patient reported attendance at movies, visiting friends, and listening to news broadcasts without difficulty. The patient's report was confirmed by his wife at termination, and again three months later.

Cautela (1965a, 1965b) presents data on four cases which are interesting because of the author's transition from "dynamic" psychotherapy to desensitization. The first case (23)[2] was a lower-middle-class factory worker who had been in treatment with Cautela's traditional approach for 2½ years. Although improvement was noted in several areas during this time, the client continued to report fear of going to work and anxiety on the job, and this difficulty was the focus of the last six months of treatment. When little progress was made, desensitization was employed as a "last resort." The contribution of desensiti-

[2] The numbers in parentheses refer to summaries of reports in Table 2–1.

zation is even less clear than in most case reports because Cautela combined "autosuggestion" and in vivo procedures with candy bars; however, after 6 sessions focused on desensitization to criticism, the client reported no more difficulty with maintenance on a six-month follow-up. Cautela's second report (24) covers the desensitization of a truck driver for anxiety while driving, a nurse for interpersonal anxiety, and a housewife for anger and anxiety related to her alcoholic husband. Specific data are sparse since the cases were presented as illustrations that "insightful-like" statements often follow clinical change from desensitization; however, Cautela reports successful reduction of anxiety and avoidance responses following 9 to 12 sessions of desensitization to single relevant hierarchies for all three cases.

Bond and Hutchison (1960) report the only case in the literature in which systematic desensitization has been purposively applied to an individual carrying a diagnosis of "sociopathic personality." The presenting problem was compulsive exposure of genitals, documented by a police record indicating 24 charges of indecent exposure, 11 convictions, and 9 prison sentences. A long history of individual and group therapy, CO_2 abreaction, "chastity belt," and hypnosis preceded desensitization attempts at a forensic clinic. Systematic desensitization was undertaken on the assumption that anxiety elicited by specific classes of feminine stimuli motivated exposure. Bond first saw the client for 20 sessions. Within a month after termination, the client was again arrested for exposure and returned to the clinic, where Hutchison continued desensitization for an additional 26 sessions over a five-month period. Treatment was again terminated, but monthly follow-ups were maintained, with reportedly excellent social and sexual adjustment for thirteen months. However, at the end of that period, several extremely stressful events, including losing his job and being turned down for financial assistance, occasioned three more episodes of exposure followed by arrest and return to the clinic. The authors note that the client never exposed in the presence of stimuli which had been subjected to desensitization, and thus considered the case at least partially successful. They further report that additional themes relating to feelings of inadequacy and women's washrooms were anxiety-eliciting stimuli which had not been desensitized, and treatment continued along those lines at the time of the report. Gold and Neufeld (1965) also report the use of systematic desensitization with a court-referred case of sexual perversion—in this instance, an active male homosexual arrested for soliciting. Treatment consisted of 6 sessions of desensitization to a 6-item hierarchy on the theme of fear of failure over a period of two weeks, followed by *imaginal* "aversive deconditioning" and "discrimination learning" for a total of 10 sessions. Follow-up interviews were held 7 times over a twelve-month period, with reported improvement and no relapse. It should be noted that this report is even less adequate in providing descriptive information than most case studies; however, it is one of the few to deal with unmotivated, court-referred cases.

Two cases reported by Cowden & Ford (1962) represent the first published attempts at knowing application of systematic desensitization to psychotic individuals.[3] Both were hospitalized males, diagnosed as "paranoid schizophrenics," who had received several years of previous hospital treatment which included shock, drugs, and "psychotherapy." Desensitization was directed only at interpersonal anxiety for one case, and at overcoming compulsive checking for forgotten articles for the other. Both remained in regular hospital treatment, including psychotherapy, and other psychotic manifestations were not treated directly. After 18 sessions of desensitization to a 24-item hierarchy involving conversations with increasingly difficult content and persons, the first patient was reported to be more relaxed, friendly, talkative, and open by ward personnel. Unusual thoughts, disturbing dreams, and ideas of reference also were reported to decrease in severity, and the patient became regular and efficient in work assignments and started taking outside passes. The second case failed to show change outside the therapist's presence, by report of ward personnel, after 56 sessions of attempted desensitization to a 19-item hierarchy consisting of "leaving" various items. In vivo practice and assertion training were also employed. The authors consider the first case a success and the second a failure, but note that the second case may well have involved an inappropriate hierarchy, and that operant factors were likely involved.

Geer (1964) also reports the use of systematic desensitization with a lower-class adolescent female who obtained a psychotic MMPI profile ($T > 70$ on six of eight clinical scales). The client was treated as an outpatient, and observers were present for over half the sessions. A multiple-intake battery was administered, but only the MMPI was given after treatment. The client obtained a full-scale WAIS-IQ (Wechsler Adult Intelligence Scale) of 85, and test data indicated pervasive anxiety; however, treatment was directed toward fear of contracting head lice, which resulted in social withdrawal. Following 11 desensitization sessions to a single 22-item hierarchy, the client reported diminished anxiety and improved interpersonal relationships. A posttreatment MMPI produced a "normal" profile, and a three-month follow-up suggested further improvement with no evidence of "symptom substitution."

Desensitization was applied as a sequential strategy in one of two cases of hysteria reported by Meichenbaum (1966c). This case was a Veterans Administration (VA) hospital inpatient with a two-year history of headaches, eye trouble, and general anxiety which had failed to respond to efforts of optical therapy, chemotherapy, and chiropractic therapy. Reports of the patient's wife and results of psychological tests suggested a generally passive adjustment

[3] Both Cowden & Ford (1962) and Lang (1964) refer to a successful study of the desensitization of snake phobias with psychotic patients by the same authors. However, that study did not appear in the reference cited and could not be found elsewhere.

with the use of exclusion and denial. The major presenting complaint, inability to keep his eyes open more than 20 percent of waking hours, resulted in loss of work, inability to drive, and hospitalization six weeks prior to treatment. After 14 daily sessions of relaxation by direct suggestion, the patient was transferred to outpatient status, and 8 sessions of systematic desensitization were carried out in the course of a month. At the end of desensitization, he returned to work and drove his car, but reported he continued to close his eyes when dominated by wife, employer, or mother. The latter problems were dealt with through assertion training over a period of three months, at the end of which the patient and his wife both reported no further difficulty with eye closure. Similar reports were obtained at a three-month follow-up, without indication of symptom substitution.

In addition to variations of treatment which cannot be considered as the individual application of systematic desensitization (summarized in Paul, Chapter 3), several uncontrolled reports within the bounds of systematic desensitization therapy employ procedures which are unusual enough to note separately. One such report is that of Agras (1965) in which the focus was on the intratherapy decrement of anxiety during desensitization proper, rather than on final results. Although the exact procedure used is unclear, Agras reports that a total of 100 items presented to six patients failed to show a GSR by the seventh session of treatment, while they presumably did show a response prior to desensitization. It should also be noted that procedural difficulties in this report preclude the authors' conclusions regarding "spontaneous recovery" during sessions; however, the suggested use of continuous physiological monitoring during desensitization is worthwhile.

Kraft & Al-Issa (1965a, 1965b) report treatment of an outpatient for a traffic phobia related to noise levels in the street, with additional complaints of insomnia and irritability, and treatment of an inpatient for a "heat phobia" involving avoidance of hot appliances, water, and foods. In both cases, the MPI and the Taylor Manifest Anxiety Scale (MAS) were administered before and after treatment. For the heat phobia, an in vivo tolerance test requiring insertion of a finger into water of increasing temperature was also included. The unusual features of their procedures have to do with relaxation and hierarchies. In both cases, relaxation was trained totally by "hypnotic induction," in three 1½-hour sessions for one (31) and four 1-hour sessions for the other (32). The hierarchies in both cases involved 16 specific stimulus situations; however, *each* item was presented at 25 different "noise levels," for the traffic phobia, and 33 to 68 different "temperature levels" for the heat phobia. Although the authors claim to follow Wolpe's (1958) procedure for desensitization proper, they report (31) that most scenes were presented only once and none were presented more than twice. In addition to the questionable ability of patients to discriminate such fine levels of temperature or noise, the expenditure of 33 to 37 hours of desensitization proper for essentially single thematic phobias appears very inefficient in comparison with other reports. The first case (31) showed a MAS reduction of 44-14, a MPI extroversion change of 34-38, and a MPI neuroticism change of 31-12 following twenty-two 1½-hour desensitization sessions over three months and ten follow-up interviews over a six-month period. All presenting problems were reportedly alleviated. The second case (32) showed no change on MAS or MPI following 37 one-hour sessions over a two-month period, but was able to tolerate water of 140° F as compared to a pretreatment tolerance of less than 118° F, and the authors report that she became completely anxiety-free in all aspects of her heat phobia. This case is further confused since the patient continued in treatment for additional problems for at least twelve months. Brough, Yorkston, & Stafford-Clark (1965) present a case to illustrate the method they have applied to a "large number" of patients. Their method appears quite similar to the procedures of Kraft & Al-Issa. The patient was a housewife who had been completely unable to leave the house during the summer for five years because of a fear of wasps. Psychotherapy, drugs, electroplexy, and prefrontal leucotomy had not been of benefit. She was initially hospitalized for treatment, but later continued as an outpatient. Relaxation training consisted of 3 sessions of hypnotic procedures only. Hierarchies consisted of 10 animals graded according to the degree of anxiety elicited, from pigeons to wasps. Scene presentations then consisted of a combined thematic and spatial-temporal approach to each animal, with only the last scene of a session being repeated. After 46 desensitization sessions over twenty-three weeks, complete relief and freedom of movement were reported, and the improvement was confirmed by the husband's report at termination and at a one-year follow-up.

Walton & Mather have reported several cases in different publications; one (1963) dealt with systematic desensitization therapy for a speech impediment based upon interpersonal anxiety. Following 9 sessions of progressive relaxation training and construction of a 20-item thematic hierarchy, 38 sessions of desensitization proper were carried out. The result was a report of no stammering and no anxiety, which was maintained at a six-month follow-up. The unusual procedure in the application was during desensitization proper; *each* session consisted of one ten-second presentation of 5 sequential items with ninety seconds between presentations. The first item from each session was also the last, and at each session, one new item was introduced and one old item was eliminated. The probability of suggestion or placebo response is especially low in this case since the same therapists had previously attempted 48 sessions of "shadowing" therapy with the patient without improvement.

Gray, England, & Mohoney (1965) present a case involving both unusual application of systematic desensitization and a unique problem for treatment. The patient was a chronically anxious female who complained of hoarseness, breathiness, and loss of voice. A laryngeal examination revealed benign vocal nodules, inflammation, and swelling, believed to result from continued hypertension of the laryngeal musculature. Surgery and vocal rest had been used before, with little lasting effect. During 7 daily half-hour sessions, the client was taught to relax "after Jacobsen," first by tape-recorded instructions, reading assignments in Jacobsen's book, and by an undescribed hypnotic procedure in which relaxation could be induced by a "slow count of three." Three hierarchies of 7, 11, and 12 items were constructed during 6- to 10-minute portions of the first 5 sessions. Desensitization proper was not described in detail; however, hierarchies were dealt with concurrently during 10 sessions over a two-week period. Further follow-ups to 10 weeks reveal "complete laryngeal recovery" by examination, and reports of reduction in pervasive anxiety and ability to handle stressful situations.

Another unusual case of application and type of problem was reported by Beyme (1964) in the treatment of hyperesthesia of taste and touch. An outpatient complaining of night sweats and insomnia was specifically treated for masseter cramps and increased saliva flow elicited by the taste or sight of acidic substances, as well as the touch of many kinds of textiles. The relaxation procedure consisted of 2 sessions of autogenic training following Schultz & Luthe (1959). A 20-item hierarchy on the acid theme and a 6-item hierarchy on the touch theme were constructed, followed by 10 sessions of desensitization proper. In early sessions of desensitization to acid, a piece of sugar was also eaten in conjunction with relaxation, and later sessions involved "imaging sugar." Description of the procedure is limited since no further data are provided with regard to procedure, and interpretation is further confounded since drugs were also administered. All problems were reported "cured" after treatment with no relapse or symptom substitution on a one-year follow-up. Data are presented on the reduction of saliva flow, but it is unclear whether saliva was measured or merely estimated from self-report.

Madsen & Ullmann (1967) report an illustrative case of the treatment of frigidity, which follows the standard desensitization procedure, but which is unusual in that the husband is involved formally as a co-therapist. The client was a female graduate student whose anxiety concerning coitus had prevented a single mutually satisfying sexual contact in two years of marriage. No benefits had been derived from four months of previous treatment by a physician or marriage counselor. A single 50-item hierarchy directed towards intercourse was constructed, and both husband and client were trained in relaxation during the first session, with early items imagined conjointly over the first 3 sessions of desensitization proper. For the remaining 8 sessions, the husband presented scenes to the wife under the therapist's direction. Orgasm was reported for the first time after 5 desensitization sessions, and at termination was occurring regularly at least twice a week. A nine-month follow-up, verified by the husband's report, revealed continued orgasm, increased mutual enjoyment of sexual contacts, and a corresponding decrease in family arguments.

In contrast to the overwhelmingly positive reports of the cases reviewed above, a few reports of questionable or negative outcome have also appeared, often in combination with unusual procedural features. Shafer & Jaffe (1965) present one such report dealing with two cases. The first was a court referral for kleptomania (habitual stealing without financial necessity) of forty-nine years duration, and the second was a male who complained of anxiety when driving faster than twenty-five miles per hour or over "certain distances." Both had received previous treatment. Although the authors refer to Wolpe (1958), no data are provided for any aspect of treatment except that total treatment duration consisted of 12 and 24 weekly sessions, respectively. The therapist is described as a "medical hypnotist," and relaxation appears to have been totally limited to hypnotic induction. The report suggests that more than one hierarchy was involved, but no information is available on number, type, or content; in fact, the little information given suggests that the treatment procedure applied was more akin to direct hypnotic suggestion of symptom removal than to systematic desensitization. For the first case, the authors report that there was no anxiety or impulse to steal while "under hypnosis," but that there was no improvement in behavior. The second case was reportedly able to drive at forty-five miles per hour without discomfort, with concurrent increased confidence at work, and no relapse on eighteen-month follow-up. It might also be noted that no evidence was presented to suggest that stealing in the first case was anxiety-motivated, and that treatment was aimed at "abolishing the urge to take articles."

Weinberg & Zaslove (1963) provide a second report of questionable outcome judgments in which no information is available concerning actual treatment procedures. The report concerns a pilot study conducted with three student volunteers, selected on the basis of "circumscribed phobias"—two about dogs, one about "squashy bugs." The students had "normal" MMPI profiles and extroverted MPI scores of 30, 36, and 40. Treatment duration was limited to the summer session at the University of California at Los Angeles, and continuous GSR recordings were attempted throughout treatment. The purpose of the article was to report the occurrence of several types of "resistance" to systematic desensitization, which actually appear to be the expected response of any unmotivated subject to experimenters who lack experience in the non-specific "clinical" skills of subject handling and in the specific skills of the experimental treatment procedure. The authors report that "slight improvements might have been made" in spite of procedural difficulties, and that GSR decreases to phobic stimuli were observed in two subjects "with complete data." In view of the lack of clarity in application, and the authors' own indecision, even as an uncontrolled case study, the outcome must be regarded as unknown.

In an early paper, Meyer (1957) mentions one case in which he was unsuccessful in applying systematic desensitization. Apparently the patient was never successfully relaxed, nor did imagined stimuli ever elicit an increase

in anxiety. No further information was provided on Meyer's use of the procedure, and it should be noted that several authors have mentioned successful
application of desensitization without further data in a similar way. The Meyer
(1957) article is listed separately as a background to a more recent report of
Meyer & Crisp (1966) in which it was stated that the authors' experience with
systematic desensitization was disappointing. The stated purpose of Meyer &
Crisp (41) was to present problems encountered with the application of general
"behaviour therapy," basing their discussion on 54 cases which appear to include all of those treated by any procedure called "behaviour therapy" at
Middlesex Hospital in London. The outcome criteria consisted of a joint rating
by the authors of the degree of change on a 3-point scale (much improved,
slightly improved, and unimproved), presumably from clinical records since
Meyer reportedly treated 36 cases, while the remainder were treated by "other
therapists." No data are presented on reliability or validity, which makes the
report of considerably less value than those reviewed above, since the rating
scale allows fewer discriminations, and the apparently retrospective use of
clinical records allows further variation and sources of bias to enter into judgments of outcome.

A further problem with the entire Meyer & Crisp report concerns the
unusual therapeutic conditions surrounding treatment, in which "behaviour
therapy" is conducted under "combined general psychiatric and behaviour
therapist supervision." On the basis of an assessment by the general psychiatrist, patients are adjudged suitable or unsuitable for "behaviour therapy."
For those judged suitable, an appropriate symptom or symptoms are selected
for treatment by such procedures. "The patient is thereafter observed by the
original clinician. . . . Meanwhile the behaviour therapist treats the specific
symptom or symptoms . . . no attempt was made to establish either intra- or
inter-group consistency for . . . method of selection for behaviour therapy"
(Meyer & Crisp, 1966, p. 367). It also appears that the definition of "symptom"
in this report exemplifies the oversimplification and narrowness of focus for
which others have been taken to task (see Lazarus, 1966a), e.g., "Behaviour
therapy was usually aimed at a symptom or one aspect of a symptom complex
(e.g. the need to avert gaze in a social anxiety state)" (Meyer & Crisp, 1966,
p. 368). In addition to the above problems with the entire report, there is no
way of determining to whom, for what, how, to how many, or by whom systematic desensitization was applied. On the basis of Meyer's previous writings
(Meyer, 1957; Meyer & Gelder, 1963), it appears that Meyer considers systematic desensitization only for classical phobias, but even here his preference
seems to be a focus on his own procedure of "practical retraining." With regard to the number and outcome of cases treated by systematic desensitization,
the authors state at one point that, "Four out of 13 phobic patients failed to
respond at all to systematic desensitization and graded practical retraining"
(Meyer & Gelder, 1963, p. 370). However, at another point they indicate that

all but 2 cases in which desensitization was attempted also received practical retraining, and further, for desensitization, there was "major success in only two cases." The problems and difficulties with attempted applications of systematic desensitization listed by the authors include those previously mentioned by Meyer (1957); namely, failure to obtain relaxation and vivid imagery, as well as patient statements that the procedure was artificial. They also reported technical problems with hierarchy construction, and difficulty in patient-therapist communications regarding the presence of anxiety. Many of the problems raised by Meyer & Crisp may indeed be important with given populations of clients or with distressing behaviors, therapists, or environments; however, the nature of their report is such that all aspects of systematic desensitization must remain in question.

Schmidt, Castell, & Brown (1965) report a retrospective study of patients treated at Banstead Hospital, Sutton, Surrey, in which an unknown portion of five patients were treated by "relaxation training and reciprocal inhibition." With the exception that these authors do not draw specific conclusions about the efficacy of systematic desensitization, their evaluation procedure and basic data are comparable to those of Meyer & Crisp, and the same comments apply.

Retrospective Studies and Other Pseudocontrolled Investigations. Retrospective studies and other pseudocontrolled investigations are included in Table 2–1 and reviewed in this section because the level of product of such designs cannot exceed that of an uncontrolled single-group study. Additionally, while some controlled experiments reviewed later (Paul, Chapter 3) may commit errors which prevent sound cause-effect relationships from being established, it seems worthwhile to distinguish such investigations from those reported in this chapter, where the word "controlled" appears in the title, but the design nearly precludes solid evidence from the outset (see Paul, Chapter 1).

In a series of three articles, Cooper (1963), Marks & Gelder (1965), and Cooper, Gelder, & Marks (1965) report retrospective studies of all cases treated by "behaviour therapy" from 1954 to 1963 at Bethlam Royal and Maudsley Hospitals in London, excluding cases of enuresis, encopresis, and school phobias. In all essential respects, their procedure is like that of Meyer & Crisp (1966), reviewed above, and all comments regarding the latter apply to these articles; however, since the current authors continually commit the lethal error of drawing cause-effect conclusions from inadequate data, a more detailed review seems appropriate.

The procedure for all three studies was nearly identical. In the first report (43), a search of hospital records found 30 cases treated by "behaviour therapy" during the period from 1954 to 1960. Having identified these cases, a further search of hospital records resulted in the selection of 16 "control cases" treated in 1956 and 1957, and "with four minor exceptions these cases were matched to within ±10% in age, ±33% in symptom duration before treatment, and for sex, nature and severity of symptoms, and for whether inpatient or out-patient" (43, p. 412).

The second report (44) similarly identified an additional 21 cases of agoraphobia and 11 "other phobias," all but one of which were treated after the first article, from 1960 to 1963. A further search of hospital records cover-ing the period 1954 to 1961 led to the selection of 31 "controls" for these cases, "matched" in the same fashion as the initial paper, although the authors state that matching of "other phobias" was "rather less complete." It appears that one case of "behaviour therapy" and an unknown number of "controls" were included in both the first (No. 43) and second (44) articles. The third article (45) combined 16 new cases of "behaviour therapy" drawn from records of 1960 to 1963, and an unknown number of "controls," with the cases from the two previous articles for a total of 77 cases of "behaviour therapy" and 55 "controls." The assessment procedure in all three reports consisted of extract-ing "relevant information" from case notes in the records before treatment, after treatment, one month later, and one year later. The second article (44) also included information extracted from three months after termination, but these data were dropped from later reports. At the one-year follow-up, of the combined total including controls, 16 cases were by direct interview, and 10 from information supplied by others. The information retrospectively extracted from records during each of these time periods were then independently rated by two "assessors" on a 5-point Symptom Severity Scale (from absent to severe) based upon the degree of interference with work or social activities. While the scale included five categories, the actual outcome criteria consisted of three categories (much improved, improved, unimproved) corresponding to changes of 2, 1, or 0 on the Severity Scale. A 4-point General Improvement Scale (from worse to much improved) was also included in the first two reports.

The first major methodological problem with these reports arises from the data source. Case notes are first of all recorded not only by different ther-apists (of an unknown number) for different cases, but by different persons in different roles over varying times for assessment within the same case. Thus, sources of error and bias are open in the patient's report to the therapist, in the therapist's frame of reference in inferring change, in the selective recording of data in the notes by the therapist, and in the possible interaction between patients and the different staff obtaining the reports. Another broad source of selection error and bias lies in the identification of "relevant information" within the notes which is extracted for rating. These sources of bias and error alone are sufficient to prevent meaningful assessment; however, this series of reports also suffers in the ratings themselves. The procedure for establishing outcome ratings was based upon the following strategy: "Agreement was as-sumed when the two assessors estimated the same degree of shift in grade of symptoms from one occasion of testing to the next. Disagreement was dealt with by first presenting the same information again, and finally, if necessary, by presenting it to a third and deciding assessor. . . . One assessor often judged the cases to be one grade higher than the other" (43, p. 412). No reliability coefficients are presented in any of the three articles, but it appears that the "assessors" were not the same across all three, and it should be noted that a difference of "one grade higher" on the 5-point rating scale actually covers two-thirds of the range of "outcome categories." Additionally, of the 132 or more assessments of change in the first article (43), comments are made about only 46 "assessments," of which 17 percent required nonindependent ratings before agreement was reached even for "shifts" from one rating period to another. The second article (44) reported 13 percent disagreements settled by a third assessor, and the third article (45) reported no information on agreement. Thus, in addition to the unacceptable data source, the ratings themselves appear to be unreliable and totally lacking in evidence of validity. The General Improvement Scale suffers from all the problems of the specific scales, and also, the first two reports (43, 44) mention that this scale was based upon such "scanty information" that only "much improved" ratings could be relied upon, and the General Improvement Scale was completely excluded by the third article (45).

Regarding the treatments supposedly being evaluated, no detailed information is provided either on treatment technique or on therapist characteristics. Of the new cases reported in the second and third papers, the majority of "behaviour therapy" cases were said to have been treated by academic psychologists "with extensive knowledge of learning theory" and student psychologists, all of whom were under the supervision of a consultant psychiatrist; the remainder were treated by psychiatric registrars. All therapists appear to have had little clinical experience and to have been inexperienced with the specific techniques to be evaluated. Additionally, the "behaviour therapy" often "was tried as a last resort, and some cases were taken on experimentally as much as therapeutically" (43, p. 413). Such cases also received, concurrently, some combination of sedatives, antidepressants, ECT, abreaction, leucotomy, and "other psychotherapy."

Although, taken alone, the above problems with these studies are sufficient to negate meaningful evidence, the use of the term "controls" is even more misleading. The obvious question is: Control for what? The "controls" were clearly selected from a different population both in terms of age and duration of disability. Additionally, the second report (44) indicates that the sex ratio of females to males in the population from which "controls" were drawn was considerably lower, such that the "matching" of even demographic variables commits a lethal error of drawing from extremes of a population known to differ at the outset (see Campbell & Stanley, 1966). The "controls" were not treated during the same time periods, and the number of sessions and duration of treatment were about half that of the "behaviour therapy" cases. The treatments themselves were no more explicit for "controls" than for "behaviour therapy," including drugs, "psychotherapy," "resocialization," ECT, leucotomy, lysergic acid diethylamide (LSD), abreaction, and for agoraphobics, "general encouragement to go out for walks." No information is provided on "control" therapists or their characteristics; however, it can safely be assumed that there was little or no overlap between groups and that there may have been more experienced clinicians in the "control group." In summary, the so-called "controls" in these reports in fact do not control for anything at all, allowing for complete confounding within all important classes of variables (see Paul, Chapter 1). The one possibility that such a group might have controlled for was rater bias; however, even this aspect is negated due to the difference in time periods, failure to obtain equal types of problems, and failure to use the same raters across all cases.

With all the above problems, questions of statistical analysis are of little importance, but it should be noted that the authors continually draw conclusions regarding differential change between groups based upon findings of significant differences on one occasion of assessment, and no significant differences on another. The latter procedure violates an elementary assumption of significance tests for which appropriate evaluations for the type of conclusions drawn require a test of the difference between differences on the two or more occasions. In only one instance was the appropriate statistical evaluation made (in that case, a test of the groups by occasion interaction in an analysis of variance) for the conclusions drawn.

It appears that the total of 77 "behaviour therapy" cases involved the application of systematic desensitization in 13 to 16 cases, which includes the one case previously reported by Meyer (40). The first article (43) reported 10 agoraphobias and other specific phobias treated by "reciprocal inhibition and desensitization," while the second (44) reported only 6 cases, all agoraphobic, who in addition to other treatments, "also had desensitization in imagination, while in a state of relaxation-hypnosis, as described by Wolpe." While it is unclear as to exactly how many of the first 10 cases actually involved desensitization, the third article summarized the use of systematic desensitization in the following way: "All phobic patients received graded practical retraining. . . . Eight agoraphobics and four 'other phobics' also had desensitization in imagination along the lines of Wolpe (1958). In the obsessives a combination of both methods was used in most patients" (45, p. 3). Thus, while the Meyer & Gelder (1963) procedure of "practical retraining" was the major focus, some 13 to 16 cases may have received something similar to desensitization. The results for these cases are not presented separately; however, the percentage "improved" at one-year follow-up, when some cases were interviewed, was 67 percent for those treated by "reciprocal inhibition and desensitization" in the first report (43), and 76 percent for all agoraphobics in the second report (44), where it was mentioned that those treated by systematic desensitization "did rather better than the rest." Unfortunately, the combined problems of this series of studies result in a level of product which cannot approach even the formulation of crude hypotheses.

The same group of investigators has reported two prospective studies specifically directed towards evaluation of systematic desensitization therapy. Gelder & Marks (1966) report a study of 20 severely handicapped "agoraphobics" treated as inpatients or day patients, in which the majority also complained of interpersonal problems and frigidity. Ten patients were randomly allocated to two groups, one of which received individual "behaviour therapy," consisting of "graded retraining . . . together with systematic desensitization in imagination as described by Wolpe (46, p. 310)." The second group, which is mistakenly called a "control group," received individual "psychotherapeutic interviews directed mainly to current interpersonal problems, relating these to past experiences" (46, p. 310). The therapists for all cases were, again, psychiatric registrars with "little previous experience." About 90 percent of the patients were on drugs during the study, and the desensitization group also received assertion training. No further details of the treatment procedure or therapist characteristics were provided, except that sessions of forty-five minutes were conducted three times weekly.

The assessment procedures included a series of 5-point (from absent to extremely severe) symptom-rating scales based upon the patient's report of fear and avoidance in an unstructured clinical interview. These "symptom ratings" included ratings for: main phobia, other phobias, general anxiety, depression, obsessions, and depersonalization. "Social adjustment" ratings were also made on 5-point scales, covering the areas of: work, leisure, sex, family, other relationships, and self-satisfaction. These "symptom" and "social adjustment" ratings were given by the therapists every two weeks during treatment and every three months during a one-year follow-up. A "second medical assessor" also rated these scales before treatment, two months later, at termination, and at six- and twelve-month follow-ups. It appears that the "second assessors'" based ratings either upon the therapists' interviews, or upon his case notes, and definitely were aware of the time and type of treatment (see 48, p. 67). It also appears that there were several different "second assessors" as well as therapists. Ratings covering the same areas at the same time as therapist ratings were also obtained from the patients; however, instead of single scales, the patients were asked specific questions (by therapists?), the responses to which were averaged to obtain a score on the 5-point scales. Patients were also required, at the beginning of treatment, at termination, and at six- and twelve-month follow-ups, to complete: a symptom checklist, checklists of phobias and social anxieties, a self-adjustment scale, and the Eysenck Personality Inventory (EPI).

The authors report random assignment to groups, and report that prior to treatment the groups did not differ significantly on a wide range of characteristics, including the ratings listed above, with the exception of depression and obsessions. Had the "control group" been a *true* control group, this study could at least have been reviewed in Chapter 3, in spite of its other faults; however, since the "control group" actually consisted of another treatment group involving the application of unknown procedures by different therapists, there was no way of establishing cause-effect relationships from the outset. If no differences were found, it might be because both treatments were effective, were ineffective, or failed to contribute at all, while any differences that might be found could result from one treatment's delaying improvement and the other having no effect, etc. (see Paul, Chapter 1). On the other hand, if the study were adequate in other respects, and if differences were found, some practical value for the conduct of hospital service might result.

For the first time, the authors do report reliability coefficients for the ratings used. It should be noted that two sources of bias and error in their previous work are removed from the ratings, but that all others remain as a function of reliance upon different therapists and patient self-reports. Further, the addition of the second assessors does not add to the validity of the ratings, nor does it reduce the possibility of bias since the assessors were not "blind." It does allow an estimate of error or agreement from the patients' report as elicited by the therapist to the rating. Unfortunately, the reliability appears to have been quite low in that the coefficients between each pair of ratings (from therapist, patient, assessors) for "symptoms" ranged from .45 to .82 with Mdn $r = .67$, and "depersonalization" reliabilities were not included. While the highest reliability accounts for less than 68 percent of the variance in ratings per se, the N reported for these ratings was 58, suggesting either that 38 additional cases were obtained elsewhere for inclusion, or that these coefficients were based upon common ratings for all five occasions, and that 42 sets were dropped for an unstated reason. The "social adjustment" ratings fared even worse, varying from .44 to .73 with Mdn $r = .62$, and these coefficients were acknowledged to include patients from another study (47). A similar question of the exact N arises, however, since that reported was $N = 140$, while the two studies together had a combined $N = 62$.

As with previous studies, "improvement" was judged on the basis of 1- or 2-point "shifts" on the 5-point scales, without evidence of reliability of change scores across patients, therapists, or assessors, and without appropriately determining the necessary degree of change from the standard error of measurement. On this basis, 7 of 10 patients in each group were judged as showing improvement. But 2 of the 10 patients in the "behaviour therapy" group did not receive desensitization: one who did not imagine scenes vividly and one who did not become relaxed. Inappropriate and incomplete statistical analyses were used throughout for the conclusions drawn, as in the previous studies, and standard deviations were not reported to allow others to compute appropriate tests. In general, it appears that only a chance number of significant mean changes across the entire data for both groups were obtained.

A number of other problems, such as lack of control for the effects of repeated testing, and differing total duration and number of sessions between groups, could be elaborated, but in view of other difficulties, this seems unnecessary.

In summary, the problems of total confounding of therapists and treatments, combined with the lack of detail regarding treatment procedures, reliability, and validity, results in this study (46) providing less contribution to even suggestive hypotheses than most case studies; at best it provides crude hypotheses concerning the rated effectiveness of inexperienced clinicians' general impact upon the self-reports of a severely disabled group.

Gelder, Marks, Sakinofsky, & Wolff (1964) report the second prospective study by the Maudsley group, which was published in greater detail by Gelder, Marks, & Wolff (1967). This study involved the treatment of phobic outpatients with an average duration of disturbance of 8.2 years. Exactly the same rating scales and procedures reported in the earlier study (46) were used for assessment, except that therapist and patient ratings were obtained at the beginning and termination of treatment, and every six weeks from the start to eighteen months after the *start* of treatment. The "second assessor" ratings were obtained only at beginning and end and every six months, while the patient questionnaire battery was completed only at the time of assessors' ratings. Additionally, a final follow-up interview was conducted by a social worker about twenty-five months after the start of treatment, including an interview with a relative or friend in 32 of 42 cases, rating improvement "thought to be related to treatment" on a 4-point scale (from worse to much improved).

A total of 42 phobic patients were assigned to three "matched groups" to receive individul systematic desensitization ($N = 16$), group psychotherapy ($N = 16$), or individual psychotherapy ($N = 10$). The desensitization group contained 8 agoraphobias, 4 social phobias, and 4 "other phobias," while both individual and group psychotherapy contained 7 agoraphobias and 3 social phobias, and group psychotherapy another 6 "other phobias." Three desensitization cases terminated before the sixth session, and another moved from the area, and all these were replaced with matched cases. The three final treatment groups were reported to be well matched on all factors except duration of distress. Patients treated by group psychotherapy were distributed among four therapy groups, each containing an additional 4 neurotic patients. One "full-time psychotherapist" and five psychiatric registrars with "at least 18 months experience" conducted individual and group psychotherapy, with only one conducting both. Desensitization, which included "other techniques" described by Wolpe and graduated retraining, was conducted by five psychiatric registrars, four of whom had "no previous experience with behaviour therapy." No further details were provided on therapist characteristics or treatment procedures.

The same problems of the absence of a true control group and questionable reliability and validity of ratings exist for this study (48) as for the earlier one reviewed above (46). In fact, the reliability data presented in this article were the identical data presented earlier. In addition to the problems of the first prospective study (46), there are further important differences between groups which prevent the establishment of solid evidence. The therapists, while relatively inexperienced, were far more qualified for "psychotherapy" than for desensitization, and it appears that a higher level of experience was maintained for the individual psychotherapy group than for others, e.g., "Sixteen patients were treated by desensitization, another 16 with group psychotherapy; only 10 were allocated to individual psychotherapy because of a shortage of skilled psychotherapists" (48, p. 54). In addition to the complete confounding of therapist effects with treatment technique, both the number and the duration of treatment sessions differed significantly: desensitization sessions were held once a week for 1 hour, for an average of 36 sessions over 9 months; individual psychotherapy was carried out once a week for 1 hour, for an average of 52 sessions over 12 months; and group psychotherapy was held once a week for 1½ hours, for an average of 80 sessions over 18 months. Of the 42 patients, 15 were also on drugs.

The difference in total duration of treatment and number of sessions is especially important due to the manner of analysis. For the first time in the series of studies by the Maudsley group, the appropriate *type* of statistical analyses for making statements about differential improvement between groups was carried out in some instances. However, the major analyses were computed on changes from the start of treatment to the "end" and "final ratings." This means the "end" point involves an average duration of 9 months for desensitization as compared to 18 months for group psychotherapy, while "final ratings" are actually follow-ups of 9 months for desensitization, 6 months for individual psychotherapy, and about at termination for group psychotherapy. Analyses of all ratings from start to 6 months assessment, when the majority of all groups were still in treatment, found desensitization significantly more improved in the main phobia ratings than the other two groups. The lack of reliability between ratings was apparent in all rating results in which several significant findings in favor of desensitization were found, but these were consistent for all raters only on the main phobia of the symptom ratings. Of the social adjustment ratings, only "leisure" showed significant differences, and these favored the desensitization group. None of the test battery scales showed significant change, except a drop in EPI neuroticism for desensitization. The latter was not appropriately tested against changes in the other groups.

The interview-based ratings of the psychiatric social worker actually constituted follow-ups of 16 months for desensitization, 13 months for individual psychotherapy, and 7 months for group psychotherapy. Her ratings indicated improvement in 12 desensitization, 4 group therapy, and 8 individual psychotherapy cases, although 5 of the 8 individual therapy cases had also "undergone important changes in circumstances." Unfortunately, the correlations of these follow-up ratings with previous ratings were not presented. The authors go into considerable detail in attempting to identify differing characteristics of improved and unimproved cases, which for the most part run the risk of capitalizing on chance differences. In general, for all groups, agoraphobics and those with more extensive disturbances appeared to have responded least.

In general, this study as well as the previous one cannot provide cause-effect data concerning systematic desensitization, nor can adequate comparisons between groups be made because of the total confounding of all variables and the lack of demonstrated reliability. Because of the inclusion of the social worker interviews with significant others, this study can provide suggestive hypotheses about the effectiveness of untrained clinicians' attempts to apply the procedure to a group of phobic patients.

Ramsay, Barends, Breuker, & Kruseman (1966) report a study which proposed to test "massed" versus "spaced" desensitization, utilizing unusual procedures in an analog study. The subjects were 20 freshman students at Amsterdam who were required to participate in an experiment. The authors note that Ss had difficulty in finding "situations" which elicited anxiety, but four situations involving a concrete "phobic stimulus" were identified for each S through an interview. These 4 "situations" were then treated as hierarchy items in which "spaced desensitization" involved 20-minute sessions every day for 4 consecutive days, and "massed desensitization" involved 40-minute sessions per day for 2 sessions separated by 4 days. Half of the Ss received "massed desensitization" of 2 items followed by "spaced desensitization" of the remaining 2 items, while the order was reversed for the remaining half. Avoidance tests and self-report fear thermometers (after Lang & Lazovik, 1963) were carried out with the 4 situations before treatment, after 2 items had been desensitized, and at termination. The "therapists" were three senior undergraduates with no clinical experience at all, given one hour of training by their instructor, who also was not experienced. Although the authors refer to Wolpe, there is no evidence that the procedure followed usual desensitization practices, and the "massed" and "spaced" desensitization proper actually resulted in each item being presented 20 times in 20 minutes for one condition, and 40 times in 40 minutes for the other, such that trials per minute of therapy really did not differentiate "massed" from "spaced," and merely resulted in unusual timing. The only significant finding was a pre-post mean reduction on the fear thermometer, which suggests "improvement," but which might have resulted from the avoidance tests as well as "desensitization." The authors also report that "spaced practice" was significantly superior to "massed practice," and offer a number of proposals for clinical desensitization on this basis. However, the latter was an incorrect conclusion based upon an inappropriate use of significance levels (a "one-tailed" *F*-test of interaction in the analysis of variance), and the unusual procedures combined with inexperienced therapists and nonanxious *S*s preclude generalization of suggestive findings to other contexts.

Two studies which are included in the present section are also unusual in that the target of treatment by desensitization was not anxiety, but "desire to smoke." Koenig & Masters (1965) report the first study in which 42 Stanford University undergraduates, who reported smoking 20 or more cigarettes per day, volunteered as *S*s in response to a newspaper advertisement. The *S*s were allocated to three groups of 14 each to receive desensitization, "aversion therapy," or "supportive therapy," with 2 *S*s in each group treated by the same 7 therapists. It should be noted that this is the first study in the present review to represent therapists factorially. The therapists included the authors, at least one of whom was experienced clinically and had received training in desensitization from Lazarus. The remaining 5 were clinical graduate students without previous training in desensitization, who were supervised by the authors. The major assessment procedure consisted of a tally sheet of smoking rate recorded by the *S*s for one week prior to treatment, and throughout the five- to six-week treatment period. A six-month follow-up was obtained by telephone. Few details were provided concerning specific procedures, except that sessions for all three treatments consisted of 3 the first week, 2 the second, and 1 per week thereafter for a total of 9 individual sessions. Relaxation training was completed in the first two sessions for the desensitization group, and a single hierarchy of no more than 20 items, graded for "increasing desire to smoke," was constructed during the first session. The criterion for moving to a new item was a thirty-second visualization of a scene without signaling a desire to smoke. A highly significant pre-post reduction in smoking rate was obtained for all groups, with no significant differences between groups. At post-treatment assessment, a significant therapist main effect was obtained, without interaction with treatments; however, there was no evidence for comparability of therapist behavior, nor description of therapists' characteristics to allow interpretation of this finding. The only significant relationship found ($r = .45$), was that the more positively the therapist was rated by *S*s, the *less* smoking change occurred. At follow-up, neither therapist nor treatment main effects were significant, although an undescribed therapist-treatment interaction was found. Unfortunately, only 27 of the original 42 *S*s either completed the study or provided usable data, resulting in a probable selection bias. In combination, the loss of *S*s and data, the absence of an untreated group, and the equation of "desire to smoke" with anxiety results in completely equivocal findings regarding systematic desensitization.

Pyke, Agnew, & Kopperud (1966) provide the second article which is presented as a pilot study on smoking. This study involved 55 undergraduates at Saskatchewan who reported smoking an average of 15 cigarettes per day and participated in the study as *paid* volunteers. The assessment procedures and assumptions of this study were similar to the previous one on smoking (50). However, in the present study (51), only 22 Ss were treated. One week of recording smoking rate was followed by 11 antismoking "group discussions" over a 10-week period, during which Ss received information on hazards of smoking and feedback on continuing daily records of smoking rate. Concurrent with these group meetings were 10 individual desensitization sessions, the first three of which were devoted to relaxation training and construction of individual 19- to 27-item hierarchies similar to those of the earlier smoking study (50). Items were presented for 15 seconds each with 3 minutes between presentations. Items were terminated if Ss signaled "desire to smoke" or if a 10-km GSR was obtained. The criterion for progression was 2 nonsignaled presentations, but a single item was continually presented each session. The records of smoking rate were continued for 3 weeks after termination, and 16 weeks later, records were again kept for 1 week for follow-up. The investigators initially included control groups but dropped them after 8 weeks; thus, 17 Ss merely recorded smoking rate for 8 weeks, and another 16 Ss were to record only during week 1 and week 8. At the 8-week period, the treated group showed both a significant overall reduction in smoking rate and a significantly greater reduction than either control group; however, post treatment and follow-up data were obtained for only 15 treated Ss and for none of the controls. In the Ss for whom data were available, smoking rate had increased by follow-up to the point that it no longer differed from pretreatment. In addition to the complete confounding of other treatment procedures, and in addition to all the problems of the earlier smoking study, the unusual procedures of desensitization in this study resulted in only 2 of 22 Ss completing hierarchies, with the result that not even suggestive hypotheses may be obtained relevant to the use of systematic desensitization.

Chapter Summary

After a discussion of the phenomena associated with anxiety, and the historical development of systematic desensitization procedures, the focus of application and specific technical operations involved were specified. A critical review of all available uncontrolled reports of individual application was presented, with the focus upon contribution to outcome hypotheses. A tabular summary of these reports is given in Table 2–1. For an overall summary of desensitization outcome, see Paul, Chapter 3.

3

Outcome of Systematic Desensitization

II: Controlled Investigations of Individual Treatment, Technique Variations, and Current Status

GORDON L. PAUL

University of Illinois, Urbana, Illinois

Review of the Literature—II

All the studies reviewed and summarized in the companion chapter (Paul, Chapter 2) are, by nature of their designs, limited to developing or strengthening hypotheses concerning the effectiveness of systematic desensitization therapy or related variables—at best allowing correlational conclusions. In contrast to the latter studies are those in which the design, usually by virtue of the inclusion of untreated or novel control groups, introduces control procedures to limit competing explanations sufficiently to allow cause-effect conclusions between treatment application and outcome. These studies are reviewed below and summarized in Table 3–1. It should be noted, however, that confounding and error may still occur in such studies and are likely to be of more importance than in obviously uncontrolled investigations, since the errors may be hidden in a mass of methodological and statistical procedures.

CONTROLLED INVESTIGATIONS OF INDIVIDUAL
SYSTEMATIC DESENSITIZATION

Lang & Lazovik. Lang & Lazovik (1963) published the first controlled study of systematic desensitization therapy, and later papers and articles have clari-

Table 3-1 Summary of Controlled Investigations of Individual Systematic Desensitization

Author	Problem treated	Clients: Characteristics — No.	Sex	Age	Other	Therapists: Characteristics — No.	Other	Assessment procedure*	No. of sessions	Treatment — Total duration	Follow-up	Outcome*
(52) Lang and Lazovik (1963) (53) Lang (1964) (54) Lang et al. (1965) (55) Lang (1965b)	Snake phobia	47	M=30% F=70%	18–24	Screened volunteer students	6	All experienced but 4 had no previous desensitization; university	FT; avoidance test; test battery	16	Average: 8 weeks	6 months (N=20)	(+)D> nov.= NT=AP
(56) Paul (1964)	Test anxiety	11	F	18–24	Students	(1)	Same as (17)	Exam. perform.	3–4	2 weeks	8 weeks	(+)D> NT
(57) Paul (1966) (58) Paul (1967)	Interpersonal performance anxiety	96	M=68 F=28	17–24 Mdn= 19	Distressed students; anxious introverts	5	All experienced; special training and supervision in desensitization; university clinic	Test battery; physiological, cognitive, observable motoric in stress; ratings	5	6 weeks	6 weeks and 2 years	(+)D> I=AP> NT> NC
(59) Zeisset (1968)	Interview anxiety	48	M	27–50 $\bar{x}$= 39.7	Psychotic VA inpatients	1+ (1)	Inexperienced (used tape)	Test battery; external observation	4	2 weeks	None	(?)D=R> AP=NT
(60) Moore (1965)	Bronchial asthma	12	M=5 F=7	5–48 $\bar{x}$= 22.7	Outpatients	1	Chest clinic	Freq. reports; Max. peak flow	18	4 months	6 months	(+)D> R= multinov.
(61) Emory and Krumboltz (1967)	Test anxiety	54	M=36 F=18	Freshmen	Screened students	9	Inexperienced; university	Anxiety Scale; self ratings under stress; grades	16	8 weeks	None	(+)D> NT
(62) Johnson (1966)	Test anxiety	33	?	"Under-grads"	Screened students	1	Inexperienced; university	Anxiety Scale; ratings; grades	5	5 weeks	"Few months" (N=27)	(+)D> R =NC
(63) Cooke (1966a)	Rat phobia	12	F	"Under-grads"	Volunteer students	1+ (1)	No desensitization experience; university	Emotionality Scale; FSS; avoidance test	4	2 weeks	None	(+)D= nov.> NT
(64) Cooke (1966b)	"Rat phobia"	50	F	"Under-grads"	Required experiment	5	1 same as (63), 4 no desensitization experience	FSS; avoidance test	5	2 weeks	None	(?)D=nov. > multinov. =NT
(65) Davison (1968b)	Snake phobia	28	F	17–35 Mdn= 18	Screened volunteer students	1	Experienced; junior college	FT; avoidance test	5–9	3–5 weeks	None	(+)D> AP =nov= NT

* See text for details; D=systematic desensitization; nov.=novel treatment or control group; AP=nonspecific attention-placebo treatment; R=relaxation-only treatment; NT=no-treatment control; NC=no-contact control; I=insight=oriented treatment.

fied and extended this investigation (Lang, 1964; Lang, Lazovik & Reynolds, 1965; Lang, 1965b). All Ss were selected from volunteers in introductory psychology classes at the University of Pittsburgh on the basis of self-ratings of "intense" fears of nonpoisonous snakes on the Fear Survey Schedule (FSS), and the fear was further confirmed in a psychological interview. Psychotics were excluded on screening by MMPI and interview. Although these studies are considered "analog" investigations by the authors, because therapists presented themselves as experimenters with an impartial attitude towards success, and because the phobias treated were not central life problems for the Ss, it should be noted that the fears experienced were very real and quite severe—to the extent found in only 1 to 3 percent of the tested population. The assessment procedures used in all studies included the 50-item FSS and the FSS-snake item rated on a 7-point self-report scale. Also the avoidance test previously used by the authors (16),[1] in which Ss were confronted with a live snake, provided assessment of approach behavior on a 19-point scale, and an absolute criterion of touching or holding the phobic object. A self-rated 10-point Fear Thermometer (FT) was also obtained from each S immediately upon completion of the avoidance test. A "blind" experimenter conducted the avoidance tests as well as tape-recorded interviews to obtain qualitative information on "symptom substitution." Originally a 3-point anxiety rating by the blind experimenter was included during avoidance tests, but this was dropped due to lack of reliability. All desensitization treatments were limited to the mimeographed procedure developed in the experimenters' earlier investigations (16), although care was taken to establish a good clinical relationship. In order to control time parameters, all treatments were limited to 5 training sessions of forty-five minutes each for relaxation training, construction of unique 20-item hierarchies, and training in hypnosis, with desensitization proper time-limited to 11 sessions, generally on a twice-weekly basis. All Ss were also administered Form A of the Stanford Hypnotic Susceptibility Scale (SHSS) following the screening interview, and Form B on completion of 5 sessions of training.

The first study (52, 53) was a modified Solomon Four Group design involving two treatment and two control groups, with random assignment to groups and attempts to balance for intensity of reaction and motivation to participate. One treatment and one control group ($N = 8$ and 5, respectively) underwent evaluation (avoidance test, FT, interview) at times corresponding to pretreatment, posttraining, and posttreatment, while the other treatment and control groups ($N = 5$ and 6, respectively) were evaluated on these measures only at posttraining and posttreatment time periods. The latter feature of the design was introduced to control for possible reactive effects of the pretreatment avoidance test. All 24 Ss also completed the FSS before and after treatment, and 11 desensitization Ss and 9 controls were available for readministra-

---

[1] Numbers in parentheses refer to tabular summaries of reports in this chapter (Tables 3–1 and 3–2) or the companion chapter (Paul, Chapter 2, Table 2–1).

tion of all measures at a six-month follow-up. A total of 5 therapists conducted desensitization in the first controlled study, each treating 2 to 4 Ss. Lang and Lazovik were two of the therapists, and the only ones with previous desensitization experience. The other three therapists, who were paid for participation, were all experienced clinicians, but obtained their first exposure to desensitization under the supervision of Lang and Lazovik in the study. It should be noted that four different time periods were included together in the first study; however, in each replication, both treatment and control Ss were included so that the assessor remained blind, and control for intercurrent life experiences was maintained.

Analyses of the results of this first study (52, 53) found no appreciable change on any measure for untreated controls, nor were significant differences found between either desensitization group and controls at the end of the training period. These findings indicate that merely undergoing the assessment procedures, even with the addition of relaxation training, hierarchy construction, and hypnotic training, did not lead to significant change in phobic response for these Ss. However, on posttreatment assessment, Ss treated by desensitization were found to show significantly greater reductions in avoidance of the phobic object than were untreated controls—for the first time establishing a cause-effect relationship between the application of systematic desensitization therapy and change in distressing behavior. The percentage increase in Ss' touching or holding the snake was also significant for the desensitization group, although this was not tested against controls. In contrast to the avoidance test, the self-report scales did not show a significant pre-post reduction in snake-elicited anxiety for desensitization Ss in comparison with controls, although the group trends were in the same direction. However, on closer inspection of the data, the authors noted that 6 of the 13 desensitization Ss had completed less than 75 percent of the hierarchy during the time-limited treatment period. When these two subgroups of desensitization Ss were compared, those Ss who had completed more than 15 of the 20 items in their hierarchies were found to show significantly greater reduction of anxiety and avoidance on all measures than Ss completing less than 15 items, and the latter did not differ significantly from controls. At the time of the six-month follow-up, while 2 desensitization Ss showed some slight "backsliding," the group as a whole showed a slight improvement to the extent that the entire experimental group obtained a significantly greater change on all measures than the controls. It should be noted that the investigators' practice of obtaining FT ratings from Ss *after* the avoidance tests actually biases results against desensitization Ss, since they reliably approach the phobic object more closely, and are thus rating in a situation which was, initially, much more anxiety-provoking than the controls who do not change in approach.

Further correlational analyses carried out on the first study (52, 53) found no significant relationship between SHSS suggestibility and improvement for desensitization Ss, which, combined with a failure to obtain change after the training period alone, argues against mere suggestion as a contributor to change. A significant relationship ($r = -58$) was found between the number of hierarchy items completed and total FSS score, suggesting that the more extensive were anxiety stimuli, the more slowly Ss proceeded through the hierarchy in desensitization proper. Unfortunately, data were not analyzed separately for the different therapists, nor were the therapists' characteristics presented in detail. The results of this first controlled study do provide significant evidence of a cause-effect relationship between the application of systematic desensitization and outcome, and the inclusion of five different therapists broadens the generality of the results; however, the possibility of within-class confounding of therapist characteristics and treatment technique was not entirely ruled out. Also, though the absence of change following the training period argues against "placebo effects," the additional time devoted to desensitization proper, and the Ss' knowledge that treatment was yet forthcoming after the training period still allowed potential confounding of nonspecific effects of undergoing treatment with specific effects attributable to systematic desensitization.

The investigators were able to overcome much of the confounding in an extension of the original study reported later (54, 55). Following exactly the same procedures as in the first study, three therapists (2 of whom were also in the first study) treated a total of 10 additional Ss by desensitization and another 10 by a "pseudotherapy" procedure. The latter treatment was included to control for placebo effects, and consisted of exactly the same procedures during the five training sessions, except that a "vaguely psychoanalytic" rationale was presented. However, for the 11 sessions corresponding to desensitization proper, the hierarchy items were not paired with relaxation; rather, Ss were hypnotized, given relaxation suggestions, and asked to visualize pleasant scenes during the first third of each session. The last two-thirds of each session of pseudotherapy was based upon hierarchy items, but rather than standard presentations, the items served as starting points for nonanxiety-evoking aspects of Ss' life. Thus, the pseudotherapy condition included the same amount of contact with the same therapists, thereby controlling for therapist characteristics, and also included the combined effects of training in hypnosis and relaxation, constructing a hierarchy for snakes, being presented a rationale, and undergoing additional procedures with the implication of improving the phobic reactions. It should be noted that this extension of the study was a "high-risk" extension since additional untreated controls were not included over the same time period. While the inclusion of two treatment procedures allowed the assessor to remain "blind," if no differences were found between the effects of the new desensitization Ss and the pseudotherapy Ss, the absence of untreated controls over the same time period would not allow exclusion of extraexperimental influences as plausible confounding factors.

As it turned out, the high risk paid off in that the new desensitization group showed significant improvement over both the pseudotherapy group and the previous untreated controls, while the latter two groups did not differ significantly. Combining all desensitization Ss with all control Ss, significant reductions in snake-elicited anxiety and avoidance were found on all measures in favor of the desensitization group. Of the total Ss treated by desensitization ($N = 23$), 13 had completed 15 or more hierarchy items. Splitting the desensitization group in this way, those Ss ($N = 13$) who completed at least 75 percent of their hierarchies were found to show significantly greater pre-post reductions on *all* measures of anxiety and avoidance than desensitization Ss who completed less than 75 percent of their hierarchies ($N = 10$), untreated controls ($N = 11$), and the pseudotherapy group ($N = 10$), while the latter three groups did not differ significantly on a single measure. Additional correlational analyses between SHSS scores and all measures of fear reduction ruled out suggestibility as a significant contributor to change in the desensitization group, although a significant correlation was found with self-report measures for the controls, suggesting that "suggestibility" may have played a part in any changes of control Ss. Further suggestive hypotheses were derived through correlational analyses, in which the number of hierarchy items completed was positively related (Mdn $r = .55$) to all measures of improvement; on the other hand, the more extensive were pretreatment sources of anxiety, the slower was progress in desensitization. The authors report no evidence of symptom substitution from the interview material, and support this qualitative finding with evidence of positive generalization of fear reduction to related items on the FSS, rather than the reverse. Lang (55) has recently summarized the above findings with the addition of 3 more desensitization cases. In 9 of a current total of 26 desensitization cases, "hypnotic" training and induction were totally excluded; progressive relaxation training alone was used for desensitization, and no differences in effectiveness was found.

In summary, the combined work of Lang, Lazovik, and their colleagues (52, 53, 54, 55) in the controlled context of the laboratory analog, has established specific cause-effect relationships between systematic desensitization and change in intense phobic reactions. Within the analog context of their investigations, nonspecific therapeutic effects appear nil, and desensitization effects were unrelated to SHSS suggestibility. Further suggestive hypotheses, at the correlational level, were found for the use of intratherapy progress in desensitization as a predictor of extratherapeutic change and for positive generalization of improvement from specific desensitization, rather than symptom substitution. Possible differences in effectiveness attributable to different therapists were not specifically analyzed; however, the inclusion of a pseudotherapy group conducted by the same therapists allowed control of these factors.

Paul.   Paul (1964) reported a small study which served as a pilot investigation for later, more extensive, and more thoroughly controlled projects. A total of 13

*S*s enrolled in an introductory psychology course at the University of Illinois requested treatment for debilitating test anxiety after participation in a validity study of the Mandler-Sarason Test Anxiety Questionnaire (TAQ) (Paul & Eriksen, 1964). Of these, 11 high-test-anxious *S*s, falling in the 70 percent middle-ability range, were assigned to treatment ($N = 5$) or control ($N = 6$) groups equated on TAQ scores and on degree of disturbance of test performance as assessed by comparisons of course examinations under relaxed versus anxious conditions. The 5 *S*s in the treatment group received individual desensitization by the author between the first and second course examination, and the control *S*s were not contacted further. In a posttreatment assessment based upon performance in the second course examination, the treated group improved examination scores from first (pre) to second (post) exams significantly more than the untreated controls. In a follow-up of performance on the final examination of the course, eight weeks later, all treated *S*s increased examination scores over those predicted ($\bar{x} = +7.5$), while all controls dropped from predicted performance, ($\bar{x} = -8.0$), and the difference between groups was highly significant. While this pilot study does provide cause-effect evidence for the effectiveness of treatment, specific relationships for systematic desensitization per se cannot be established due to the possibility of within-class confounding of therapist characteristics and general nonspecific treatment effects. Further, while self-reports of treated *S*s, as well as other empirical research, strongly suggest that a reduction of anxiety was responsible for the improved performance of treated *S*s (see Paul & Eriksen, 1964), direct posttreatment assessments of anxiety were not employed.

In a later monograph, Paul (1966) presented the first extensive factorial study of systematic desensitization therapy in the literature, and the only well-controlled investigation to date comparing desensitization with traditional psychotherapeutic techniques. Interpersonal-performance anxiety was selected as a treatment target on the assumption that classes of anxiety-eliciting stimuli were sufficiently delimited to allow rigorous experimental methodology, yet broad enough to allow more direct generalization of findings than is possible in analog studies. Additionally, since public performance situations provide prototypic stress conditions for eliciting interpersonal-performance anxiety, standard external "work sample" assessments were possible. The investigation was conducted at the University of Illinois, where a graduation requirement of successful completion of a course in public speaking resulted in even greater distress for a large group of students in whom social-evaluative anxiety was a central life problem.

Of 380 *S*s who requested treatment following the administration of a battery of personality and anxiety scales to students enrolled in required public speaking courses, 96—the most debilitated by anxiety—were included in the study. The test battery included scales to assess distressing target behaviors, relatively stable personal-social characteristics, and anxiety in other interpersonal-evaluative situations, in order to provide both descriptive data on the population and information concerning possible "symptom substitution" or generalization. Demographic data and information regarding motivation for treatment were also obtained on the pretreatment administration of the test battery. Additional screening by psychometric and interview procedures excluded Ss with high falsification scores, low motivation, evidence of psychotic behavior, previous treatment, or interpersonal-performance anxiety that was not a central life problem. The resulting sample of 96 Ss were "good bets" for psychotherapy, being young, intelligent, middle-class, highly motivated, with strong to severe interpersonal-performance anxiety of two to twenty years standing. In most cases, pretreatment anxiety was reported to occur in nearly any social, interpersonal, or evaluative situation and to be most severe in a public speaking situation. As a group, the Ss also obtained significantly higher scores on general anxiety and emotionality, and were more introverted than the normal student population.

Following the pretreatment administration of the test battery and initial screening, 74 Ss were contacted individually and brought in for additional stress assessment, in which they were required to present a speech before an unfamiliar audience under standard conditions. Four minutes prior to the stress speech each S completed the Anxiety Differential to provide a cognitive assessment of anxiety, and physiological measures (pulse rate and palmar sweat) were obtained ninety seconds and thirty seconds preceding the stress speech. During the stress speech, four trained observers recorded the presence or absence of 20 specific manifestations of anxiety every thirty seconds on a Behavioral Checklist developed for the study. It should be noted that the latter instrument is *not* a rating scale, but an objective frequency count of the occurrence of observable manifestations of anxiety, for which the interobserver reliability exceeded $r = .95$ prior to S contact. The Ss were then randomly distributed to four treatment and control groups from stratified blocks based upon pooled Behavioral Checklist scores. The groups were equated on sex, class time, course instruction, stress assessment group, and observable performance anxiety $\bar{x}$ and standard deviation. Each of these Ss was then seen in a short interview by the investigator, during which appointments with therapists were arranged, and common expectations of benefit, as well as rationale and course of treatment to be undergone, were presented in a standard manner.

The four groups to which the Ss were assigned after the stress assessment included three treatment groups ($N = 15$ each) who were to receive individual (1) systematic desensitization, (2) insight-oriented psychotherapy, or (3) an attention-placebo treatment; there was also (4) a no-treatment "waiting list" control ($N = 29$). A fifth group ($N = 22$) constituted a no-contact control, whose members were equated with the other groups but were never contacted individually for stress assessment, and were in fact unaware of their inclusion in the therapy study.

The treatments were conducted concurrently by five psychotherapists who had six to eighteen years of experience and were paid for their time. Each therapist treated 3 randomly assigned *S*s in each of the three treatment groups. Prior to *S* contact, therapists underwent intensive training in both systematic desensitization and attention-placebo procedures based upon detailed manuals. Every treatment hour was individually supervised by the investigator via tape recordings and weekly meetings with each therapist. In contrast to the latter two treatment procedures, all therapists were highly experienced with insight-oriented psychotherapy, and this treatment was controlled by having each therapist complete a Therapist Orientation Sheet (TOS) which included detailed frequency of usage of 20 specific techniques in insight-oriented psychotherapy. Each session of insight-oriented treatment was also individually monitored by the investigator via tape recordings and weekly meetings, to ensure that the therapists followed the procedures detailed on the TOS. The TOS also included 24 items regarding relatively stable personal-social characteristics of therapists, as well as nonspecific treatment-related influences, attitudes, and practices. In general, these scales revealed the therapists to be representative of national samples of traditional psychotherapists, with major influences from Neo-Freudian and Rogerian schools, and with preference for treatment of interpersonal-performance anxiety through helping *S*s to gain "insight" into the historical bases and interrelationships of the problem.

Since insight-oriented treatment, as presented in most textbooks and case reports, appeared usually to involve a much longer period of time than systematic desensitization as used by the investigator, the therapists were provided with all details of the investigation, including the target of treatment and the criteria to be used for evaluation. On the basis of these data, the therapists were asked to specify the number of sessions and the duration of treatment in which they would be confident of successfully treating interpersonal-performance anxiety in the population by the insight-oriented procedures used in their daily practice. While therapists varied by a few sessions in their estimates, both the mean and mode were 5 weekly sessions of one hour; this figure was taken as the time limit for all three treatment groups, in order to control for duration of contact. Prior to the start of treatment all five therapists rated themselves as quite confident of effecting change during this period with their usual insight-oriented procedures. It should also be noted that, while the treatment duration was brief, diagnostic work was completed prior to therapist contact, and the actual duration of treatment is representative of about 80 percent of reported practices for comparable problems in outpatient clinics and counseling bureaus, although it is considerably shorter than psychoanalysis or other treatments when more extensive problems are involved (see Paul, 1968).

Four weeks after the initial contact, treatments were begun. They were counterbalanced for order of treatment sessions among therapists, and all three treatments were conducted equally at the University Psychological

Clinic, the Guidance and Counseling Center, and the Student Counseling Bureau. Since therapists were factorially represented in all three treatment groups, not only the amount of attention and the duration of contact were controlled, but also potentially important effects of therapists' prestige, personality, and physical attributes. In all three treatments, care was taken to establish rapport, to present a meaningful rationale, to maintain a positive attitude toward outcome, and to include all "nonspecific" aspects of any therapeutic relationship. The content of the rationale and techniques of treatment proper were the only procedures differing, with the attention-placebo treatment involving a stylized procedure which allowed therapist attention during treatment proper, but prevented Ss from discussing their problems by requiring them to listen to a recorded tape of auditory signals through headsets during "treatment" sessions. The inclusion of the latter group allowed assessment of improvement resulting only from nonspecific relationship and "placebo" effects of "undergoing treatment" with the therapists involved, against which specific effects of desensitization or insight-oriented procedures could be evaluated.

In the week following treatment termination, Ss in all three treatment groups and untreated waiting-list controls again underwent a stress assessment, with the same physiological, cognitive, and observable measures of anxiety obtained under standard and "blind" conditions. A follow-up administration of the test battery was obtained six weeks after termination on Ss in all five groups, by administering the battery to the entire speech course population. Several self-ratings of improvement and therapist characteristics were obtained from treated Ss at this time. Therapists also provided ratings of improvement and prognosis for each S, as well as several other ratings on characteristics of treatment. The inclusion of the waiting-list control group allowed assessment of treatment effects over and above possible effects of the diagnostic and assessment procedures, while the no-contact control provided for assessment of possible effects of undergoing the latter procedures, and being placed on a waiting-list.

Group and individual differences on all data were evaluated by complex analyses of variance, t-tests of the difference between differences, and individually significant changes on each measure for each S. Changes observed under stress conditions were the most stringent test of treatment effects, since the measures used were most reliable and objective, and were based upon a situation in which the maladaptive anxiety was most likely to occur. On all three classes of measurement (cognitive, physiological, and observable) the group treated by systematic desensitization showed significantly greater reduction of anxiety under stress conditions than did the untreated controls. Desensitization was also consistently superior to either attention-placebo or insight-oriented treatments, while the latter two treatment procedures did not differ significantly from each other. Both insight-oriented psychotherapy and nonspecific treatment did show significant gains over the untreated waiting-list controls; however, the desensitization group was the only one showing a significant reduction on physiological measures. The effects produced by the various therapists over all treatments, or within individual treatments, did not differ, as each produced more gain through systematic desensitization than with either insight-oriented or attention-placebo procedures. Essentially the same results were again obtained on analysis of the six-week follow-up battery, although the untreated waiting-list controls were found to show a slight but significant improvement over the no-contact controls.

Not even suggestive evidence of symptom substitution was found at the six-week follow-up. Rather, the data indicated that desensitization to a single spatial-temporal hierarchy of the most threatening public-speaking situation imaginable resulted in generalized reduction of anxiety in several other social-evaluative situations. With the exception of physiological data, which was related only to observable behavioral change, consistent evidence of convergent and discriminative validity of "improvement" was found among all measures. Standardized therapists' ratings of specific improvement and prognosis were significantly related to the external criteria at termination and follow-up (r's in the .40's), but "other" improvement ratings were unrelated. The only measures which failed to show significant differences between groups were Ss self-ratings of improvement, in which all Ss rated themselves as improved. Numerous analyses were carried out on other factors involved in the treatments; however, the only results of importance to the present review are that none appeared to contribute to differential outcome, and that improvement was not predictable from either therapist or S characteristics.

The results of this study, then, establish specific cause-effect relationships between systematic desensitization and change in severe maladaptive anxiety which was a central life problem of treated Ss. These effects were in addition to significant "nonspecific" effects of undergoing treatment with experienced therapists (which can account for the improvement seen following insight-oriented psychotherapy) and in addition to improvement resulting from the additional exposure and attention involved in assessment procedures.

While the above cause-effect relationships were established for systematic desensitization under stress conditions and were maintained on six-week follow-up, the differing theoretical rationales from which insight-oriented psychotherapy and desensitization were derived suggested the desirability of a long-term follow-up. Specifically, traditional psychodynamic theory would predict the occurrence of relapse or symptom substitution in desensitization and attention-placebo groups, with corresponding increases in improvement for the insight-oriented group, after "insights" had "consolidated." Learning theory, on the other hand, would predict no greater relapse for one group than another, and additional change in untreated areas only to the extent of generalization from the specific treatment. While findings favored the learning interpretation at the six-week follow-up, it was possible that the first follow-up was too short for the processes expected from psychodynamic theories to show their effects. Therefore, a two-year follow-up was undertaken (Paul, 1967).

The procedure for the two-year follow-up (58) involved contacting treatment and control Ss from the earlier study (57) for a third administration of the test battery, augmented to obtain specific frequency data on the occurrence of stress during the posttreatment period, and on external behaviors which might reflect predicted symptom-substitution effects of increased dependency, anxiety, or introversion. Additionally, data were obtained on further psychological treatment or the use of drugs during the follow-up period. Stress assessments could not be obtained due to the fact that 64 percent of the population was no longer in the area. Starting exactly twenty-four months after treatment termination, packets were sent to all Ss from the earlier study, excluding a group of untreated controls who participated in a different treatment program in another context (Paul & Shannon, 1966). All but 3 Ss were contacted during a period of twenty-five to twenty-seven months after treatment termination, and complete data were returned by 100 percent of treated Ss ($N = 45$) and 70 percent of controls ($N = 31$). However, in addition to 3 controls who could not be located, and 10 who were located but failed to return data, 12 returning controls had to be excluded from follow-up analyses because they had received two or more sessions of psychological treatment during the follow-up period, and 1 had to be excluded because of an extreme falsification score. Of treated Ss, a total of 5 were excluded on the basis of additional psychological treatment during the follow-up period (3 insight-oriented, 1 desensitization, 1 attention-placebo), and 1 desensitization S was excluded because she was undergoing chemotherapy for a thyroid deficiency.

Although no differences were found on earlier data between treated Ss who obtained additional treatment and those who did not, there was no question that the retained controls constituted a positively biased subsample of the original control groups. The nonreturning controls were found to show both a higher rate of academic failure and significant increases on several anxiety scales, from the first to second assessment, than retained controls. Similarly, controls excluded for receiving treatment showed significantly greater increases on all specific anxiety scales, and lower extroversion scores, than retained controls. Thus, the controls available for analyses at the two-year follow-up were those who had improved more from pretreatment to the six-week follow-up, raising the probability that 2-year follow-up comparisons would underestimate the effects of all three treatment groups.

Results were again analyzed by complex analyses of variance, t-test of the difference between differences, and individually significant change scores on each measure for each S. Correlations over the two-year period from the first to the second follow-up found a relatively high degree of stability over all scales, ranging from .51 to .72 (Mdn $r = .64$). Questions of "relapse" and "symptom substitution" were analyzed by individually significant changes from the first to the second follow-up, in which *all* Ss in all three treatment groups were found to maintain status in the focal area without a single case of relapse, while 11 percent of the positively biased untreated controls showed significant relapse. Of all other comparisons in which a change in nonfocal scales might be interpreted as "symptom substitution," none of the groups, including controls, differed from chance-level changes, nor were significant differences obtained between groups on the frequency data. Further analyses substantiated essentially the same findings and the same order of results as were found at the six-week follow-up, with even greater evidence of significant generalization effects. Focal improvement at the two-year follow-up was reliable ($r = .78$), and was predictable from stress condition improvement on different instruments two years earlier ($r = .61$). Basing computations only upon Ss retained at the two-year follow-up, including the positively biased group of controls, the percentages of Ss showing significant improvement from pretreatment to two years after treatment termination were: systematic desensitization—85 percent; insight-oriented psychotherapy—50 percent; nonspecific attention-placebo—50 percent; untreated controls—22 percent.

While the exclusion of Ss at the follow-up causes some difficulty in interpretation, the results of this study (58) were clear in substantiating the cause-effect relationships for systematic desensitization found earlier (specific superiority of desensitization over nonspecific and insight-oriented procedures) and in extending the evidence that the effects produced were lasting. No differential contribution was found for either therapist or S characteristics within the homogeneous group of skilled therapists and anxious, introverted Ss involved.

Zeisset.   Zeisset (1968) reported the first attempt at a controlled investigation of systematic desensitization with psychotic Ss. The study was a laboratory analog in the sense that Ss were all treated for a common situational anxiety (interview anxiety) that was not a central life problem or the reason for hospitalization. All Ss were selected on the basis of observable anxiety in a criterion interview from a population of open-ward inpatients in a VA hospital, with an average of 64.6 months total hospitalization, and a minimum current hospitalization of 1 month. Only patients who were cooperative and communicative were included, and none were currently receiving psychotherapy, although all were under medication.

Pretreatment assessment procedures included a test battery consisting of half of Welsh's *A* and *R* scales, Eysenck's short-form Introversion and Neuroticism Scales, a shortened version of the FSS used by Lang & Lazovik (52), and the Ullmann & Giovannoni Process-Reactive Scale. Following the pretreatment administration of the test battery, each S underwent a five-minute criterion interview before two observers who recorded the presence or absence of 13 observable manifestations of anxiety on a Checklist for Anxiety Behavior

Observation (CABO) which was adapted from Paul's Anxiety Checklist (57). The 48 Ss finally selected had demonstrated the presence of anxiety in these criterion interviews, which involved a total of four interviewers and four sets of observers, all of whom were "blind," with interobserver reliabilities on the CABO ranging from $r = .88$ to $r = .96$. At the end of the criterion interview, each S rated his own anxiety on a 10-point Anxiety Thermometer, adapted from Lang and Lazovik's FT (52), and global anxiety ratings on a 5-point scale were obtained from the interviewer and the two observers. An additional performance measure, percentage of "sick talk," was obtained from tape recordings of the criterion interviews. Continuous GSR recordings were obtained during the second and fourth treatment sessions for all treated Ss, but not during criterion interviews. In order to assess possible generalization of treatment effects, McReynolds' Anxiety Behavior Checklist (ABC) was completed by two nurses on the ward for each S, two weeks prior to the start of treatment.

After completion of the pretreatment test battery and criterion interview, Ss were randomly assigned to one of four groups ($N = 12$ each) to receive (1) systematic desensitization, (2) relaxation plus application, (3) attention-placebo treatment, or (4) no treatment. All treatments were time-limited to four sessions of forty to fifty minutes duration, with at least one day between sessions. All treatment sessions were conducted by the investigator, who had some clinical experience with the population but was inexperienced with systematic desensitization.

For the systematic desensitization treatment, the first two sessions were devoted to relaxation training, with hierarchy arrangement during part of the second session. Three hierarchies with standard items were used ("being observed"—6 items; "being interviewed"—9 items; "speech"—5 items), with Ss only allowed to arrange the order within hierarchies. The remaining two sessions were devoted to sequential desensitization proper, following Paul's (57) procedure. The relaxation plus application group also received relaxation training during the first two sessions, but sessions 2 to 4 consisted of specific instruction and practice in the use of differential relaxation in the interview situation, in order to compare the efficacy of imaginal presentation of anxiety eliciting stimuli with the direct application of relaxation responses in the criterion situation itself. The attention-placebo treatment was included to control for nonspecific effects of merely undergoing treatment, the impact of the therapist irrespective of technique, etc., as discussed above. Paul's (57) attention-placebo tape, and similar rationale were used for this purpose; however, the rationale and the possible plausibility of the procedure were modified by not including an actual within-treatment placebo capsule.

An unusual feature of both the desensitization and the relaxation groups was that relaxation training was carried out through the use of taped instructions, recorded by *another* therapist, who had participated in a previous desensitization study (Paul, 1966). The relaxation instructions on the tape followed Paul's (57) order and timing for the most part, but with a few modifications of specific muscle groups and manner of presentation after the recorded relaxation instructions of Lazarus and Abramovitz (1962a). Unfortunately, the use of this tape introduces confounding into the design, since the "second therapist" was not involved in the attention-placebo group.

One to four days following treatment termination, a "blind" posttreatment criterion interview was obtained on all Ss, including untreated controls, with the same measures included as in the pretreatment interview. The test battery was also readministered at this time, excluding the Process-Reactive Scale, and including "parallel forms" of the Welsh A ($r = .89$) and R ($r = .72$) scales. The ABC was again obtained from ward personnel within a week of termination. It should be noted that the "blind" interviewers and observers were held constant over the pre and post criterion interviews (which were two weeks apart); however, of the 96 ABC ratings, only four pairs of nurses did 10 pre or post ratings, with the interrater reliabilities ranging from $r = .28$ to .65. Thus, in contrast to the high reliability of the CABO, over half of the ABC ratings were done by different persons, and those by the same persons were unreliable. Also, the gross anxiety ratings achieved an average interrater reliability of only $r = .61$.

Group differences on all data were evaluated by complex analyses of variance, by multiple comparisons, by appropriate t-tests, and by extensive correlational analyses. Changes observed within the criterion interviews were the most stringent test of treatment effects, since the measures used were more objective and reliable than any others. The observable manifestations of anxiety on the CABO revealed no significant differences between the desensitization group and the applied relaxation group, although both produced significantly greater reductions in anxiety than either attention-placebo or untreated controls. The attention-placebo group and the untreated control group did not differ significantly on a single measure, nor did either of these two groups show any significant change from pre to post assessment, except that the percentage of sick talk dropped in all groups. The two treatment groups combined showed significant improvement as compared with the two control groups combined on: 8 of 10 criterion-related items of the FSS, Welsh Anxiety Scale, Eysenck Neuroticism, and FSS total, while the Anxiety Thermometer showed significant improvement over the untreated group. No other overall or intragroup changes were found to be significant.

In addition to the lack of reliability of the gross anxiety ratings and the ABC, several problems in interpretation of this study arise from the lack of consistency across measures, in which the most reliable assessment of change (CABO) was unrelated to any of the other instruments. Within the self-report measures, low but significant correlations (r's in the .30s) were obtained between changes in scores on the Welsh Anxiety Scale, the Eysenck Neuroticism, and the FSS, but the Anxiety Thermometer was unrelated to any other measure. While the significant differences between treatment groups and controls on the self-report and observable measures do establish cause-effect relationships between the "active" treatments and change in target behaviors, these effects cannot be identified as a specific result of desensitization. Few Ss completed the hierarchies during the two sessions allowed, and there was no evidence that 11 of the 20 items were relevant to the criterion. The author reports that, unlike previous studies (52 to 55), no relationship was found between improvement and number of items completed, number of anxiety signals, or GSR deflections during visualization. However, over half of the desensitization Ss gave "less than 2" (i.e., 0 or 1) anxiety signals and only 1 S showed GSRs to the majority of tested items. These latter findings, combined with the fact that the taped relaxation instructions by another therapist were included in both "active" treatments but not in the other groups, suggest that the only effects actually found may be attributable to the taped training procedure.

The investigator himself raised the possibility that relaxation training alone was all that either the desensitization or the relaxation group actually received, but discounted this alternative on the basis of further analyses in which he found long-term patients changed most with desensitization, while short-term patients changed most with applied relaxation. However, a detailed inspection of the original data reveals that these latter findings may be attributed to unfortunate inequalities in the composition of the two treatment groups, in which the desensitization group was found to include twice as many Ss with a diagnosis of "paranoid schizophrenia" as the relaxation group. More importantly, a highly significant difference ($p < .001$) was found between the length of hospitalization of Ss in the two treatment groups, with the desensitization group including many more long-term patients, and the relaxation group weighted with short-term patients.

In summary, this study (59) provides evidence that brief, taped relaxation training may be of benefit in a psychotic population; however, the confounding of a "second therapist" through the introduction of taped instructions prevents comparative cause-effect relationships from being drawn with regard to systematic desensitization. By attempting a controlled investigation of desensitization within the inpatient group, this study does strengthen hypotheses that the procedure need not be restricted to a "neurotic" population without first evaluating possible effectiveness directly with psychotics.

Moore. Moore (1965) also reports a small controlled study of desensitization with unusual characteristics, the only study to date achieving control without the inclusion of an untreated group. Three treatment procedures (A, relaxation only; B, relaxation plus direct suggestion; C, systematic desensitization) were applied in a balanced incomplete blocks design, which combined an equivalent time-samples procedure and the use of a single therapist in such a way as to allow cause-effect conclusions to be established in the absence of a true control group. The Ss were six adults and six children selected from consecutive patients consulting a chest clinic, who met the following criteria: history of severe asthma attacks (one to seven per week; $\bar{x} = 3$), absence of x-ray evidence of emphysema, no cardiac lesions, not on steroids, and diagnosis of reversible airways obstruction. Assessment procedures consisted of Ss' self-reports of number of attacks, plus measurement of maximum peak flow (MPF) at the beginning and end of each session. MPF was also tested at the beginning, middle, and end of treatment after inhalation of a test dose of isoprenalin to establish optimal flow.

All treatments were conducted by the investigator, who appeared to have previous clinical experience but no special training in desensitization. After pretreatment assessment, all Ss received two half-hour sessions of relaxation training, which involved an unusual combination of Jacobson's procedure with gradual release of muscle groups (arms and shoulder girdle; neck and face; masseters and swallowing; legs and pelvic girdle; abdomen; respiration) and Schultz's autogenic training. After the two training sessions, relaxation was induced by "monotonous repetitive patter," although "hypnosis" was not mentioned. Following the initial relaxation training sessions, the three treatment procedures mentioned above were conducted in a balanced incomplete blocks design, with one adult and one child in each "block" receiving eight half-hour weekly sessions of each of two treatments in the following combinations: AB, AC, CB, BA, CA, BC. Thus, a total of eight Ss received desensitization, with two each receiving an additional eight sessions of relaxation before, relaxation after, direct suggestion before, direct suggestion after. The remaining four Ss received only relaxation and direct suggestion in counterbalanced order. The desensitization procedure was also somewhat unusual, involving three thematic hierarchies covering (1) the attack itself, (2) anxiety-eliciting stimuli, (3) presumed traumatic events associated with the onset of asthma. During desensitization proper, hierarchies were covered sequentially, with each item presented three times (not apparently contingent upon Ss' response) and with all completed items again presented at the beginning of each session.

Comparisons both with the own-control equivalent time-sample involving other treatment procedures, and with Ss receiving only the other treatments, found the desensitization procedure to produce significantly greater MPF improvement than any of the other procedures. The frequency of reported attacks fell with all procedures and intergroup differences were not significant, although only one desensitization S failed to show improvement.

In general, this study (60) provides cause-effect evidence for the application of systematic desensitization to change in tension-produced respiratory obstructions, with controls for both direct suggestion and continued relaxation. While the use of a single therapist always allows for the possible entry of therapist bias as a confounding factor, the plausibility of the latter as an influence is low due to the counterbalanced, time-sample nature of the design.

Similarly, although generality is restricted due to a lack of description of therapist characteristics, the same therapist across all treatments holds these characteristics constant for the study in question.

Emery & Krumboltz. Emery & Krumboltz (1967) report an investigation of systematic desensitization with test-anxious university students. All *S*s were selected from a population of 96 Stanford University freshmen who responded by letter to an offer of treatment sent to 240 students after screening on an 18-item test-anxiety scale constructed for the investigation. The stated purpose of the study was to evaluate the comparable effectiveness of standard versus individualized hierarchies. Therefore, 36 males and 18 females were randomly selected from respondents and randomly assigned to one of three groups ($N = 18$ each) to receive: (1) desensitization with an individualized hierarchy, (2) desensitization with a standard hierarchy, or (3) no treatment. After assignment, no pretreatment differences were found between groups on test-anxiety scores, age, sex, GPA, or ability scores.

Treatment was conducted by nine graduate students in clinical and counseling psychology on a twice-weekly basis through completion of the hierarchy, to a maximum of 16 sessions total treatment, with each therapist treating two *S*s in each experimental group. In addition to an assumed lack of general clinical experience, these therapists were also inexperienced with the desensitization procedure. Although it was stated that the therapists were "trained in the desensitization technique" for the study, no information is provided on the extent or nature of the training, and the therapists do not appear to have been supervised. No data are provided regarding the exact procedures used, except that *S*s in both groups started with a standard 16-item spatial-temporal hierarchy constructed on the basis of individual hierarchies collected in a pilot study. The desensitization treatment with a standard hierarchy followed the original one, while the individualized hierarchy group used the same 16 items, but were asked to order the items themselves.

Posttreatment assessment procedures consisted of a readministration of the test-anxiety scale, as well as *S* self-ratings of anxiety on a 7-point scale before and during each final examination at the end of the quarter during which treatment was conducted. Additionally, exam grades from a common freshman course (history) were obtained for the quarter before and after treatment. Results were analyzed by analyses of covariance for both exam and test anxiety scores, while the self-ratings were analyzed by one-way analysis of variance. Both on self-ratings of anxiety before and during final exams, and on pre-post text-anxiety scales, the two desensitization groups showed significant improvement over the no-treatment controls, with no significant differences being obtained between the two treatment groups. Performance on the history exam showed similar trends, but did not achieve significance. However, as the authors note, this exam grade was an inappropriate criterion for this study, since the population fell at the 90 percent ability level on national norms, placing the experimental group in a restricted range of talent in which the given level of anxiety does not appreciably interfere with examination performance (see Spielberger & Katzenmeyer, 1959; Paul & Eriksen, 1964). Additionally, these grades were obtained from four essay questions graded by 26 different instructors without standardization.

No data were presented concerning therapist characteristics or differential therapist effectiveness. The results of this study, then, provide cause-effect evidence for the effectiveness of treatment, but specific relationships cannot be established for systematic desensitization per se due to intraclass confounding, and due to the absence of details of procedures. Additionally, the absence of external validity data for the self-report scales limits the generalizability of the data, and no evidence is provided regarding standard versus individualized hierarchies because of the overlap of 60 percent in order, in addition to the common items between groups.

Johnson.   Johnson (1966) reports an analog study of treating test anxiety in which the above problems of examination performance criteria were overcome. The Ss were selected from undergraduate psychology courses at Northwestern University on the basis of course grades as well as debilitating Alpert-Haber test-anxiety scores obtained from all classes, in order to use examination performance as an external criterion of improvement. Additional assessment procedures were developed by the investigator, based upon the appearance of examination papers. The latter, rather unusual, procedures included (1) counting the number of nonessential marks on IBM answer sheets, and (2) rating the "messiness" of papers by specific criteria. Validity data were presented in terms of significant differences between extreme groups ($N = 20$ each) on the Alpert-Haber scale. No reliabilities were presented for the "discrete marks" score, but interater reliabilities for "messiness" were adequate ($r = .81$ to $.83$); however, the validity data were not presented in terms of correlations, and the variances, even between extreme groups, were heterogeneous; presumably, the high-anxiety group showed a wide spread. The investigator also reported the use of a Behavior Checklist during examinations; however, this was not a "checklist" in the sense of the original instrument used by Paul (57), but a series of gross rating scales for which no reliability was obtained, with reported lack of confidence from raters.

The Ss were drawn from three consecutive psychology courses, in which the test-anxiety scale was administered by another investigator. Those Ss meeting criteria on both prior course examinations and the text-anxiety scale (10 percent of students) were then contacted by telephone and asked to participate in treatment. Those agreeing to participate ($N = 23$) were randomly assigned to one of two treatment groups to receive five weekly sessions of (1) systematic desensitization or (2) continued relaxation training. An additional 10 students meeting other criteria served as a no-contact control group which was unaware of its participation.

The investigator served as therapist for all *S*s, and was apparently inexperienced both clinically and with desensitization at the start of treatment. The desensitization procedures were detailed in a manual after Paul (56), but with procedural changes including muscle order for relaxation training, in which the legs followed the arms and other groups were in reversed order (see Table 3-3), and with timing changed to 8 seconds of tension and 10 seconds of release. Two standard spatial-temporal hierarchnes were used (a 7-item quiz hierarchy and an 11-item major exam hierarchy), with some unusual procedures in desensitization proper. The first hierarchy was completed during sessions 2 and 3, with a minimum of 2 presentations (5 seconds and 10 seconds) without response, with 10 seconds between visualizations. In session 3, the entire first hierarchy was again presented once per item, and the second hierarchy was started. During session 4, *S*s were moved to a school desk, and desensitization proper continued there. The latter procedure was also followed in session 5. The *S*s in the relaxation group received the same relaxation training as desensitization *S*s; however, in sessions 2 to 5, after inducing relaxation, the therapist left the room after instructing *S*s to continue relaxing for the remainder of the session.

Following treatment termination, *S*s completed the final examinations with the regular course, and the pretreatment assessments were again obtained from these examinations. "A few months later" the test-anxiety scale was mailed to all *S*s, 27 of whom returned the completed scale. The results were evaluated by analyses of covariance and multiple comparisons, revealing significantly greater improvement in performance on a standardized multiple-choice examination for the desensitization group than either relaxation or no-contact control groups, but no other significant intergroup differences were found. An interesting trend was obtained over the three consecutive groups of *S*s; all three desensitization *S*s who failed to improve grades were in the first group of 4 *S*s treated. Unfortunately, this first group not only constituted the first attempt at desensitization by the therapist, but also differed from the two later groups in course instructor and in the use of an overstuffed chair rather than a recliner—thus totally confounding all possible sources of influence.

While this study, again, demonstrates cause-effect relationships between systematic desensitization and improved target behavior, interpretation is clouded by the failure to find corresponding differences in the test-anxiety scale, and failure to obtain the posttreatment assessment with the latter scale *prior* to the criterion examination. The other measures included were sufficiently unusual, unreliable, or lacking in demonstrated validity that no information could be obtained from them. The inclusion of the relaxation group partially controls for therapist characteristics, and for nonspecific treatment effects, although the amount of attention and "ritual" were not controlled. The author also notes that selection bias may have been operative, since 8 potential Ss declined the offer of treatment, while controls had no such opportunity. However, the declining students did not show significant differences in improvement over controls. In summary, this study cannot be taken as independent evidence for the reduction of test anxiety by systematic desensitization, although improved examination performance can be attributed to undergoing the treatment.

Cooke. Cooke (1966a) reported a small analog study which was similar to Zeissett's (59) in comparing relaxation with in vivo exposure to fearful stimuli with systematic desensitization. The Ss were selected from 34 introductory psychology students at the University of Iowa who volunteered to participate in a study on "fear of laboratory rats" after a classroom administration of the Bendig Emotionality Scale and a modified form of the FSS (Lang & Lazovik, above, 52). Additional screening was carried out in an in vivo avoidance test, following the snake-avoidance test of Lang & Lazovik (52). However, a 3-point avoidance score (look-touch-hold) was used, rather than the 19-point score of Lang and Lazovik, presumably because all Ss were able to approach the cage containing the rat. Additionally, a modified version of Paul's (57) Behavior Checklist, called a Fear Behavior Checklist (FBC), was completed by three "blind" observers behind a one-way window. The 12 Ss with the highest FBC scores were selected for study and were further dichotomized as "high and low anxiety" on the basis of Emotionality Scale scores. Two Ss within each level of anxiety were randomly assigned to groups to receive (1) systematic desensitization, (2) in vivo desensitization, or (3) no treatment.

The therapists were two graduate students who were reported to have had previous experience in client-centered therapy but no experience or training with the current treatment procedures. Both treatments were conducted for a total of four sessions at three-day intervals, with the two therapists seeing Ss equally in all groups. The desensitization treatment was conducted according to a manual, which in a later study (Cooke, 1966b) was shown to be taken directly from Paul's (57) procedure, but with a standard 14-item hierarchy arranged by each S. The in vivo procedure involved the same hierarchy and relaxation training during the first sesson, but sessions 2 to 4 were conducted in the avoidance-test context, with Ss proceeding toward the caged rat, stopping at points included on the hierarchy until no fear was reported. Five days following termination of treatment (three weeks after pretest), all Ss were again administered the Emotionality Scale, FSS, and avoidance test, and "blind" FBCs were obtained.

The reliability of the FBC scores was quite acceptable ($r = .95$), and significant intercorrelations were found between all rat-specific anxiety scores (FBC, avoidance test, rat item of FSS) ranging from .35 to .54, with none of the rat-specific items being related to the FSS total or the Emotionality Scale.

The latter two measures were positively related ($r = .41$). Appropriate tests of the difference of differences found both treatment groups to show significantly greater reduction in anxiety and avoidance than the untreated controls, while the two treatment groups did not differ between themselves. Of the 8 treated Ss, 7 showed significant change on all three measures, and 1 on two measures. No significant changes were found on the FSS total or the Emotionality Scale. As in Lang & Lazovik (52), Ss with higher pretreatment Emotionality Scale scores were found to complete fewer hierarchy items; however, the high-emotionality group was found to show greater improvement with systematic desensitization than the low-emotionality group, while no differences were found with the in vivo procedure. Pre-post data are not presented, so that it is impossible to judge whether this finding might be a result of group inequalities, or whether the high emotionality scores of the present study were "high" in comparison with other samples.

While therapist characteristics were held constant across the two therapy groups, therapist differences were not analyzed. This study (63), then, shows effective cause-effect relationships between undergoing treatment and change in phobic reactions; however, specific effects cannot be directly attributed to systematic desensitization because of the possible within-class confounding of therapist characteristics and nonspecific treatment effects. Other suggestive hypotheses concerning the level of anxiety are unclear due to the absence of pretreatment data and due to indications that the degree of anxiety and avoidance evidenced by Ss in this study prior to treatment was much less severe than that even of other analog studies.

In a later investigation, Cooke (1966b) attempted to extend the above report to a factorial study involving more novel control groups. Unfortunately, concessions to practical problems and instrument changes within the investigation resulted in essentially uninterpretable findings. In an attempt to gain large enough numbers of Ss, the FSS was administered to all females enrolled in an introductory psychology course at the University of Iowa ($N = 484$). These students were then rank ordered on the FSS total score, and the 66 students with highest scores on the FSS rat item were brought in for the same avoidance test used in the earlier study (63), with each receiving credit for required participation as experimental Ss. During the avoidance test the same 3-point approach score was obtained as before; however, a different form of the FBC was used, involving a single rating of the presence or absence of observable manifestations of anxiety by the three judges. Following the avoidance test, the 50 Ss rated highest on the FBC were selected as Ss for the therapy analog study, with each receiving course credit for required hours of experimental participation.

The Ss were then randomly assigned to one of five groups ($N = 10$ Ss each) to receive: (1) systematic desensitization, (2) desensitization with relaxation training but without specific relaxation induction during desensitization proper, (3) relaxation only, but with an initial ranking of a hierarchy which was not presented, (4) hierarchy ranking only, or (5) no treatment. For all treatment groups (1 to 4), a few minutes of the first session were devoted to rank-ordering 15 items of a standard hierarchy relevant to laboratory rats. The hierarchy-only group was then discharged, while Ss in the other three treatment groups (1 to 3) were seen for a total of five sessions at three-day intervals. During the first session, Ss in groups 1 to 3 were provided a rationale for treatment and initial relaxation training, in addition to ranking the standard hierarchy. The remaining four sessions were devoted to desensitization proper for group 1 (systematic desensitization), while group 2 followed exactly the same procedures, including timing and item presentation until no response was obtained, except that relaxation was not specifically induced by the therapists in sessions 2 to 5. Group 3 received four sessions of relaxation by suggestion in which the hierarchy was not included after the initial ranking.

The therapists consisted of five graduate students who were currently enrolled in practicum training, one of whom had treated two desensitization cases in the earlier analog study (63), while the other four had no previous experience. The therapists were trained by reading a manual taken directly from Paul (57), with two practice sessions in which the investigator "role-played" a client. Group 2, desensitization without continued relaxation treatment, followed the same procedure, but allowed Ss to relax themselves after the first session. Therapists were not apparently supervised during the study. Additional therapist characteristics were not assessed or described, but control was provided by factorially representing therapists across all treatment groups, with each therapist treating 2 Ss in each of the four groups. Several of Paul's (57) ratings were also completed by therapists for treated Ss.

Two weeks after termination of treatment, all Ss were again brought in for administration of the FSS and the avoidance test. However, for unstated reasons, the FBC assessment at posttest was again modified from that used for pretest. Presumably because of the latter change in instrumentation, the results were *not* analyzed appropriately by comparisons of pre-post change between groups, nor were pretreatment data presented to allow others to perform appropriate analyses. Rather, data were presented and original analyses conducted only on posttreatment differences among groups, for which no significant differences were found between any of the groups on any measure.

A number of problems were apparent in this study (64) which result in a failure of the reported findings to provide any useful information. The analyses based only upon posttreatment data were justified by the investigator on the basis that "Ss were initially randomly assigned." However, that justification assumes that randomization had achieved its purpose of equating groups prior to treatment, which (1) was not demonstrated, (2) was unlikely with such small numbers of Ss, (3) appears, in fact, *not* to be the case on the basis of limited pretest data which were presented. Perhaps an even greater difficulty with the investigation was the use of available Ss from a required-participant subject pool, which appears to have resulted in a group of Ss who were not particularly anxious even in the presence of the "phobic stimulus," as indicated by the report that 70 percent of the untreated controls and 90 percent of the hierarchy-only groups could touch or hold the rat without treatment. Further, while the additional changes in the FBC still resulted in reliable ratings ($r = .95$), the validity data of the previous study (63) could not be used. The actual data presented for the current study (64), in fact, found no relationship between the self-report measures and either of the measures from the avoidance test, and only a slight relationship ($r = .25$) between the FBC and the 3-point approach measure, probably a result of the lack of anxiety and avoidance in the S sample, even in comparison to the volunteers of the previous study (63). Cooke (64) further reported that only 4 of 10 desensitization Ss and only 6 of 10 desensitization-with-self-relaxation Ss completed hierarchies, and that analyses of the Ss who completed hierarchies showed significantly lower posttreatment scores on 5 of 6 comparisons with control groups, and on all comparisons with Ss who did not complete hierarchies. While these findings are suggestive, the differences could have resulted from pretreatment differences which were not included in the analyses. Therefore, contrary to the author's conclusions, this study must be considered as providing no evidence for or against the effectiveness of systematic desensitization.

Davison. Davison (1968b) also reports an analog study with novel controls. The purpose of the investigation was to evaluate the mechanisms of change involved in desensitization, utilizing target behaviors and assessment procedures patterned after Lang & Lazovik (52). All Ss were drawn from female volunteers at a Junior College who reported themselves to be very much afraid of nonpoisonous snakes. As in the Lang & Lazovik study, suggestion and placebo effects were reduced to a minimum by presenting the project as an experiment, rather than a clinical study; however, severe reactions were dealt with by prescreening Ss in an avoidance test and excluding all those who could touch the phobic object. Pretreatment assessment consisted of a modified form of the Lang & Lazovik avoidance test, scored for 13 items corresponding to progressively greater approach and intimate interaction with the snake. Self-ratings on a 10-point scale, similar to the FT, were obtained from each S after each discrete step of the avoidance test, rather than after completion of the entire test. The avoidance tests were conducted by a second "blind" experimenter, who never approached the snake more closely than 2 feet, in order to control modeling effects.

On completion of pretreatment assessment, Ss were grouped into matched clusters on the basis of avoidance-test scores, and were randomly assigned to 1 of 4 groups to receive: (1) systematic desensitization, (2) pseudo-desensitization, (3) exposure only, or (4) no treatment. Treatment was time-limited to a maximum of 9 sessions, with 8 Ss in each treatment group and 4 Ss in the no-treatment control. The investigator served as therapist for all Ss and was not only experienced clinically, but was also experienced with desensitization, having previously been trained by Lazarus. Desensitization Ss were trained in relaxation during the first session by a thirty-minute tape of instructions previously recorded by the therapist. A standard 26-item hierarchy was used, with Ss arranging unique order at the beginning of the second session. Desensitization proper began thereafter and continued through completion of the hierarchy, or to a maximum of 8 more forty-five-minute sessions. The pseudodesensitization group was conducted in the same manner, except that the hierarchy consisted of 16 snake-irrelevant items drawn from common childhood experiences, with an appropriate rationale. The exposure group was like the desensitization group, except that the first session was excluded and these Ss were never trained in relaxation at all. Each of the pseudodesensitization and exposure Ss was yoked to her matched desensitization S, whose progress then defined the number of treatment sessions, the length of each session, and the number and duration of each visualization. Thus, exact controls of all time and procedural parameters were included, except that one control group dealt with an irrelevant hierarchy and the other did not pair relevant hierarchy items with relaxation.

Three days after treatment termination, all Ss again underwent the "blind" avoidance test, with self-ratings of anxiety obtained at the pretreatment avoidance level to prevent confounding of ratings with the degree of exposure. Detailed records were also kept regarding frequency of anxiety signals during treatment, and item completion. The investigator notes that the yoking requirement for the exposure group resulted in a procedure which was not optimal for allowing self-controlled extinction to take place (see also Lang, Chapter 4); however, for outcome evaluation, the pseudodesensitization and exposure groups provide both an attention-placebo control and a novel control. These controls allow assessment of nonspecific treatment effects and do much to rule out any effect of bias which might have been operative in the use of a single therapist.

Results were analyzed by analysis of variance of change scores and appropriate *t*-tests of all data. Ss treated by systematic desensitization showed both significant pre-post change and significantly greater reduction of avoidance scores than pseudodesensitization, exposure, and untreated controls, while the latter three groups did not differ significantly on a single measure. Only the systematic desensitization group showed significant improvement on the self-report scales which, although greater than the other three groups, did not reach statistical significance. However, a highly significant relationship ($r = .81$) obtained between reduction in self-rated anxiety and closer approach to the phobic object suggests that the self-report scales were meaningful and showed essentially the same results. Inspection of individual data provided also revealed significant improvement for 7 of 8 desensitization *S*s, although only 5 totally completed hierarchies, as compared to 1 significantly improved *S* for pseudodesensitization, and none for the exposure and untreated groups.

In summary, this study (65) in the controlled context of the laboratory analog replicates the specific cause-effect relationships previously found by other workers (52 to 55) with a different therapist, assessor, and population. Within the analog context of the investigation, nonspecific treatment effects appear to be nil, based upon two additional novel control groups and upon control of therapist characteristics. Highly suggestive correlational data were found in favor of the validity of change and the usefulness of intratherapy measures for predicting success.

INVESTIGATIONS OF SYSTEMATIC DESENSITIZATION APPLIED IN GROUPS

While the reports reviewed above and in the companion chapter (Paul, Chapter 2) have dealt with the usual practice of systematic desensitization in a one-to-one therapeutic relationship, a few studies have appeared in which desensitization was applied simultaneously to two or more clients. In most cases, it should be noted that economy was the major rationale for group desensitization, and that treatment was typically *in* rather than *by* groups, in the sense that communications were most frequent from therapist to clients rather than among clients. Because group desensitization is a relatively recent innovation, involving only a few published reports, all studies applying systematic desensitization in groups are summarized in Table 3–2 and reviewed below, whether they are controlled or uncontrolled investigations.

Lazarus. Lazarus (1961) published the first report in which desensitization was applied in groups. All *S*s were selected from a group of white, middle-class, urban South Africans who requested treatment following announcement of a study of phobic disorders. The *S*s were further screened to ensure inclusion of only those whose reactions "imposed a severe limitation on their social mobility, jeopardized their interpersonal relationships, or hindered their constructive abilities." Those currently or previously receiving other psychological treatment were excluded. In addition to Lazarus's (9) usual assessment by interview and external report, obtained for impotent men ($N = 5$) and "mixed" phobias (1 *S* each for sharp objects, physical violence, travel, dogs), all acrophobics ($N = 11$) and claustrophobics ($N = 15$) were subjected to an in vivo tolerance test conducted by the investigator. Acrophobics were individually urged to climb as high as possible on a metal fire escape, and the *S*s accepted for treatment did not go higher than 25 feet. Claustrophobics were individually tested by placing them in a small cubicle, closing French windows before them, and moving a screen toward the center of the cubicle until it was

Table 3-2 Summary of Investigations of Systematic Desensitization Applied in Groups

Author	Clients (subjects)					Therapist		Treatment				
	Problem treated	Characteristics				Characteristics		Assessment procedure*	No. of sessions	Total duration	Follow-up	Outcome*
		No.	Sex	Age	Other	N	Other					
(66) Lazarus (1961)	Acrophobia; claustrophobia; impotence; mixed phobias	35	M=12 F=23	$\bar{x}$= 33.2 SD= 9.9	Distressed volunteers	(1)	All Lazarus; Medical school	External reports; tolerance tests; self-report	$\bar{x}$=20.4 (10.1)*	$\bar{x}$=7 weeks	$\bar{x}$=9 months	(+)D> nov.
(67) Lazarus (1968)	Impotence	3	M	26-32	Outpatients	(1)	Lazarus; clinic	Wife's report	5	7 weeks	2 years	+
	Frigidity	3	F	24-33	Outpatients			Husband's report	14	14 weeks	6 months	+
(68) Burnett and Ryan (1964)	Mixed*	(100)* 25	M=33 F=67	$\bar{x}$=42	"Rural" hosp. day care	2	No desensitization experience	T-ratings	? $\bar{x}$=25	$\bar{x}$=5 weeks	1 year (N=25)	+
(69) Rachman (1965) (70) Rachman (1966a)	Spider phobia	15	F	?	Volunteer students	2+ ?	University	FT; avoidance test; EPI; ratings	11	6 weeks	3 months	(+)D> NT+ multinov.
(71) Rachman (1966b)	Spider phobia	3	M=1 F=2	?	Volunteer students	?	University	FT; avoidance test	50	?		+
(72) Paul and Shannon (1966) (73) Paul (1968)	Interpersonal performance anxiety	50 (72)*	M	19-24 Mdn= 21	Distressed students	(2)	Experienced; university clinic	Test Battery; grades	9	9 weeks	6 weeks and 2 years	(+)D> nov.> NT
(74) Katahn et al. (1966)	Test anxiety	43	M=57% F=43%	"Under-grads"	Psychology students	3	No desensitization experience	Anxiety Scale; grades	8	? 8 weeks	6 months (N=7)	(+)D> NT+ nov.
(75) Shannon and Wolff (1967)	Snake phobia	36	F	18-24 Mdn= 19	Volunteer students	(1)	Experienced; university clinic	FSS; avoidance test	4	4 weeks		(+)D> NT

* See footnote, Table 3-1.

no longer tolerated. All claustrophobics accepted for treatment were unable to tolerate the screen at a distance of less than 20 inches.

After pretreatment assessment, pairs of claustrophobic, acrophobic, and impotent Ss were matched on sex, age (within four years), and type and severity of phobia, and were randomly assigned to one of two homogeneous groups, one of which always received systematic desensitization. Five replications over sequential time periods were involved. The first three periods involved groups of acrophobic, impotent, and claustrophobic Ss, respectively, with 2 to 3 Ss treated together in each group by systematic desensitization, while the other members of each pair were treated concurrently in groups of 3 by interpretive group therapy. The fourth and fifth time periods included additional groups of acrophobics and claustrophobics in which systematic desensitization was applied in groups of 3 and 4, respectively, while the other members of each pair were treated concurrently in groups of 3 and 5 by interpretive group therapy plus relaxation training. The 4 Ss with "mixed" phobias were treated in a single group by desensitization. A total of 18 Ss were initially treated by group desensitization, 9 by group interpretation, and 8 by group interpretation plus relaxation.

The investigator served as therapist for all groups, conducting sessions three times a week. Each desensitization group was limited to 1½ sessions of relaxation training, followed by desensitization proper, involving a single hierarchy directed toward the major phobia. All hierarchies, except for the mixed phobias, were group hierarchies constructed by the therapist extracting common elements from pretreatment questionnaires. The acrophobic group was desensitized to an 11-item combined hierarchy, the impotence group to a 10-item spatial-temporal hierarchy, and the claustrophobic group, whose sessions were conducted out of doors, to a 16-item thematic hierarchy. Relaxation and desensitization proper followed the investigator's usual procedure, except that new items were introduced only when all Ss in each group could visualize a given item for ten seconds without response. Unlike usual practices, no explanation of rationale was included, in order to limit any possible contribution from that procedure. Desensitization groups were terminated when all Ss within a group could visualize the final item without response, and interpretive groups were given the same number of sessions as the corresponding desensitization groups. Unlike the homogeneous desensitization groups, members of the mixed phobic group each had individual hierarchies which were presented by typewritten instructions for each scene, rather than verbal instructions.

While the procedures for the interpretive groups were described in more than usual detail, including the addition of group relaxation during the last fifteen minutes of each session for interpretation-plus-relaxation groups, the author notes the relevance of possible experimenter bias in this study. The latter issue is somewhat clouded due to the therapist's greater experience in and theoretical preference for desensitization but personal preference for treatment conduct which were "decidedly in favor of the interpretive methods."

Because of these problems, it seems best to consider the interpretive groups as novel controls for nonspecific treatment effects involving the therapist and group meetings, rather than as representative insight-oriented group treatments.

On termination of the original groups, members of the interpretive groups who did not report recovery were provided the opportunity to continue with group desensitization. All interpretive group Ss who wished to continue then immediately undertook group desensitization, except for the impotence group who continued with interpretive procedures "a while longer" before undertaking desensitization. The result was a slight difference in total number of sessions for the original treatments, with an average of 20.4 sessions for desensitization groups, and 22 for interpretive groups. A mean of 10.1 desensitization sessions was required to complete hierarchies for Ss previously attending interpretive groups.

Posttreatment assessment was in terms of a dichotomized criterion of unimproved versus recovered, rather than change. The initial criterion was by Ss' self-reports of recovery. Acrophobic and claustrophobic Ss who claimed recovery were brought in for further stress-tolerance tests one month after treatment termination. As at pretreatment, the tolerance tests were conducted by the investigator, but in front of a witness in an attempt to rule out further experimentor bias. Like self-reports, the tolerance tests were evaluated on the basis of an absolute criterion, rather than change. Thus, acrophobic Ss were classified as "recovered" only if they could accompany the investigator to a roof garden, eight stories above street level, and count the number of passing cars for two minutes. Claustrophobic Ss were required to remain in the test cubicle for five minutes without distress with the screen "a few inches away." Follow-up reports were obtained from "recovered" Ss by means of a 7-item questionnaire requesting self-reports of relapse and symptom substitution from $1\frac{1}{2}$ to 15 months ($\bar{x} = 9.05$ months) after treatment termination. No reliability or validity data were reported, except that all but 2 Ss in the acrophobic and claustrophobic groups who claimed "recovery" were able to complete the tolerance test.

Results were first analyzed by comparison of the total proportion of cases "recovered" in desensitization groups versus interpretive groups, with findings significantly in favor of group desensitization (13:18 versus 2:17). Additional analyses comparing the proportion recovered within matched pairs of Ss found desensitization to produce significantly more recoveries than interpretation, and also found a trend, which did not achieve statistical significance, in favor of desensitization over interpretation plus relaxation. Of the 15 Ss classified as unimproved following interpretive group therapy, 10 were later classified as recovered following group desensitization, yielding an overall posttreatment classification of 23 recoveries in 33 cases treated by group desensitization. Of the 23 recoveries following desensitization, 5 were considered "relapses" on the basis of follow-up questionnaires, while 1 of the 2 recoveries following interpretation plus relaxation was considered a relapse; no *S*s treated by interpretation alone were classified as recoveries, and thus there was no opportunity for relapse. No evidence of symptom substitution was found for any group.

While the absence of a no-treatment control group prevents the establishment of cause-effect relationships between systematic desensitization and outcome in this study, problems of instrumentation and design also limit the interpretation of results. The use of an absolute criterion for recovery and the use of dichotomized analyses do not allow for assessment of change and rely upon more exact pretreatment equation of groups than was possible with the small numbers of *S*s available. Additionally, the practice of subjecting only those *S*s claiming recovery to the tolerance tests biases results against the desensitization group, plus allowing confounding of additional stress exposure which may have influenced findings at follow-up. The classification of relapse at follow-up cannot be accepted at face value since there was no demonstrated relationship between the posttreatment and follow-up criteria, with the follow-up data based solely upon subjective reports of change by treated *S*s. However, the inclusion of additional groups treated by the same therapist and the use of a rigorous objective criterion for assessing the acrophobic and claustrophobic *S*s have considerable practical value. Further, the scientific value of this study should not be underestimated due to the creative introduction of new procedures and the strengthening of hypotheses concerning the effectiveness of desensitization in both homogeneous and heterogeneous groups.

Lazarus (1968) has recently provided case reports to illustrate the use of group desensitization combined with other procedures in the clinical setting with homogeneous sexual problems. One group consisted of three impotent men for whom interview and test materials suggested that a common basis of sexual incompetence lay in anticipatory fears of sexual failure. A total of five group meetings was held over a seven-week period. The first two sessions were devoted to training in relaxation and to didactic instruction in sexual physiology and technique. The clients' sexual partners were seen before the second session and instructed in foreplay techniques. Desensitization proper began with the third session, and two of the three clients completed a common 6-item spatial-temporal hierarchy during the third and fourth sessions. The third client was unable to complete the final item as rapidly as the other group members, and was consequently seen for two brief individual sessions the same week. In the fifth and final session, two weeks later, all three clients reported a series of highly successful sexual performances, which were verified by their sexual partners. Follow-up information could be obtained from only one couple in which both partners "reported a sustained level of sexual adjustment more than two years later."

The second illustrative group in this report (67) involved three women who had been married less than a year, all of whom reported sexual contacts to be frightening and repulsive. Two of the clients consulted the author for problems of frigidity within a two-week period, and they were conjointly trained in relaxation for four sessions on a weekly basis. The third client had been in treatment for general anxiety over a two-month period, with frigidity left as the remaining problem, and she was added to the group after relaxation training was completed. A fourth client started group treatment, but was withdrawn after three sessions to undergo conjoint treatment with her husband. A total of 10 weekly one-hour sessions of desensitization proper were needed to complete a common 8-item spatial-temporal hierarchy. Concurrently, about half of each session was devoted to discussions of attitudes toward sex and didactic instruction on biological, psychological, and sociological aspects of sexual functioning. All three clients reported improvement in sexual pleasure, reaching orgasm from 50 to 100 percent of the time, with maintenance at six-month follow-up (at which time all were at least three months pregnant). Like previous case reports, these illustrative groups cannot provide cause-effect evidence, but do further strengthen hypotheses of the usefulness of group desensitization.

Burnett & Ryan.   Burnett & Ryan (1964) present the first published report of the large-scale use of desensitization in groups in regular hospital service. Over a period of eight months the authors reported group desensitization of 100 day-care patients at St. John's Mental Hospital, Newfoundland. The patient population came from rural areas and fishing villages, and were generally of low educational and intellectual levels. Problems treated were not reported in detail, nor were pretreatment assessment procedures delineated. Rather, the group as a whole was described as "anxious, tense, phobic and lacking in self-confidence. . . ." Unfortunately, no details are provided regarding specific procedures of desensitization, except to reference Wolpe (1958). The length of treatment was reported only to the extent that average stay at the day-care center was five weeks. During this period, concurrent group meetings were also held for "education regarding the effects of emotion on the body" and for "motivation towards relaxation when in fear-provoking situations." Additionally, the authors report that assertion training was used regularly and that the "usual electro-convulsive therapy, insulin subcoma and coma, and drug therapies" were used with an unknown number of patients.

Although the authors report treatment of 100 patients, data are presented on only 25 who could be followed up by "regular interviews" for one year. The only assessment procedure used for these patients was a 5-point rating (from unimproved to apparently cured) based upon Wolpe's criteria. No reliability or validity data were obtained. Of the 25 patients, none were rated unimproved, 2 were rated slightly improved, 15 (60 percent) apparently cured or much improved, and 8 (32 percent) moderately improved.

While the report of group desensitization with a low socioeconomic population provides an interesting attempt at extending the procedures, with which the authors were pleased, the complete confounding of variables in all domains and the lack of adequate criteria limit the findings of this report to the development of crude hypotheses.

Rachman. Rachman (1965c, 1966a, 1966b) published a series of analog studies in which Ss were treated in groups of 3 purely for efficiency. The purpose of the investigations was much the same as Davison's (65) study, utilizing assessment procedures patterned after Lang and Lazovik (52), but focusing on Ss reporting themselves to be intensely afraid of spiders. The first study (69) involved 12 Ss selected from 84 students who completed a short questionnaire. Pretreatment assessment procedures consisted of the administration of the Eysenck Personality Inventory (EPI) followed by a modified form of the Lang-Lazovik avoidance test, scored on a 10-point scale corresponding to progressively closer approach to a live spider in a plastic container, with the Lang-Lazovik FT completed at the point of closest proximity.

On completion of pretreatment assessments, Ss were assigned to 4 groups of 3 each, equated on avoidance scores, to receive (1) group desensitization, (2) group desensitization without relaxation, (3) group relaxation, or (4) no treatment. The first three groups were all treated for 10 sessions on a twice-weekly basis during the same six-week period, with group 1 (desensitization) receiving 1 additional session for relaxation training at the start of treatment. A common 20-item hierarchy was developed through group discussion by the 6 Ss in the first 2 groups prior to the start of treatment. In addition to the group application, unusual timing procedures were invoked in which all hierarchy items were presented three to five times, whether or not a response was obtained, with an average of 2 items covered each session for both group 1 and group 2. The Ss in the relaxation group were merely relaxed for 10 sessions with no hierarchy involved. Even with the small number of Ss, the design of the study potentially could have provided solid factorial data; unfortunately, the investigator reports that practical factors necessitated the use of two therapists, which may have introduced unnecessary confounding. While the investigator was experienced with desensitization, no information is provided concerning the characteristics, training, or supervision of the therapists used in the study. Nor is information provided concerning which groups were treated by different therapists. If the novel control groups were treated by a different therapist than the desensitization group, therapist characteristics would be completely confounded with treatment effects.

At termination of treatment, all Ss were again reassessed on the same measures obtained at pretreatment, with the FT completed at the pretreatment approach point. Additionally, each S completed a 5-point self-report rating of change (from substantially worse to substantially better). Three months after termination, the avoidance test, FT, and self-ratings were again obtained, as well as a modified version of the symptom-substitution questionnaire used by Lazarus (66).

Results were presented primarily for qualitative evaluation. On all measures except EPI, group desensitization appeared to produce greater improvement than novel controls or no-treatment controls, without indications of relapse or symptom substitution at follow-up. The EPI Neuroticism Scale showed a drop of 3 points for both group desensitization and no-treatment controls, with no change on the Extroversion or Lie Scales. The only statistical evaluation made found that group desensitization Ss showed significantly greater reductions in anxiety (FT) and avoidance than the combined novel and no-treatment controls.

In the second paper of this series, Rachman (70) drew 3 more Ss from the same population, matched to the previous groups. The same avoidance tests and FTs were obtained at comparable points in time, while this group received 10 sessions of "flooding." The latter procedure consisted of the imaginal presentation of two items corresponding to the top of an anxiety hierarchy for two-minute durations, about 10 times per session. The Ss in this group reported no change in their fear of spiders at posttreatment and follow-up. These Ss were then combined with the no-treatment controls of the earlier study and evaluated against the earlier desensitization Ss; again, significant improvement was revealed for the desensitization Ss over the combined controls on both the FT and the avoidance test.

The author notes that the small number of Ss involved in these studies restricts the findings to suggestive results. While significant differences were found between group desensitization and the combined controls, the possible confounding of therapist characteristics in all groups and the addition of possible environmental confounding in the "flooding" group further restrict interpretation. Although a direct test of desensitization versus no treatment was not evaluated, the data presented suggest that group desensitization would be shown effective if an adequate number of Ss were included.

The third paper in this series (71) was entirely directed at a study of mechanisms, and provides little direct data on outcome or treatment procedure. In fact, it is not entirely clear from the report that the three spider-phobic students were actually treated in a group, except for a suggestive statement that the treatment ". . . was conducted in the manner described in the first study of the present series." The purpose of the study was to investigate the "speed of generalization" from desensitization in imagination to real-life stimuli. Hierarchies were individually ranked by each S, excluding items which could not be reproduced in vivo. A total of 50 sessions were conducted, with avoidance tests and FTs obtained immediately before and after each session, one day later, and either three or seven days after the session. On 6 occasions with each S, the assessments were carried out with a rest period interposed instead of desensitization, in an attempt to control for extinction effects of assessment. Unusual timing procedures in which two or three items were usually presented three times each, whether or not a response was obtained, impose severe limitations on the generalization of findings regarding suggested transfer effects to the usual practice of desensitization. However, all three Ss were evidently able to hold the spider before treatment was completed, and they reported a reduction in anxiety responses, providing further suggestive data for the effectiveness of the desensitization procedure.

Paul & Shannon. Paul & Shannon (1966) report the first investigation of group desensitization involving both central life problems of Ss and a no-treatment control group. The purpose of the study was to evaluate the feasibility and effectiveness of extending Lazarus's (66) group innovation to the treatment of social-evaluative anxiety in the context of intensive group therapy. All Ss were drawn from the larger groups initially involved in Paul's comparative study, reviewed earlier (57, pp. 111 to 116). Following the second administration of the test battery, at the completion of the earlier study, 10 chronically anxious males were selected from the "waiting-list" controls of the earlier study, to receive the group treatment. These Ss were those who showed *no* anxiety reduction over the waiting period, equated on pretreatment performance anxiety scores with the male Ss receiving earlier individual treatments ($N = 10$ each, individual desensitization, insight-oriented psychotherapy, attention-placebo treatment). A fifth group ($N = 10$) was drawn from earlier untreated Ss to serve as a no-treatment control group for assessing effects of the group treatment on college grade point average (GPA). The Ss in group 5 were therefore equated with group desensitization Ss on college, class, and age as well as on all scales of the test battery. Group desensitization was started four weeks after the second administration of the test battery and continued for 9 weekly sessions. The same test battery and ratings used in the earlier study were then obtained from group desensitization Ss 6 weeks following treatment termination. Thus, Ss treated by group desensitization formed an "own-control" group, plus allowing comparisons over equal time intervals with the earlier individual treatments on personality and anxiety scales, and a matched no-treatment group on pre-post GPA, obtained from the university registrar.

The authors served as therapists for the group desensitization treatment, each being experienced with both group therapy and individual desensitization. One therapist had been an individual therapist in the earlier study, and the other had supervised all previous individual treatments. The TOS, completed by both group therapists, revealed them to be similar in orientation to each other, as well as to the individual therapists, with primary "school" identification being eclectic. Each therapist treated one group of 5 Ss, with subgroups formed on the basis of homogeneity of age and anxiety and on the basis of heterogeneity of extroversion scores within the restricted range of introverts.

Comparability of the two desensitization groups was ensured by following a schedule which detailed the amount of time to be spent in various activities during each successive treatment hour, and tape recordings of each session followed by weekly discussions of procedure and progress.

Prior to the first group meeting, each S was seen in a short interview during which appointments were arranged, and common expectations of benefit, as well as rationale and course of treatment to be undergone, were presented in a standard manner. During the first session, the first twenty minutes were devoted to introductions, statement of problems, and presentation of rationale. The remainder of the session was devoted to relaxation training and discussion of the relaxation experience. The first hierarchy for each group was constructed during the second and third sessions by group discussion, resulting in 14 items for one and 18 for the other. In both groups, this was a combined hierarchy concerning speaking situations, on the assumption that less threatening interpersonal experiences would respond via generalization. Relaxation training was completed by the end of the second session, and desensitization proper began during the third. In all cases, relaxation and desensitization procedures were the same as those described earlier by Paul (57) but were paced to the "slowest" responding member, and each desensitization session was started with coverage of all new items from the previous session. Sessions 4 to 8 each consisted of forty minutes of desensitization proper, with the first fifteen minutes of each session devoted to reeducative discussion. During session 7, a spatial-temporal test-anxiety hierarchy was constructed for both groups, involving 7 items for one and 9 items for the other. For one group, both hierarchies were completed during session 8, while one group needed part of session 9 to complete the test-anxiety hierarchy. The ninth and final session was devoted to a discussion of treatment, future plans, and goals.

Group and individual differences on all data were analyzed by analyses of variance, *t*-tests of the difference between differences, and appropriate nonparametric statistics. On evaluation of test changes between the wait and treatment periods, group desensitization Ss were found to show significant anxiety reduction after treatment not only in the specific "target" areas of desensitization, but on related interpersonal-anxiety scales as well, suggesting significant generalization effects. A trend toward increased extroversion and decreased emotionality was obtained, but could not be attributed to group desensitization as it was also evident over the waiting period. General anxiety, as well as interpersonal-performance anxiety, also showed a reduction over the treatment period. The most stringent test of treatment was with regard to GPA, where a highly significant difference was found between no-treatment controls and group desensitization Ss. The latter group showed a gain in academic performance from pretreatment to posttreatment semesters, while the former lost nearly a full grade point. On comparison with the earlier individual treatments, the group desensitization procedure was found to be as

effective as individual desensitization in all areas, even though the group treatment was not aided by concurrent enrollment in the speech course. Additionally, the group procedure produced significantly greater anxiety reduction than
either individual insight-oriented psychotherapy or attention-placebo treatment, not only in focal treatment areas, but other areas as well. As with the
earlier comparative study, no differences were found among therapists, nor
was any evidence of symptom substitution obtained.

Paul (1968) has recently completed a two-year follow-up of the above
Ss (72), following exactly the same procedures as those in the long-term
follow-up of the comparative study reviewed above (58, pp. 116 to 117). As with
the comparative follow-up, 100 percent return of test batteries and frequency
data was obtained from treated Ss ($N = 40$). Of all remaining untreated male
Ss, only 69 percent ($N = 22$) returned data, and these were, again, a biased
subsample who had improved most over the initial treatment period. The untreated group was further biased by the necessary exclusion of 10 Ss for receiving treatment during the follow-up period, and 1 for a high falsification
score. Of the male Ss in treatment groups, excluded for receiving additional
treatment during the follow-up period, 2 were in the insight group, and 1 was
in individual desensitization. No Ss were excluded from the individual attention-placebo treatment or from group desensitization. Again, no differences
were observed between treated Ss who were retained and those who were excluded, but retained controls were definitely positively biased. GPA data, on
the other hand, were obtained from the university registrar on all matched
no-treatment controls, as well as group desensitization Ss, two years after
treatment termination, or for the final semester in the case of Ss who were
dropped from the university or graduated.

Results were again analyzed by analyses of variance, t-tests of the
difference between differences, and individually significant change scores on
each measure for each S. Correlations for the group desensitization Ss over
the two-year period of the follow-up found reliability and stability of scores
comparable with that found on the comparative follow-up (58). Analyses of the
group desensitization data, alone, revealed not only maintenance of improvement in focal areas of treatment but further significant reductions in test-
anxiety and other interpersonal-performance situations, as well as general
anxiety and emotionality over the follow-up period. Questions of "relapse"
and "symptom substitution" were analyzed by individually significant changes
from the first to the second follow-up. As previously found for individual
treatments, not a single group desensitization S showed evidence of relapse,
with all Ss maintaining status on focal scales. Similarly, of all other scales in
which a change might be interpreted as "symptom substitution," changes in
the "worse" direction did not exceed chance expectation. On comparison with
individual treatment and control groups, no differences were found on the
frequency data, and the earlier superiority of both individual and group desensitization over individual insight-oriented psychotherapy and attention-

placebo treatments was not only maintained, but the group treatment was also found to show even greater reduction in emotionality than any individual treatment. Basing computations only upon the male Ss retained at the two-year follow-up, the percentage of Ss showing significant focal improvement from four weeks prior to treatment to two years after termination were: group desensitization—80 percent; individual desensitization—89 percent; insight-oriented psychotherapy—50 percent; nonspecific attention-placebo—50 percent; untreated controls—27 percent. On test anxiety, which was a focus of treatment for group desensitization but not for other groups, similar percentages were: group desensitization—70 percent; individual desensitization—44 percent; insight-oriented psychotherapy—25 percent; nonspecific attention-placebo—20 percent; untreated controls—9 percent. On the test anxiety scale, both the insight-oriented and the nonspecific treatment groups did show significant increases in anxiety in 13 and 10 percent of cases, respectively.

The academic performance of group desensitization Ss as compared with the matched untreated control group, again found highly significant differences in favor of group desensitization two years after treatment termination, with posttreatment and follow-up GPAs correlating significantly ($r = .62$). Of even greater interest was a significant difference in academic success (graduation or still enrolled in good standing) versus academic failure (dropped from the university) for the last two groups. Two years after treatment termination, 90 percent of group desensitization Ss were successful academically versus only 40 percent of controls matched for college, class, age, and personality variables. As with the original group study (72), no differences were found for therapists, nor was improvement predictable from any S or therapist characteristic. Similarly, the only measures which failed to show significant differences between treatment groups were Ss' self-ratings of improvement, in which all groups yielded mean ratings indicating improvement.

In summary, these two studies (72, 73) provide cause-effect evidence for the effectiveness of the group treatment and for stability of resulting client changes. However, due to the confounding of reeducative group discussion and therapist characteristics, specific cause-effect relationships cannot be established directly for systematic desensitization per se. The comparison with individual treatment programs produces highly suggestive results, with strong hypotheses of specific effectiveness; however, it should be noted that the group treatment involved four more hours of client contact than the individual treatments, as well as possible beneficial effects of group discussion. On the other hand, comparison with other group treatments of any sort in which GPA has been used as a criterion suggests that group desensitization may well be both more effective and more efficient (see Paul, 1968).

Katahn, Strenger, & Cherry. Katahn, Strenger, & Cherry (1966) also report a study of group desensitization for test anxiety involving additional group procedures. All Ss were drawn from second-year psychology courses taught by

Katahn at Vanderbilt University. On the basis of scores in the upper 25 percent of the distribution on Sarason's Test Anxiety Scale (TAS), administered to each class at the start of the course, 45 students were selected. Of these, 22 students indicated a desire to participate in group desensitization for test anxiety after the program was described in class, and 16 were assigned to treatment groups. The remaining 6 had conflicting schedules and formed a "volunteer control group," by default. The 23 students who did not wish to participate were considered a "nonvolunteer control group." The Ss were selected over two consecutive semesters, and one group was treated each semester; however, the distribution of control Ss over semesters was not detailed in the report.

Pretreatment assessment for all Ss included administration of the TAS in class at the beginning of each semester, and determination of cumulative GPAs up to the semester prior to treatment. Posttreatment TASs were apparently obtained on all treated Ss, but the second TAS was reported for only 8 control Ss who were in the same class as the first desensitization group. The posttreatment TAS was administered to these controls at the time of the final exam. Posttreatment GPAs were also determined for all Ss; the GPAs for treatment and controls selected in the first semester consisted of the average of two semesters GPA, while Ss selected during the second semester provided post-GPAs only for that semester.

The first treatment group was composed of 8 Ss (4 male, 4 female), and the second treatment group of 6 (2 male, 4 female). The second group also was initially composed of 8 Ss, but 2 withdrew after the first group meeting, and these Ss were excluded from the study. Both groups were time-limited to 8 one-hour sessions with a therapist and a co-therapist. The senior author was a therapist in both groups (as well as professor in the course) and was described as psychoanalytically oriented. The junior authors each served as co-therapist for one group, and both were graduate students with some previous group experience. None of the therapists had previous desensitization experience. In addition to the use of co-therapists, a number of unusual procedures were involved in the group treatment. The initial twenty-five minutes of the first session was devoted to introductions, discussion of test anxiety, and presentation of rationale. During the next ten minutes, Ss were asked to list individually 10 experiences related to test anxiety, and to rank-order the items in a hierarchy. The last fifteen minutes was devoted to relaxation training. The first twenty minutes of the second session was again devoted to discussion, and it was suggested that the students buy a book on problems of college students and ways of overcoming them. The following ten to fifteen minutes was devoted to completing the individual 10-item hierarchies, and the last twenty-five minutes to completing relaxation training. It should be noted that both hierarchy construction and relaxation training were most unusual. The treatments were conducted in a seminar room around a table. The Ss essentially constructed their own hierarchies, which were limited to 10 items, and which appear to include multiple themes involving study, class attendance, fear of professors, etc., as well as examination items. The relaxation was not group relaxation, but individual relaxation in the group, in which "the leaders circulated around the room holding ankles, knees, etc. in order to illustrate the difference in feeling between tension and relaxation." Muscle groups proceeded "from the toes to the head," with about 5-seconds tension, exerting pressure against the therapists, followed by instructions to "relax slowly." No further details were provided on relaxation training.

In the remaining sessions (3 to 8) the last twenty minutes of each session was devoted to desensitization proper, while the first forty minutes was devoted entirely to discussion of the way professors view education, and to discussion of study skills. The brief periods of desensitization proper were also unusual, in that each *S* picked 3 items from his individual hierarchy. These individual items were then visualized 3 times each for five to ten seconds, whether or not anxiety was elicited, although *S*s were instructed to start each session with the last item which still elicited anxiety. By the third or fourth sessions, *S*s were also instructed to use in vivo differential relaxation.

Results were analyzed by appropriate analyses of variance only for the combined desensitization groups versus combined controls on pre-post GPA, in which the treated group showed significantly greater improvement on GPA than controls. A highly significant reduction on TAS scores for the overall treatment group was also obtained. When TAS reduction was compared to that of controls for the *S*s on which data were available (8 treatment *S*s, 8 controls), the treated *S*s showed greater anxiety reduction at the 10 percent level of significance. A semester later, follow-up GPAs on 7 treated *S*s were still higher than pretreatment GPAs, but no analyses were performed.

The authors note a number of problems with this study which place serious limitations on the findings: Since the major therapist was also a full-time professor and the instructor of the *S*s, considerable additional influence may have entered into the sessions. Further, desensitization procedures were completely confounded with nonspecific treatment effects, and with bibliotherapy and the study skills discussion, which actually constituted a greater part of the therapeutic contact, with the result that no cause-effect conclusions could be drawn about desensitization per se. In addition to the above problems noted by the authors, a clear selection bias was present in the control groups, as control *S*s were those who were unmotivated or less acquiescent, or who had unusual schedules. The latter methodological difficulties preclude the establishment of solid evidence even for the combined treatments, so that the study can, at best, be taken as providing suggestive hypotheses of the effectiveness of group desensitization.

Shannon & Wolff. Shannon & Wolff (1967) have recently completed an analog study of group desensitization following many of Davison's (65) procedures. The purpose of the investigation was to evaluate the contribution of modeling and expectancy in desensitization. From several hundred entering freshmen at the University of Illinois who rated themselves as intensely afraid of nonpoisonous snakes, 36 Ss were selected. The Ss were administered the Lang-Lazovik FSS and a snake-avoidance test conducted and scored in the same manner as Davison's (65). Three experimental groups ($N = 12$ each) were formed, equating pretreatment avoidance scores, to receive (1) group desensitization (2) group desensitization with a model, or (3) no treatment. After four weekly fifty-minute treatment sessions, all Ss again underwent the avoidance test conducted by a "blind" experimenter, and the FSS was also repeated.

Treatments were all conducted by the senior author, who was experienced clinically, as well as with individual and group desensitization, in closed groups of 6 Ss each. The only difference between the "regular" and "model" conditions for group desensitization was that the latter groups included a "plant" who continually reported high expectations and success with all treatment procedures. Relaxation training and induction throughout treatment was by means of instructions recorded on tape by the therapist (the same tape used by Zeisset, 59). During the first session for each group, a standard 17-item hierarchy was established, taken from Davison's (65) items. The other sessions always included a ten-minute group discussion of snake phobias, with the remainder devoted to desensitization proper, following the rules of timing presented by Paul (57) and Paul & Shannon (72), with all Ss completing hierarchies.

Results were analyzed by analyses of variance and t-tests of differences between change scores on the avoidance test. The FSS data had not yet been analyzed at the time of this review. Analyses of the group data found that both group desensitization and group desensitization with a model produced significantly greater reductions of snake avoidance than were found in the untreated controls, and no differences were obtained between the desensitization groups. Individual data showed that all desensitization Ss significantly increased approach to the phobic object on posttest, while only 5 untreated Ss did so. Ratings of the recorded treatment sessions revealed that the model had performed adequately, and that the number of positive statements by group members with the model were significantly higher, starting with the second treatment session; however, desensitization groups without a model gradually and spontaneously increased positive statements over sessions, so that there were no differences between groups by the final session.

Six weeks after termination of the above groups, 6 Ss from the untreated group were brought in for group desensitization with a different modeling procedure. Treatment and assessment were conducted with the same timing as for the earlier groups, except that the phobic object was in the treatment room for all sessions. Additionally, the therapist himself modeled for the Ss, by picking up the snake and holding it for about five minutes each session during the discussion of phobic reactions. The Ss in this group showed a significant reduction in avoidance behavior in comparison to their "own-control" period, and all *Ss* showed significant improvement. The degree of improvement for this "intensive-model" condition was no different from that of the desensitization groups.

In summary, this study does provide cause-effect evidence for the effects of undergoing treatment, and the inclusion of additional modeling procedures strengthens hypotheses concerning the specific effect of desensitization. However, nonspecific effects and therapist characteristics are confounded with desensitization in such a way as to prevent solid evidence for desensitization per se.

Summary of Outcome, Related Factors, and Future Research Needs

The 75 available papers reviewed above and in the companion chapter (Paul, Chapter 2) report data on the application of systematic desensitization therapy by more than 90 different therapists with nearly 1,000 different clients. While the majority of these papers are uncontrolled case reports and single-group studies which, alone, cannot provide evidence of effectiveness or ineffectiveness, the historical development of the evaluation of systematic desensitization as a specific treatment procedure is striking. Even though more than 70 different authors and investigators have reported on work with systematic desensitization, the cumulative progress in knowledge has more closely approximated ideal tactics in behavior modification research, albeit unsystematically, than for any other treatment procedure (see Paul, Chapter 1). Thus, from Wolpe's early laboratory studies leading to the development of the basic procedures, modification and trial with a wide range of problems and clients in 55 separate uncontrolled reports resulted in positive correlational conclusions or strengthened hypotheses of effectiveness in all but 9 reports. Of the latter, 6 were sufficiently ambiguous in results or reporting that either the author or the reviewer was unable to make even a subjective estimate of outcome, and in only 3 reports were the authors' conclusions negative. At the second level of evaluation, in which nonfactorial experimental designs may provide cause-effect evidence for treatment effectiveness but allow intraclass confounding, 10 reports have appeared. All 10 reports found treatments including systematic desensitization to be more effective than no treatment (56, 61 to 63, 69, 70, 72 to 75), although one study (74) may be discounted because of questionable no-treatment controls. Finally, 10 reports involved designs which could potentially evaluate specific cause-effect relationships between systematic desensitization therapy and change in clients' behavior, although two of these (59, 64) fail to provide information because of methodological problems. Of these 10 reports, the work of Lang and his colleagues (52 to 55), Paul (57, 58), Moore, (60), and Davison (65) were all sufficiently controlled experimental studies to rule out intraclass confounding, and all found solid evidence for the specific effectiveness of systematic desensitization. Paul's (57, 58) investigations have been the only ones to date that adequately compared desensitization with traditional therapeutic procedures, and the results were clearly in favor of desensitization.

It should be noted that the scientific evaluation of systematic desensitization is still a recent development. After Wolpe's first report of the technique in 1952, only 13 reports appeared during the following 10 years. In contrast, 46 reports included in the combined review chapters have appeared since 1965, with only 3 controlled investigations appearing before 1965. In fact, it is only since 1966 that controlled investigations of systematic desensitization have outnumbered uncontrolled studies. Thus, while systematic desensitization is the first psychotherapeutic procedure in history to withstand rigorous evaluation, future research should focus upon the wealth of hypotheses and questions present in the current literature.

RANGE OF CLIENT PROBLEMS, CHARACTERISTICS, AND ENVIRONMENTS

The majority of controlled research on systematic desensitization has dealt with homogeneous classes of eliciting stimuli, due to the greater ease of establishing reliable assessment and control operations. Many studies have involved concrete "phobic stimuli," such as snakes, rats, spiders, heights, and enclosures, characterized by high states of anxiety, avoidance, and inhibition of adaptive behavior in the absence of objective danger. Others have dealt with more generalized social and evaluative situations, such as interviews, exams, and public performance, which result in similar distressing maladaptive behaviors, but which are not normally considered "classic phobias." A few have focused upon homogeneous response classes, such as impotence, frigidity, or asthma. While controlled studies have established the effectiveness of desensitization with "classic phobias," more generalized social-evaluative anxiety, and some psychophysiological disorders, suggestive positive results have been reported across the full range of distressing behaviors in which the direct treatment of anxiety could be considered of fundamental clinical importance (see Paul, Chapter 2). Unfortunately, current assessment procedures are sufficiently individual and unreliable that no valid comparisons can be made between various reports, although both the range of eliciting stimuli and the range of maladaptive responses appear to be nearly unrestricted.

The only suggestive evidence of poorer differential success with desensitization, where the direct treatment of anxiety would appear appropriate, was with problems described as "panic" and "pervasive anxiety." These latter problems seem to arise through difficulty in constructing appropriate hierarchies, but have also been confounded with the extent and duration of disability. Conflicting data have also been reported in which duration and severity of disorder were apparently unrelated to treatment response (see Wolpe; Hain,

Butcher, & Stevenson, 1966). Lang and his colleagues (52 to 55) have found the extent of eliciting stimuli to be related to the rapidity of desensitization, but not to effectiveness once desensitization has been accomplished. Cooke (63) reported that higher-emotionality Ss took longer to complete hierarchies, but showed greater improvement; however, Rachman (personal communication) has reported a failure to replicate Cooke's findings, and there is considerable question about the degree of anxiety or emotionality in Cooke's study as compared to others. Additionally, Paul's research did not find these factors to be of importance. While a few uncontrolled case studies report negative or questionable results, many more report positive results with similar distressing behaviors. It is interesting that both of the two negative reports which provide data deal with response-defined problems (compulsion, kleptomania) in which the presence of anxiety appeared to be reactive to other maladaptive behaviors, rather than central to the complaints.

Aside from the possible suggested relationship of general anxiety level, other client characteristics and environmental settings have not been seriously considered. Approximately 60 percent of the clients treated by desensitization have been female, but no differential response between sexes is suggested. The great majority of cases have fallen in the fifteen to fifty age range, although cases as old as seventy have been treated, with no differential response suggested. Only four children (aged twelve, eleven, nine, and five) were reported in the literature, presumably due to difficulty in relaxation training; however, systematic exploration with children has not been done. The problem of client motivation appears to be no more or less a problem than with any psychotherapeutic procedure. Three cases were specifically noted to be court or police referrals, and two were considered successes by therapists, while the third appeared to be a reactive anxiety case in which desensitization was inappropriate. A small number of failures are reported due to difficulty in imagery, in which avoidant thinking patterns precluded responses to visualization. These difficulties do not appear related to any identifiable characteristic of clients and often respond to training. Most reports of problems with imagery, and with relaxation, appear to come from inexperienced therapists and may be more a technique or communication problem than a client characteristic.

Remarkably little concern has been shown with assessment or description of client personality characteristics. Where assessment procedures or descriptions were provided, nearly all appeared to be anxious introverts, although four cases described as anxious extroverts, hysterics, or sociopathic were reported as treatment successes. One report involved three extroverted student volunteers (39), but other difficulties were sufficient to preclude even suggestive evidence from being obtained. "Suggestibility" has been evaluated and found to be unrelated to outcome. Perhaps the greatest question regarding client characteristics is with regard to the presence of psychotic behavior.

Wolpe & Lazarus (1966) specifically exclude cases diagnosed as psychotic from treatment with desensitization; however, two case reports have appeared (27, 28) in which persons labeled psychotic were treated, and one study (59) focused entirely on psychotics. While the latter study had methodological flaws, the evidence is at least as strong in favor of desensitization with psychotics as against it. In fact, Davison, Shannon, and Paul (separate personal communications) all report successful use of desensitization with schizophrenic patients over the last two years.

As with client characteristics, little descriptive information has been included concerning life environments. The great majority of cases have been white, urban, middle-class individuals, and nearly all controlled studies were conducted in university communities. One report (68) involved, entirely, a rural lower-class population. While, again, no solid comparisons can be made, no obvious differences in response appear to be attributable to clients coming from South Africa, from Canada, or from the Southeast, Middlewest or West Coast of the United States. In general, reports from England are less favorable, but nearly all of these are confounded with unusual treatment procedures, inexperienced therapists, and questionable methodology. In those reports with better methodology, no differences are suggested.

In summary, the greatest needs for future research in these areas first focus upon the development of adequate instruments for reliable assessment and description of clients' distressing behaviors, characteristics, and life environments. Within these areas, controlled investigations are needed to evaluate the specific effectiveness of desensitization across types and levels of these classes of variables, with important factors treated as independent variables. The most pressing questions do not appear to be related to the type of distressing behavior, as long as anxiety may be identified as the central factor (see Paul, Chapter 2); however, the more stimulus and response classes involved, the greater the generalizable knowledge. Rather, questions of interactions between successful treatment of distressing behaviors and other client characteristics appear to be more important at the present stage of knowledge: Can desensitization be effective when psychotic behavior is present? Is it useful with children? Are there limits or differential response depending upon the extent of anxiety-eliciting stimuli, IQ, verbal skills, habitual patterns of behavior or manner of dealing with stress? Other than the presence of depression or reactive anxiety, are there contraindications for desensitization? In general, the needs at this stage seem to be for factorial studies which "test the limits" of effectiveness across all classes of client variables.

RANGE OF THERAPIST CHARACTERISTICS AND TREATMENT SETTINGS

Even less concern and care has been demonstrated with regard to description of therapist characteristics and treatment settings than with regard to client variables. Only one series of investigations has assessed and described these characteristics in detail (57, 58, 72, 73), although several studies have controlled for them. The settings in which desensitization has been conducted seem to cover the full range of settings in which any psychological treatment might be conducted. These have included public and private clinics and hospitals, hospital clinics and day-care centers, university clinics and counseling bureaus, departmental seminar rooms, experimental rooms, offices in medical schools and universities, and clients' homes. Again, no meaningful comparisons can be made across treatment environments because of the total confounding of all other factors; however, no suggestive evidence exists for interactions between environments and effectiveness, and the one study involving three similar, but physically different, environments found no difference among them (57). It should be noted that the few negative or questionable outcome reports involving hospital settings all came from the English groups in which methodological problems and unusual hospital procedures were involved. One study (39) in which treatment was conducted in an experimental room of a university resulted in questionable outcome reports, but more important factors appeared to have contributed to this difficulty than the setting.

Of the more than 90 therapists involved in these reports, only 7 were identified as females. While 2 of the latter were involved in reports with negative or questionable subjective outcome evaluations, these possible results appear attributable to other factors, and no suggestive evidence of differential response according to sex was seen in other reports. The orientations of therapists were seldom reported, but the ones that were included only a few who were avowed "behavioral therapists," with most considering themselves "eclectics." Several therapists of psychoanalytic and client-centered orientation were involved in various investigations, but these orientations did not appear to have influenced outcome when use of desensitization procedures was carefully programmed and supervised. Similarly, in those studies in which therapist expectation of success was evaluated, no differential rates of effectiveness were found as long as the procedures were appropriately applied.

While no direct comparisons of experienced versus inexperienced therapists were reported, all authors reporting negative or questionable outcomes used therapists without previous desensitization experience, and all but two of these studies involved therapists with little general clinical experience. Similarly, studies involving therapists without previous desensitization experience appeared to report more difficulties with imagery, relaxation training, and construction of appropriate hierarchies. It should be noted that controlled studies in which experienced therapists were intensively trained in desensitization have found them to be effective (e.g., 52 to 55, 57, 58); however, in every case, the therapists were carefully supervised in the application of the procedures, and the assessment of target stimuli and hierarchy construction were not tasks they undertook on their own. If any suggestive hypotheses can be drawn concerning therapist characteristics, it appears that the major one is that nonspecific clinical skills should be present and that the major liability of inexperience in systematic desensitization may be in the identification and construction of appropriate hierarchies. However, essentially no solid evidence exists in the literature concerning the interaction of therapist characteristics with outcome of desensitization, and the evidence available shows no differences between experienced therapists when desensitization is appropriately applied.

Of the reports reviewed in this chapter and the companion chapter (Paul, Chapter 2), four have moved in directions which partially remove interpersonal therapist characteristics by using taped instructions for relaxation training (9, 59, 65, 75). While no comparison of effectiveness has been reported to date, the reviewer has a study in progress to evaluate the use of tapes. Additionally, Lang (1966) reported the introduction of a "device for automated desensitization" (DAD) in which desensitization proper is conducted by a machine without out a live therapist present, and Migler & Wolpe (1967) report the use of a modified tape recorder for conducting all of systematic desensitization except hierarchy construction. These cases were not included in the reviews because they are essentially experimental and only at the case study stage; however, success with such automated procedures further suggests that specific therapist characteristics are not essential.

In summary, at our present stage of knowledge, future research on therapist characteristics and treatment settings is entirely open. Within the normal limits of research and practice, the treatment setting does not appear especially important, but care should be taken to provide adequate description. Questions to which research might best be directed would seem to be those involving possible interaction between therapist characteristics (such as sex, age, experience, likability, prestige, expectancies, and habitual patterns of behavior) and client characteristics—again, "testing the limits" of effectiveness. But it should be noted that care to ensure standard and appropriate applications of the procedures must be maintained in such research, lest therapist characteristics have a spurious effect on outcome through modification of techniques.

RANGE OF PROCEDURAL VARIATION

Even limiting the term "systematic desensitization" to the treatment package involving relaxation, hierarchies, and imaginal presentation, a wide range of variation is possible (see Paul, Chapter 2). A careful definition of procedures is of major importance, since the procedures define the independent variable. Running through the 75 separate reports are four identifiable procedural "packages" which account for the great majority of procedures used in both uncontrolled and controlled investigations, and these are summarized in Table 3–3.

Table 3–3 *Summary of Major Time and Technique Parameters within Systematic Desensitization Therapy*

		Authors		
Operation and parameter	Wolpe (1) (2) (3) (4) (5)	Lazarus and Rachman (6), Rachman (18), Lazarus (7) (8) (9) (10) (11) (12) (13) (14) (1964c) (1967b)	Lang and Lazovik (16), Lang (19), Lang et al. (52) (53) (54) (55)	Paul (17) (56) (57) (58) (73), Paul and Shannon (72)
Relaxation training:				
Within session time ...	"About half"	"About half"	15–30 min.	10–35 min.
Total no. of sessions ..	"Usually 5–7"	"Usually1–3", "seldom > 6"	5	1–3 (see below)
Muscle sequence	Arms and forearms; head and facial; tongue, jaws, eyes, neck; shoulder; back, thorax, abdomen; thighs and legs	Right hand and forearm; left hand and forearm; biceps; triceps; forehead; eyes; jaws; tongue; neck; shoulders; chest; abdomen; back; hips and thighs; calves and feet	Left forearm, arm; right forearm, arm; left leg, right leg; abdomen, forehead; neck and shoulders; eyes	Dominant hand and forearm; upper arm; nondominant hand and forearm; upper arm; forehead; eyes and nose; mouth and cheeks; neck; chest and back; abdomen; dominant upper leg, calf, foot; nondominant upper leg, calf, foot
Duration of tension ...	30 sec.	5–10 sec.	30–60 sec. small groups; 5–15 sec. large groups	5–7 sec.
Duration of release	"a few–20 min."	10–15 sec; lengthened later	1 min; 2 min; 5 min.– small-large groups	20–30 sec.
Manner of release	Gradual	Abrupt	Abrupt	Abrupt
No. of tension-release cycles	1–2	2–3	2 (each group reviewed each session)	2–4
Use of suggestion	Direct; "hypnosis" in 1/3; some drugs	Direct; some "hypnosis"; some drugs	Training in hypnosis; 1/2 of 3 sessions	Indirect only ("hypnosis" in one case—17)

Table 3-3 *Summary of Major Time and Technique Parameters within Systematic Desensitization Therapy (cont'd)*

Operation and parameter	Authors			
	Wolpe (1) (2) (3) (4) (5)	Lazarus and Rachman (6), Rachman (18), Lazarus (7) (8) (9) (10) (11) (12) (13) (14) (1964c) (1967b)	Lang and Lazovik (16), Lang (19), Lang et al. (52) (53) (54) (55)	Paul (17) (56) (57) (58) (73), Paul and Shannon (72)
Relaxation training:				
Other features	New muscle groups introduced sequentially over sessions	As many muscle groups as possible each session; all groups in one session by end; pleasant image; sometimes by recorded instructions	2 new muscle groups introduced each training session; later by suggestion only	All muscle groups covered each session; phase to larger groups as skill acquired; later by imagery alone
Hierarchy construction:				
Within session time ...	"About half"	"About half"	15 min.	15–30 min.
Total no. of sessions ..	"Typically 5–7"	"Usually 1–3"	3; 10 for No. (19)	1–3: Mdn=1
No. per client	1–36: Mdn=2	1–6; Mdn=2	1; 7 for No. (19)	1; 2 for (72), (73)
Items per hierarchy ...	3–25	4–25	20; 10–13 for No. (19)	7–25
Usual type	Thematic or combined	Thematic; spatial-temporal; combined	Thematic	Spatial - temporal (combined in some)
Other features	Based upon Willoughby FSS, interview, self-listing	Same as Wolpe, but additional psychological tests often used	Based upon interview and self-listing; (16) had many problems of inexperience	Based upon interview and self-listing; care to establish equal-interval just-noticeable differences

Desensitization proper:

Within Session time ...	"15–30 min."	"Usually 20–30 min."; up to 90 minutes	"30–60 min." for (16) & (19); 45 min. for others	"30–45 min."
Items per session	"Usually 2–4"	"Usually 2–4"; up to 15	2–4 maximum	2–10
Presentations per item..	"Usually 3–4"	"Usually 2–4"	"At least 2"	2–12
Sessions per hierarchy..	1.6–72.3: Mdn=8	"2–50: mean=10"	6–8 for (16); $\bar{x}$=8.6 for (19) 11 for others	2–6
Manner of progress	Concurrent	Concurrent and sequential	Sequential	Sequential
Duration of scenes	1–10 sec: "usually 5 sec."	3–60 sec; "usually 8 sec."	3–10 sec.	10 sec.
Interval between scenes.	4–20 sec.	"10–20 sec."	30 sec.	30–45 sec.
Criteria for progression.	No response after 2–4 presentations	10-sec. tolerance; 20–60 sec. if response	2–10 sec. presentations	2–10 sec. presentations; 20 sec. if response
Other features	About 1/3 relaxed by "hypnosis"; 2–3 sessions per week; 1-min. interval after anxiety elicited	Usual practice is to lengthen duration of scenes; 2–3 min. relaxation if response; 2–3 sessions/week—usual; range 4/day–1/mo.	Study (16), no S completed hierarchy in time limit of 2 weeks; 2–3 sessions per week; terminated if anxiety elicited; (52)–(55) about half completed	If response to 10 sec. presentation, 1 min. relaxation, 3–5, 5, 10, 20 sec. same item; continued response drop to lower item

No investigations have directly evaluated possible differences in effectiveness of the four major approaches, and differences in clients, problems, and criteria are sufficient to preclude direct comparison across studies. It is unfortunate that several studies merely refer to Wolpe, but provide little or no data on the exact procedures followed (15, 21 to 26, 68), while others refer specifically to the Lazovik & Lang (27, 28) or Paul (20, 29) manuals. A number of reports (40 to 48) merely refer to Wolpe and provide no data on specific procedures, yet do indicate unusual features. Others report sufficiently unusual variations to be detailed in the text above (30 to 39, 50, 51, 60, 61, 69 to 71, 74). Three studies (59, 65, 75) provide details on procedures which combine the Lazarus and Paul relaxation methods, while one (65) combines the Lazarus and Paul procedures for desensitization proper. Five studies providing details followed the Paul manual (59, 62 to 64, 75). While no solid comparative evidence exists, both the Lazarus and the Paul relaxation procedures appear to be more rapid than those of Wolpe or Lang. Additionally, Wolpe reports a few clients whom he is unable to relax, while the other authors seldom mention this difficulty. The relaxation differences might be accounted for by client characteristics; however, this difficulty is mentioned more frequently in case reports with inexperienced therapists than with experienced desensitization therapists. In general, the features of the major variations appear sufficiently similar to allow generalization from one to the other, and there is no evidence of significant differences between the effects produced. However, having established the effectiveness of systematic desensitization, future research may well focus upon delineating the most effective time and technique parameters. Additionally, the promise and efficiency of group desensitization make it seem worthy of considerable research effort.

While research now needs to focus specifically on questions of "how" desensitization works (e.g., Lang, Chapter 4), there are specific technique variations which pose empirical questions of effectiveness. With regard to relaxation, the question is whether the effects produced by progressive relaxation, "hypnosis," and drugs are indeed similar; there is also the question posed above regarding taped relaxation instructions. Lang (1965b) reports no difference in effectiveness of desensitization when "hypnosis" is or is not used in combination with progressive relaxation training, but Barber & Hahn (1963) report that "hypnotic induction" was no more effective in reducing physiological arousal than instructions to sit quietly. I am currently making a comparative evaluation of progressive relaxation and "hypnotic" procedures.

The question of using drugs to induce relaxation is also open. Wolpe and Lazarus (1966) report the use of meprobamate, librium, chlorpromazine, and other phenothiazines to aid in relaxation, while I have regularly found interference with relaxation in several cases with the same drugs. Costello (1964) reports three cases of desensitization under the effects of lysergic acid diethylamide (LSD), while Wolpe & Lazarus (1966) report that three attempts at LSD desensitization were unsuccessful. Although all work to date is only at the case study level, more generally positive results have been reported with desensitization under the effects of intravenously administered barbiturates than with other drugs. Cooper (1964) and Walton & Mather (1964) report a total of three cases using intravenous sodium amytal with positive results; however, all three of these cases also involved very unusual desensitization procedures, and were confounded with a number of other treatments. Friedman (1966a, 1966b) reports a total of 26 phobic cases who were desensitized while relaxed by intravenous methohexitone sodium in an average of 12 sessions. Unfortunately, no information at all is provided on other procedures or on criteria of evaluation. Brady (1966) also reports the use of intravenous metho-hexitone sodium, combined with suggestions of calm and relaxation, for de-sensitization of five frigid women to single spatial-temporal hierarchies of 4 to 14 items, using scene presentations two to three minutes long. Four of the five cases reported success, verified by the husbands, in 10 to 14 weekly sessions. On the other hand, Reed (1966) reports the same drug-induced relaxation to be of limited value, and Reed & Cohen (1966) report six cases in which treatment initially included intravenous injections of methohexitone sodium, but later was switched to progressive relaxation training without drugs. The authors report that all six cases were successful and that progressive relaxation was preferable to drug-induced relaxation, because it was "equally simple and quick . . . the relaxation was as profound, could be maintained longer, and was more acceptable to the patient." Further difficulties are suggested by studies with both animals (e.g., Barry, Ethredge, & Miller, 1965; Davison, 1966a) and humans (Turner & Young, 1966) which suggest that counter-conditioning and extinction fail to transfer directly from drug to nondrug states. At the present level of knowledge, it appears that therapists who prac-tice and do research with systematic desensitization should ensure that clients are not concurrently taking drugs; however, parametric investigations of types and dosages of drugs in combination with the presence and absence of progres-sive relaxation training are certainly called for.

In addition to the quality and method of inducing relaxation, several case reports have appeared with variations in procedures which did not specifically train relaxation, but relied upon self-relaxation or simply the presence of the therapist to reduce anxiety. While these studies are not to be equated with systematic desensitization, they do provide alternative treatments to be con-sidered in future evaluations. Wolpin & Raines (1966) report on 6 cases which did not involve direct relaxation training, but did involve imaginal presenta-tion of items. The Ss were snake-phobic females, 2 of whom visualized items without relaxation training, 2 of whom visualized items while tensing muscles, and 2 of whom visualized only the items at the top of the hierarchy. After four to five sessions, all Ss were reportedly able to pick up the snake. How-ever, no evidence of anxiety reduction is presented, and neither standard desensitization nor no-treatment controls were included, with the result that these findings, alone, are not impressive. Additionally, in the studies reviewed above, both Davison (65) and Rachman (69) included groups who visualized hierarchies without relaxation. These groups were found inferior to desensitization groups and no different from controls. Rachman (70) similarly found a "flooding" group inferior to the desensitization group and no different from controls.

On the other hand, a large number of positive case reports have appeared involving in vivo presentation of hierarchy items without specific relaxation training. These have included pictorial or in vivo presentations in the therapist's office (e.g., Freeman & Kendrick, 1964; Murphy, 1964; Haslam, 1965; Leventhal, 1968) as well as therapist-accompanied exposure outside the office (e.g., Schmidt, 1964; Grossberg, 1965; Garvey & Hegrenes, 1966), but all involved one or two cases without appropriate controls. Similarly, case reports have appeared with in vivo presentation of hierarchy items in which relaxation was trained, with equally positive results (e.g., Clark, 1963a; Meyer & Gelder, 1963), although the latter are also without controls. Only one small pilot investigation, by Davison (1965b), has attempted to compare the effects of in vivo hierarchy presentation with and without relaxation training. In that study, 2 Ss with relaxation and 3 Ss without relaxation were compared with 2 untreated controls in an avoidance test for "beetle phobias." Both treated groups showed more approach than the controls, with 2 of 3 exposure-only Ss and both exposure-with-relaxation Ss achieving criterion; however, the Ss receiving relaxation showed more anxiety reduction. Of the studies reviewed above, Zeisset (59) and Cooke (63) included groups with relaxation training and both imaginal and in vivo item presentations. Both of the latter studies found significant improvement over untreated controls for either treatment procedure, with no differences in the type of presentation; however, both studies also involved confounding sufficient to preclude establishment of cause-effect relationships specifically for the presentations themselves.

Some of the most pressing needs for future research concern the identification, construction, calibration, and type of hierarchies to be employed. Little can be drawn from the current literature, except to point out that spatial-temporal hierarchies, in general, appear to allow more rapid construction and desensitization than thematic hierarchies, and that inexperienced therapists report more difficulty here than with any other desensitization procedure. The major problem appears to lie in the fact that identification of important dimensions and consequent construction of hierarchies is much less operationalized than any of the other procedures, and still relies mainly on the "clinical sensitivity" of the assessor or therapist. Current investigations, especially those of Paul and Lang, do suggest that desensitization to the most stressful anxiety-eliciting stimuli results in generalization along related dimensions; however, the means of identification of central dimensions in the clinical setting is still more "art" than "technology" and relies upon a broad basis of knowledge (see Paul, Chapter 2). Questions of both theoretical and empirical importance need to be answered regarding the inclusion of endogenous stimuli versus external stimuli, especially when endogenous stimuli compose a part of the anxiety response. More reliable methods need to be developed for distinguishing between stimuli which are appropriate for hierarchy items and stimuli which consist of maladaptive behavior that should be altered rather than desensitized, lest therapists inadvertently reinforce inappropriate behavior.

In addition to the above questions concerning hierarchies, a few case reports have appeared in which relaxation has been paired with visualizations of one or more scenes without lower hierarchy items (e.g., Clark, 1963b; Geer & Katkin, 1966), and several authors report the use of "differential relaxation" or some method of relaxation training applied in vivo by clients, without hierarchical programming (e.g., Wolpe & Lazarus, 1966; Davison, 1966b; Snider & Oetting, 1965). While the latter should not be confused with systematic desensitization and have not been evaluated in controlled studies, they do provide promising alternative treatments which should be considered in future evaluations, as do direct "hypnotic" treatments not involving hierarchies (e.g., Hussein, 1964; Larson, 1966).

Future research on desensitization proper might, again, best be focused on development of appropriate assessment procedures, although additional questions concerning parametric variations (see Paul, Chapter 2) are far from being answered. On the basis of current controlled research, it appears that the rules of timing presented by Lang, Paul, and Lazarus, relying upon a minimum criterion of two 10-second exposures without response, are sufficient to obtain reliable results. Entirely too much "random variation" in timing appears in individual case reports, and it would seem that future studies should follow procedures which have been found effective, or vary them systematically in order to identify possible differences in effectiveness. No suggestive evidence exists in the literature regarding an optimal number of presentations or the duration of sessions of desensitization proper. The duration of sessions has been determined primarily by client tolerance, and on occasion, I have conducted desensitization proper for as long as three hours at one sitting. No differences in effectiveness appear attributable to concurrent versus sequential progress when multiple hierarchies are involved, but it appears that sequential progression may be more efficient, possibly because positive generalization may reduce the number of items ultimately included. The majority of questions concerning desensitization proper are now more of concern for determining mechanisms of change than for outcome, and are summarized by Lang (Chapter 4).

However, there are a few reports of imaginal item presentation following relaxation training which were sufficiently unique that they are not considered reports of systematic desensitization, but which may be of interest for future comparative investigation. Lomont & Edwards (1967) report a complex analog study involving two groups ($N = 11$ each) of snake-phobic volunteers, each treated individually by stylized procedures. The stated purpose of the investigation was to determine the role of extinction and counterconditioning in systematic desensitization, but in fact, no Ss received standard desensitization. Rather, they visualized hierarchy items, in response to buzzer signals from therapists who were physically removed, while tensing muscles in a special chair and halter arrangement. One group relaxed on termination of visualization, while the other continued tensing for fifteen seconds after termination of the image. Assessment procedures were adapted from Lang & Lazovik (52), including FSS, FT, avoidance test, and number of items completed, with the addition of GSR measurement during the avoidance test. While this study has a number of serious flaws which prevent its acceptance as solid evidence, including lack of a no-treatment control and the fact that only one S completed treatment, the authors report a significant difference on the FSS snake item in favor of the group who relaxed on termination of images. Differences on the avoidance score and the FT approached significance, and no differences were found on other measures. However, the suggestive value of this study is further reduced by the fact that pre-post changes were not significant on any measure for any group. Three reports (Wolpin & Pearsall, 1965; Cautela, 1966b; Geer & Silverman, 1967) have appeared which involve the continuation of images in the presence of anxiety, with various attempts to bring about relaxation concurrently. Since all are uncontrolled case reports and only Geer & Silverman restricted treatment to the specific procedure, only suggestive hypotheses are possible. These last procedures may be useful alternatives in problem cases or in future investigations on mechanisms of change.

Chapter Summary

A critical review of all available controlled studies of individual desensitization (see Table 3–1) and all reports of group desensitization (see Table 3–2) was presented.[2] In this and the companion chapter (Paul, Chapter 2), a total of 75 papers were reviewed in detail, excluding multiple reports of the same data.

These reports covered the application of systematic desensitization therapy to nearly 1,000 different clients in the hands of over 90 different therapists. While 55 of these papers were uncontrolled case reports or group studies without sufficient methodological controls to establish independent cause-effect relationships, 20 of the reports were controlled experiments, and 10 of the controlled experiments included designs which could potentially rule out intraclass

[2] See Paul, Chap. 2, Footnote 1.

confounding of therapist characteristics and treatment techniques. The findings were overwhelmingly positive, and for the first time in the history of psychological treatments, a specific therapeutic package reliably produced measurable benefits for clients across a broad range of distressing problems in which anxiety was of fundamental importance. "Relapse" and "symptom substitution" were notably lacking, although the majority of authors were attuned to these problems. Investigations of equal quality and scope have not been carried out with other treatment techniques deemed appropriate for similar problems, and cross-study comparisons where control is absent have little meaning. Only one set of investigations to date (57, 58) may be considered adequate comparative evaluations of desensitization with more traditional procedures, and the reviewer has, therefore, taken the liberty of presenting further details concerning that comparison in order to correct recent misconceptions (see Strupp, 1967; Rachman, 1967).

The range of client problems, characteristics, and environments and the range of therapist characteristics and treatment settings were summarized with suggestions for future research, as were the details of procedural variations within systematic desensitization therapy (see Table 3–3). Note was also made of 30 additional case reports of procedural variations which are related to systematic desensitization. In general, while specific research needs were identified, systematic desensitization has been established as an effective treatment package for given distressing conditions. Future research might best focus upon: (1) "testing the limits" of desensitization, by comparative factorial studies, across domains of clients, problems, therapists, and environments, (2) appropriate "process studies" including outcome to determine the mechanisms of operation, (3) parametric studies to standardize and operationalize the most efficient procedures for individuals and groups, and (4) the development of standardized assessment procedures with adequate reliability and validity.

4

The Mechanics of Desensitization and the Laboratory Study of Human Fear*

PETER J. LANG
University of Wisconsin, Madison, Wisconsin

The study of fear and anxiety in human beings has long been a central theme of psychological research. In general these investigations have followed either of two strategies: the first and more direct approach is to instigate fear in the laboratory. An animal, usually a white rat, is the preferred subject, and electric shock prompts the fear response. The paradigm is occasionally employed with human beings. However, for ethical reasons the stressors are comparatively mild, or the study takes advantage of chance events which cannot be exactly replicated. Either condition devaluates the resulting data. The alternative strategy is to ask human beings about their fears. We may inquire into the antecedents of fear, recollections of first experiences, the breadth or depth of fear, according to the informants' insight and narrative skill. The procedure may be more or less structured, and it can be carried out with both clinical and normal populations. I would include here questionnaires, and data from traditional therapy sessions or interviews.

Both of the above strategies involve severe limitations for the scientist— the first, because of uncertainties in generalizing across species, and the second, because of the failure to gain real experimental control of the phenomenon.

* The writing of this review was supported in part by grants from the National Institute of Mental Health (MH–10993, MH–35, 324) and the Wisconsin Alumni Research Foundation.

The advent in the clinic of a direct method of fear reduction has stimulated a third approach to the experimental study of fear. Systematic desensitization has been demonstrated to be an effective technique in the treatment of fear and anxiety (Wolpe, 1958; Lazarus, 1963b). Futhermore, it may be defined independently of the specific patient under treatment, and it consists of a specific set of repeatable operations. Thus, unlike methods derived from dynamic psychology, desensitization and other similar techniques lend themselves to laboratory analysis and control, and are potentially important research tools. The concern of this chapter will be with the laboratory study of these behavioral techniques of fear reduction. Much of this research was undertaken to demonstrate the effectiveness or the mechanism of the treatment method, and these implications will not be ignored. However, it is well to consider that some of the most important information growing out of this work concerns the nature of fear itself.

Before describing attempts to analyze and assess desensitization, we must consider the general probem of fear measurement. At this stage of our knowledge it is wise to make relatively few preliminary assumptions. It is both convenient and parsimonious to consider fear a response, or more properly a complex of responses (as opposed to energy, drive, a phenomenal event, or a psychic structure). These responses may be evidenced in the main, expressive modes of the body. Thus, we expect to find verbal fear responses, overt motor-fear behavior, and relevant somatic responses (cortical, neuromuscular, and autonomic). Fear change should appear in all modes. However, correlations between separate measures of fear or fear change are surprisingly low (Lang, 1966). Thus, subresponses of the complex must be measured separately and, at least initially, assessed separately. Furthermore, we must be careful not to assume that one system is more important or fundamental than the others—not to assume that what people say about their feelings is emotion, or that polygraph changes show true feelings. Avoidance behavior may appear when the subject professes no distress; despite a verbal report of intense fear, the subject may seek out fearful stimuli. These response systems can be shaped and controlled independently. It is reasonable to assume that treatment may be similarly specific. Change in one behavioral mode does not automatically signal change in an overall organismic set.

The main fear contents that have been studied in the laboratory are fear of snakes, rats and other small animals, test anxiety, and social anxieties (e.g., fear of authority figures or public speaking). The choice of fear content has generally been dictated by frequency of occurrence (Can a sufficiently large experimental sample be obtained?) and the ease with which multiple measures of fear (including overt behavior) can be gathered.

The analysis of desensitization may proceed by a number of alternate strategies. Perhaps the most prevalent approach involves a sequential dismantling of the basic treatment unit. This approach is rather like that of a curious aborigine who hopes to understand a modern automobile. Clinical reports tell him that it runs. He has even taken it out for a spin. But he does not understand what makes it go. His plan is to start pulling things off it (perhaps starting with the shiny hood ornament) until it stops, hoping that he will come to know what parts are critical to its functioning—and that the owner will not mind too much the mess he has made of things.

A parts list of desensitization therapy is easily arrived at. It includes the therapist; the client; the fact of a therapeutic relationship (two people have come together for the purpose of reducing the client's fear); training in muscle relaxation and hypnosis; construction of an anxiety hierarchy (a graded list of objects or events related to his fear, starting with the least intense stimulus and extending to the most frightening situation); actual desensitization, which usually includes the hypnotic presentation of hierarchy items in sequence; concurrent muscle relaxation; and finally, the subject's control via distress signals of the frequency of individual items and/or their length.

In this chapter we will first assess the current harvest of the dismantling strategy. Theories purporting to explain desensitization will then be considered, along with related methods of fear reduction and supporting laboratory studies.

Desensitization and Generalization in the Laboratory

The entire desensitization unit clearly produces a positive reduction in fear behavior. Figure 4–1 presents data for 37 snake-phobic subjects seen in our laboratory over a six-year period. All desensitization and all control conditions have been combined to define these two groups. Desensitization subjects show significantly greater reduction in snake avoidance, and report less fear on these two verbal measures than do control subjects. Furthermore, gains are maintained at follow-up testing (approximately eight months after posttest). These basic data have been replicated by Paul (1966), who used students anxious about public speaking as subjects, and more recently by Schubot (1966), who also studied snake phobics and employed fear measures very similar to those used in our laboratory. Positive changes in avoidance behavior have been obtained by Davison (1965a) in another study of snake phobics, and Lazarus (1961) found significant fear reduction in a group desensitization study of acrophobics, claustrophobics, and miscellaneous fear. The above experiments affirm the replicability of positive desensitization effects. The variety of fears treated indicates that results are not limited to specific contents.

No experiments have been reported in which desensitization led to a significant increment in fear, in response either to the treated stimulus or to other stimuli. On the contrary, research suggests that successful desensitization is associated with a generalized reduction in anxiety (Lang & Lazovik, 1963) and improvement in overall adjustment (Paul & Shannon, 1966).

The reduction of untreated fears appears to be a direct function of their similarity to the desensitized fear stimuli. In our own experiments conducted

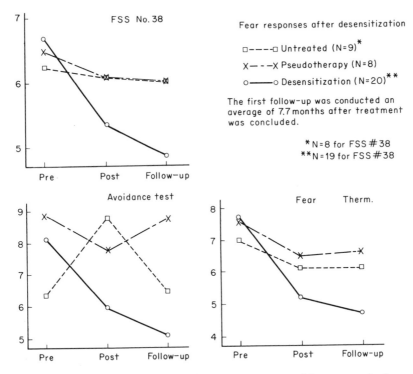

Figure 4–1. *Changes in snake-phobic behavior occasioned by systematic desensitization therapy, compared with changes resulting from placebo treatment and with changes observed in untreated control subjects. The avoidance test involved an actual confrontation of the phobic object. The FT is the subject's rating of his own anxiety during this encounter. No. 38 is the snake item taken from the FSS.*

at the University of Pittsburgh, all subjects rated the degree of fear elicited by each of 50 stimuli. This Fear Survey Schedule (FSS) was filled out before desensitization, after treatment, and again at the follow-up testing. Correlations between FSS items were subsequently obtained from an independent sample of 114 college students at the University of Wisconsin. Items were then ranked, from the one displaying the highest correlation with fear of snakes to the one displaying the lowest.

These 49 stimuli were then ordered into item groups, determined by the percentage of variance that could be accounted for by the snake item. The percentage of variance for each item cluster is given on the abscissa of Figure 4–2. For the snake-phobic students treated at the University of Pittsburgh, the mean changes for each group of items, from pretherapy to posttherapy, were then computed. These data are presented on the ordinate of Figure 4–2 for the combined control group (pseudotherapy and untreated) and for desensitization subjects. It will be noted that greater fear reduction is associated with desensi-

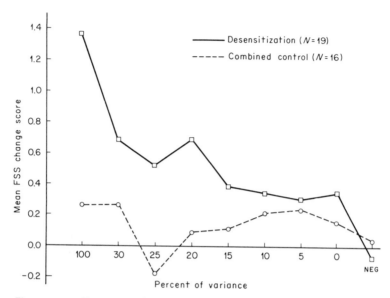

Figure 4–2.   *Treatment changes in the FSS items according to the correlative relationship of these items to snake fear. The change depicted is from just prior to desensitization to just after treatment was discontinued.*

tization. This levels effect was significant at the .05 level. Furthermore, while the curve for the control subjects is relatively flat, the desensitization subjects show a monotonic gradient of generalization. For this latter group, the degree to which a subject reports an item to be less fearful is directly related to the percentage of variance attributable to the snake-fear item. The interaction in the appropriate analysis of variance was significant at the .01 level. A similar analysis of pretherapy to follow-up changes was undertaken, and the data are illustrated in Figure 4–3. The same effects persist and are significant at comparable levels of confidence.[1] These data clearly argue against the symptom-substitution hypothesis and affirm that successful desensitization results in positive generalization along empirically determined gradients of generalization.

Therapist and Therapeutic Relationship

The first component of desensitization that must be considered is the fact of therapy itself and the placebo effects that may be associated with a continued

---

[1] The interpretation of these data is somewhat less clear than it might be because of an obvious tendency among snake phobics, for items closely correlated with the snake item have higher initial values than other items. It could be argued that the tendency to show greater reduction is an artifact of differential initial levels. Nevertheless, it is also true that despite equally high initial levels, a similar drop on high percentage of variance items is not seen among control subjects.

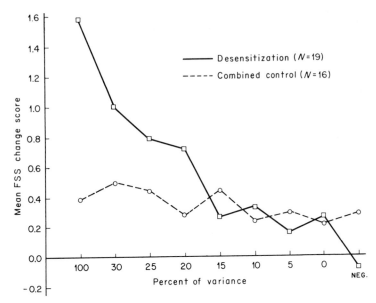

Figure 4–3. *Treatment changes in the FSS items according to the correlative relationship of these items to snake fear. The change depicted is from just prior to desensitization to the follow-up evaluation (an average of 7.7 months after the conclusion of treatment).*

treatment relationship. In an early study, we found no significant fear change to be associated with the training and instruction sessions which precede laboratory desensitization (Lang & Lazovik, 1963). In a subsequent experiment (Lang, Lazovik, & Reynolds, 1965), a group of phobic subjects were administered a psychotherapeutic placebo. This pseudotherapy followed the standard training sessions and included all the main elements of desensitization. Thus, subjects were hypnotized, visualized scenes, received instructions in relaxation, and utilized the hierarchy. However, these parts were mixed up in ways that, beyond the fact of the relationship, were theoretically neutral, i.e., only pleasant scenes were visualized and the hierarchy items provided a starting point for conversations unrelated to the fear. To make it all hang together, a plausible, vaguely psychoanalytic theory was provided. No differences in pre-post test scores were apparent between no treatment and pseudotherapy for any of the fear measures, and the follow-up scores are about the same as at the end of the experiment. Desensitization subjects, on the other hand, showed a significant positive change with treatment and maintained the improvement at the follow-up testing.

Paul (1966) employed what may have been a more powerful placebo drug-suggestion therapy as a control condition. He found that while the placebo yielded greater changes than untreated subjects, both groups changed significantly less than the desensitization group. Davison (1965a) also compared desensitization with a placebo treatment involving relaxation and visualization. Instead of imagining events from an anxiety hierarchy, Davison's group ranked a series of previously prepared scenes from childhood, which were then visualized during treatment. While verbal measures did not distinguish the two groups, a significantly greater reduction in overt avoidance was found for the desensitized subjects.

The attitudes, interests, and convictions of the therapist seem to be important to the process and perhaps to the success of traditional insight therapies. In our own desensitization research we have made every effort to minimize the effect of these variables. Thus, the experimenter-therapist's communications are in the main read from a prepared mimeographed script. Details of procedure—number of items, time of visualization, etc.—are arbitrarily controlled. In the course of our largest outcome experiment (involving almost 50 subjects), six different therapists were utilized. All of them learned the method specifically for this experiment. Despite varied theoretical convictions and personalities, all were able to apply the desensitization method successfully. Paul (1966) has since used a similar procedure of training professional therapists to act as experimenters. His careful analysis of the therapists' and the subjects' attitudes supports the hypothesis that these therapist variables (given an average level of clinical skill and competency) are not significant in the success of desensitization. These findings are consistent with the experience of those who have trained others in desensitization. It is a frequent occurrence to allow a trainee to "sit in" in the middle of therapy and administer the procedure (Geer & Katkin, 1966), or to have a colleague take over when the responsible therapist is ill. This practice seldom interferes with the course of treatment.

Mrs. Melamed and I are currently undertaking an even more rigorous test of the therapist variable. This is accomplished by comparing his performance with a programmable apparatus that can conduct desensitization sessions. This mechanism, which is known in our laboratory as DAD (Device for Automated Desensitization), stores hierarchy and relaxation instructions on magnetic tape. In use, it automatically presents instructions in hypnosis and relaxation and the items of the prerecorded hierarchy in sequence. The apparatus may be programed to present each item a preset number of times before a subsequent item is administered. The subject's signal of distress terminates the item and automatically initiates instructions to stop visualizing the scene, followed by the muscle review according to a modified Jacobson (1938) procedure. If the subject signals that anxiety is decreasing with repeated presentations of an item, the apparatus will continue to present the same item until he reports no further distress on two successive repetitions of the image, and only then go on to the next item. If the subject reports an increase in anxiety, the preceding item is repeated, and the subject must work his way back up the hierarchy, following the usual rules of the game. The subject's response to automatic inquiries on the clarity of imagery are recorded, along with four channels of bioelectric information. It will be noted in Table 4–1 that DAD is about as effective as the live therapist in producing fear reduction. This is true both when the automated group is compared with previous samples and when other subjects are treated concurrently by a live therapist. Subjects who have experienced desensitization with DAD are not in the least distressed by the absence of a human therapist. The therapy process appears to be little altered, with the advantage that much greater control over method is obtained. In future experiments we plan systematic investigation of a variety of procedural and therapist variables with this apparatus. In our current research, a human experimenter conducts the first training sessions—hierarchy building and the initial relaxation instruction. During desensitization, DAD conducts the entire session, with the exception of the posttherapy inquiry. The fact that a pro-gramed device can "sit in" for the experimenter during a fundamental part of the therapy process is the strongest kind of evidence that it is the specific pro-gram of instruction, and not therapist or relationship variables, that is the viable aspect of desensitization therapy.

Hypnosis and Suggestibility

The fact that the pseudotherapy procedure which includes hypnosis did not lead to a significant reduction in fear (Lang, Lazovik, & Reynolds, 1965), argues that hypnosis does not produce the desensitization effect through a simple placebo enhancement or transference. However, it leaves open the question of whether hypnosis is a necessary or useful component of the desensitization process. In 1959, at the outset of the desensitization project, our assumption was that it might enhance visualization and thus facilitate treatment. In order to assess the hypothesis, desensitization treatment has been given to a group of 10 subjects, without hypnotic induction at the beginning of each session. These subjects were compared with a concurrently run sample

Table 4–1 *Mean Pretreatment to Posttreatment Change Scores*

Group	Avoidance test	Fear Thermometer
Wisconsin sample		
Desensitization (N=14)	.33	3.21
DAD (N=7)	.32	4.29
Therapist present (N=7)	.34	2.14
No treatment (N=7)	−.09	− .57
Pittsburgh sample		
Desensitization (N=23)	.27	3.58
No treatment (N=11)	−.19	1.00

SOURCE: P. J. Lang. Fear reduction and fear behavior: Problems in treating a con-struct. In J. M. Shlien (Ed.). *Research in Psychotherapy. Vol. III.* Washington, D.C.: A.P.A., 1968, pp. 90–102.

who were regularly hypnotized. The similarity in fear change of the hypnosis and no-hypnosis desensitization groups is readily apparent (see Table 4–2). For one measure, the latter group actually shows greater mean change.

These data suggest that hypnotic induction is not a significant aspect of the desensitization process. It must be pointed out that all subjects in this sample had been exposed to hypnosis during previous training and suggestibility assessment sessions. Furthermore, they were all trained in muscle relaxation, which was employed during desensitization. Thus, the data pertain only to the presence or absence of standard trance-induction procedures during treatment. Nevertheless, the results led us to eliminate hypnosis from our procedure, with no apparent change in rate of success.

For most theorists the induction procedure is a less important criterion of hypnosis than an actual "altered state of consciousness," which is held to be indicative of the trance state. It may be argued that relaxation training produces such a state, which is in turn the vehicle for fear change in desensitization. I will not dwell on the problems of objective measurement when this definition is employed (Barber, 1965), but will simply describe what appear to be relevant data.

Cautela (1966a) cites a variety of case studies in which hypnotic procedures produced a reduction in phobic behavior. He argues that visualization and graduated approach were employed, and thus, the results can be explained as desensitization. However, there are few laboratory experiments comparing hypnotic fear-reduction procedures with each other or with nonhypnotic desensitization. Larsen (1965) studied the effects of hypnotic therapies on snake-phobic behavior. In two of the groups assessed, subjects were instructed to visualize previous frightening experiences with snakes. In one case they were told to remain relaxed and calm during this experience, and in the other, to vividly relive the emotion. A third group was simply given a posthypnotic suggestion not to be afraid. Immediately after testing, all three of the experimental groups were superior to controls in approach behavior increase and reduction in reported fear of "harmless reptiles." However, because of relapses in the other groups, only the "relaxation" group had a significantly higher

Table 4–2   *Mean Pretreatment to Posttreatment Change Scores for All Fear Measures*

Group	Fear measures			
	Thermometer Fear	FSS, 38	Fear survey	Avoidance test
Desensitization:				
Hypnosis (N=17)	2.38*	1.58	14.8	.24
No hypnosis (N=9)	2.78	1.56	22.3	.35†
Combined control (N=21)	1.14	.48	12.1	−.03

* N=16 for this measure.
† N=10 for this measure.

approach score than controls at the follow-up test (nine to thirty-four days later). Experimental and control subjects did not show differential change in generalized anxiety or other fears.

One hesitates to draw conclusions for the desensitization of fear from an experiment in which neither graduated approach nor subject control of the visualized scenes was involved. Nevertheless, it would appear that direct suggestion is as efficient as scene visualization in producing short-term reduction in fear behavior. Whether this effect was specifically enhanced by hypnotic induction procedures cannot be determined, as no nonhypnotic therapy was included. On the other hand, there is a suggestion, in the differential relapse rate, that visualization with relaxation and perhaps the presence of a competing response lead to the most persistent change.

The importance of hypnosis may be assessed indirectly by studies of the relationship between hypnotic susceptibility and therapy change. In our own experimental program, the Stanford Hypnotic Susceptibility Scale (SHSS) has been routinely administered to desensitization and control subjects before and after training. Table 4–3 presents a matrix of correlations between the two SHSS forms, their difference score, and all measures of fear change used in

Table 4–3 *Pearson Correlations between the SHSS and the Initial Measures of Fear and Fear-change Scores**

Fear measure	SHSS form		
	A	B	Change
Total sample (N=44) (initial score):			
Avoidance test	−.34†	−.47‡	−.06
FT	−.14	−.22	.04
FSS, 38	.10	.19	.11
Fear survey	.00	−.10	−.13
Control group (N=21) (change score):			
Avoidance test	.00	.12	.06
FT	.33	.46†	.15
FSS, 38	.47†	.48†	−.02
Fear survey	.29	.36	−.23
Desensitization group (N=23) (change score):			
Avoidance test	−.16	.11	.28
FT	−.16	.18	.39
FSS, 38	.07	.02	−.19
Fear survey	.08	.07	.02

* All correlational statistics were computed on the IBM 7090 at the University of Pittsburgh Data Processing Center.
† $p<.05$
‡ $p<.01$
SOURCE: P. J. Lang, A. D. Lazovik, & D. J. Reynolds. Desensitization, suggestibility, and pseudotherapy. *Journal of Abnormal Psychology*, 1965, **70**, 395–402.

our study of snake-phobic subjects. It will be noted that avoidance-test change is unrelated to suggestibility for both the desensitization and the control subjects. For control subjects alone, the Fear Thermometer (FT) and FSS change are positively related to these measures of suggestibility, and the snake item (FSS, 38) shows a tendency in this direction. However, there is no signficant relationship between the desensitization group's SHSS scores and any fear-change measure. The above findings imply that while suggestibility may be a meaningful variable in fear research, the positive effects of desensitization therapy are so great that no variance assignable to suggestibility can be detected.

Larsen (1965) also reported correlation coefficients between fear measures, fear change, and hypnotic susceptibility. In general, verbal reports of anxiety tended to correlate negatively with hypnotic susceptibility, a finding which is consistent with studies of the general college population (Lang & Lazovik, 1962). A significant positive relationship between the SHSS (Form A) and snake-approach behavior was found for the posttest but not for the pretest. Larsen (1965) suggests that this indicates a relationship between hypnotizability and improvement. However, the actual correlations between approach-change scores and the SHSS were insignificant and close to zero.[2]

Schubot (1966) studied the desensitization of snake phobics and also examined the relationship between the SHSS and approach behavior (he reports no correlations for verbal measures). He found very high positive correlations between change in approach behavior and the SHSS for subjects who were desensitized using a hypnotic-relaxation procedure, but essentially no relationship for subjects who were desensitized without using hypnosis. Schubot suggests that his results differ from our own because he used Form C of the SHSS. This scale contains more cognitive items than A or B. Form C is thus "more related to the acquiescence tendency than responding to sensorimotor items" (Hilgard, 1965, p. 335), which predominate on the other forms of the SHSS.

It is possible to reconcile these findings along different lines. Schubot's (1966) and Larsen's (1965) subjects were tested during the initial experimental session, prior to the establishment of any extended therapeutic relationship. No positive correlation between this test and the SHSS was found. It is reasonable to suppose that the subsequent therapeutic contacts potentiate such a relationship, particularly if the subjects were continually hypnotized. In point of fact, SHSS suggestibility and the posttests (and in Schubot's study, change) were positively related.

In our own research, the relevant pretest was administered to experi-

[2] Larsen found a positive relationship between the subjects' reported depth of hypnosis during therapy sessions and their behavior test change. However, this measure is not independent of the therapy process and may well be confounded with the subject's own perception of change.

mental subjects just before actual desensitization, but after five training sessions in hypnosis and relaxation, plus initial interviews, personality testing, and hypnotic evaluation. Thus, it may be assumed that whatever contribution hypnotic susceptibility might make to change, it had already been potentiated. In fact, the correlation between this pretest and the SHSS for the combined sample is positive and significant. However, it is also clear that the subsequent increment in approach behavior (and decrement in reported anxiety), which is specific to the period of the desensitization sessions, is unrelated to SHSS score.

In summary, the data suggest that hypnotic experience in the context of therapy may produce fear change, in part related to individual hypnotic susceptibility. They also indicate that hypnotic susceptibility is not related to the specific desensitization effect. We shall need to be sensitive to future attempts at replication, to determine whether these conclusions continue to be warranted.

I should strike a note of caution here in reference to the population studied in our own research and some of the other experiments reviewed here. While the sophomore may be a good laboratory subject for studying fear or desensitization, the college population is probably much too homogeneous to warrant the serious assessment of interactions between treatments and personality. In the experiment described above, the range of suggestibility was relatively narrow. College students who volunteer to participate in experiments are cooperative, and in this sense they are all moderately suggestible (Orne, 1962). Patients vary from the compulsively suggestible to the frankly hostile and negative. This variable, even as measured by the SHSS, may be much more important in a clinical population or in the normal population at large, and needs to be assessed in that context.

Relaxation

The importance of relaxation in desensitization is difficult to assess. In our research we have obtained a consistent positive correlation between the number of hours subjects spend in relaxation practice and fear reduction in desensitization. However, relaxation is here hopelessly confounded with the subject's motivation to change. The experiment by Larsen (1965) just cited suggests that visualization with relaxation may lead to more persistent change than visualization with emotional involvement. However, it does not constitute an evaluation of the relaxation component as it is used in desensitization.

Recently Davison (1965b) attempted a more specific test of the relaxation hypothesis. He compared fear change following desensitization with fear change resulting from a procedure in which hierarchy items were presented in the correct order but no relaxation training or instructions were given. Only the desensitization subjects showed significant positive change. However, this still does not provide crucial evidence for the role of relaxation. As part of his design, exposure time to the imagined stimuli was held constant for both groups. The times were determined by the performance of the desensitization subjects, who signaled item termination when they experienced anxiety. Thus, as Davison points out, the nonrelaxation subjects actually did not proceed through the hierarchy at their own pace. Failure to progress may have resulted from an aversion to therapy built up by the procedure, which required subjects to expose themselves to threatening stimuli for longer periods than they would have wanted. This same fact could account for Davison's other finding, that nonrelaxation subjects signaled anxiety more frequently than control patients.

Schubot (1966) addressed himself to the relaxation issue with an improved experimental design. In his study, subjects who were trained in relaxation and who experienced desensitization under hypnosis were compared with a group who received no relaxation training and were desensitized in the waking state. No differences between the two groups in overall fear change were apparent. However, when subjects were divided into subgroups, determined by degree of initial approach to the phobic object, it was found that the more frightened subjects showed greater change when hypnosis and relaxation were part of the desensitization procedure. No difference in amount of improvement was apparent for low-approach subjects. Like Davison's study, these results pertain only to overt behavior, and not to reported fear. Some support for the importance of relaxation is provided, but the experiment is difficult to interpret because of the confounding of hypnotic and relaxation procedures.

Cooke (1966) also compared relaxation and nonrelaxation procedures of desensitization. However, he failed to find a clear difference in fear change between treatment and control conditions. When those subjects who had completed the hierarchy were compared to noncompleters or controls, significant improvement was demonstrated. However, no significant difference, was found between the relaxation and nonrelaxation subgroups. Lomont & Edwards (1967) did find evidence which favored desensitization with relaxation, but significant differences were obtained on less than half of the measures studied. Rachman (1965c) has also compared relaxation and nonrelaxation variants of desensitization, with results which favored the former. However, the sample was so small (group $N = 3$) that the results are quite tentative.

None of the above experiments included measures of the physiological responses of subjects, and thus there is no information about the actual success of the relaxation or hypnotic-relaxation instructions employed. Schubot (1966) did find that hypnotized subjects reported significantly lower states of bodily tension than did the waking subjects. However, this response was strongly suggested to the former group, and subjects are notoriously inaccurate in their ability to report on their own physiology (Mandler & Uviller, 1958).

While Jacobson (1938) found that his extended relaxation training produced marked reduction in autonomic and neuromuscular arousal, there is little evidence that the brief relaxation training advocated by Wolpe has this effect. Barber & Hahn (1963) failed to find any differences in physiological tonus levels when hypnotic relaxation instructions were compared with simple instructions to sit quietly. Grossberg (1965) analyzed the autonomic and muscular responses instigated by brief relaxation training. He found no overall differences in arousal level between relaxation subjects and a group that simply listened to music. Some effects of relaxation were suggested by GSR trends, and differences in activity among specific muscle sites, but it is not clear how these relate to the main hypothesis.

In a recent experiment, Folkins et al. (1967) compared the effects of three brief treatments on autonomic and verbal responses to a stress-producing motion picture film. One group listened to a tape recording of relaxation instructions; a second group practiced imagining frightening scenes similar to those used in the film (concerned with shop accidents). Both of these factors were combined in a third group, analog desensitization, while members of a fourth group, control, simply listened to tape recordings on improving study habits. Treatment was completed in three sessions. The only stress evaluation was conducted at the end of the last session when the film was presented.

All treatment groups yielded anxiety scores lower than controls on an adjective checklist, although two other verbal report measures did not generate significant differences. Skin conductance during the film was higher for controls than for treatment groups, and there was a tendency, not always significant, for the relaxation and the visualization-only groups to show lower conductance than desensitization subjects. No significant differences between groups were found for heart rate. Again, measures of stress failed to show high intercorrelations.

The fact that no pretest was administered makes the data difficult to interpret. We must assume that small, randomly chosen groups were equal in stress response prior to treatment, and that treatment effects may be assessed by analysis of this one session. The failure to record physiological responses during the first two training sessions means that we again have no evidence that training in muscle relaxation actually produced the intended reduction in autonomic activity and muscle tonus. Furthermore, the desensitization treatment was extremely brief, and while the scene-presentation order appeared to follow the film sequence, it was not tailored to the subject's unique stress response, nor was it a graduated-approach sequence similar to that used in clinical desensitization. It must also be pointed out that, as in the Davison experiment, the subject had no control over length of scene presentation.

Ignoring these limitations, the data imply that both the relaxation component and the "cognitive rehearsal" aspects of the desensitization treatment are viable elements in fear reduction. The relatively lower values obtained for the combined treatment could well arise from the design problems described earlier. In point of fact, Folkins et al. (1967) report that the desensitization subjects showed an increase in reported subjective discomfort during desensitization, which may have augured the sensitization effects that Wolpe (1958) holds are occasioned by overexposure to stressful scenes. In further support of this hypothesis, the presented graphic data suggest that the desensitization subjects may have shown a greater relative increment in skin conductance with scene visualization than the rehearsal only group.

The dismantling strategy has produced data which on the whole favor the use of relaxation in desensitization. However, relaxation has not been established by these studies as a generator of fear-competing physiological responses. Progress in resolving this issue will demand yet more refined experimental design and a closer look at the autonomic and neuromuscular responses in both treatment process and change.

Visualization and the Anxiety Hierarchy

Conditioning theories of desensitization postulate that the visualized scene is an adequate representative of the actual fear stimulus, and explanations of the desensitization effect (with illustrations from the animal laboratory) make no distinction between in vivo desensitization and that based on imagined material.

Both methods appear to produce reductions in the fear behavior of human subjects (Meyer, 1957; Cooke, 1966). The latter author has attempted a test of these two methods in the experimental reduction of a rat phobia. No difference in the effectiveness of these methods was found when generalized anxiety was ignored. However, the visualization technique proved to be more effective for high-anxious subjects, while the in vivo treatment was more successful with the low-anxious. The sample is small, and the experiment bears replication before it can be accepted without reservation. However, it is interesting to recall that Schubot (1966) found a difference in effectiveness for his relaxation and nonrelaxation treatments when subjects were divided into high- and low-fear groups. Similar factors may be involved. It is also possible that in treating anxious subjects, one needs to start "farther back" with the less powerful imagined stimuli, and that the low-anxious can be confronted more rapidly with strong medicine.

Kirchner & Hogan (1966) also studied rat phobics, instructing them to visualize maximally frightening scenes, with little preliminary anxiety hierarchy. They report significantly more approach behavior after treatment than for untreated controls. Neither Larsen (1965) nor Folkins et al. (1967) employed anxiety hierarchies in treatment analogs, and both were able to show some positive change in phobic behavior. However, desensitization treatments with and without graduated approach have not yet been compared.

In most of the desensitization experiments considered in this paper, subjects reported individual scenes as frightening. However, from the counter-conditioning point of view advocated by Wolpe and others, it is important that the visualized scene also evoke the physiological responses associated with fear. Folkins et al. (1967) reported increased skin conductance when subjects visualized frightening events, and similar but larger increases when these events were presented on a motion picture film. In our own laboratory, we have been studying the autonomic activity associated with imagined fear stimuli in the context of desensitization. Figure 4–4 presents heart rate and skin conductance responses yielded for sequential items during desensitization. It will be noted that both heart rate and skin conductance peak on item VI-1, the only one to which the subject signaled anxiety. For roughly half the subjects that we have followed in this manner, distress signals are associated with a reduction in heart rate and with conductance changes. It is not yet clear why some sub-jects display these phenomena while others do not. While adequacy of visuali-zation is sometimes involved, it is not always. We are still assembling data to determine whether the presence or absence of these process, autonomic changes are related to desensitization outcome.

In a related experiment, spider-phobic subjects were instructed to visual-ize hierarchy items presented in a randomized order. The items were presented in the context of muscle relaxation, and the setting was similar to that for desensitization. Figure 4–5 presents the heart rate changes seen in the first four

Figure 4–4. *Skin conductance change and heart rate activity for the visualization periods of successively presented hierarchy items during a single desensitization session. The subject signaled that she was anxious only on the first presentation of item VI.*

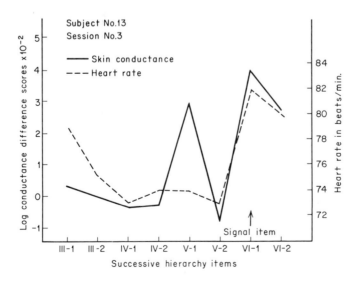

*S*s run, for items at five hierarchy levels (increasing from I to V). It will be noted that all these subjects show greater heart rate increments for high- than for low-hierarchy items, and that for two of the subjects the curves are monotonic. Figure 4–6 presents the results obtained for five subjects with public speaking anxiety. Here the data are less clearly ordered. However, it will also be noted that these subjects reported less distress on the high items. Thus, verbal report of fear for high-hierarchy items (IV and V) is not significantly greater than that reported for low items (I and II). It would appear that this is in turn attributable to the difficulty these subjects had in visualizing the public-speaking scenes. The spider phobics reported a statistically significant, greater vividness of imagery. It is not yet clear whether this difference is intrinsic to these specific items used, or a function of this particular subject sample.

The data available for review suggest that imagined fear stimuli do evoke autonomic as well as verbal fear responses and, furthermore, that the visualization of anxiety hierarchy items may produce similarly ordered autonomic responses. In addition, there is evidence that progress in the hierarchy is

Figure 4–5. *The heart rate responses of spider-phobic subjects during the nonsequential presentation of individual anxiety hierarchies. The order of items on the abscissa is from lower-anxiety (I) to high-anxiety (V).*

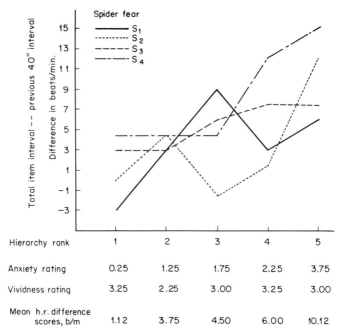

Hierarchy rank	1	2	3	4	5
Anxiety rating	0.25	1.25	1.75	2.25	3.75
Vividness rating	3.25	2.25	3.00	3.25	3.00
Mean h.r. difference scores, b/m	1.12	3.75	4.50	6.00	10.12

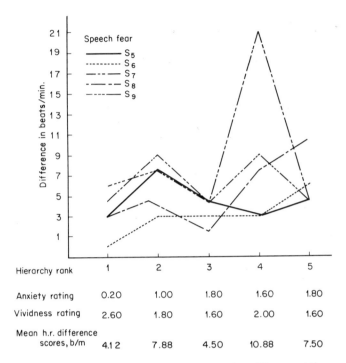

Figure 4–6. *The heart rate responses of public speaking phobic subjects during the nonsequential presentation of individual anxiety hierarchies. The order of items on the abscissa is from low-anxiety (I) to high-anxiety (V).*

related to the degree of fear change. In our studies of snake-phobic subjects, we have always used a hierarchy of 20 stimuli, with similar beginning and end items. As the number of sessions is always held constant, the total items completed during treatment is a good measure of therapeutic progress, independent of therapeutic change. A high positive relationship between items completed and all measures of fear change has been a consistent finding. Furthermore, with the fear measures used in our research, a certain degree of progress appears necessary before significant change is observed. Nearly all subjects completing more than 15 items show markedly reduced fear, while those completing less are not significantly different from controls (Lang, Lazovik, & Reynolds, 1965). Number of items completed is thus a good measure of therapy process, a meaningful prognostic sign, and if not crucial to successful desensitization, highly related to it.[3]

[3] Another way to conceptualize these data is simply to say that subjects who are less willing to confront frightening, imagined stimuli are the same ones who avoid the actual fearful events. In any case, the data argue for a parallel between the two stimulus categories.

Extinction and "Traumatic Approach"

Experimental extinction is the simplest explanation of the desensitization effect. Skinner first raised this hypothesis in an effort to explain all psychotherapeutic cures (1953). The verbal representatives of anxiety stimuli which occur in treatment are not reinforced by the therapist (e.g., do not lead to the social disapproval, moral castigation, or physical punishment the patient has led himself to expect), and thus the anxiety response may be expected to decline with stimulus repetition. London (1964) suggested that this may explain the results obtained in desensitization, and Stampfl (1961, 1967) has developed a streamlined treatment paradigm based on extinction theory. He holds that both relaxation training and the development of a graded anxiety hierarchy may be dispensed with in treatment. The client is presented only with the final, most frightening scenes, and every effort is made to instigate maximal anxiety. These contents are repeated over and over again. No real, negative reinforcement occurs, and it is assumed that the anxiety response will simply extinguish. As with desensitization, the unlearning which has taken place to imagined scenes is held to transfer to the life situation. While there is considerable interest in this approach, and a number of clinical reports have been made (London, 1964; Hogan, 1966), little laboratory evidence for its effectiveness is available. Kirchner & Hogan (1966) studied 35 college students who initially refused to approach a live laboratory rat. Control subjects imagined pleasant scenes, while the extinction subjects were presented with imagery concerning rats, "designed to induce a high level of anxiety" (p. 103). Significantly more members of the latter group than of the control sample picked up a rat during posttesting. No effort was made to assess any other components of the fear response (verbal and physiological), either during therapy or as part of the pretests and posttests. Thus, it is difficult to be certain whether the imagery produced the anxiety responses demanded by the theory, or changed anything more than this specific, overt posttest response.

Stampfl argues that his extinction treatment paradigm is not only more efficient, but also a necessarily more effective technique than desensitization. The degree of fear is believed to be proportional to the number of cues presented to the subject. These cues are organized to some extent in a serial order, extending away from a focus of maximum fear (as with Wolpe, the model is the laboratory runway). Stampfl (1961) holds that following the extinction of anxiety responses to peripheral cues, movement forward leads to the introduction of further stimulus elements. Thus, more anxiety is experienced, which then "*renews* the anxiety eliciting potential of the cues to which extinction has taken place" (p. 2). For Stampfl, the effect of such piecemeal treatment as desensitization is in sum negative, and the subject soon finds himself back where he started. In response, the desensitization advocate may say that this rarely occurs, and he can point to considerable laboratory evidence that his procedure produces positive results. However, it must also be stated that effects very like that described by Stampfl have been observed. Subjects do proceed through the hierarchy, run upon an item which evokes unusual distress, and then find themselves afraid of items which were successfully dealt with in the past. Wolpe (1958) argues that it is only the hierarchy which is at fault. A stimulus has been essayed which is out of place, involving too great an increment on the anxiety gradient. While Stampfl emphasizes the backward generalization of anxiety elicited by stimuli further along on the gradient, Wolpe stresses the forward generalization of the new competing responses, which have replaced anxiety on items lower down. To some extent the argument is tactical, and we may find that individuals should be treated differently —some pressed forward as rapidly as possible despite the generation of considerable distress, and others moved slowly, avoiding anxiety at all costs.

Malleson (1959) preceded Stampfl in applying this technique of traumatic approach. He employed a hierarchy similar to that used in desensitization. However, instead of encouraging relaxation, the client was instructed to feel more and more frightened as he proceeded through the items. Malleson reported that following an initial increase in distress, the client showed rapid recovery and complete cure. In practice, Stampfl and his associates (Levis, 1967) also use a gradient approach, albeit truncated. Thus, in the Kirchner & Hogan study (1966), initial material describes the "approach of a rat." "In each successive stage of the taped material there was an increase in the number and depth of descriptive cues" (p. 103). Stampfl (1961) begins treatment by presenting cues "by way of the symbolic value of certain objects or animals" (p. 5), which he feels then make other, higher anxiety eliciting stimuli more accessible. Furthermore, Stampfl does seem to provide practice with alternative responses during treatment. Thus, a girl with social anxieties not only visualizes herself castigated by others, but also visualizes that she is fighting back, hurling insults and physically attacking her adversaries. While Stampfl is inclined to interpret this as an extinction of anxiety responses to her own aggressive impulses, the alternate interpretation is obvious.

Perhaps the most important issue raised by Stampfl's technique concerns the presence of the anxiety response itself in treatment. Should the subject experience intense anxiety? Does this enhance fear reduction or retard it? The therapeutic format used by Stampfl involves a massive, compelling, and persistent evocation of dreadful stimuli. His use of fear imagery is very like that described by Sargant (1961). Sargant began treating war neuroses by an abreactive technique, but soon (p. xxv):

> ... found that a patient could sometimes be restored to mental health not by his re-living a particular traumatic experience, but by stirring up in him, and helping him to discharge strong emotions not directly concerned with it. ... Outbursts of fear or anger thus deliberately induced and stimulated to a

crescendo by the therapist, would frequently be followed by a sudden emotional collapse. The patient would fall back inert on the couch—as a result of this exhausting emotional discharge, not of the drug—but he would soon come round. It then often happened that he reported a dramatic disappearance of many nervous symptoms."

Stampfl is similarly inexplicit in the cues presented—"experiences of rejection, deprivation, abandonment, helplessness, guilt, shame, and sex" (1961, p. 5), to name a few—and is similar to Sargant in the emphasis on stirring up the patient—"at each stage of the process, effort is concentrated by the therapist to attain a maximal level of anxiety" (p. 6). Sargant suggests that this procedure induces a temporary emotional collapse, in which the individual is hypersuggestible, and altered behavior has a protective function. He compares the therapeutic process with the art of religious conversion as practiced by Wesley and the other evangelists—the evocation of the terrors of hell, leading to emotional collapse, followed by a revival and redirection of the convert. Sargant returns to the animal laboratory for his theoretical concepts, describing this process as analogous to Pavlov's ultraparadoxical phase in canine conditioning, in which behavior patterns are reversed by intense emotional stress. While elements of extinction may be involved in Stampfl's method, much more seems to be going on, and the definition of discrete elements will be difficult.

   A test of the extinction process in the laboratory is not readily achieved. Studies of desensitization without relaxation (Cooke, 1966; Davison, 1965b; Lomont & Edwards, 1967; Rachman, 1965c; Schubot, 1966) have not produced consistent results. Furthermore, this approach cannot be crucial for extinction, because other interpretations of the change occasioned by nonrelaxation treatment have equal presumptive validity (e.g., reinforcement of approach or cognitive theories). Only Larsen (1965) has attempted to evaluate the importance of "getting out the response." Her data favor the evocation of fear stimuli without attendant emotion (and are thus inconsistent with an extinction hypothesis), but this was only true for the follow-up relapse rate and not for the initial treatment differences. This issue deserves considerably more attention, both because of its relationship to theory and because of what its resolution can tell us about the mechanics of desensitization.

Counterconditioning and the Competing Physiological Response

Guthrie (1935) proposed that the unlearning of habits could be accomplished by training the subjects to do something else, while he attended to the eliciting stimulus. From his contiguity framework, extinction is not a withering of the response from lack of reinforcement, but a positive substitution of some new behavior which inhibits the former response. When applied to the treatment of fear, this formulation suggests that responses which are incompatible with fear should be encouraged in the presence of phobic stimuli, e.g., that subjects should approach rather than avoid, report less rather than more fear. The theory is deceptively simple, and if conceived in a general way, it appears to explain the desensitization process adequately. However, when an effort is made to be explicit about the fear or counterfear responses postulated by the theory, many thorny conceptual and experimental problems emerge.

Wolpe (1958) holds that the essence of desensitization is "reciprocal inhibition," that subjects learn to substitute incompatible physiological responses for anxiety or fear. Fear is identified with high levels of autonomic activity and neuromuscular tension. It is argued that the treatment involves the substitution of muscle relaxation and lowered autonomic tonus for this Hull-Spence type of anxiety. Wolpe is not exact in specifying the physiological responses, but in this relatively simple form of the theory it may be presumed that they are direct increments in heart rate, skin conductance, blood pressure, muscle potentials, which are held by Malmo (1958), Duffy (1962), and others to indicate drive and arousal. The first experimental issue raised by this theory concerns the dependence of overt, fearful behavior (e.g., avoidance) and verbal report of anxiety on the covert responses described above. Jacobson (1938) clearly holds that such dependence exists. He reports a variety of anecdotes and experiments which suggest that verbal or cognitive events are invariably accompanied by peripheral striate activity. Gellhorn (1964, p. 467) stresses "the modulating rather than the causative role" of muscle activity in emotion. However, proprioceptive stimulation of the posterior hypothalamus is held to maintain a sympathetic autonomic balance of the organism. Thus muscle tension may help to instigate, and maintain or extend, emotional behavior. Furthermore, Gellhorn argues that the voluntary assumption of competing postures or muscle states will alter or inhibit overt emotional responses. Similarly, it may be argued that the effects of tranquilizing drugs are achieved by reducing peripheral muscular and therefore proprioceptive feedback (Gordon, 1964).

A variety of experiments do suggest that when drugs are used to block proprioceptive feedback, a reduction in cortical activity and sympathetic hypothalamic responsiveness occurs. However, Davison (1966a) considers the research cited by Gellhorn and concludes that the effects may have been due to a confounding reduction in exteroceptive stimulation. Furthermore, the literature on learning in curarized organisms (Solomon & Turner, 1962) clearly shows that avoidance training which occurred when the muscles were curarized transfers to the normal state. If mediating anxiety is assumed to be important to such learning, emotion clearly was not inhibited by muscular immobility.

While the data may be equivocal for striate muscle activity, there is more explicit evidence that autonomic feedback effects higher centers. Bonvallet and her coworkers (1954) have shown that distension of the carotid sinus alters the frequency and amplitude of cortical activity and, by implication, the arousal level of the organism. Lacey & Lacey (1958) argue that variability in blood pressure and heart rate influence both the cortex and the neuromusculature, and are thus determinants both of persisting temperamental characteristics of the individual and of the moment-to-moment responsivity of the organism. Coquery & Lacey (1966) have shown that reaction time depends in part on the heart rate during the foreperiod. Birren, Cardon, & Phillips (1963) and Calloway (1965) present data indicating that speed of response varies with the period of the cardiac cycle in which stimuli are presented. Furthermore, a recent study of men with severed spinal cords (Hohman, 1966), finds that reports of feeling intensity diminished in these individuals, with greater effects the higher the lesion on the spine (and therefore the less autonomic feedback). Thus, upward autonomic effects seem to be present, explicitly in neurophysiological studies with chronic preparations, and by implication from the laboratory studies of intact human organisms and the interview of clinical cases.

The above data pertain only obliquely to the second issue raised by the theory of desensitization effects proposed above. Does the peripheral imposition of the competing autonomic state produce an immediate attenuation of the emotional response, and furthermore, can this response be learned? Does the repeated contiguity of fear stimulus and muscle relaxation produce a persisting bond? It would appear that a direct test of this hypothesis could be undertaken using tranquilizing or muscle-relaxant drugs. However, here psychopharmacological studies suggest that responses learned under the influence of this medication may not transfer to the nondrug state. Otis (1965, p. 121) states that "drug treatments may result in an internal milieu sufficiently different from the non-drugged state to cause dissociation of behavior when a drug is discontinued." Thus, psychotherapy undertaken while the patient is on such medication often does not generalize. Furthermore, laboratory research provides no examples in which a drug- or surgery-imposed UCS was transfered to an external CS. The absence of an external UCS, or more importantly, its cortical representative, is undoubtedly critical. The literature then suggests that if the reduction in muscle tonus is in the main peripheral in effect (as with curarae), inhibition of cortically mediated fear does not occur. If, on the other hand, the drug does have greater CNS effects (and thus inhibits fear), transfer of training may not occur.

In some measure, the above equivocations can be considered irrelevant: drugs are not normally employed in desensitization. However, if they are truly ineffective stimuli in this context, it does suggest something important about the mechanism of desensitization: The mere imposition of relaxation and lowered autonomic tonus is insufficient. Davison (1966a) suggests that the efferent activity of muscle relaxation is the critical factor, a decrease or cessation of discharge in the motor neuron that is the anxiety inhibitor. Such neurophysiological speculations are not currently amenable to test. However, it would appear that if muscle relaxation plays any effective role in desensitization, it is as the self-imposed response of an intact organism.[4]

The clearer role of autonomic activity in modulating and maintaining emotional responses in other behavioral systems suggests that it should be dealt with directly, rather than going through the uncertain medium of muscle relaxation (Lang, 1966). Recent research indicates that autonomic events can be brought under operant control. A variety of studies have indicated that rewards and punishment may be employed in altering sweat gland activity (Crider, Shapiro, & Tursky, 1966), heart rate (Engel & Hanson, 1966), blood volume (Lisina, in Razran, 1961), and even the cortical electroencephalogram (EEG) (Kamiya, 1966). In our own laboratory we have been studying the effects of feedback on cardiovascular activity. The data strongly encourage the thesis that human subjects can develop considerable facility at controlling autonomic responses, with relatively brief training (Hnatiow & Lang, 1965; Lang, Sroufe, & Hastings, 1967). Furthermore, it is reasonable to suppose that this may be achieved without the aid of the striate musculature. Recently Trowill (1967) and Miller & DiCara (1967) demonstrated operant conditioning of heart rate in curarized laboratory rats, which were being artifically respirated. Results from our own studies of human subjects indicate that respiration is not a key factor in control. Work now under way is designed to explore the possibility of direct neural effects.

The above findings suggest that an explicit test of the competing-response hypothesis might be accomplished by presenting stressor stimuli to individuals who had learned to reduce the autonomic components of arousal. If verbal reports and performance measures of anxiety were attenuated, a competing response mechanism would be suggested.

Up to this point we have been considering a relatively simplified version of reciprocal inhibition theory, in which only two alternative organismic states are hypothesized, arousal and quiescence. However, many researchers argue for a multiplicity of psychophysiological states appropriate to different emotions or motivational conditions. Thus, Ax (1953) and Schacter (1957) reported autonomic differences between fear and anger. Lacey (1959) suggested that in addition to the fact that specific stimuli evoke reliable patterns across subjects, individuals often show patterns that are reliable across stimuli. Thus the autonomic nervous system does not appear to operate in a unitary manner, in

---

[4] Recently, Friedman (1966a) has reported success in desensitizing patients with injections of methohexitone sodium (Brietal; known in the United States as Brevital) substituted for the usual training in muscle relaxation. He states that this drug induces muscle relaxation without interfering with the subject's ability to imagine stimuli and presumably to learn new responses. No laboratory studies are yet available, and it is thus not clear whether his result constitutes an exception to the conclusions stated here.

which any response is a monotonic indicant of anxiety. Rather we are faced with a "somatic sea of responses," controlled by a variety of interacting winds and currents. Wolpe (1958) has explicitly adopted the specificity hypothesis in his approach, but his description of opposing sympathetic and parasympathetic events lacks precision. Thus, assertive behavior and eating are assumed to produce organismic states which compete with anxiety. Recently, this approach has also been used in desensitization by Lazarus & Abramovitz (1962b) who propose that positive "emotive imagery" be employed as an anxiety competitor rather than relaxation. Some researchers (Folkins et al., 1967) have employed this variant in studies of desensitization.

The specificity theory of desensitization is considerably more complex than the unitary arousal interpretation. The fact must be faced that psychophysiologists are not at all ready to define explicitly the physiology of different emotional states, and a test of the theory demands that this is clear beforehand. Data relevant to this issue were collected by Silverman & Cohen (1960). They reported a significant interaction between personality and response to high-gravity stress. Subjects able to tolerate high g's were generally more aggressive, active, and independent, while low-g subjects tended to appear more anxious, dependent, and conscience-oriented in interviews and on thematic personality tests. Furthermore, urinary bioassays indicated that high-g subjects had higher noradrenaline levels while low-g subjects showed high adrenaline output. Differences in the blood pressure response to mecholyl were also found for anxious and aggressive subjects. Of particular significance for the present discussion is the fact that an effort was made with some subjects to alter the affect state and then to check the consequences in a subsequent test of high-g tolerance. These data indicate that shifts in the direction of increased aggression or anxiety resulted in heightened or lowered g stress tolerance, respectively. Unfortunately the sample is quite small, and no effort was made to measure physiological changes coincident with affect change. While these data clearly show that tolerance for stress is associated with explicit physiological events, it does not suggest that the most efficient way to increment stress tolerance is to produce these changes. It is also possible that the shaping of verbal behavior is the important part of desensitization, that cognitive set is the controlling element, and that the physiological concomitants are a simple peripheral consequent.

Desensitization and Cognitive Set

Up to this point we have been considering upward effects on cortically mediated verbal and motor behavior. It is important that we also consider the downward effects of cognitive events. This has been the royal road of traditional psychotherapies, and it is undoubtedly an important path to consider for desensitization.

Folkins et al. (1967, p. 29 of preprint) speculated "that subjects exposed to our experimental condition of cognitive preparation [scene visualization without relaxation] spent the one-week intervals from session to session developing and working through some adequate way to cope psychologically with the subsequent film induced threat." Postexperiment interviews with their subjects yielded a variety of explanations of how the training sessions contributed to change. These were coded according to "coping strategies" (mastery, ego defense, aggression) and noncoping responses. Those who reported no effective coping behavior showed greater stress reactions on all verbal measures than did those who felt they had been able to use the training sessions to reduce fear. Subjects reporting efforts at "mastery" (e.g., "I imagined scenes so I knew exactly what was coming") showed the least stress response. The relationship of these responses to physiological reactions during the film was not reported, nor did the authors report that specific strategies were related in any explicit way to the experimental treatments.

It could be argued that the relationship between coping behavior and stress response is tautological, as the interviews and anxiety scales constituted nearly coincident measures of the same verbal response set. It would be strange indeed if subjects who reported that the training had no value were the same subjects whose responses on the more formal anxiety scales indicated the procedure's positive effects. However, this does not explain significant differences between strategies. It has been our impression that desensitization subjects interpret change in the context of their own personalities and unique notions of psychological theory. The Folkins et al. data further suggest that a specific class of explanations is associated with positive change. At least three alternative hypotheses fit this fact: (1) People of a particular personality type (ie., those who explain their behavior change in terms of a specific strategy) are more likely than others to change when exposed to desensitization; (2) any one, regardless of personality type, may show fear reduction, and although not causative, explanation in terms of a particular strategy is highly correlated with success; (3) if the subject hits on a particular explanation strategy, it will precipitate positive change (the Folkins et al. hypothesis). The data now available do not suggest that these "coping" verbalizations are causative in desensitization, nor, on the other hand, can they be dismissed at this time as simply epiphenomenal.

Research does provide clear evidence that cognitive set can attenuate verbal and somatic components of fear behavior. In other experiments, R. S. Lazarus and his colleagues (1962) have found that subjects who view a frightening film with an accompanying sound track or following a preorientation that encourages fear-competing attitudes (e.g., intellectualization or denial), report less fear on a variety of paper and pencil tests and show reduced heart rate and skin conductance during the film. Here at Wisconsin, Hart (1966) found that snake-phobic subjects showed a significant increase in approach to a live snake after they had prepared a taped speech, supposedly for use in teaching others to be less afraid. We may assume that the rehearsal of reasons for being unafraid altered the subjects' set, which in turn had effects on avoidance behavior. The various studies of fear reduction through imitation, beginning with Jones (1924) and, more recently, with Bandura et al. (1967) and Geer & Turteltaub (1967), can be similarly interpreted. The action of the model may simply be a nonverbal instruction: "This object may be approached or touched without harm"—with results varying according to the age, suggestibility of the subject, and the prestige of the model. It must be pointed out that these laboratory effects are often quite transient, and readily changed by new information. In the cognitive dissonance experiment described above, Hart found that fear reduction was not a consequence of his procedure when subjects observed a confederate, who had supposedly heard their tapes, fail to approach in the avoidance test.

In point of fact, the effects of threatening stimuli may be both accentuated and reduced by manipulation of set or instructional variables. Sternbach (1966) shows that subjects vary systematically in their report of shock aversiveness, depending on preliminary instructions about the nature of this stimulus. Stomach motility is altered in the expected way, depending on whether subjects are told that a drug administered early in the experiment is a relaxant, is a stimulant or has no effect (Sternbach, 1964). Experiments by Graham, Kabler, & Graham (1962) show that specific emotional attitudes, induced by hypnotic instructions, are reliably associated with specific physiological response patterns. Thus, subjects told to feel "unjustly treated" tended to show the relatively high skin temperature of patients with hives; those told that they "had to be on guard against bodily assault" showed the high diastolic blood pressures found in hypertension.

For many theorists, cognitive set is a master system which dominates other emotional behavior. Schachter & Singer (1962) argue that emotion is a two-component event; consisting of somatic arousal and an accompanying cognition. They present data which suggest that despite somatic arousal, overt components of emotion will not occur if there is no coincident emotional attitude. Thus, uninstructed subjects aroused by epinephrine readily entered into aggressive or related behavior stimulated by a film or modeled by a stooge, but such a consequent was not obtained when subjects were instructed in the physiological effects of the drug.

The experiments reviewed above indicate both that instructional set (including self-instructions) will reduce verbal reports of stress intensity, as well as autonomic responses usually associated with fear arousal. Furthermore, despite the direct instigation of autonomic activity, overt emotional behavior may be blocked by an explanatory statement to the subject. While this suggests that verbal set has tremendous power for emotional control, we must be careful not to overgeneralize from these data. The Schachter & Singer experiments, for example, represent short-term effects, obtained within the laboratory. Explanation is frequently much less effective in the life situation. Thus, a knowledgeable female physiologist, who experiences marked autonomic arousal associated with the menstrual cycle, persists in being tense and irritable at her "time of the month." The individual with chronic muscular tension and peripheral vasoconstriction has headaches, trembles, and partly as a consequence, is socially vulnerable and withdrawn. Neither a physiological explanation nor an analytic insight may do him any good. For many individuals seen in the clinic, it is the autonomic and muscular symptoms themselves which are anxiety cues. Thus, one woman who managed to maintain control in the face of stress reports that she finally broke down completely when she noticed that her chin was trembling. Anxiety over tachycardia is hardly uncommon. In these cases the patient is caught up in a cyclical interaction of physiological and behavior events which mutually enhance each other.

Given the complex interactions described above, how might the cognitive events occasioned by the desensitization procedure account for the observed fear reduction? It is clear that a schedule for shaping verbal behavior is in effect. Subjects are encouraged to visualize, without distress, progressively more frightening scenes. Reporting that a scene no longer evokes anxiety is reinforced by the therapist implicitly, if not explicitly. In addition, the subject certainly rewards himself verbally (Kanfer & Marston, 1963) as each hurdle is passed. This is essentially the method of successive approximation described by Skinner (1953), which has been used so successfully by his disciples in the animal laboratory. From this perspective, desensitization is an operant training schedule, designed to shape the response "I am not afraid" (or a potentially competing response such as "I am relaxed" or "I am angry") in the presence of a graded set of discriminative stimuli. When well learned, the response could have the status of a "set" or self-instruction, which can then determine other related behaviors in the manner already described.

If all that desensitization is doing is shaping verbal behavior, the available data suggest that the effects would not transfer to other systems. Yadoff (1958) failed to find transfer to other behavior from such simple verbal-shaping schedules. However, more than this seems to be going on in desensitization. The subject vividly visualizes scenes in which he is closer and closer to the fear stimulus. This process could be conceptualized as a progressive reinforcement of implicit approach responses. If the visualized approach mediates behavioral approach, effects on the overt avoidance behavior of subjects could be anticipated. In this light, it is interesting to note that increases in approach behavior have been the most reliable findings of the animal phobia studies. Changes in verbal estimates of fear either have not been obtained or have temporally lagged behind the other response. Considering that the hierarchies used have been organized around actual approach (rather than around changing fear statements), this is a kind of presumptive evidence for the above interpretation. Little experimental work has been devoted to attempts at manipulating the reinforcement contingencies in desensitization. If combined with a systematic exploration of hierarchy content (e.g.: Is the subject passive or active in the scene? Is the base dimension temporal or spatial?), much more might be uncovered about the mechanism of desensitization.

The subject's control of the imagined fear stimulus—its length, frequency, and sequence of presentation—is another important cognitive element in the desensitization procedure. When this control element was eliminated in Davison's experiment, positive reduction in fear was not obtained. It may be that the aversiveness of phobic stimuli lies in the helplessness of the subject, the fact that he has no organized response except flight and avoidance. Hebb (1949) has suggested that the essence of fear is a cerebral disorganization evoked by stimuli for which no adequate response is available. These stimuli elicit partial responses which are incompatible either with each other or with the reactive properties of the stimulus. Thus, behavioral sequences cannot be smoothly completed. The central processor becomes disorganized, energy is mobilized which cannot be appropriately discharged, and the result is the uncoordinated, helpless behavior we associate with fear.

In desensitization the subject learns to control the presentations of stimuli and perhaps in turn to control the responses that they evoke. He is encouraged to make discriminations in degree of threat within a stimulus class that previously only generated a generalized avoidance. The individual thus develops a controlled transaction with the environment, in which behavior is modulated according to stimulus intensity and variety of other associated semantic or structural factors. It is not clear that the development of such a control system is best conceptualized as exclusively cognitive (Hebb, for example, stated his theory in neurophysiological terms). In any event, this conception of fearful and fearless behavior as it applies to desensitization therapy deserves attention.

Conclusions

As the preceding review and theoretical discussions suggest, there is presently no facile explanation of desensitization that is well buttressed by research findings. Nevertheless, considerable progress has been made. It is clear that the laboratory successes are not attributable to placebo effects or transference, in the tradition of dynamic psychology. It is equally clear that we can discard the notion that fear changes only when it is understood by the subject in terms of a specific psychological theory, or when first experiences with the thing feared are examined. We know that there is something about the desensitization process itself, the bald mechanics of the procedure, which instigates change. However, consistent positive results are obtained despite wide variations in procedural details. Thus, desensitization may be successfully applied by therapists of varying experiences and theoretical persuasion—even by an anonymous machine. Hypnotic induction procedures are not vital and have been dispensed with by most researchers and many practitioners. While the use of relaxation training and instructions have increased the frequency or persistence of fear reduction, it is not clear that such training is necessary. Most laboratory workers have employed anxiety hierarchies in treatment analogs of desensitization, and the data suggest that visualized scenes tend to evoke both the verbal and autonomic components of fear. However, some researchers have observed positive effects, even when intense fear stimuli are presented without preamble.

Most of the theories that have been advanced involve controversial speculations about the basic laws of behavior, in addition to a dearth of evidence specific to their role in desensitization. We have already discussed in detail the psychophysiological lacunae and controversies implicit in Wolpe's reciprocal inhibition hypothesis. While extinction theories seem less complicated, many scholars would deny that this process is the simple withering of response strength that its advocates describe. Extinction is held by many to occur because of response substitution, and the issue is hardly resolved in the animal laboratory, much less in the clinic. I do not mean this statement to sound pessimistic; on the contrary, these controversies highlight a most encouraging and exciting stage for psychology. The important practical problems and the vital theoretical issues are in conjunction, and results obtained in the laboratory have import both for the basic and for the applied segments of our science.

The laboratory study of desensitization has already enhanced our basic understanding of fear and anxiety. In the first place, it is very difficult to bend the evidence being gathered in these experiments to the traditional phenomenal constructs. Despite preliminary disclaimers, most clinical theorists and many research psychologists have tended to treat fear as a direct experience, which is indirectly assessed through behavioral or physiological indicants. As if we already knew what anxiety is, we ask questions such as: Is the GSR a good measure of anxiety? Thus, if an experiment yields a relationship between a laboratory stressor and GSR, it is assumed that the inner man has been measured. On the other hand, if no relationship is observed, the psychological investigator takes it that he has a poor indicant of anxiety, and may casually discard the data. Desensitization research generally involves multiple measures of fear, which all seem to have considerable face validity. Nevertheless, they do not all occasion change, or if they do, not at the same time or to the same degree. The intercorrelations among measures of fear are consistently low and often insignificant. Furthermore, the data suggest that specific behavioral systems may be separately manipulated. In the Davison (1967) and Cooke (1966) studies, overt approach behavior changed, but the subjects did not report less fear. Individual subjects in our own experiments have shown this effect; we have also remarked subjects who showed change in verbal but not overt fear responses. These data imply that fear is not some hard phenomenal lump that lives inside people, which we may palpate more or less successfully. On the contrary, the implication is that fear is a loosely woven fabric of responses, with many edges where an unraveling process may be initiated.

I do not mean to suggest that fear responses are unrelated to each other. On the contrary, the evidence reviewed here indicates that one response system can have profound effects on another. However, we need to study these relationships, unprejudiced by our introspective preconceptions. We must develop the integrating concepts that are demanded by the data, rather than picking and choosing among the output of the organism for those responses we think are indicants of feelings.

Current research suggests that both the organization of fear responses and the order of their change is idiosyncratic to the subject and perhaps to the treatment method employed. This has implications for the acquisition as well as the reduction of fear. Thus, disrupting autonomic responses may be evoked in the presence of specific discriminative stimuli. The organism may learn to avoid these stimuli. Subsequently, the fact of coincident avoidance and somatic arousal may be remarked and the unit self-labeled as fear. However, such a process could as well start with the verbal or overt behavioral components, and it need not necessarily involve all the organism's potentially expressive systems or subsystems. It seems to me very unlikely that most fears are initiated by the traumatic conditioning of the total behavioral output of the organism. Fears may develop piecemeal, as I have suggested above.

There are now clear data which show that autonomic responses may be operantly shaped by environmental events (see p. 183). Thus, we need no longer assume that the autonomic components of fear are established only by their contiguous association with aversive stimuli, nor that there is likely to be one immutable pattern of autonomic events which must underlie the avoidance behavior of animal or human being. If responses innervated by the autonomic nervous system can be shaped by the environment, we can more easily understand the slow development of fear via social learning, and the frequent absence of traumatic experience with the phobic object in the reports of very fearful subjects.

The systems of behavior that we are considering undoubtedly influence each other, to the extent that events in one system become both initiating cues and terminating responses for other systems. Thus, peripheral vasoconstriction, alterations in stomach motility, or acid secretions may prompt avoidance behavior which terminates the autonomic sequence. However, positive feedback loops also can develop in which awareness of autonomic events precipitates avoidance, that is a cue for further autonomic and verbal distress responses. Thus, the important therapeutic changes depend on training programs designed to eliminate specific response components and to interrupt mutually augmenting feedback between response systems.

The success of desensitization may very well lie in the fact that it is a multiple-level treatment, designed to modify the somatic, overt, and verbal responses of subjects. Therefore, the relevant responses for a specific individual are more likely to be altered, and a more reliable reduction in the fearful behavior is more likely to be obtained. The continued study of desensitization will force us to pay closer attention to its consequences for specific behavior, rather than attempting to assess vague concepts. This procedural demand of the laboratory will force us to explore the relationship between behavioral systems and to develop integrating emotional constructs which are based on data rather than on subjective experience. This enterprise will lead us to the creation of a more powerful technology and ultimately to a scientific theory of fear.

Chapter Summary

This chapter is a critical review of laboratory research on systematic desensitization and related techniques. Evidence for the general effectiveness of this method in reducing fear is considered, followed by an analysis of experiments designed to assess the importance of separate elements in the desensitization procedure or to test the major hypotheses raised to explain treatment effects. Evidence relevant to the following procedural factors is considered: (1) the contribution of the therapist or the therapeutic relationship, (2) hypnosis and suggestibility, (3) relaxation training, (4) visualization and the anxiety hierarchy. The following theoretical interpretations of desensitization are then evaluated: (1) extinction and catharsis, (2) counterconditioning and competing physiological response formulations, (3) cognitive explanations of desensitization. The concluding section provides an overview, describing our present knowledge of the fear-reduction mechanism, as well as the many lacunae in our understanding that laboratory research has not yet filled. Finally, the author proposes some changes in our conception of fear and its treatment, prompted by findings from this area of investigation.

5

Appraisal of Operant Therapy Techniques with Children and Adults

JAMES A. SHERMAN
DONALD M. BAER
University of Kansas, Lawrence, Kansas

Introduction

If psychology is the study of behavior, then psychotherapy is the modification of problem behavior, usually through environmental manipulation. In most conventional psychotherapies this environmental manipulation has been attempted in regularly repeated therapy sessions during which the therapist and patient interact. Traditionally this interaction is verbal; its purpose is to establish a "relationship" between the two through which the deviant behavior of the patient eventually will be changed. The techniques of traditional psychotherapy, in general, are based upon four assumptions: (1) Deviant problem behavior grows out of a maladaptive personality state (commonly anxiety). (2) The maladaptive personality state is a result of faulty early interpersonal relationships. (3) Since the personality state is causal to behavior, durable modification of that behavior cannot be obtained without prior changes in this state. (4) Verbal behavior is an expression of the underlying personality state and also can serve as a medium for the modification of it.

Recently, unconventional psychotherapies have appeared under the label of "behavior therapy" or "behavior modification." Many of these therapies result from the work of investigators who are students primarily of what people do, not what they think, feel, or wish. Consequently, a very different set of assumptions underlies the behavior therapies: (1) An individual may be viewed simply as the sum total of the behaviors which he emits. (2) There are general principles which describe the relationship of those behaviors to the environment; these principles emphasize the power of current environmental events. (3) Deviant, problem behavior is not different in quality than behavior in general, and thus it can be changed by the techniques already known to be applicable to other more ordinary behaviors. (4) Somewhat redundantly with the preceding three assumptions, it is neither necessary nor realistic to hypothesize a deeper level of behavioral function than the environmental events known to operate in current behavioral techniques. Behavior modification thus is a changing of overt behavior, not of an underlying personality state; the environmental manipulations applied typically are performed directly upon the deviant behavior.

The purpose of this chapter is to review that portion of the behavior therapy literature which has employed operant conditioning procedures to modify various examples of deviant, disruptive, or maladaptive human behavior.

Relevant Principles of Operant Behavior

An *operant* is a behavior which can be controlled by its environmental consequences. That is, whether the operant remains stable or changes over time depends upon the specific nature of the environmental events which follow it, when it does occur. Clearly enough, there are two general ways in which a response can have stimulus consequences: new stimuli may be added to the environment, or current stimuli may be subtracted from the environment. Some stimuli, when added to the environment, strengthen the immediately preceding response; these are termed *positive reinforcers*. Some stimuli, when subtracted from the environment, strengthen the immediately preceding response; these are termed *negative reinforcers* or, quite often, *aversive stimuli*. *Reinforcement* means the strengthening of a response; thus, there are two reinforcement contingencies.

Obviously, not all stimuli have reinforcing functions. There are stimuli which, when added to the environment, weaken the immediately preceding response. These stimuli are termed *punishing stimuli* (Azrin & Holz, 1966); quite often, but not necessarily, punishing stimuli prove to be negative reinforcers as well. (That is, it is typically found that punishing stimuli, when subtracted from the environment, strengthen the immediately preceding response.) Similarly, there are stimuli which, when subtracted from the environment, weaken the immediately preceding response. There is no widely accepted single term to label such stimuli. Often, but not necessarily, they will prove to be positive reinforcers (that is, when added to the environment, they strengthen the immediately preceding response). The contingency is sometimes referred to as "response cost" (Weiner, 1962), that is, what is costs in current environmental stimuli to perform the response. In very specialized situations, the contingency greatly resembles the "time out from positive reinforcement" operation of the animal laboratory. "Time out" is a complex operation; it will be discussed as such later in this chapter. Response cost, on the other hand, is thoroughly descriptive and has fairly good connotations in the everyday language. Consequently, contingencies in which the subtraction of a stimulus from the environment weakens the immediately preceding response will be referred to as *response cost contingencies;* the stimuli themselves may be termed *costs. Punishment* means the weakening of a response; thus, response costs and the addition of punishing stimuli constitute two punishment contingencies.

A response may be altered by reinforcement or punishment. Often, if the responsible contingency is discontinued, the effect of that contingency disappears some time after. That is, the response returns to the level of strength characterizing it before it was altered by the reinforcement or punishment contingency. This undoing of the effects of such contingencies, frequently observed when they are discontinued, is termed *extinction.*

In summary, then, it appears that there are five basic environmental manipulations which can be applied to the development, maintenance, or change of operant behavior: two reinforcement contingencies, two punishment contingencies, and extinction. Thus, operant therapy is primarily an enterprise in programming reinforcing consequences for desirable behaviors and eliminating the reinforcement for or punishing undesirable behaviors. Correspondingly, the bulk of this review of behavior therapy studies will be organized in terms of these elemental contingencies, as they encompass the most functional logic of operant behavior therapy available.

Reinforcement, punishment, and extinction contingencies, although basic to a technology of behavior modification, by no means exhaust the known principles of behavior upon which that technology is built. Of extreme importance is the principle of *discrimination.* This principle describes a frequent observation: the effects of reinforcement, punishment, and extinction contingencies typically are not widespread; rather, they are restricted to the stimulus settings in which they take place. Of course, if a response is reinforced everywhere, it will be strong everywhere. If, however, it is reinforced in one setting, say at home, but extinguished elsewhere, it will be strong at home but weaker elsewhere. That is, the reinforcement contingency being in effect only in one stimulus setting, its results often are seen only in that setting. In all other settings, the behavior should show a strength characteristic of whatever contingencies operate on it in those settings. This ability to give control over an operant to stimuli which precede it and mark the occasion of its usual reinforcement, punishment, or extinction consequences makes the operant extremely flexible in its pattern of relationship to the total environment. This flexibility is typically evident since few contingencies operate uniformly throughout the environment. Where there are stimuli correlated with the typical consequences which a response will meet, should it occur, those stimuli usually acquire a controlling function over the response. They are termed *discriminative stimuli*. When discrimination fails—that is, when a response shows a strength in a stimulus setting not characteristic of the contingencies which actually operate in that setting, but instead characteristic of contingencies operating in some other setting—the result is usually termed *generalization*.

The relevance of these two processes to operant behavior therapy is frequent. Typically, the behavior therapist wishes to produce certain behavior changes, and wishes these changes to function in the total range of his subject's environment. Unfortunately for such an ambition, experience suggests that discrimination is more likely an organization of behavior than is generalization, since generalization is usually transitory in settings where the maintaining contingency consistently fails to operate. In most of the studies to be reviewed in this chapter, the behavior therapist has concentrated first on demonstrating that the problem behavior under study is indeed amenable to modification through operant techniques. The problem of extending the behavioral change produced in his office, laboratory, preschool, ward, or clinic to other settings in which the subject lives and behaves remains a largely unattacked problem, as far as the printed literature of this field reveals. Current systematic investigation of this problem is ongoing, but little can be offered to the reader by way of inspectable data at this point in time.

There is, of course, a great deal more to the principles which describe the functioning of operant behavior, and to the technology developed from those principles. Some of this will be developed later in this chapter, where its specific application arises. For a thorough exposition, the reader is referred to Skinner (1953), Keller & Schoenfeld (1950), and Honig (1966). The brief account offered here is meant to organize only those principles most basic to operant therapy: they explain much of its character as a behavioral technology, and they explain the fundamental organization of this chapter.

Selective Review of Operant Therapy Studies

Most of the studies reviewed here embody the deliberate manipulation of critical stimulus consequences of the behavior under study, and thereby they approach remediation of the problem which these behaviors constitute. Some of these studies have demonstrated experimentally that the stimulus manipulations performed were in fact responsible for the behavioral changes produced. These studies are, of course, the fundamental demonstrations on which operant behavior therapy is built and validated. Other studies cited have employed operant techniques in a nonexperimental manner. They are included only to exemplify other possible uses of operant procedures to modify deviant behavior. They exemplify possibilities; they do not demonstrate that the reinforcement techniques involved were functional in causing the behavioral change noted.

A considerable number of studies, many of which do represent well-demonstrated operant processes, are not included because they exemplify research within institutional settings, and are to be reviewed elsewhere in this book.

Thus, it should be made clear that the studies reviewed in this chapter are illustrations, but are not exhaustive of research in the area of operant behavior therapy.

TECHNIQUES OF STRENGTHENING BEHAVIOR

Positive Reinforcement.   The most commonly used technique of operant behavior modification has been positive reinforcement. The use of positive reinforcement to strengthen one behavior has often been combined with other procedures, such as extinction, designed to weaken incompatible behavior. Typically, it is then impossible to evaluate the relative contribution of each technique to the final result; however, the therapist has usually focused first on achieving maximum effectiveness and later on experimental analysis.

Two techniques frequently used in conjunction with positive reinforcement are shaping (Skinner, 1953) and fading (Terrace, 1963a, 1963b). *Shaping* is used to develop behavior not currently exhibited by a subject, perhaps because of the complexity of the behavior desired. In shaping, the experimenter' at first reinforces responses which may have little similarity to the desired behavior, but which are clearly within the subject's current behavioral repertoire. The variability of the subject's behavior allows the experimenter to reinforce successively only behaviors which are increasingly similar to the desired behavior. Finally only the desired behavior is reinforced, until it attains suitable strength.

Fading is used to develop new discriminations, i.e., to change the discriminative stimulus conditions controlling the behavior. Initially the behavior is maintained with reinforcement in those stimulus conditions where the behavior is already highly probable. Gradually, at a rate which produces no disruption in performance, the desired changes are introduced in these stimulus conditions (the behavior must be maintained, meanwhile). Eventually the behavior will come under the control of these new discriminative stimuli. The new stimuli may be of greater complexity, of lesser complexity, or totally different from the former stimuli.

Positive reinforcement and its related techniques have been employed to strengthen behaviors which have had markedly different prior histories of reinforcement. They have been applied to the problems of increasing behaviors currently occurring at low rates, reinstating behaviors once present but no longer exhibited, substituting appropriate responses for avoidance behavior or "anxiety" responses, and building completely new behavioral repertoires.

A series of studies conducted in preschool settings has exemplified the basic mechanism of positive reinforcement as a technique for strengthening weak but desirable behavior (Allen, Hart, Buell, Harris, & Wolf, 1964; Baer & Wolf, 1968; Harris, Johnston, Kelley, & Wolf, 1964; Johnston, Kelley, Harris, & Wolf, 1966). In these studies, the basic reinforcement applied was social, consisting of the various ways of displaying positive attention that different preschool teachers could generate. This reinforcement was applied to diverse behavior problems: for example, the development of increased social interaction with other children (Allen et al., 1964; Baer & Wolf, 1968), the increase in climbing and other forms of active play (Johnston et al., 1966), and the increase in noncrawling behavior (Harris et al., 1964).

The studies uniformly incorporated an experimental examination of the procedures used. Typically, this was accomplished by recording a base-line rate of the behavior under study; then, when that baseline appeared stable, applying the reinforcement contingencies until a desirable change was obtained; then reversing the contingencies just long enough to demonstrate that the newly produced behavioral change would not be maintained without reinforcement; and finally reinstating reinforcement long enough to accomplish behavioral changes of desirable strength and durability.

The emphasis of these studies was on positive reinforcement; however, in each case, reinforcement of one class of behavior was implicitly coupled with extinction of incompatible classes of behavior. The possibility of separating the two processes has been approached in recent work. In a preschool girl showing extreme attachment to adults, social interaction with children was increased greatly simply by reinforcing it more consistently than interaction with adults (Baer & Wolf, in press). In this case, extinction of the incompatible response was not essential.

An extremely valuable development in positive reinforcement technology is the "token system," sometimes referred to as a "currency system." Such a system sets up a convenient stimulus, or token, as discriminative for a variety of reinforcers. The token is made discriminative by allowing subjects to exchange it for any other reinforcer available. Thereby, the reinforcement function of that variety of reinforcers is acquired by its discriminative stimulus, the token, in the familiar mechanism of conditioned reinforcement. Thus, the token can be used to reinforce behavior with much the same effectiveness as any of the reinforcers for which it can later be exchanged. Tokens may be presented to subjects as they perform the behaviors being developed or maintained; later, perhaps at the end of a session, a day, or a week, they are able to exchange their tokens for whatever reinforcers they may choose (or can afford, if different reinforcers have different token prices, as is common). In effect, the discriminative token becomes a currency, i.e., a medium of exchange for a variety of goods. It is a close analog in miniature to money in normal society. Indeed, some token systems use money. (It may be pointed out that the authors, the editor, and the reader all operate on a token system involving money, and that the usual function of that token system is indeed to maintain a wide range of normal behavior patterns in us all. Nevertheless, it is rare to see the business world reviewed as a behavior therapy. Clearly, this is an arbitrary omission.)

The token is usually chosen for ease of dispensing. Poker chips have been used, as have points marked on a subject's tally sheet, numbers recorded on an electric counter, holes punched in a ticket, and plastic slips from the Peabody Language Development Kit clipped onto a safety pin in a child's clothing. The reinforcers for which such tokens are exchanged have ranged from money through food, privileges, toys, and special trips to movies, shows, pools, etc. Such reinforcers are usually called "backup" reinforcers.

Token systems have a number of advantages. (1) The tokens are usually much easier to present to a subject than some of the backup reinforcers for which they can be exchanged. Food, for example, is a messy and not always sanitary reinforcer if dispensed experimentally. Indeed, certain backup reinforcers, such as trips to a swimming pool or a wrestling match, can hardly be dispensed in experimental settings at all. (2) A very single potent reinforcer may be used to support a great deal of behavior, as when a child "saves up" for a bicycle or a camera. The lengthy time before actual delivery of such single reinforcers is filled with tokens, which transform the single very potent reinforcer into many quite potent reinforcers, and thereby may be used to develop a correspondingly great amount of behavior. (3) When dealing with a large number of subjects, as in a ward or classroom, token systems can overcome much of the variability in effectiveness of reinforcers which the individual subjects are likely to display. A sufficient variety of backup reinforcers makes it probable that there is at least one potent reinforcer available for virtually every subject whose behavior is to be reinforced. (4) When it is necessary to offer relatively mild reinforcers, as when offering small toys to children, a token system backed up by a variety of such mild reinforcers may function more strongly than any one of the mild reinforcers alone might, over a period of time.

There are, of course, certain disadvantages to token systems. They require establishment. The token is not automatically a stimulus with discriminative function for the backup reinforcers; it must be discriminated by the subjects as such before it will function. With some subjects a simple verbal explanation will suffice; with others, however, such as retardates, actual shaping in the use of the token system may be required before its full reinforcing effectiveness is achieved. Furthermore, the token system is no better than its backup reinforcers. If these do not include stimuli of sufficient variety and potency, then few of the advantages of the token system will be realized. This places a considerable burden on the experimenter: in effect, he must maintain a store. (By using money as the tokens, he may exploit the already existing stores of the community, of course; but with some subjects, such as retardates, it will be necessary often to escort them to, through, and from the store.)

Perhaps the most fundamental disadvantage of the token system is that it is not the reinforcer system which should maintain most therapeutic behavior changes—the social environment in which the behavior eventually must survive. However, this consideration may not apply to some problems (such as permanently institutionalized subjects). When it does apply, nevertheless, token reinforcement may serve as an initial tool to establish new behavior, which later can be transferred to social control.

On balance, the advantages of token systems increasingly seem to outweigh their disadvantages, and they are steadily increasing in application. Some of the most extensive and ingenious applications of token reinforcement to the development of behavioral repertoires are found in the work of Ayllon & Azrin, who applied such systems to the inmates of a mental hospital. Their work also contains some of the best examples of experimental analysis of the effects of this reinforcement system to be found in the literature; however, since their programs are described in another chapter of this book, no further reference to them will be made here.

Birnbrauer, Bijou, Wolf, & Kidder (1965) have described a procedure in which token reinforcers, exchangeable for food, toys, and school supplies, have been used in conjunction with programmed instruction procedures to develop and maintain academic study behavior in retarded children. In a subsequent report (Birnbrauer, Wolf, Kidder, & Tague, 1965) experimental manipulations were performed to investigate whether the token reinforcement system was essential to the maintenance of accuracy of work and rates of studying behavior of these children. When the tokens were no longer delivered to the 15 children in this experiment for academic study behavior, 5 showed little change in behavior. The remaining 10 showed decreased accuracy of work, and 4 of the ten also showed an increased amount of disruptive behavior during the no-token period.

Wolf, Giles, & Hall (1968) also employed a token reinforcement system to increase the rate of academic study behavior of low-achieving fifth and sixth grade children. In this system points were given contingent upon a variety of student behaviors such as work completed in regular school, grades obtained on school report cards (higher grades in school resulted in a higher number of points), and work completed in a remedial classroom. Points were exchangeable for a variety of events such as field trips, snacks, money, candy and other small items available in a "store," and a variety of items available from department stores. After a year of these procedures, the students showed gains on standardized achievement tests and school grades above that seen in comparable children who did not participate in the remedial program. Within the remedial classroom itself, experimental manipulations were performed to assess the effects of the point reinforcement system. It was found that choice of study materials could be manipulated by assignment of a differential number of points for completed work on a particular task, showing that the point contingencies were functioning as reinforcers.

The importance of imitation for the development of complex behavior in children is well appreciated (e.g., Bandura, 1962). Recent experimental work with normal, retarded, and autistic children has indicated two important effects when these children are reinforced for matching the behavior of a model. First, after an adequate history of matching specific behaviors of a model, the children begin to match new behaviors of the model even though they have never been reinforced for these imitations. Second, imitations which have never been reinforced are maintained for extended periods as long as other imitative behaviors are reinforced (Baer, Peterson, & Sherman, 1967; Baer & Sherman, 1964; Metz, 1965; Peterson, 1966; Lovaas, Berberich, Perloff, & Schaeffer, 1966). A procedure common to all these studies was teaching a series of responses, each of which was topographically similar to a response just demonstrated by a model. This training apparently was sufficient to create conditions in which diverse new behaviors could be established and maintained merely by demonstrating them.

Thus, one of the most efficient techniques for establishing many and various new behaviors in subjects with behavioral deficits could be first to establish general imitative skill, and then to employ demonstration, or modeling, to generate new behaviors. In this manner, it would seem possible to develop a wide variety of new behaviors without the necessity of extensive shaping procedures for each new response.

In spite of the apparent usefulness of imitation procedures in behavior development, they have not been extensively used to modify behaviorial deficits. Jones (1924a) supplied one of the few examples of such a use in a case of a young boy who exhibited avoidance responses to fuzzy objects. The first therapy procedure which was employed with this child involved bringing him into a play situation in which three other children and a rabbit were present. The three other children were particularly chosen because of their fearless attitude toward the rabbit. In the play situation, it was observed that the subject first touched the rabbit immediately after having watched the other children pet the rabbit. Unfortunately, further employment of this technique was prevented by the subject's illness. Jones (1924b) reports the use of similar imitation techniques in other cases to modify children's behavior, but the descriptions are extremely limited. Further, in none of the examples Jones presents is an attempt made to examine or evaluate the specific usefulness of employing the other children as models.

Lovaas, Freitas, Nelson, & Whalen (1967) trained autistic children to imitate the behavior of adult models in an initial series of nonverbal tasks. After some initial imitative repertoires had been established in these children, these repertoires were utilized, in conjunction with shaping and fading procedures, to develop new behaviors such as washing hands, brushing hair, making beds, playing games, drawing, printing, and so forth. The authors assert that the use of imitation then facilitated training these new behaviors, which otherwise could have been difficult to establish. (However, the extent to which the imitative training facilitated the acquisition of these new behaviors was not measured in an experimental manner.)

In the area of verbal development there have been several studies which indicate the usefulness of the development of imitative repertoires for subjects who exhibit verbal deficits (Hewett, 1965; Lovaas, Berberich, Perloff, & Schaeffer, 1966; Risley & Wolf, 1967). In each of these studies one of the first steps in verbal training was to establish a verbal response (usually employing shaping procedures) under the stimulus control of the same word said by the experimenter. In each study it was observed that once stimulus control over a few of the subjects' words was established, it was quite easy to obtain new words from the subjects without extensive shaping, merely by presenting an appropriate demonstration from the experimenter. Once the new response occurred, it was possible to reinforce it and eventually to change the stimulus conditions in which it was emitted.

In the Risley & Wolf study, the subjects were retarded and autistic children who had periodically exhibited some rudimentary but unreliable mimicking behavior prior to experimentation. In these cases the experimenter said a word or sound, and then delivered food and social reinforcement if the subject repeated the word or sound immediately after the experimenter. Any disruptive or inappropriate behavior of the subjects produced a brief period in which the experimenter did not attend to the subject. After these procedures resulted in a number of reliably mimicked words, the subjects were taught, through fading procedures, to name objects and to use phrases employing the words previously mimicked. In addition, the parents of these children were trained to capitalize on the children's newly developed mimicking repertoire, and by fading out their verbal prompts, were able to establish functional language phrases in the children.

In the study by Lovaas et al., the subjects were two autistic children who did not initially display any imitative vocal behavior. For these children any vocalization was reinforced with food until a high rate of this behavior was established. Then the experimenter periodically said a word to the subjects and reinforced behaviors of the subjects which were successively closer and closer approximations to what the experimenter had just said. In this manner several verbal responses were brought under reliable imitative control.

In the Risley & Wolf and the Lovaas et al. studies, it was demonstrated that the contingency relationship between reinforcement and verbal behavior was instrumental in maintaining the newly developed verbal behavior. In the study by Lovaas et al., when reinforcement was presented in a basically noncontingent manner instead of contingent upon verbal imitations, the subjects' imitative behavior deteriorated but increased again when contingent reinforcement was resumed. Risley & Wolf performed several manipulations to demonstrate the functional role of the food reinforcement contingencies in maintaining already established verbal behavior and in developing new verbal behavior. They showed that when the contingency relationship between food and the subjects' verbal behavior was removed (by noncontingent delivery of food, or by reinforcement of behavior other than verbalization), the rate of verbalization fell, but that it rose again when the food contingency was reinstated. They also demonstrated that learning of new verbal responses was faster when food and praise were contingent upon correct verbal responses than when praise alone was contingent upon responses, although the percentage of words recalled in later tests did not differ with respect to the two learning conditions.

Hewett (1965) established imitative vocalization in an autistic boy by reinforcing successive approximations. He then paired questions with their answers, reinforced the boy for imitating only the answer, and then faded out the answer, so that the child answered questions put to him. Finally, the child was required to respond verbally in phrases outside the experimental situation before he received items such as candy, juice, and crackers.

Kerr, Meyerson, & Michael (1965) established vocal responses in a previously mute retarded girl by reinforcing any vocalization which the child emitted. However, the child would stop when the experimenter vocalized. To eliminate this, the experimenter at first vocalized softly enough to avoid stopping the girl; gradually, the volume and number of experimenter vocalizations were increased, until normal vocalizations no longer caused a drop in the subject's vocalizations. Subsequently, the child was reinforced only when she vocalized shortly after the experimenter had.

Rickard, Digman, & Horner (1960) and Rickard & Dinoff (1962) increased the relative rate of appropriate speech in a patient who frequently engaged in delusional verbal behavior, by reinforcing appropriate verbal behavior with social stimuli and ignoring delusional speech.

Rickard & Mundy (1965) increased the rate of fluent speech in a stutterer by requiring successively more complex verbal behavior and by programming social and material reinforcers contingent upon a gradually increasing proportion of speech without repetition errors.

In many cases extensive behavioral repertoires which once were exhibited by subjects are, for unknown reasons, no longer present or are present in only fractional form and rate. Several studies have demonstrated the use of positive reinforcement procedures to reinstate these behavioral repertoires.

Isaacs, Thomas, & Goldiamond (1960) employed shaping procedures, with chewing gum as the reinforcer, to reinstate verbal behavior in two psychotics who had been mute for a number of years. One subject then spoke only in response to questions by the experimenter in the experimental situation. Another subject would speak both in the experimental situation and on the ward, but only to the experimenter. His verbal behavior was then generalized to another person by bringing the other person into the experimental situation. Sherman (1963) reinstated verbal behavior in a mute psychotic who previously communicated with ward attendants by writing notes. The experimenter refused to read the subject's notes and used a shaping procedure to establish a vocal response. The reinstatement of one vocal response was accompanied by an almost total reinstatement of full-blown language behavior in response to the experimenter. In addition, once ward attendants refused to read the subject's notes, he would speak to them on the ward.

Sherman (1965) reinstated some verbal behavior in three previously mute psychotics and then examined the role of the contingency between the recently developed speech and reinforcement. In this study, shaping and fading procedures, using food as a reinforcer, were used to establish a number of verbal responses to questions by the experimenter. Once some verbal responses were established, the subjects were no longer reinforced for speech, but only when they were not responding verbally. Verbal responses decreased markedly, but increased again when the contingency was reinstated between reinforcement and verbal responses.

Brady & Lind (1961) reported the recovery of sight in a patient who for two years had claimed he was blind. In this study, both social and material reinforcers were used to establish a self-timed button-pressing response. Visual stimuli were then introduced which if employed by the subject, facilitated timing discriminations. After extensive training and clear reliance on the visual stimuli, the subject reported the recovery of sight.

Grosz & Zimmerman (1965) have argued that the Brady & Lind study hardly exemplifies operant behavior therapy. They maintain that the study demonstrates only the extent to which visual stimuli controlled the behavior of a patient who claimed to be blind. Grosz & Zimmerman (1965) and Zimmerman & Grosz (1966) later reported that the clinical improvement described by Brady & Lind was very short-lived; shortly afterward the patient again claimed to be blind. These authors once more demonstrated that the behavior of this patient could be controlled by visual stimuli in an experimental situation, but that suggestions by an experimental assistant were effective in remodifying the patient's behavior so that his performance once again looked like that of a blind person.

The questions raised by Grosz & Zimmerman clearly have some merit. However, it should be noted that at least one of the patient's behaviors of therapeutic interest was his verbal report of blindness. According to Brady & Lind this behavior was changed, however briefly, in the course of their manipulations in the experimental situation. The important questions would seem to be how to extend such changes to a wider range of environments, how to make them durable, and how to prevent reshaping of the "blind" complaint in the outside environment.

There also have been demonstrations of changes in behaviors which somehow have become a fraction of their former rate or form. Bachrach, Erwin, & Mohr (1965) increased the rate of eating in an anorexic patient by making many environmental reinforcers, such as visitors, television, and magazines, contingent upon food ingestion.

Wahler, Winkel, Peterson, & Morrison (1965) trained mothers in a clinic setting to provide differential social reinforcement for certain desirable and problem behaviors of their own children. Initial observation of the mother-child interaction in a playroom setting demonstrated the problem behavior and the mothers' typical ways of responding to these behaviors. Following this, the mothers were given instructions to attend with approval to certain desirable behaviors and to ignore problem behaviors. A cue light, visible in the playroom, was used (1) to signal mothers when to attend to the child and (2) to reinforce the mothers for accurate performance. Three cases, exemplifying three different types of behavior, were examined in this manner. In one, imperative and nonimperative behaviors towards the mother were manipulated; in the second, dependent or independent responses; in the third, oppositional and cooperative behaviors. In the first two cases, alternating periods of social reinforcement and extinction of specific behaviors demonstrated that these contingencies exerted substantial control over them. In the third case, extinction of oppositional behavior was not sufficient to reduce its rate, even when cooperative behavior was being reinforced. Consequently, an added contingency was imposed in which the mother left the playroom contingent upon oppositional behavior. Following this, oppositional behavior decreased while cooperative behavior increased. Further procedures were performed to replicate this effect with the child.

Extensive shaping procedures were employed by Wolf, Risley, & Mees (1964) with a young autistic child. Although this child had an eye condition which made wearing glasses necessary, he refused to do so. Wearing glasses was shaped by presenting portions of his meals contingent upon increasing approximations to this behavior. Once the wearing of glasses was established, it was maintained by making other everyday reinforcing events, such as going on a walk, contingent upon the child wearing his glasses. In a similar manner, some appropriate verbal behavior was shaped.

Several studies have used positive reinforcement to toilet-train children. Gelber & Meyer (1965) trained a thirteen-year-old boy who had never displayed appropriate toilet defecation. They allowed the boy a period of time away from his ward whenever he defecated in the toilet, or whenever his pants were found to be clean during periodic checks. Giles & Wolf (1966) established appropriate defecation and urination in several retarded males by reinforcing approaches to, then sitting on, and then successful elimination in the toilet. When positive reinforcement alone was not completely effective, mild aversive events were applied contingent upon inappropriate toilet behavior, whereupon it was suppressed and replaced by appropriate behaviors. Wolf, Risley, Johnston, Harris, & Allen (1967) toilet-trained a five-year-old autistic boy by placing him on the toilet and reinforcing him with candy and praise whenever he displayed proper urination behavior. Bowel training was accomplished by placing the child on the toilet at times of the day when he frequently defecated and then reinforcing all bowel movements which occurred in the toilet.

Patterson (1965b) decreased the rate of inappropriate or disruptive classroom behavior in a young hyperactive boy by delivering points on a counter (which later were converted to candy and pennies divided among the class) contingent upon each ten-second period in which the boy did not exhibit these behaviors. Similar procedures were used in a second study by Patterson, Jones, Whittier, & Wright (1965) to modify the behavior of another hyperactive child.

Positive reinforcement and extinction were used by Zimmerman & Zimmerman (1962) to increase the productive behavior of two subjects in a special classroom. In one case appropriate spelling behavior was reinforced with teacher attention; concurrently, abortive and bizarre spelling responses were ignored. In the other case, appropriate classroom work behavior was attended to, while disruptive behaviors, such as tantrums and irrelevant questions, were ignored.

A common use of positive reinforcement is to develop desirable behaviors as substitutes for current behavior which is undesirable. These undesirable behaviors frequently appear to be avoidance, "anxious," or phobic behaviors. Avoidance behavior is behavior which is maintained simply because it prevents the occurrence of an aversive stimulus. In clinical cases it is rarely possible to determine whether specific behaviors are in fact avoidance responses, since the occurrence or nonoccurrence of aversive stimulation contingent on that behavior cannot easily be established. In practice, an aversive history is likely to be assumed if a patient reports anxiety in a situation, or cries, or is reluctant to enter a situation, even when a specific aversive history is not reported. This assumption is obviously open to question, since it is possible that such behavior is due not to a history of aversive stimulation in the situation, but rather to positive reinforcement (such as attention and sympathy) produced by the behavior. Despite this reservation the studies below are presented as examples in which positive reinforcement is used to substitute other behavior for avoidance responses.

In one of the earliest behavior therapy studies reported, Jones (1924a) used a fading-in procedure to eliminate avoidance behavior in a situation. A child exhibited crying and avoidance when presented with various fuzzy objects, including a white rat, cotton wool, feathers, and a rabbit. The child was seated in a chair and fed a food which he liked. Simultaneously, the experimenter brought a rabbit as close to the child as possible without evoking crying or avoidance. Gradually the rabbit was brought closer, until the child no longer cried even when touching it. Correlated with this change, the crying and avoidance responses to other fuzzy objects (and even new animals) were reduced.

Bentler (1962) described a child who avoided bath water. The child's toys were so placed that to play with them, she first had to approach an empty bathtub, then a sink filled with water, and so forth, until the behavior of bathing was reestablished. Neale (1963) toilet-trained three of four children presumably inhibited by fear of the toilet. The children were periodically placed on the toilet, and candy, pennies and social approval were presented when they defecated there. Lazarus (1960) apparently used shaping procedures to reestablish automobile riding in a child who showed strong avoidance of moving vehicles. Lazarus first reinforced positive comments about vehicles with chocolate; later the child received chocolate when he played with toy vehicles, and finally when he rode in an automobile.

Patterson (1965a) dealt with a child who refused to stay in school unless one of his parents remained with him. The initial procedure was to present a series of situations to the child, each of which involved longer and longer periods of time without the parents while the child was engaged in doll play. The child was reinforced with candy and approval for not asking about parents and for talk indicating he was not fearful. Then the child was taken to school and left there alone for longer and longer periods of time each day. Spending time in school alone produced praise and approval from the child's family. Eventually, the child returned to school fulltime without displaying fearfulness.

The general features of the last five studies cited include: (1) A systematic series of stimuli to present to subjects is arranged. As the series progresses the stimuli more and more closely approximate the ones which are "fearful," or evoke avoidance behavior. (2) As this series is presented, the subject's nonavoidance or nonfearful behavior is maintained, first by gradually progressing through the series of stimuli at a rate which produces no sudden increases of avoidance behavior, and second by positive reinforcement when the patient displays approximations to desired alternative behaviors.

These features are similar in many respects to the procedures described by Wolpe (1958), Wolpe & Lazarus (1966), and many others, used in eliminating phobias and other abnormal human behaviors. In such application, procedures are labeled *psychotherapy by reciprocal inhibition*. This general term includes a number of specific techniques such as systematic desensitization, assertive training, and use of sexual response. They are discussed in detail elsewhere in this book, and will be described here only to note procedural similarities to operant behavior modification techniques.

The most widely used technique of reciprocal inhibition is that of systematic desensitization by relaxation. In this technique, the patient lists a hierarchy of stimuli which make him anxious. Deep relaxation is then induced in the patient, and the therapist instructs him to imagine the least fearful item on the list. If deep relaxation can be maintained under these conditions, the therapist goes into the next item. If the patient reports a loss of relaxation and a feeling of anxiety, the therapist assists him in recovering his relaxation, and then starts up the list again, first with an item to which the patient reports no loss of relaxation. Usually the therapist's techniques are verbal. Wolpe's frequent finding is that once the patient can maintain deep relaxation when told to imagine a fearful situation, he will be able to respond appropriately when faced with the actual situation. Others (e.g., Clark, 1963) use similar techniques, but employ stimuli other than verbal ones in the therapy situation; they also instruct patients gradually to come into contact with previously fearful situations outside the therapy situation, but only so long as they do not become fearful. In other techniques of reciprocal inhibition (using assertive and sexual responses) patients are given instructions to substitute appropriate responses gradually in situations where they previously behaved inappropriately.

The therapeutic effect of reciprocal inhibition is presumed to result from the inhibition of the anxiety previously aroused in the relevant situations. This inhibition supposedly occurs because responses such as relaxation are established which are incompatible with anxiety. Wolpe defines anxiety as a group of observable potentially measurable overt responses. Although some anxiety responses such as respiration rate and muscular tension are observed during therapy, the observation is done in an unsystematic manner. The primary criterion for anxiety is the patient's verbal report. Thus, following therapy, a reduction in anxiety is inferred from the patient's claim that he is better. Certainly the patient's verbal report has changed. In the absence of systematic measurement, however, there is no demonstration that the anxiety responses have changed. Further, even if systematic attempts were made to record all responses called anxiety before and after therapy, that alone would not establish their causal role in producing avoidance behavior, nor would it establish their reduction as causal in reducing avoidance behavior. If changes in two (or more) behaviors are functionally related to an environmental manipulation (such as therapy procedures), causality may be assigned to that manipulation.

However, that one behavior is functional in producing the other is not established thereby. (In fact, it is as reasonable to suppose that avoidance behavior produces the anxiety responses as it is to suppose the reverse. Alternatively, the environmental manipulation may have affected both behaviors similarly but independently.)

In systematic desensitization two major operations are performed. One is the development of responses presumably incompatible with anxiety. The second is the presentation (or self-presentation) of a series of stimuli of increasing fearfulness. Either one or both of these operations may be functional in producing the therapeutic changes reported by Wolpe and others.

An operant analysis emphasizes the therapist's instructions as discriminative stimuli; attention and approval are used as reinforcers to create and maintain relaxation responses, while stimuli previously discriminative for avoidance behavior are introduced in the therapy situation. In addition, it is apparent that the therapist often expresses warm approval when the patient reports behaving appropriately outside the therapy situation. This contingency should strengthen primarily verbal reports of improvement; the actual behavior outside the therapy session is temporally quite distant from the therapist's approval. However, several studies (Lovaas, 1961, 1964a, 1964b; Sherman, 1964) have demonstrated that control of verbal behavior sometimes yielded partial control over related nonverbal behavior.

The contingencies between the therapist's approval and the patient's report of behavior outside the therapy situation become even more evident in techniques which involve the therapist instructing the patient in ways of behaving outside the therapy situation. However, by no means does it appear that all the relevant stimulus consequences are under the control of the therapist. Certainly the environmental stimulus consequences of certain of the techniques, especially the use of assertive and sexual responses, would appear to play an important role.

The use of a graded series of stimuli is quite similar to operant procedures involving verbal training (Risley & Wolf, 1967; Sherman, 1965) and the development of academic skills (Birnbrauer, Bijou, Wolf, & Kidder, 1965; Birnbrauer, Wolf, Kidder, & Tague, 1965), deficits presumably not a result of avoidance behavior. The effects of the gradual presentation of stimuli may be regarded in at least two ways. The first, related to the preceding discussion, emphasizes the maintenance of some type of desired behavior through the use of the therapist's instructions and approval while gradual changes are made in the stimulus conditions in which this behavior occurs. For this analysis it is not necessary to assume that "anxiety" is aroused by the stimuli in the series, nor is it necessary to assume that the behavior established is incompatible with anxiety. The primary question here is one of assessing the stimulus situations in which a patient has a behavioral deficit (e.g., inability to enter situations where certain stimuli are present), of generating appropriate responses (verbal and nonverbal), and then of gradually shifting the stimulus control of these responses to appropriate stimulus situations. The other possible effect of the graded presentation of stimuli is extinction. This assumes that avoidance responses are discriminated to certain stimulus situations, and that the major effect of presentation of the series of stimuli is to extinguish these responses gradually by the presentation of the stimuli in situations where aversive events do not occur. Possibly, the graded series of stimuli facilitate extinction by allowing reduction of avoidance responses a little at a time. Lomont (1965) and Rachman (1967) have presented thorough discussions of this latter point.

Negative Reinforcement. When aversive stimuli are used for behavior modification, the results are often difficult to categorize: negative reinforcement (escape and avoidance), or punishment? Dinsmoor (1954) has shown that the major distinction between escape-avoidance and punishment studies lies in which response class precedes the aversive stimulation. In avoidance studies the response class potentially is very broad; it may include all behaviors with the exception of the few which avoid or escape the aversive stimulus. In punishment studies the response class is narrow, consisting of only those specific behaviors which produce the aversive stimulation. The studies included in this section are those in which a relatively narrow class of responses has been strengthened by contingent escape or avoidance of aversive stimuli. However, in several of the studies to be described, punishment procedures as well as escape and avoidance procedures have been used in combination to produce behavioral changes.

An effective technique for the treatment of nocturnal enuresis has been in use for some years. It involves an apparatus first devised and employed for therapeutic purposes by Mowrer (1938) and Mowrer & Mowrer (1938). Electrically sensing moisture, the device wakes the patient by some auditory stimulus (usually a bell) whenever nocturnal micturition occurs. Following the suggestions of the Mowrers, the technique commonly has been analyzed in terms of respondent conditioning in which detrusor tension becomes a CS, eliciting waking and sphincter contraction (see Jones, 1960). Recently, however, Lovibond (1963) has presented an argument that an analysis in terms of respondent conditioning does not account for the maintenance of noctural continence. Rather, Lovibond analyzed the technique in terms of avoidance conditioning. The bell presumably serves both as an aversive stimulus and as a stimulus eliciting sphincter contraction. Lovibond reasoned that a shock component rather than a bell would facilitate continence training due to the greater aversiveness of the shock stimulus. He further reasoned that if the response of sphincter contraction could escape as well as avoid an aversive stimulus, it would result in more rapid establishment of nocturnal continence. An "escape" condition was added by an apparatus which presented a loud noise just as the child urinated. This noise was timed to last just long enough for the sphincter contraction elicited by the sound to occur as the sound ended. The data from Lovibond's comparisons of three different training apparatuses support his analysis.

Walton & Black (1959) have used avoidance of mild aversive stimulation to strengthen the amplitude of verbalizations in a case of functional aphonia. In this case the S was required to read aloud for fifteen-minute periods from an uninteresting book. Every time the S failed to maintain volume, or to improve volume on successive fifteen-minute sessions, an extra two minutes was added to the session, until improvement had been made. In addition, if the S made improvements during the fifteen-minute session, the time required was reduced by two minutes as long as the improvements were maintained. During later periods of treatment, encouragement and fading-in procedures were employed to establish audible verbal behavior in the presence of several people.

Blakemore, Thorpe, Barker, Conway, & Lavin (1963a) applied punishment and escape procedures to a man who exhibited transvestite behavior. The patient was instructed to dress in his favorite female clothing while standing barefoot on an electric grid. As the patient dressed, pulsing shock was periodically introduced, and it was continued until the patient had completely removed all female clothing. Fourteen months later the patient had reported only one further instance of transvestite behavior (Blakemore, Thorpe, Barker, Conway, & Lavin, 1963b).

Feldman & MacCulloch (1965) employed escape and avoidance training to treat male homosexuals. They projected pictures of males for the patient; the patient could switch off the pictures. If after eight seconds the patient had not switched the picture off, shock was delivered until the picture was switched off. If the picture was switched off before the eight seconds had elapsed, the shock was avoided. Later, the switching response was effective only intermittently. Feldman and MacCulloch also presented pictures of females on some trials contiguous with the removal of the male. When the picture of the female had been removed (by the experimenter) the patient could obtain its return (on a random schedule) by pressing a switch. Since the absence of a female picture meant that a picture of a male (with the shock contingency) might reappear, the response of re-presenting the female pictures constituted a further extension of the avoidance procedure. The authors report that these procedures were effective in modifying the homosexual behavior of the patients outside the laboratory situation, the majority of the patients reporting that they had given up homosexual practices and were more interested in heterosexual activities.

The use of verbal reports exemplified in the two preceding studies requires comment. Verbal behavior may, of course, be viewed in at least two contexts: expressive and instrumental. The authors of these—and many other —studies apparently attend primarily to its expressive function, in that they accept verbal report as a reflection of behavioral improvement in the patient. If they were to consider his verbal report as instrumental, however, considerable scepticism would seem only reasonable. The patients in each case—and in many other similar studies—are being subjected to a treatment procedure involving stimuli chosen as aversive. It is hoped that, because these stimuli are aversive, the patient will lose the undesirable behavior which leads to them and gain the desirable behavior which avoids them. But verbal behavior can avoid these stimuli just as effectively, if not more effectively. Thus, when a patient reports that he is better, he is reinforced for that report, if he thereby stops or reduces further treatment. Therefore, any therapist using aversive stimuli should expect escape and avoidance behavior of any and every sort; when the one measure of the patient's improvement is the patient's own report, it should be assumed that his verbal behavior is certainly as sensitive to escape and avoidance contingencies as is his transvestite, homosexual, or anxious behavior.

Lovaas, Schaeffer, & Simmons (1965) used shock escape and avoidance to increase the social behavior of two autistic children. Each child was placed barefoot on an electric grid, and the experimenter requested the child to approach him. When the children did not respond to these requests, the grid was electrified until the child did approach the experimenter (usually assisted at first by a gentle push from a second experimenter). In later sessions the shock was withheld if the child approached the experimenter within five seconds following the request. If they did not, the shock was turned on until the child did approach. Both children quickly learned to approach the experimenter and continued to do so upon request for a nine-month period without further shock. Then there was a sudden decrease in the children's responsiveness; however, one noncontingent shock immediately reinstated the children's approach responses when requested. The authors further explored the conditions in which the children followed other simple requests of the experimenter. They found that the children had a high probability of following other simple requests when in the room where the original procedure took place, but not in a different room. However, once the children were presented with a brief shock-avoidance procedure in the different room, they then responded to the experimenter's requests there, too.

A series of case studies by Yealland (1918) exemplify the use of escape and avoidance procedures, although certainly Yealland did not regard them in these terms. His main concern was with patients who exhibited hysterical disorders resulting from war experiences. A case of mutism (pp. 7–15) is an example of his approach. The patient was informed that he would not be permitted to leave the therapy room until he was talking normally again. A strong electric current was applied to the patient's throat, apparently with pauses only when the patient attempted vocalizations. In addition, Yealland constantly told the patient that leaving the room was contingent upon recovery of normal speech. In this case, as in others of stammering, functional deafness, tremors, and functional blindness, quick amelioration of the disorders was achieved.

TECHNIQUES OF WEAKENING BEHAVIOR

Response Cost.   Simple response costs for reducing a behavior have not been used extensively in behavior therapy studies. In a study by Baer (1962) thumb-sucking in three young children was markedly reduced in a laboratory situation by turning off an ongoing movie cartoon contingent upon thumb-sucking. Thumb-suckers in a yoked control condition showed no such reduction in rate. In a similar manner, Barrett (1962) reduced a man's rate of multiple tics by interrupting ongoing music contingent upon the tics. This reduction was greater than that obtained when music was played continuously. It should be noted that in these two studies the reinforcement contingencies not only included the subtraction of a presumed positive reinforcer but, once a subtraction had been made, the contingent re-presentation of the stimulus. In the Baer study the re-presentation of the cartoons was contingent upon thumb withdrawal from the mouth; in the Barrett study the re-presentation of the music was contingent upon the absence of tics for 1.5 seconds. The double contingency of both subtraction and readdition of presumably positive reinforcement thus makes it difficult to interpret the results simply as the effects of response cost (as Baer pointed out in his report).

Wetzel (1966) employed response costs to reduce stealing by a young boy. He removed the opportunity to visit the home of a friendly person each time articles belonging to other people were found in the boy's possession. But in addition, after the operation had been in effect for some time, the boy was reinforced for socially appropriate behavior as long as he had not stolen anything.

Several studies have employed a time-out procedure to reduce the frequency of an undesirable behavior. Wolf, Risley, & Mees (1964) greatly reduced tantrums and self-destructive behaviors in an autistic boy by placing him in his room alone with the door closed contingent on these behaviors. This procedure removed all possibility of social reinforcement for the period of time the child was in his room. The door was opened ten minutes after the tantrums stopped. Wolf, Risley, Johnston, Harris, & Allen (1967), in a follow-up study of this same child, employed a similar time-out procedure to eliminate self-slapping and pinching others in a nursery school situation. Risley & Wolf (1967), in establishing functional speech in echolalic children, report the use of time-out procedures to eliminate behaviors such as leaving the chair, autistic mannerisms, and mild temper tantrums, all of which were disruptive to verbal training. In these cases the experimenter either looked away or, in extreme cases, left the room when the child engaged in the disruptive behavior. Looking back at the child or returning to the room was contingent upon the child's not emitting the disruptive behavior for a brief period of time.

The time-out contingency employed in these three studies was a complex one, possibly involving four different components: (1) If the current environment provided positive reinforcement, then the procedure constituted subtraction of positive reinforcement. (2) Since the child was returned to the environment only after the undesirable behavior had ceased (plus the passage of a specified period of time), the time-out procedure may have reinforced behavior incompatible with the undesirable behavior. (3) During time out the child was placed in a situation where others did not attend to him. If the undesirable behavior had been maintained, totally or in part, by social reinforcers, the time-out contingency removed all possibility of this reinforcement, and thereby contributed to their extinction. (4) If isolation for a period of time was a punishing stimulus, then the time-out procedure included a punishment component.

In the three uses of time out cited above, it is difficult to evaluate which of these possible operations produced the reduction in frequency of the undesirable behavior. Perhaps the power of the technique stems from the effect of all four operations.

Punishment Stimuli.   In the behavior therapy literature there are relatively few studies in which stimuli have been delivered contingent upon some behavior and the probability of that behavior reduced thereby. Recently, the natural reluctance to consider punishment as a proper therapeutic technique seems to be undergoing cautious review.

Flanagan, Goldiamond, & Azrin (1958) made a one-second blast of loud tone contingent upon the stuttering responses of three male stutterers. For all three subjects there was a marked decrease in stuttering rate during the period while this contingency was in effect. When the contingency was removed the stuttering rate initially rose above its usual rate but then fell back to that rate. It further was demonstrated that the loud tone was an aversive stimulus: its contingent removal produced higher rates of stuttering.

Goldiamond (1965c) reduced stuttering in several chronic stutterers by presenting periods of delayed auditory feedback contingent upon their disfluencies when they read. With one subject who had shown decreased stuttering under these conditions, delayed feedback was then presented continuously while he read. The immediate effect was to reduce reading rate but to leave stuttering rate relatively unchanged. After the initial effects, both reading and stuttering reverted to their usual (no-delayed-feedback) levels. The conclusion is that, for this subject, the contingency between stuttering and delayed feedback caused the reduction in stuttering, rather than the mere presence of delayed feedback. Goldiamond also subtracted delayed feedback contingent upon disfluencies. There were initially increases in disfluencies, but the long-term effect was a decreased amount of stuttering. Goldiamond noted the development of new patterns of speech which both minimized the disruption produced by delayed auditory feedback and were incompatible with stuttering.

Barrett (1962) presented contingent periods of white noise to reduce the rate of tics in a patient. However, subtraction of the noise was contingent upon the patient's not exhibiting tics for a brief period of time, thus involving possible escape and punishment procedures. The reduction in tics obtained under this condition was slight compared to the reduction obtained under parallel conditions using music, and was similar to that obtained when the subject was instructed to employ "self-control" to reduce his tic rate.

Liversedge & Sylvester (1955) describe techniques involving shock to modify writer's cramp. They observed that most cases of writer's cramp involve two components: tremors and muscle spasms. For the treatment of tremors patients were instructed to insert a metal stylus into holes in a metal plate. If the stylus touched the plate, the patient received a shock. Another metal plate had strips of insulating tape arranged in various patterns. When tracing over the tape, the patient received a shock anytime the stylus touched the plate. Spasms were assumed to result from excessive thumb pressure. A pen was constructed such that excessive pressure of the writer's thumb produced a shock.

The authors reported that six cases of writer's cramp were treated by having the patients practice with these pieces of apparatus. In two of the cases there was a total elimination of the cramps; in the remaining four cases, appreciable reduction was obtained. In a later article Sylvester & Liversedge (1960) present further data on using this method of treatment for writer's cramp and related functional disorders. They treated 39 cases, 29 of which showed marked improvement. Beech (1960), however, has reported an attempt to treat four cases of writer's cramp with these methods in which a therapeutic effect was obtained in only one case.

Lovaas, Schaeffer, & Simmons (1965) shocked two autistic children when they engaged in self-stimulatory and/or tantrum behaviors. This procedure greatly reduced these behaviors over an extended period of time without further shock.

In addition to studies exemplifying punishment, there have been a number of studies in which stimuli often presumed to be aversive have been paired with relevant discriminative stimuli. For example, Kushner (1965), dealing with sexual fetish, delivered a shock to a subject in the presence of stimuli associated with the fetish. Subsequently, the subject reported a decreased amount of fetish behavior. No attempt will be made here to review these studies, as they are detailed elsewhere in this book. However, it should be noted that the procedure of pairing aversive stimuli with particular discriminative stimuli closely resembles a procedure effective in developing conditioned punishing and aversive stimuli. Thus, the pairing of aversive and discriminative stimuli may give these discriminative stimuli additional properties which will now reduce the frequency of certain previously likely behaviors (e.g., looking at the stimuli, approaching them) and support behaviors which avoid these stimuli.

Other Procedures. There have been attempts to reduce the strength of behaviors by other techniques. Only two such studies will be cited.

Wolf, Risley, Johnston, Harris, & Allen (1967) attempted to develop "substitute" behaviors in an autistic boy which would replace behaviors of pinching others in a nursery school situation. During the nursery school a teacher showed the child how to "pat" instead of pinching another child. After this, the teachers encouraged the child to "pat" others instead of pinching them, and praised the child when he did so. Although the child exhibited a moderate rate of "patting" others, this had little effect upon his rate of pinching them. It was only after the time-out contingency, described earlier, was imposed that pinching others decreased.

Ayllon (1963) reported the use of *stimulus satiation* to eliminate towel-hoarding behavior in the case of a hospitalized woman. During the procedure, nurses periodically brought towels to the patient's room and left them. This continued until approximately 600 towels were stored in the patient's room and she spontaneously began to remove them. At this point no more towels were brought to her room. During a twelve-month follow-up, it was observed that the patient no longer hoarded towels. However, while Ayllon terms the procedure "satiation," it does not appear to be analogous to satiation procedures employed in the animal literature. Rather, it appears to be a technique for establishing an excess of towels as an aversive stimulus, in that the patient's room was so crowded with towels that she could not effectively live in it.

EXTINCTION

There have been only a few studies in which explicit extinction procedures have been used; in all these cases, extinction represented the discontinuation of positive reinforcement and the behavior was therefore weakened. Williams (1959) programmed extinction for bedtime tantrum behavior in a young child. When the child cried at bedtime, his parents usually would remain in the bedroom until he had fallen asleep. During the extinction period, the parents put the child to bed and left the room, whether the child cried or not. Under these conditions the child's crying at bedtime was completely eliminated.

Walton (1960c) used extinction procedures to eliminate a skin condition associated with compulsive scratching. Prior to the study, the patient, because of her skin condition, had apparently received a great deal of attention from her family and her fiancé. Therefore, to accomplish extinction the family was instructed not to discuss her skin condition, and her fiancé was stopped from rubbing ointment on the afflicted area (the back of the neck) as he usually did.

Under these conditions, the scratching stopped within two months, and the skin condition had disappeared within three months.

In most instances when extinction procedures have been employed, it has been in combination with reinforcement of incompatible behavior. An example is reported by Wolf, Birnbrauer, Williams, & Lawler (1965) with a young retarded girl who frequently vomited in the classroom situation. Ordinarily the child was returned to her hall when she vomited. For extinction, this contingency was discontinued: the girl was not returned to her hall when she vomited, and the classroom continued to operate normally. In addition, praise and candy were used as reinforcers in an attempt to shape desirable classroom behavior. The girl's vomiting rate showed a spurt upward at the start of extinction, then dropped to zero and remained there. To demonstrate the functional role of the extinction operations, the original contingencies were reinstated: if the girl vomited she was allowed to return to her hall. After an extensive period of time, a vomiting response finally occurred and was followed by the planned contingencies. Thereafter, vomiting rose to its former rate. Final extinction procedures were then reinstated successfully.

A study by Hart, Allen, Buell, Harris, & Wolf (1964) demonstrated the extinction of crying in two preschool children who showed a high rate of this behavior during the preschool morning. Since it seemed possible that teacher attention was maintaining this crying, crying was ignored by the teachers. In addition, if the children made more appropriate responses (e.g., verbal behavior) in situations in which they usually cried, they were attended to by the teachers. In both cases crying decreased markedly. With one child, further experimental manipulations clearly established the functional role of the procedures in producing this change. In the other case this was not as clearly established.

There are some studies of desensitization which can be interpreted as examples of extinction, and in particular, extinction of punishment effects ("anxiety"). In these cases, the effect of extinction is, of course, an increase in the strength of the response as it returns to its presumed prepunishment level. The reader is reminded of the previous discussion of these studies.

Concluding Discussion

When operant procedures are applied to the modification of problem behavior, a consistent problem recurs despite the diversity of behaviors attacked. This is the problem of proof: the demonstration that the particular environmental manipulation applied was indeed responsible for producing whatever behavioral change was noted subsequently. In short, it is always important to show that operant modification procedures are functional.

This kind of demonstration is important in any kind of research, of course. However, it seems particularly important in operant behavior modification studies. First of all, operant techniques diverge markedly from conventional therapeutic techniques in many instances; thus, they are properly viewed with scepticism. Furthermore, many of the techniques employed were developed originally in the animal laboratory, and now are being extended to a new population, humans. Even without the precedent of different techniques being applied to human behavior problems, it would be only basic research logic to insist upon a thorough investigation of that extension. Indeed, these techniques, when applied to humans, often become modified; thus, they are not even exact replications of the familiar animal laboratory techniques.

Despite these considerations, experimental demonstration of the function of operant behavior therapy has not often been attempted. In large part, this seems due to the clinical need to produce a therapeutic outcome, when the behavior under study is problem behavior. A therapeutic goal seems to require choosing procedures with greatest probability of success rather than procedures with the greatest theoretical purity. And achievement of success militates against further investigation of the procedures which achieved it, for the following reason: Such investigation requires experimental manipulation of the elements of those procedures; investigation requires that manipulation, when relevant to the behavior, will alter the behavior. Once a successful therapeutic outcome has been achieved, there is usually only one way for the behavior to change—undesirably. Thus, experimental investigation of a therapeutic procedure will often appear antitherapeutic.

Nevertheless, short-term subservience to the apparent and most proximate therapeutic goal may in fact accomplish a long-term antitherapeutic outcome. The therapist may have just accomplished only one of a number of behavioral changes which his client requires. Unless he investigates the functional nature of the technique which has just apparently worked, he is failing to achieve the potential efficiency for the future work that this demonstration can give him. A good part of that technique may be irrelevant to the behavioral changes desired (indeed, the whole technique may be irrelevant—coincidence is no rarity in clinical work). Experimental manipulation of the technique could show whether or not it does contain truly functional elements; further experimentation could narrow down those elements to their functional core (and thereby probably increase the efficiency of their application).

Furthermore, the therapist using a novel technique needs to be able to convince not only himself, but also other therapists, that the technique is an effective one; similarly, he needs to convince his client, or his client's parents or caretakers. These are primarily clinical goals rather than research goals; they are likely to be served best by experimental investigations of novel therapies as they are ongoing in particular cases.

There is thorough precedent for such clinical practice in medical applications. The well-trained allergist, for example, when he suspects a certain allergen as the critical offender of his patient, will remove that allergen from the patient's environment, and hope to note a decrease in allergic symptoms. If this decrease is found, the allergist nevertheless is quite likely to reintroduce

the allergen to the environment, to see if the allergic symptoms will be recovered. He is, of course, merely checking against the possibility of coincidence: allergic symptoms (like problem behaviors) do occasionally decrease
for unknown reasons, and reappear later. Thus, the allergist is making certain
of his identification of the allergen. In doing so, he is making his patient worse,
briefly, after he had succeeded in making him better. But it is hardly likely that
the allergist would be accused of antitherapeutic practice. He means to advise
his patient to rearrange his environment so as to minimize all future contact
with the allergen. Such rearrangements typically are difficult, drastic, and expensive. The allergist wishes not to advise such a difficult course until he is
certain that it will be a functional course. The analogy to behavior therapy is
close; thus, temporary manipulation of behavioral change, even for the worse,
is not antitherapeutic if it leads the therapist to take wise action in the future
for the client-subject and for other client-subjects with similar problems.

A number of studies cited in this chapter have employed experimental
manipulation to investigate the functional role of their procedures in producing
behavioral changes. One class of techniques employed to accomplish this
demonstration is often referred to as *reversal techniques*. For example, in cases
where a particular set of stimulus consequences appears to have been effective
in developing or maintaining a desirable behavior, this stimulus consequence
may simply be removed from the environment (e.g., Birnbrauer, Wolf, Kidder,
& Tague, 1965); or it may be presented in a noncontingent manner (e.g.,
Risley & Wolf, 1967); or it may be presented contingent upon behaviors incompatible with the desirable behavior (e.g., Sherman, 1965). If the desirable
behavior change is developed or maintained under the original conditions, is
decreased ("reversed") when these changes in procedures are performed, and
is recovered when the original conditions are reinstated, support is added to
the conclusion that the procedures employed, rather than some unspecified
variable, are responsible for the behavior changes.

A possible alternative approach to reversals is the *sequential analysis*.
This type of analysis can be used in cases where a subject exhibits two or more
similar problem behaviors. An environmental manipulation can first be performed on one of the behaviors, then upon the next, and so on. If changes in
each behavior within this one subject are sequentially related to the manipulations applied to them, then the effect of that particular manipulation has been
demonstrated.

The establishment of a functional relationship between a procedure and
a behavior in an individual case does not, of course, establish the generality
of applicability of that procedure for different behaviors of the same subject,
for similar behaviors in different subjects, or for different behaviors in different
subjects. However, the accumulation of many individual cases in which the
functional efficacy of a particular technique has been established for each case
does gradually document generality (Sidman, 1960).

Chapter Summary

This chapter defines operant behavior, describes the general mechanisms of environmental control that are so far known to be applicable to operant behavior, and develops a minimal vocabulary for the systematic discussion of a therapy based on such mechanisms. Therapy is considered to be the process of changing behaviors identified as "problem" behaviors in the environmental context of the subject-client. Thus operant therapy differs from the general area of the experimental analysis of operant behavior only in that the topography of behavior under study has some special social significance. In that this approach constitutes a marked contrast to several of the more traditional concepts and techniques of psychotherapy, its special character is developed in some detail.

Subsequently, that portion of what is considered the behavior therapy literature which embodies operant techniques is reviewed. The review is organized in terms of the basic mechanisms of behavior change known and applied, rather than in terms of the specific behaviors involved. Thus the studies reviewed are grouped primarily as exemplifying controlling contingencies: two reinforcement contingencies, two punishment contingencies, and extinction in its various forms. Techniques of reinforcer development are considered, notably conditioned reinforcement techniques, especially as exemplified in token reinforcement systems. Discrimination and generalization mechanisms are considered in terms of therapeutic applications, discrimination primarily as a method for building desirable new behaviors suitably restricted to appropriate stimulus settings, and generalization as a problem of extending desirable behavior changes beyond the stimulus settings in which they were brought about. Stimulus fading techniques are found to be useful in both problems.

The range of behavior topographies considered includes social interaction skills, language, stuttering, motor abilities, activity level, academic and preacademic accomplishments, imitation, hysterical inabilities, dependence, enuresis, toilet training, self-help and personal care in general, disruptive and aggressive behaviors, transvestite behaviors, deviant sexuality, thumbsucking, stealing, tantrum behaviors, tics, fetishes, writer's cramp, scratching, vomiting, and crying.

The chapter also includes a discussion of the requirements for a believable demonstration that behavioral change did indeed take place and that it took place because of the techniques applied (rather than because of extraneous or unidentified factors). The importance of such demonstrations is emphasized because of the relative novelty of operant techniques in clinical and therapeutic contexts, their related lack of widespread acceptance for such purposes, and the general ethical problem facing any clinical practitioner who needs to be confident of his techniques. Several designs of procedure suitable for both research and clinical application are presented in outline.

6

Appraisal of Behavior Modification Techniques with Adults in Institutional Settings*

GERALD C. DAVISON

State University of New York at Stony Brook

Introduction

Since Lindsley & Skinner's (1954) report of the successful application of operant conditioning procedures to certain very limited behaviors of severely regressed[1] psychotic patients, a lively interest has developed in generalizing to mental hospital populations the techniques and general orientation of Skinnerian psychology. In fewer than a dozen years afterwards, one is aware of attempts, some ambitious, others more restricted, to approach the hospital patient with the same "set" as one would approach a laboratory rat in a Skinner box. In view of the limited usefulness of other therapeutic methods, operantly oriented "behavior therapists" or "behavior modifiers" have been allowed by medical staffs to see whether these new "conditioning procedures" could do any better than the succession of hospital therapies that have ranged

* To David Anderson, Thomas J. D'Zurilla, Cyril M. Franks, Marvin R. Goldfried, Arnold A. Lazarus, Paul Lehrer, K. Daniel O'Leary, and David Pomeranz, the author expresses his thanks for critical reading of preliminary drafts of this chapter. The review of relevant literature was completed in January, 1967.
[1] *Regressed* is used to denote a return to earlier patterns of behavior, without necessary relation to psychoanalytic stages of psychosexual development.

from cold baths and lobotomies to electroconvulsive shocks and chemotherapy. To the dilettante, Skinnerian procedures have at least two powerful attractions: They appear easy to implement, and they seem to work. The intent of this chapter is to cast some constructive doubt on these assumptions.

In the spirit of this book, I (who identify myself with the general area of behavior therapy) will examine critically the clinical and experimental behavior modification research which has been published so far with adults in institutional settings. As others have pointed out (e.g., Breger & McGaugh, 1965), it is indeed time that behavior therapists subjected their own work to the analytic (small "a") scalpel which some have rather intemperately wielded on other therapeutic bodies. Not the least of the favorable features of behavior modification is its amenability to being criticized and to profiting from it.

A few general remarks seem in order at the outset. The present writer takes issue with definitions of "behavior therapy" which limit the field to applications of "modern learning theory" to clinical problems. As Breger and McGaugh (1965) have rightfully pointed out, there is no body of thinking which can be viewed as "modern learning theory." Furthermore, issue is taken also with those who have modified their positions to the extent of stressing instead the empirical commonalities which the various learning theories share: for example, to increase the strength of a response, one should make contingent upon its occurrence a positively reinforcing stimulus (compare with Eysenck, 1964). Issue is taken with such shifts because they do not go far enough in merely acknowledging that there is agreement on the facts of conditioning and disagreement on the explanations. My orientation has been succinctly stated elsewhere (Davison, 1966b, pp. 177f.):

> To the extent that a psychiatric case is considered qualitatively different from so-called normals, afflicted with organic and/or psychic diseases which underlie the observable deviant behavior, one might tend to overlook in therapy the various procedures in general experimental phychology for modifying behavior.... [On the other hand, one can assume] that "mental illness" entails a categorization made in relation to social norms (cf. Bandura and Walters, 1963; Szasz, 1960; Ullmann and Krasner, 1965).... Perhaps it is more fruitful to characterize [this approach as one] ... which makes no assumptions about organic or psychic disease processes, and which therefore can, with some optimism, employ procedures analogous to experimental manipulations from the general area of *psychology*, as opposed to *psychopathology*.

This position appears much closer, then, to that adopted recently by Goldstein, Heller, & Sechrest (1966) than to that held by such writers as Eysenck, Wolpe, Skinner, and Ayllon. Many of those who have spent hours in the consulting room are often painfully aware of the constraints of a conditioning model. It is probably not too soon to stop writing our articles as if these "nonspecifics" (which would include nonconditioning variables) do not exist (compare with Lazarus & Davison, in press).

It will be well to make another bias explicit. While most of the work to be reviewed focuses on overt behavior, one need not limit behavior modification to overt muscular movements. Dollard & Miller (1950) long ago presented a convicing case for regarding covert responses as "little r's" which obey the same laws as do "the big R's" that the operant conditioner sees as his only legitimate domain of investigation (see Hefferline, 1962, for an exciting exception). Many "hard-nosed" learning theorists have since that time provided reviews and arguments in favor of this mediating behavioristic view (e.g., Miller, 1959; Mowrer, 1960a; Osgood, 1953; Staats & Staats, 1963). Provided that one anchors his intervening variables securely on both the antecedent and the consequent ends, there seems little reason to shy away from conceptualizing the human being—especially a hospital patient—as operating in such a fashion as to be understandable, predictable, and controllable on the basis of functional relationships which go beyond the immediate observables. In other words, a mediational SR position will be taken in this chapter.

Operant conditioning. The general features of operant conditioning have been described in many places and will not be reviewed here. The reader is referred to, *inter alia,* Skinner (1953), Ferster & Skinner (1957), Lundin (1961), Staats & Staats (1963), Sidman (1962), and Bachrach (1964). A passing comment, however, would seem to be in order with regard to terminology: strictly speaking, *negative reinforcement* increases the probability of a response via *removal* of an aversive stimulus, while *punishment* decreases the probability via *presentation* of an aversive stimulus; these terms are often confused in the behavior modification literature.

Operant techniques have the singular virtue of being aimed at the manipulation of the behavior of an individual organism (compare with Bachrach, 1964; Lindsley, 1960; Sidman, 1962) rather than restricted to drawing conclusions about group averages. Moreover, when working within an operant framework, one is compelled to specify very carefully what he is interested in observing and manipulating. Thus, "hostility" is defined in terms of the frequency of responses which typically inflict pain on another; and as shall be seen, "problem eaters" are defined as people who engage frequently in behaviors such as arriving late in a dining room and spilling food on other patients. Indeed, the use of operant procedures in institutional settings rests on the assumption that the most important aspects of the patient are clearly observable acts, in contrast with inferred internal states (compare with Ayllon, 1963; Ferster & DeMeyer, 1961; Skinner, 1953).

Outline of Chapter. Variables other than the degree and nature of deviant behavior play an important role in determining whether a person becomes a mental hospital patient, e.g., availability of hospitals and financial circumstances. Furthermore, the populations of mental hospitals are heterogeneous to a very marked degree. For these reasons, focusing on "behavior modification with adults in institutional settings" might be considered a rather arbitrary and irrelevant categorization. Nonetheless, within the past fifteen years enough studies have been done under this rubric to render worthwhile a critical examination of behavioral work with hospitalized adult patients. Moreover, as has been suggested by many writers (e.g., Fairweather, 1964; Goffman, 1961), the institutionalization of an adult human being seems to create problems of desocialization and even dehumanization which can neutralize or outweigh any therapeutic effects thought possible through hospitalization.

This review will be divided into four segments: operant conditioning of specific target nonverbal behaviors, verbal conditioning, operant conditioning of ward-wide behaviors ("token economy"), and other behavioral approaches. Clearly, the literature could have been divided in any number of other ways.

Moreover, much that will be said here will have obvious implications for work outside institutions, as well as for work with children. Several other chapters in this volume review such research in depth (see Sherman & Baer, Chapter 5; Patterson, Chapter 9).

A general theme of the present chapter will be the limitations imposed by following a particular model. Most of the work, it will be seen, is most readily cast in operant conditioning terms, and it is so construed by the overwhelming majority of the authors. However, in many instances adherence to this model has blinded investigators to what appear to me to be crucial issues, both theoretical and practical. Pushing a given model to the fullest is an excellent way to assess its utility; yet, at the same time, this procedure makes salient often glaring inadequacies and limitations. Even this effect is much to its credit.

Operant Conditioning of Selected "Target" Nonverbal Behaviors

In this section we shall review those clinical and experimental studies which are characterized by the selection of specific nonverbal patient behaviors for manipulation through extinction procedures, incompatible response procedures, positive reinforcement, negative reinforcement, or punishment. Studies in verbal conditioning will be considered in a separate section.

Fuller (1949) reports what is probably the first deliberate attempt to apply operant procedures to an institutionalized human being. Via successive approximations with warm sugar-milk as reinforcer, he shaped the movement of the right arm in an eighteen-year-old "vegetative idiot." Subsequent withdrawal of the milk resulted in the expected extinction of the response.

The experimental analysis of the behavior of psychotic patients can probably be said to have begun in earnest with Lindsley and Skinner's (1954) report of the adaptation of the Skinner box to experiments with adult mental hospital patients. In this report, and in subsequent ones (Lindsley, 1956, 1960), the utility of this technique was amply demonstrated: even severely regressed schizophrenics[2] were able to learn a simple lever-pulling response in order to obtain a wide variety of reinforcements, from cigarettes and candy to giving milk to hungry kittens (as a measure of "altruism"). The advantages of this procedure, as pointed out by Lindsley, are (1) the high degree of experimental control, (2) the exclusion of observer bias through automatic recording and scheduling, (3) the high generality made possible through varying the drive state of the subject, as well as the manipulanda and reinforcements, (4) the feasibility of obtaining vast amounts of data from a single subject, and (5) the very minor role played by verbal instructions, particularly advantageous with regressed psychotics. This Massachusetts Metropolitan State Hospital work firmly established operant conditioning principles and technology as appropriate to the measurement and manipulation of psychotic behavior.

The work is significant furthermore in making explicit an assumption which underlies virtually all the operant work reviewed here, namely, that "If psychosis is what makes, or has made, this person psychotic, then psychosis is the behavioral deviation that caused this person to be hospitalized, or that is keeping him hospitalized" (Lindsley, 1960, p. 66). Thus, the focus is on observable, measurable, overt operant behaviors, with little attention paid to mediating processes. After showing how marked decreases in rate of responding tended to correlate with observations of psychotic behavior (hallucinating, destructive outbursts, etc.), Lindsley (1960) proposed that such behavior be characterized as responding in such a manner as to compete with task requirements in a given situation. Thus, the important aspect of psychotic behavior might be not its content, but rather the fact that it occurs frequently and in competition with "normal" behaviors.

The words "operant" and "response contingent" are not used once in an early article by Peters & Jenkins (1954), but their study is clearly relevant to this chapter, as well as being one of the more clinically significant pieces of work. On the assumption that "schizophrenia" entails a replacement of adaptive responding by stereotyped, frustration-induced behavior, these investigators set out to test the global clinical effects of extended "guided problem-solving motivated by hunger." The rationale was that if the patient could be motivated to deal realistically with graded problems, this successful interaction would generalize to variables such as nurses' ratings of ward behavior.

The crux of the therapy for their long-term male schizophrenics was making food reinforcement contingent upon successes on graded problem-

[2] The word "schizophrenic" and its variants are used to designate individuals so labeled; the use of such psychiatric terms will not, in this chapter, imply an acceptance of the traditional nosology.

solving tasks, beginning with simple mazes and culminating in problems as complex as interpreting proverbs; the later tasks were reinforced with approval and praise. A control group was given similar doses of insulin to provoke ravenous hunger; this drive state, however, was reduced by simply serving food noncontingently.

During the six months immediately following this three-month experimental phase, each of the patients was measured on a variety of variables, including (1) incidence of negative events recorded in folders, e.g., fighting with another patient, (2) being granted partial privileges, (3) being sent home on a trial visit, and (4) performance in occupational therapy (OT).

The results provide strong evidence in favor of the hypothesis that the guided problem solving led to significant clinical improvement on all measures. Moreover, the group which served as control for attention and insulin injections did not differ significantly from a no-treatment group. That these differences showed up on measures quite remote from the specific reinforced behaviors constitutes striking data on generalization effects.

Unfortunately, there are two methodological problems which warrant considerable caution in interpreting these very convincing and important results. First, there is no indication in the article that the behavior ratings were done by people who were unaware of which treatment group a given patient was in. Second, while the insulin control group did receive at least as much personal attention and insulin as did the experimentals, it would have been preferable had these controls been provided with some sort of meaningful task with noncontingent, personally administered fudge rewards instead of merely being ushered into a room for breakfast. Be that as it may, this experiment is extremely provocative evidence of the general and important kinds of improvement which may be possible through carefully planned, reinforced problem solving.

In a similar study, King, Armitage, & Tilton (1960) report the use of the Multiple Operant Problem-Solving Apparatus (MOPSA) with severely regressed, largely mute male schizophrenics. Proceeding from the observation that the behaviors still intact were motor, these investigators arranged for both primary and secondary reinforcements (praise) to be contingent on increasingly complex motor interactions with an automated apparatus that presented manageable problems similar to the machines created by Lindsley & Skinner (1954). Patients were matched with Ss in three control groups: recreational therapy, verbal psychotherapy, and no particular therapy. Three times weekly over 3½ months, for about half an hour a day, patients in the "operant-interpersonal" group were encouraged by an experimenter to respond appropriately to various problems presented on the apparatus; ultimately other patients were introduced, making cooperative behavior necessary to obtain rewards in a manner similar to the work of Azrin & Lindsley (1956) with normal children. Ss in the recreational and verbal therapy control groups met for equivalent amounts of time with other therapists, while the no-therapy controls merely continued to participate in the usual ward activities. The effects of these interventions were assessed by various rating scales of ward behavior, filled out by ward personnel who did not participate in the treatment phases of the study. Results showed that the increased goal-oriented activity with the MOPSA was accompanied by clinical improvement on the ward, to a very significant degree. Less controlled observations attested further to the changes effected in the operant group; e.g., one morning a long-term mute patient greeted the experimenter with "Good morning. Got a match?" This study furnishes strong additional data in support of the suitability of this primarily nonverbal procedure for helping withdrawn patients establish meaningful contact with the environment, with indications of beneficial generalization to extratherapy situations.

Brief mention can be made of two articles in which hospitalized schizophrenics were used far more as available subjects to investigate theoretical matters than as patient-subjects to explore clinically relevant behavior modification techniques. Hutchison & Azrin (1961) describe the development of plunger pulling on a Lindsley-type apparatus for various fixed-ratio schedules of reinforcements. In spite of the patients being chronic, the usual high rates of responding were gradually built into each man with successively increasing response-reinforcement ratios. Holz, Azrin, & Ayllon (1963), using a similar apparatus, except with two different manipulanda instead of only one, found that a response which led to a time-out from positive reinforcement on a well-learned habit was eliminated significantly more quickly and thoroughly if an alternative response was available for obtaining positive reinforcement. It is interesting to the present writer that in both studies very specific verbal instructions and even demonstrations of the contingencies were given to patients in order to accelerate the responding; more will be seen of this.

Mertens & Fuller (1963) effected improvement in shaving by regressed psychotic patients with a combination of instructions and reinforcers such as chewing gum. In an attempt to control for the importance of the contingency, they included a group which likewise received rewards, albeit in a noncontingent manner. Although their results are equivocal statistically, the contingent reinforcement seemed to lead to significant improvement in the target behavior.

Bachrach, Erwin, & Mohr (1965) report an operant approach to severe eating problems in a female medical patient. This thirty-seven-year-old moribund woman had been losing weight for about the previous seventeen years, and the prognosis was extremely poor. Apparently because of the failure of medical intervention, permission was obtained for the implementation of an operant program which required the cooperation of the entire staff of the psychiatric ward to which she had been transferred in desperation.

Therapy entailed depriving her of niceties such as visitors and flowers in the room; these events were made contingent upon approximations to eating and ultimately to gaining weight (this change in target behavior being made because of suspicions that she had been privately vomiting the food she had ingested for reinforcement). Weight gain was continued on an outpatient basis, with both her family and the "normal" reinforcing environment apparently serving to foster noninvalid behavior. The orderliness of improvement after many years of steady deterioration would seem to argue well against a "placebo" interpretation of these striking clinical results.

Probably the most extensive, original, and widely quoted work in the area of behavior modification in institutional settings has been done by Teodoro Ayllon and his associates at the Saskatchewan Hospital in Canada and, more recently, at Anna State Hospital in Illinois. Because references to Ayllon's work are becoming more and more frequent, it is worthwhile to examine it closely and very critically. For purposes of exposition, comments will be made only after describing all pertinent studies.

Ayllon & Michael (1959) report several different cases of mostly long-term schizophrenic patients hospitalized on a ward managed almost entirely by psychiatric nurses. Training involved an undoing of the usual psychiatric nursing instruction which stresses noncontingent care while leaving specific tactics pretty much up to the individual nurse. The behavioral strategies employed were varied: extinction, extinction combined with reinforcement for incompatible behavior, reinforcement of incompatible behavior, escape and avoidance training, and stimulus satiation. An example can serve to illustrate the straightforward and clever extrapolation and application of simple conditioning principles. One female schizophrenic refused to eat unless spoonfed by a nurse. Noting that she cared about keeping her clothes neat, Ayllon and Michael instructed the nurses to spill small amounts of food on her dress while feeding her, while at the same time praising her for any self-feeding attempts. Over a period of eight weeks, self-feeding became fairly steadily the rule. It is significant that the success of this program led to her discharge, for her admission nine months earlier had been based on her refusal to eat, combined with concerns about poison in the food. The implication of the authors is that the delusional thinking about food dropped out when the overt behavior was changed.

Ayllon & Haughton (1962) report three field experiments on controlling the behavior of hospitalized patients with food. In the first study, patients who had consistently had to be spoonfed or otherwise goaded into eating were denied access to the dining room if they failed to enter within a given period of time following the announcement of the meal. After missing a few meals, most of the 32 chronic schizophrenics learned to enter the dining room within five minutes of the announcements, a significant change from their previous behavior. Without paying attention, then, to the "mental condition" which the psychiatric staff had assumed underlay the reluctance to eat unassisted, Ayllon

& Haughton altered a very significant "psychotic" behavior simply by treating it like any other operant.

Next, some of these patients had to drop a coin into a can in order to gain access to the dining room. Finally, food reinforcement was effective in getting patients to cooperate: two buttons were placed 7 feet apart, and the task was to depress both of them simultaneously in order to obtain the penny required for gaining access (compare with Azrin & Lindsley, 1956; Hingtgen, Sanders, & DeMeyer, 1965). An interesting incidental finding is that situation-appropriate verbal interaction increased among the patients as they dealt with this new problem-solving situation. Also noteworthy is the use of simple verbal instructions from the nursing staff on the nature of each task, viz., "Give this penny to the nurse when you go to eat" (Allyon & Haughton, 1962, p. 346). This anticipates the study of Ayllon & Azrin (1964), to be discussed below.

Another incidental finding, mentioned in passing by the authors, is that one patient failed to learn to cooperate with another in the two-button experiment in order to obtain the pennies needed for entrance into the dining-room. Instead, she "continued paying for meals by finding pennies, and even dimes, which she exchanged for pennies" (Allyon & Haughton, 1962, p. 349). While the authors report this instance as failure to set up the contingencies with enough care (which is true), it seems likely that this task required considerable ingenuity and "nonpsychotic" behavior, which might be seen as even more impressive than the cooperative social responses learned by the other patients.

A concentrated application of operant procedures to the "crazy" behavior of a single patient is provided in an interesting case report by Ayllon (1963). A female patient, hospitalized for nine years, exhibited three principle undesirable behaviors: stealing food, hoarding towels, and wearing too many clothes. Each of these behaviors was treated separately and consecutively, with follow-up ranging up to a year: there was no evidence of "symptom substitution" or return of the behaviors. The stealing of food was eliminated simply by removing her from the dining room when she attempted to steal. The hoarding of towels was checked by providing her with excessive supplies of towels, making her room quite crowded and hence uncomfortable. The wearing of too many clothes was handled by setting limits on how much she could weigh prior to obtaining entrance to the dining room. Although she was still in the institution at the time of the writing, she nonetheless was reported to have made a better social adjustment within the hospital and was even taken out on pass by relatives for the first time since admission.

Ayllon & Azrin (1964) studied the relative contributions of verbal instructions and positive reinforcement in modifying psychotic behavior. In their first experiment, 18 female patients (15 classified as schizophrenic, 3 as mentally defective) with a median duration of hospitalization of thirteen years were observed with reference to the frequency of picking up all the usual eating utensils prior to entering the cafeteria line. Since they had been selected from the ward on the basis of a virtual absence of this behavior, it was not surprising to find a near zero percentage of patients performing the target behavior, which entailed picking up a knife, fork, and spoon, during the 10 base-line meals. The reinforcement procedure was then introduced, i.e., if a patient performed the response, she was given an extra milk; explanations offered by the attendants took the form of: "We have some extras today." The percentages went up only slightly during this operant reinforcement period, primarily because so few patients performed the response at all. Finally, each patient was told: "Please pick up your knife, fork, and spoon, and you have a choice of extra milk, coffee, cigarettes, or candy" (p. 323). The percentage of patients doing so in this instruction-plus-operant-reinforcement period went up dramatically. Although long-term change was not the purpose of the study, 6 of the 18 patients were reported to be still performing the response one year later, after the experiment had been terminated.

In order to ascertain whether instructions alone could effect such behavior change, a second study was conducted with a similar sample of patients. This time the operant consequences were immediacy of access to the serving line; i.e., if the appropriate response was not made, a delay was imposed. After base-line observation, the same instructions as above were given to each patient, but with no differential consequences. After 100 meals of instructions alone, the aforementioned consequences were applied contingent upon following the verbally presented instructions. Results showed that instructions alone boosted the percentage of patients performing the response to between 40 and 70 percent, with considerable variability. When the consequences (i.e., extra food) were added, the percentage increased to between 90 and 100 percent, thus indicating the superiority of the combination of procedures.

CRITIQUE OF THE AYLLON STUDIES

The extensive series of studies reported by Ayllon & Azrin (1965) will be described in a later section on ward-wide operant reinforcement procedures. A critical examination of the work thus far summarized will now be presented, for many of the issues raised here are crucial and relevant to work yet to be reviewed.

In the study by Ayllon & Michael (1959), an example is given of a female schizophrenic patient whose refusal to eat, apparently based upon a belief that the food was poison, was eliminated by having the nurse spill food on the clothes which the patient liked to keep clean. After eight weeks of this intentionally messy spoonfeeding, the patient finally began to feed herself in order to avoid having her clothes soiled by the "careless" nurse. When the problem in eating was thereby eliminated, Ayllon and Michael assumed that the "psychotic" belief about food had likewise been changed. If one accepts their Skinnerian assumption that any mediator such as "crazy belief" or "anxiety" is eliminated through eliminating the avoidant behavior (compare with Skinner, 1953; Lundin, 1961), then, indeed, the woman no longer believed that her food was being poisoned. The only problem is that this definition of the patient's inappropriate attitude towards food may be too narrow in this instance. We must speculate, inasmuch as the data relevant to the issue are not provided in the article, but surely a relevant question is: What did the patient think about food after she had begun to feed herself without coaxing from the nurse? The present writer's own bias would have led him to ask the patient about this, as well as to observe her behavior in other situations to see whether, in some way, her "crazy belief" about food (or people) might reliably be inferred. It is possible, moreover, that more basic than her fears of being poisoned was a distrust of strangers. This being the case, her subsequent discharge (because of the elimination of the eating problem) may not have been the wisest decision. Because the suggestions being made here are verifiable in terms of observable situations, the author is not simply offering the kind of argument frequently made by insight-oriented therapists whose inferences are not always testable by appeal to public data (compare with the critical discussion of "insight therapy" by London, 1964).

The essence of this objection, then, is that by assuming that a particular behavior constitutes a completely adequate definition (or behavioral analysis) of a particular mediating process (such as believing that food is poisonous), Ayllon & Michael perhaps have overlooked the failure of their behavior modification technique to alter another class of even more important behaviors. It is interesting also to note that the authors obviously paid attention to the patient's verbalizations about food prior to the conditioning procedures —how else could they know that the patient thought the food was poison?— but did not rely on verbal report following the change in eating behavior to the extent of asking the patient outright about her thoughts in relation to food.

A not unrelated problem stems from the assumption being made by Ayllon and his colleagues that the behaviors they are dealing with, no matter what their topography, are operant in function (see Ferster, 1965). This assumption leads them to focus on events which follow a given behavior, to the virtual exclusion of other variables that may be playing an important role in maintaining the behavior in question. This is easily illustrated in their own work, although, once again, some speculation will be necessary to fill in the gaps caused by their failure to report possibly relevant material. One of the cases reported by Ayllon & Michael (1959) is of a violent patient whose outbursts they tried to eliminate by ignoring them as well as by reinforcing an incompatible response, in this instance, squatting on the floor. After establishing the squatting response (which eliminated the violent behaviors), the staff then attempted to develop a more appropriate behavior, namely, approaching the nurse. This change in procedure precipitated such violence that the patient was dropped immediately from the investigation. It is unfortunate that Ayllon & Michael did not take advantage of this negative result to learn more about the patient's violent behavior. The assessment which they made was clearly inappropriate and/or incomplete, and, I contend, this error is probably attributable to their overly simplified conception of "psychotic" behavior. First of all, it is not known what kinds of situations triggered the violent outbursts initially. Simply that the attention of the staff usually followed such behaviors does not necessarily mean that the attention was the only variable maintaining the behavior. To say that attention was the only variable would be analogous to saying that atomic tests in Nevada are maintained solely by the attention they receive from reporters, and that, if one withdraws this attention, the atomic devices (which we know are set for other purposes) will soon no longer be detonated. To return to the patient, it does not seem unreasonable to hypothesize that the violent outbursts were triggered by tensions built up by disturbing thoughts. Certainly the extensive clinical evidence from "behavior modifiers" such as Wolpe & Lazarus (1966) indicates strongly that a wide variety of deviant behaviors are a function of antecedent conditions such as anxiety and tension and only partly, if at all, a function of their consequences. Without a more complete behavioral analysis of a problem such as violent behaviors, one is simply asking for trouble, which is precisely what Ayllon & Michael encountered in this instance. Furthermore, before making the decision to teach a social response such as approaching a nurse, one would have advised these workers to find out something about the patient's attitudes toward the staff. Of course, there could also have been neurophysiological factors operating. Or perhaps the initial violence was related to that observed when this last shaping procedure was instituted. Again, one can only guess at the reasons for this unexpected finding; but no guesswork is involved in inferring that the procedures employed were quite inappropriate to the particular instance.

Another case from the Ayllon & Michael (1959) article, along with one (Ayllon & Haughton, 1964) from a study to be mentioned in the verbal conditioning section, will serve as a springboard for a related issue. Ayllon & Michael instructed the staff to ignore the incessant "psychotic" talk of one female patient; hitherto, nurses had been paying considerable attention to her speech in their attempts to get to the "root of the problem." These extinction procedures, when combined with positive reinforcement for nondelusional talk, resulted in markedly reducing the frequency of the inappropriate verbalizations. Once again, however, we find ourselves asking whether the "crazy talk" was not part of another functional class of behaviors, for example, behavior that serves to reduce subjective distress.[3] Removal of this behavior without

[3] This concern has been independently voiced in an excellent paper by Simkins (1966).

taking care that its antecedents had been eliminated might lead to what looks like "symptom substitution," which might better be regarded as incomplete treatment (compare with Lazarus, 1965b).

Fortunately, Ayllon & Haughton (1964) provide some data which remove the need for merely engaging in speculation. The staff were extinguishing the somatic verbal complaints of one of the patients. During this procedure, however, when such verbal responses were approaching zero frequency, the authors observed a sudden and surprising increase in frequency. They then report (pp. 93–94):

> ...an instance where an extraneous event temporarily influenced the frequency of somatic responses. This occurred when a relative visited Suzy at the hospital and informed her that she had to sign some property over to her.... During this period the patient was particularly distressed because she regarded her relative's insistence on having the patient's property signed over as evidence that the family planned to leave her in the hospital.

Their integrity in reporting this event is exceeded only by what seems to this writer their blindness to an alternative, and probably more valid explanation. While the writers do not state that the sudden increase was a function of different reinforcement contingencies by the relatives (as they do state in a very similar case, Helen, in Ayllon & Michael, 1959), I will, for the sake of argument, infer that they regarded the change in this way. Even if this is not the case, however, it is clear that they do omit from consideration the possibility that Suzy's "crazy talk" was a function of tension or anxiety, in addition to being maintained to some degree by social reinforcement. The fact that such talk increased after an occurrence which the authors, themselves, describe as distressing, supports this notion.

Paying attention to deviant behavior, while it probably serves in some degree to reinforce it, is often necessary in eliminating the behavior. This point is illustrated in both clinical and experimental studies from an area of behavior modification which is seldom associated with studies in institutional settings (but see later section on Other Behavioral Approaches). For example, Lazarus, Davison, & Polefka (1965) report the case of a school-phobic child, who, while hardly psychotic, did become so anxious as sometimes to report dissociated feelings. These authors suggest that, when avoidance behavior is mediated by high levels of anxiety (as inferred from degree of avoidance, self-reports, and easily observable signs such as whining, shivering, and blanching), a counterconditioning procedure is needed to reduce the anxiety, *even at the cost of reinforcing the avoidance behavior.* And, in addition to numerous clinical reports, there is a growing body of experimental evidence demonstrating the efficacy of Wolpe's technique of systematic desensitization (Wolpe, 1958) in significantly reducing often very extreme anxiety and avoidance behavior (e.g.,

Davison, 1968b; Lang, Lazovik, & Reynolds, 1965; Paul, 1966). If one examines the details of this procedure, it is clear that considerable attention is paid to "sick talk," for much time and care are expended in drawing up anxiety hierarchies. If therapy were seen as nothing but the elimination of verbalizations centering around unrealistic fears, and if, furthermore, one proceeded immediately, as does Ayllon, to extinguish such talk through nonreinforcement, one would not draw up such hierarchies. The only problem is that, even if the given client were to stop talking about his fears, he would probably still be afraid: there is yet to be reported an experiment demonstrating the elimination of a neurotic fear through verbal conditioning procedures.

The case study of Ayllon (1963) will serve nicely in examining a problem which is central to the whole area of behavior modification. Recall that a technique termed "stimulus satiation" was employed to eliminate the crazy behavior of hoarding towels. As Simkins (1966) points out, this concept is taken over from experimental psychology with infrahuman organisms, in which there is ample evidence that making a reinforcing stimulus freely available to a subject ultimately renders the stimulus incapable of functioning as a reinforcer. In the case of a hungry rat, for example, food pellets cease being reinforcers for that animal when his drive state is reduced. Whether one subscribes to a drive-reduction view of reinforcement or not is irrelevant. The central issue is that "stimulus satiation" makes sense only if it has been independently demonstrated that the particular stimulus was once a reinforcer. There is no such evidence in Ayllon's article. Simkins suggests that Ayllon should have tried to strengthen some behavior other than towel hoarding; to the extent that other behaviors could be increased in frequency or amplitude, he would have had better justification for describing his technique as he did (cf. Meehl, 1950).

The study by Ayllon & Azrin (1964) assesses experimentally the relative contributions of verbally presented instructions and response contingencies. Hints of the use of "discriminative stimuli" such as instructions can be found in some of his earlier work. The recognition of the central role played by presumably covert responses (compare with Dollard & Miller, 1950) such as "thoughts" and "feelings" takes the operant conditioner considerably beyond the original work of Lindsley & Skinner, in which, like the laboratory animal in the Skinner box, the subject was not informed of the steps which he could take to obtain reinforcements. A similar development is readily seen in the operant work with severely disturbed children, where one can compare the early more strictly Skinnerian work (e.g., Ferster, 1961) with later more clinically oriented work (e.g., Davison, 1964, 1965c) in which contingencies were liberally spelled out in considerable detail. The role of "covert thinking responses" in operant conditioning has been well described by Hefferline (1962), Staats & Staats (1963), and, more recently, Homme (1965). Whether one conceptualizes the operations of telling the subject what you want him to do and what he will get if he does it as "in accord with the theory and practice of operant conditioning" (Ayllon & Azrin, 1964, p. 330) or whether one adopts a cognitive position (Peterson & London, 1965; Davison, 1966b) seems to me less important at this juncture than the establishment of verbal communication of contingencies as part of the behavior modifier's armamentorium. This will be seen again in the discussion of large-scale operant programs.

Before leaving the study by Ayllon & Azrin (1964), mention should be made of a methodological flaw. It is possible that these authors are dealing at times more with the effects of wrong instructions than with no instructions, for "on a few occasions during a no-instruction-operant-reinforcement period," patients inquired about why they were not obtaining extra food, and were misinformed that this change in procedure had nothing to do with their behavior, i.e., that it was entirely fortuitous. This, of course, was not true, and the deception may have contributed to the poor performance observed in the reinforcement-only condition. Human beings are different from rats and pigeons in sometimes vexing ways.

CLOSING NOTE

In these studies we have seen the effective application of response contingencies in measurably altering behavior that had been designated as "psychotic," usually by virtue of the person's status as a mental hospital patient. Several studies have even provided suitable evidence that, in fact, it is the response-contingent reinforcements or lack thereof which are mediating the observed changes. A few of the studies, e.g., Peters & Jenkins (1954), have demonstrated the apparent power of restricted shaping in effecting generalization to other behaviors, such as adjustment on a ward. The work of Ayllon and his colleagues, Haughton, Azrin, and Michael, illustrates courageous and ambitious attempts to tackle long-standing and obviously resistant behavior problems in severely regressed patients.

On the other hand, many of these studies have been shown to have methodological and conceptual shortcomings. Although it is sometimes speculative, evidence has been provided from many of the studies themselves to indicate the inappropriate application of a strictly operant model to behavior which is probably not only topographically more complex than a lever press, but also functionally more complex as well. Looking at their patients with a particular set, Ayllon et al. seem to have been overlooking other very important variables which might play a part in determining the occurrence of given "psychotic" behaviors. More specifically, the Skinnerian orientation followed by all the workers seen so far appears to have prevented a consideration of emotional antecedents to some of the behavioral difficulties, viz., the example of Suzy (Ayllon & Haughton, (1964). In a later section, behavior modification strategies that others have employed with patients similarly disturbed will be examined; the contrast will be evident in that these other workers, after entering a hospital setting, have not forgotten the clinical and experimental research done with nonhospitalized people.

Verbal Conditioning in Institutional Settings

Since Greenspoon's (1951) dissertation, which demonstrated a significant increase in the frequency of plural nouns when various stimuli ("mm-hmmm," a red light, and a tone) are made contingent on their occurrence, numerous studies have been reported to replicate and extend this primary finding. Since most of the work has been with nonpsychiatric subjects, it will not be considered here. Several reviews have already been published (Greenspoon, 1962; Kanfer, in press; Krasner, 1958a, Salzinger, 1959b; Williams, 1964), and whether the outcomes are due to the subject's formation of hypotheses on the contingencies (e.g., Spielberger & DeNike, 1966; Dulany, 1961) or whether conditioning is occurring without awareness (e.g., Krasner, Weiss, & Ullmann, 1961), the phenomenon has nonetheless been firmly established: the verbal responses of human subjects can be significantly altered by contingent administration of both primary and secondary reinforcers. For our purposes, we shall adopt the generally accepted definition of "verbal conditioning" as "the systematic application of social reinforcements to influence the probability of another person emitting a specifiable verbal behavior (Krasner, 1965, p. 213)." It might further be noted that the actual responses reinforced are usually already in the subject's repertoire, but so long as one regards the conditioning process as effecting a shift in the probability of making a predetermined response via response-contingent reinforcement, we may continue to regard the paradigm as operant (Greenspoon, 1962, p. 516).

This general approach to language is readily traced to Skinner's (1948b, 1957) conceptualization of speech as behavior which follows the same laws as the motoric behavior studied extensively in infrahuman organisms. The studies to be reviewed below are to be seen within this framework. Although I agree completely with the general behavior modification position that research with nonclinical populations is relevant to patient populations, the review will, in keeping with the title of this chapter, be restricted to experiments carried out with hospitalized psychiatric patients.

AFFECTIVELY TONED WORDS

In the same year, Krasner (1958b) and Salzinger & Pisoni (1958) reported the first successful application of operant conditioning techniques to the verbal behavior of hospitalized mental patients. Krasner reinforced two male "schizophrenic reactions in remission" for any references to "mother" during a free operant story telling situation. Salzinger & Pisoni, in a similar situation, increased the verbal output of self-referred affect statements in newly admitted schizophrenics. In both studies decreases were noted during extinction trials. Moreover, the latter study furnished evidence that the results were due to specific reinforcement effects: classes of self-referred statements other than that being reinforced did not increase significantly, and the number of reinforcements during acquisition was significantly correlated with the number of self-referred statements in extinction.

Similar results have been reported by Hagen (1959, as cited by Greenspoon, 1962), Ullmann, Krasner, & Sherman (1963), and Weiss, Krasner, & Ullmann (1963).

MUTISM

Isaacs, Thomas, & Goldiamond (1960) reinstated verbal behavior in two schizophrenics who had been mute for nineteen and fourteen years. Verbal behavior was shaped via the method of successive approximations, beginning with eye movements, facial movements, lip movements, and grunts, and proceeding to intelligible speech. It is of interest that the first real utterance of one man was emitted all at once, to wit: after making the chewing-gum reinforcer contingent upon any spontaneous vocalization at all, the experimenter verbally urged the patient to say "Gum"; after several unsuccessful sessions, the subject suddenly said "Gum, please," after which other verbal behaviors could be elicited by the experimenter. Generalization to other ward personnel was effected without difficulty by instructing them to refrain from interpreting the man's nonverbal requests, as had been done for the previous nineteen years. A similar case has been described by Sherman (1963).

In a more recent study, Sherman (1965) has reported a carefully controlled experiment on the role of various operant procedures over extended periods of time (more than 100 sessions) in instating verbal behavior in mute hospital patients. His three subjects were all long-term state hospital patients, with mutism ranging from sixteen to forty-five years. Three techniques were used, as appropriate: shaping of responses (beginning sometimes with lip movements, vide Isaacs et al., 1960), reinforcement for imitating the experimenter, and fading (gradually changing the stimulus conditions that control a response so as to bring the behavior under different discriminative stimulus control with few if any errors, cf. Moore & Goldiamond, 1964). The reader is referred to Sherman's article for excellent detailed descriptions of how these techniques were applied in each individual instance. It should be mentioned that the role of reinforcement contingencies was convincingly demonstrated by reinforcing nonverbal behaviors for a while after verbal responses had been instated: the expected decrease in frequency of the latter was observed.

Sherman's use of imitative procedures should be described here. One of the patients exhibited practically no verbal behavior (not even grunts) after

35 experimental sessions of trying to shape up any sort of vocalization. In order to establish behavior for shaping, the experimenter rewarded the patient for imitating some simple nonverbal behaviors, such as standing up. These behaviors were gradually changed to approximate verbal behaviors (e.g., hissing), and, within 20 sessions, verbal behavior of suitable variability was being emitted for differential reinforcement. All Ss maintained their respective new verbal behavioral repertoires when a second experimenter duplicated a few of the later sessions, and generalization was likewise noted, in some degree, to the ward.

Wilson & Walters (1966) have also successfully employed modeling procedures, with and without complementary reinforcement, to increase verbal output in severely regressed predominantly mute schizophrenics. Their results indicate that the combination of model plus reinforcement for imitation effected significant increase in output, as did just the use of a talkative model; both groups were superior to a control group, which received equal amounts of attention and reinforcement (noncontingently).

No appreciable generalization to the ward, however, was observed. It is interesting to note that the introduction of a talkative model had been made following pilot work which had shown the failure of shaping alone to increase output in the patients used. Furthermore, in a more clinical spirit, several of the schizophrenics were given more extended training involving no modeling, only prompt and contingent reinforcement: having been brought up to some level of verbal output via the modeling procedures, these patients then dramatically increased in output even more. These data, then, suggest the peculiar appropriateness of modeling when operant levels are especially low; once occurring, the behaviors can then be effectively strengthened even further with the usual operant reinforcement (cf. Bandura & Walters, 1963).

"SICK TALK"

Rickard, Dignam, & Horner (1960) report the application of differential reinforcement to delusional and rational speech in a sixty-year-old chronic neuropsychiatric male patient, hospitalized continuously for twenty years. The operant level of delusional talk, e.g., "Stars have metal bottoms and exert a magnetic pressure on the earth," was about forty-three out of forty-five minutes. When it occurred, the experimenter looked away; he paid attention and expressed interest only when rational speech was emitted. In thirty-five sessions, rational speech was occurring about half the time. In a second experiment, another experimenter interacted similarly with the same patient over a period of six months, this time actively interrupting delusional talk and eliciting rational talk. This procedure was replicated by a third experimenter. During these studies also, ward staff were instructed to engage the man in similar fashion. With this intensive and manipulative approach, the experimenters were able to maintain rational speech nearly all the time. Decrements in non-delusional speech were observed when social reinforcement was made inter-mittent and noncontingent. It should be noted, however, that the authors seem to be unaware of the significance of altering the contingency relationship be-tween rational talk and social rewards, for they term "minimal" or "partial" those sessions in which the experimenter expressed interest only rarely and irrespective of the content of talk. At any rate, considerable generalization was found from the "maximal" (100 percent contingent reinforcement) to the "minimal" reinforcement sessions, as well as to the ward, and it is of course plausible to assume that the contingencies set by the ward staff were generaliz-ing also to the experimental sessions. A two-year follow-up is reported by Rickard & Dinoff (1962), in which two 30-minute sessions showed the man responding almost all the time with rational speech. The results are, indeed, impressive, although their limitations are obvious in view of the fact that the patient was still available in the hospital for the two-year follow-up.

Ullmann, Krasner, & Edinger (1964) demonstrated significant increase in common associations to words in 20 chronic long-term schizophrenic VA patients, replicating an earlier finding by Sommer, Witney, & Osmond (1962). The latter investigators had used cigarettes as reinforcers, while Ullmann et al. used the familiar "mmh-hmm" with accompanying smile and head nod. Generalization to another task, the Sarbin-Hardyck Stick Figure Test (Sarbin & Hardyck, 1955), was not obtained. The significance of the study clearly lies in its demonstration that, after only a single verbal conditioning session, a possibly primary aspect of schizophrenia, namely unusual word associations, can be measurably altered even in long-term hospital patients.

In a clinical demonstration of verbal conditioning over an extended period of time (more than three months), Ayllon & Haughton (1964) report the cases of three psychotic female patients, each of whom served in an own-control design. The agents of reinforcement here were nursing personnel, who were instructed by the authors to record base-line frequencies of crazy verbal behavior, and then to deliver or withhold reinforcements contingent upon delusional or hypochondriacal talk. The expected changes and reversals were observed, and perhaps because psychotic talk never returned to base line, one of the patients was even taken home by relatives, and remained there after three years. An important problem with this study has already been discussed in the section above on the operant conditioning of selected target behaviors.

Ullmann et al. (1965) investigated the shaping of "healthy" versus "sick" talk during a twenty-minute structured interview. Subjects were 60 male schizophrenics with an average hospitalization of about seven years. The classes of verbal behavior reinforced were considerably more complex (and hence, less reliably scorable) than the plural nouns and positive affect words which we have seen thus far. "Healthy" talk was defined as verbalizations re-lating to comfort, liking, good physical or mental health, personal assets, presence of motivation, enthusiasm, etc. "Sick" talk was the converse. A control for speech content was provided in a group which was reinforced for emission of plural nouns; this furnished response-contingent reinforcement which would not be likely to differentially affect healthy and sick talk. The principal results showed that the reinforcement of sick talk led to a significant increase in this response class, while reinforcement of healthy talk led to a significant decrease in sick talk. Moreover, psychometric measures indicated that as sick talk decreased, self-reports about mental and physical condition became more optimistic.

In a pair of related studies, Meichenbaum (1966a, 1966b) has investigated effects of different kinds of secondary reinforcement on abstract thinking in mostly acute, short-term schizophrenics. The first study was concerned primarily with the contingency of the reinforcement, over and above any nurturance or fear reduction which frequent nods, positive comments, etc., from an experimenter might have on improving task performance. Using a yoked design, he found that only a contingent-positive group improved significantly on a proverbs task, the noncontingent-positive group not differing from a control in which the experimenter maintained a nonevaluative attitude. This important difference generalized also to a new but related conceptual task. In the second study he examined the effects of more extensive training (11 half-hour sessions) with contingent social ("mm, hmm") and token reinforcement aimed at two aspects of verbal and conceptual behavior, namely performance on proverbs and amount of nonpathognomic talk. In addition, the contingencies were spelled out to each patient beforehand. He also examined the problem of generalization to other interview situations. The results show that the reinforcement contingencies effected significant improvement as manifested by more abstract proverb responses and less "sick talk," as well as generalizing to response classes other than those directly reinforced during the training. For example, Ss who had been reinforced for "healthy talk" improved not only on this dimension but also on abstraction in the proverbs task on test interviews run both by the experimenter and by a patient confederate who was unaware of the purposes of the study. These very impressive effects stood up well on a follow-up one week later. One additional result is especially noteworthy: post treatment proverb performance of this sample of schizophrenic patients did not differ significantly from that of an untreated control group of medical patients with no psychiatric history or known CNS pathology, indicating that the verbal conditioning procedures improved the schizophrenics' performance on the very central dimension of abstract thinking to a degree indistinguishable from "normals."

GROUP THERAPY BEHAVIOR

In two very closely related studies, Dinoff, Horner, Kurpiewski, & Timmons (1960) and Dinoff, Horner, Kurpiewski, Rickard, & Timmons (1960) present evidence that specific classes of verbal behavior can be effectively shaped within a group-therapy-like setting. In both studies, Ss were male VA patients, all with prior hospitalizations, and the target responses were either self- or group-referent statements. In the first study, operant levels were ascertained in a leaderless discussion-group setting, and then patients were divided into two experimental groups, in each of which an examiner actively elicited and reinforced statements which referred either to the patient himself or to the group. The effects of this manipulation were then assessed in the original, larger group. The operant and extinction phases were each three 50-minute sessions, and the experimental phase was carried out over six 50-minute meetings. The results were somewhat disappointing, in that the hoped-for mean differences in frequencies of the respective target behaviors did not reach significance; however, sign tests did show a significant trend in the expected direction. An interesting and valuable additional manipulation was what the authors call "counterconditioning": after the posttreatment assessments, Ss were returned to their smaller groups, where the experimenter reinforced that class of reference statements which had not been reinforced earlier, i.e., Ss initially reinforced for self-referent statements now were rewarded for group-referent statements, and vice versa. Here, too, very suggestive trends were found with the sign test.

Because in this first experiment the groups in which effects were measured were different from the settings in which reinforcement had occurred, Dinoff, Horner, Kurpiewski, Rickard, & Timmons (1960) ran a similar study in an attempt to make the posttreatment test less a measure of generalization than that which appeared to hold in the first study. Essentially, the design was the same, except that (1) the assessments and manipulations all occurred within the same group setting and (2) the experimenter was absent during the assessment meetings. As predicted, statistically significant changes were found this time.

Before regarding these studies as contributing anything of significance to the fruitful relationships between verbal conditioning and group therapy, one should keep in mind that Ss were reinforced in a group-therapy-like setting only to the extent that the experimenter conditioned each patient in the presence of fellow patients. No direct attempt was made to manipulate interpersonal behavior, and the assessments of change (done during a leaderless group discussion) were likewise directed to individual responding, in contrast to the Ullmann et al. (1961) study below. Perhaps more important than group therapy variables is the likelihood that each patient unwittingly served as a model for his peers in talking about certain subjects. The study by Wilson & Walters (1966), discussed above, relates to this.

On the assumption that an increase in emotionality would improve interpersonal relationships in group therapy, Ullmann, Krasner, & Collins (1961) set out to determine whether verbal conditioning sessions aimed at emotionally toned words would have a measurable effect in a separate group therapy situation. The subjects were 30 male "continued treatment" patients at a VA hospital (it is not specified how many were diagnosed as psychotic). In each of the three experimental conditions S was asked to make up five-minute stories in response to line drawings of situations such as purchasing a necktie or fishing. Each subject was seen individually for four sessions over two weeks. In the "positive-personal" reinforcement condition, the experimenter reinforced all emotional words with head nods and "mmm-hmm." In the "impersonal-unstructured" condition, the experimenter reacted to such words by pressing a button which advanced an electric counter, the dial of which was placed so that S was able to see it. Finally, in the "no-reinforcement" condition, the experimenter made no responses to the stories. The dependent measure was Finney's (1954) Palo Alto Group Therapy Scale (GTS), and it was filled out on these patients by therapists who did not know which condition the subjects had been assigned to. The groups had been equated for GTS scores prior to the experimental manipulations. The results showed that the therapy group composed of patients who had undergone the "positive-personal" verbal conditioning sessions improved significantly ($p = .05$, one-tailed test) over its pretreatment level, while the other two groups did not. Furthermore, the post-treatment GTS scores of this group were very significantly higher than those of the other two groups. Thus, through attention contingent upon expression of emotional words, the experimenters were able, in a very short time, to affect significantly and beneficially the interpersonal behavior of psychiatric patients in an independent group therapy setting. In evaluating their results, the authors remind us that the experiment was carried out within the context of an ongoing hospital program, with many uncontrolled variables that probably worked against the experimental effect.

It would have been helpful, in evaluating this study, to know whether the output of emotional words increased during the verbal conditioning sessions. Since these data are not reported, one can only speculate about the nature of the generalization, if any, which was measured in this study. Recall that the "positive-personal" and "impersonal-unstructured" groups were designed to differ only in the nature of the response-contingent reinforcement, in the former case mediated by examiner interest and in the latter case doled out by the movement of the examiner's finger to activate a counter. If we assume that the increases in emotional output were significant within both these groups (and this is a safe assumption in view of many reports of successful verbal conditioning via such response-contingent stimuli as red lights and buzzers; cf. Greenspoon, 1951; Atkinson & Robinson, 1961), then to what can we attribute the interpersonal gains made by the first group in therapy? Upon reflection, it appears to me that the main variable on which the groups differed appreciably is degree of human interest and warmth, irrespective of whether it was contingent on the emotional responses made during the verbal conditioning sessions. Thus, only in the "positive-personal" group did the examiner act humanly and kindly towards the subject. Surely in the no-reinforcement condition the examiner did not appear interested, and in the "impersonal-unstructured" condition the extent of the examiner's verbal interactions seems to have been limited to conveying misleading information about the clicking counter, viz., "Questions about the meaning of the counter were answered with the phrase that it was one of the experimental measures" (Ullmann et al., 1961, p. 130). Thus, from the data which Ullmann et al. report, it remains questionable whether the increase in emotional output from verbal conditioning generalized to group therapy. It might have been possible, indeed, to obtain the same results simply by having an interested examiner spend an equal amount of time with each patient talking about the weather. In fact, given the limited amount of individual attention which hospital patients as a rule enjoy from professional staff, this would be an interesting study to run.

This important issue of what is generalizing to what was examined in a subsequent study which collected the data on increase in emotional verbal output which are seen to be missing in the study just above. Ullmann, Krasner, & Ekman (1961) included two trials of no-reinforcement in a replication of the personal-positive reinforcement group; this yielded a measure of operant output against which changes as a function of reinforcement might be measured. This study also used a different-sexed experimenter as well as patient-subjects who were considerably more "acute" than the "continued treatment" patients in the earlier study. A further change entailed dropping the impersonal-unstructured and the no-reinforcement control groups, substituting a no-verbal-conditioning group.

The results are quite puzzling, in that they run *counter* to expectation. First, with these shorter-term patients, Ullmann et al. did not replicate the earlier finding that GTS scores could be significantly improved by verbal conditioning of affect words. When, however, they selected out those patients in both experimental and control groups who had been in the hospital at least three months, the differences were, in fact, statistically significant. Naturally, this result would require cross-validation with a different set of subjects. Of even more interest is the finding that, within the experimental group, there was no significant positive correlation between increase in emotional verbal output and increase in GTS scores, a relationship which, as we have already pointed out, would be needed to support the notion of generalization from verbal conditioning to group therapy. In fact, the correlation was negative ($r = -.24$). In sum, the very intriguing and important hypothesis which was explored by Ullmann, Krasner, & Collins (1961) did not receive confirmation in a subsequent study which provided the measure necessary for making any conclusion about generalization from verbal conditioning to interpersonal performance in group therapy.

OVERALL EVALUATION OF VERBAL CONDITIONING STUDIES WITH HOSPITALIZED MENTAL PATIENTS

In addition to the specific issues and problems already noted within the discussion of the respective studies, there are several more general issues which should be examined. These include the matter of generalization, the use of instructions, the instatement of modeling procedures, and the general appropriateness of directly manipulating a patient's verbalizations.

The question of generalization of effects is of obvious importance in the application of verbal conditioning to mental hospital patients, especially if one is interested in therapeutic applications. Most of the studies above did concern themselves with this problem. Several investigators trained ward staff to provide consistency in the new contingencies set for patients' verbal behavior. Thus, Isaacs, Thomas, & Goldiamond (1960) report considerable generalization in the reinstatement of some forms of speech in their long-term mute schizophrenics by instructing the staff to refrain from interpreting the nonverbal requests as they had been doing for so many years. Rickard, Dignam, & Horner (1960) employed a similar strategy in extinguishing the delusional talk of their twenty-year continuously hospitalized patient, to the extent even of raising questions as to which behavior modification procedures were generalizing to which. Ayllon & Haughton (1964), as one would expect, made extensive use of attendants and nurses in reducing delusional and hypochondriacal talk. Sherman (1965) reports generalization to the ward even without specific measures to ensure maintenance of contingent reinforcement by the staff.

Perhaps a more significant kind of generalization was investigated by workers concerned with the effects of verbal behavior changes on other aspects of the patient's behavior, occurring more "spontaneously," as it were. Ullmann, Krasner, & Collins (1961) and Ullmann, Krasner, & Ekman (1961), it will be recalled, analyzed effective group therapy behavior as entailing expression of emotions, and then attempted to affect such behavior by direct manipulation of emotional words in an entirely separate setting, namely, a verbal conditioning situation in which emotional words were reinforced in the context of telling a story. As pointed out earlier, there are problems in isolating the variables responsible for the observed improvement in group therapy; the idea is nonetheless interesting and worthy of more research. Ullmann, Krasner, & Edinger (1964) failed to obtain generalization from successful increase in common word associations to a scale of the Sarbin-Hardyck Stick Figure Test designed to measure the degree to which a subject describes a figure as labeled by a normal standardization group. As they point out, it would probably be necessary to train such long-term patients directly on such a conceptual task. On the other hand, Ullmann et al. (1965) report some generalization from increase in "healthy talk" to questionnaire measures of mental and physical condition; no doubt the verbal nature of the generalization measure contributed to this outcome. If one could demonstrate related changes on a non-verbal dimension, e.g., discharge from hospital, the findings would be even more impressive.

By far the most significant work in this area has been reported by Meichenbaum (1966a, 1966b). Accepting the several conceptualizations of schizophrenia as largely a thought disorder (cf. Buss & Lang, 1965), he demonstrated significant beneficial change in conceptual tasks via explicit explanations of the responses desired and the rewards to be earned by approximating them, and then via the reward of such verbalization. Moreover, he achieved significant generalization to related but discriminably different conceptual tasks, viz., his finding that patients reinforced for "healthy talk" improved not only on this dimension but also on the level of abstraction on a proverbs task. Furthermore, he found that after intensive verbal conditioning of proverb performance, his sample of schizophrenics performed at as high a level of abstraction as a control group of nonpsychiatric patients; to the best of my knowledge, this is the first demonstration with hospitalized adults of change effected via operant procedures to such a degree as to render the behavior indistinguishable from normals—a very significant finding, indeed.

There is little reason to assume that the problems of generalization in verbal conditioning will be qualitatively different from what holds in normals (compare with Drennen, 1963). If anything, progress is likely to be even more difficult. When the assumption is being made that behavior is maintained by its consequences, and when, furthermore, the consequences are mediated primarily by agents other than the individual himself, it is to be readily expected that efforts must be made at least in either or both of two directions: (1) to shape the patient's behavior in such a manner that it will, by the nature of things, be reinforced by the environment and/or (2) to change the environment in such a manner as to maintain a change effected in a limited conditioning setting. Meichenbaum's work can be seen as illustrative of the first strategy, while Ayllon & Haughton's (1964) work amply demonstrates the second. That the verbal conditioning research has only begun to yield significant generalization data is an understatement (compare with Lanyon, 1967).

As we have already seen in the application of operant techniques to other-than-verbal behaviors, workers are beginning to realize that making use of the patient's verbal (cognitive) repertoire is an effective short cut to eliciting the desired behaviors. That interesting and important theoretical issues are involved in whether verbal conditioning does, in fact, fit into the operant paradigm is not being disputed. Whatever model best fits the data, however, one need not continue to follow doggedly and inappropriately the Skinner-box paradigm in refraining from informing the patient exactly what is expected of him and what he can obtain by trying. This writer is reminded of McConnell's humorous but, at the same time, sobering tale of the psychologist caught in an outer-space version of a Skinner box: "If only I could communicate with Him! I don't mind being subjected to tests nearly as much as I mind being underestimated. Why, I can solve puzzles hundreds of times more complex than what He's throwing at me. But how can I tell Him?" (McConnell, 1957).

One of the most intriguing research efforts which this writer can conceive of would be to replicate those verbal conditioning studies which did not use instructions to the patients, adding appropriate verbal directions on the target behaviors and the contingencies (cf. Ayllon & Azrin's 1964 article on instructions relating to motoric behavior, discussed above).

As in other areas, the use of models in verbal conditioning appears to be a fruitful and as yet little-explored variable. The studies by Sherman (1965) and Wilson & Walters (1966) illustrate well the peculiar appropriateness of modeling procedures, that is, when the target behavior does not occur with enough frequency for contingent reinforcement to have an effect. A review article by Bandura (1965) provides a lucid summary of the research which he and his collaborators have engaged in over the past few years, and there seems little doubt that an extension of such work in verbal conditioning with mental patients can prove at least as valuable as in other areas.[4]

That much verbal behavior of hospitalized, often psychotic patients can be significantly altered with verbal conditioning procedures has been amply demonstrated. While most of the studies reviewed above were not intended to provide therapeutic benefit to the patient-subjects, the implication is clearly present in virtually every instance, if not always explicit. An example of an open statement of what seems to me to be the prevalent orientation can be found in the article by Ullmann et al. (1965, p. 211):

> The present experiment probably has its greatest value as an addition to the web of evidence showing that meaningful clinical behaviour may be affected rapidly and significantly by direct methods of training. The concepts and procedures of behaviour therapists may be compared with the indirect or neoanalytic approach exemplified by a widely disseminated pamphlet (Baruch, 1945) in which the reader is told, "Misbehavior is one way a child has of getting out his bad feelings. *He has to learn better ways of getting them out.*" The parent is counseled to help his child by encouraging, prompting, and illustrating the expression of negative feelings, for *"As the bad feelings come out the good feelings sprout!* This is something to print in big letters and underline in your thoughts" (Baruch, 1945, p. 19). Within the limits of the present data it is likely that this procedure will not only be ineffective but also have an effect opposite to the one intended.

Ullmann et al. seem, unfortunately, to be implying that the only (or at least most fruitful) alternative to extinguishing "sick talk" and reinforcing "healthy talk" is to do nothing but elicit "sick talk" within a hydraulic model of dammed-up libidinal energy which must be drained off in order for any improvement to occur. This writer's contention, however, is that there are many alternatives, not the least of which is to take care initially to find out what is wrong and only then to proceed with behavior modification techniques. As has been discussed in relation to some of Ayllon's work, the designation of verbal behavior as nothing but operant manipulation by the patient of his social en-

---

[4] A dissertation by S. Wilder (1967) at Columbia University, New York City, is a step in this direction.

vironment runs the grave risk of committing real mistakes. One need not be inclined to make a psychoanalytic prediction of "symptom substitution" in order to be concerned about merely removing a behavior without having first made a satisfactory behavioral analysis of its functional role in the behaving organism. For better or for worse, behavior therapists are not dealing with an animal whose developmental and interactive history is as simple as that of even the most highly sophisticated Skinnerian pigeon. This orientation is well explained and illustrated by Wolpe & Lazarus (1966) and Lazarus (1965b). Further, the research of R. S. Lazarus (1966) makes graphically clear the importance of not attending solely to what a person is saying or even overtly doing.

Interestingly enough, Greenspoon, whose work was a major factor in triggering research in verbal conditioning, seems very much aware of the problem: "Though the verbal conditioning paradigm has provided the clinical psychologist with a seemingly valuable research tool, it should be viewed and examined with great caution. It should be recognized that efforts to reduce behavior disorders to some facet of verbal conditioning may represent a great over-simplification of the many variables that may be involved in the development and maintenance of a behavior disorder" (Greenspoon, 1962, p. 547).

Even if the research thus far done in conditioning the verbal behavior of hospitalized patients falls far short of the clinical benefits which have been reported for neurotic patients from such techniques as systematic desensitization and assertive training (cf. Wolpe & Lazarus, 1966), there would still seem to be considerable utility in these procedures, namely, rendering these people more amenable to perhaps superior behavior modification procedures (or, to court heresy, other kinds of therapies). Thus, in discussing the considerable and rapid change effected via the now-familiar "M & M therapy" of the operant conditioner working with severely disturbed children, I have observed: "It is hard to conceive of a therapy which does not presuppose at least that the patient pay attention to the therapist and follow his instructions, whether they be to press levers or to free-associate. Especially with psychotic children does this pose a problem, and any procedure which enables the therapist to achieve a working measure of control over his patient's behaviour merits consideration from practitioners of any persuasion" (Davison, 1964, pp. 158–159).

Thus, like any conditioning procedure which provides for the therapist's mediation of primary and/or secondary reinforcements, the verbal conditioning paradigm seems well suited to establishing the therapist and other staff members as people to be listened to and, in some instances, obeyed.

Operant Conditioning of Ward-wide Behaviors

There is considerable interest lately in organizing, within mental hospitals, experimental wards run on a "token economy." This notion grew out of a series of studies, to be described shortly, by Ayllon & Azrin (1965), which suggest the feasibility and efficacy of making easily available "reinforcements" such as sitting in the dayroom, access to the canteen, more desirable beds, etc., contingent upon behaviors which are considered desirable. Thus, for example, to be allowed to watch television, a patient would have to earn a certain number of tokens; this could be done by performing any variety of "healthy" behaviors, such as shaving or regularly attending an industrial-therapy assignment. The range of behaviors designated worthy of tokens, the number of tokens earned for performance of a given behavior, the numbers of tokens needed for various desired activities, and the kinds of activities to be made contingent upon tokens—all these variables give to the reader some idea of the complexity and richness which is possible within this simple paradigm. Let us see how appropriate the idea is.

Although one hears of many token-economy projects, this writer has been able to find only three formal reports: Ayllon & Azrin (1965), Atthowe & Krasner (1968), and Gericke (1965). In addition, there is an unpublished preliminary report from Steffy, Hart, Craw, Torney, Marlett, & Fenz (1966).

AYLLON & AZRIN (1965)

The experiments reported by Ayllon & Azrin (1965) constitute one of the most impressive pieces of work in the behavior modification literature to date. These workers have independently followed the exhortations of such writers as Goldstein, Heller, & Sechrest (1966) in going directly to the relevant material in the real-life setting, rather than remaining at the analog level of research. Executing controlled research in the situation which is the ultimate focus of the conclusions to be drawn puts one far ahead of the less intrepid researcher who limits his work to subject, situation, and/or behavior analogs, with the resulting need to limit his generalizations (compare with Maher, 1966).

To review even cursorily the intricacies of this article would require too much space; the interested reader is urged to avail himself of the "reinforcement" (both as information and as gratification) of reading the paper himself. Only the main features will be described here.

The behaviors to be strengthened, the criteria for reinforcement, and the nature of the reinforcements were such as to make it possible to train non-psychologists (nurses and nurses' aides) to implement the program. An entire ward was set aside for the series of experiments. The behaviors which were intentionally strengthened and eliminated throughout the six experiments were socially significant, e.g., making beds, combing hair, working in a laboratory, cleaning up the kitchen—a far cry from the plunger pulling of ten years earlier. The patients were all long-term hospitalized females who had been receiving only tranquilizers as treatment. A unique feature of the program was the intentional use of Premack's (1959) principle of reinforcement, whereby, of two behaviors which can occur in a given situation, the more probable will function as reinforcer for the less probable one. This principle extends considerably the variety of reinforcements which can be found for a given organism, especially the chronic hospital patient who often exhibits relatively little interest in what goes on around him.

In order to bridge the gap between performance of a target behavior and the presumably reinforcing higher-probability response, Ayllon & Azrin introduced distinctive tokens, which were delivered by an attendant right after a given performance. These tokens could later, in various amounts, be exchanged for the right to engage in the higher-probability behavior. For example, working in the hospital laundry for six hours daily earned 70 tokens; attending religious services cost ten tokens.

Investigation of the reinforcing properties of the tokens took various forms, and in all, six related experiments were conducted over a period of almost three years with selected subgroups of patients. In each study an A-B-A design was employed, in which each subject served as his own control: after measuring response frequency under reinforcement contingency A, decrease in the response was attempted by reversing the contingencies (B), after which the original contingencies were reinstated in order to reestablish the original behavior. This procedure will be illustrated below.

Experiment I in the series can be examined in greater detail to obtain a better idea of the general strategies employed. In order to determine whether the tokens and high-probability behavior could, in fact, function as reinforcers, Ayllon & Azrin first assessed which off-ward job assignments each patient was attending for tokens. The experiment began with a suspension of the automatic rotation of jobs among the patients and the presentation of verbal instructions provided by an attendant, stating that, while the people for whom the given patient had been working were pleased with her efforts, other patients wanted to work there also; moreover, tokens would no longer be provided in this preferred job location, but only in a nonpreferred job. Thus, the authors set themselves the task of demonstrating that the tokens which they had been providing patients for performance of certain activities could, in fact, function as reinforcers, i.e., could, by virtue of their discontinuance, eliminate behavior which they had been following (maintaining?), and shape up hitherto unperformed behavior by being made contingent upon its occurrence. The results of this change in token contingencies revealed a dramatic and sudden shift to nonpreferred but token-reinforced jobs. In the spirit of the own-control designs of all the studies run, the experiment did not end until it was demonstrated that reversing the contingencies effected a reversal in behavior; this was done by informing patients that tokens would now be given only for the originally chosen job.

One of the valuable features of the report is the inclusion of patients' verbal reports. Thus, while many patients were heard to be explaining their attendance at token-reinforced jobs on the basis of job satisfaction and social contact, the shift of the contingency to another job, led, as has been said, to a shift in job choice, which was accompanied by such statements as, "No, honey, I can't work at the laundry for nothing, I'll work at the lab. I just couldn't make it to pay my rent, if I didn't get paid" (pp. 363, 365).

The above experiment was done with those patients who were sufficiently adjusted to attend off-ward activities. To ascertain the effectiveness of the token economy with more regressed (behaviorally) patients, a similar experiment was executed with those women who could not leave the ward; in this case, the job choices manipulated were on-ward activities, e.g., cleaning pot and pans. The results in this instance were largely the same as those for the off-ward assignments, except that a few very regressed patients remained unaffected by the changes in contingencies. Moreover, some behaviors, such as self-care (combing hair, bathing, making bed), seemed almost entirely impervious to the tokens, indicating a considerable amount of intrinsic reinforcement or pleasure, or, as the authors more cautiously put it, ". . . the self-care behaviors for all patients did not change appreciably when the tokens were made non-contingent. The reason for this is not known" (p. 374).

The general results of all the experiments can be summarized at this point: (1) The tokens were effective in changing voluntary job choices from initially preferred to nonpreferred jobs. (2) The administration of the tokens noncontingently led to a decrease in job attendance, showing the crucial nature of the response-reinforcement relationship. (3) The removal of the tokens from the ward economy while still leaving the "back-up reinforcers" (compare with Premack, 1959; Staats & Staats, 1963) freely available led to significant decline in job performance. (4) The contingencies could be set both by oral and by written instructions from the staff. Furthermore, the model of nonprofessional staff working under the aegis of a psychologist was again confirmed as practicable and effective.

Anyone who has worked in a mental hospital (except perhaps for a few private ones) is painfully aware of the shortage of psychologists, psychiatrists, and more recently, psychiatric social workers. The "treatment" to which the patient is usually exposed entails the use of drugs, ECT, occupational and industrial "therapy," plus any "milieu therapy" which (sometimes) pleasant surroundings and staff can provide. Unfortunately, most of the hospital patient's time is spent either alone or in the company of others who have not coped on the outside. The chronicity which the hospital engenders has been documented elsewhere and need not be discussed here (e.g., Fairweather, 1964; Goffman, 1961). What the Ayllon & Azrin (1965) work, as well as the other studies already reviewed, indicates is the possibility of making far more effective use of those personnel who have extended contact with the patients—i.e., the aides—and of the usual hospital facilities which provide opportunities for the mental patient to "act normally" but little incentive to do so.

Critique of Ayllon & Azrin (1965).   I have not tried to conceal my enthusiasm about these studies. At the same time, however, there are problems with which, it is believed, Ayllon and Azrin have not come to grips.

As has already been seen in the earlier work by these same authors and other collaborators, the assumption is being widely made that the "psychotic" behavior exhibited by these mental hospital patients is a function of its consequences. This bias is seen quite clearly in the Discussion section of the article: "Eight patients . . . were relatively unaffected by the reinforcement procedures. Statistical comparison of them with other patients [who conformed to the operant mold] revealed no difference in diagnosis or age. It appears that their failure to modify behavior appreciably stemmed from the relative absence of any strong behavior patterns that could be used as reinforcers" (pp. 381–382). These patients are not the difficult cases who were subjected to an additional experimental manipulation to draw them away from the performance of various chores after the token contingencies had been eliminated. Rather, these eight patients are the few who, in spite of repeated and ingenious efforts by the experimenters, remained unaffected.

I believe that Ayllon & Azrin would do well to break set and at least consider the possibility that the behavior (both overt and covert) of some chronic hospital patients is regulated by processes which have little if anything to do with operant conditioning. Their "explanation" for the failure of these patients to respond to their program is, unfortunately, not unlike the similarly unsatisfactory "explanations" which are invented by psychoanalytically oriented therapists for those patients who do not respond to that treatment; such patients are called "resistant." Rimland (1964) has very convincingly shown the all-important difference between plausibility and validity in scientific interpretation. To relate Rimland's point to the conclusions of Ayllon & Azrin, one would want the authors to make clearer their appreciation of the fact that post hoc explanations of puzzling data are no substitute for experiments which are designed with the possibility of disconfirming a particular hypothesis. To be specific, one should take these eight patients and set out to build, perhaps via primary reinforcements, certain classes of behavior, so as to *create* high-probability behaviors where previously there were none. *Then* one would make these newly acquired "reinforcers" contingent on infrequent behaviors and see whether the infrequent behaviors increased in frequency or vigor. At some point in the process, one would have to resolve to forsake the operant model for another.

The question here, as with the majority of operant conditioning work, is how far the model can be pushed (Davison, 1965c). This question is explored in the next study.

ATTHOWE & KRASNER (1968)

In an extension of the experiments of Ayllon & Azrin (1965), Atthowe & Krasner (1968) have published an interim report of a token-economy program on a closed ward in a VA hospital, designed to encompass virtually every important aspect of hospital life, viz., bed-wetting, attendance at assignments, making beds, going out on pass. Sixty predominantly chronic schizophrenic male patients were chosen as a core sample to be studied over two years' time. Their base-line performance was measured over a period of about six months, after which eleven months of the token economy was instituted. Patients were provided explicit instructions about the radical change in routine, including very specific explanations of the contingencies for various behaviors, for example, one token for making the bed in the morning, two tokens for attending industrial therapy (IT) assignments, etc. These tokens could later be traded in for the "good things in life," e.g., sitting in the dayroom watching TV, buying things at the canteen. As men progressed, considerable delay in reinforcement was instituted (compare with Mischel, 1965), viz., tokens were distributed on a weekly basis, in much the same manner as a weekly paycheck, rather than immediately following an activity. The ultimate in reinforcement was, ironically, buying oneself out of the system and obtaining a "carte blanche," which functioned in the place of tokens.

In the own-control design, very significant increases were observed in such behaviors as attendance at group activities, going out on passes, following rules against antisocial behavior, and engaging in social interaction. Although discharge was not part of the design, twice as many men were discharged from the hospital as in the preceding eleven-month period; however, half returned within nine months.

In discussing their results, the authors mention that for 10 percent of the sample the tokens had no appreciable effect. Moreover, little, if any, individual shaping was attempted. In arguing against a Hawthorne Effect, they refer to the controls instituted by Ayllon & Azrin (1965), showing the crucial role of the contingencies. Moreover, they are also able to point to an increase in activity following an increase in number of tokens for performing the given activity. And, perhaps most importantly, they point out that their experimental ward did not have more of the "good things in life" than other wards; indeed, as those who have worked in VA settings can readily appreciate, the token ward represented a sharp reversal from the usual state of affairs in which patients are literally paid by the federal government for being "sick."

As Atthowe & Krasner point out, their project was limited to a ward-wide manipulation of only certain important behaviors. This focus has certain limitations of which the present writer became aware in visiting the ward. Although the psychologist took pains to spell out to each man why he was obtaining the respective number of tokens, it is probable that many undesirable behaviors were likewise being reinforced, e.g., a patient engaging in typical mannerisms while being handed the tokens for his weekly performance (an occurrence which I witnessed). While the authors' statement that the ward was "jumping" is no doubt true, we must keep in mind that, due to the admittedly limited nature of the program, much of this "jumping" can be taken quite literally. Though this program was effective in attaining its limited but ambitious goals, it nonetheless falls far short of rendering these difficult patients indistinguishable from normals.

A further criticism of the study is the fact that the token economy was administered by staff psychologists and trainees who had considerable interest in trying out other behavior modification methods, e.g., systematic desensitization, relaxation, aversive conditioning, etc. Perhaps because of the nature of the token program, this ward tended to attract such staff (who, moreover, may have been more enthusiastic than the usual VA personnel). Whether the application of these other behavior modification techniques contributed appreciably to the significant improvement observed with the patients is unclear. However, it is a distinct possibility and does justify caution in attributing the favorable changes solely to the token-contingency program.[5]

GERICKE (1965)

In a lucid article written for psychiatrists and other professionals relatively unfamiliar with the behavioral sciences, O. L. Gericke (1965), superintendent of the Patton State Hospital in California, describes the initial clinical results from a token economy built primarily upon the work of Lindsley, Skinner, Ayllon, and Azrin. The general outline is very much like that described by Ayllon & Azrin (1965) and Atthowe & Krasner (1968), although it appears that at Patton State Hospital more responsibility was placed upon nurses and attendants for finding behaviors to reinforce, and for deciding on the most meaningful reinforcer for any given occasion. Nursing personnel were lectured on the general principles of operant conditioning, with special emphasis on the different "set" which the approach warranted and on the responsibility which accrues to a person when he is told that his own behavior can have marked effect on the actions of another human being. The training seems closely analogous to that which I used in training undergraduates to function as social reinforcers for severely disturbed children (Davison, 1964, 1965d). Each nurse was assigned to follow three patients throughout their stay in the hospital. The reinforcers ranged from food to privileges like sleeping in a more comfortable room. Tokens were also used in the same manner as in the aforementioned token economies. The kinds of behaviors reinforced included cleaning hands and fingernails, arriving on time at the dining room, working in jobs off the ward, and so forth. Patients were admitted to the experimental ward provided that they evidenced no signs of brain damage, had been hospitalized for more than six months, and appeared able to function on an open unit.

[5] At the Kankakee State Hospital in Illinois, G. L. Paul is instituting just such a ward, i.e., providing for individual behavior modification treatment within the context of an ongoing token economy.

It is interesting that even early in the program, Gericke and his staff attempted to make token reinforcement intermittent, so as to "wean the patient away from . . . [this] artificial support" (Gericke, 1965, p. 6). Friendly praise and other generalized reinforcers were seen as preferable.

Gericke has made no attempt in this article to supply quantitative data or to arrange different experimental conditions in order to assess the "active ingredients." Taking the report at the descriptive level, however, one can appreciate the enthusiasm generated in the staff by this radically new program: sometimes sudden and dramatic changes were observed in hitherto unresponsive patients. At the very least, the demands made upon patients eliminated the problem of passivity, even if this meant some initial rebelliousness. But, as Gericke says, "While such rebellion is obviously not a desirable response to any therapeutic technique, it is better to have a patient react even negatively than not to react at all" (Gericke, 1965, p. 6).

Changes wrought in a few patients are reported in some detail. The case of Susan, a twenty-six-year-old Mexican girl, will serve well to illustrate the problems that an apparently uncritical and careless acceptance of the general idea of operant conditioning may create. The rather harsh criticism which follows is directed at the specific instance reported, not necessarily at the overall program.

Susan had been repeatedly hospitalized after exhibiting destructive behavior at home, including tearing her own clothing. She is also described as expressing "paranoid ideation" and many somatic complaints. The token program had succeeded in moving her slightly from her customary solitary sitting in a corner, but no other progress was being made. Her "behavioral engineer" noticed that the patient would take only milk as nourishment and would dress only in white or light-colored clothing. It was, therefore, decided to use white clothing as incentive and reinforcement. The patient's white dress was consequently taken away from her, and olive-drab institutional clothing was substituted. As expected, she became quite violent and tore the dress. Instead of attending to this tantrum and furnishing different (white) clothing, the nurse rightly ignored her; three hours later, Susan asked the nurse for a needle and thread, and proceeded to repair the dress she had ripped. Reinforcement was a white scarf to wear with the dark dress. "The resulting change in Susan's behavior was dramatic. After she had mended the clothing, she asked for odd jobs in the kitchen. Each time she completed a task, she received a token and some of her white clothing back. . . . The next goal was to condition her to wearing dark clothing and to eating foods that were not white" (Gericke, 1965, p. 8).

Thus far it would appear that the staff had acted with compassion and ingenuity, all to good effect. However, from the fact that no report is really given as to whether Susan learned ultimately to wear dark clothes, the present writer is concerned about a bit of clinical information which is later provided on Susan: we are told that white had rather an unusual significance for the patient, namely, that (as they learned after using it as reinforcer) she associated it with purity and goodness, while associating black with the devil, sin, and other undesirable things. She felt, furthermore, that God had punished her by giving her black hair. It would appear, therefore, that, in their zeal to find an effective reinforcer for shaping other behaviors, the staff made use of and perhaps strengthened an apparently important portion of her "pathology," namely the "paranoid" notions about white and black. Recall that the staff made white clothing contingent on good behavior. Presumably other generalized and perhaps also primary reinforcements were delivered to Susan along with the white clothing. Regardless of what language one wishes to use, the staff undoubtedly underlined for Susan even further the special significance of white things.

It is for this reason that one would like to have learned what happened to the "crazy" notion which Susan had about white. And if the staff *did* succeed in acclimating her to dark clothes, did her "crazy" ideas about white and black disappear? That considerable beneficial changes were effected in Susan is surely not being denied here. Rather, an effort is being made to point up the kind of problem which the application of operant procedures might create if one does not carefully assess the individual situation.

STEFFY, HART, CRAW, TORNEY, MARLETT & FENZ, (1966)

Steffy et al. (1966) have been running a token economy on a closed ward at Lakeshore Psychiatric Hospital in Toronto, Canada. Their preliminary report encompasses only a portion of the total program, namely the elimination of problem behaviors in very severely regressed patients at mealtime and at bedtime. With the nurses' cooperation, they were able to get patients into the dining room in the same manner as reported by Ayllon & Haughton (1962). They were also able to teach the patients to hold onto an admissions token for a half hour prior to mealtime. This change represents no mean achievement in the patient-population with whom they worked. Problems centering around sleeping (undressing, retiring at proper time, dressing, etc.) were handled by making a token contingent upon following the instructions; sometime during the day those patients who had earned such tokens were able to "purchase" special afternoon culinary treats. However, the principal concern of these investigators has been with the generalization of effects from such restricted behaviors as arriving in the dining room on time to other response classes that were not directly manipulated. One of their findings is that patients who were exhibiting improvement within the token program also improved on the Minimal Social Behavior Scale (Farina, Arenberg, & Guskin, 1957), which measures appropriateness of responding to such questions as, "What year is it?" and "What month is it?" Other analyses are in progress, and it seems likely that this program will add considerably to our evaluation of token economies as vehicles for meaningful retraining of severely regressed hospital patients.

FAIRWEATHER (1964)

If one includes under the rubric of behavior modification any procedures that explicitly attempt to change behavior through techniques and programs which look to general experimental psychology for hints and rationale, then the social psychological work of George Fairweather and his associates at the Palo Alto VA Hospital is quite relevant. While he does not express himself in the conditioning jargon which we have encountered thus far, it will be readily apparent that the operations which he performs are, without any strain, translatable—and fruitfully so—into conditioning terminology.

Fairweather et al. (1964) have described a project on two wards for evaluating the effectiveness of small patient-run, task-oriented groups in treating "mental illness." Their assumption is that "mental illness" has more to do with the lack of social skills than with any inherent "pathology." Noting that the usual tendency is for patients to become dependent on the hospital and, therefore, all the more ill-suited to act independently on the outside, as demanded by society, Fairweather set up one ward divided into four groups managed by patients and responsible for handling many behavior problems which are typically the province of the professional staff. He very carefully matched the two wards on diagnostic categories, length of hospitalization, and demographic variables, as well as daily routines, so that the principal difference lay in the experimental ward being run primarily through patient groups in which the burden of responsibility was on the ward members for improving each others' social behavior. In effect, the experimental groups were designed to maximize the resemblance between the demands made on the outside and those within the hospital.

The central difference is illustrated by tracing the intake procedures. On the traditional ward, a man would be interviewed initially by the psychologist, who would explain what his job assignment would be and outline his treatment program for him; all requests for passes and money, as well as consultation over personal problems, would be handled by staff. By contrast, a man entering the small-group ward was informed immediately that he was a member of one of the small groups, and it was further explained that the members would orient him to the ward. The respective group was notified of the new member by means of a note in a message box. Since the groups met every day, the man was quickly initiated into the ward. The small groups met alone four out of the five days, with the psychologist available only to answer questions of fact that bore on recommendations to be made by the group. On the fifth day each group reported to the staff on what plans they had in regard to passes, money, and any problems of the member (e.g., arriving late for drugs). At this juncture the staff acted upon the specific recommendations.

The contrast should be clear. Whereas the man on the traditional ward was in a subservient role, with little to say in the conduct of his hospital affairs, the small-group member was forced into a situation which required the exercise of independent judgment and collective responsibility in regard to his own affairs as well as those of his fellow patients. The action of the staff upon the group recommendations presumably provided reinforcement for task-oriented, reasonable thinking, relating ultimately to plans for discharge.

The actual operation of the small groups should be examined more closely. The funds of each man were controlled, that is, each man received increasing amounts of money per week depending on which step-level he had attained, and the step-levels, in turn, required increasingly responsible, "normal" behavior. In order, moreover, to encourage "healthy" group functioning, the group was rewarded with promotions contingent upon the soundness of the recommendations they made for each patient. In this way, the staff was able to maintain ultimate control over the ward, while, at the same time, allowing for a maximum of participation of each man in his group and rewarding such involvement with promotions, or punishing irresponsible behavior with demotions, with corresponding denial of privileges and money. Of particular importance in the group's functioning was planning for the discharge and employment of patients in the highest step-level. Dissatisfied with existing liaisons between the hospital and the community, the patients even set up their own employment service, which placed more men on jobs than did the hospital machinery.

The experiment ran for twenty-seven weeks, with a six-month follow-up beginning on the day that each man left the hospital. Assessments took place continually throughout the program. Time-sampled observations were made of patients' behavior at various times during the day, and it was found, for example, that the small-group patients were more physically active, participated in more social events, talked more frequently, and exhibited more initiative and humor in ward meetings. Questionnaire data revealed that small-group members felt more frequently that they had been helped, seeing their fellow patients as instrumental in improving their behavior to a greater extent than did the men on the traditional ward who, if they saw any improvement at all, attributed it to staff. Small-group patients were also more optimistic about future employment. Moreover, the experimental patients spent significantly fewer days in the hospital, stayed out longer, and achieved better employment records. They also ingested less medication daily. However, as predicted, recidivism was not affected by the small-group program, presumably because, once on the outside, the patients lost the social contacts which had apparently formed the basis of their superior hospital adjustment.

In evaluating Fairweather's work, it should be borne in mind that, like other good researchers, he is concerned with testing the limits of a particular model—in this case, the view that what people term "mental illness" is fruit-fully defined as behavior which lacks the social skills necessary for surviving in our society. He is unconcerned with "real causes," either in a psycho-analytic sense or even in a social-learning sense. Moreover, the program is not organized to provide much in the way of individual or other professional psy-chological and psychiatric treatment. While, as has been said elsewhere in this paper, most hospital patients receive very little individual attention from pro-fessionals aside from prescribed drugs, one can see, at least ideally, a program such as Fairweather's containing within it provisions for other specific ther-apeutic interventions. Thus, for example, if the admitting clinician noticed that a given patient was debilitatingly anxious about specific social situations, he might arrange for desensitization therapy to be done at certain times of the day when the patient was not busy with his small-group assignments; it is possible that even greater success could have been realized had more individual attention been paid to certain patients.

It should also be borne in mind that the patients in this study were not the chronic, regressed people typical of almost all the operant work we have seen.

OVERALL EVALUATION OF THE WARD-WIDE PROGRAMS

These studies certainly demonstrate the effectiveness of ward-wide response-contingent tokens and back-up reinforcers in increasing the frequency of many desirable hospital behaviors. Moreover, to the extent that the responsible be-havior aimed for in these programs resembles that which contributes to a satisfactory outside adjustment—and it seems that such similarities do exist—one would look with some optimism at this sort of procedure; judicious appli-cation of operant methods such as these would seem capable of reducing or even eliminating many of the institutionalization problems discussed by such writers as Goffman (1961). Especially in a VA setting would it appear crucial to reverse the sometimes exasperating contingencies which exist for many of the patients, especially those with so-called "service-connected disabilities." An additional advantage, as has already been mentioned, is the excellent use to which the psychologist can put the nursing staff, who, after all, are closest to the patients and are in the best position to control their reinforcing environment.

The studies reported by Ayllon & Azrin (1965) provide the much-needed evidence that the observed changes do appear to be due to the various con-tingencies being set by the staff. Although the sharp reversals in response frequencies do not resemble the gradual acquisition curves that the experi-mentalist is used to seeing, it does nonetheless seem justified at this point to conclude that the various stimulus events which workers call "reinforcers" do function in this way at least to the extent that they exert definite effect upon response frequencies through their relationship to the emission of a given response. Then again, it does not seem at all clear whether, in looking at individual acquisition data as opposed to group data, one does not find the sudden stepwise shifts in experimental studies of learning that one finds in the graphs of Ayllon & Azrin (compare with Bower, 1961).

My main reservation about these studies has already been made clear in this section, as well as in the discussion of "target behaviors" in an earlier section. There is perhaps a natural tendency to concentrate on those problems which best fit the model one is working with, especially if that model is proving fruitful. It seems to this writer that behavior modifiers working in institutional settings are especially open to the risk of committing grave errors simply because of their successes. Indeed, if one is to take most learning theories seriously and apply them to the behavior of behavior modifiers—is there a willingness to do this?—then it is to be expected that successes with operant conditioning will lead to still greater efforts in the same area. Enough examples have been cited from the published reports to indicate where this narrow perspective has limitations. In the next section we shall be examining other behavior modification work to illustrate techniques that seem to fit better into different behavioral models—and that occasionally seem also to manifest greater clinical sophistication.

Other Behavioral Approaches

The work to be reviewed in this section consists almost entirely of case studies. While the lack of controls makes it impossible to derive scientifically respectable conclusions, the studies do, nonetheless, serve the crucial heuristic function of suggesting what variables might be operating to produce the observed changes. The history of science is replete with incidental, relatively uncontrolled observations which lead the way to more controlled and systematic investigations of nontrivial phenomena. It is in this spirit that the following reports are discussed.

There is another reason for this section. These case reports reflect the writer's strong bias that admission to a mental hospital, even with some kind of "psychotic" diagnosis, conveys little information to the therapist other than that the behavior problems have become so severe that admission seemed to the person, his family, to the courts, or to some other agency the most expedient way of dealing with the difficulties. This is not to deny that there are, indeed, real differences between schizophrenics and nonschizophrenics, or among various subtypes (e.g., Silverman, 1964). It is, rather, to say that such differences have had as yet little bearing on what to do with the suffering human being sitting on the other side of one's desk.

Many of the case studies in Eysenck's (1960a) collection deal with institutionalized individuals in England (e.g., Bevan, 1960; Meyer, 1957; Walton, 1960a, 1960b; Walton & Black, 1958, 1959). The techniques employed and the rationale suggested to explain the clinical results contrast strikingly with most of the work already reviewed. Perhaps the title of the volume—*Behavior Therapy and the Neuroses*—does not contribute to making the connection between these studies and the behavioral work being done in hospitals in the United States. The reports to be discussed in this section, all of them published after 1960, may be seen as representative of a synthesis and elaboration of these two mainstreams of behavior therapy.

One of the few clinical reports of systematic desensitization with hospitalized patients is by Cowden & Ford (1962). Explicitly rejecting Wolpe's (1958) assertion that his techniques are unsuitable for psychotics, they employed the procedure with two very disturbed, chronic "paranoid schizophrenics," both of whom displayed avoidance reactions whose elimination seemed to promise a considerable improvement in their overall functioning. One man, whose behavior included extreme tension, excessive drinking, hallucinations, and delusions of persecution, was desensitized to speaking with other people. The other man was desensitized to leaving things behind in rooms, being psychologically crippled by the compulsion to keep rechecking.

Cowden & Ford experienced with these men the kinds of problems that can "drive a desensitizer back to the couch" (compare with Davison, 1968b; Lazarus, 1964c; Wolpe & Lazarus, 1966): there was reluctance to practice relaxation; hierarchies were slow in building because of the patients' difficulties in picking out anxiety stimuli; visualization of the items was difficult to achieve; and the signaling of anxiety was considered to be unreliable.

Nonetheless, after upwards of 50 sessions, the results were heartening. While neither man was discharged, the first patient improved so much—not only along the dimension that he was desensitized to but also in regard to hallucinations and his other "paranoid symptoms"—that he could have left the hospital if his parents had accepted him at home.

It is significant that both men had undergone various other kinds of therapies, with no improvement. As has been argued elsewhere (e.g., Grossberg, 1964), this not atypical datum lends some support to the notion that improvement did not occur "spontaneously." While neither case would classify as a "clinical cure," this question seems less important than the very real changes effected.

Meyer & Gelder (1963) describe "in vivo desensitization" (compare with Meyer, 1957) of five hospital patients who, though highly idiosyncratic in respect to other problem areas, were all extremely agoraphobic. Each had also undergone other kinds of therapy, including ECT, various drugs, and "intensive psychotherapy." The content of some of the fears was so unusual, in fact, that, in my opinion, some of the patients might have been diagnosed as psychotic had they been seen in this country. Be that as it may, the treatment method employed was training the person to relax in the presence of the therapist and then gradually reexposing him to more and more fearful agoraphobic situations in the therapist's company. The results showed that at least three of the five maintained improvement outside the hospital.

Kennedy (1964) has reported several highly provocative and successful cases with hospitalized adults. She directly attacked the primary delusional structures of three chronic paranoid schizophrenics, after gaining their confidence in several nonjudgmental sessions. Therapy in each case lasted no longer than three months, and the patients were seen a few times a week. During the sessions most of the time was spent disagreeing with delusional statements and positively reinforcing reality-oriented remarks. Ward personnel cooperated also, in order to provide as consistent a hospital environment as possible. In each instance the delusional ideas disappeared, followed by satisfactory extrahospital adjustment.

Meyer (1966) reports the cases of two highly obsessional women admitted to a teaching hospital. Both had rather severe and prolonged histories of psychiatric problems and hospitalizations, with treatments including leucotomy, ECT, and systematic desensitization. The crux of therapy was to urge them strongly to resist performing their obsessive rituals; the author reasoned that by exposing the patients to the experience of not going through with the act, he could change their expectations about the dire consequences of not doing so. This straightforward, rather commonsense approach appears to have greatly alleviated the principal complaints, at least making it possible for them to live productive lives outside the hospital.

Davison (1966b) has presented a case study involving a combination of Wolpian-type procedures with direct attempts to change inappropriate cognitions ("delusions") about physical sensations. The case material bears some resemblance to White's (1956) well-known account of L. Percy King. The patient was a forty-four-year-old truck driver, admitted for the first time to a VA hospital complaining of "pressure points" over his right eye. He interpretated these sensations as being caused by spirits inside or outside his body, helping him make decisions. In addition, he expressed feelings of being misunderstood and persecuted. His admissions diagnosis of "schizophrenic reaction, paranoid type" had been changed within several weeks to "paranoid state," apparently because he did not appear quite so crazy once he got away from a troubling home situation.

A maintenance dosage of acetophenazine ("Tindal"), 20 mg three times a day, reduced his tensions somewhat, but his principal complaints of "pressure points" persisted, even though the psychiatric staff had allowed him an operation to remove a cyst over his right eye in the explicit hope of eliminating the sensations. He was referred to the author for "behavior therapy" two months following his admission.

Direct questioning quickly revealed that the "pressure points" occurred in decision situations which were very anxiety-provoking. Deciding in the first session that therapy should aim at changing this unusual belief about what were probably simple muscle tensions, the author presented to the man this alternative explanation of the sensations, in the spirit of a scientific hypothesis which the two of them would test together. It was demonstrated to the patient that sensations very similar to his "pressure points" could be readily generated by clenching one's fist, extending the arm, and bending the closed hand down toward the inside of the wrist. The next step was intensive relaxation training to try to control the sensations. Over a period of eight sessions, the therapist continued to explore the implications of interpreting the pressure points in a naturalistic fashion, and the man was soon perceiving them in this way and controlling their intensity and frequency by differentially relaxing his forehead in difficult decision situations.

Therapy included also assertive training to enable the patient to handle himself in otherwise anxiety-provoking interpersonal situations. He was also told to reflect more on how other people would view certain actions taken in the heat of emotion; as he became more relaxed, he grew increasingly capable of appearing less "paranoid."

Following the publication of this case report, a nine-month follow-up was obtained independently of the therapy, i.e., from a questionnaire which the patient filled out at home for a research study he had been participating in on his ward with a research psychiatrist. He was gainfully employed, considerably less tense, and, most importantly, reported infrequent and controllable occurrences of the "pressure points" (his quotation marks).

The therapy bears some similarity to Kennedy's (1964) work, as well as to the suggestions of Cameron (1959), Salzman (1960), and Schwartz (1963), who, from much different theoretical viewpoints, propose that paranoid ideas be subtly challenged by alternate explanations. Clearly, had the therapist not taken care to establish a trusting relationship, it is likely that the man would have placed him among those who were persecuting him. Moreover, what appears to this writer to have been of paramount importance was the strategy employed to persuade the man that an alternate interpretation was more plausible. In short, the implications of construing the "pressure points" were explored via engaging in specific behavioral tests, in a manner that might be fitted into George Kelly's (1955) system.

Meichenbaum's (1966c) account of two "conversion reactions" illustrates nicely how techniques from various subareas of behavior therapy can be applied effectively and ingeniously within the framework of a particular idiographic instance. Both his VA patients had long psychiatric histories. In one case, the man complained of an inability to keep his eyes open, but this problem had been preceded by familial tensions arising from religious differences with his wife. Initially steps were taken, via tranquilizers and relaxation training, to reduce his tensions; it was also strongly suggested to him that taking a deep breath and exhaling would make his eyes open. After his first stage of therapy, which, within eight hours, had him keeping his eyes open much of the time, he was desensitized in imagination to situations which were making him maladaptively tense. Finally, because the therapist had taken care to ascertain that the man had most difficulty keeping his eyes open in situations with domineering people, the patient was given training in assertive behavior (Salter, 1949; Wolpe, 1958) in order to substitute a more adaptive behavior for the "escape" and "denial" afforded by the "hysterical symptom." A three-month follow-up after discharge found him functioning effectively.

Hogan (1966) has reported some preliminary results from clinical trials with Stampfl's "implosive therapy" (cf. London, 1964). The crux of this technique is the elicitation, via disgusting imagery, of high levels of anxiety and antipathy in fearful patients, under the assumption that many of the problems are avoidance reactions mediated by unrealistic anxiety. By having the person confront the feared situation (CS) without untoward consequences (UCS), extinction of the fear is presumed to occur. The procedure has some interesting similarities to and contrasts with Wolpe's (1958) more benign procedures for exposing anxious individuals to their neurotic fears; the reader is referred to London's (1964) excellent discussion for particulars. Although controls for enthusiasm and personality of therapists are lacking, Hogan does report very suggestive evidence that hospitalized psychotic patients improve significantly more from such therapy than roughly matched controls, as judged by higher discharge rates. Controlled studies with implosive therapy are just beginning to reach publication (e.g., Kirchner & Hogan, 1966). As personally aversive as the procedure may be to some clinicians, it certainly deserves evaluation with respect to the same criteria as are applied to less extreme techniques.

Lazarus & Davison (in press) report the case of a young man who had been repeatedly hospitalized with various diagnoses: paranoid schizophrenic, character disorder, psychopathic personality, and antisocial reaction. He had also been jailed for armed robbery. Having proved refractory to other treatment methods, he was referred for "behavior therapy" (a practice which is becoming more and more prevalent). An initial step was to explain that, whereas hostility meets with negative consequences, appropriate assertive behavior is adaptive. Several sessions were spent establishing a working relationship with the man and assessing the steps which might be taken to change his aggressive, "paranoid" behavior. It was noted that underlying the violent outbursts were various irrational fears and hypersensitivities, especially in regard to guilt over his mother's accidental death and in regard to being scrutinized by authority figures. Systematic desensitization, therefore, was executed with a 90-item hierarchy designed to reduce his sensitivities to numerous social situations. He was seen twice a week for three months, after which he was discharged from hospital. A two-year follow-up revealed that he had obtained several salary increases at the job which the therapist had helped him obtain, and had also married one of the secretaries. This case, like the preceding ones, illustrates well the effectiveness of making a thorough behavioral analysis of the presenting problems before plunging ahead with therapy.

Two pilot studies have been reported by Wolpin and his colleagues from Camarillo State Hospital in California (Wolpin & Pearsall, 1965; Wolpin & Raines, 1966). The first article is a case report of a middle-aged woman hospitalized for "neurotic depression." She also reported herself to be fearful of snakes. Within seven sessions a student-therapist under Wolpin's supervision desensitized her to this fear, enabling the woman to hold a snake and even to want it as a pet at a three-week follow-up. A most intriguing aspect of the report is that the actual desensitization (pairing of relaxation with imaginal aversive stimuli) was carried out in one session. Since several hours had been spent earlier in intensive exploration of personal problems with an enthusiastic young therapist, it is difficult to be sure what contributed to the elimination of the phobia. The second study attempted to assess the relative contributions of gradual but forced imaginal exposure without relaxation, gradual but forced imaginal exposure with tensing of muscles, and forced exposure to the top of the hierarchy. Five of the six hospitalized subjects handled the snake, with no difference among the conditions. Unfortunately, there was no independence between assessments of avoidance behavior and the actual treatment conditions. Nonetheless, the study does provide further confirmation of the appropriateness of variants of systematic desensitization with institutionalized patients, provided, of course, that a relevant fear dimension is isolable.

I am aware of only one desensitization study with hospitalized patients (Zeisset, 1968) which attempts to institute satisfactory controls. For details of the experiment, refer to Paul (Chapter 3, pp. 117ff.). I would like to mention several problems, however, which seem to justify some caution in interpreting the results. There were only four treatment sessions for both desensitization (D) and relaxation-plus-application (RPA) subjects. These included both the training in relaxation (total for D Ss, differential for RPA Ss) and, for the D subjects, the actual pairing of imaginal aversive stimuli with relaxation. Even if the majority of Ss completed their hierarchies (this information is lacking in the write-up upon which I am basing this discussion), one is faced with a considerable disparity between the speed with which desensitization was completed by Zeisset and that found by earlier workers (Lang & Lazovik, 1963; Lang, Lazovik, & Reynolds, 1965; Davison, 1965a). Lang reports the need for at least 10 sessions with snake-phobic college volunteers, and Davison allowed 9 sessions; it is significant that in neither of these three earlier studies did all Ss complete their hierarchies. Zeisset is aware of this difference, as well as the significantly smaller number of anxiety signals during desensitization itself (as compared with the frequencies reported earlier by Agras, 1965, and Davison, 1965a). Since the assumption is that vivid images and anxiety signaling are crucial in the procedure, it is possible that Zeisset's subjects were not as capable of performing in these respects as the college Ss used in former studies. It is conceivable, therefore, that the requisite pairing of relaxation with imaginal aversive stimuli (compare with Davison, 1968b) did not take place. If this is the case, as I am hypothesizing, then the beneficial results reported by Zeisset may not be due to desensitization at all. My own clinical experience in trying to relax and desensitize VA patients confirms the possibility that Zeisset's desensitization procedure may have been problematical (compare with Cowden & Ford, 1962, discussed above).

An additional difficulty is found in the RPA group. Recall that these Ss were trained in differential relaxation with strong suggestion that they could learn to control their emotional reactions thereby. No specific application was made, however, to the target-behavior situation. To what can we attribute the significant reduction in interview anxiety, a reduction which did not differ from that measured in the D group? Since the attention-placebo Ss did not improve, one would tend to rule out mere suggestion factors in the RPA subjects. Since no attempts had been made directly to desensitize these Ss in vivo (as done by Davison, 1965b), such counterconditioning effects can also be ruled out (as Zeisset himself does). I would like to suggest that the suggestion about "control of emotional reactions" contributed importantly to the reduction in anxiety. If the differential relaxation training was at all successful, then subjects, during the four treatment sessions, were no doubt able to feel themselves reducing their own anxieties. This element of self-control could have contributed to the results in at least three ways: (1) the subjects could have applied the procedures in the actual posttreatment assessment situation, although not specifically instructed to do so by the therapist; and/or (2) in practicing the relaxation in vivo between treatment sessions, they could have been desensitizing some related anxieties in vivo on their own; and/or (3) the treatment experiences of having some control over their own internal reactions could have led to a beneficial reevaluation of themselves as "individuals who can control anxiety."

In spite of these questions of method and interpretation, the experiment (which should be replicated) is an important one in providing further evidence to suggest that, whatever the nature of the hospital patient's problems, significant alteration of certain anxieties can be effected via desensitization and training in relaxation. One would expect such changes to have greater or lesser effects in other areas (including discharge) depending on the role played by the anxiety dimension in each individual case.

Evaluation. The operations followed by the therapists in these studies clearly differ from most of those reviewed earlier: more was done than applying differential consequences contingent upon particular behaviors. Whether the processes underlying the observed changes were due to other than operant factors cannot, of course, be proved. In most instances, however, the therapist carefully appraised the situation in respect to as many relevant variables as he could point to, not limiting himself to procedures which appear to fit the operant paradigm. For example, Davison (1966b) made use of relaxation both as a means of testing the alternate construction of the "pressure points" and as a means of lowering the patient's general anxiety level. In addition, he trained the man in assertive behavior in the hopes of avoiding the violent, "crazy" outbursts which, in the past, seem to have been the result of failing to express himself appropriately in a given situation. Meichenbaum (1966c) likewise made use of several procedures in his two cases of "conversion reactions." The case reported by Lazarus & Davison (in press) illustrates what Lazarus (1966a) has referred to as "broad spectrum behavior therapy," that is, the application of several techniques, as appropriate, to as many areas of sensitivity and deficit as seem necessary to render the individual better able to function. Thus, assertive training was undertaken in the same spirit as already seen in Davison (1966b); numerous fears and hypersensitivities were handled by systematic desensitization; and a job was obtained for the patient after discharge so as to maximize the chances of his coping effectively outside the hospital.

As has been argued elsewhere (Lazarus, Davison, & Polefka, 1965), complex problems frequently require attention to be paid to both respondent and operant factors, as well as to the so-called "nonspecifics" (Lazarus, 1963b), i.e., those probably crucial variables in the interpersonal therapeutic situation which, at least thus far, are outside the purview of "modern learning theory." My experience has been that many behavior modifiers who have a strong clinical commitment are all too aware of the limits of contemporary behavior modification—while, to be sure, making effective use of its very real strengths.

A further characteristic which seems to differentiate this work from the operant studies is the deliberate appeal to mediational processes such as "anxiety" and "cognition." To be sure, in each instance the nonobservable is tied to observables. Nonetheless, taking into consideration a client's imaginal processes (e.g., in systematic desensitization) is considerably more inferential than, for example, plotting on a graph the frequency of verbal somatic complaints (Ayllon & Haughton, 1964). This writer's argument is that such inferences are *necessary* and *appropriate* to behavior modification, involving at times what is thought to be "underlying causes," albeit conceptualized in behavioral terms readily verifiable by observables (compare with Dollard & Miller, 1950). This point of view is fruitfully contrasted with that of Ullmann & Krasner (1965), who, in the historical introduction to their case studies book, appear to categorize such inference making as "disease model." The clinical data seem at this point to justify and even to require mediational approaches; it is an important task of future research to determine the circumstances under which reliance upon these mediators provides more useful explanatory concepts than are available in nonmediational approaches.

A SUGGESTION REGARDING THE USE
OF ASSESSMENT AS A THERAPEUTIC TOOL

Traditionally, assessment and diagnosis are seen as analytical-descriptive activities engaged in by a professional for purposes of specifying what is wrong and, at times, what should be done to alleviate the problem(s) assessed. Following this initial step, decisions are made on whether changes should be attempted; and finally, therapy, as such, begins. This orientation, indeed, is institutionalized in the separation between "intake" and "therapy" interviews, often conducted by different clinicians.

From a reading of the behavior therapy literature, as well as from personal experience, I discern a fascinating tendency toward the breakdown of the split between assessment and therapy. For example, Mischel (1968) and Goldfried & Pomeranz (1968) seem to be furthering the trend that one's assessment procedures should be tied quite closely to the therapeutic maneuvers that are conceivable following the problem description. It is beyond the scope of this chapter to explore fully the implications of this approach for the conduct of clinical activities.

However, there is another side to this issue which is quite relevant to behavior modification in general, and to behavior modification in institutional settings in particular. This writer has been "doing behavior therapy" (as the saying goes, unfortunately) in hospitals, outpatient clinics, and private settings. With virtually every client, he has had occasion to explain exactly the procedures which would be followed and, as far as is known at this point, the reasons for doing so (see Goldstein et al., 1966, for discussion of this characteristic of behavior therapies). The explanation almost always begins with a statement of the assumptions made by behaviorally oriented therapists on the nature of the psychological processes presumed to underlie the problem(s). These assumptions have already been summarized, in part, in the first section of this chapter (see pp. 220–222). In essence, the argument (obviously buttressed by the prestige of the therapist role) presented to the client is that, while his feelings may appear very odd, peculiar, crazy, and "sick," such feelings can be produced in "normal" people as well by subjecting them to certain environmental-developmental situations. Furthermore, his feelings are explicable in terms of the same psychological processes which psychologists invoke to explain such human behavior as rote learning, acquisition of sensorimotor skills, and sensory deprivation experiences. In other words, the client's own experiences are brought within the framework of general experimental psychology rather than being excluded by virtue of being due to an "illness" or "disease" which sets the individual apart in a qualitative—and often pejorative—fashion. Furthermore, the client is told that labels such as "sick" and "mentally ill" are constructions imposed by social animals rather then traits inherent in the client/patient. Naturally, whether these preliminary statements are true or not is irrelevant; we have, in fact, already cast doubt on portions of the foregoing in this chapter. What is relevant is that the behavior therapist, by and large, construes psychological "ills" in this nondisease fashion and, in so doing, can have occasion to communicate this orientation to the client. If you will, it is as if the client is qualified to understand the implications of such recent books as Ullmann & Krasner (1965) and Goldstein, Heller, & Sechrest (1966).

Returning now to the client, I have observed clinically that, provided the client/patient is able to understand this orientation and accept it, at least provisionally, he is frequently very much relieved and encouraged at the very outset, and is sometimes enabled later on to use this information to good advantage in important interpersonal relationships.

Two case reports that illustrate this "assessment-therapy" technique have recently been published. Part of the therapy with the "paranoid schizophrenic" (Davison, 1966b) described earlier entailed just such a preliminary "spiel" to a VA patient who was beset with delusional beliefs regarding the nature of bodily sensations: he felt that spirits were telling him what to do in difficult decision situations by means of "pressure points" in his forehead. Furthermore, because of the manner in which he talked about these experiences, he was being regarded as a "mental case" and had, of course, most recently been admitted to a mental hospital with a medical label certifying this. A part of the first session was devoted to an antidisease argument in the manner already described. It was observed clinically that the man was, simply, very happy to have someone in authority tell him that his admittedly strange behavior could be regarded as "normal" in respect to the processes causing it, and "sick" only in respect to social judgments (compare with Szasz, 1960). Therapy as traditionally conceived then proceeded as already outlined.

In a second case (Davison, 1968a), a college student presented himself for private therapy with the complaint "I'm a sadist." It turned out that, since age eleven, he had found only fantasies of torturing girls sexually stimulating and could not recall ever having been titillated by a culture-appropriate image or activity. Once again, the initial step was to remove the stigma and concern from this problem by describing the kinds of unusual experiences that can be induced in normal human beings by certain psychophysiological manipulations, and by stating the working assumption that his own odd experiences had come about in like fashion and would be approached therapeutically in a manner consistent with this construction of the problem. The relief and encouragement afforded by this viewpoint were likewise readily observable clinically, viz., "Boy, am I glad to hear *that*!" It should be stressed that, in both of these cases, the presumed benefits of these orienting remarks appeared to be separate from any assumption that the client could have made in regard to the efficacy of the therapy to follow. Indeed, in years to come, a diagnosis even so disturbing as "lung cancer" will hopefully be no more troubling than the statement that one has a sprained wrist.

What is being suggested, then, is that behavior therapists may have within their very orientation and diagnostic practices (the "behavioral analysis") a potentially useful therapeutic tool, especially with hospitalized patients, who suffer not only from the problems which lead to institutionalization, but from the very *effects* of institutionalization, especially the stigma and despair which go with a mental hospital admission (compare with Goffman, 1961).

Two studies in institutional settings illustrate related possibilities. From the Houston VA Hospital, Rothaus, Hanson, Cleveland, & Johnson (1963) report an experiment in which patients were taught to play two different roles in interviews with prospective employers. In the "mental illness" condition, patients were told to talk about their "nervous condition" and "illness," with stress on the hospital aspects of their most recent life, e.g., their "medications" and their hopes for "cures." In the "problem" condition, these same patients talked about such things as being shy, having difficulty in handing responsibility, and being lonely (these being less inferential descriptions of why they were in the hospital). The interviewers, ignorant of the ruse, rated subjects in the problem condition as better job bets than the (same) patients in the illness condition. In discussing the results, the authors speculate that focusing on the problems being experienced rather than on the presumed underlying "illness" set the stage for the interviewer to regard the patient more as a human being struggling with human problems than as a mental patient afflicted with an illness. More recently, Rothaus & Hanson (1965) have provided suggestive evidence that the lines of questioning after a problem-centered description differ from those elicited by an illness description.

In another study, Jones, Kahn, & Wolcott (1964) compared the attitudes of both patients and staff on two matched wards in a university psychiatric hospital. On the experimental ward, all hospital personnel wore street clothing instead of their usual hospital uniforms. Preliminary results indicate that the patients on this ward favored the change, finding that it facilitated communication with staff and made the setting more similar to real life. The staff likewise expressed preferences for this arrangement. Interestingly enough, the only opposition came from the medical administrative staff. There are no reports on clinical improvement, nor are there data on what might have operated to produce the attitudes—perhaps the nursing staff behaved differently when in street clothes, in addition to patients perceiving less distance from them. Whatever the reasons, however, the study is very exciting and, no doubt, has been and will be attempted in other hospitals.[6] Of course, what the staff does with

---

[6] I have recently become aware of more research of this nature, conducted by Paul Rothaus and his colleagues at the Houston VA Hospital. In their Human Relations Training Laboratory, efforts are made, wherever possible, to divest the ward of mental illness connotations. For example, patients are called "participants"; staff wear civilian clothes, as seen in the report of Jones et al. (1964), and are on a first-name basis with the ward members; and participants even administer their own

any possible increase in patient contact, or with any beneficial change in the patients' self-concept, is a separate question.

Concluding Remarks

A problem which can be said to be relevant to almost all the operant work reviewed here is really quite simple, yet does not seem to have received the attention which it merits. As London (1964) has already pointed out, this research has really yet to prove itself effective in "curing" the hospitalized patient: "It is marvellous to induce psychotics to ask for gum after years of total silence, even if months of effort are required. But it is not clear exactly when or how or whether this kind of maneuver will equip them to leave a hospital and function again in society. And great as the promise of operant therapy is there, a Scotch verdict is still in order—not proven" (London, 1964, p. 117).

Although many of the studies we have examined were not executed in a clinical spirit, enough of them have been—and many more will be—to justify applying to them the criterion against which any therapeutic technique ought to be evaluated, namely, how effective the procedure is in changing the individual so that he can function as a "normal" person in the outside world. To be sure, one does not declare modern dentistry as ineffective simply because most of us have to make annual corrective therapy visits. In regard to behavior modification, however, this should be our worst problem!

Optimism about one's theories and methods can be carried perhaps too far if one concludes too much from statements such as: "From these preliminary results one can appreciate the long-term potentialities of this approach" (Davison & Krasner, 1964). That the general approach has potential has been amply demonstrated; that it is truly effective in altering the problems encountered in institutional settings has not. Whether a general psychological approach can make an impact on the ever-growing mental hospital population will no doubt provide a focus for exciting clinical and experimental work in the future.

Perhaps one of the more important and exciting implications of the general operant approach is the possibility it offers to extend "psychotherapy" to the hours which the hospital patient spends outside the therapist's office—

---

drugs (Rothaus, Morton, Johnson, Cleveland, & Lyle, 1963). Similar attempts have been made for some time on an acute ward at the Palo Alto VA Hospital, where J. Shelton, M.D., along with a succession of like-minded ward psychologists (I was one), tries to create a nonmedical, nonillness atmosphere by such means as referring to medications as "drugs" and/or "perceptual regulators"; stressing responsibility for "sick" behavior; and focusing on "problems in living" (Szasz, 1960) rather than on "symptoms of illness."

meaning, in most cases, all of his hours. As has been pointed out by many workers (e.g., Ayllon & Haughton, 1964; Davison, 1964; Ullmann & Krasner, 1965), the chief merit of behavioral approaches lies with the explicitness and concreteness with which they can be implemented, even by so-called "nonprofessionals," including members of the patient's own family. Even if the studies reviewed above have not demonstrated the "cures" which one should set as a goal in designing behavior change techniques, they surely provide impressive evidence for effectiveness in radically altering often long-standing "crazy" behaviors, many of which form the basis for hospitalization itself. It is also likely that, whatever the original causative factors, some "psychotic" behavior is maintained and perhaps even further shaped by well-meaning hospital personnel who are unaware of the role which their own attending behaviors can have in manipulating "sick" responding. As Ayllon & Haughton (1964, p. 97) have put it:

> Therapy must be couched in a set of objective techniques which can be easily taught and implemented by relatively untrained personnel. Whereas therapy is presently discussed at hospital staff meetings, ward meetings, and sundry meetings, the actual step-by-step method of influencing the patient's behavior is left to the imagination of nurses and attendants. All the sophisticated professional staff composed of psychiatrists, social workers, psychologists, counsellors, recreational therapists, etc., will not suffice if the dynamics of therapy are not translated into a practical down-to-earth form to be used by the very personnel entrusted to care for the patients. This personnel is at present made up of attendants and nurses whose day-to-day treatment of the patient is primarily based on common sense and sometimes outright superstition. The techniques illustrated in this investigation constitute an objective therapeutic tool which can be used effectively by relatively untrained hospital personnel. Hence, irrespective of theoretical persuasion and clinical conviction, this too represents a powerful instrument in the development of normal behaviour and the elimination of maladaptive behaviour in schizophrenic patients.

SEVERAL IMPORTANT ISSUES

Perhaps *because of* the effectiveness of various conditioning procedures in changing behaviors that had hitherto been recalcitrant to other therapeutic intervention, there are discernible in the behavior modification literature certain tendencies to go further than is warranted either by data or by logic. This is perhaps compounded by the relative ease with which a clever learning theorist or practitioner can devise rather compelling "explanations" for how a given behavior has come about. To take but one area in the animal learning literature, one recalls the heady controversy engendered by Tolman & Honzik's (1930) classic study on latent learning, and how diehard Hullians found "secondary reinforcement" lurking in hitherto unsuspected corners of the T-maze (compare with Kimble, 1961).

A study by Ayllon, Haughton, & Hughes (1965) can serve as a spring-board for discussion of many of these problems. In this demonstration, Ayllon and his colleagues taught, via the familiar operant procedure of successive approximations, a chronic female patient to hold a broom with considerable tenacity and vigor. After firmly establishing this unusual behavior in the patient's repertoire, they invited two unsuspecting psychiatrists to comment upon the phenomenon. Their psychoanalytic interpretations contrasted sharply —and, of course, ridiculously—with the true reasons for the behavior. The conclusions of these authors is that what are termed "psychotic symptoms" may, in fact, be acquired by analogous shaping, through accidental reinforcement (compare with Skinner, 1948a). This experiment makes explicit a theme which runs through much of Ayllon's work, as well as through the theoretical writings of other operant conditioners who have ventured forth bravely from the animal laboratory into the clinic and hospital (e.g., Ferster & DeMeyer, 1961). This study, however, bears closer examination:

1. The most obvious question that can, and must, be raised is how good an analog the conditioned broom holding is for a behavior occurring in nature without the artificial shaping carried out by Ayllon et al. The only empirical evidence furnished in this study is the willingness of the two psychiatrists to comment upon the etiology of the behavior. One wonders what the patient herself might have said if she had been queried. Might she not have responded to the effect that she was carrying the broom in hopes of obtaining more cigarettes and attention? If so, is this madness? This issue has already been touched upon, but it bears repetition. A concept such as "psychotic symptom" may possibly be definable not only in terms of what a patient can be observed doing but in terms of what he says about what he is doing. By ignoring the patient's reports on her own behavior, one may be extending too faithfully a model that has been developed from work with nonverbal organisms.

2. "The etiology of many so-called psychotic symptoms exhibited by hospitalized patients or those in need of hospitalization does not have to be sought in the obscure dynamics of a psychiatric disturbance" (Ayllon et al., 1965, p. 5). This conclusion suggests that an operant conditioning explanation renders unnecessary, even fictional, another type of explanation because it has been shown possible to produce a psychotic-looking behavior by means of an operant procedure. Unfortunately, these authors run the risk of committing a logical error known as "affirming the consequent," that is, concluding that *A* always causes *B* on the basis of the observation that *A*, in a given situation, causes *B* (compare with Maher, 1966). It is, in short, unjustified and even dangerous to adduce such data as these as anything more than barely suggestive evidence in favor of a conditioning explanation of other behavior labeled as psychotic, or even of instances of broom holding in other situations. Indeed, it would be relatively easy to produce broom holding by an entirely different means—e.g., asking a cooperative patient to hold a broom. It seems doubtful

to me that one would then be inclined to generalize to the statement that psychotic behaviors are the result of people acceding to the explicit requests of others.

3. There is, in the field generally, an undesirable and poorly justified tendency to infer etiology from treatment effectiveness. As an example, let us take the study by Ayllon & Haughton (1962). After demonstrating convincingly that problem eaters could be taught to eat unassisted simply by withdrawing the "social reinforcement" which had been observed to follow upon the refusal to eat, these authors conclude: "Indeed, this assistance appeared to produce whatever eating problems existed" (p. 345). Ayllon & Haughton really have no empirical support for such a contention, unlike, for example, the evidence provided in numerous other studies, among which is work of their own (Ayllon & Azrin, 1965). Reference is being made to successful reversals in the familiar operant A-B-A design, which do lend support to the notion that contingencies can be important in maintaining deviant behavior. In the example with the eating problems, however, their inference that the nurses' assistance produced the refusal to eat has as much validity as concluding that, because aspirin eliminates a headache, the headache was caused by a lack of aspirin. Rimland (1964), from whom this analogy was taken, deals with this issue in his compelling and comprehensive treatise on infantile autism. In a discussion which bears also on the previous point ("affirming the consequent") he draws long overdue attention to the fact that the various psychogenic theories of autism, while they may be parsimonious and plausible, may at the same time be unsubstantiated.

Let us stay with infantile autism for a moment, for it can serve as a fruitful example. In the late 1950s, C. B. Ferster conducted several experiments to see whether children diagnosed as schizophrenic or autistic could acquire simple habits through shaping procedures. In a now classic article (Ferster, 1961), he constructed an elaborate and likewise very compelling hypothesis about the development of such deviant behavior in terms of the retardation, through nonreinforcement at the primary level, of the development of secondary and generalized reinforcers in controlling the child's behavior. To be sure, this conceptualization has fostered intensive and exciting clinical research in therapy. However, it also perpetuates, albeit in different language, the unproved notion that the parents or guardians of these children caused the behavior disorder through their unwitting ("unconscious") patterns of behavior. In striking contrast is Rimland's hypothesis of autism as a genetically based illness, revolving about a dysfunction in some part of the brain (perhaps the reticular formation) which plays a role in the processing of incoming peripheral stimulation. To bring the discussion back to the etiology-treatment issue, it must be stated that *knowledge about how to change a phenomenon is not tantamount to knowing how it originated.* That a given behavior change technique can be compatible with two radically different notions about etiology can be appreciated by referring to my observation (Davison, 1965c) that Rimland's physiological orientation leads him to a point regarding psychological treatment which is hardly different from Ferster's. Thus, the child, according to Rimland (1964, p. 182) is largely unresponsive to social stimuli because there is a ". . . failure in association (via the reticular formation or some other structure), a failure to associate biological rewards (food, warmth, etc.) with social (mainly maternal) relationships . . . a failure to associate stimulus and reward." Furthermore, the important implication for treatment is ". . . that since *meaning* cannot serve its usual role in guiding the learning of autistic children, it may be necessary to rely on the use of lavish praise and other forms of overt reward to provide direction as well as incentive for the child's efforts. Discovering ways of making optimum use of the autistic child's limited ability to learn, and especially discovering ways of increasing the child's ability to generalize what he has learned, would appear to offer challenging problems for future research." (p. 138).

While Rimland, because of his biogenic bias, looks to biochemical research for an answer to the prevention and cure of autism, his recent interest in efforts to condition such children is not at all inconsistent with his conviction about the etiology of the problem (Rimland, 1965).

I deem this issue of sufficient importance to merit further discussion. Ullmann & Krasner (1965) preface their collection of case studies with a scholarly review of the so-called "medical" and "psychological" models of abnormal behavior. They state: "Maladaptive behaviors are learned behaviors, and the development and maintenance of a maladaptive behavior is no different from the development and maintenance of any other behavior" (p. 20). I find it significant that this thesis is put forth in a collection of case studies which, except for a preliminary report of the Ayllon et al. (1965) study already described, illustrate the modification of already existing behavior, with very little attention paid by any of the contributors to the etiology of the respective behavior problem. Nowhere in their review of the literature can I find justification for the assertion quoted above.[7]

In a similar vein, Wolpe (1958), on the basis of animal experiments on conditioned fear and the counterconditioning of this fear, as well as various clinical reports purporting to demonstrate the efficacy of counterconditioning techniques in eliminating human fears, asserts that neurotic anxiety is the result of conditioning. In a more recent book (Wolpe & Lazarus, 1966), it is stated that: "A basic premise about neuroses is that they are persistent, unadaptive learned habits of reaction" (p. 12). The assumption seems to be operating that in order to justify the application of conditioning procedures to

---

[7] These writers have recently published an abnormal psychology textbook (Ullmann & Krasner, 1969) which rests entirely upon this highly questionable assumption regarding treatment and etiology.

change a given behavior, one must be reasonably certain that the behavior is a product of conditioning. This insistence is all the more surprising in view of the paucity of experimental data on the acquisition of stable fear responses in human beings by conditioning procedures. To be sure, as Wolpe & Lazarus point out, ethical considerations preclude concentrated efforts at conditioning long-standing fears in humans, and they are able to cite only three studies which can provide evidence for their thesis (Watson & Raynor, 1920; Krasnogorski, 1925; and Campbell, Sanderson, & Laverty, 1964). However, examining the Campbell controlled study, one finds a highly atypical conditioning situation, in which the unconditioned response is suspension of breathing and other muscular movements for almost two minutes from an injection of a paralytic drug. It seems to me quite unlikely—and it would appear that Wolpe's clinical reports bear this out—that such high-level fear reactions can be found in real life. In other words, except for the rare "traumatic neuroses," this particular behavior analog seems quite unsuitable for drawing conclusions about human neuroses.

Furthermore, the acquisition of stable conditioned fear in humans is nowhere reported in the experimental literature (aside from the Campbell et al. study); once the classical reinforcement is no longer forthcoming, human Ss typically extinguish very quickly (e.g., Mowrer, 1938b; Wickens, Allen, & Hill, 1963). In reporting an experiment which provides strong confirmatory evidence in favor of Wolpe's contention that the beneficial effects of systematic desensitization are due to a process of counterconditioning, I have stressed (Davison, 1968b) that the findings allow *no* conclusions to be drawn about how the fears originally came about.

4. One last related issue merits consideration. In a review of verbal conditioning and psychotherapy, Krasner (1965) takes a behavior modification position that psychotherapy can be seen as a behavior influence process and thus is genotypically similar, in some respects, to experiments in verbal conditioning. He justifiably states: "How these operants first came about, what gradual shaping, acquisition, one-trial learning, or no-trial learning were involved in their acquisition is, for purposes of modification, irrelevant" (p. 215). So far, his assumption, one that I have shown is valid, is that the mode of acquisition of a behavior is logically irrelevant to techniques which might work to modify it. But he continues: "Irrespective of how the behavior developed, it was learned in a lawful way. The same can be said of the individual's behavior in psychotherapy. Patients have learned the 'sick' role, which determines to a large extent their performance in psychotherapy" (p. 215). This statement, in my opinion, is misleading if taken for more than an assumption, and is incorrect if it excludes the operation of nonlearning variables. There is a crucial difference between the *development* of behavior and the *learning* of behavior. While, as Hebb (1953), among others, has correctly pointed out, it is fallacious to speak of a particular behavior as "learned" or

"innate," it does make sense to speak of the relative contributions of nurture versus nature in a given (class of) behavior. In the area of eyeblink conditioning, for example, whether one aligns himself with the Iowa camp (Spence & Taylor, 1951; Spence, 1964) or the Maudsley group (Eysenck, 1965c; Franks, 1960b), the data do show undeniably that eyeblinks occur to a hitherto neutral stimulus (CS) only if the subject has undergone a conditioning procedure. In addition, however, there is strong evidence that differences in conditionability can be predicted from an independently measured trait, whether "anxiety" as defined by the MAS or "introversion" as measured by the MPI, both of which are thought to be largely genetically determined. Thus, the actual eyeblink is probably a function both of genetic and conditioning variables. Indeed, this would be the case even if no measurable genetic factors such as introversion could be isolated, for one must have eyes and a conditionable nervous system to be a suitable subject!

In their zeal, behavior modifiers would do well to reflect that learning and conditioning may not be the whole answer.

FUTURE RESEARCH

There is hardly an article which does not conclude with a plea for more research; this chapter is no exception. It should be clear that we are just beginning to understand the kinds of problems for which behavior modification techniques may be appropriate, as well as the reasons for their efficacy. From the present review, moreover, it is also clear that much of the data in institutional settings are of an uncontrolled, "clinical" nature, while many studies which are presented as experimental tests sometimes suffer from serious methodological flaws. One hopes that an initial step by researchers would be to rectify procedural errors where they exist so as to provide a better foundation for what we hope is a cumulative science.

A direction for future research would also seem to lie in coordinating behavior modification investigations with studies into the nature of the various disorders themselves. To take but one example of many, might it not be fruitful to attempt to train paranoid schizophrenics on certain perceptual tasks in the direction of nonparanoid performance, so as to take advantage of some of Silverman's (1964) research into perceptual styles among paranoids? If paranoids tend to scan excessively, would it be possible to reduce this scanning, and would this affect the total clinical picture?

A recurrent theme in this chapter has been the limitations of an operant model, a model which currently dominates the field of "behavior modification in institutional settings." While tactics which look to this body of experimental literature for justification and procedural clues have already shown themselves to be surprisingly effective in altering long-standing psychotic behaviors, the appraisal of these techniques must, as already mentioned, be one of hopeful skepticism. Moreover, it has been suggested that, perhaps in their zeal to apply response contingencies, many hospital operant conditioners are overlooking clinical data and procedures which might fruitfully complement their brave efforts (see section on Other Behavioral Approaches). Perhaps the nonclinical background of most operant workers is, at the same time, their greatest advantage and their greatest disadvantage.

In line with my own definition of behavior modification as an approach which looks to experimental psychology as a whole rather than to conditioning studies alone (see p. 221 above), reference is made once again to the recent book of Goldstein, Heller, & Sechrest (1966) as a wonderfully rich source of clinical research ideas for both hospital and outpatient populations. With their focus on resistant clients, these authors present a multitude of interesting hypotheses to make such individuals more malleable. For example, from data which suggest that limited sensory and social deprivation increases the persuasiveness of communications and the positive attributes of stimuli (compare with Adams, Carrera, Cooper, Gibby, & Tobey, 1960), they suggest that certain patients/clients be isolated for varying periods of time before attempting to influence their behavior. To take just one more example from many, reinforcements for desirable behaviors might perhaps be made only so great as to maintain the discrepant behavior, so as to generate the greatest amount of cognitive dissonance (Festinger, 1957), which, in turn, may lead to greater attitude and overt behavioral change than under conditions of more generous reinforcement.

There is an obvious need for both "basic" and "applied" research in behavior modification. One would hope, however, that in the search for basic learning processes in techniques which purport to rest upon them, workers will remain cognizant of the crucial difference between analog studies and those which test out notions in the actual area to which one aims to draw conclusions. The institutional work reviewed above seems to be evolving from analog research (Lindsley & Skinner, 1954) to field research (Ayllon & Azrin, 1965; Atthowe & Krasner, 1968). It is to be hoped that future research will be characterized by the maximum possible control consistent with asking clinically relevant questions. Poor control is not intrinsic to clinical research—satisfactory controls are only a good deal more difficult to achieve. We would do well, in sum, to remain mindful of cautionary notes such as Festinger's (1953, pp. 141, 169–170): "It should be stressed . . . that the problem of application of the results of . . . laboratory experiments to the real-life situation is not solved by a simple extension of the result. Such application requires additional experimentation and study. . . . Experiments in the laboratory must derive their direction from studies of real-life situations, and results must continually be checked by studies of real-life situations. The laboratory experiment is a technique for basic and theoretical research and is not the goal of an empirical science." This caveat is of particular relevance to research in behavior modification.

Chapter Summary

This chapter has reviewed behavior modification research, both clinical and experimental, carried out with adults in institutional settings. Probably for historical reasons, most of this work has been couched in operant conditioning terms, and a prevalent theme of the chapter has been the apparent limitations of rigidly adhering to this particular model. Several subareas were examined critically and evaluated for their contributions toward significantly altering those patterns of behavior, both overt and covert, which seem to underlie the wasteful institutionalization of an alarmingly large proportion of the adult population:

1. Investigators have succeeded in markedly affecting various nonverbal "psychotic" behaviors, e.g., refusing to enter the dining room on time (Ayllon & Haughton, 1962), hoarding towels (Ayllon, 1963), and have sometimes demonstrated beneficial generalization to areas not directly manipulated (e.g., Peters & Jenkins, 1954).

2. The verbalizations of hospital patients have also been directly changed through response-contingent reinforcements such as chewing gum, nods, smiles, and words of approval. Affectively flat patients have been conditioned to emit more emotionally toned words (e.g., Salzinger & Pisoni, 1958); mute patients have been goaded into speaking (Isaacs et al., 1960); "sick talk" has been drastically reduced via extinction combined with reinforcement of "healthy talk" (e.g., Rickard et al., 1960; Ullmann et al., 1964; Meichenbaum, 1966a, 1966b); and performance in group therapy has been influenced by selective reinforcement of certain classes of verbal behavior in separate situations (e.g., Dinoff et al., 1960; Ullmann et al., 1961). Unfortunately, some of these studies were shown to suffer from serious methodological and conceptual flaws, justifying some caution in interpretation. Generalization to other behaviors was seen to be problematical and occasionally trivial, with the significant exception of Meichenbaum's work. Special caution was suggested also in attacking directly the verbal repertoire of a given individual without first ascertaining the functional role of the behavior(s) in the overall clinical picture.

3. Several "token economies" were described, and it was seen that by judicious and resourceful use of generalized reinforcers, many socially significant hospital behaviors could be influenced in the direction of "healthier" functioning (e.g., Ayllon & Azrin, 1965; Atthowe & Krasner, 1968).

4. Finally, behavior modification approaches were reviewed to illustrate a "broad-spectrum approach" (Lazarus, 1966a) to various maladaptive behaviors, such as intense irrational fears (Cowden & Ford, 1962; Meyer & Gelder, 1963; Zeisset, 1968; Lazarus & Davison in press) and "paranoid" ideas (Kennedy, 1964; Davison, 1966b). These reports were characterized by a willingness to regard certain behavior problems in other than operant terms (cf. Lazarus, Davison, & Polefka, 1965).

It was suggested also that the general psychological, nonillness orientation of behavior modification might prove therapeutic to clients/patients within the context of the assessment of a given problem, thereby eliminating what may well be an unnecessary division between assessment and therapy (Davison, 1968a; Mischel, 1968).

The overall evaluation of behavior modification in institutional settings was less than completely enthusiastic, primarily because of the failure of at least the operant approaches, thus far, to make an appreciable contribution to the goal of equipping adult mental hospital patients with the means to cope successfully in the outside world. At the same time, however, the very real accomplishments of these attempts were noted, especially the opportunity they offer for so-called "nonprofessional staff" to play a more than custodial role in their dealings with hospitalized people.

Finally, several issues of logic and interpretation, relevant not only to the topic of this chapter but to the field in general, were examined in the hope that fellow researchers may maintain scientific perspective in their theorizing about the very encouraging and exciting findings which are being reported.

7

Aversion Therapy: An Appraisal

STANLEY J. RACHMAN AND J. TEASDALE

Institute of Psychiatry, University of London, London, England

Introduction

The surprising thing about aversion therapy is not that its effects are uncertain, but rather that it works at all. First, the connections among aversion therapy, psychological theory, and verified experimental data are tenuous. Second, the techniques currently in use are rudimentary. Although they nearly all involve the administration of some unpleasant stimulus, the means and methods employed are usually selected by their resemblance to some observation or procedure described in animal experiments. This borrowing from the laboratory is both understandable and justifiable, but, unfortunately, the shortage of appropriate analogs means that, in practice, aversion therapy procedures are an untidy collage. A third factor which militates against success with aversion therapy is our ignorance of the learning processes involved. For example, are we attempting to develop classical or instrumental conditioning? Last, and this is a serious puzzle, why should the patient refrain from carrying out the deviant behavior after he has left the clinic? He knows that if he cross-dresses (for example) in the safety of his home, no shock will be incurred.

Even so, for long periods after the termination of treatment, many patients do not carry out their deviant acts.

For these reasons we consider it surprising that aversion therapy is effective. Before discussing these difficulties in detail, however, a few general observations are worth recording.

We have already implied it is our view that the available evidence permits one to conclude that aversion therapy is often effective. The evidence is scanty and rarely meets the strict standards which must be applied in assessing therapeutic effects with most types of disorder. It is our contention, however, that the disorders which have been the prime target of aversion therapy are so rarely responsive to treatment, and probably have such a low rate of spontaneous remission, that our standards of judgment must be tailored accordingly. Stated bluntly, any treatment procedure which produces even a modest success rate with sexual disorders is an improvement on existing treatment alternatives. Naturally, we are not advocating a general reduction in standards, and the accumulation of more substantial evidence will allow a mature assessment to be made at a later date. In the present circumstances, however, we are willing in this interim assessment to err on the side of optimism.

Aversion therapy is used predominantly for the treatment of those behavior disorders (alcoholism and sexual deviations) in which the patient's conduct is undesirable but nevertheless self-reinforcing. The appetitive characteristics of these disorders frequently involve the therapist in problems concerning the introduction of other suitable forms of satisfying behavior. Sometimes it is not sufficient only to eliminate the unsuitable behavior. This observation is one of the most important themes of the present chapter, and we hope to show that both on clinical grounds and as a deduction from general experimental psychology, the aim in aversion therapy should be twofold: we should attempt to eliminate the deviant behavior, and further, we should attempt to generate satisfactory alternate (and preferably incompatible) forms of behavior. This necessity for generating alternate forms of behavior is not often encountered in the treatment of neurotic disorders (Eysenck & Rachman, 1965).

In essence, aversion therapy is an attempt to associate an undesirable behavior pattern with unpleasant stimulation or to make the unpleasant stimulation a consequence of the undesirable behavior. In either case, it is hoped that an acquired connection between the behavior and the unpleasantness will develop. There is a further hope that the development of such a connection will then be followed by a cessation of the target behavior.

After a brief account of the present status of the treatment, we will discuss the theoretical basis of aversion therapy, describe the available methods and their effects, and, finally, attempt a synthesis of theory and practice.

Present Status

The three most commonly used methods of behavior therapy are desensitization, operant conditioning, and aversion therapy. Although aversion therapy is the oldest of the three methods, it is not the best-established or most refined procedure (Eysenck & Rachman, 1965; Rachman, 1965a, 1967). Aversion therapy has been used intermittently over the past thirty years but has never quite caught on. The limping progress of the technique probably can be attributed to the mixed results which have been reported over the years (see Franks, 1963b, 1966b, for a full account). The renewed interest in aversion therapy is a reflection of the *Zeitgeist* which has involved, among other events, a reappraisal of accepted ideas of psychopathology and treatment. These changes are associated with the emergence of behavior therapy.

After a period of considerable activity during the forties,[1] research workers appeared to lose interest in the therapeutic possibilities of aversion conditioning. The resurgence of interest in aversion therapy (in Britain at least) can be traced to some extent to the publication of Raymond's (1956) account of the treatment of a fetishist by apomorphine conditioning. The response to this paper was enhanced by the general development of behavior therapy, and in the past few years many successes with aversion treatment have been reported (see the reviews by Rachman, 1961, 1965; Franks, 1958, 1963b, 1966b; Eysenck & Rachman, 1965).

Anyone who contemplates using this form of treatment must first make a decision about the type of noxious stimulus which he is going to employ. To date most of the cases reported in the literature have been treated by chemical aversion methods but there are sound reasons for believing that electrical methods may be preferable (Eysenck, 1960; Rachman, 1961, 1965a). For present purposes, some of the alternate noxious stimuli which have been explored (such as intense auditory stimulation will not be discussed; the emphasis instead will be placed on chemical and electrical techniques.

CHEMICAL OR ELECTRICAL?

Aversion treatment, particularly chemical aversion, can be an unpleasant and arduous form of therapy, and this fact, coupled with the often equivocal results obtained in the treatment of alcoholics, probably contributed to its decline in popularity. Franks (1958, 1963b) has drawn attention to the poor quality of much of the early work on aversion treatment of alcoholism. "Unfortunately not all modern practice is sound . . . for example, some clinicians advocate

---

[1] Miller, Dvorak, & Turner (1964) traced 169 references to conditioning procedures in the literature on alcoholism.

giving the alcohol after the patient reaches the height of nausea. This, of course, is backward conditioning since the unconditioned stimulus of the apomorphine or emetine is preceeding the conditioned stimulus of the alcohol and backward conditioning, if it occurs at all, is at best very tenuous" (Franks, 1963b). In any conditioning situation, the time intervals which elapse between the presentation of the various stimuli and the response are of considerable importance, and some aversion therapists appear to have been ignorant of this fact or have tended to ignore it. Franks writes that ". . . under such circumstances, it is hardly surprising that reports of evaluation studies range from virtually zero success to 100 percent success."

The choice of nausea-producing drug has also given rise to difficulties. Some of the drugs which have been used to produce nausea also act as central depressants. This type of drug would interfere with the acquisition of the conditional response. There is, furthermore, some confusion about the nature of the particular responses which one is attempting to attach to the sight, smell, and taste of alcohol. In some of the earlier studies, therapists stressed the action of vomiting rather than the feeling of nausea. As Raymond (1964) has shown, however, the action of vomiting is not the important event; apparently it is the feeling of nausea which influences the acquisition of an avoidance reaction to alcohol. The failure to distinguish between the feeling of nausea and the actual vomiting is a prominent feature of the majority of reports on chemical aversion treatment, and this confusion increases the difficulty of assessing the effectiveness of various series of case reports.

The problems involved in chemical techniques of aversion conditioning are multiplied by the existence of individual differences in reactivity to the various nausea-producing drugs. People differ in the speed and extent of their reactions to the various drugs, and furthermore, the same person may react differently to the same quantity of drug on different days or even at different times on the same day. Individual differences in reactivity, therefore, make the planning of a carefully controlled form of conditioning treatment extremely awkward. The use of chemical noxious stimuli also precludes the possiblity of making accurate measurements of the unconditioned responses which are being elicited. While it is possible, of course, to obtain measurements of reaction latency, it has proved extremely difficult, if not impossible, to obtain measures of magnitude of the responses produced.

Because of the arduous, complicated, and unpleasant nature of the chemical aversion conditioning sessions, it is impractical to provide frequent repetitions of the association between the conditioned stimulus and the unconditioned stimulus. The number of conditioning presentations and the number of sessions which can be provided are therefore inherently restricted. These restrictions not only increase the duration of the treatment period but also limit the number of conditioning trials which can be carried out.

The treatment is unpleasant, not only for the patient but also for the therapist and the nursing staff. It is not uncommon for attendants to object to participating in this form of treatment, and there can be no doubt that it arouses antagonism in some members of the hospital staff. Complaints that the method is unaesthetic and even harrowing are not without justification—it is certainly a method which does not lend itself to popularity. The nature of the treatment also makes it rather difficult to arrange for patients to be treated on an outpatient basis.

There is also some clinical evidence to suggest that chemical treatment brings about increased aggressiveness and hostility on the part of the patient (Morgenstern & Pearce, 1963). It should be pointed out that some of these reactions to chemical aversion therapy are not entirely surprising; it has been observed experimentally that the administration of aversive stimulation of various kinds can give rise to an increase in aggressive behavior (see below). It may indeed prove necessary to develop special methods for managing the increased aggression if and when it occurs. A second difficulty which may be anticipated in most forms of aversion therapy concerns the anxiety which it arouses in some patients. On the one hand, it has been suggested by Eysenck & Rachman (1965) that there is a possibility that highly anxious patients may respond unfavorably to aversion treatment, whereas Bancroft (1966) has postulated that a high level of anxiety is necessary for successful treatment. Finally, it should be mentioned that some of the drugs which have been used in chemical aversion treatment have unpleasant side effects and can be dangerous. Certainly, chemical aversion cannot be used for the treatment of patients with gastric ailments or cardiac complaints.

Despite the difficulties enumerated above and the indifferent quality of a great deal of the work on chemical aversion therapy, some remarkable successes have nevertheless been achieved. Voegtlin and his colleagues (Voegtlin & Lemere, 1942; Lemere & Voegtlin, 1950) obtained creditable results in their treatment of over 4,000 alcoholic patients. Raymond (1964) has reported successes in treating alcoholics, sexual deviates, and drug addicts; Morgenstern & Pearce (1963) have obtained encouraging results in their treatment of transvestites. Although the value of this method is decreased by the size of the relapse rate, there is no escaping the fact that many otherwise untreatable patients have obtained substantial benefit from chemical aversion treatment. It should also be emphasized that the types of disorders that have yielded successes are precisely those kinds of abnormalities which are ordinarily resistant to change. Certainly, until the advent of aversion therapy there was very little that could be offered to patients with sexual perversions such as fetishism and transvestism.

One of the earliest reports of an electrical aversion method was a brief account given by Max (1935) of the elimination of a homosexual fixation by the administration of brief electric shocks. This suggestive paper was apparently ignored. In view of the extensive use made of electrical stimulation in conditioning experiments, it is curious that therapists neglected to apply these findings until fairly recently.

The bulk of the available laboratory evidence on conditioning (and there is of course a considerable amount of such laboratory evidence) concerns experiments in which the aversive stimulus was an electric shock. This is the first, and potentially the most important, of all the advantages offered by electrical methods of aversion treatment. Over the past few decades psychologists have accumulated much detailed information about the effects of electrical stimulation on behavior, and while it is true that there are still many problems which have yet to be resolved, there is also little doubt that the information which is already available can assist in the design and conduct of aversion treatment. A start in this direction was made by Feldman & MacCulloch (1965), who attempted to construct a therapeutic program from findings in the field of avoidance conditioning. Recently, important theoretical contributions to the understanding of the effects of aversive stimulation on behavior have been made by Solomon (1964), Church (1964), and Azrin & Holz (1966).

The effectiveness of electrical stimulation depends on numerous factors such as the intensity of the stimulus, the amount and kind of previous training, the person's drive level, the time relations between the administration of the stumulus and the occurrence of the response (see below).

Electrical stimulation can be precisely controlled. The therapist is in a position to administer a discrete stimulus of measured intensity for an exact duration of time at precisely the required moment. In this respect, electrical aversion stimulation is clearly superior to chemical aversion. Each of these variables can be manipulated according to requirements, and the entire treatment process becomes considerably more flexible. Variations in the patient's subjective reaction to the shock and general adaptation effects are, however, continuing problems. Nevertheless, the greater control which is possible with electrical stimulation should permit more effective treatment, closer definition of the treatment process, and increased theoretical clarity.

Chemical techniques do not provide much scope for modifications which might be introduced on the basis of the patient's personality. Individual differences tend to be blotted out because the chemical aversion procedures cannot be manipulated with precision. For example, the observation that extroverts have a greater tolerance for pain than introverts (Lynn & Eysenck, 1961) could not be used to advantage. Additionally, individual differences in reactivity to and tolerance of electric shocks can be incorporated in electrical aversion treatment. When the relationships between personality and these factors have been worked out in greater detail, it should be possible to design treatment schedules which will meet the needs of the individual patient.

The increased therapeutic control provided by electrical stimulation permits the therapist to make accurate measurements of the progress of the treatment. For example, Rachman (1961) gives a brief account of the technique of measurement which he used in tracing the effectiveness of electrical stimulation on sexual images of a fetishist. It was found that, as the number of associations between fetishistic-transvestite impulses and electrical stimulations increased, the patient found it increasingly difficult to conjure up the images. The duration of the images showed a concomitant decrease. It was found possible to make accurate measurements of both latency and duration of the response (the image). This enabled the therapist to plot the course and progress of the treatment. More precise and detailed observations were recently added by Marks & Gelder (1967). Similar measurements have also been reported by McGuire & Vallance (1964) and Feldman & MacCulloch (1964). Measurements of the patient's reactions at each stage of the treatment are valuable in their own right and also because of the information which they provide about the relationship between imagery and action. With the accumulation of research on this topic, it should be possible to work out in some detail the relationship between, say, images of sexual perversions and the real act.

Unlike chemical aversion treatment, electrical stimulation permits frequent repetitions of the association between the unwanted behavior and the noxious stimulus. It is perfectly feasible to present a large number of trials to the patient during one session and also to provide for numerous conditioning sessions within the same day. This should enable treatment to progress more quickly.

It is also feasible to construct portable apparatus which would allow the treatment to be carried out on an outpatient basis. In some cases the patient can even administer the noxious stimulus to himself, if and when the necessity arises. This procedure was used by McGuire & Vallance (1964), and a recent example of self-administered treatment was also reported by Wolpe (1965). In this report, he described the partially successful treatment of a patient who was suffering from a drug addiction. It was possible to bring about a temporary suppression of the drug craving by getting the patient to administer the electric shock to himself whenever the craving arose.

Experience with chemical aversion methods leads us to expect a rather high relapse rate in aversion treatment generally. A similar situation has, of course, been encountered in the conditioning treatment of enuresis (Jones, 1960; Turner, Rachman, & Young, 1967). Lovibond's (1963) work on enuresis introduced the feasibility of employing intermittent reinforcement schedules. Although it is not yet possible to reach a conclusion about the long-term effectiveness of this type of schedule, there are grounds for believing that it might provide a means of reducing relapse rates in various forms of treatment. Certainly, intermittent reinforcement is much simpler to program if one employs an electrical stimulus rather than drugs. Another possible technique for reducing the relapse rate is the use of booster treatments, and this technique, too, is more feasible with the electrical method.

Another difficulty which can be overcome by the substitution of electrical methods concerns the staff problems mentioned earlier. Electrical treatment does not require more than one therapist to be present, and it is considerably less arduous and cumbersome to administer than other techniques. With the possible exception of patients with cardiac complaints, there is virtually no danger involved in the application of electrical stimulation, providing that the equipment is well designed and well constructed.

Unlike drug treatment, electrical stimulation does not give rise to unpleasant side effects. Electrical stimulation also avoids the possibility of inducing an unwanted suppression of the developing conditioned response by depressing central nervous activity. The hypnotic effects produced by the administration of the commonly used nausea-producing drug apomorphine can be avoided.

Electrical techniques are also likely to have a wider range of application than chemical methods. For example, it would be impossible to employ chemical aversion in the treatment of writer's cramp.

It will be some time before all the disadvantages of the electrical method become apparent. It is worth drawing attention, however, even at this early stage, to some of the practical difficulties which have been encountered in chemical aversion treatment and which may be expected to arise when the electrical method is fully developed. First, the administration of aversive stimuli in laboratory experiments can give rise to aggressive behavior (Ulrich, Hutchinson, & Azrin, 1965). In clinical practice, aggressiveness, negativism, and hostility have already been encountered during the conduct of aversion treatment (Rachman, 1965b). Second, there can be little doubt that most people have a fear of electric shocks and that the method may prove to be exceedingly unpopular with some patients. The anxiety level of many patients certainly increases with the introduction of electrical stimulation and this may in turn interfere with the development of conditioned avoidance reactions. An example of this type of difficulty is reported by Beech (1960), who found that some patients reacted unfavorably to the administration of electric shocks involved in the treatment of writer's cramp (see discussion below). If the presence of a high degree of emotionality does prove to be a stumbling block in the application of electrical aversion treatment, the experimental work of Turner & Solomon (1962) may be of some assistance. They concluded, on the basis of an interesting series of experiments on avoidance conditioning in human subjects, that the conditioning of ". . . a highly emotional subject will proceed most rapidly if we start off with a short CS–UCS interval and then lengthen it, at the same time that we start with an intense UCS level then lower it to produce longer latency escape responses. When these procedures are combined, we should be able to produce rapid learning. . . ." The possible application of these findings is discussed in Eysenck & Rachman (1965). It should be noted, however, that one of the recommendations offered by Turner & Solomon, namely the progressive reduction in UCS intensity, is apparently contrary to Azrin & Holz's (1966) view that the UCS intensity should not be altered. Whether Turner & Solomon are correct in regard to the management of highly anxious subjects will need general confirmation, and this specific point can be given particular attention.

A major problem which looms in the background is that of relapses. Here again techniques will have to be developed to overcome the relapses or to prevent their occurrence. Two possible methods which might be used, intermittent reinforcement and booster treatments, have already been mentioned. A third possibility is the use of stimulant drugs during the progress of electrical aversion treatment, as there is some evidence that these drugs facilitate the acquisition of conditioned responses (Eysenck, 1964).

Thus far we have been considering the selection of a suitable aversive stimulus primarily from the clinical point of view. In 1966, Azrin & Holz discussed the qualities of an "ideal" punishing stimulus—from the point of view of experimentalists. Interestingly enough, many of their conclusions parallel those which we have derived from a consideration of the clinical data presently available.

Among the properties which Azrin & Holz regard as being desirable in an aversive stimulus are the following: In the first place, "the punishing stimulus should have precise physical specification. Unless the relevant dimensions of the stimulus can be measured accurately and in physical units, we have imposed limits on studies from the outset in terms of replicability and reliability" (p. 384). To this we may add that an aversive stimulus also needs to be controlled for specified periods of time. In all these respects, of course, electrical aversion is superior to chemical aversion. The second important feature mentioned by Azrin & Holz is ". . . the constancy of the stimulus in terms of the actual contact it makes with the subject. . . ." Here again, electrical aversion (while not entirely satisfactory on this point) is superior to chemical aversion. The third characteristic of a satisfactory stimulus concerns "the ability of a subject to escape or minimize the stimulation by means of some unauthorized behaviour." In this respect neither chemical nor electrical aversion appears to have an advantage. The fourth characteristic in the list given by Azrin & Holz is that there should be few skeletal reactions to the stimulus. The elicitation of strong and enduring skeletal reactions may physically interfere with the emission of the behavior under study. Once again electrical aversion is preferable to chemical aversion. The fifth characteristic is that the stimulus should be of a kind that can be "varied over a wide range of values" because a limited range prevents a full investigation of the effectiveness of the stimulation being employed. In this respect electrical aversion is obviously superior.

From both the clinical and the experimental points of view, therefore, electrical aversion is preferable to chemical aversion. It is worth mentioning that in their consideration of the different types of aversive stimuli, Azrin & Holz argue that noise has a number of desirable features (e.g., it can be precisely specified, varied, and controlled). The main disadvantage, according to these writers, is that noise cannot be used over a particularly wide range of effectiveness; furthermore, even when used at high intensity, noise has not "resulted in complete response-reduction." This observation parallels the information which we can derive from clinical attempts to use aversive auditory stimulation. In no case has it proved to be entirely satisfactory as a therapeutic agent for engendering prolonged behavioral changes, and its use is further complicated by the appearance of adaptation effects.

THEORETICAL CONSIDERATIONS

Suppose that a behavior therapist was presented with one of the dogs from the experiment of Solomon & Wynne (1953). In this experiment the dogs were trained to make an avoidance response of jumping a hurdle to avoid traumatic shock. The behavior was extremely resistant to extinction, and for the purposes of our example we shall assume that it is for some reason considered undesirable and that the therapist is asked to eliminate it, without knowing its "case history."

A naïve approach, which simply regards the problem behavior as undesirable without attempting to obtain an adequately tested formulation of the mechanism maintaining it, is likely to lead to an attempt to eliminate the hurdle-jumping response by a punishment procedure, i.e., shock is delivered to the dog as he lands in the second compartment, after making the hurdle-jumping response. Solomon & Wynne (1953) applied this procedure and found that, far from suppressing the response, the punishment procedure actually enhanced the hurdle jumping. This result, surprising if one had made no theoretical formulation or an inadequate one, would have been quite expected if one had made an accurate "behavioral diagnosis" of the disorder as an avoidance response in terms of a Mowrer-type two-process theory; the response is anxiety-mediated, and punishment increases the level of anxiety, thereby enhancing rather than suppressing the avoidance response.

A clinical example of this situation is provided by Beech (1960), who found that a punishment procedure had an adverse rather than beneficial effect on writer's cramp in anxious patients. In a later case of writer's cramp and stuttering (Beech, 1963), a closer investigation of the problem revealed that the undesirable behavior appeared to be motivated by anxiety attached to authoritarian figures. Elimination of this anxiety, by systematic desensitization, led to the disappearance of the writer's cramp and stuttering, without the necessity to resort to aversion techniques.

Adequate formulation of the mechanisms maintaining the problem behavior is probably best attempted by interviews, combined with some form of single-case study (Shapiro, 1961). Learning theory models have been suggested for several commonly occurring problems, and these would provide a useful basis for one's model of each particular case (e.g., for alcoholism: Conger, 1956; Franks, 1963; Kepner, 1964; for sexual disorders: McGuire, Carlisle, & Young, 1965).

Three main learning-theory paradigms seem to be of interest in formulating models for the aversion therapy procedures used to date:

1. Punishment
2. Avoidance conditioning
3. Classical conditioning of anxiety or "aversion" responses

Each of these will be considered separately.

Punishment. Azrin & Holz (1966) define punishment as "a reduction in the future probability of a specific response as a result of the immediate delivery of a stimulus for that response." This definition clearly differentiates punishment from avoidance and escape training, which attempt to generate new responses.

As Solomon (1964) has pointed out, there has been current in psychology a myth to the effect that punishment is ineffective in producing lasting suppression of the punished response. This myth seems to have originated in a paper by Estes (1944) who found that punishment of a bar-pressing response in rats led to only temporary suppression of the response. That this myth has no foundation is dramatically demonstrated by the finding that it is possible, by punishment of feeding responses in experimental animals, to suppress the feeding response permanently, to the point where animals will die from self-starvation (Masserman, 1943; Lichtenstein, 1950). This myth has led, until recently, to a relative neglect of punishment procedures as potential therapeutic maneuvers. Another factor contributing to this neglect has been the apparently inconsistent effects of punishment; in most cases suppression of the punished response is obtained, but in other cases no effect, or even an enhancement of the punished response, is obtained, as in the example of Solomon & Wynne (1953) described above. Further examples of such paradoxical effects of punishment are provided in the papers of Church (1963), Martin (1963), Sandler (1964), and Solomon (1964).

It is thoroughly understandable that clinicians have been reluctant to employ a therapeutic method which produces apparently unpredictable effects. However, the situations in which punishment will produce effects other than the desired suppression of the response seem now to be reasonably well defined (Church, 1963; Azrin & Holz, 1966). This clarification of the effects of punishment has led to therapy procedures specifically based on a punishment paradigm (Kushner & Sandler, 1966).

For an excellent review of parametric studies of punishment, the reader is referred to Azrin & Holz (1966). By way of summary of a most valuable contribution to the field of punishment, we shall quote their conclusions on how they would set about eliminating a behavior pattern by punishment (pp. 426–427):

> We have seen above that punishment can be quite effective in eliminating behaviour. Let us imagine that we are given an assignment to eliminate behaviour by punishment. Let us summarize briefly some of the circumstances which have been found to maximize its effectiveness: 1) The punishing stimulus should be arranged in such a manner that no unauthorized escape is possible. 2) The punishing stimulus should be as intense as possible. 3) The frequency of punishment should be as high as possible; ideally the punishing stimulus should be given for every response. 4) The punishing stimulus should be delivered immediately after the response. 5) The punishing stimulus should not be increased gradually but introduced at maximum intensity. 6) Extended periods of punishment should be avoided, especially where low intensities of punishment are concerned, since the recovery effect may thereby occur. Where mild intensities of punishment are used, it is best to use them for only a brief period of time. 7) Great care should be taken to see that the delivery of the punishing stimulus is not differentially associated with the delivery of reinforcement. Otherwise the punishing stimulus may acquire conditioned reinforcing properties. 8) The punishing stimulus should be made a signal or discriminative stimulus that a period of extinction is in progress. 9) The degree of motivation to emit the punished response should be reduced. 10) The frequency of positive reinforcement for the punished response should similarly be reduced. 11) An alternative response should be available which will not be punished but which will produce the same or greater reinforcement as the punished response. For example, punishment of criminal behaviour can be expected to be more effective if non-criminal behaviour which will result in the same advantages as the criminal behaviour is available. 12) If no alternative response is available, the subject should have access to a different situation in which he obtains the same reinforcement without being punished. 13) If it is not possible to deliver the punishing stimulus itself after a response, then an effective method of punishment is still available. A conditioned stimulus may be associated with the aversive stimulus and this conditioned stimulus may be delivered following a response to achieve conditioned punishment. 14) A reduction of positive reinforcement may be used as punishment when the use of physical punishment is not possible for practical, legal or moral reasons. Punishment by withdrawal of positive reinforcement may be accomplished in such situations by arranging a period of reduced reinforcement frequency (time-out) or by arranging a decrease of conditioned reinforcement (response cost). Both methods require that the subject have a high level of reinforcement to begin with; otherwise, no withdrawal of reinforcement is possible. If non-physical punishment is to be used, it appears desirable to provide the subject with a substantial history of reinforcement in order to provide the opportunity for withdrawing the reinforcement as punishment for the undesired responses.

Two points made by Azrin & Holz seem particularly relevant to the clinical application of punishment procedures. The first of these is the importance of providing an alternative rewarded response, motivated by the same drive as and followed by similar reinforcement to the undesirable response being punished. The dramatic enhancement of the effects of punishment produced by provision of an alternative response has been described by Solomon (1964) and Azrin & Holz (1966). The latter cite as an example an experiment by Herman & Azrin (1964). These workers showed that punishment of a manipulandum response (maintained by a cigarette reinforcement schedule) by a loud unpleasant sound produced only a slight degree of suppression. However, if another manipulandum, responses to which produced only positive reward and no noise, was available, the response rate on the punished manipulandum was reduced completely and almost immediately.

This result will surprise no one, and clinicians have long recognized the importance of providing alternative desirable responses to the undesirable target responses of treatment. It is known, for example, that in the sexual disorders, prognosis for elimination of aberrant sexual behavior is far better if normal heterosexual interests are present (Feldman & MacCulloch, 1967).

It seems unfortunately true that the great importance of providing rewarded responses which can act as satisfactory alternatives to the undesirable response is matched by the great difficulty of providing such responses (see p. 308 below). This seems to underline the point that aversion therapy should only be one item in a battery of therapeutic procedures, and that it is important to devote time and research to the problem of providing alternative responses as well as to investigate the parameters involved in the aversion procedure itself. The second point of Azrin & Holz's we shall discuss seems to pose even greater difficulties for the clinician. This problem is that of the generalization of the suppression of the punished response; there are many experiments to show that if, in a punishment procedure, one provides rats with a stimulus to indicate when they can make the otherwise punished response without receiving punishment, the rats can make the discrimination and perform the response in the presence of the safety signal and refrain from making the response in the absence of the safety signal (Azrin, 1956; Brethower & Reynolds, 1962; Dinsmoor, 1952; Hunt & Brady, 1955).

If rats are able to make this discrimination, it seems extremely likely that human subjects can do the same. We are forced to ask the question: Why, once the shock electrodes have been removed from the patient, and he has left the hospital situation in which he has received the shocks, should the patient refrain from making the punished response, as he "knows" that he will not receive shock if he makes that response? This poses the whole problem of the extent to which the patient's "cognitive control" can undo the effects of aversion therapy. A salutary example of the extent to which the patient can, if he decides to, overcome the effects of his aversion treatment is provided in a patient described by Hammersley (1957). This patient had been subjected to a punishment procedure as an incidental feature of the use of traditional chemical aversion therapy, and had acquired a conditioned aversion to alcohol. After his discharge from hospital, he set about undoing the effects of his treatment and persisted for four hours in drinking and vomiting, until he had successfully "broken his conditioning." Although he succeeded in "breaking" his conditioned aversion by deliberate effort, it must be remembered that he was in the first place "conditioned" despite his apparent resistance.

The general problem of the patient's "cognitive control" will be discussed later (see p. 314). For the moment we will return to the problem in the case of punishment. In an attempt to elucidate why punishment should have any permanent suppressive effect on patients once they leave the hospital, we shall consider the actual "responses" punished in four patients reported in a paper by Kushner & Sandler (1966). These writers deliberately adopted a punishment model for their procedure. The "responses" punished in their four patients were:

1. Arousal, fantasy, and masturbation in response to fetish stimuli
2. Obtaining a mental image of self performing exhibitionist behavior
3. Suicidal ruminations
4. Typing cramp

It is obvious that some of these "responses" differ quite considerably from the typical operant behavior, such as bar pressing, studied in investigations of the effects of punishment on animals; e.g., responses 1, 2, and 3 consist largely, if not exclusively, of covert "mental responses" rather than overt behavior.

One reason one could suggest for the lack of interference from "cognitive control" is that, at least in patients 3 and 4, we are dealing with "responses" which themselves are not apparently within the scope of "cognitive control."

The success of punishment procedures in the case of "sexual responses," such as those in patients 1 and 2, could be explained by postulating that a different process is operating during the punishment procedure here than in the case of punishment of operant behavior maintained by food reward.

In discussing the factors contributing to the level of a drive, Kimble (1961, p. 399) distinguishes the contributions of deprivation, stimulus properties (desirability of food, attractiveness of sexual lure), and the past history of the organism. In the case of sexual arousal, the importance of the learned elements of the drive seems particularly high. As Ford & Beach (1952) have pointed out, in man the arousing properties of sexual stimuli are largely dependent on learning. On this view, sexual perversions can be thought of as examples of classical conditioning of sexual arousal responses to inappropriate stimuli. It is known that a mutually inhibitory relationship appears to exist between sexual arousal and anxiety (Masters & Johnson, 1966; Wolpe, 1958;

Gantt, 1949). If, then, we countercondition anxiety to the sexually arousing stimuli, we remove their arousal properties and remove a significant element in the drive to perform the aberrant sexual behavior.

What is being suggested is that a punishment procedure, consisting of punishment contingent on the report of an image or fantasy of aberrant sexual behavior, is effective in reducing that behavior by virtue of the counterconditioning of anxiety to the aberrant sexual stimuli, thereby reducing their sexual arousal properties. If the usual punishment paradigm were the only process operating, one would expect that the actual response being punished, reproducing an image of the aberrant sexual behaviour, would be eliminated and nothing else would happen. An inability to produce the punished image generally does occur in cases treated in this way (Marks & Gelder, 1967) but it is usually accompanied by reduction in deviant behavior other than the deviant fantasies. It is suggested that this generalization of the suppressive effects of the punishment procedure is mediated via the generalization of the anxiety conditioned to the fantasy stimuli to the real-life stimuli. In this way the deviant sexual stimuli are "devalued" of their arousal properties. Relevant to this discussion is the fact, pointed out by Solomon (1964), that consummatory responses are peculiarly susceptible to the suppressive effects of punishment. Solomon's discussion of this phenomenon is best conveyed verbatim (p. 242):

> The interference with consummatory responses by punishment needs a great deal of investigation. Punishment seems to be especially effective in breaking up this class of responses, and one can ask *why*, with some profit. Perhaps the intimate temporal connection between drive, incentive and punishment results in drive or incentive becoming conditioned-stimulus (CS) patterns for aversive emotional reactions when consummatory acts are punished. Perhaps this interferes with vegetative activity: i.e. does it "kill the appetite" in a hungry subject? But, one may ask why the same punisher might not appear to be as effective when made contingent on an *instrumental* act as contrasted with a consummatory act. Perhaps the nature of operants is such that they are separated in time and space and response topography from consummatory behaviour and positive incentive stimuli, so that appetitive reactions are not clearly present during punishment for operants.

The whole topic of the effect of punishment on consummatory responses is a fascinating one, requiring considerable elucidation. Relevant to the practical problem of eliminating consummatory responses by punishment procedures are the studies of Solomon (1964) and Lichtenstein (1950). These workers attempted to answer the question: Where is the most effective point in the response sequence of the consummatory act at which to apply the punishment stimulus? The famous experiment of Solomon, on punishing puppies by swatting them with a rolled-up newspaper, showed that greater suppression of the feeding response was obtained if punishment was administered as the puppies were approaching the food than if it were administered as they were actually feeding. Lichtenstein showed that conditioning fear to food stimuli had little effect in reducing feeding behavior, whereas punishment of the initiation of the feeding behavior itself was extremely effective. It seems that punishment of a consummatory response is most effective when the punishing stimulus is contingent with the proprioceptive stimulus associated with the initial responses of the consummatory act. Eysenck & Rachman (1965) mention studies with children in which essentially similar results were obtained.

It is not yet possible to assess the relative therapeutic contributions made by classical and instrumental factors in the punishment paradigm. However, most therapists who have used electrical aversion have employed a punishment model, although few of them acknowledge this explicitly. There are, of course difficulties in extrapolating from animal experiments to human behavior, and these difficulties are particularly great in situations where noxious stimuli are involved. As we have suggested, the existence of "cognitive control" in patients would limit the generalization of suppression of the punished response from hospital to everyday life. It would seem that the usefulness of punishment procedures can be evaluated, and the processes involved understood, only by investigations of the specific phenomena occurring in the treatment situation itself.

Avoidance Learning.   Avoidance training is defined as "A training procedure in which the learned movement circumvents or prevents the appearance of a noxious stimulus" (Kimble, 1964, p. 477).

The case, both theoretical and clinical, for the use of the avoidance paradigm in aversion therapy has most noticeably been made by Feldman & MacCulloch (Feldman & MacCulloch, 1965; MacCulloch, Feldman, & Pinschof, 1965; Feldman, 1966). These workers have applied their technique (which is described in detail on pp. 308–309) with considerable success to the treatment of homosexuality (Feldman & MacCulloch, 1965; MacCulloch, Feldman, & Pinschof, 1965) and without success to the treatment of alcoholism (MacCulloch, Feldman, Orford, & MacCulloch, 1966).

Their choice of an anticipatory avoidance paradigm for their therapy procedure was made on the basis of the well-known resistance to extinction often observed in responses established by anticipatory avoidance learning. It is obviously highly desirable to attempt to make the responses trained in aversion therapy as resistant to extinction as possible. Feldman & MacCulloch reject the use of "classical Pavlovian conditioning" on the grounds that, "This technique results in unstable learning and easy extinction." Anticipatory avoidance training, unlike punishment, acts in the direction of generating new responses; it can eliminate undesirable responses only by training new responses, incompatible with the undesirable responses, to the stimuli which previously led to the undesirable responses. Furthermore, the striking resistance to extinction of responses trained by avoidance conditioning seems to be mainly at the level of motor response. Animals performing a well-established avoidance response characteristically show little sign of anxiety. Also, Black (1965) has shown that, while the occurrence of a conditioned heart-rate change (an autonomic response) is essential to the occurrence of avoidance responses during the acquisition phase, no correlation appears between the occurrence of changes in heart rate and the occurrence of avoidance responses in extinction, suggesting that the autonomic components may not show the same resistance to extinction as the motor avoidance responses.

To obtain a lasting suppression of undesirable behavior by avoidance conditioning, then, we must use the avoidance procedure to train a motor response which will prevent the occurrence of the undesirable behavior. When we look at the response trained by Feldman & MacCulloch, we find that it is the depression of a button to remove a colored slide of a naked male from a back-projection screen. On the face of it there is not the slightest reason to think that this response is in any way incompatible with the homosexual behavior which it is desired to eliminate. Further, as the homosexual is not provided with a button to carry around with him, it is not possible for the patient to make the actual trained response outside the hospital situation. It would seem that only by generalization of a fairly massive kind could the button-pressing response lead to a response such as shunning of homosexual haunts and acquaintances. Such shunning would seem to be a reasonable motor response incompatible with the undesirable behavior. While such generalization may occur, experimental reports of similar generalization are not known to the writers, and it seems a little unlikely.

It would seem that there is a danger inherent in the use of the term *anticipatory avoidance learning* to denote a certain paradigm of behavior. This danger is that one may assume that because an "avoidance response" (which can be any type of response one chooses) to a particular CS has been established, the subject will "avoid," in the sense of shunning, the CS after training. There is no reason why this should occur.

Another problem in the use of an avoidance conditioning paradigm is that, for most effective conditioning, the avoidance response trained should be of an operant "emitted" nature (Turner & Solomon, 1962), i.e., in humans, under a fair degree of voluntary control. (MacCulloch, Feldman, & Pinschof, 1965, mention this point: the button-pressing response they employ is of an operant nature.) We are presented with the problem: Why, if the response is under the subject's voluntary control, should he continue to make it after he has left the hospital?

However, the fact remains that Feldman & MacCulloch's procedure is impressively effective in eliminating homosexual behavior. In the light of what we have just said, we must ask why.

The work of Black (1965) seems to suggest that the classical conditioning of anxiety to the CS is an essential prerequisite to the emergence of the
motor avoidance response. MacCulloch et al. claim that only those patients
who developed conditional cardiac responses to the CS of the male slides also
developed consistent motor avoidance behavior and showed improvement from
treatment. We have then, as an inevitable concomitant of the development of
the motor response, the classical conditioning of anxiety to the CS. This
classical conditioning will be even more pronounced in the procedure employed
by Feldman & MacCulloch, in which, in its main phase, shock is delivered on
one-third of the trials whether the patient makes a button pressing response
or not. Thus, one-third of the trials are actually classical conditioning trials.

We are suggesting that the effective process operating in the Feldman
& MacCulloch procedure is not the development of a motor avoidance response, but the classical conditioning of anxiety to the homosexual stimuli,
thus "devaluing" them of their sexual arousal properties.

Since formulating this suggestion, we have learned that Feldman & Mac-
Culloch (1967) in fact are conducting a comparative trial between their original
anticipatory avoidance procedure and a classical conditioning procedure, in
which the subject makes no avoidance response. Unfortunately, the results of
this study are not available at the time of writing.

As mentioned above, Feldman & MacCulloch rejected the use of classical
conditioning procedures on the grounds that they produced "unstable learning
and easy extinction." While this may be true for classically conditioned motor
responses, it is most definitely not true for classically conditioned autonomic
responses. Solomon & Brush (1956) make this point in their extensive review
of the literature on avoidance conditioning: "We are led to conclude from the
experimental studies concerning the relative effectiveness of classical aversive
conditioning and avoidance training procedures that the latter produces better
and more stable aversive motor behaviour, while the former produces more
anxiety or emotion."

Many studies are available which show the retention of classically conditioned emotional responses for very long periods, e.g., the literature on
"experimental neurosis" resulting from noxious stimulation (Wolpe, 1958).
The distinction between the motor and autonomic aspects of classical conditioning is dramatically demonstrated in a study reported by Gantt (1964). This
study demonstrated the formation of a conditioned cardiac response in the
dog, which was extremely resistant to extinction and was retained over at least
thirteen months, following a single reinforcement with faradic shock. The
motor conditioned reflex did not even appear at the small number of reinforcements given.

We suggest that the classical component was the effective component
of Feldman & MacCulloch's procedure. The devaluation of the sexual stimuli
would have the effect that, even when exercising "cognitive control," the

homosexual would not choose to make the homosexual response; the devaluation of the homosexual stimuli has removed the gratification attached to the homosexual act.

Feldman & MacCulloch reported a failure to obtain any therapeutic improvement when applying to alcoholism essentially the same technique as they had found successful in the treatment of homosexuality (MacCulloch et al., 1966). On their hypothesis that they are training the patient to "avoid" the stimuli that trigger the undesirable behavior, their technique should be equally applicable to this behavior as it is to homosexuality. Feldman & MacCulloch suggest that the reason for this failure may have been the inconsistent pattern of development of the avoidance response, and the failure to develop a conditioned cardiac response to the CS, both of which were indicators of poor prognosis among their homosexual patients. An alternative hypothesis would be that the reinforcement value of alcohol is determined to a lesser extent by its "lure" qualities, which we can "devalue" by conditioning anxiety to them, than is the case with sexual stimuli. If sexual stimuli are rendered affectively neutral, they lose most of their motivating and reinforcing qualities; rendering stimuli associated with alcohol affectively neutral has no effect on its physiologically reinforcing properties, such as anxiety reduction and relief of a specific "alcohol hunger."

What Feldman & MacCulloch were trying to do with alcoholics is comparable with the procedure applied to the dogs in Lichtenstein's experiment, mentioned above, when they were shocked in the presence of food stimuli. This experiment demonstrated that while the animal might be afraid of the food, it was not afraid to eat it.

A recent paper by Menaker (1967) leads to the suggestion that conditioning anxiety to stimuli associated with alcohol, instead of reducing drinking, might actually increase it. This study showed that in alcoholics who have not received aversion therapy there is an initial anticipatory rise in anxiety before drinking followed by a return to lower levels of anxiety after the ingestion of the alcohol begins. One can hypothesize that the vicious circle diagrammed below would serve to perpetuate the drinking behavior. Conditioning anxiety to the stimuli associated with drinking might only serve to intensify the vicious circle.

Again, as in the case of punishment, we have encountered the problems

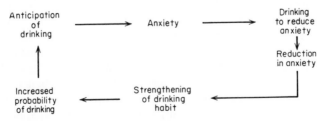

inherent in extrapolating from the behavior of animals in artificial experimental settings to the behavior of human beings in real life. That which we call "cognitive" or "voluntary control" would seem to limit the applicability of much of the experimental literature, e.g., we have seen that, for ease of acquisition, the avoidance response trained should be of an operant "voluntary" nature; if performance of the trained response is under the patient's volitional control, why should he perform it outside the hospital situation?

From such considerations, we would suggest the limited usefulness of avoidance techniques. This position stands in contrast to that of Feldman (1966); indeed we have suggested that his therapy procedure is effective by virtue of its classical conditioning component, rather than its anticipatory avoidance component.

Classical Conditioning. The majority of the early attempts at aversion therapy would seem to be based on a classical conditioning paradigm: the intention of the therapist appeared to be to condition feelings of "aversion" to the previously attractive stimuli. In this way it was hoped: (1) to change from positive to negative the sign of the "lure" component of the drive to perform the undesirable behavior; (2) in the case of alcoholism, actually to change the nature of the reinforcement of the drinking response; by conditioning aversion and nausea to the sight, smell, taste, etc., of the alcohol, the drinking response would immediately be negatively reinforced, whereas, before treatment, the response would immediately have been positively reinforced. Alternatively, the conditioning of anxiety to the situation in which the undesirable response appeared might disrupt the smooth performance of the undesirable response, thereby interfering with its reinforcement value. This would be especially true in the case of sexual disorders.

It has been suggested that the extent to which one can modify a deviant behavior by "devaluation" of the attractiveness of the stimuli triggering the undesirable behavior varies from one class of behavior to another. Thus Marks & Gelder (1967) have shown that it is only necessary to change the "affective value" of deviant sexual stimuli from highly positive to neutral in order to achieve elimination of the aberrant sexual behavior; it is as if one "titrated" sexual arousal against anxiety until a point of neutrality was reached at which the stimuli provoked neither sexual arousal nor anxiety. Lichtenstein, however, showed that conditioning of anxiety to food stimuli, though it made the dogs afraid of food, did not make them afraid to eat it. In the case of food it would seem more effective to condition anxiety to the proprioceptive stimuli associated with approach to the food, etc., in a punishment procedure.

This raises an important point: The replacement of chemical methods of aversion by electrical methods probably has led to a change in the nature of the response being classically conditioned; chemical aversion leads to the conditioning of an "aversion response" to the conditioned stimuli, whereas electrical aversion leads to the conditioning of an anxiety response. It seems likely that the two conditioned responses may have different effects on the frequency of the responses they are associated with. For example, Ullmann (1951) has shown that anxiety leads to increased feeding behavior, whereas one would expect feelings of nausea and aversion associated with feeding to lead to a decrease in feeding behavior. Similarly, there is some reason to think that anxiety may be a drive motivating alcoholic drinking (e.g., Franks, 1966) and that conditioning anxiety to stimuli associated with drinking might lead to an increase rather than a decrease in drinking behavior. (However, the work of Blake, discussed below, seems to suggest that electrical aversion may be quite successful in the treatment of alcoholism). On the other hand, it would be expected that feelings of nausea or aversion associated with the ingestion of the alcohol would lead to a reduction in the drinking behavior, as the alcohol would augment, rather than reduce, the nausea.

It would seem that a case can be made for use of a greater range of noxious unconditioned responses than the shock-induced anxiety employed in electrical aversion. This particular unconditioned response seems especially effective in eliminating arousal properties of sexual stimuli. The use of covert sensitization and other methods discussed below would seem to be one means of providing a wide variety of unpleasant responses on which conditioning therapies could be based.

As has been pointed out above, classical conditioning seems to play an important part in both punishment and avoidance training procedures. This, coupled with a consideration of the therapeutic possibilities of a straightforward classical conditioning procedure, leads us, in contrast to Feldman (1966), to advocate the exploitation of classical techniques.

We will not discuss here the parametric studies investigating the most effective conditions for the development of conditioned responses, such as the effect of varying the interstimulus interval, as these form the subject of standard texts (e.g., Kimble, 1961).

The problem we will consider is that of establishing conditioned responses that are resistant to extinction and are independent of the subject's voluntary control. Several studies have investigated the effects of assuring the subject that he will receive no more shock, after developing a conditioned autonomic response [psychogalvanic response (PGR) or heart rate] to a conditioned stimulus (Cooke & Harris, 1937; Bridger & Mandel, 1964, 1965; Chatterjee & Eriksen, 1962; Grings & Lockhart, 1963; Wickens, Allen, & Hill, 1963). These experiments, typically, showed that assuring the subject that he would no longer receive shock, often accompanied by removal of the shock electrodes, led to a very rapid extinction of the conditioned autonomic response.

In contrast to the extreme transience of the autonomic response conditioned in these situations stand studies where an extremely resistant change in autonomic reactions has been conditioned in humans. Thus, Sanderson et al.

(1962), with a one-trial conditioning procedure employing the extremely traumatic UCR of respiratory paralysis, obtained autonomic CRs which, far from extinguishing over time, actually increased in strength. A considerable number of patients treated for alcoholism by the early chemical methods actually acquired a conditioned "nausea reaction" to the stimuli associated with drinking. This conditioned nausea persisted for some time (Hammersley, 1957). Further, the learning-theory model of the neuroses (Eysenck & Rachman, 1965) depends on retention of conditioned autonomic reactions for considerable periods, although extinction of these reactions is included in the model as an explanation of spontaneous remission. Our hypothesis of the efficiency of aversion techniques depends on the assumption that the classically conditioned change in autonomic response is persistent and is independent of the patient's "cognitive control." A discussion of this problem is given on p. 314 below.

In connection with the problem of bypassing "cognitive control" and thereby increasing the resistance to extinction of the conditioned response, we suggest that a paper by Razran (1961) is of extreme interest. In this paper Razran discusses "interoceptive conditioning" which he defines as "classical conditioning in which either the conditioned stimulus (CS) or the unconditioned stimulus (US) or both are delivered directly to the mucosa of some specific viscus."

Selected quotations from Razran's summary and conclusions will indicate the direct relevance of the phenomenon of interoceptive conditioning to the problems of obtaining classically conditioned responses which are resistant to extinction and independent of the subject's voluntary control (p. 97):

> **1.** Unlike the continuum of exteroceptive stimulation, which is the body-material of all our conscious experience, the continuum of interoceptive stimulation leads largely to unconscious reactions.
>
> **2.** Interoceptive conditioning, whether involving conditioned or unconditioned interoceptive stimuli, is readily obtainable and is by its very nature largely unconscious in character.
>
> **4.** Interoceptive conditioning is somewhat slower in formation than exteroceptive, but once conditioned, it is more fixed and irreversible (less readily extinguished).
>
> **5.** When equal but opposing interoceptively produced and exteroceptively produced reactions are juxtaposed, the interoceptive reactions dominate the exteroceptive ones, with the final result that preceding exteroceptive stimuli become conditioned stimuli for succeeding interoceptive reactions, whereas preceding interoceptive reactions become strengthened by exteroceptive reactions succeeding them.
>
> **6.** The juxtaposition of conditioned interoceptive and exteroceptive stimuli of the same conditioned reaction, unlike similar juxtapositions of exteroceptive stimuli of different modalities, produces a certain amount of conflict and decrementation of conditioning.

Only one of the many examples of interoceptive conditioning cited by Razran will be given: an experiment by Okhuyanakaya (Razran, 1961, p. 92), in which the experimenter noted that when human subjects were told to inhale they showed arm vasoconstriction in addition to changes in their pneumograms. This vasoconstriction appears to be a visceroviscerae vasomotor reflex evoked by the respiration. If the experimenter then told his subjects not to inhale when the word "inhale" was given, the vasoconstriction to the word "inhale" persisted although the pneumogram showed that the subject had obeyed the instructions "not to inhale when the word 'inhale' was given." Razran concludes: ". . . it [the vasoconstriction] was, presumably, 'naturally conditioned' to the word 'inhale' and was not deconditioned—or inhibited—by the instructions 'not to inhale when "inhale" is uttered.' "

We feel that the study of interoceptive conditioning is highly relevant to the problems of aversion therapy, and we suggest that exploitation of the findings in this field would be extremely worthwhile.

Recent Clinical Findings

The effects of aversion therapy have been the subject of a number of reviews in the past few years (Franks, 1966b; Feldman, 1966; Eysenck & Rachman, 1963; Rachman, 1961, 1965a), and in this chapter we will concentrate mainly on the more recent work in the field.

A valuable addition to our understanding of the processes involved in aversion therapy was recently made by Marks & Gelder (1967). They described the results obtained from five patients who were suffering from fetishism and/or transvestism and who were each submitted to a concentrated course of therapy. The importance of their contribution lies in the fact that they made careful quantitative and qualitative assessments of the behavior, physiological reactions, and attitudes of the patients before, during, and after treatment. In addition to undergoing a full psychiatric examination prior to treatment, all the patients were assessed on the semantic differential test, and their penile reactions to appropriate and deviant sexual stimuli were gauged.

All the patients were treated on an inpatient basis over a two-week period during which they received two aversion therapy sessions per day, each lasting approximately one hour. After their discharge they were given booster sessions, first weekly and then monthly, for several months. The aversive stimulus was produced by a simple shock-box run by batteries; the electrodes were attached to the patient's forearm or leg. At the commencement of each treatment session, the patient was asked to select a shock level which was just above the pain threshold. In the initial stages of treatment, the shock was delivered when the patient imagined himself in a sexually provocative and arousing situation which incorporated some features of his sexually deviant behavior. In the second stage of treatment, which usually commenced on about the third or fourth day of treatment, the patients were shocked when they actually carried out the deviant behavior in reality. The shock was delivered on an intermittent schedule; and approximately one-quarter of all trials were not shocked. Throughout the treatment the patient was required to wear the penile plethysmograph (a refined version of Freund's original instrument). The plethysmograph recordings were used to monitor the progress of treatment throughout. The effects of the treatment were assessed by reported changes in the patient's behavior, plethysomographic recordings, concept changes, and the reports obtained from members of the patient's family (especially their wives).

All five patients had relatively sound personality and were highly motivated and cooperative, and three of them were able to engage in heterosexual relations prior to the commencement of treatment. All five patients masturbated while cross-dressing or while in contact with the fetishistic object, and all of them had commenced this deviant sexual behavior in childhood or early adolescence. All but one had engaged in deviant sexual behavior for at least twenty years.

One of the first observations to emerge from this study was that, with increasing exposure to the electrical aversion treatment, the patients experienced increasing difficulty in conjuring up the required images. The time taken

Figure 7–1. With treatment, patients take increasingly longer periods to obtain the deviant images. (Reproduced from Marks & Gelder, *British Journal of Psychiatry*, 1967.)

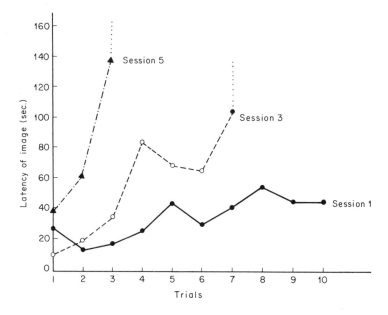

to obtain the image increased, and in numerous instances the patient eventually reached a point where he was unable to obtain images at all. This increase in latency is clearly illustrated in Figures 7–1 and 7–2.

It will be seen from Figure 7–5 that Marks & Gelder checked the effect of simple repetition of the image and found that no change in latency occurred *except* when the image was followed by the delivery of electric shock. In other words, the change in ability to obtain the abnormal sexual image can probably be attributed to the effects of aversive stimulation and is not a simple habituation effect. The increase in latency observed was paralleled by an increase in the time which elapsed before the abnormal stimulus produced an erection in the patient. In the early stages of treatment (and certainly before treatment commenced) patients generally produced fairly rapid and substantial erections when presented with the abnormal sexual stimuli. As the treatment progressed, however, the erectile response was increasingly delayed until, in many cases, the stimulus failed to produce any reaction. Figures 7–3 and 7–4 illustrate the increasing erection latency observed in one of their patients (a transvestite).

Another interesting aspect which is illustrated in this figure is the remarkable specificity of the erectile changes which occurred during treatment. It can be seen that the erection latency observed in response to a particular stimulus was fairly strictly related to the type of aversion treatment which had been administered. The first item which was treated in the case of this patient was panties, and it will be observed from the figure that erections in the presence of panties were totally eliminated after a few sessions of treatment. Notice, however, that the other sexual stimuli (skirt, slip, pajamas) re-

Figure 7–2. Increased latencies of image production are restricted to items which have been shocked. (Reproduced from Marks & Gelder, *British Journal of Psychiatry*, 1967.)

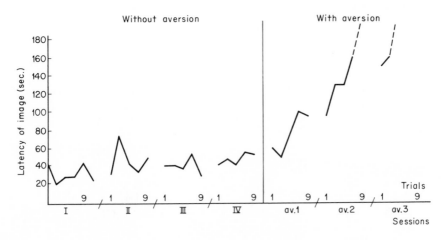

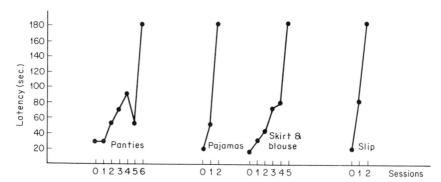

Figure 7–3. The selective effect of electrical aversion: reductions in sexual reaction are restricted to treated items. (Reproduced from Marks & Gelder, *British Journal of Psychiatry*, 1967.)

mained unaffected until they in turn were subjected to the treatment. The patient continued to show erectile responses to the specific stimuli until they had been associated with electrical stimulation. The second item which the therapist knocked out was pajamas, and again, by referring to the figure, one can see that the effect of treating this item was highly specific. The next items to be eliminated were skirt and blouse, and then the therapist had to deal with the last item—a woman's slip.

The selective effect of the treatment is consistent with some laboratory findings (Azrin & Holz, 1966). At the same time, however, it introduces another paradox: How can we reconcile the specificity observed during the treatment process with the general clinical outcome in these cases? The inhibition or suppression of normal sexual reactions does generalize to external circumstances and specific (but untreated) deviant sexual stimuli. It is evident that during the treatment only a very limited number of deviant stimuli can be dealt with—nevertheless, the effects of aversion therapy appear to be widespread. These effects spread from the clinic to the external world and from a few selected sexual items to a very wide range of stimulating conditions.

Figure 7–4. The selective effect of aversion treatment: changes in attitude are restricted to treated items. (Reproduced from Marks & Gelder, *British Journal of Psychiatry*, 1967.)

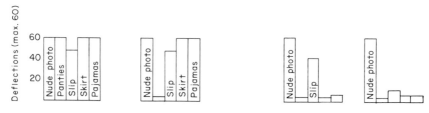

Marks & Gelder also observed that the patient's sexual and other concepts changed in a way which paralleled these physiological alterations and imaginary productions. The patients' attitudes, erectile reactions, and images all changed in the same direction but "at rather different speeds." The main attitudinal change observed in this group of patients was that the abnormal sexual stimuli became "devalued" or "neutralized" as the treatment progressed. For example, the attitudes of transvestities to items such as silk panties and corsets changed from "favourable" at the beginning of treatment to "not favourable" at the end of treatment. It should be noted, however, that in the main the patients' attitudes changed from favorable to neutral rather than, as might have been expected, to intensely unfavorable. Contrary to expectation, the patients did not develop aversive attitudes towards the previously stimulating objects. In this sense, the aversion therapy did not produce aversion—but, rather, a neutralization of sexual affect. It was also noted that the patients' changed attitudes were, like the plethysmographic changes, highly specific to each phase in the treatment. The selective attitudinal changes are neatly illustrated in Figure 7–5.

Figure 7–5.   Evaluative change with selective aversion.

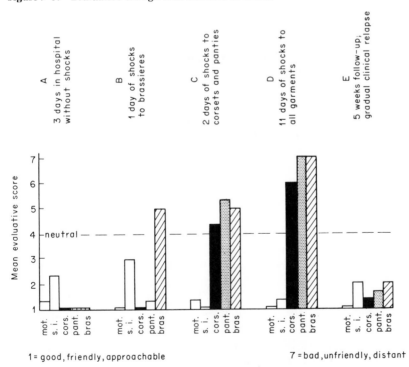

1 = good, friendly, approachable   7 = bad, unfriendly, distant

mot. = mother; s. i. = sexual intercourse; cors. = corsets; pant. = panties; bras = brassieres

Another point which emerged from this study was the comparative independence of the patient's normal and abnormal sexual activity. In no instance was the successful application of aversion to the abnormal sexual behavior associated with, or followed by, untoward changes in the patient's normal sexual outlets where these existed. In fact, in at least two cases, their normal sexual behavior was noted to improve shortly after the treatment had been completed. In general, the therapeutic outcome in these cases was encouraging. In all five cases the abnormal sexual behavior was eliminated by the end of the concentrated course of treatment. Unfortunately, two of the patients showed some measure of relapse within a year of discharge.

Of all the techniques of electrical aversion which are currently in use, the one described by Marks & Gelder appears to be the most satisfactory in bringing about a termination of deviant behavior. It appears to be clinically effective and, except on some points, would seem to be entirely reasonable and justified in terms of our current knowledge regarding the effects of punishment, avoidance training, and similar topics. The only two queries which might be raised at this point concern Marks & Gelder's use of an intermittent schedule of reinforcement (a 100 percent schedule may be more efficacious; see Azrin & Holz, 1966) and their use of the appearance of the image as a signal for the administration of the shock. This may very well prove to be the most efficient procedure to use, but on the other hand, it can be argued that one should administer the shock when a plethysmographic reaction to the abnormal stimulus occurs. One of the features of this treatment which recommends itself most strongly is the very careful assessment techniques and, in particular, the use of the semantic differential and the penile plethysmograph. The continued use of these monitoring instruments is strongly recommended. Ideally, the patients' other autonomic reactions should be recorded both during and after treatment, e.g., cardiac rate and respiratory rate. The purpose of including these autonomic measures would be to ascertain whether or not the patients acquired conditioned aversive reactions of an autonomic type.

Another important study was recently completed by Bancroft (1966), who made a detailed examination of the effects of electrical aversion treatment on seven homosexual patients. The treatment sessions were given two to four times per week and lasted for approximately an hour, and each patient was given between 30 and 40 such sessions. Five other patients who were offered the treatment declined to accept it, and two others defected before treatment commenced. The nature of the disorder meant that the treatment had to deal wtih fantasy material only, and the subjects were shown photographs of sexually provocative males. In addition, at the beginning of every session they were asked to look at photographs of sexually provocative women in order that their plethysmographic reactions to these stimuli might be assessed throughout the course of the treatment.

Bancroft's treatment differed from that of Marks & Gelder in one important respect. He administered the shock when the patient showed an erectile response of a certain predetermined amplitude. In Bancroft's (1966, p. 102) own description "when the threshold is reached a shock would be given. This would be repeated at 15 second intervals for the next minute provided that each time the amplitude was still above threshold and not actually falling. Thus a maximum of five shocks was given." The patients were also required to complete self-rating forms at the end of each treatment session, in which they gave an account of their feelings of sexual arousal and anxiety. Apart from the therapeutic sessions, the patients were given no specific instructions other than being encouraged to masturbate to heterosexual fantasies between sessions. This instruction plus the "practice" which the subjects had with heterosexual pictures during the sessions constituted the main attempts to facilitate the growth of heterosexual behavior as a replacement for the homosexual activities.

From a clinical point of view the outcome in these seven cases was not quite as satisfactory as might have been hoped. "In every case behavioural changes have resulted which have been relevant to the therapeutic goal but in at least two of the seven patients these changes have been insufficient or too impermanent to produce long-term significant effects" (Bancroft, 1966, p. 231). Bancroft noted that in those cases where the homosexual interests were substantially decreased, the treatment was associated with considerable anxiety. These and related observations lead Bancroft to postulate that "the suppression of homosexual interest is dependent on a high level of anxiety being generated or being maintained." The mixed clinical results obtained in the study, while disappointing, are not altogether surprising in view of the special difficulties associated with the treatment of homosexuality. In homosexuality the therapist is faced with a double problem. In the first place he is attempting to suppress or eliminate the sexual behavior and, second, he hopes to assist the patient in redirecting his sexual drive along heterosexual lines. The latter object is, of course, immensely difficult to achieve, and in a sense, one of the most interesting.things to emerge from Bancroft's study is the suggestion that certain types of practice may facilitate such an adjustment. A second difficulty which arises in the treatment of homosexual patients is the fact that one is obliged to restrict the aversion training to imaginal and photographic representation.

A disturbing feature of Bancroft's study, however, is that his subjects appear to have been simultaneously trained to make homosexual responses. An examination of the plethysmographic recordings indicates that the patients, for the most part, continued to produce marked erectile responses to the homosexual material. In fact the main change that seems to have occurred (judging from the plethysmographic recordings) is that the patients began to respond sexually to photographs of females as well as males. There seem to be two possible explanations for the failure of the electrical treatment to reduce erectile responses to male photographs. In the first place it is possible that the shock intensity was not sufficiently great to produce suppression of the response. Second, Bancroft might inadvertently have been habituating the subjects to the administration of shock by his method of reapplying the electric shock even when the erectile response remained unchanged. It will be remembered that he continued to apply the electric shock on up to five occasions during a one-minute period if the plethysmograph response showed no signs of declining. In this sense, he was conditioning or training his subjects to endure the electric shock and causing them to maintain their erections despite the administration of shock. One is reminded here of Miller's (1960) finding that, under certain conditions, exposing animals to repeated mild shocks may induce in them an immunity to the effects of shock. It is possible, therefore, that one should avoid using repeated shocks when the erectile response fails to decrease. Additionally, one can increase the intensity of the shock if the plethysmographic reactions do not decrease after the first few sessions.

On the positive side the plethysmographic records indicate quite clearly that most of the patients developed erectile responses to the heterosexual photographs as a result of the treatment. The possibility that this improved reaction to heterosexual material was obtained as a result of encouraging the patients to masturbate in response to heterosexual fantasies and/or repeated exposure to the female photographs should be explored further because of the potential value which they offer in the development of the normal heterosexual reactions. These possibilities are of particular importance in view of the likelihood that the best way of establishing a permanent elimination of unadaptive sexual behavior is to suppress the undesirable response and then to generate a more satisfactory alternative response.

Feldman & MacCulloch (1965) made one of the first systematic attempts to apply the evidence on the experimental application of aversive stimulation to clinical problems. As mentioned earlier, the attempt, although admirable in many ways and apparently of considerable therapeutic effect, unfortunately contains a number of difficulties.

We feel that Feldman & MacCulloch have paid insufficient attention to the role of cognitive factors. This is perhaps best made by presenting a full description of their treatment and technique.

After undergoing fairly extensive psychological investigations, the patient was asked to assess a large series of slides depicting males both clothed and unclothed and then to arrange them in a hierarchy of attractiveness. The hierarchy usually comprised about eight slides, and treatment was commenced with the slide which was least attractive. The patient was then worked up through the hierarchy in ascending order. The patient was also asked to compile a hierarchy of female slides; in this case the highest slide, i.e., the most attractive, was presented first, and the patient then worked down the hierarchy in descending order. Feldman & MacCulloch then established a level of shock which was described by the patient as being very unpleasant. The treatment was carried out in a dark and quiet room at the hospital. The description continues (pp. 170–171):

> The patient is told that he will see a male picture and that several seconds later he might receive a shock. He is also told that he can turn off the slide by pressing a switch, with which he is provided, whenever he wishes to do so, and that the moment the slide leaves the screen the shock will also be turned off. Finally he is told that he will never be shocked when the screen is blank. It is made clear to him that he should leave the slide on the screen for as long as he finds it sexually attractive. The first slide is then presented. The patient has the choice of switching it off or leaving it on the screen. Should he switch it off within eight seconds he is not shocked and this is termed an avoidance response. Should he fail to turn it off within 8 seconds, he receives a shock. If the shock strength is not sufficiently high to cause him to switch it off immediately, it is increased until he does so. In practice this has hardly ever been necessary. The moment a patient performs the switching off response the slide is removed and the shock is terminated. This is termed an escape trial. In addition to switching off, the patient is told to say "No" as soon as he wishes the slide to be removed. It is hoped that a further increment of habit strength will accrue to the avoidance habit by means of this further avoidance response. The usual course of events is: (i) several trials in all of which escape responses are made; (ii) a sequence of trials in some of which the patient escapes, and some which he avoids; (iii) a sequence of trials in which the patient avoids every time.

After the patient has successfully avoided on three successive trials he is placed on a predetermined schedule of reinforcement. In addition to the attempt at suppressing sexual responses to nude males, Feldman & MacCulloch tried to make the patients more responsive to female photographs. This was attempted by introducing a female slide contiguous with the removal of the male slide. "That is we attempt to associate the relief of anxiety with the introduction of the female." They go on to say that the female slide was always removed by the therapist and never by the patient "so that his habit of avoiding females is not strengthened in the training situation." It is evident from this description that we are here dealing with a situation which is a long way removed from Solomon's dogs jumping from one compartment to the next. As an example we would draw particular attention to Feldman & MacCulloch's comment about the removal of the female slides. Their insistence that the patient should never remove the female slides seems to us to be stretching the analogy. We cannot see that there is anything but a very remote resemblance between pushing a button to remove a photograph of a female from a screen and what they describe as "his habit of avoiding females."

Had we been asked to predict, on purely theoretical grounds, the likelihood that such a treatment procedure would effect a major change in homosexual behavior, we would undoubtedly have given it a low chance of success.

Such a prediction, of course, would have been entirely wrong—for the fact of the matter is that a substantial number of the patients treated by Feldman & MacCulloch did respond to this treatment. Nonetheless, we feel that it might be worthwhile to consider substituting some other stimulus representation in the treatment technique. As a possibility we would suggest that more effective results might be obtained by the use of imaginal stimulation in which the patient could be asked to produce fantasies concerning the sexual behavior in which he indulges—in the manner of Marks & Gelder (1967).

We opened this chapter with the remark that the surprising thing about aversion therapy is that it works at all. One of the reasons which we gave for making this observation was the fact that patients know perfectly well that when they leave the clinic and approach the abnormal sexual object or indulge in the deviant sexual behavior they will no longer receive electric shocks. In the present case, the patients treated were undoubtedly aware that when they left the hospital they would no longer receive electric shocks—for any reason, let alone for making homosexual approaches or even, for that matter, when looking at photographs of attractive males. Nevertheless, a high proportion of their patients did make the generalization from this highly artificial situation to the outside world. The operation of cognitive factors in aversion therapy is of crucial significance. Closely related to this problem is our need to understand what happens to the patient's autonomic reactions during a course of aversion therapy. The clinical effectiveness of the procedure used by Feldman & MacCulloch is satisfactory and offers considerable encouragement. In the first place it should be noted that they offered treatment to all patients who were referred, which in itself is, as they comment, a very unusual procedure. In the report made in 1965 they had completed the treatment of 19 patients. Of these, 3 defected from treatment, 11 were improved at the end of treatment, and the remaining 5 made very little response. At the time of publication the follow-ups on these patients were of short duration, and it was therefore impossible to assess the persistence of the observed changes. The original sample has now been extended (without altering the selection procedure), and a more recent report (Feldman, 1967) indicates that the early successes are being maintained. Treatment of 43 patients has now been completed, and of these, 25 were improved at termination, 11 were unsuccessful, and 7 defected from treatment. These results are exceptionally promising, and there can be little doubt that Feldman & MacCulloch have made an important contribution which needs to be extended and repeated. Incidentally, we feel that this report by Feldman & MacCulloch is an amusing example of the divergence between theory and practice in that, although the theoretical basis for their model is far from satisfactory, its clinical effectiveness is very encouraging. In a later report (MacCulloch, Feldman, & Pinshoff, 1965) these workers provided some additional information about the physiological changes which occurred during treatment. Unfortunately, however, the data are almost all qualitative in nature, and as the sample involved is very small, it is extremely difficult to draw firm conclusions.

Other clinical reports on the effects of aversion treatment in the handling of sexual disorders include the work of Kushner (1965), Kushner & Sandler (1966), and Solyom & Miller (1965).

ALCOHOLISM

After the encouraging results reported by McGuire & Vallance (1964), Blake (1965) described his experience with a comparison trial between electrical aversion treatment and electrical aversion combined with relaxation training (carried out as a preparatory step). The 37 patients who received aversion therapy combined with relaxation underwent a three-part program. The three phases of the program were: relaxation training, motivation arousal, and aversion conditioning proper. After the patient had acquired the ability to relax successfully he was given a few sessions of what appears to be counseling, and during these periods, he was forcibly reminded of the undesirable consequence of his alcoholism. Attempts were also made to increase his desire to participate in the treatment and to rid himself of the disorder. The final phase of the treatment consisted of the aversion conditioning procedure. The treatment was carried out with the subject and therapist in separate rooms. Each subject was supplied with a glass, water, and alcohol of his choice and was instructed to mix his drink according to taste.

The method is descibed by Blake as follows: "He is told to sip his drink but not to swallow. A shock of increasing intensity randomly starting above the threshold reported by him in a pre-aversion test to be unpleasant, is delivered contiguously with his sip on reinforced trials. He is instructed to spit out the alcohol (into a bowl provided) as a means of having the shock terminated." The conditioning treatment extended from four to eight days and the whole program took an average of 4.93 hours per subject. This aversion treatment procedure was also used in treating the patients in the aversion-therapy-only group. Attempts were made to see each subject at intervals of one, three, six, nine, and twelve months. The success of the treatment was assessed in terms of five criteria proposed by Knight where these were applicable. In addition, follow-up information was obtained wherever possible, from at least one independent person. The abstinent category included those individuals who were known to be abstinent during the one-year follow-up period. The improved category included "those people whose drinking was now of a social order . . . and appeared to be in no danger of pathological escalation. . . ." The majority of the patients in this study belonged to social classes 1 and 2. The full results available at the completion of the one-year follow-up were presented by Blake in a later paper (1967). Of the 37 patients treated by relaxation and aversion, 46 percent were abstinent, 13 percent were improved, 30 percent had relapsed, and 11 percent were unaccounted for. The 22 patients who were treated by electrical aversion therapy alone yielded the following outcome: 23 percent were abstinent, 27 percent were improved, 27 percent had relapsed, and 23 percent were unaccounted for. Although the differences between the two groups in terms of the abstinent and improved categories were not statistically significant it would appear that the relaxation combined with aversion therapy produced substantially more patients who succeeded in abstaining for at least one year. Blake very fairly points out that the results give no grounds for complacency but that they are far from being discouraging.

It is of course very difficult to sort out the factors involved in the relaxation-plus-aversion-therapy group, as the patients were also receiving something akin to counseling. Nevertheless, this treatment program would appear to deserve replication, especially with a more representative sample. In regard to the actual procedure itself, it is possible that Blake's method of increasing the intensity of the shock is undesirable. Blake also recorded GSR changes during the conduct of therapy, and while he has yet to give a detailed report of these findings, it is interesting to note that the great majority of his patients did in fact develop conditioned reactions during the course of treatment.

In 1966, MacCulloch, Feldman, Orford, & MacCulloch reported on their unsuccessful attempt to treat four alcoholic patients by their technique of "anticipatory avoidance learning," earlier used with some success in the treatment of homosexuals. They state that one of the main purposes in presenting their results was to introduce "into the discussion a salutary note of caution." In fact, what they have done is to indicate that their treatment technique does not appear to hold much promise for the treatment of alcoholics. In view of Blake's comparatively encouraging findings, it would appear that his procedure is the one which would best repay further investigation at this stage.

Although MacCulloch et al. (1966) state that the treatment procedure used with their four alcoholic patients was essentially similar to that employed in the management of their homosexual patients, it is not stated what instructions their patients were actually given. As we have suggested, the subject's cognitive appraisal of the situation may be of considerable importance, and the absence of this information is unfortunate. Their patients appeared to have difficulty in developing the anticipatory avoidance response of switching off the slide before the eight-second danger period had elapsed— and it is difficult to understand why they failed to do so. They were not permitted to drink during the treatment sessions and were merely exposed to photographs of alcohol, the sight of an open bottle, and the sight of alcohol in a glass. None of these stimuli appeared to be particularly reinforcing, and the patients would have gained nothing by permitting the slide to stay on beyond the eight-second danger period. It is in this light that their failure to develop the anticipatory avoidance reaction of switching off the slide appears to be so puzzling. Pulse-rate recordings were obtained for two of the four patients but, as in their earlier reports, the authors did not provide a quantitative analysis of these observations. In consequence it is not possible to ascertain whether or not a conditioned cardiac response did in fact develop in either of the patients. Certainly, the graphic samples which they present indicate that there was, at least in one of the patients, if not in both, considerable fluctuation in pulse rate. In view of the difficulty of assessing this information (both in the report on alcoholics and in the earlier one on homosexuals), we are unable to accept at face value their conclusions that the pulse-rate findings obtained from their alcoholic patients are "in direct contrast to our homosexual patients." It is of course perfectly possible that such a distinction can be made, but in the absence of further information their conclusion cannot be supported at this stage.

In 1965, Hsu described a new variant of electrical aversion therapy in which his alcoholic patients received a powerful shock within .5 to 5 seconds after swallowing alcohol. The shocks were administered to the head and lasted for 30 seconds. The initial treatment consisted of five daily sessions and was boosted by two daily sessions given one month and six months later. Great anxiety was (not surprisingly) provoked by this unpleasant method, and less than half the original 40 volunteers completed the first and second treatments. Quite reasonably, Hsu has refrained from giving detailed results until a prolonged follow-up is completed. In our view, however, the results would have to be extraordinarily good in order to justify a technique of this type.

The selection of studies discussed here illustrates the point made earlier that there is no single and generally accepted method of conducting aversion therapy. It is not surprising that a procedure of such recent origin should not yet have solidified into a single method of treatment. While this has many disadvantages, most obviously the difficulty of replication, it also has the advantage of allowing various therapists and experimenters to explore the wide range of possibilities which are now open. With increasing knowledge, and particularly with the conclusion of acceptable field trials, we will be in a better position to assess the merits of the versions of therapy described to date. At this stage, however, it seems that the most promising technique for treating sexual disorders is the one described by Marks & Gelder (1967) and that the most promising technique for treating alcoholism is the one described by Blake (1966). The Feldman-MacCulloch method for treating homosexuality has produced very useful clinical improvements, and when the difficulties discussed above have been clarified, it may make an even larger contribution. It is also desirable that workers in this field should make every attempt to obtain reliable physiological recordings during the course of treatment—whether the treatment is being conducted in an experimental or purely clinical setting.

COGNITIVE FACTORS

We must constantly bear in mind that patients know perfectly well that drinking whisky or cross-dressing outside the treatment room is not followed by an electric shock. Why do they refrain from the deviant behavior outside treatment sessions? The fact that the patient is aware of the distinction between the stimulus contingencies in the treatment room and the rest of his world compels us to look for at least part of our explanation "below the neck."

It has become increasingly clear over the past few years that cognitive factors can influence autonomic functioning in a surprising fashion. It is, of course, quite possible for people to acquire conditioned autonomic reactions without awareness and/or without parallel changes in their overt behavior. Work from Gantt's (1964) laboratory indicated some years ago how this process (which he calls *schizokinesis*) can occur. "I also want to emphasize this difference between the formation of the cardiac conditional reflexes, the visceral conditional reflexes and the more easily observable motor ones; but here we have a split between the functions of the organism so that the organism may be in adaptation with some of its organs and some of its reactions, but not with others. This phenomenon I term schizokinesis." Gantt has provided numerous examples of this phenomenon.

In regard to aversion therapy, all we can do here is to raise the possibility that these patients are acquiring cardiac (and other) autonomic reactions to the deviant stimuli and that these are related to, or even mediate, the overt behavioural and attitudinal changes. At the very least we feel that full autonomic recordings should be taken during the experimental investigations of aversion therapy. Any explanation which relies exclusively on presumed cognitive changes seems to us likely to fail. Similarly, an explanation which relies too heavily on the conditioning of behavior that is under voluntary control seems likely to be inadequate.

Nowadays it is commonplace that the setting and instructions which are given to a subject undergoing a course of conditioning may have a profound effect on the development of these responses (e.g., Spence, 1965; Grings, 1966). As far back as 1937, Cook & Harris reported that the magnitude of a GSR was increased when the subject was told that he would receive a shock, and decreased when he was told he would not receive a shock. The dramatic effect of the threat of shock on the GSR is clearly illustrated in a report by Bridger & Mandel (1964). Other illustrations of the effect of instructions on the course of the conditioning are seen in the work reported by Spence & Goldstein (1961) on eyeblink and Chatterjee & Eriksen (1962) on heart rate. In a way the most impressive and important aspect of the research which has been conducted on the relationship between cognitive factors and conditioning relates to the data on the effect of instructions and expectancy on the extinction of conditioned reaction. These findings are central to the apparent paradox involved in aversion therapy. In addition to demonstrating the facilitation of conditioning by means of instructions, Cook & Harris (1937) also showed that the GSR is considerably reduced when the subject is told that he will not receive any more shocks. Bridger & Mandel (1965) demonstrated very rapid extinction of a conditioned GSR when the subjects were informed that they were to receive no further shocks. Similar results were reported by Grings & Lockhart (1963).

The significance of this work on the relationship between cognitive factors in conditioning and extinction for an understanding of aversion therapy is twofold. In the first place, it highlights the paradox which has been observed in the administration of this treatment. It is, of course, possible that this paradox arises from the fact that patients who undergo aversion therapy receive not (as is customary in most of the experiments described) 10, 20, or 30 conditioning trials but something in the region of 300 to 750 conditioning trials. Nevertheless, these experimental findings demonstrate the profound influence which cognitive factors have on conditioning and extinction, and serve to emphasize the need for a detailed and careful examination of the cognitive and autonomic changes which occur during aversion treatment.

We should, however, bear in mind the fact that virtually all the available evidence on cognitive control relates to GSR conditioning. We need confirmation that conditioned cardiac and respiratory changes (for example) are as vulnerable to cognitive control as the GSR—and it is these reactions which are likely to have a more important role in aversion therapy. One of the central features of neurotic conditions (most notably, anxiety states) is their resistance to cognitive control. Even when the patient is convinced that he is not in danger, he continues to experience strong autonomic reactions. Cognitive control conspicuously fails to extinguish neurotic anxiety reactions.

ETHICAL CONSIDERATIONS

The use of aversion therapy raises ethical problems which need to be examined—particularly as the method appears likely to be adopted extensively.

Our views on these matters are, of course, an expression of a personal attitude. We feel that psychologists, like other scientists, have a general responsibility to other people and that this responsibility must be exercised. Detachment in scientific matters should not be confused with a detachment in ethical matters. In the first place we feel that the existence of a problem must be recognized. Aversion therapy involves the deliberate application of painful or unpleasant stimulation—it involves punishment in a technical sense, but this should not be allowed to become punitive in the everyday sense. We have little sympathy with the argument that aversive therapy does not raise ethical problems because other types of therapy also involve pain or discomfort (e.g., electroshock therapy [EST] in psychiatry, surgical procedures). Apart from the intrinsically fallacious quality of the argument ("One good abuse deserves another."), it is a counterargument which is irrelevant in the particular case. We doubt that a patient who is about to undergo an unpleasant form of treatment derives much comfort from being reminded that there are other experiences which are even more unpleasant.

It is true that aversion therapy is unpleasant, but psychologists must avoid becoming punitive agents. To do so would be both inherently objectionable and contrary to the nature and traditions of the discipline. In our opinion the treatment can only be given with the knowledge and consent of the patient. In addition, we feel that aversion therapy should only be advised if there are no alternative methods of treating the patient.

He must be informed of the detailed nature of the treatment and must be given an honest appraisal of the chances of success. Also, it is unthinkable that any form of coercion should be used in an attempt to induce a patient to accept the treatment. While we agree that coercion comes in various packages, we nevertheless feel that in practice there is little difficulty in recognizing "undue influence." We can illustrate this point by referring to two instances of what we regard as undue influence: (1) making a prisoner's release or parole contingent on his agreeing to undergo aversion therapy, (2) using aversion therapy without giving the patient an opportunity to refuse treatment. The experiment reported by Sanderson et al. (1964) would seem to be an example of this type. In this study the patients were given an injection of a curare-like drug which brings about total paralysis for between 30 and 150 seconds. During this period, breathing ceases, and there is no doubt that it is a terrifying experience to undergo. Although Sanderson et al. have reported a degree of success in treating alcoholics with this method, we have reservations about its use. Our specific objections are underlined by the fact that Sanderson et al. apparently did not give all their potential patients a full explanation of the nature of the treatment which they were to be given. As we have suggested, there are good reasons for recommending complete candor in describing the nature of any treatment which has been offered to a patient. In this instance, the reasons are more compelling because the experience is so harrowing. As a precaution against enforcing compliance in a patient, it is advisable to insist that he consider his decision for at least a week after the therapist has explained the procedure to him. In the long term, however, perhaps the best ethical solution is to find an effective substitute for aversion therapy. With this aim in mind we will now consider some of the alternatives.

BEYOND THE AVERSION PRINCIPLE

Some of the variations of aversive stimulation which have been explored include isolation, verbal punishments, the withdrawal of reinforcement, intense auditory stimulation, time out from reinforcement, and aversive imagery. Here we propose to discuss aversive imagery in some detail and also to suggest a possible application of the extinction phenomenon which we feel may prove to be of some value in the treatment of specific types of sexual disorders.

The successful reduction and elimination of responses by the technique known as *errorless extinction* may provide an alternative to aversion therapy and could be applied along the following lines (or some variation). In the case of what we might call surplus and misdirected sexual behavior, notably fetishism and transvestism, the possibility seems worth considering that repeated unreinforced presentations of the stimulus may produce decrements in response strength. To particularize, the following method is one which appears to us to have some promise but which we have unfortunately not yet had an opportunity to explore. A thorough analysis of the patient's misdirected sexual responses would be carried out by means of the penile plethysmograph. Once a large range of imaginal, pictorial, and real stimuli had been isolated, the patient would be exposed to each of the stimuli on a number of occasions in order to establish base rates of the magnitude of his sexual reactions. Once these base rates had been established, the stimuli which produced the milder sexual reaction would be presented for a very brief duration. Each stimulus would be withdrawn before a plethysmographic change became apparent. After a particular stimulus had been repeatedly presented at gradually increasing exposure duration without eliciting a reaction, the next stimulus in the hierarchy would be presented in the same manner. The second but mild stimulus would likewise be presented for a very brief period to begin with. Providing that no sexual reactions were evoked at the rapid exposure time, the stimulus presentations would be gradually lengthened. When the second stimulus was no longer capable of producing a sexual reaction, even at long exposure times, then the next most provocative stimulus would be presented in the same gradually extended manner. The therapist would work through the entire range of sexually arousing stimuli in this way until no plethysmographic reactions were obtained in the presence of the deviant stimuli. It would of course be necessary to prevent the patient from elaborating a provocative image after the brief stimulus presentations. This could be achieved by making him do arithmetic problems as soon as the sexual stimulus was withdrawn (and before the penile reaction occurred).

Obviously this technique would be time-consuming, but if successful, it would provide an acceptable alternative to painful aversive stimulation. Naturally, other types of extinction procedures are also worth considering.

COVERT SENSITIZATION

An alternative to aversion therapy which has already undergone some development is the technique which is sometimes described as "covert sensitization" or "aversive imagery." This procedure is actually an attenuated type of aversion therapy but one which is undoubtedly less unpleasant. Instead of presenting the deviant stimulus and then administering an aversive consequence such as shock, the sexual stimulus is followed by an imaginary event. In developing this procedure, Gold & Neufeld (1965) "did a Wolpe" with aversion therapy. That is, they attempted to substitute an imaginal event instead of relying on overt occurrences just as Wolpe did when he developed the therapeutic technique known as systematic desensitization—in this procedure the patient is exposed gradually to increasingly more disturbing phobic stimuli of an imaginal type. Gold & Neufeld successfully treated a sixteen-year-old boy who had been convicted for soliciting men in the toilets of a railway station. The patient was relaxed and then asked to imagine a rather unpleasant image (that is, to visualize himself in a toilet alongside a most unprepossessing old man). Further images were then given and were slowly changed to a more attractive form, but at the same time they were surrounded by prohibitions such as the image of a policeman standing nearby. "With this technique the patient quickly learned to reject an otherwise acceptable and attractive young man even in the absence of prohibition. . . ." Later the patient was presented with imaginary alternatives in the form of an attractive young man and an attractive young woman. The image of the woman was associated with pleasant suggestions, and the image of the man was associated with unpleasant imaginal stimulation. After 10 treatment sessions the patient reported feeling considerably improved and said that he had been able to avoid homosexual contacts. After another 7 interviews, carried out over a period of twelve months, the patient retained his therapeutic improvement and successfully formed a relationship with a girl which involved petting but not intercourse.

Although it is impossible to be certain about the direct effect of the aversive imagery in this case, the report opened up a very promising treatment possibility. More recently another interesting case history was described by Davison (1967) in which a sadistic fantasy was eliminated by a combination of positive counterconditioning and covert sensitization. Kolvin (1967) also obtained two successes with aversive imagery in treating adolescents. The first patient was a fourteen-year-old fetishist and the second a fifteen-year-old boy who was addicted to sniffing petrol. Cautela (1966c) obtained success in the treatment of two patients by a treatment technique which had some similarity to that described by Gold & Neufeld. In a later paper, Cautela (1967) described the method in detail and reported some early successes in managing obesity, alcoholism, homosexuality, and conduct disorders. The importance of getting the patient to "practice" at home is emphasized. In his discussion of the technique and its effects, Cautela expressed an optimistic view about the possible applications of covert sensitization. If the recent clinical report by Anant (1967) is anything to judge by, Cautela's optimism is well grounded. Anant described the successful treatment of all his 26 alcoholic patients by a type of covert sensitization in which they were asked to imagine themselves drinking and then feeling sick and vomiting. Like Cautela, Anant instructed his patients to practice imagining the same type of scene at home. Anant's results are remarkable. Certainly they are the best which the present writers have ever seen in the treatment of alcoholism, and for this reason the technique deserves close investigation and early replication. Further experiments along this line, however, should control for the effects of suggestion and brief counselling. The deliberate insertion and exclusion of these factors should not be difficult to arrange.

A striking thing about covert sensitization is that, like desensitization, it appears to produce results despite its apparent simplicity. To date, covert sensitization appears to have been successfully used in the treatment of sexual disorders, alcoholism, addiction, and compulsive behavior. Admittedly, very few patients in all have received this treatment. Nevertheless it would seem that, in some instances at least, it is effective, and the substitution of this attenuated form of aversion therapy would, of course, be extremely welcome. Some encouragement can be drawn from the success which is now being achieved with Wolpe's method of systematic desensitization (Rachman, 1967). This procedure relies on imaginal evocations of anxiety-provoking stimuli and situations. It can be argued that if evoking the "negative" emotional reactions of anxiety by direct verbal instruction is possible, there is no reason to suppose that similar verbal provocation should not be capable of eliciting "negative" emotional and physical reactions such as nausea, embarrassment, and disgust.

Chapter Summary

Aversion therapy is classified as one of the methods of "behavior therapy." It consists of the administration of an aversive stimulus after an abnormal act is performed or imagined. Stimuli which are associated with the abnormal activity, and particularly those which elicit such activity, are also presented to the patient and coupled with, or followed by, an aversive stimulus.

The two main types of aversion therapy, chemical and electrical, are described and compared. It is argued that, at present, the theoretical and practical considerations indicate that the electrical method is preferable. The qualities of an "ideal punishing stimulus" are considered in the light of views proposed by Azrin & Holz.

Aversion therapy is used primarily for the treatment of sexual disorders and alcoholism. The effects of such applications are described and evaluated in terms of recent clinical reports, and it appears that selected types of sexual disorder respond well to aversion therapy. Alcoholism responds only moderately well. On the clinical side, the actual techniques need to be refined and evaluated and their range of applicability explored. There are clear indications that a proportion of successfully treated patients relapse—usually within six months of treatment termination. The need to reduce the frequency of relapses is discussed.

Some ethical considerations involved in the use of aversive stimulation are noted, and certain safeguards are proposed. It is also argued that these ethical considerations increase the urgency of the search for more acceptable alternative treatment techniques. Some possible alternatives are discussed, and two of these are recommended for early investigation.

In addition to the need for careful evaluations of the overall effects of aversion therapy, there are serious deficiencies in our comprehension of the changes occurring during treatment which also require study. The most pertinent variables are the influence of cognitive factors and the autonomic changes which occur during treatment.

On the theoretical side, there has been a welcome phase of clarification. The manipulation of aversive stimulation and its effects are better understood —largely due to the analyses undertaken by Solomon, Church, Azrin & Holz, and others. Aversive stimulation usually suppresses behavior; this suppression can be enduring. The parameters which influence suppression effects include stimulus intensity, CS and UCS intervals, and reinforcement schedules. We also have data about the conditions under which aversive stimulation will not suppress behavior.

This type of experimental and theoretical information is of some value and can be employed in the design and evaluation of aversion therapy. There is, however, a great need for "transitional" investigations, that is, experimental studies which approximate the treatment situation more closely. These investigations need to be specifically designed to explore the problems which arise clinically. In this way, we will be able to advance beyond our exclusive reliance on experimental findings which, by chance, provide us with useful information. The type of research which we have in mind would include, for example, studies of the role of cognitive control in punishment training and studies of the autonomic changes which accompany prolonged aversive stimulation.

On the practical, clinical side there is sufficient evidence to support the further exploration of aversion therapy. In particular, we may be approaching the establishment of a viable method for the treatment of sexual disorders and, possibly, alcoholism. The range of effectiveness of aversion therapy now has to be demonstrated by properly controlled clinical trials. In addition, we need to obtain detailed and precise measurements of the variables involved in treatment and of the changes induced by electrical stimulation (see Marks & Gelder, 1967, for example). Until this information becomes available, it will be impossible to design a maximally effective treatment procedure.

At the same time, we have to extend the search for suitable and less unpleasant substitutes for aversion therapy. Of the possibilities suggested, we feel that covert sensitization is the most promising alternative.

PART TWO

New Directions and
Related Developments

8

Behavior Therapy and Self-control:

Techniques and Implications

JOSEPH R. CAUTELA

Boston College, Boston, Massachusetts

Although investigators in behavior therapy have consistently demonstrated the effectiveness of their procedures by therapeutic applications (Lazarus, 1963b; Wolpe, 1958) and substantiated their claims with experimental evidence (Davison, 1965a; Lang, 1964; Paul, 1966), the behavior therapist has not, to any extent, attempted to make the individual less susceptible to the development of future maladaptive behaviors; neither has he provided means for the individual to eliminate any such maladaptive behavior without the aid of the therapist. For the most part, the behavior therapist has concentrated exclusively on removing the maladaptive behavior present in the individual when he comes for treatment. Only recently, by relying on basic research in the area of self-control (SC) and extending such techniques as desensitization, thought stopping, and covert sensitization, have behavior therapists begun to teach their patients self-control procedures. Some patients are now taught to work out their own treatment strategy and apply a behavior therapy technique to themselves (Ferster, Nurnberger, & Levitt, 1962; Goldiamond, 1965b; Homme, 1965).

A major goal of psychoanalysis and nondirective therapy, on the other hand, has been the preparation of the patient to obtain a high control over his own behavior whenever necessary, without the continuing aid of the therapist, in conjunction with the elimination of any undesirable behavior. Shaffer (1947) expresses this point of view when he states that psychotherapy is a learning process through which a person acquires the ability to speak to himself in appropriate ways so as to control his own behavior. Unfortunately, other evidence (Wolpe, 1958; Eysenck, 1966) indicates that these therapeutic procedures are not sufficiently effective in achieving either therapeutic purpose.

It is, of course, too soon to conclude that the self-control techniques of behavior therapy will succeed where other approaches have been found inefficient and inadequate. However, describing some of the procedures may be worthwhile so that other workers may begin to submit them to experimental and clinical tests. Furthermore, this presentation may lead some investigators to expand upon those techniques already in use and to develop new ones.

The Concept of Self-Control

The term *self-control* is used to describe a response repertoire in which an individual can make responses to increase or decrease a response probability that is perceived as injurious to the individual himself or to others. It is said that an individual lacks SC if he is not able to change the probability of undesirable responses. It is said that he has good SC if he is able to make responses to inhibit undesirable responses which are likely to occur under certain conditions.

It can be said of a heavy drinker, for instance, that he lacks self-control because he is not able to make responses to reduce the frequency of his drinking behavior. A student who says he just can't make himself sit down and study is simply not able to increase the frequency of study responses (i.e., sitting at his desk and reading a text). In other words, he has no self-control in that situation. If an obese individual is presented with great amounts of delectable food at a party but eats little or none of the food, observers at the party may remark that, at the moment, the obese person is exerting good self-control.

In each of these examples, self-control is conceptualized as the response of an organism made to control the probability of another response. Concepts such as volition, inner direction, and will power are not viewed as scientifically useful since they are not as testable as hypotheses couched in terms of controlling response probability.

In this chapter, rationale, procedures, and experimentation concerning SC will be discussed within the framework of an individual initiating responses to control the probability of other responses. Although such a framework could be used to analyze any class of responses, special emphasis will be given here to responses labeled "maladaptive."

In a typical dyadic therapeutic situation the therapist initiates the self-controlling responses (SCRs) in order to change the frequency of maladaptive behavior, or the responses to be controlled (RCs). By means of proper instruction, repetition, and other devices of the therapist, the self-controlling responses introduced within the therapeutic hour will eventually be maintained by the patient outside the therapeutic hour.

In behavior therapy the identification of the SCRs and the RCs are usually quite specific (e.g., the thought to be controlled is "I am going crazy"; the SCR is "Stop"). This is not the case with conventional dynamic therapy in which the therapist does not clearly specify the SCRs and the RCs.

In some instances SCRs may themselves be RCs. Drinking alcohol (SCR) may be effective in reducing anxiety (RC), but it becomes a response to be controlled itself if it occurs at such a high rate that it becomes harmful to the organism. In phobias the SCR of avoidance is effective in reducing the fear but is itself an RC. Sometimes maladaptive approach behaviors such as drinking alcohol, overeating, homosexual behaviors, and aggression may be effective in modifying the anxiety response (the RC) but may themselves be RCs.

Advantages in Teaching Self-Control

There are certain advantages in providing the patient with responses (SCRs) that he can initiate whenever necessary. (This is called *teaching self-control.*)

1. Many more conditioning trials can take place within a time period. As a result, there should be a more rapid elimination of the undesirable behavior, thereby conserving time, money, and the therapist's services.

2. If anxiety (defined as an avoidance response, labeled as a fear response by the individual, and accompanied by high sympathetic nervous system activity) is the response to be eliminated, its rapid elimination can prevent further stimuli from becoming attached to it, thereby making the formation of new faulty habits less likely. Also, since the anxiety response has been prevented from occurring in the presence of particular stimuli that elicit (respondent) or are the occasion for (operant) the anxiety response, deconditioning can then occur. Other responses will then become attached to the stimuli. This can be viewed as a method of counterconditioning à la Guthrie (1952).

3. Often, once the patient has demonstrated to himself that he has effective SCRs available, his anxiety level is reduced. In nonlearning terms we can say that the patient has obtained self-confidence (the awareness that SCRs are available when needed).

The concept of "self-reinforcement" as a SC procedure has special relevance in this regard. Recently there has been a series of experiments and studies (Bandura & Kupers, 1964; Kanfer, 1966b; Kanfer & Marston, 1963a, 1963b; Marston, 1965) concerned with the effects of self-evaluative statements on behavior. If the statements are self-evaluating in a positive way they are designated as "self-reinforcing." Kanfer & Marston (1963a, 1963b present evidence to support this assumption. Self-reinforcement may be administered overtly to oneself (e.g., buying an ice cream) or covertly by making a positive self-evaluating statement (e.g., "I had the audience in the palm of my hand"). Covert self-reinforcements are considered to have the same influence on behavior as do overt self-reinforcements (Marston, 1965).

The behavior therapist can influence covert self-reinforcing responses in two ways. He can reinforce positive self-evaluation when it is overtly expressed by the patient, or he can modify behavior in such a manner that the patient is more apt to make self-reinforcing responses after he observes his own behavior. Effective behavior modification increases the number of possible alternative responses available to the individual. The reduction of fear responses increases the individual's response repertoire in that he is now able to approach the previously feared object if he so desires. After compulsive behavior is modified, the individual now has a choice of approaching or not approaching the object (alcohol, homosexual). The increase in behaviors available to the organism is likely to increase positive self-evaluative statements and decrease self-punitive statements. A person who makes a significant number of positive self-evaluating statements will perceive himself as worthwhile. A person who perceives himself as worthwhile is said to have dignity. Also, when an individual feels that whenever necessary he can make responses that are adaptive in most situations, he is said to have self-confidence. Therefore, effective behavior modification will result in an increase in personal dignity and self-confidence. It is also apparent that if the behavior modification procedures involve self-control techniques the feeling of personal "dignity" and "self-confidence" is more likely to occur.

4. Reconditioning (relapse) can be prevented if the patient initiates the relevant SCRs under conditions that were originally responsible for the occurrence of the faulty response (RC).

5. Within the behavior therapy model, SCRs can be taught to large numbers of individuals to prevent the occurrence of faulty behavior on a large scale (a sort of behavioral hygiene).

6. In addition to the advantages noted above, it is the author's contention that new behavior is more apt to be maintained when the individual perceives that he is responsible for the behavior change. The study by Secord & Backman (1964) in cognitive dissonance lends some support to this assumption.

Disadvantages of Teaching Self-Control

There are, of course, some possible disadvantages in teaching effective SCRs:

1. The individual who is taught the self-control procedures may not be

as effective in observing his own behavior as would a trained therapist in observing that same behavior.

2. Decisions have to be made concerning the identification of the responses to be controlled, the method and time they are to be controlled, and the extent. If the decisions are incorrect, further strengthening of the response to be controlled may result, or new faulty responses may be formed.

3. By removing self-control procedures from the therapist's influence and jurisdiction, several avenues of misuse may open. An individual may remove the SCR that acts to inhibit an RC; (e.g., a bank clerk may eliminate the anxiety that is preventing him from stealing from the bank). Also, misapplication of the procedures is more apt to occur in the hands of the layman (e.g., an individual may apply covert sensitization to his drinking behavior without attempting to eliminate a strong anxiety component of the behavior).

The major question which arises from the consideration of these theoretical examples and issues is that of whether, on the basis of possible harmful consequences, the behavior therapist can attempt to keep the self-control procedures from the general public despite the advantages of teaching self-control. If data accumulate indicating that instruction in self-control techniques can effectively eliminate maladaptive behavior, the behavior therapist may have to decide that a negative response to such a question is insufficient to prevent large-scale instruction in schools, clinics, and workshops for the betterment of a greater number of people.

The following behavior therapy procedures are described and analyzed in terms of their use as self-control devices.

Reciprocal Inhibition Techniques

RELAXATION

For the most part, relaxation has been used mainly as part of the desensitization procedure and not as a self-control procedure in itself. This lack is due to a combination of factors. Jacobson's (1938) use of relavation as a therapeutic procedure in its own right took as much as several hundred hours of training. Such intensive training was not thought practical in modern therapeutic practice. Wolpe himself has not put much emphasis on the use of relaxation as a therapeutic approach. Studies by Davison (1965a) and Lang, Lazovik, & Reynolds (1965) have indicated that relaxation itself (without desensitization) was as effective as the no-treatment groups in the modification of phobic behavior (i.e., of no therapeutic value whatsoever). The studies of Lang & Davison do not necessarily argue against the use of relaxation as an effective therapeutic procedure, however. Their experiments merely present evidence that relaxation instruction alone did not have any specific therapeutic effect in their study. Graziano & Kean (1967) found relaxation training alone effective in modifying the behavior of autistic children ranging in ages from five to nine years. They concluded that (1) carefully structured training in physical relaxation, without formal desensitization, significantly reduced generalized response of high excitement and (2) the resulting relaxation generalized beyond the training situation. In these studies the S was not given instructions on how to extend the use of relaxation in a therapeutic manner. A study by Zeisset (1968) does present evidence that relaxation paired with specific instructions on how to use it therapeutically is effective. Zeisset employed four experimental conditions in the treatment of male psychiatric patients who complained of interview anxiety. One group was given treatment by the traditional desensitization procedure. Another group was given relaxation plus application training. The relaxation-plus-application-training group was given progressive relaxation training, followed by illustration and discussion of the use of relaxation in everyday activities with particular emphasis on stressful interpersonal relations. Attention and no-contact control groups were also employed. The results show that the desensitization and relaxation-plus-application-training groups were superior to the attention and no-contact control groups in treatment outcome.

The desensitization groups and the relaxation-plus-application-training groups did not differ from each other. Similarly, no difference was found between the attention control and the no-contact control. The author concludes that relaxation plus application training can be useful in many situations where desensitization is not feasible. He also concludes that the relaxation procedure has the added advantage of providing the patient with a procedure he can use to "treat" himself in future situations involving the presenting complaint, or in other areas.

Relaxation, then, can be considered a self-control technique in its own right: first, when it is used to reduce the overall anxiety level, and second, as a means of decreasing anxiety or tension whenever the patient is either involved in a readily identifiable anxiety-provoking situation, or is experiencing anxiety without being able to discern the antecedent conditions.

When a patient enters therapy he is given training in relaxation and informed that the procedure will be useful to him whenever he feels it necessary to control his own behavior, particularly when he is very anxious during the day or evening. For example, if he is upset about a forthcoming speaking engagement, the use of this technique will enable him to relax before he is to speak. The relaxation procedure will also be helpful in minimizing any disturbing aftereffects of a distressing event.

After the patient is able to relax himself completely, he is told, while relaxed in a sitting position in the office, to say "relax" aloud 10 times. He is then instructed to repeat this procedure twice every day on his own until the next session. If he followed instructions, 10 more trials are given in which the patient says "relax" to himself. The patient is then taught to relax in a standing position and told to practice relaxation at home once a day in both positions. He is also instructed to say "relax" 10 times each time he relaxes in both these positions, thereby associating the word with the relaxation response. After the therapist determines that the patient can relax well in either position, he again emphasizes the necessity of employing the technique whenever the patient feels upset about a forthcoming event. At the next session, when inquiry is made about the utilization of the technique, patients usually report that the procedure was very effective and that they are enthusiastic over their own ability to obtain control over their fears. They are then told to say "relax" to themselves any time they feel tense during the week. By this time, the word itself has become an occasion for eliciting the relaxation response. In this technique two SCRs are employed—the response of relaxing and the word "relax." Dean (1966) has provided some experimental support regarding this approach.

Dean conducted an experiment in which 30 Ss received 30 conditioning trials in which the words "tense" and "relax," projected on a screen, were paired with shock onset and shock offset respectively. The Ss were instructed to say the words aloud when they appeared on the screen. The experimental Ss performed significantly better than the control Ss when instructed to say the word "tense" or "relax" (SCR) to avoid shock [i.e., the GSR (RC) of the experimental subjects tended to increase with the word "tense" and decrease with the word "relax"]. Dean concluded that classically conditioned mediators can be employed in the voluntary management of autonomic responses.

Relaxation, as is true with other SC techniques, can be combined with other procedures for effective behavior modification (Cautela, 1966b).

DESENSITIZATION

In the use of desensitization as a self-control procedure the anxiety-producing stimulus is presented to the S by the S himself while he initiates the SCR of relaxing. The S is taught the procedure so that the SCR will have maximal effect. The author has found the following format useful:

1. The principles behind desensitization are explained to the patient. The level of explanation depends upon the patient's level of sophistication.

2. Special care is taken to teach the patient hierarchy construction.

3. After the first desensitization session, the patient is asked to practice the same procedure at home as was practiced in the office. He is assigned the task of going through the hierarchy to the same point achieved in the office at the last treatment session (i.e., the point at which no anxiety was signaled).

4. After some experience in "homework," the patient is taught to desensitize himself at night, or on a weekend, to events which may have been disturbing during the day or week.

5. He is then taught to desensitize himself to anxiety-provoking events which will occur that day or the next day.

6. At the termination of therapy, the complete desensitization procedure

is gone over again in detail. It should be noted that the therapist is particularly concerned with thoroughly explaining the rationale for desensitization and preparing the patient to apply the technique on his own whenever necessary.

Kahn & Quinlan (1967) developed a "do-it-yourself" desensitization kit for use with phobic patients which proved therapeutically successful. Even though these investigators were not primarily interested in self-control techniques per se, the results of their study provide some indication of possible self-control applications.

THOUGHT STOPPING

Thought stopping, within the reciprocal inhibition framework, is usually taught as a self-control procedure. I have found this technique particularly valuable in treating cases of obsessive thinking, hallucinations, and compulsive behavior. In the thought-stopping procedure the word "stop" (SCR) prevents the undesirable response (RC) from occurring.

The thought-stopping procedure consists primarily of simple instructions and demonstrations by the therapist. The most typical conversation is presented almost verbatim below so that the reader may obtain an accurate understanding of the procedure.

The patient is asked to close his eyes and to deliberately think of the thought which is troubling him (e.g., "I want to kill my children"). He is then asked to signal with his right index finger when he begins to think that particular thought. At the signal, the therapist shouts "stop!", at which point a startle reaction is usually elicited from the patient. When asked what happened to the thought when the therapist shouted at him, the patient usually replies that it "went away." He is then told: "See, you can't think of two things at the same time. Now close your eyes again and deliberately think of the thought as you did before." The therapist again shouts "stop!" and then says: "As you noticed before, you stopped thinking of wanting to kill your children when I said 'stop.' " Next the patient is told to close his eyes and imagine that he is yelling "stop!" to himself. If, upon inquiry, he reports that the imagery is clear (i.e., that he can actually hear himself yelling "stop!", he is again told to close his eyes and think of the undesirable thought and immediately yell "stop!" to himself. When he has done this and reported that the thought went away, he is told to say "stop" to himself every time the thought occurs. In this way, the thought-stopping procedure is entirely under the patient's control and available for use whenever he needs it.

COVERT SENSITIZATION

Covert sensitization (Cautela, 1966c, 1967) is a relatively new technique based on principles of aversion therapy for use in cases of maladaptive approach responses. In the covert sensitization procedure the maladaptive approach responses (RCs) such as stealing, inappropriate sexual arousal, excessive alcoholic intake, and smoking are prevented from occurring by preceding them with an imagined noxious stimulus (SCR). Despite its novelty, experimental evidence indicates that covert sensitization has been effective in successfully modifying alchoholic behavior (Anant, 1966, 1967), smoking (Mullen, 1967), overeating (Stuart, 1967), and in eliminating sadistic fantasy (Davison, 1968a), and pedophilia (Barlow, Agras, & Leitenberg, 1968). Because it is not as widely known as the other reciprocal inhibition procedures previously discussed, the covert sensitization method will be treated here in greater detail than the other techniques.

In this procedure, the patient is taught to relax in the manner used in desensitization. When the patient has learned to relax completely, treatment strategy is clearly explained to him. He is told that he is unable to stop drinking (or eating, or whatever is the problem to be treated) in excess because it has become a strongly learned habit which now provides a great amount of pleasure. He is also told that by associating the pleasurable object with an unpleasant stimulus (SCR), he will be able to eliminate his compulsion (RC). The patient is then asked (while relaxed, with his eyes closed) to visualize very clearly the pleasurable object (e.g., liquor). When he signals that the image is clear, he is told to imagine a sequence of scenes leading up to the commission of the compulsive act: looking at the glass; holding the glass in his hand; bringing it up to his lips. When he can visualize the glass about to touch his lips, he is told to imagine that he begins to feel sick to his stomach. In imagination, he begins to vomit. The vomit goes all over the floor, the drink, his companions, himself—any aspect of his particular drinking situation. He is then asked to visualize the whole scene by himself and actually feel nauseous when he has the intention of drinking, gradually getting sicker as he touches the glass, raises it, etc.

Alternate scenes are presented in which the patient abstains from the liquor and experiences a relief sensation. He is told to imagine, for instance, that as he "rushes outside into the fresh, clean air" or "home to a clean, invigorating shower," he no longer feels ill. Other relief scenes contain the patient's refusal to drink and the subsequent elimination of the nauseous feeling.

In this procedure, an aversive stimulus is made to follow the response to be reduced (i.e., the individual imagines an aversive situation as soon as he thinks of drinking or is about to take a drink). Supportive evidence is mounting (Kushner & Sandler, 1966) indicating that punishment can effectively reduce the frequency of response in a long-lasting or permanent way.

By telling the patient that the nausea and vomiting behaviors immediately decrease and that he feels better when he turns away from the undesirable object, the therapist is involving him in an escape procedure (which occurs when a particular behavior terminates the presentation of a noxious stimulus). Eventually, avoidance behavior takes place and the patient reports that he no longer has the "urge" for the particular stimulus. The cues, which were previously associated with the noxious stimulation of nausea and vomiting, become discriminatory stimuli for avoidance behavior.

This explanation is essentially similar to the two-process theory of avoidance learning first proposed by Mowrer (1947) and later elaborated upon by Solomon & Wynne (1954) and Turner & Solomon (1962).

After several practice trials in the therapist's office, the patient is instructed to continue treatment on his own by means of "homework" assignments, consisting of 10 to 20 repeats of the office trials. He is also carefully instructed to imagine immediately that he has just vomited on his drink whenever he is tempted to take one, about to order, or about to ingest one. As therapy continues, the use of this procedure as a self-control technique progresses as well. Through conscientious use, the patients eventually become effective monitors of their own behavior in their particular problem area. Patients are also instructed to use the covert sensitization procedure in any other instance of maladaptive approach behavior which may develop later.

If the patients intend to employ the covert sensitization procedure after therapy has been discontinued, they are cautioned to examine their own physical well-being constantly for problems which could be produced by frequently imagining vomiting experiences. Although the problem has never arisen in the author's therapy sessions, it still remains a theoretical possibility. Patients are also made aware of the possibility of satiation which may arise if the same aversive stimulus is constantly used. One way to ensure against satiation is to employ a variety of stimuli aversive to the patient (e.g., spiders, snakes, or open wounds) instead of vomit.

ASSERTIVE TRAINING

In teaching assertive training the individual is instructed to assert himself whenever he feels an injustice has been done to him. Persons who need assertive training are inhibited by anxiety from asserting themselves in appropriate situations. The SCR is the assertive response and the RC is anxiety. If instructions alone are not sufficient to have the individual make the SCR, then behavioral rehearsals (Salter, 1949; Wolpe, 1958) and desensitization (Cautela, 1966b) can be used to facilitate the assertive response.

Operant Procedures

This section will deal with the work of various representative investigators who have developed and applied operant methods of self-control-training. The work of Ferster, Nurnberger, & Levitt (1962) and Goldiamond (1965b) provides a rationale and basis for future work in this problem area and demonstrates the actual utilization of these techniques. The work of Lloyd Homme (1965) furnishes an especially simple and easily adaptable method of changing the frequency of responses. At the same time, Homme's technique forms a supplement to both operant and reciprocal inhibition procedures.

FERSTER

According to Ferster et al. (1962), self-control refers to the manipulation of certain influential conditions which will lower the disposition to emit the behavior which the patient wants to control. Using eating behavior as an example, Ferster presents some self-control methods, based on elementary principles of reinforcement theory.

One of Ferster's major techniques concerns the identification and use of the "ultimate aversive consequence" (UAC) of the behavior to be controlled. Typically, when an individual performs a particular behavior, desirable or undesirable, he is immediately reinforced for it and usually does not consider any aversive consequence of the behavior at that time. For this reason, Ferster feels it is difficult to develop control of undesirable behavior. If the UAC (SCR) can be made to occur at the same time the undesirable behavior (RC) occurs, then that behavior may also become aversive. For pairing the UAC (e.g., heart trouble, obesity, social criticism) with the RC (e.g., overeating), Ferster has developed the following methods to help the patient identify the UAC: frequent repetition, written examinations, and rehearsals in which the consequences of the undesirable behavior can be readily observed. The purpose of these methods is to extend the active verbal report of the UAC so that it can be brought into use when the RC occurs.

Another method designed by Ferster is one which interrupts the chain of responses leading to the undesirable behavior. He recommends extension of the chain to such a length that the disposition to begin the chain is weakened and interference is thereby facilitated. In trying to control eating behavior, for example, an individual can arrange to buy food on a daily basis; he can buy food which requires a great deal of preparation; or in other ways he can arrange for certain behaviors to occur prior to eating. In this procedure a series of SCRs are employed.

The chain can also be broken by designing simple conditions to precede the final behavior. For instance, the therapist can tell the patient to completely swallow the food in his mouth (SCR) before putting any more food on his fork. This procedure can be expanded in still other ways (e.g., by requiring the patient to wait five seconds between mouthfuls) until the chain is broken.

Ferster has expanded upon the notion of stimulus control for self-control purposes. He aims at having the patient gain control over stimuli which were present at the time the undesirable behavior occurred. For example, if one has a habit of eating while watching television, the occasion of watching television may gain control over eating behavior to the extent that whenever the person watches television he will tend to eat something. The practice of reading in bed is another example we can consider. In this situation, the stimulus of reading occurs in the presence of tired or sleepy behavior. In such a case, reading at any other time may be an occasion for the same type of sleepy behavior. By ensuring that the RC does not occur in the presence of a wide variety of stimuli, an individual can manipulate stimulus control. For example, eating should be permitted only in the "pure" eating situation (the kitchen at mealtimes). It should not occur while watching television or pleasantly conversing with others, for example. The SCR in this case is the performance of the RC in a minimum-stimulus situation.

Still another method of self-control concerns the establishment of responses incompatible (SCR) with the responses the patient wants to control (RC). Ferster calls this the establishment of a "prepotent repertoire." Activities such as telephoning a friend after breakfast, washing the floor, going to a movie, or taking a walk may become prepotent over eating because of the temporary aversive consequences arising from their interruption. Prepotent responses can be weakened by emotional responses, however—a fact which necessitates careful monitoring of this procedure.

In developing these various self-control techniques, Ferster has found that specific self-control responses can be treated as any other response because they are influenced by the same variables. Almost any person can shape the smallest bits of self-control behavior and achieve control over a strong habit. If reinforcement is not applied properly, self-control can be extinguished, especially in the early stages of learning. For this reason, it is usually wise for the behavior modifier to proceed with some performance already present in the individual's response repertoire and gradually progress in successive stages to more complicated performance. As the individual notes a new gain in self-control, eventually it may be necessary for the behavior modifier only to inform the subject which behaviors should be controlled and the subject will be sufficiently motivated to control them. Ferster strongly emphasizes the importance of establishing a set of behaviors for the individual which will occur with sufficiently high probability in spite of competition from the individual's other repertoires, as well as teaching him the potential techniques of self-control.

GOLDIAMOND

Goldiamond (1965b) has based his self-control procedure on the assumption that behavior is best described as a functional relationship between the organism and the environment. The behavior which an individual desires for himself can be achieved by the application of the same methods used to control the behavior of other people.

Goldiamond recommends two primary approaches to the attainment of self-control: first, training the individual in the functional analysis of behavior and permitting him to develop his own control techniques; and second, instructing the person in procedural methods for environmental change which thereby bring his behavior under his own control. Both procedures involve the identification of RCs and SCRs. After this is done, procedures are arranged whereby SCRs can be performed in optimal temporal and spatial relationships to the RCs. This ensures that the RCs will be emitted at a low rate.

The first approach is essentially one of self-report in which the patient regularly informs the therapist of the results he has achieved from session to session. At this time, both the therapist and the patient analyze the data and discuss procedural changes. Eventually, the patient becomes his own therapist. In this case, it is assumed that the patient is the one person most concerned with his behavior and most familiar with the conditions and consequences of that behavior. Because individual tutorials in behavior analysis are given, together with homework assignments and readings, one stipulation for the employment of this procedure is a certain minimal intellectual ability.

When a person is incapable of learning this type of self-analysis, the therapist must take a more active part in rearranging certain relevant functional relationships between the patient and his environment. If the second approach is used, however, the patient will not be as well trained to develop new self-control procedures if future need arises as he would be if the first approach were utilized.

Within these approaches several methods can be exercised to change behavior. One method deals with the alteration of conditions under which the behavior (RC) usually occurs. This is called "stimulus change" or the "effects of novel stimuli." These novel stimuli are combined with new behavioral contingencies (SCRs) designed to produce new behavior. This technique attempts to eliminate some of the stimuli which would ordinarily generate the old undesirable behavior and at the same time introduce new stimuli which are apt to generate new, more desirable behavior in the same situation. For instance, Goldiamond (1965b) refers to a marital case in which there was frequent quarreling. The husband and wife were instructed to completely rearrange the household furniture and the use of the rooms, which acted as stimuli for the old behavioral responses (RCs). (The wife carried the technique one step further by buying herself a new outfit.) In this method, the stimuli become occasions for new responses.

In this same case, the therapist was also able to bring the husband's "sulking behavior" (RC) under stimulus control. Any time the husband felt like sulking he was instructed to sit on a special "sulking stool" (SCR) and "sulk and mutter over the indignities of life as long as he wished" (p. 857).

When he finished with his sulking, he was permitted to leave the garage and rejoin his wife. A daily record of such behavior indicated that the sulking time gradually decreased and finally disappeared altogether.

Goldiamond also makes use of the chaining method to elicit new behavior. He distinguishes between a "chaining sequence" and a systematic sequence." In the former, a chain of behavior is maintained by the consequences attached to the last element in the chain. Goldiamond states: "In this type of sequence, the order of training is the reverse of the chronological order in which the sequence of behavior is performed" (p. 866). In teaching children to tie their shoes by the chaining procedure, for example, the child would be taught to start with the last behavior element which ties the bow.

In the systematic sequence the acquisition of one behavior depends upon the prior existence of another. For example, to learn algebra a person must first know how to read. In modifying a present behavioral deficit which was caused by the nonacquisition of an earlier behavior, it is necessary to first initiate the earlier behaviors. A mentally retarded child cannot learn to identify letters of the alphabet, for instance, until he can first discriminate between horizontal and vertical lines.

The research work of Goldiamond has been, to date, necessarily restricted to the laboratory. As a result, his work is characterized by a simplicity of procedures and concepts. Recognizing these limitations, Goldiamond has emphasized that the extension of these laboratory techniques to the solution of complex human problems requires careful examination and considerable precaution. Goldiamond places more emphasis on the manipulation of the external environment than does Ferster. In this situation the SCR is rearranging the environment.

HOMME

Employing as a basis Premack's (1959) differential probability hypothesis (DPH), which states: "For any pair of responses, the more probable one will reinforce the less probable one," Homme (1965) has developed a method for the self-control of private (mental) events. His technique overcomes the past experimental difficulties of detecting the occurrence of such events or responses and of developing a range of reinforcers for them.

In order to apply the DPH, the therapist has only to determine the low-probability event (RC) whose frequency he wants to increase and a high-probability event (SCR) to make contingent upon the low-probability event. For example, if studying an assignment is a low-probability event for a student and smoking is a high-probability event, by making the lighting of a cigarette contingent upon studying a chapter of an assignment, the behavior can be controlled. This same technique can be applied to covert behavior as well. By making the experience of drinking coffee (the high-probability event) contingent upon thinking the thought "I am a worthwhile person" (low-probability event), the thought will increase in frequency.

The primary difficulties involved in this technique center around persuading the patient to follow the instructions carefully and maintaining the application of the self-controlling response (the DPH).

In employing this technique, it is well to recognize the following precautions:

1. Since "contingency management" (i.e., the use of the DPH) has no technology for the direct elimination of the response, its main use lies in strengthening behavior incompatible with the response to be eliminated.

2. It is important to avoid pairing an incompatible low-probability event with the high-probability event. For example, if smoking is the behavior the patient wants to eliminate, a response antagonistic to smoking could be: "If I smoke I'll get lung cancer." This response would be a low-probability event. In this case, the high probability event should not be smoking itself.

According to Homme, it has been empirically established that when the high-probability event is made contingent upon an antagonistic response, adaptation is more apt to occur. The individual may, for example, typically report: "Smoking, which seemed so horrifying to me when I first began to follow your instructions, doesn't bother me any more." If adaptation does occur, Homme suggests that it be mitigated by the following methods:

1. The use of a variety of low-probability events antagonistic to the behavior to be eliminated (e.g., statements such as: "If I smoke, I'll get cancer," "Smoking is making my teeth yellow," and "Smoking is expensive").

2. The use of a reinforcing consequence event (e.g., "The money I save by not smoking will help pay for my vacation") to follow an aversive consequence event (e.g., "If I smoke, I'll get cancer") and then permitting the occurrence of the high-probability event.

Comparison of Reciprocal Inhibition and Operant Techniques of Self-control

In reciprocal inhibition procedure, the response antagonistic to the undesirable response (SCR) is made to occur in the presence of the stimulus which usually elicits the undesirable response (RC). In a reciprocal inhibition self-control procedure, the *S* himself arranges conditions so that reciprocal inhibition occurs. In this same procedure, it is assumed that anxiety acts as both a response and a stimulus which results in maladaptive avoidance behavior and, in some cases, maladaptive approach behavior.

It is evident in the techniques of relaxation, desensitization, assertive training, and, in some respects, thought stopping, that their purpose is the elimination of the maladaptive behavior (RC). Also in these four procedures, responses other than anxiety are made to occur in the presence of the anxiety-provoking stimulus. Although anxiety is one component of the faulty approach behavior, a motor component which may become independent of the anxiety after a great number of trials is also present. The use of aversive procedures such as covert sensitization provides the response (SCR) antagonistic to the undesirable response (RC). The approach response is changed to an avoidance response by substituting the antagonistic response. These conditions are also arranged by the *S* himself.

Although the primary method of the operant procedure involves reinforcing the incompatible response, it is similar to the reciprocal inhibition technique in that its purpose is to make an antagonistic response occur under certain environmental conditions. Homme's (1965) method can also be regarded as a means of providing antagonistic responses under certain conditions. The other operant methods of self-control involve the establishment of new responses by shaping and chaining techniques in which the client must arrange environmental contingencies in relation to his own behavior. In the operant techniques, "anxiety" is not considered a manipulative variable necessary for effective self-control.

It has been the author's experience that for effective use, operant SC procedures require a greater level of intellectual functioning on the part of the *S* than the reciprocal inhibition procedures. The reciprocal inhibition procedures seem to provide more immediate SCRs than the operant techniques. In relaxation, thought-stopping, and covert sensitization procedures, the RCs can be immediately removed in the presence of the eliciting stimulus. In the operant methods, on the other hand, the arrangements of environmental contingencies in relation to individual behavior results in a gradual change in the frequency of the undesirable behavior which is not as immediately evident to the client. The client who uses the reciprocal inhibition procedures seems to feel he has greater control over his own behavior than the client taught the operant self-control techniques.

Research on Self-control

Although ample anecdotal evidence exists indicating the effectiveness of self-control procedures in the modification of behavior (Cautela, 1966c, 1967; Ferster et al., 1962; Goldiamond, 1965b; Homme, 1965; Madsen & Hoffman, 1967; Tooley, 1966), experimental investigation is necessary to determine the validity and extension of present self-control procedures. Though the purpose of this chapter is to present a rationale and description of some established self-control procedures, it is essential that basic research provide the data for optimal effectiveness of existing procedures and for the development of new techniques. Many important questions relating to the effective use of self-control procedures remain unanswered (e.g.: What SCRs are the most effective in modifying certain RCs? At what rate are the SCRs to be employed? Should the SCRs be made 100 percent of the time, or at some fixed percentage or at varying percentages less than 100? What is the optimal time interval between the SCR and the RC?). Some basic research is already available on some of these questions.

A study by Kanfer & Goldfoot (1966) is illustrative of an experiment designed to determine the most effective SCR in the tolerance of noxious stimulation. Kanfer & Goldfoot performed an experiment on the effect of different kinds of self-control (the effect of different SCRs) on tolerance of noxious stimulation. Five groups of female Ss were told to keep their dominant hands in ice water as long as possible. A control group was given only the above instructions. A verbal negative set group was also told it would find the experience painful. A verbal talk group was asked to visualize all sensations and thoughts they had pertaining to the situation. An external distraction clock group was given a clock and told they could use the clock to help keep their hand in the water by knowing how long they were doing so. The Ss in an external distraction slide group were provided with a slide projector in which they could present slides and describe them. They were also told they could change slides as often as they wished.

The slide and clock groups showed superiority over all groups. The authors conclude that self-controlling behaviors (SCRs) that provide some external stimulation effect greater facilitation (are more effective in modifying RCs) than verbal devices. The conclusion seems unwarranted based only on the data of the experiment. The experiment does indicate what SCRs are more effective than other SCRs in the RC of hand withdrawal. [In some situations verbal SCRs can be developed to effectively control some RCs (Cautela, 1966b; Dean, 1966). It would have been more informative if the authors had included another group in which the presentations of the slides were controlled by the experimenter.]

At the present time, we are not quite sure how self-control procedures will affect the future probability of a particular maladaptive behavior. If, however, a few months after the S has tested a procedure, he notices that response probability is increasing or decreasing to the point of incapacitation, he can then reapply the procedure.

Though it appears relatively easy to test the efficacy of self-control procedures to eliminate ongoing maladaptive behavior, it is another matter to test how the knowledge of self-control procedures will affect a lifetime of adjustment. Effective teaching of self-control will give an individual high control over his own behavior for his entire life span.

Chapter Summary

The term self-control (SC) is used by the author to describe a response repertoire in which an individual can make responses to increase or decrease response probability of undesirable behavior. An individual is said to lack self-control if he is not able to change the probability of undesirable responses.

Teaching self-control involves: (1) Providing the individual with responses he can initiate whenever necessary to change the probability of undesirable responses; (2) instructing the individual when and under what conditions to make the self-controlling response (SCR).

A number of advantages of teaching SC are presented. More conditioning trials can occur within a given time interval than with other treatments, thereby conserving time, money, and the therapist's services. Further maladaptive behavior can be prevented by not allowing the undesirable responses to increase in strength. Further reconditioning can also be prevented. Other advantages are also discussed. Disadvantages such as faulty use of self-control procedures are explored.

Some reciprocal inhibition and operant self-control procedures are described. Though some of the reciprocal inhibition procedures have not been generally used as self-control techniques, the author describes how they can be used as such. Relaxation, desensitization, thought stopping, covert sensitization, and assertive training are described as self-control procedures, and relevant evidence is presented. The attempts of Ferster & Goldiamond to utilize operant procedures in self-control are also discussed. Homme's work is presented as a method which involves both respondant and operant features in the use of self-control. Reciprocal inhibition and operant procedures of self-control are compared. It appears to the author that greater intellectual level is needed on the part of the S when learning operant self-control procedures as compared with reciprocal inhibition procedures. Implications for research are explored, together with an illustrative study.

9

Behavioral Techniques Based upon Social Learning:
An Additional Base for Developing Behavior Modification Technologies*

GERALD R. PATTERSON

*Oregon Research Institute and School of Education,
University of Oregon, Eugene, Oregon*

Thus far, the major impetus in the development of behavior modification technologies has been provided by the association theories of learning. The dramatic developments in desensitization procedures,[1] aversive conditioning, and instrumental conditioning draw heavily from the concepts and laboratory procedures related to the learning theories outlined by Guthrie (1952), Hull (1943), Pavlov (1928), and Skinner (1953). The productiveness of the applications from these theories is witnessed by the sheer volume of empirical findings generated in the last decade of research in behavior modification. However, it would indeed be surprising if these same theories also constituted a set

* I gratefully acknowledge the financial assistance provided by the National Institute of Mental Health research grant, MH 08009-03 in making the necessary time available for preparation of this manuscript. I also wish to acknowledge a special debt owed to my colleague-mentors, J. Straughan and W. Bricker, for their contribution to the bead game.

[1] It was pointed out to the writer in a personal communication that the concept of reciprocal inhibition was not drawn directly from theories of learning such as Guthrie (1952) with which it would have been in close agreement. Rather the procedure developed in the context of laboratory studies of escape and avoidance learning (Masserman, 1943).

of finite boundaries which contained the *only* structure from which data productive principles might be sampled in developing future behavior modification technologies.

When I consider the direction which these developments might take, it seems to me that future trends will of necessity involve a greater reliance upon principles available from social learning. The term *social learning* as used here refers to the loosely organized body of literature dealing with the changes in learning, or performance, which occur as a function of contingencies which characterize social interaction. This body of literature reflects two rather broad areas of activity and speculation. By and large, the greater empirical effort has been made relevant to questions concerning "how" it is that the behavior of one person might alter the behavior of another. Many of the mechanisms which have been described for bringing about these changes have been based upon principles from social psychology rather than learning theory; they would include such processes as persuasion, conformity (Asch, 1948; Janis, Hovland, Field, Linton, Graham, Cohen, Ruge, Abelson, Lesser, & King, 1959), and modeling (Miller & Dollard, 1941; Bandura & Walters, 1963). Another set of mechanisms for behavior control has been based upon laboratory studies investigating reinforcement principles as they might apply to social interaction (Greenspoon, 1954). These studies have adapted principles such as reward, punishment, and contiguity to a social learning matrix (Skinner, 1953; Rotter, 1954; Bijou & Baer, 1961).

Because of the different paradigms from which they have been drawn, these statements about the mechanisms associated with behavior change show marked differences in concepts about the determinants governing human behavior, differences in procedures, data forms, and even differences in publication sources. Consequently, proponents of one paradigm tend to ignore data from other sources which also relate to the problem. For example, the publication by Miller & Dollard (1941) particularly stressed modeling procedures, while the publications of Skinner (1953) and Rotter (1954) placed particular emphasis upon reinforcement principles.

The second major area of speculation in social learning concerns the content of the interaction occurring among persons in the social environment. What are the behaviors which are actually modeled for the deviant or the normal child? What are the behaviors which social agents positively reinforce or punish? In what situation might the parent or the peer culture attempt to persuade or influence judgments being made by the child?[2] Partial answers to the

[2] Although I am somewhat knowledgeable in the general area of behavior modification, I have had, until very recently, a profound ignorance of social psychology. For this reason, the patient efforts of friends and colleagues are gratefully acknowledged: R. Buehler, R. Littman, and, more recently, R. Ziller. To minimize somewhat the effects of my excursion in the unfamiliar, the comments and references which follow will be directed primarily to the literature in child psychology. Most of my experience and data-collecting activities have been oriented toward this subject population.

question of HOW it is that one person influences the behavior of another might provide a blueprint for improving the present applications of modeling, persuasion, or reinforcement principles to the behavior modification enterprise. Data relevant to questions about the content of this interaction could explicate the relative contribution of social interactions to the acquisition and maintenance of deviant behaviors. For example, it is entirely possible that the major antecedents to deviant behavior are to be found not in the preschoolers' sensitive foreskin (or total absence of same) but rather in their more prosaic day-by-day social interactions. It is possible that deviant behavior is modeled and reinforced in these interactions. Furthermore, it is likely that this process of altering behavior in the matrix of social interaction continues throughout the life of the individual. Data will be presented which demonstrate that the social environment provides contingencies which support the maintenance of deviant behavior prior to, during, and following the advent of most treatment enterprises. Whether the "true believer" espouses desensitization procedures, aversive conditioning, or operant conditioning, in some large part the final outcome of his efforts will be determined by the effect which the alterations in deviant behavior have upon the content of the child's interaction with his social environment. If the parents or the peer culture provide intensive efforts to persuade, model, and reinforce deviant behavior, the outcome of even the most powerful treatment program may be sabotaged by the very people who initially complained about the deviant behavior.

The first section briefly reviews the concepts and the literature associated with the question of HOW the behavior of one person may function to alter the behavior of another. In that context the procedures relevant to persuasion, modeling, and social reinforcement will be examined for any relevance which they might have for application to existing behavior modification procedures. In the second section, the implications raised by questions about the content of social interaction will be examined together with the innovations which they suggest.

Principles of Behavior Control Based upon Social Learning Literature

Probably one of the most significant, and least explored, aspects of the process of socializing the child is to be found in the first stage of development. This is the period in which the child is taught to respond to social stimuli. If, for some reason, this process is omitted or incomplete, the child will fail to develop social behaviors. Perhaps the most dramatic instance of such a failure and the resultant limited behavioral repertoire is to be found in the description of the autistic child (Kanner, 1944; Ferster, 1961). The fact that a child has been trained to respond to the eliciting and reinforcing aspects of the behavior of other people provides a basis for training him in the acquisition of both adaptive and deviant behaviors. By the same token it can also provide a basis for constructing procedures altering the deviant behaviors once they are present in the repertoire of the child.[3]

The most traditional mode of conceptualizing this training in responsiveness to social stimuli is to assume that the child is first trained to respond to the eliciting and the reinforcing properties of the behavior of the mother. It is assumed that from this training the responsiveness generalizes to other important social agents. Such an account oversimplifies in several important aspects. First, the data suggest that the process of training for responsiveness to social stimuli is carried out over a considerable period of time. Second, while it may be true for early age that responsiveness is generalized across classes of social agents, the data suggest that the particular experience which a child has with agents of a specific class determines how responsive he will be to their behavior. Finally, it also seems to be the case that there is not a highly generalized trait of responsiveness to social stimuli.[4] Rather, the data suggest that the con-

---

[3] Although the literature on the acquisition of responsiveness to social stimuli was certainly germane, covering it in the space allotted for this review was not feasible. The recent publications of investigators such as Schaffer & Emerson (1964), Gewirtz & Gewirtz (1965), and Cairns (1966) exemplify the exciting investigations being carried out in this area.

[4] A series of studies has shown low magnitude but positive correlations holding between various operational definitions of responsiveness to social stimuli. For example, one set of studies showed positive correlations between measures of suggestibility and measures of responsiveness to social reinforcers (Weiss, Ullmann, & Krasner, 1960; Greenspoon, 1954; Das, 1958a).

Cairns (1962) failed to obtain a positive correlation between measures of responsiveness to social reinforcement and a measure of persuasibility; the latter was based upon a procedure comparable to that described by Abelson & Lesser (1959). However, the lack of relationship was probably due to the presence of a variable which he failed to take into account. Our own data show this variable to be a major determinant of the variance in change scores measuring the effect of the behavior of social agents. This variable mediates both responsiveness to social reinforcers and responsiveness to models. In our laboratories the variable has been labeled "negative set." Under conditions of negative set the child attends very poorly to the behavior of the model. If he does attend, the behavior of the model is not reflected in the subject's immediate performance. On those occasions when he *must* perform and the set is negative, the behavior of the child is the opposite of the model displayed by the model (Patterson, Littman, & Littman, 1967).

The data showed that this variable accounted for about 60 percent of the variance in behavior change scores based upon a problem-solving type of modeling procedure and 50 percent of the variance in an object-preference procedure. This strongly suggests that a significant amount of the variance in modeling procedure may be a function of the general set adopted by the child toward the model. The presence of such a contextual, or set, effect has also been noted in both social reinforcement literature (Weiss, Krasner, & Ullmann, 1960, 1963; Simkins, 1961; Sarason, 1964) and in the literature concerned with persuasion (Bauer, 1964; Berenda, 1950).

The possible existence of this, and other sets, in measures of persuasion, modeling, and social reinforcement would suggest that the effect of such variables should be partialled out of the various measures of social responsiveness when investigating the convergence among measures. In the report by Patterson, Littman, & Littman (1967), it was clear that the negative set and task variables contributed

tingent arrangements described under the rubrics social reinforcement, persuasion, and modeling represent related but somewhat different operational definitions of the term "social responsiveness." Because of these findings the procedures associated with the eliciting effects of social behavior (persuasion and modeling procedures) will be considered separately from the procedures investigating the effects of the consequences provided by the behavior of another person (social reinforcement).

In each of the following sections an attempt will be made to review data pertinent to questions about the major determinants of responsiveness for a given procedure, the generality of responsiveness across classes of social agents (female, male adults, peers), and the relation between responsiveness and deviant behavior. Finally the contribution of these findings will be related to the development of behavior modification procedures.

ELICITING PROCEDURES FOR PRODUCING BEHAVIOR CHANGE

There are a number of contingencies which will elicit changes in the behavior of the observer. In one procedure the subject is first presented with a stimulus which, of itself, does not have any particular response associated with it at high strength. He is then required to indicate his "judgment" of whether, for example, a spot of light is in fact moving or stationary (Jakubczak & Walters, 1959). Or, for example, he may be asked to indicate whether or not a line is different from a standard (Berenda, 1950). The subject might also be required to indicate which of n alternatives constitutes a correct answer for an extremely difficult vocabulary item (Hugo, 1956), or to indicate an opinion about a topic for which he has no strong preference (Janis et al., 1959). In these situations the stimulus is presented first, then the behavior of the social agent is presented, and finally the subject indicates his judgment or preference. Following this, the subject makes his decision. His behavior may, or may not, result in a match with the previous behavior of the social agent. The paradigm might be described as:

S_1	S_2	R
Presentation of stimulus to be judged	Judgment or preference indicated by agent	Judgment or preference of subject

The characteristics of the stimulus at S_1, the agent at S_2, and the subject at R are significant determinates of the frequency with which the behavior of

---

more variance than did the procedural class (modeling versus instrumental conditioning) variable. The data did show covariation among measures of responsiveness to social reinforcers and responsiveness in a modeling task, but only after the effect of negative set had been partialled out.

the subject will match the behavior of the agent. In this procedure there are usually no explicit reinforcing contingencies.

These and similar procedures were derived from a social psychology which emphasized an implicit assumption that behavior is determined, to some important extent, by values and attitudes. Consequently the persuasion tasks were deemed important contributions to behavior control technologies in that they seemed to offer an analog by which the social environment could alter values and attitudes. More recently the same contiguity-based paradigm has been applied to behaviors which are of even greater relevance. For example, such innovations have demonstrated that observing a model display aggressive behaviors increased the probability that these behaviors would be manifest in the behavior of the observer (Bandura, 1965b). It was also demonstrated by Berger (1962) that observing a number of sequences of neutral stimuli (CS) paired with an apparent delivery of a shock (UCS) and then observing the emotional responses of the subject was effective in establishing the CS as an eliciting stimulus for autonomic responses in the observer. Thus, the paradigm can serve as an analog for discussing an impressive array of social behaviors ranging from values, attitudes, and aggression to emotional responses.

More recently, further extensions have been made, the effect of which is to increase both the flexibility and the complexity of the rubric.

S_1	S_2	S_3	R
Situation	Behavior of the model	A negative or positive consequence is attached to the behavior of the model.	The observer responds.

The addition of S_3 provides for an additional element of control over the effect of these manipulations upon the performance of the subject. There are extensive data from studies such as those carried out by Bandura (1965a) and by Kanfer & Marston (1963) which indicate that making positive consequences contingent upon the behavior of the model increase the probability that the child will imitate those behaviors. Negative consequences decrease the probability of modeling.

Each of the components in each of these rubrics can be manipulated to increase behavior control. For example, the data are consistent in demonstrating that when the situation (S_1) demands some form of judgment, it is more advantageous to provide a stimulus which is ambiguous (Marinho, 1942; Hugo, 1956; Berenda, 1950). To the extent that these stimuli elicit preexisting responses which are already at high strength, it will be increasingly difficult to alter the behavior of the subject. For example, if he has already indicated preferences for one member of a series of alternatives and is then exposed to preference selections by a model, the observer will tend to display few changes in his behavior (Janis et al., 1959; Deutsch & Gerard, 1955).

Extensive studies have been carried out in the persuasion-influence tradition which demonstrate that the characteristics of the social agent are significant determinants of the magnitude of the alterations in behavior. For example, the more prestige and status attributed to the social agent, the greater the effect upon the overt behavior of the observer (Asch, 1948; Lefkowitz, Blake, & Mouton, 1955; Lippitt, Polansky, & Rosen, 1952). The adult model who was friendly and reinforcing to the child observers increased the likelihood that imitation would occur (Bandura & Huston, 1961; Henker, 1964). It is also true that some characteristics of the model are associated with no immediate change in the behavior of the observer but rather produce a significant delayed effect upon performance. For example, Harlow (1963) noted that the subordinant monkey would observe the behavior of the dominant monkey but not reproduce the behavior until the dominant monkey had left the area. In a like manner Patterson, Littman, & Littman (1967) observed that some characteristics of a model seemed to elicit a negative set in some of the children. Under conditions of such a set, three outcomes could occur: (1) the child might do the opposite of what the model was doing, (2) the observer might attend to the models' behavior only in the most peripheral fashion, (3) the performance of the observed behavior might be delayed until the model was absent. A preliminary analysis by Brown (1966) showed that, with young boys as subjects, adult female models elicited this set if they were distant and "efficient" but not if they were warm and friendly. The effect of a set akin to negative set has, of course, been noted frequently in the literature associated with this paradigm (Bauer, 1964).[5]

At this point there are no generalizations which can be made about the relative contribution of sex of the model or the relative efficiency of adult versus peers as social agents. With regard to this point, a review by Bandura (1966) cites several studies which showed that the adult models were more effective; however, these findings are not in agreement with the results obtained by Duncker (1938) and Berenda (1950). For the present, there is also only a limited set of data available which evaluate the generalization of responsiveness across classes of social agents. For example, in one of the classic studies on persuasibility the data showed that only the younger children were equally responsive to persuasion by peers and by parents (Abelson & Lesser, 1959). The correlation between the two sets of persuasion scores was .42 for seven-year-old subjects, .54 for nine-year-old subjects, and approximately zero

---

[5] There is an interesting possibility that deviant children might represent a sample of subjects many of whom have such a set in conjunction with their interaction with adult models. A laboratory assessment of the presence of such a set in a preschool boy with markedly deviant behaviors indicated that he was 100 percent consistent in doing the opposite of what his mother was doing. Following behavior modification there was a marked reduction in the posttest assessment score (Patterson, Hawkins, McNeal, & Phelps, 1966).

for older subjects. Data from the same study showed these procedures to be reliable; the split half reliabilities ranged from .73 to .79, while the test-retest reliabilities ranged from .41 to .61.

Another major contribution to the variance in change scores is to be obtained from a consideration of the characteristics of the observer. When children are observers, the data are surprisingly consistent in showing the younger child to be more responsive than the older child (Duncker, 1938; Berenda, 1950; Hugo, 1956; Schwartz, 1953). The more recent review by Bandura (1969) suggested that the dependent child and the anxious child are those likely to be more responsive to these manipulations, as is the child who has experienced repeated failure. However, it seems likely to be the case that the relation between the personality characteristics of the observer and the magnitude of change brought about in these situations will vary as a function of a complex interaction between the age and sex of both the observer and the model. For example, it seems reasonable to believe that the kind of personality trait behaviors which might accompany a boy's nonresponsiveness to his mother would be quite different from the social behaviors likely to accompany nonresponsiveness to the father. The data from several studies show that this is in fact the case.

If a boy is particularly responsive to communication by female adult agents, he is more likely to be described as deviant. In the study by Abelson & Lessor (1959), boys most responsive to females' (teacher) persuasion were most likely to be described on peer sociometrics as submissive (correlation of .33) and isolated (correlation of .43). The data also showed them to have lower self-esteem. These findings were also supported by data from a study using modeling procedures with boys as subjects and mothers as models (Patterson & Littman, 1965). In that study, the boys most responsive to the modeling behaviors of their mothers were rated by teachers as being high on a set of items with positive loadings on the factor *Aggression*. The correlation between the measure of responsiveness and the factor score was .32 (P less than .05). While Abelson & Lesser (1959) found a negative correlation between aggressiveness and responsiveness to teachers, the general pattern of findings suggests that high responsiveness to either the persuasive or the modeling behaviors of *female* agents is associated with the occurrence of deviant behaviors in boys.

One would expect, however, that responsiveness of boys to persuasion and modeling behavior of male models would be associated with socially adaptive behaviors. In the studies reviewed by Patterson & Littman (1965) the correlations between the measure of responsiveness to fathers as models and the factor scores summarizing the teachers' ratings of the boys were −.35 for the Hostile and Withdrawn factor, and .50 for the Nonaggressive factor. These findings are also corroborated in the study by Cairns (1962) who used the same persuasion task as Abelson & Lessor (1959). Cairns found a correlation of −.39 (P less than .05) between teachers' ratings of aggression and the scores assessing the responsiveness of the boys to a male experimenter. In the same study, boys more responsive to the male model were also rated by the teacher as displaying more conforming and suggestible behaviors and less negative attention-getting behaviors.

Contribution of the Eliciting Procedures to Behavior Modification. There are at least two important respects in which the persuasion and modeling procedures could contribute to the behavior modification enterprise. One contribution lies within their explanatory power in handling some of the traditional questions about what determines deviant behavior. The second lies in their ability to generate innovations (past and present) which facilitate the practical engineering aspects of the behavior modification effort.

When considering the application of eliciting procedures as explanatory devices for deviant behavior, a problem immediately presents itself. Given a deviant behavior, from this framework one would quite naturally assume one of two antecedents. Either the child has been exposed only to models who elicited deviant behaviors or he has been exposed to models who elicited both deviant and nondeviant behaviors and selected one set of behaviors over the other. Casual observation would suggest that for most children the latter is the case. The child occasionally observes some deviant behavior in most of his adult and peer models. The child also observes that even the most deviant model occasionally displays nondeviant behavior. Thus, it seems evident that before an "eliciting theory" can be used as an explanation for deviant behavior, it is necessary to explain the process by which the subject selects which judgments or behaviors to imitate. This situation has, of course, been recognized by investigators and a number of studies have been carried out to explicate the variables which determine modeling effects. These studies, which were reviewed by Bandura (1966), represent an impressive beginning in outlining such determinants.

An understanding of these variables could explain the initial occurrence of that "first" deviant response. Any one of these eliciting manipulations could function to produce the first occasion on which a sibling hits his younger brother, or the first occasion upon which he reacts with fear to being left alone. However, the eventual strength of this response is obviously a function of much more than these contingencies. If the first occurrence is reinforced as is the subsequent series of responses, then it will become part of the child's repertoire of social behaviors. If the first few responses are ignored or punished, the response will simply not exist at high strength and will probably be of little concern to anyone. Knowledge of variables such as the frequency of occurrence of deviant-model behaviors, the characteristics of the model, the characteristics of the subject, and the reinforcement schedules provided for the model would simply not account for the repeated occurrence of these behaviors in the repertoire of the child. It may be that deviant models also tend to reinforce deviant behaviors positively in observing subjects, but unless this is the case, variables associated with modeling per se are neither necessary nor sufficient determinants for many types of deviant behaviors. Whether or not modeling and persuasion procedures occupy the position of necessary and/or sufficient determinants, the possibility that such a set of variables could account for the initial appearance of deviant behaviors in the performance of the child places the variables in a position of great importance.

When conceptualizing their contribution to the acquisition of deviant behaviors, the eliciting procedures have been assigned the role of "catalyst." A similar role is assigned to these procedures in considering their contribution to behavior modification technologies. In altering deviant behavior, the introduction of a model who displays socially adaptive behavior could affect the repertoire of the deviant child if the child received extensive positive reinforcement when he performed the adaptive behavior. Given that the model possessed characteristics which enhanced the status as eliciting stimulus and given that the model's behavior was observed to have been reinforced repeatedly, then these contingencies should serve to accelerate the possibility of the deviant child's "trying out" similar behavior. The catalytic effect of these procedures should be most apparent for deviant children who do not have the terminal behaviors, or even gross approximation of them, in their existing hierarchies. To the extent that the child has previously acquired these behaviors but they are simply at low strength, the eliciting procedures would probably provide only a slight acceleration in the modification program.[6] The eliciting procedures should produce a major impact in cases representing extreme deficits in socialization.

Probably the most impressive demonstration of the contribution of modeling in extreme deficit cases is illustrated in the dramatic procedures innovated by investigators providing speech training for autistic children (Lovaas, 1956; Metz, 1964; Bricker, 1965; Straughan, 1965). Some autistic children will imitate simple motor behaviors when nonsocial reinforcers such as food or M & M candies are made contingent upon the child's imitating the experimenter. For these *S*s, operant procedures were used initially to shape specific speech sounds to occur at a reasonably high rate. Once these behaviors existed in the repertoire of the child, the contingencies were shifted so that the verbal behaviors of the experimenter served as discriminative stimuli eliciting these verbal behaviors from the autistic child. These speech sounds were gradually lengthened to words, e.g., ma-ma, ba-ll. Later in the program, visual representations of the words were presented in conjunction with the verbal

---

[6] I believe that most of the children and adults coming to outpatient facilities already possess the adaptive behaviors in their repertoire. For example, even the most dependent or aggressive child occasionally displays nondependent or nonaggressive behaviors. Typically, the "therapist" does not have to "condition" adaptive behaviors *de nouveau*.

behavior of the experimenter to elicit the response from the child. Gradually the verbal behavior of the experimenter was faded out until just the visual stimulus (written word, picture, or object) elicited the behavior. In Bricker's (1965) work, only those autistic children who initially showed evidence of learning to imitate the simple motor movements of the experimenter showed progress in the language-training program. An informal survey of other investigators who are developing language-training programs for autistic children confirms the notion that an "ability" to learn to imitate is a necessary basis for language training in the autistic child.

Thus far, unfortunately, there have been only a limited number of studies investigating the effect of these eliciting procedures in altering deviant behaviors. Only a few of these studies have attempted to follow a design in which these procedures have been compared with traditional behavior modification procedures. What is required is a series of studies across various types of deviant behaviors in which the catalytic effect of eliciting procedures could be used in conjunction with traditional behavior modification procedures.

Among the studies available, there is the oft-quoted report by Jones (1924b) which described an ingenious eliciting procedure. In that study, a child fearful of white, furry animals observed peer models interacting with such animals. Though the child's behavior changed following this training, the effect was somewhat confounded due to the fact that other procedures were also introduced. However, a more carefully controlled study has recently been completed by Bandura, Grusec, & Menlove (1967) which showed that modeling effects per se can produce a desensitizing reaction to feared objects. In this latter study, young children who were afraid of dogs observed models interacting with dogs under various conditions. The group of subjects which observed nonfearful models interacting with dogs showed marked reductions in its avoidance reactions. Just in passing, it might be noted that eliciting procedures which produce responses which compete with fear reactions can be further improved by using reinforcers to strengthen the adaptive responses. The data provided by Lazarus, Davison, & Polefka (1965) showed that eliciting procedures plus reinforcement were more effective than eliciting procedures alone. In the study by Bandura et al. the reduction in fear reactions might have been even greater if the nonfear behaviors had been systematically reinforced by either social or nonsocial stimuli.

I have been able to locate only two studies which provide data showing the catalytic effect of introducing eliciting procedures. One such study was carried out by Hawkins (1964), who used adult schizophrenic patients as subjects. In that study the dependent variable was the rate of occurrence of affectively toned verbal statements which occurred during group sessions. In one group the patient-models tended to avoid affectively toned material; in another group the patient-models frequently used such words. The "therapists' in both of these groups were programmed to reinforce these words positively whenever they occurred. In a third group, there were no new patient-models introduced into the group, but the therapist positively reinforced words denoting affect whenever they occurred. After a series of base-line sessions, the experimental manipulations were introduced. The results showed an impressive contribution of both modeling and reinforcement effects. The group with the models who used few affective words showed a significant decrease in the occurrence of affective words during the experimental period. The group with no models present but with a reinforcing therapist showed a positive increase in affective words; however, the increase was not of the same order as found for the group which had both the models who frequently used such words and the reinforcing therapist.

In a study reported by Nixon (1966), hyperactive children were assigned to various experimental manipulations. Some of them participated in reinforcement procedures to strengthen attending behaviors in the classroom setting. Another group participated in reinforcement training in addition to being exposed to movies of child models attending and studying. Another rather clever innovation included reinforcing the subjects with M & M candies whenever the model attended properly. Various control groups were also included. An effective comparison of reinforcement and modeling could not be made because there was an inadequate sampling of the observation data which served as the criterion for evaluating treatment outcomes. The base-line estimates of deviant classroom behavior were based upon only sixteen minutes of observations, whereas five or six times that amount of data would probably constitute a minimally reliable estimate.[7] I hope that further studies of this kind will be carried out in the near future both with subjects who display severe deficits (psychotic, aphasic, severely retarded, autistic) and garden variety outpatients.

In summary, then, it seems that the traditional eliciting procedures such as persuasion and modeling have only begun to make a contribution to explanations of deviant behavior and perhaps have made even less contribution to the current technologies involved in altering deviant behavior. However, it is my impression that these techniques will come to play a major role as "cata-

---

[7] There is also some reason to believe that the conditioning procedures were not as powerful as they might have been. In the Nixon study sixty seconds of attending behavior was required before the subject received a reinforcer. In our own laboratories we have found it necessary to begin with as low as five-second intervals and gradually increase to thirty to sixty seconds. With the more extreme cases of hyperactivity it is only after several hours of conditioning that intervals of sixty seconds are reached. Also, the Ss in Nixon's sample received an average of only 11 or 12 M & M candies for a trial. In our own studies we have found that we lose control of the behavior if the "earnings" drop much below 40 or 50 M & M candies. In addition, Nixon used only 8 trials, in contrast to our findings that 10 to 15 are required before the effects become noticeable (Patterson et al., 1965; Anderson, 1964).

lytic procedures" in the future systems which deal with either the problem of explanation or alteration.

In the following section a more recent addition to the mechanisms available for control of social behaviors is considered. Social reinforcers are evaluated both for their contribution to explanations of deviant behavior and for the innovations which might be suggested by the empirical literature which has developed in the past decade.

SOCIAL REINFORCEMENT PROCEDURES
FOR PRODUCING BEHAVIOR CHANGE

The general analog for the social reinforcement procedures was drawn from operant conditioning (Skinner, 1953). The research by Greenspoon (1954) represented a landmark in the development of the social reinforcement literature in that it confirmed the assumption that social behavior could function as a reinforcer in an operant procedure. Prior to this, it had been clear that information about "correct" or "wrong" responses when provided by another person could function as a positive reinforcer or as a mildly aversive stimulus. However, the innovation established by Greenspoon was that the more subtle aspects of social interaction were potential reinforcers. From this point on there was a marked increase in the studies which investigated the effect of a smile, attention, gestures, or verbal approval in controlling behavior. The general paradigm for the operant analysis of social learning has been as follows:

S	R	s^r
The eliciting components of social situations are generally not specified social	The subjects' response	The consequence provided by the social environment

In this situation the social consequences elicited by the response has an effect upon the probability that the response will occur again. These are conditional probabilities in that they are a function of characteristics associated with the subject, the characteristics associated with the structure of the response being manipulated, the agent dispensing the reinforcer, and, partially, the kind of reinforcer used.

The first variable to be considered in this complex interaction among determinants of responsiveness to social reinforcers is the effect of response structure. The data relevant to the eliciting procedures had shown that certain classes of responses ("dislikes" in contrast to "likes") are more difficult to manipulate. The data from social reinforcement also show that it is more difficult to alter some classes of responses than others with reinforcing contingencies. For example, if the subjects have already indicated that they strongly dislike a class of responses, it is more difficult to alter the frequency of occurrence of these responses than if they had indicated that they "liked" the class of responses (Cushing, 1957; Ekman & Friesen, 1960).[8]

When considering the effect of the characteristics of social stiumuli as reinforcers, there is good reason to believe that for many children these are not powerful reinforcers. For the kinds of procedures followed in most studies, as a rough guess only 55 to 75 percent of the children show changes in their behavior which demonstrates the impact of positive social reinforcers. There are also a set of consistent findings that suggest that positive social reinforcers were not as effective in controlling behavior as were aversive social stimuli (Brackbill & O'Hara, 1958; Meyer & Seidman, 1961; Starr & Patterson, 1961). It is also true that, in massed trials in which social stimuli are used as positive reinforcers, control is quickly lost over the behavior of the child (Jessor, 1951). Similar rapid satiation effects for social reinforcers have been demonstrated for young infants by Landau & Gewirtz (1967), and for older children by a number of investigators (Erickson, 1962; Shallenberger & Zigler, 1961; Stevenson & Knights, 1962; Gewirtz & Baer, 1958). As indicated in the extensive review by Stevenson (1965) the reinforcing value of social stimuli may be enhanced by brief periods of social isolation.

The characteristics of the social agent dispensing the social reinforcers determine a significant portion of the variance associated with behavior change scores. A number of studies have shown that critical or hostile behaviors on the part of the social agent reduce the effectiveness of social reinforcers dispensed by him (Simpkins, 1961; Sarason, 1965). As with the eliciting procedures, the social reinforcement literature showed that the high-prestige agent was the more effective in altering behavior (Prince, 1962). A number of studies showed that, with adults as social agents, the male is more effective in altering the behavior of girls than boys. Just the opposite effect is obtained when using female adult agents (Gewirtz & Baer, 1958; Stevenson & Knights, 1962; and Patterson, Littman, & Hinsey, 1964; Stevenson, 1961).

[8] There is one additional problem which should be noted in the context of response classes. The problem involves the well-known difficulty in defining the boundary of a response class. To the extent that there is some ambiguity in the definition of the class of behaviors, it is difficult to make precise predictions about the outcome of reinforcing contingencies.

A simple example of the difficulties involved was presented in an investigation of the effect of reinforcing contingencies upon a "simple" two-choice preference situation (Patterson & Hinsey, 1964). In the study the reinforcers were contingent upon the occurrence of one of the choices. For most of the subjects this produced an increase in the reinforced response. However, for many the response class being reinforced was not A or B but rather some unit of a series. For example, some of the children showed highly consistent patterns of alternation. For such subjects, the response "class" was some unit of the series ABAB. . . . Reinforcement of A or of B produced only an increase in alternation. Very likely the effect of reinforcement contingent upon more complex chains of responding introduces even more severe limitations upon the precision of the predictions which can be made.

The data for the eliciting procedures had shown only a limited generalization of responsiveness across classes of social agents. A similar finding was obtained when considering generalizaton of responsiveness to social reinforcers across classes of social agents. Unpublished data from a series of three studies at the Oregon laboratories showed that there are no significant correlations in responsiveness to positive social reinforcers among mothers, peers, and female adults. In one study (Patterson & Fagot, 1967), 40 boys were conditioned in an instrumental task by mothers and in a later trial by peers. The correlation between the preference change scores was −.09. In another study, 13 boys were reinforced first by their mothers and later by a female adult. The correlation between the preference-change scores produced by the reinforcement effects was .04. In a third unpublished study, by G. Lerner (1963), preschool girls were reinforced first by their mothers and in a later trial by female adults. The correlation between the preference-change scores was .02. The same apparatus was used in all three studies. A previous report presented data showing that the preference-change scores were highly reliable; the test-retest reliability for the preference-change score for this procedure was .75 (Patterson & Hinsey, 1964).

The next set of determinants which account for significant amounts of the variance in distribution of change scores is provided by characteristics of the subjects whose behavior is being altered. Again, as with the eliciting procedures, it was the younger children who were more responsive to social stimuli. In the present case the review by Stevenson (1965) showed that the younger child was more responsive to social reinforcers. There was also a consistent trend for the firstborn child to be more responsive to social reinforcers (Walters & Ray, 1960; Patterson, Littman, & Hinsey, 1964; Patterson & Fagot, 1967).

In the review by Stevenson (1965), several studies were cited which indicated that the more dependent child was more responsive to social reinforcers. However, as with the findings relevant to eliciting stimuli, it also seems that the particular social behaviors which relate to responsiveness are, in part, a function of the particular class of social agent involved. Apparently, nonresponsiveness to social reinforcers is correlated with one set of social behaviors if the agent is a peer and quite another set of traits if the agent is a father or a mother.

As pointed out in the publication by Janis et al. (1959), there is no clear way of evaluating correlational relations between social behaviors on the one hand and responsiveness to social stimuli on the other. It is equally reasonable to consider either one as being the cause and the other the effect. For heuristic purposes the present writer chooses to impose a series of assumptions about these correlations (Patterson, 1965b). First it is hypothesized that a variety of determinants produce broad individual differences in responsiveness to positive and negative social stimuli, which provides a basis for a socialization process that is likely to produce deviant behavior. Such an outcome can be brought about by a number of processes. For example, if the child were nonresponsive to social reinforcers, by definition his behavior would reflect massive deficits in social skills. Probably the best examples of this relationship are to be found in the literature describing the autistic child (Kanner, 1944; Ferster, 1961). These children are deviant in the sense that social behaviors are absent. The data are clear in demonstrating that such children are not responsive to social reinforcers (Lovaas et al., 1964; Ferster, 1961; Straughan, 1965; Bricker, 1965; Davison, 1965d). In working with an autistic child one obtains the definite impression that a lack of responsiveness to social stimuli is the causal agent producing the massive deficits in social behaviors. Whether the lack of responsiveness is produced by faulty learning or by some impairment in physiological process is, of course, not clear at this stage. But whatever the determinants, it is conceivable that nonresponsiveness is a matter of degree and that it is a "condition" which is to be found in nonautistic children. It may be that individual differences in responsiveness to contingent social stimuli (persuasion, modeling, social reinforcers) will relate to deviant behavior in nonautistic samples.

There are various ways of conceptualizing such a relationship between deviant behavior and nonresponsiveness in the nonautistic children. At the simplest level it could be that the individual who is primarily under the control of *non*social stimuli develops behaviors which are somewhat at variance with the remainder of society; the "Hermit" is a case in point (Olson, 1966). The fact that the individual is less responsive would be of little import if society ordinarily provided for massive overlearning of most social behaviors. However, to the extent that many of the socialization contingencies are relatively infrequent in occurrence or nonsystematic in application, even minor variations in responsiveness could result in omissions in socialization training.

It is more likely, however, that a child is not equally responsive to all social agents. The data reviewed earlier from laboratory measures of responsiveness in persuasion, modeling, and social reinforcement procedures suggested that responsiveness is learned somewhat independently for each major group of agents. This being the case, a child might be highly responsive to his peers but only minimally responsive to either or both of his parents. It is also hypothesized that to some extent each major group of social agents is responsible for training somewhat different social behaviors. For example, the kind of behaviors which are most likely to be modeled, to elicit positive social reinforcers, or to elicit persuasive communications from peers are likely somewhat different from the behaviors most likely to elicit such behaviors from the mother. Undoubtedly there is some common "core" of social behaviors which are both trained and maintained by all the social agents. However, it is assumed that particularly for the younger child, there are some behaviors for which various classes of social agents are uniquely responsible.

These speculations suggest that the kinds of deviant behaviors associated with nonresponsiveness vary as a function of the class of social agent involved. To the extent that any one of these classes of agents makes a unique contribution to socialization, selective nonresponsiveness to that group of agents could result in serious distortions or omissions in socialization training. In summary, it is hypothesized that nonresponsiveness to social reinforcers will be associated with deviant social behaviors. The class of social behaviors will vary as a function of which agents are involved.

Responsiveness to Adults. Children who are referred by adults to guidance clinics because of their deviant behavior are relatively nonresponsive to adult-dispensed social reinforcers. A study by Levine & Simmons (1962a) showed that a group of boys referred to a child guidance clinic were relatively nonresponsive to adult-dispensed social reinforcers in an instrumental conditioning task. A later study (Levine & Simmons, 1962b) showed that these same subjects were responsive to nonsocial reinforcers. Similar findings have been reported in a series of individual case studies where the data showed that the deviant child was nonresponsive to adult-dispensed social reinforcers (Patterson, 1965a; Patterson, Hawkins, McNeal, & Phelps, 1967). A recently completed doctoral dissertation by Perkins also showed that a group of boys referred for deviant behavior were comparatively nonresponsive to adult-dispensed social reinforcers.

When considering more limited ranges of deviant behaviors found in samples of boys[9] who have not been referred to child guidance clinics, the findings are not so clear-cut. For such samples, there are few, if any, consistent relations between teachers' ratings of deviant behavior and laboratory measures of a boy's responsiveness to positive social reinforcers dispensed by mothers (Patterson, Littman, & Hinsey, 1964; Patterson & Fagot, 1967), fathers, (Patterson, Littman, & Hinsey, 1965) or neutral adults (Cairns, 1962; Rawley & Stone, 1964). However, the study by Patterson & Fagot (1967) showed that, for boys (from nondeviant samples), the variable which relates to a deviant behavior is selective responsiveness. For example, if a boy is nonresponsive to his mother but responsive to his peers he tends to be described as nondeviant. However, if he is described as nonresponsive to peers and fathers and responsive only to his mother, he tends to be described by teachers as being characterized by behaviors such as nervous, tense, unsociable, and distrustful.

Peers. There are only a very limited number of studies testing for a relation between responsiveness to peers and deviant behaviors. The two studies which have been carried out (Patterson & Anderson, 1964; Patterson & Fagot, 1967)

---

[9] Because of the limited number of appropriate studies which are available, no attempt will be made to review the comparable research findings for girl subjects.

showed that the measure of preference change is correlated with teachers' ratings for behaviors described in such words as excitable, strong-willed, adventurous, and noisy. These cross-validated findings suggest that such behaviors may be among those for which the peer group provides intensive training. A lack of responsiveness to peers might mean a deficit in training for these "boylike" social behaviors.

Tagiuri (1952) showed that maladjusted boys received fewer sociometric choices by peers. The literature reviewed by Lott & Lott (1965) also suggested that sociometric choices are heavily influenced by deviancy of many kinds. For example, an individual tends to be less preferred if he is known to be "sickly," to have frequent accidents, or to be disciplined a good deal. Such findings imply that many social environments seem to have a low tolerance for deviancy. In such an environment, the deviant child is likely to have fewer interactions with his peers; he is also likely to be perceived as having "lower status" and to be less similar to themselves (Newcomb, 1956; Lott & Lott, 1965). Any one of these variables could operate as a determinant for lowered responsiveness to peer-dispensed social reinforcers. It is also quite possible that within a family the deviant member occupies a similar position so that eventually the family has increasingly limited control over the deviant child.[10]

Whatever the initial determinants, the existence of deviant behaviors may well lead to the child's occupying a special status in the immediate group which further reduces his responsiveness to social controls. This reduced responsiveness might in turn lead to the acquisition of other sets of deviant behaviors. At some point the child could reach a stage where only high-amplitude deviant behaviors elicited positive social reinforcers; but at that point, the schedule is likely to be so lean that he would be placed upon constant deprivation schedules with their concomitant emotional upheavals. This kind of cycling could conceivably be initiated by relatively innocuous training procedures. The cycle could be broken by altering some particular deviant behavior which leads to his unique status in the group. On the other hand, it is equally reasonable to consider the possibility of increasing either his general responsiveness or the range of social agents to which he responds.

Contribution of Social Reinforcement Procedures to Behavior Modification. The imprint of the empirical literature investigating social reinforcement contingencies has already been made in a number of ways. In the general case,

---

[10] A recently published series of studies identifies a new and exciting area of research within the province of social learning (Hastorf, 1965; Oaks, 1960, 1962). One such study, reported by Weiss (1965, 1966), investigated the variables associated with one person reinforcing the behavior of another. A related group of studies using observation data has identified changes in schedules of social reinforcement provided by peers for the behavior of other children in natural settings (Charlesworth & Hartup, 1967; Harris, 1966). Both of these latter studies showed significant increases in the frequency of social reinforcers as a function of increasing age.

the major impact of this literature was to establish a point of emphasis; however, the effect of such an emphasis has been to produce major innovations in the development of technologies for changing behavior. The obvious implication of these studies for behavior modification was that social agents could alter deviant behavior by systematically making social reinforcers contingent upon the occurrence of adaptive behaviors. This was such an obvious innovation that in retrospect it is amazing that it had been overlooked by the traditional therapies. While the earlier approaches might have occasionally stressed the need for the parent, the teacher, or the therapist to "recognize" adaptive behaviors when they occurred, such attention was not considered a major determinant of behavior change. In addition to identifying social reinforcement contingencies as major determinants in treatment programs, a functional analysis approach also stressed the need for systematic control over these contingencies. For example, in one of the classic papers by the "Washington group," the child who isolated herself from peers was reinforced (by the adults) only when she was in close proximity to other children (Allen et al., 1964).[11] One aspect of the same program required that the adults terminate the social reinforcements which they had previously made available for the peer-isolate behaviors. Ordinarily when an adult had observed the child to be alone they would approach the child and begin to interact with him. The effect of these behaviors was to strengthen "peer-isolate" behaviors. This careful programming of the social agents to reinforce adaptive behaviors consistently and to ignore deviant behaviors consistently constitutes one of the hallmarks of this group of investigators. Similar procedures have been described for regressed-crawling behavior (Harris et al., 1964) and vomiting (Wolf, et al., 1965), crying (Hart, et al., 1964) and to alter some of the deviant behaviors of an autistic child (Wolf, Risley, & Mees, 1964). Also, as Krasner (1962a) pointed out in his excellent review of the social reinforcement literature, there is reason to believe that traditional interviewing procedures could become a more effective base for changing deviant behavior if the therapist were more carefully programmed in the way in which he dispenses social reinforcers.

Another set of speculations has recently emerged from the empirical investigations of social reinforcement, this set with specific import for the development of behavior modification technologies. As noted in an earlier section, the data from a number of studies suggested that a lack of responsiveness to social reinforcers (or selective responsiveness) tended to covary with the occurrence of deviant behaviors. Conceivably, this could imply that the focus of the behavior modification program might be that of conditioning the

[11] These social reinforcements were initially not contingent upon terminal behaviors, e.g., playing with other children. The contingencies were arranged so that the terminal behaviors were gradually shaped. The notion of shaping behaviors was not contributed by social learning research but by the developments within operant conditioning.

child to become responsive to the social reinforcers dispensed by the major groups of social agents. Such a formulation would assume that if the child's behavior were brought under the control of a wider range of social agents, he could be taught adaptive social behaviors.

The first, and clearly the most significant, set of studies which has been carried out in an effort to alter responsiveness was designed for autistic children. In the classic studies carried out by Lovaas and his colleagues, procedures were initiated which were designed to change the status of previously neutral (social) stimuli. Drawing concepts from several different association-based learning theories, Lovaas first established that stimuli associated with the termination of electric shock would establish the presence of the experimenter as a secondary reinforcer (Lovaas, Schaeffer, & Simmons, 1964). He later used words as discriminative stimuli in an instrumental conditioning setting in which food was used as primary reinforcer. After a large number of pairings the words could then be used as secondary reinforcers in shaping new behaviors (Lovaas, Freitag, Kinder, Rubenstein, & Schaeffer, 1964).

To constitute a test for the present hypothesis, data would be required which showed a commensurate decrease in deviant behaviors for these children. Twelve months after the initiation of an operant training program at the University of Oregon laboratories, the laboratory data showed that several of the children were partially under the control of social reinforcers. Observations of the occurrence of adaptive social behaviors were made in the homes of the autistic children during a three-month period in the intervention program. During that interval the data showed little change in social behavior (Ray, 1965; Jones, 1965). Presumably if these observations had been made at the very beginning and at the close of the program the data might have shown the expected changes in social behaviors.

Attempts to work with autistic children in the laboratories at Orgeon have provided data which replicated some of Lovaas' findings (Bricker, 1965; Straughan, 1965). The outcome was also instructive in several other respects. As part of the program, one child was seen every day over a period of a year and a half.[12] During an early stage in the program his nonresponsiveness to the initiations of the five people in our group quickly extingiushed our enthusiasm. This effect was replicated when he was later placed in a detention home and provided with sixteen hours a day of tender loving care. He was assigned to shifts of adolescent girls who literally carried him around all day, fed him, and slept with him. For the first two days these "mother surrogates" were models of enthusiastic motherhood. By the fourth day, they asked to be relieved. Even mother surrogates must be reinforced by the infant. This experi-

[12] I particularly wish to acknowledge the efforts of Dorothy King of the Child Welfare Department, who transported this child daily to the laboratory and arranged foster home care for him. We are also indebted to J. Jacobson, his staff, and some of the clientele of the Skipworth Detention Home.

ence and the data provided by Ray (1965) and Jones (1965) leads this writer to believe that the chronic nonresponsiveness of the autistic child produces the "refrigerator parent" described by Kanner (1944). This is in contrast to Kanner's claim that it is the refrigerator parent that produces the autistic child. These children are, of course, an extreme case in point, but the experience reiterates the hypothesis that the nonresponsive child has an impact upon the social environment.

It is quite feasible to construct programs which will alter the responsiveness of the nonautistic child. One of the first children in behavior modification programs at our laboratories was a mute six-year-old girl referred because she was continually wandering about the neighborhood; she could not be controlled by her parents and would not talk to people other than members of her own family. She had been brutally beaten throughout much of her life. She was thought to be retarded and perhaps autistic. During her wanderings about, she had gone into a home and begun playing with the baby while the mother was absent. The baby was scalded to death.

It quickly became apparent that the only stimuli which functioned as reinforcers for her behavior were paper dolls. These reinforcers were used to shape vocalizations and also "approach" behaviors, e.g., standing close to one of the experimenters. She spent several weeks in this program with modest changes in her behavior. One day she and I were standing by the window waiting for the second experimenter (S. Fahrion) to join us. As he turned the corner and came toward the clinic, her whole face lit up. During this session, and those which followed, doll reinforcements were not necessary. Social approval, interest, and physical contact functioned as powerful reinforcers for her behavior. It was reported at about this point that she was much more responsive to people in the detention home and, later, with her foster parents. Once under the control of social stimuli, this child was found to be eminently trainable. I would like to mention, in passing, that she was later tested and found not to be retarded; nor was she autistic. She remained in the foster home rather than going to an institution. Undoubtedly, the most significant aspect of this program was the training to respond to social stimuli, at which point she came under the control of the behavior of other people within her environment.

Our next encounter with changing responsiveness, an accidental one, occurred in conjunction with the treatment of a school-phobic child (Patterson, 1965a). A series of 23 brief (fifteen- to twenty-minute) sessions were held in a playroom setting. At the beginning of the sessions, the child seemed responsive only to the reinforcers dispensed by the mother. Presumably, separation from the mother constituted a deprivation state for social reinforcers and resulted in intense fear. Findings from the laboratory procedures for measuring the effect of social reinforcers showed that he was nonresponsive to social reinforcers dispensed by the experimenter. During the total series of structured play sessions, about 500 to 700 M & M's were dispensed contingent both upon socially adaptive behaviors displayed by puppets and upon the child's report about his own adaptive behaviors. Following this, he was again conditioned by the same experimenter. On the second trial, the social reinforcers had a marked effect in altering his behavior. A second, untreated, deviant child did not show an increase in responsiveness. Nondeviant children conditioned by the same adult on two trials separated by a week showed a slight decrease in responsiveness on the second trial (Patterson & Hinsey, 1964).

A more direct attack upon the hypothesis was provided in an interesting doctoral dissertation recently completed by M. Perkins at the University of Illinois (personal communication, 1966). In his study, Perkins selected a group of 27 boys between the ages of six and eleven who had been referred because of their deviant behavior. The marble box procedure was used to assess their responsiveness to social reinforcers. They were then randomly assigned to one of three possible treatment groups. Each of the "therapists" participated in each of the three treatment conditions. One group was a control, and the second group used traditional play-therapy procedures. Children in the third group participated in a set of play sessions in which M & M candies were dispensed contingent upon the adaptive behaviors. These were similar to the sessions previously used by Patterson (1965a) to treat school-phobic children. Each of the children met with their "therapists" for 9 twenty-minute sessions; then the child and the therapist again participated in the laboratory assessment procedure. The data showed that there was little change in responsiveness for the members of the control group. The differences in responsiveness between this group and the group which had received the traditional play therapy was not significant. However, for the group that had received contingent reinforcement with M & M candies, there were significant increases in responsiveness to social reinforcers. It might be noted, in passing, that there were also more symptom changes reported for this group.

The Perkins study is important in several different contexts. Of immediate interest is the fact that the data confirm what had only been suspected previously. For children, responsiveness to social stimuli seems to change dramatically as a function of a short series of interactions with an adult. These interactions, however, must be "more than" just warm and nurturant. The additional characteristic found in all of the studies is that the adult must dispense quantities of social and nonsocial reinforcers in conjunction with a clearly defined set of contingencies.

The evidence suggests that social reinforcement procedures provide a powerful tool in the hands of the behavior modifier. However, it is equally true that the same procedures create a situation in which the best efforts of the behavior modifier may be either sabotaged or short-lived. Even the most agile behavior modifier provides only an infinitesimal portion of the social reinforcers accruing in the daily life of any child. In a sense, the modifier and his cohorts are continuously being outnumbered by unknown social agents who create unknown contingencies in shaping unknown social behaviors. In the face of such an accumulation of unknowns, it seems legitimate to raise the question of what programs of reinforcement, punishment, and modeling are provided by the social environment in which the deviant child lives.

It is entirely possible for the social environment to provide inadequate models before, during, and following the advent of a "successful" behavior modification program. It is equally possible that a social system such as a family or a peer group could provide massive schedules of positive reinforcement for nonadaptive social behaviors and that these programs could be in force before, during, and following the advent of a "successful" program. The outcome of a successful program in such an instance would mean that the effects were not only short-lived, but also restricted to a few, narrowly defined, social settings. I propose that, for these reasons, the focus of the behavior modifier should be less upon the direct manipulation of deviant behavior and more upon the reprogramming of the social environment in which the individual lives. The function of the professional should be to train the teacher, the peer group, the parent, or the spouse. The actual manipulation of the deviant behavior should be carried out by the social agent with whom the deviant individual lives. By definition, then, a successful program involving key social agents in the life of the child should ensure both generalization and persistence of treatment effects.

The Content of Social Interaction: The Irrational Social System

It is assumed that the social environment provides positive reinforcement for deviant behavior. The rather exaggerated heading above alludes to the fact that if the general hypotheses are supported, then, on the face of it, the social system is behaving in an irrational fashion. On the one hand, it is a representative of the social system, such as the parent, who complains of the deviant behavior of the child. According to the assumption stated here, it is this representative and the others who interact with the deviant child who are responsible for the maintenance of the deviant behaviors. It is the mother who is placed under great tension because of the deviant behavior of her child. However, in this Kafka-like quadrille, it is also she who is expending enormous amounts of her time in providing reinforcing contingencies for the very behaviors which generate the tension.

A satisfactory explication of the general assumption would require a host of data and the testing of a number of hypotheses. At the present time, only a very limited set of data, testing a restricted set of hypotheses, is available. In the discussion which follows, these data will be examined to determine whether they support the hypothesized relation between deviant behaviors and positive social reinforcers. The last section will outline the treatment programs which have been developed to alter the programs of social reinforcement provided by the social environment.

MAINTENANCE OF DEVIANT BEHAVIORS

This first group of studies showed that some special subcultures provide support for some classes of deviant behaviors. This conclusion, of course, has been a part of the conventional wisdom for some time. For example, subgroups have been described which teach and presumably maintain such deviant behaviors as homosexuality (Caprio, 1954), drug addiction, delinquency (Sutherland, 1937), and prostitution (Greenwald, 1958). However, no data have been provided which show what the mechanism involved in this kind of behavioral manipulation by the subcultures might be, let alone whether the processes bear any relation to reinforcement, modeling, or persuasion procedures.

A series of three observation studies was carried out to demonstrate that social reinforcement was being provided by a delinquent subculture for deviant behavior. All three studies showed that in an institutional setting, there was a massive reinforcement schedule for delinquent behavior (Buehler, Patterson, & Furness, 1966). The behavior classed as deviant covered a wide range of responses including verbal criticisms of the staff, breaking rules, destroying property, and positive statements about delinquent behaviors. In the pilot study, on 70 percent of the occasions when such responses occurred, they were reinforced postively by at least one peer. Consequences classed as positive reinforcers were such behaviors as verbal approval, agreement, interest, attention, smiling, and laughing. In the second study in the series, the comparable figure was 88 percent. Interesting enough, a large proportion of the social consequences provided by this peer culture were nonverbal. This same culture tended to provide aversive consequences for a majority of the behaviors which would be classed as "middle-class conforming."

Though the observation that deviant cultures do "something" to maintain deviant behavior may be commonplace, one would not necessarily expect to find such contingencies in "nondeviant" subcultures. A general hypothesis was invoked to explain the process whereby a "normal" parent or peer could find himself positively reinforcing deviant behavior. The hypothesis was labeled the "coercion hypothesis" and states that many deviant behaviors have one (at least) common characteristic in that they coerce a limited set of reactions from the social environment. Most adaptive social behaviors do not have this "demand" characteristic. When an adaptive behavior occurs, the other individual has a wide range of responses which will be appropriate (reinforced). However, most responses which are labeled as deviant permit only a limited set of reactions. For example, the hypochondriacal patient continues to respond until he elicits a sympathetic statement about his symptoms. The suicidal threats of the depressed patient force the other person to be sympathetic. The prolonged whining of the child eventually produces the glass of water at night, or the ice-cream cone on the Sunday drive. Presumably, if this type of coercion becomes too frequent, or if the responses demanded are aversive, then the responsible agents in the environment bring the individual to see the psychologist and the individual is labeled "deviant."

If the audience-responder ignores the first few responses in such a deviant chain, the behaviors are likely to show an immediate increase in either rate or amplitude. The "coerced" behavior of the audience-responder is reinforced because it produces the temporary termination of an aversive stimulus which is the deviant withdrawal of an aversive stimulus or the avoidance of even more intense aversive stimulation. Listen to Aunt Maud's complaints about her wayward bowels and you avoid the hurt silence which will follow if you neglect to do so. In such a situation, behaviors of both the "deviant" individual and his audience-responder are being mutually maintained. It seems likely that the particular set of coerced responses would vary depending upon the type of deviant behavior involved.

The studies which provided data relevant to this hypothesis were carried out as a part of a series of programs designed to alter hyperactive behaviors in children. Certainly, most adults find hyperactive behaviors to be rather aversive. It is one of the behaviors most likely to elicit a referral to an agency for professional help from both teachers and parents. However, a dissertation completed by Ebner (1967) showed that in a classroom for the retarded, both the teacher and the peer group provide contingent positive reinforcement for hyperactive behaviors. For three children observed over a two-month period, the data showed daily fluctuations in the schedule of reinforcement varying from 8 percent to as high as 70 percent (percentage of deviant responses reinforced). Similar data have been obtained by Anderson (1964), Grindee (1964), and Hotchkiss (1967) showing that the teacher frequently reinforced hyperactive behaviors. Not only did they tend to provide positive reinforcement for deviant behaviors, but the data showed that they were most likely to provide these reinforcers during periods of high-rate or high-amplitude deviant behaviors. Anderson, for example, found a correlation of .80 between the rate of output of deviant behavior and the amount of time spent by the teacher at the desk of one deviant child. While these data do not permit a direct test, they would be in keeping with predictions which would be made from the coercion hypothesis.

It follows from these findings that parents too might provide positive reinforcers for deviant behaviors. Thus far, the best support for this is provided in a study by Hawkins, Peterson, Schweid, & Bijou (1966). Their observation data showed a positive correlation between the frequency of output of deviant behavior by the child and the frequency of occurrence of positive social reinforcers provided by the mother. Within the home of the deviant child, it is not necessarily just the parent who provides the positive social reinforcers for deviant behavior. Unpublished observation data from a family that had trained a hyperaggressive child showed that several younger siblings seemed to function as giggling sycophants dispensing positive reinforcers for much of the deviant behavior which was so upsetting to the parent.

There is also another series of studies which provides indirect support for the hypothesis. In these studies the behaviors of social agents significant in the life of the subject are programmed in such a way that they no longer positively reinforce the deviant behavior of the subject. The classic studies by Ayllon & Michael (1959) are an excellent example. The data showed that altering the reinforcement program being provided by the nurse produced dramatic reductions in the incidence of some forms of deviant behaviors in psychotic adult patients. The findings provide indirect support for the hypothesis that it was the presence of these social reinforcers which maintained the deviant behaviors. Similar indirect support was provided for the effect of social reinforcers upon the output of deviant child behaviors in the studies by Allen et al. (1964), and Wolf, et al. (1965).

These data represent only the most preliminary sort of support for the hypothesized relation between deviant behavior and positive social reinforcers. However, thus far, the findings are consistent; the social environment does indeed seem to provide maintenance schedules for an impressive array of deviant behaviors. The findings suggest that many, or most, deviant behaviors are probably maintained by schedules such as these. In passing, it should be noted that several other kinds of supporting evidence are also needed to establish the hypothesis. For example, do the contingencies which are labeled, a priori, as positive social reinforcers in fact increase the probability that a deviant response will occur in the future? The limited data now available suggest that they do; for example, the data from one study showed that positive social reinforcers increased the probability of occurrence of aggressive responses in a nursery school setting (Patterson, Littman, & Bricker, 1967). The same set of data provided support for another hypothesis which must be investigated: that normal peer interaction provides reinforcing contingencies which result in the acquisition of deviant behavior in children who did not previously display these responses at high strength.

While such findings may be of some general interest to those who are interested in questions concerning the antecedents of deviant behavior, they should be of immediate concern to the behavior modifier who is interested in developing efficient programs for altering deviant behavior. To me, the findings suggest that the persistence and generalization of modification programs will be determined by the extent to which the reinforcement programs provided by the social environment are altered.

When the problem of maximizing the effect of modification programs was first being considered, it seemed to some that the most reasonable course would be to embed the program in the social environment and thus maximize transfer effects. Many of the earlier programs were in fact carried out in the classroom rather than in the laboratory (Hart et al., 1964; Harris et al., 1964; Patterson, 1965c; Patterson et al., 1965; Anderson, 1964; Grindee, 1964; Hotchkiss, 1966; Nixon, 1966). The data in fact showed that the effects of such modification programs did generalize to occasions on which the experimenters were not present and that the effects generalized across social settings (Ebner, 1967). However, it is possible to have perfect generalization across a large number of social settings and to have at one and the same time an extremely inefficient behavior modification program. The reason for this is clear. Granted that the effects of the modification program generalize, it is the reaction of the social environment to the behavior which determines how long the generalization effects will persist. If the "generalized" behaviors are not reinforced, they will cease to "generalize."

The study by Ebner (1967) showed that the peer groups in special classrooms did not consistently alter the reinforcement programs for deviant behavior following the advent of successful modification of deviant behaviors for a child in the classroom. For most subjects, even when their deviant behavior decreased, the peer group continued to reinforce them for deviant behavior. A study by Grindee (1965) showed that although the procedures apparently produced some changes in the reinforcement programs provided by the peer group, the changes did not persist beyond the termination of the experiment. This fact would lead to the prediction that, for such subjects, the long-term outcomes for the successful modification program would be limited indeed. If these considerations are correct, then it is the social environment which should be the focus of the behavior modification program. The reinforcement programs being used by the family and the peer group should be altered. If this is done, then these social agents will change the deviant behavior of the child. In doing so, one ensures that they will provide for the maintenance of these gains. The section which follows outlines some preliminary techniques and data to demonstrate the feasibility of such an approach.

REPROGRAMMING THE SOCIAL SYSTEM

In the brief review which follows, only those studies will be discussed which present procedures for altering schedules of reinforcement provided by members of the peer group, or parents, or teachers.

Peers. There have been several attempts to provide an indirect effect upon the reinforcement programs being provided by members of the peer group (Patterson, 1965c; Straughan, 1965). In such attempts the members of a classroom were informed that they could earn more candy if they would ignore

368 New Directions and Related Developments

the deviant behavior of the subject. Presumably their compliance with these instructions would place some of the deviant child's behaviors on a partial extinction schedule. The behavior of the peers would be reinforced not only by the M & M candies which they received at the end of the trial but also by the reduction in rate of aversive behaviors. No data were collected which showed that the instructions actually changed the schedule of positive reinforcement provided by peers for deviant behaviors. But a more direct intervention should be more profitable; for example, it should be possible to provide both more systematic and more immediate (rather than delayed) reinforcement contingent upon the adequate use of reinforcers by the peer group.

The first case which provided an occasion for attempting such a procedure involved a hyperaggressive boy named Karl, who had succeeded in training members of the peer group to avoid him (Patterson & Brodsky, 1966). As a result, the peer group was ineffective in shaping socially adaptive behaviors in Karl. To alter this situation, it was necessary to train the subject to initiate some positive social behaviors *and* at the same time train the peer to respond with a positive social reinforcer rather than with avoidance responses. Second, it was necessary to train the peers to initiate positive social behaviors to which the subject would respond with social reinforcers rather than with an attack. A successful program would require the (almost) simultaneous alteration of these four events within the social system. However, if the program was successful, the behavior of the subject would be under the control of the peer group, who could then socialize him.

Earlier in the program, Karl had been conditioned to respond to a signal from a buzzer as a secondary reinforcer. The buzzer had been backed up by M & M candies. The signaling device was brought to the playground and the child was told that he could earn candy in this setting. He was told that the buzzer would sound upon each occasion that "he could play with another kid without hurting him." He then walked over to a girl on a swing and picked up a long rope attached to the swing. Very gently he pulled the rope. The buzzer signaled and he stood for some time smiling and pulling on the rope. Periodically the girl on the swing smiled and talked to him. He probably received about five such reinforcers from the girl and at least that many from the buzzer. The experimenter then called him over and told him that all the candy which he earned would be divided among the other children. He then walked back to the playground and said to the first child he met, "Hey, I'm earning candy for you" (buzz). Often, this remark elicited a smile from the other child. He then ran through the playground touching children and telling them that he was earning candy for them. The buzzer signaled on each such occasion. On this journey he also rescued a fair maiden being trampled in a cardboard box prison by two young ruffians. For this he received two buzzes and a smile of gratitude from the maid.

On the following day, the other children had received their M & M's from his previous day's work and they were curious when the experimenter again appeared with the box. They asked what it was, and the experimenter told them that it was a "Karl box." They asked, "What is a Karl box?" The experimenter said, "It is a box that makes a noise, and gives candy whenever you talk to Karl." Immediately several children said "Hi, Karl" to the box. The experimenter said, "No, you must say it to Karl; not to the box." The peers then received 150 reinforcers for initiating social contacts with Karl. During this day and the two days which followed, the members of the peer group and the subject were reinforced by the signal whenever they reinforced each other for positive social initiations. The observation data showed a two- or threefold increase in such initiations for both the subject and the members of the peer group (initiations directed toward the subject); these increases were maintained for the three months following termination of the procedures. Little more than three training sessions and a total of about sixty minutes of the psychologist's time were involved in this aspect of the treatment program for this child.

The changes brought about by this procedure should be maintained because the behaviors of the subject and the peers are now mutually reinforced. In this sense, the behavior modifier initiates the changes in interaction behaviors by reinforcing alterations in the reinforcement programs used by the subject and by his peers. The eventual outcome of the program is a function of the mutual reinforcers supplied within the social system. In this sense the behavior modifier is cast in the role of midwife as it were; he is present as a facilitator, but only during the opening scenes of the play. The final outcome is a function of the social agents who live with the child.

The limited number of studies and the limited range of procedures described attest to the fact that little consideration has been given as yet to the problem of reprogramming the peer group.

Reprogramming Teachers and Parents. One of the first attempts to reprogram the social reactions of significant persons living in the same social environment as the patient was described in the important study by Ayllon & Michael (1959). In that study, carried out in an institutional setting, the social reactions of the nurse constituted a significant portion of the patients' social interactions. In the cases described, the behaviors of the nurses were "programmed" in such a way as to provide no social reinforcers contingent upon deviant behaviors and maximal reinforcement for the occurrence of socially adaptive behaviors. The data provided demonstrated dramatic changes in the behavior of a number of adult patients.

Similar procedures have been used to "teach" professional adults working with children to use their behavior in systematic programs designed to alter the deviant behavior of the child. The reports by Allen et al. (1964) and Harris et al. (1964), described earlier, demonstrated the efficiency incurred as a result of using the teachers' social reinforcements in systematic programs designed to alter regressed crawling and isolated behaviors of preschool children. Similar programs have also been described which are appropriate for older and "more deviant children." James (1965) and, more recently, Hotchkiss (1966) described programs in which the teachers' behavior functioned as an important component in programs designed to alter the deviant behaviors of groups of hyperactive children. Lindsley (1966) at the University of Kansas and Becker at the University of Illinois are constructing programs for training teachers to use these principles. From the initial reports describing the results of such teacher training, it appears that this is a highly efficient application of social learning principles.

Straughan (1964) described a procedure that was a step toward more direct retraining for parents. The parent observed a psychologist interacting with her daughter. Following this, the parent interacted with the child in the playroom, providing examples of the contingencies being used by the mother to shape the deviant behavior. The parent reported changes in the behavior of the child; however, again no criteria were presented for evaluating the reports and no attempt was made to partial out the effect of retraining the parent from the other techniques used with the child.

Several reports have recently presented a description of techniques developed to reprogram the social reinforcers used by the parent in the home (Wolf et al., 1964; Hawkins et al., 1966; Patterson et al., 1966). In most instances, the training occurred in the home, and observation data are provided which demonstrate the effectiveness of the parent as a social agent in altering deviant behaviors. A similar procedure was described in the report by Patterson & Brodsky (1966) in which the parent, the teacher, and the experimenters all served as agents in modifying deviant behavior. A similar intrusion into the social environment of the child was also described in a report by O'Leary, O'Leary, & Becker (1967) in which the parents and the sibling functioned as behavior modifiers.

It seems quite reasonable to suppose that future studies will replicate these general findings and demonstrate the utility attached to such invasions of the social environment. The critical test of developments involving the reprogramming of the peers, teachers, and parents should be found in their relative increased efficiency in maximizing generalization and persistence of treatment effects. One of the problems attached to this kind of approach concerns the expenditure of time used in travelling to and from the classroom and the home, and in training the relevant social agents. It seems reasonable to believe that a more efficient use of the professionals' time might be found in utilizing teaching techniques for training groups of parents. Such programs are in fact currently being developed in several settings such as the University of Kansas (Lindsley), the University of Tennessee (Wahler et al., 1965), and the University of Illinois (Becker). Preliminary reports of the effects of such parent-training programs indicate that this is a promising technique (Wahler et al., 1965). It seems that for many types of cases, it may not be necessary for the experimenter actually to make the observations and carry out the manipulations, but that on both counts the parent can function as an able assistant. It may also be possible to accelerate the process of teaching parents to utilize these concepts and procedures by providing them with programmed texts which outline the concepts and the procedures for altering behavior (Patterson & Brodsky, 1966).

An interesting question has been posed as a result of these preliminary attempts to manipulate the reinforcement programs of the social agents who are crucial in the life of the child. The question concerns the "psychological M & M" to be invoked, which maintains the behavior of the agent. Specifically, the question is: What is it that maintains the altered behavior (reinforcement programs) of the social agent? While the social reinforcers of the experimenters might provide support for the initial alterations in the behavior of the parent, it is clear that the successful program must in some sense alter the mutual reinforcement systems of both the parent and the child. In several of the cases reported thus far, it is apparent that the behavior of the child is extremely aversive to the parent. In that context, the manipulations of the parent which result in a decrease in the frequency of such behaviors are strongly reinforced by the withdrawal of the aversive stimuli (deviant behavior of the child). For some other parents, however, the initial stages of the program might reduce the incidence of child behaviors which were not necessarily intensely aversive to the parent. For example, one parent considered the presence of the deviant child as a potential threat to the life of a newly born infant. The "isolated" and withdrawn behaviors of this deviant child were maintained both by the positive reinforcing of the parent and by the child's isolation being made an occasion for the withdrawal of the parent's aversive behaviors (Patterson et al., 1967). In such an instance the parental manipulations which resulted in the child's coming out of isolation would not necessarily be maintained by the reduction in incidence of his "isolated" behavior. For this particular family the behavior of the parents was initially maintained by reinforcing their behavior with $1; the money earned was subtracted from their fee schedule. In the process of "earning" $50 or $60 the parents produced marked changes in the behavior of their child.

However, the eventual fate of such manipulations is a function of the reinforcement contingencies provided by the social environment. An effective program would require that the adaptive behavior of the subject be sustained by a maintenance schedule provided by a parent or a peer and that either the subject or some other member of the environment provide a maintenance schedule for the reinforcing agent.

These kinds of speculations confront the reader with an infinite regression; for there must obviously be someone who reinforces the person reinforcing the reinforcer, who in turn reinforces the deviant child, etc. It is equally clear that what is involved in understanding such interactions is some analysis of the social system. In a sense, successful behavior modification programs involve some alterations in the complex web of mutual reinforcements provided by the deviant child and the persons with whom he lives. In some instances it may be necessary actually to teach individuals to reinforce each other because such interactions have long ago been extinguished in that particular social system (Patterson et al., 1967).

It is equally reasonable to suppose that occasionally when one produces a "slight" change in the reinforcement schedules or deviant behavior of one member of such a system, this change in turn will produce an impact upon the behavior of some other member of the system, which in turn will produce an effect upon some other unit of the system. In effect, a small initial ripple can produce wide-ranging effects upon several members of a system. This kind of exponential effect has been noted both by traditional clinicians and by behavior modifiers. In one such case training a mother to use a time-out procedure resulted in her obtaining immediate control over the behavior of a hyperaggressive child. Brief training in techniques of positively reinforcing socially adaptive behaviors not only provided additional control over a wide range of the child's behavior but also produced a marked reduction in her shrill Xanthippe-like behaviors. This in turn produced a household which was more pleasant to be around, and the husband began to spend time at home and to reinforce his wife positively. This change in the behavior of the husband altered in turn a deprivation state which had existed for the wife for years. She began to report that she "felt less anxious and less angry"; later her family physician recommended that she no longer take the tranquilizers she had been using for years.

Until we better understand the parameters which govern the behavior of the members of a social system, there is no reason to believe that fortuitous sequential reactions of the kind described here will invariably be beneficial. Nor should we expect that other social systems or other families will change, with just a minimum of effort on our part. It seems likely that unless efforts are bent to analyze these complex reinforcement programs, occasional apparently "successful" cases will suddenly revert or prove to be intransigent. To me it seems that the utility provided by future modification programs will be largely determined by the outcomes of investigations which purport to explain, or manipulate, social systems.

Chapter Summary

It was proposed that the literature relevant to social learning could provide a base from which behavior modification technology could be further expanded. As a preliminary outline, a limited set of data was explored to determine what contributions, if any, might be made to the behavior modification enterprise. Three general areas were reviewed: the traditional social psychological research in persuasion and modeling, the social reinforcement literature, and the literature which describes the "programs" of reinforcement provided by the social environment.

A review of the findings from the eliciting procedures (modeling and persuasion) for producing behavior change suggested that these techniques could be considered as catalytic mechanisms. Presumably, the effect of such procedures could be that of accelerating both the acquisition of social behaviors (e.g., deviant behaviors) and the alteration of these behaviors once they had been established. The major contribution of modeling, for example, was considered to be that of providing a basis for altering the initial probabilities that a deviant response would occur. For example, under certain conditions, the behavior of the model could produce an increase in the probability that a behavior would be performed by the observer. However, the fact that these behaviors are performed by the child relates only in a limited sense to the question of whether the behaviors become a part of his permanent repertoire of social behaviors. The behaviors will become an important part of the repertoire only if the child has been reinforced by the social environment for their performance. In this context, modeling and persuasion accelerate the process of acquiring deviant behaviors under conditions where these behaviors are then reinforced. By the same token, for programs designed to alter deviant behaviors, modeling procedures should accelerate change in behavior by increasing the probabilities that the appropriate behaviors will be performed. If the modification program also provides for reinforcement contingencies for these behaviors, then socially adaptive behaviors should become an important part of the child's repertoire. This catalytic effect should be most marked in the modification of deviant children who display massive deficits in their repertoire of social behaviors.

The literature relevant to the social reinforcement procedures suggested that the systematic application of reinforcing contingencies by key social agents such as teacher, peers, and parents should provide a powerful technology for altering the deviant behavior of children. This kind of emphasis upon utilizing social agents available in the social environment has characterized the behavior modification literature from its earlier beginnings. There is a second set of findings from the social reinforcement literature which suggested that the deviant child is less responsive to adult reinforcers. There are also some preliminary data suggesting that the deviant child may be selectively responsive to only a few classes of social agents. These findings in turn suggest that one approach to such children may be that of altering their selective responsiveness in order to bring their behavior under the control of a wide range of social agents. Studies were reviewed which attested to the feasibility of altering the responsiveness of deviant children to social stimuli.

The third area of discussion dealt with the implications of the hypothesis that the social environment provides positive social reinforcers for deviant behaviors in children. Data were reviewed from observation studies investigating the contingencies provided by peers, teachers, and parents for deviant behaviors ranging from "hyperactive" to delinquent. The fact that these contingencies exist poses a problem in that some observation data also showed that the social environment does not necessarily terminate these maintenance schedules for positive social reinforcers during the course of a "successful treatment" program. In several such cases the observation data showed that even though the output of deviant behavior significantly decreased, the peers and teachers continued to reinforce the deviant behavior on the same schedule. This suggests that, in a long-term follow-up, the eventual outcome of such reinforcement schedules could very well be to increase the output of the deviant behaviors to their preintervention level. It was hypothesized that the persistence and generalization of behavior modification programs are a function of the changes in contingencies provided for adaptive and deviant behaviors by the social system. Furthermore, it is assumed that the most "efficient" modification programs would consist of systematic efforts to reprogram the social system in which the child lives. Several studies were discussed which demonstrated the feasibility of such an approach.

10

The Place of Operant Conditioning of Verbal Behavior in Psychotherapy *

KURT SALZINGER

Biometrics Research and Polytechnic Institute of Brooklyn, New York

The fact that psychotherapy involves learning has become a truism. It has become widely accepted, even by psychodynamic therapists, in large measure due to such hybrid psychologists (hybrid because their writings are based on both learning theory and psychodynamic psychotherapy) as Dollard & Miller (1950), Mowrer (1953), and Shoben (1949). Important as was the contribution of these psychologists to learning theory, however, close inspection of the bridge they built between learning theory and psychodynamic therapy shows that it is strictly one way. They began by accepting the psychoanalytic terms describing the course of psychotherapy and then directed most of their energies toward finding analogs in the animal learning literature. The acceptance of learning theory by the conventional psychotherapist thus turned out to be a Pyrrhic victory for behavior theorists. Acceptance merely gave conventional psychotherapists still another reason for continuing what they were doing already. It is therefore no wonder that learning theory had no impact

* This paper was supported in part by Research Grant MH 07477 from the National Institutes of Health. The author is grateful to his wife Suzanne Salzinger for careful editing. Special thanks are due to J. Zubin for his constant support and interest.

upon psychotherapy until techniques derived from the former were applied directly and independently of conventional therapy to the psychopathology itself. Outside the United States this took the form of applying Pavlovian (respondent) conditioning (Eysenck, 1960a; Wolpe, 1958). In this country it consisted primarily in the application of operant conditioning. The major impetus for applying operant conditioning came, perhaps predictably, from the descriptive behaviorism of Skinner (Skinner, 1938, 1953, 1957; Ferster & Skinner, 1957; Holland & Skinner, 1961) and of Keller & Schoenfeld (1950) who did so much to promote and extend it. It should come as no surprise that the seemingly antithetical approach to psychodynamics should lend itself to therapeutic purposes when one remembers that descriptive behaviorism, much more than the work of Hull, Guthrie, or Tolman, concentrated on the study of the individual organism, the *sine qua non* of clinical practice. The success and vitality of this approach has shown itself in a series of books (Honig, 1966; Krasner & Ullmann, 1965; Millenson, 1967; Sidman, 1960; Staats, 1964; Staats & Staats, 1963; Ullmann & Krasner, 1965; Ulrich, Stachnik, & Mabry, 1966; Verhave, 1966) and in a major journal (*Journal of the Experimental Analysis of Behavior*). Descriptive behaviorism has come a long way since Skinner's (1938) initial work on the laboratory rat in his *Behavior of Organisms*. Even superficial inspection of the literature today shows that this approach to psychology has now not only been extrapolated but, even more important, widely applied to human subjects.

The aim of this chapter is to show in what way descriptive behaviorism can be utilized in the analysis and control of the verbal behavior emitted during the course of psychotherapy, the conduct of which is purportedly determined by different models for bringing about change in a patient.

Before pursuing the above-stated aim, it might be well to delineate the scope of this chapter, and give the reasons for including the material found here. At first glance, one is inclined to think that verbal behavior, no less operant conditioning of verbal behavior, is important only in conventional psychotherapy. However, it plays a critical role in the newer types of behavior therapy as well. Moreover, it tends to be ignored as much in the one type of therapy as in the other.

Conventional Psychotherapy

Let us look first at conventional psychotherapy. The many studies on the conditioning of verbal behavior, which were most recently stimulated by Greenspoon's (1955) experiment on the conditioning of plural nouns, have in large measure addressed themselves to the problem of setting up a model for conventional psychotherapy. Essentially these studies have given rise to two inferences: First, the verbal behavior of the therapist influences the verbal behavior of the patient so as to make questionable the validity of the information obtained from the patient. This means that under the typically uncontrolled conditions of conventional psychotherapy one can never be certain of a patient's report about his state, whether subjective or objective. Thus it becomes difficult to use the psychotherapeutic interview to evaluate either a patient or a theory of personality or treatment. The second inference from the verbal conditioning literature is that the therapist who is interested in modifying the verbal behavior of his patient now has available to him reliable and well-tested techniques for doing so. We now have the means for putting the effectiveness of conventional psychotherapy to empirical test in a more detailed and therefore more useful way. A patient whose verbal behavior has not changed (has not been conditioned) during the course of conventional psychotherapy would certainly not be expected to change his verbal and nonverbal behavior outside the therapy session. For example, one can test the hypothesis, generated by a certain school of psychotherapy, that a patient must learn to label his emotional responses accurately (Dollard & Miller, 1950). Although we now have available conditioning techniques for instating such labels, such techniques have not yet been incorporated in actual therapeutic practice.

In a recent paper, Kanfer (1966a, p. 173) expresses a note of pessimism, saying, "In contrast to the wealth of information available in the literature [of verbal conditioning], the behavior of interviewing therapists and the format of interview therapy seems to be essentially unaffected by these findings and continues to follow closely the framework of the traditional dynamic theories of personality." Kanfer goes on to say that extensive application of the results of studies on the operant conditioning of verbal behavior will be made only when behavior theory provides more concrete guidelines to the general strategy in psychotherapy. It is hoped that this chapter will move us along the way, but that, if we do not get to the ultimate goal of a general strategy immediately, conventional therapists will still be willing to try those techniques which are well worked out.

Lack of planning or, in the vocabulary of behavior theory, lack of programming, gives rise to important consequences for conventional therapy. Reinforcement in interaction between two or more people is not something which can be laid aside to be used only when one wishes. Reinforcers form a very important aspect of any conversation: their presence maintains it and their absence terminates it. What are the implications of the abnegation of the use of reinforcement? It means that the control over the emission of reinforcers becomes unknown. It has been suggested by some that under these conditions the distribution of reinforcers is random and can therefore be ignored. That reinforcers are not distributed at random under such conditions will be demonstrated below, but in point of fact there is very little evidence that any verbal behavior is really random. There are, after all, many response biases which all of us learn, and there are a great many determinants of verbal behavior, as the literature on verbal behavior well demonstrates (Salzinger & Salzinger, 1967). Thus some of the determinants of the interviewer's reinforcing behavior reside in his own reinforcement history (how he was conditioned to reinforce others), and some of the determinants reside in the behavior of the patient (in the discriminative stimuli and in the reinforcers he emits) whose behavior the therapist is in fact trying to change. A study by Heller, Myers, & Kline (1963), although not based upon behavior theory, investigated the effect of different kinds of client behavior upon interviewer behavior and found it to be significant. They concluded that both interviewer and client "are variable responders, each alert to the incoming cues from the other and each in turn acting as a partial cause of the other's behavior" (p. 121).

The importance of planning therapy sessions stems from other considerations as well. Some time ago I reviewed the interview literature (Salzinger, 1959a) and pointed out the many sources of distortion of the information given by the patient, i.e., distortion arising from the way in which the interviewer questions and reinforces the patient, as well as distortion occurring as an integral part of the interviewing procedure. Looking upon the interviewer-patient interaction as a communication system, a list of five potential filters and noise generators was postulated: (1) the process of observation, i.e., what the interviewer attends to when he listens to his patient; (2) memory, i.e., what the interviewer remembers of the interview; (3) record, i.e., what the interviewer considers important enough to write down; (4) method of analysis, i.e., how he combines his information; and finally, (5) summarizing measure, i.e., how he labels the combined information in a diagnostic category, prescription for treatment, etc. These filters and noise generators function in terms explainable by behavior theory, since the behaviors of observing, remembering, recording, and synthesizing of information are also susceptible to reinforcement contingencies. Thus, with regard to observation, Holland (1958) showed that meter-monitoring behavior is controlled by the number and pattern of significant meter deflections observed, i.e., the observed event controlled the act of observing and therefore what the subject would observe next. Another study of interest with respect to errors in observation was carried out by Chapman (1967). Allowing subjects to observe the cooccurrence of various pairs of words, he presented them in such a way that each pair occurred one-third of the time. When the subjects were later asked to estimate how frequently the various pairs occurred, they overestimated the cooccurrence of words which had strong associative connection, and perhaps even more interesting, they overestimated the cooccurrence of words which had in common only the fact that both members of the pair were distinctive in the series. Along similar lines, Goldiamond & Hawkins (1958) showed that "perception" can be explained completely in terms of response bias (number of superliminal exposures to a given stimulus before being asked to guess what one sees) when no relevant stimulus is shown. Finally, Portnoy, Portnoy, & Salzinger (1964) showed that association value of a verbal stimulus determines search time even when response bias is effectively ruled out, thus showing that even when a stimulus is clearly there to be observed, past experience with that stimulus influences its rate of detection. The potential difficulties inherent in obtaining and retaining information on the basis of interviewing make the planning of its conduct even more important and provide an additional reason for the behavior therapist's distrust of the technique.

What, then, is the fatal fascination that the interview has for the conventional psychotherapist? If we discard the fact that he is simply used to it as a way of dealing with patients—the tradition of interviewing—we are left with one significant argument for the interview, its value in evoking the patient's subjective experiences. Put into somewhat different terms, the conventional therapist embraces the interview because it allows him to evoke and evaluate the patient's reactions to private events, where a private event may be defined as a stimulus to which one person only can be exposed at a given time.

Private events which conventional therapists find so important in their work are very difficult to get at, both because of their nature (the fact that only one person is exposed to each of them) and because of the many possibilities for different reinforcement contingencies acting upon these verbal responses (Skinner, 1945). Although no studies have been undertaken specifically to compare the conditionability of verbal response classes under the control of private and public stimuli, related investigations would seem to indicate that conditionability of verbal responses under the control of private stimuli will be more influenced than those under the control of public stimuli. Judgments of extent of movement in the experiment with the autokinetic effect (a private event) appear to be more easily modified by the judgments of a fellow observer (Sherif, 1935) than are the judgments of which of three obviously different-sized lines is largest (Asch, 1952). This difference in susceptibility to influence has two implications. One is that responses ostensibly under the control of private events should be used as sources of information only if additional corroborative evidence is available and if the reinforcement conditions surrounding the evocation of the responses are known. The other implication is that if the conventional psychotherapist wants to modify such responses, he could not have selected a happier response class.

It should have become clear by now that there are both strategic (effective therapeutic techniques) and methodological (reliable techniques for obtaining information) reasons for applying descriptive behaviorism to conventional psychotherapy. There are negative reasons which motivate the application of a new model to conventional psychotherapy and we will present these briefly now.

The foremost reason for reevaluating conventional psychotherapy is of course the fact that its effectiveness is equivocal (Eysenck, 1952, 1960b; Levitt, 1957, 1963).

Another reason for reevaluating conventional psychotherapy is that the typical psychodynamic terms are simply inappropriate for description of what goes on in the course of psychotherapy. As Haley (1963, p. 69) recently pointed out, "A problem in describing psychoanalysis, as well as other schools of psychotherapy, is the fact that reports of therapists emphasize the theory of a school rather than what actually happens between therapist and patient." He points out that the typical psychodynamic ideas of repression, orality, ego, oedipal conflict, etc., cannot possibly form the basis for describing patient-therapist interactions. He further takes nondirective therapy to task by saying: "To state that any communication between two people can be nondirective is to state an impossibility" (p. 71).

Bandura & Walters (1963) have made an additional criticism of conventional psychotherapy by pointing out that attempts to modify deviant behavior have been based on the school of the particular therapist rather than on the problem of the patient. They state: "School affiliations not only determine the range of techniques of psychotherapy that a given therapist will employ but even define the client's central conflict or distrubance that the techniques of the school are designed to resolve" (p. 249).

Behavior Therapy—Pavlovian Type

Although it has been suggested by behavior therapists that conventional psychotherapy is all talk while behavior therapy deals directly with pathology, behavior therapy is also involved with talk. As Mowrer (1965) pointed out, it, like conventional psychotherapy, is based upon the notion that to remove abnormal behavior, one must remove underlying emotions. Wolpe (1958) states that improvement in the course of conventional psychotherapy must be attributed to the interviewer's eliciting an emotional response from the patient which is antagonistic to anxiety and strong enough to inhibit it. The technique most frequently used for that purpose in behavior therapy is Wolpe's (1958) systematic desensitization procedure.

Let us look more closely at the procedure. Verbal behavior first comes into the inquiry which is designed to establish one or more anxiety hierarchies. These hierarchies consist of the verbal responses to the private event of feelings of anxiety. Later, when the behavior therapist presents parts of the anxiety hierarchy as scenes, public stimuli are presented as private events. Presumably, to the extent that the private events of a given patient differ radically from the public events in his hierarchy, this kind of therapy is ineffective for him. At this stage, the patient's verbal responses are responses to the private event of anxiety evoked by the private event that is the scene conjured up by the therapist for the patient to imagine. Presumably part of what the patient does is to respond subvocally to the therapist's injunction to imagine a given scene. The fact that a patient's verbal response is not always under the control of his private events was reported in at least one study (Lazarus, Davison, & Polefka, 1965, p. 226), where "it was obvious that his [the patient's] verbal reports were aimed at eliciting approval rather than describing his true feelings."

One of the important classes of behavior which the therapist must successfully train the patient to emit is self-regulative behavior. The patient has to learn to associate to the stimuli presented to him by the therapist and to cease associating to them when told to stop. One would certainly think that here might well be a place for the operant conditioning of a verbal behavior paradigm. Is it possible that what Wolpe calls a Pavlovian conditioning design is in fact an operant conditioning design? Wolpe's interpretation of the systematic desensitization procedure is that the therapist presents stimuli which gradually become more like the anxiety-eliciting stimulus and that with each successive stimulus, part of that anxiety is inhibited by relaxation. Essentially this process depends on *stimulus* generalization. But is it not possible to view this procedure as being dependent on *response* generalization in an operant conditioning paradigm, whereby the patient is positively reinforced by feeling relaxed and by the verbal and nonverbal approval of the therapist to think of responses more and more like the response he fears to make? We are not suggesting that the autonomic nervous system is not involved in the procedure. We know, however, that muscle relaxation can be produced directly by means of operant conditioning. We know also that response generalization is used in the process of shaping responses not yet in the repertory of an organism. The procedure of shaping has an uncanny similarity to the systematic desensitization procedure. Simply substitute response for stimulus. Both procedures are gradual ones, and in both, the organism emits a response he did not emit before.

In an experiment (Salzinger, Feldman, Cowan, & Salzinger, 1965) with a speech-deficient boy who was afraid to leave the ward to come into the experimental room, an operant conditioning procedure was used to shape the response of getting him ever closer to the feared room. A very important aspect of the reinforcer consisted of terminating the progress toward the feared room once the child had approached it somewhat. Thus approach to the room was reinforced by candy (delivery of positive reinforcement) and by allowing him to return to the ward (termination of mildly negative reinforcement). When the child finally ventured into the experimental room he was allowed to pick up a piece of candy on the table and immediately to leave the room and return to the ward. Is it possible that the procedure in which the behavior therapist presents the patient with a neutral or relaxing scene acts the same way as allowing the boy to leave the feared experimental room? Is the act of change in the patient's verbal behavior from aversive to neutral responses reinforcing?

It is of some interest to note that there are dangers in shaping procedures. It is possible to reinforce, and therefore to condition, behavior which might be directly opposed to the desired behavior; it is therefore important to know which kind of behavior will turn into what other behavior before reinforcing it. Another danger in a shaping procedure consists of reinforcing a given response which, though it is not initially incompatible with the desired response, might become so because it has been reinforced too often. This implies that to the extent that systematic desensitization is an operant conditioning situation, too large a number of presentations of a given scene might be deleterious to the therapeutic process; to the extent that it is a respondent conditioning process, a large number of presentations of the same scene should have *no* deleterious effect. Thus we have here a possible experiment to test which of the two types of conditioning better describes the process.

What of the role of the relaxation procedure? Hefferline (1962) has suggested that the differential activity of muscles may act as a controlling stimulus for the so-called higher mental processes. Is it possible that the proprioceptive stimulation stemming from the normal but nonrelaxed state controls responses incompatible with the ones the therapist is trying to evoke, while the proprioceptive stimulation coming from the relaxed state of the muscles has no such controlling stimulus function? In other words, we are suggesting that the relaxed state of the muscles offers the patient the opportunity to emit responses which he does not ordinarily emit and which would otherwise be difficult to instate. Certainly, the procedure of training assertive behavior is a case of operant conditioning. Here therapist and patient go through role playing such that the patient's assertive verbal behavior is positively reinforced by the therapist in order to transfer the increased frequency of it in one stimulus situation, where it can easily occur, to another stimulus situation where its probability of occurrence is initially low. It seems reasonable to consider that behavior therapy à la Wolpe is very much an overlap situation in which both kinds of conditioning take place and that the therapist should pay more explicit attention to both types of conditioning so as to use both to better advantage.

Let us look at two studies in which operant and respondent conditioning procedures were combined in an explicit way. Lazarus, Davison, & Polefka (1965) found it necessary to reinforce certain operant behavior, namely, going to school, while carrying out extinction of anxiety along classical conditioning lines. Although the operant conditioning was mainly of nonverbal behavior, this experiment showed clearly the benefits which could accrue from the combination of the two conditioning procedures. Schmidt (1964) combined three behavior modification procedures: the operant conditioning of verbal behavior, the operant conditioning of nonverbal behavior, and Wolpe's systematic de-sensitization procedure in vivo. Although Schmidt used only one patient in her experiment, her experimental design, which included well-thought-out controls, along with her results, require that this study be generally read and replicated on a sample of other patients. Taking one of two series of anxiety-provoking situations, she designed a verbal conditioning task for it, followed by the desensitization in vivo procedure. Then she took the other, matched series of anxiety-provoking situations and subjected it only to in vivo desenitization. Her verbal procedure included a shaping technique which specified that the patient be reinforced for statements gradually expressing less anxiety. The statements varying in degree of anxiety were made up by the patient himself under the therapist's instruction, and were then typed on 75 cards. The patient's task was to select one of 4 statements about a given anxiety stimulus (e.g., a bus), with the statement varying in degree from great anxiety to feeling of ease. This verbal conditioning procedure (verbal reinforcers were success-fully employed under some conditions and nonverbal ones under others, but the former were most effective) was continued until the patient chose the "recovery" (feeling at ease) statement for every one of the 75 cards. Although significant conditioning effects were obtained, subjective evaluation by the patient of the original anxiety-provoking situations after conditioning showed no statistically significant change from the preconditioning evaluation. The actual behavior-shaping procedure (desensitization) was then instituted for all anxiety hierarchies, with the result that those anxiety hierarchies which were preceded by the verbal conditioning procedure required a mean of 4 hours for successful treatment, while those hierarchies not so preceded required a mean of 7 hours for successful treatment. To take one example, the effectiveness of the verbal conditioning procedure with statements about the bus showed itself by requiring fewer nonverbal behavior-shaping sessions for the patient to be able to travel on a bus without fear. Furthermore, the subjective evaluation by the patient showed a greater effect of the nonverbal behavior sessions in reduc-ing the anxiety when the nonverbal behavior conditioning was preceded by verbal conditioning. Finally, follow-up one year after treatment showed that those anxiety hierarchies treated by both conditioning procedures elicited sig-nificantly less anxiety than before treatment, while those hierarchies treated only by conditioning nonverbal behavior elicited the same amount of anxiety as before treatment. Schmidt (1964, p. 26) summarizes part of her findings by stating "that though verbal conditioning cannot produce behavioral changes it may facilitate their induction by other methods and their maintenance." Here, then, is an example of how a focused verbal conditioning procedure by itself, i.e., without an equally focused nonverbal conditioning procedure, is unsuccess-ful in producing a behavioral change. This can be taken to be analogous to current conventional psychotherapy. Its enhancing power when coupled with nonverbal behavior conditioning may account for that apparently small number of conventional psychotherapy successes. The operant conditioning of non-verbal behavior, or, for that matter, the systematic desensitization procedure, without the verbal conditioning may well fail to produce lasting therapeutic effects.

We would like to note, as did Schmidt, that there is direct evidence for the usefulness of conditioning verbal behavior in influencing nonverbal behavior. Lovaas (1961, 1964a, 1964b) showed that the reinforcement of verbal aggressive behavior causes an increase in nonverbal aggressive behavior, that differences in verbal and nonverbal rates of responding can be controlled by conditioning discriminative verbal responses, and finally that children's food intake can be controlled by conditioning appropriate verbal responses. Contrary to Freud's notion of catharsis, the emission of aggressive responses induces the further emission of aggressive responses (Bandura & Walters, 1963). The general problem of transfer to which so many investigators have referred, but about which so few have done anything, must finally be dealt with in a paradigm like Schmidt's. It may be that the verbal behavior which Schmidt conditioned was not similar enough to the kind of verbal responses which in daily life control an individual's nonverbal behavior for transfer to be most effective. Perhaps a focused interview situation in which such responses were reinforced would have better served the purpose. Therapists must begin to make their therapy sessions more like the situations in which the behavior they want to change is likely to occur.

Programmed Psychotherapy

This bring us to a third therapeutic approach which has recently come into use. An article by Kanfer (1966a) suggested a name for this kind of therapy, *instigation therapy*, but it might more appropriately be called *programmed psychotherapy*. It consists essentially of setting up a program for the patient to follow, a program which involves his cooperation in providing basic information about his state and environmental conditions, in following the procedures suggested, and in bringing back news of the effects of the program. It also involves the application of a series of techniques for the purpose of instating self-regulatory behavior which can control the patient's behavior between sessions and after these sessions have ended. Finally, it proposes to train the patient in the skill of behavioral analysis, that is, in the analysis of the environmental conditions, present or potential, which influence his behavior. In the ideal case, the successful patient of programmed psychotherapy should be able to set up his own program the next time he encounters a crisis. This technique involves both the interview and its attendant problems as well as some form of operant conditioning.

Fox (1962), in his work on poor study habits, first presents an analysis of poor "study responses" as being those under poor stimulus control, i.e., neither time nor place sets the occasion for studying without also setting the occasion for other incompatible responses. Furthermore, the responses emitted by the poor student are also often inappropriate, e.g., underlining of material does not prepare the student for reciting material in the absence of the underlined material. Fox's program, therefore, consisted of having the student do all his studying of one subject in one room. He did not require the student to remain in that place for a specified time because the resultant danger of daydreaming during or toward the end of a session would have allowed him to learn to make responses incompatible with studying. Instead he used a procedure based on behavior theory. The student was required to go to the "study" room and required to leave if he found himself daydreaming. However, at the point at which he decided to leave he was required to read one page of text or do one easy problem and then leave. The act of leaving the study room for other activities was regarded as a positive reinforcer and was therefore utilized in such a way that it followed the response which was to be strengthened, in this case studying. Fox then applied a shaping procedure by requiring the student to increase the number of pages or problems to be solved before he was allowed to leave the study room. He also used the concept of approximation conditioning by applying the general procedure first to one course, then to one additional course, then to two, and so on. Following the advisor's instructions was under the reinforcement contingency of the advisor's potential withdrawal of help. The advisor monitored the extent to which the student followed the instructions as well as his success by interviewing him periodically for five to ten minutes. Using this general procedure, Fox was able to raise the grades of some five students; the smallest average change was 1 letter grade, and the highest was 4, that is, from an F average to a B average.

Programmed therapy has also been applied to the medical problem of overeating. Ferster, Nurnberger, & Levitt (1962) reported on setting up a program for the instatement of self-control of eating. These authors present a detailed report of the concepts underlying their behavioral program. First in their behavioral analysis is determination of the variables which control eating; second is determination of how these controlling variables can be manipulated; third is identification of the unwanted effects of overeating—these being the Ultimate Aversive Consequences (UACs)—which are the variables that bring the subjects in for help and maintain their determination for going through this procedure; the fourth point consists of programming the acquisition of self-control, by a procedure which employs approximation training.

Since the UACs are by definition not immediate, the first step was to make them so. This was accomplished by pairing the information (verbal responses) about the UACs with various kinds of verbal responses about eating. In other words, the first task was to establish the mention of food as a discriminative stimulus for verbal responses with aversive consequences, i.e., with responses which are also related to the UACs. (It is interesting to note here that Staats, 1967, views this kind of association as an example of respondent rather than operant conditioning.) To this end the authors established group discussions, rehearsals, frequent repetitions, even written examinations—all calculated to produce an active, readily available, well-discriminated *verbal* repertory which would set up conditioned aversive stimuli which could then be avoided or escaped from by the self-control behavior. In all the above techniques the operant verbal conditioning paradigm was used even though perhaps not stated as explicitly as it might have been. Concurrently, a program of self-control was initiated which consisted, in the main, of having the subject follow verbal instructions outside the therapy sessions. Thus the person himself was required to manipulate the occasions when he ate and the stimuli present on these occasions (such as the presence of others, books, and music); he had to modify the length of the chains leading to eating (such as shopping on a day-by-day basis); he had to produce behavior incompatible with eating; and so on. In other words, the person undergoing programmed psychotherapy must develop a verbal repertoire which will regulate the nonverbal behavior required by his program. Such a process is a further use of the verbal conditioning paradigm.

A fairly recent paper on producing self-control in patients was written by Goldiamond (1965b), who presented cases on study problems and marital problems. Here too, in a program employing the concepts of behavior theory, verbal operant conditioning was utilized in order to teach the patients the program and sometimes even some behavior theory by means of interview type of encounters.

Other psychologists have also used programmed psychotherapy. Sulzer (1965a) set up a program to eliminate alcoholic drinking and in one case reinforced the verbal report of nondrinking behavior during the interview. In a second case he dealt with a student who had difficulty in studying, poor relations with his boss and his wife, and a belief that he was an inadequate father to his child. The therapist set up a program in which he prescribed a different study environment, a different pattern of behavior toward his wife, more contact with other families like his, and a change of job. The patient's reports of his actions in following the program were approved by such verbal reinforcers as "That was wise." When the patient reported occasional discomfort with the new required behavior, the therapist put the patient on an extinction schedule, i.e., did not respond to those comments at all. Mertens (1964a, 1964b) wrote manuals for both alcoholics and their therapists about carrying out behavior programs, and finally Berlin & Wyckoff (1963), as seen in Krasner & Ullmann (1965), devised a program to improve communication in marriage.

In summary, programmed psychotherapy employs the interview technique to obtain information on the basis of which a program can be constructed, to present the program and to teach essential verbal self-control techniques, to monitor the extent to which the program was carried out, and to instate further programming when required. Relying as much as it does upon verbalization, the importance of the verbal conditioning paradigm in programmed psychotherapy appears to be as great as it is in conventional psychotherapy or in behavior therapy à la Wolpe.

Review of Some General Principles Involved in the Operant Conditioning of Verbal Behavior

Now that the ubiquity of the verbal conditioning paradigm has been shown in a number of different types of psychotherapy, it might be well to review some of the principles underlying the effective operant conditioning of verbal behavior.

The most important principle of behavior theory is the notion of reinforcement contingency, namely, that behavior is controlled by its consequences. In the past dozen years or so this fact has been extensively demonstrated for verbal behavior (see reviews by Krasner, 1958a; Salzinger, 1959b; Greenspoon, 1962; Williams, 1964; Holz & Azrin, 1966). No attempt will be made here to embark on a further review. Instead we will discuss a number of the outstanding issues in the area that have particular relevance for therapy.

Perhaps because of the great attraction which the verbal conditioning paradigm had for clinicians, many of whom lacked the requisite training in behavior theory, a number of studies in this area quickly focused on so-called cognitive variables such as "awareness," which cannot be directly observed, instead of on the observable and manipulable variables of discriminative stimuli or response-produced stimuli specified by the theory. At the same time, in a naïve attempt to "control all the relevant variables," these experimenters resorted to a multiple-choice paradigm in which the subject was reinforced for reading 1 to 2 out of 4 to 6 personal pronouns in conjunction with a verb. While such a paradigm may be useful for answering some questions, it should not be viewed as a typical operant conditioning paradigm. First, it is not a free operant situation and thus is not like the psychotherapy session to which these experimenters are trying to extrapolate. Second, it makes use of a response class consisting at the most of two members. After a subject has chosen the pronouns "I" and "we" for even a small number of trials, the task reduces itself to a memory exercise in which all he has to do to obtain reinforcement is to remember two items. He can emit one of them only once per trial so that maximum learning is achieved very rapidly and control over the response is rapidly taken over by variables other than the experimenter's reinforcement. This paradigm raises issues relevant to the problem of awareness and will be discussed below. At this point it is important to call attention to the more serious problem of responses class, a concept of moment with respect to conditioning in psychotherapy, but one which is completely ignored by the typical multiple-choice design.

A recent paper of mine (Salzinger, 1967) reviewed this problem in some detail. A response class was essentially defined as "a group of responses which have in common the fact that any one of them can be substituted for any other, according to some criterion." This criterion can be any of the following: a common effect, i.e., all the different verbal responses which have the same consequence; a common discriminative stimulus, i.e., all the verbal responses evoked by a verbal or a nonverbal stimulus; a common response, i.e., all the verbal responses which, as stimuli, evoke some particular response, e.g., a galvanic skin response or a response on the semantic differential (Osgood, Suci, & Tannenbaum, 1957); a common topography of the responses in question, e.g., ending in a common sound, having the same number of letters, fluent versus nonfluent speech; correlation to an identified response class, i.e., cooccurrence of certain responses with certain response classes like those revealed in a content analysis or in a syntactical analysis; a state of the organism, e.g., state of deprivation or private events caused by drug intake.

Knowledge of class membership of different responses is of course critical in modifying behavior, since by reinforcing some responses one can cause a desirable shift in behavior, whereas by reinforcing other responses one can condition undesirable behavior. Thus, knowing whether crying is an elicited response or one under operant control would determine how the behavior therapist would respond, i.e., whether he would comfort the child or ignore him. It is important also for the psychotherapist to know, for example, whether a patient's verbal complaint about his wife is a member of the same response class as a complaint about his boss, or, put another way, whether the variable which determines the complaint regarding his wife is the same as the one which determines the complaint regarding his boss. If the two types of complaints are members of the same response class, then the therapist need only instate verbal responses to one of these complaints, utilizing generalization to effect an amelioration of the other responses as well.

Knowledge of class membership of a patient's verbal responses is also of importance in terms of the problem of transfer from the therapist's office to the outside world. Topographical criteria for response classes are certainly the most tempting ones to be used but need not be the most critical. The therapist, very much like the experimenter, must determine class membership on an empirical basis; he must rely on grouping the verbal responses of his patient on the basis of functional, not formal, similarity. Some psychotherapists may see this as an argument for interpretation of the manifest content of the patient's verbal behavior. It is important to note here, however, that we are emphasizing the empirical validation of response classes, not how these classes are initially proposed.

Let us look at some experiments dealing with the subject of response class. The discovery that it is possible to condition verbal behavior gave rise to a number of studies whose major import was that many different classes can be conditioned and that some appear to be more resistant to conditioning than others. Wilson & Verplanck (1956) found that they could not condition adverbs because of too low an operant level. More analytic studies such as that of Estes (1945) have been rare. In that study response generalization from one class to others was such that it obscured the increase in rate of response of the class being reinforced. It may be of interest here to quote my description of this study some years ago (Salzinger, 1959b, pp. 68–69):

> Estes was able to condition the general thematic class of food words by reinforcing the word 'eat' but was unable to achieve conditioning when reinforcing all food words. Such an effect might be explained by the generalization of the word 'eat' to a thematic class of food and the generalization of other food words to responses outside the general thematic class of food. The word eat might generalize to vegetables where the experimenter reinforces the word eat; the word vegetables which would be reinforced when the experimenter reinforces all food related words, might generalize to the response plant. The former is a member of the response class of food words; the latter, however, does not belong to that class. In other words, the generalization of a representative and restricted subset of responses would aid in the increase of the general class while the generalization of all members of the general class would cause an increase in responses outside the general class. The emission of these responses would forestall an increase in the general response class reinforced by the experimenter.

If this interpretation is correct—and further research on this question is certainly called for—the therapist should be very careful in his decision of which members of a response class he will reinforce. Certainly one conclusion that can be drawn on the basis of the above discussion is that a therapist should not reinforce peripheral members of a response class. The fact that the nature of the response class in question must be considered was shown by an experiment with young children (Salzinger, S., et al., 1962) in which reinforcement of first-person pronouns produced an increase not only in that class but also in speech in general. On the other hand, an experiment in which we tried to condition the response class of plural nouns (Salzinger, Portnoy, Zlotogura, & Keisner, 1963) resulted in what appears to be an increase in a subclass marked by a particular sound, /z/.

Our investigations of the conditioning of the response class of self-referred affect (Salzinger & Pisoni, 1958, 1960, 1961; Salzinger & Portnoy, 1964; Salzinger, Portnoy, & Feldman, 1964) have shown that the reinforcement of that class first results in an increase in speech in general, then in general self-referred statements, and finally in self-referred affect statements. Further evidence for the integrity of that response class comes from an experiment (Portnoy & Salzinger, 1964) in which subjects were confronted with a choice of pairing one of three pronouns with one of three verbs (one of which was a positive affect verb, one negative, and one nonaffect). Reinforcement of either affect response class showed an increase primarily at the expense of the nonaffect class, while reinforcement of the nonaffect class reduced each of the affect classes equally, thus showing that the two different affect classes were in fact related to each other by way of response generalization to form one response class of affect.

The alert therapist can also take advantage of response class membership to produce more general changes. Salzinger, Feldman, Cowan, & Salzinger (1965) reinforced the utterance "Gimme candy" in a child who had practically no sentences at all, and found that other members of the response class to which candy belonged were also used in the sentence frame, with the result that the child began to use sentences more generally.

The relative conditionability of different response classes is another matter of interest to the therapist who uses verbal conditioning procedures. The study by Portnoy & Salzinger (1964) already mentioned showed that positive, negative, and nonaffect response classes conditioned equally well although they differed in frequency of occurrence in operant level. Further analysis showed that the response class of positive affect had the highest frequency during operant level but that, in contrast to the other two classes, it increased in frequency during the course of operant level. This suggests that certain response classes will increase by their own response-produced positive reinforcement. Ullmann, Krasner, & Gelfand (1963) found similar effects in that, as conditioned emotional words increased in frequency, the new responses which were emitted were more pleasant. In other words, all a therapist needs to do to increase certain response classes is to provide the occasion (the discriminative stimulus) for them to occur. It would be worthwhile to see whether a patient's depression could be lifted by asking him to describe happy experiences, first perhaps about others and eventually about himself. The fact that a response class which decreases in frequency of occurrence over time might have associated with it a negative reinforcement which is response-produced must also be considered by the therapist. In relation to this, Weiner (1962) manipulated such negatively reinforcing effects through the variable of response cost, where each response made costs 1 point and each positive reinforcement consists of 100 points.

The differential conditionability of verbal and nonverbal behavior was empirically tested by Salzinger, Feldman, & Portnoy (1964). As might be expected, verbal behavior was more easily conditionable. Whether the relative ease of conditionability of verbal behavior is caused by an inborn factor or is due to the greater amount of reinforcement which verbal behavior receives, is not as important here as the fact that the superior conditionability of verbal behavior could be turned to advantage by a psychotherapist. Certainly this greater conditionability of verbal behavior should be considered when programming for a patient.

Another factor related to response class is the size of the response unit. The size of any behavioral unit must be determined empirically and the point at which one response ends and another begins is not always clear. With respect to verbal behavior this problem is further aggravated since response unit size varies from one situation to another. It is important to remember that the unit, like the class of a response, is determined by functional arrangements and not by topography. For a more detailed discussion of this issue see Salzinger (1962).

At a recent meeting of the American Psychological Association Psychotherapy Conference, I (Salzinger, 1968) discussed another related phenomenon, namely, complexity of behavior. Among the sources of response complexity mentioned were response class and response unit. Of special interest here as another source is the kind of response class whose occurrence has a much greater payoff than the typical response class. Such a response class makes possible an entirely new series of responses and their concomitant positive reinforcers and elimination of negative reinforcers. Thus a child who is conditioned to emit the verbal response class whose members are, "Can I play with you?" or "Come look at my blocks!" or "Do you want to play with me?" is obviously optimizing the positive reinforcements he might get for playing with those children and minimizing the negative ones he might receive for simply intruding into a game of some other children.

The phenomenon of response incompatibility has not been made use of often enough in verbal conditioning experiments, but it obviously has a place with respect to such clinical phenomena as obsessive thinking. Conceivably, the therapist might more easily influence such thinking by reinforcing verbal responses which will compete with the undesirable responses than by trying to extinguish them.

New Developments in Behavior Theory

Among the principles which have been used very sparsely are those involved in programmed instruction. Its techniques would be quite useful in the area of verbal conditioning. The first step in any programming venture is the specification of the terminal behavior, i.e., the behavior the therapist is interested in having the patient emit at the end of therapy. Specification of this behavior must be much more detailed than is usual for psychotherapists. Statements such as "He should have a healthy personality" or "He should be able to get along with others" are grossly inadequate. Response classes and their discriminative control must be described in detail.

The next step calls for cataloging the entering behavior, i.e., current response classes and the discriminative stimuli which control their occurrence. A comparison of the entering behavior with that of the terminal behavior sets the task for the therapist. At this point he has to do a behavioral analysis of the behavior to be instated, the behavior to be eliminated, the chains of responses to be instated or eliminated, and the discriminative control to be established, increased, reduced, or eliminated.

The next step consists of planning the strategy to be followed in bringing about the requisite changes. A staple series of techniques is used here: shaping of responses, which has already been mentioned, and prompting followed by fading. Prompting procedures are used to produce responses whose operant level is close to zero. Direct instruction, leading questions, and imitation procedures, sometimes called modeling (Bandura, 1965a) and sometimes vicarious reinforcement (Kanfer, 1965b), are called for here. A modeling design for increasing the response class of self-referred affect statements was recently used. In that design, the interviewer modeled the response class to be learned by the interviewee (Wilder, 1967). Programmed instruction generally changes the prompting stimulus slowly by gradually fading it out. This is in contrast to the prompting procedures now used in psychotherapy. Like shaping, the removal of a given type of stimulus control must be accomplished gradually. What this means for the conduct of the interview is that the questions and other discriminative stimuli used by the interviewer must be slowly faded out over a number of sessions so that other stimuli, possibly response-produced ones, assume control over the desired responses.

One of the new developments in the literature on the operant conditioning of verbal behavior has been what might be termed the pseudoproblem of awareness. The issue has been reviewed by Krasner (1967), and, earlier, a symposium was devoted to it (Eriksen, 1962). Perhaps the most unfortunate aspect of the controversy is that some psychologists of the "cognitive" school of thought have drawn the unwarranted conclusion that where one finds "awareness" the operant conditioning model is inappropriate for human behavior. Considered quite differently, awareness means that at some point in the experiment the subject emits a verbal response which takes over some or all control of subsequent conditioned responses. In the case of some experiments this may be rapid, in others slow, and in still others nonexistent. The fact that a discriminative stimulus assumes control over a response class is of course not surprising; it is in fact a well-studied phenomenon in animal and in human work, with a history perhaps as long as that of learning itself.

In verbal conditioning studies the phenomenon of awareness is "revealed" by means of interviewing the subjects after they have gone through a conditioning procedure. That the process of interviewing itself may in fact produce "awareness," i.e., may condition the subject to emit "awareness responses," was stated by Spielberger (1962), who found six subjects admitting to awareness and yet could not separate them from a control group which received no reinforcement at all. It is also true that most studies which find awareness to be correlated with amount of conditioning are carried out with response classes of one or two members, with instructions so designed and types of subjects so selected as to maximize curiosity, and therefore increase the probability of verbal responses that might serve to control subsequent conditioned responses.

Before leaving this topic I might just mention one study (Dixon & Oakes, 1965) which showed, using a design common among the "awareness" psychologists, that even here one can structure the experiment to produce either a positive relation or no relation between a postconditioning interview and conditioning.

With respect to the implications for psychotherapy, the following may be said: Typically, experimental designs which call for continuous speech, such as interviews or story descriptions, do not result in verbal responses which completely control further emission of the conditioned responses. It may also be true that some response classes are more easily changed if the subject develops no such verbal responses. Such responses often take the form of "I don't want him to control me" or "Is he trying to trick me?" They have a conditioned aversive quality which can be terminated only when the patient ceases to emit the conditioned responses. On the other hand, carefully achieved verbal control over a patient's own responses, together with the therapist's reinforcement, may be an even more powerful way of modifying the patient's behavior.

Behavior theory is a changing field in which new discoveries are still being made. It is therefore important for the psychotherapist to apply the current principles of behavior theory and not those of yesteryear to his practice. An important new discovery with respect to stimulus generalization, for example, was recently made by Terrace (1966), namely, that stimulus generalization appears to be a function of the original training procedure rather than a phenomenon simply related to physical stimulus properties. The training procedures for conditioned reinforcement, which seemed completely clarified some fifteen years ago, now appear to be in a state of ferment again (Wike, 1966). These and other developments must be monitored so that the verbal conditioning procedures can be improved as new knowledge is acquired.

On the Future of Verbal Conditioning

When Krasner (1962a) delivered a paper entitled "The Therapist as a Social Reinforcement Machine," much of the subsequent discussion was an attempt to refute completely the applicability of the verbal conditioning model to psychotherapy. Such claims were made as that the changes in operant conditioning are not deep, lasting, or extensive; that the changes occur in people who want to change; that "change in psychotherapy is mediated quite differently"

(Luborsky & Strupp, 1962); and even that the definition of reinforcement is too general and that it is not clear what is being reinforced. Answers to these criticisms are available in the foregoing discussion. Furthermore, the presence of reinforcement and its effect in actual non-behavior-theory-oriented therapy sessions has been made manifest. In some studies, such as that by Murray (1956), objective content analysis revealed a clear relationship between frequency of occurrence of "approval" and "disapproval" in conjunction with the categories these reinforcers followed. In another content analysis of psychotherapy, Truax (1966, p. 7) argued that, having found the presence of reinforcers in Carl Rogers' own therapy sessions, "the finding that empathy and warmth act as reinforcers suggests that the evidence relating empathy and warmth to patient outcome is open to a behavioristic interpretation, based in part on the therapist's use of differential reinforcement."

We have come a long way. Not only have psychologists developed new techniques of psychotherapy on the basis of behavior theory, but even conventional psychotherapy appears to have included, unbeknownst to the therapist, differential reinforcement. As Moliere's character discovered that he had been speaking prose all his life, so the conventional psychotherapist has discovered that he has always used reinforcement on his patients.

Chapter Summary

An attempt was made to describe the place of operant conditioning of verbal behavior in three different types of psychotherapy: conventional psychotherapy, behavior therapy (therapy based on classical conditioning), and programmed psychotherapy (therapy based on operant conditioning). It was pointed out that none of the three types of therapy makes sufficient, explicit use of verbal conditioning data and techniques. A number of specific suggestions for the application of verbal conditioning to therapeutic procedures were presented.

With regard to conventional psychotherapy, I traced the historical relationship between therapy and behavior theory, pointing out that only when the relationship's independent usefulness was established was the field of psychotherapy ready to profit from it. The danger and futility of disregarding reinforcement of any verbal interaction were underscored by showing that it is an integral part of any such interaction. It was also shown that the lack of success of conventional psychotherapy, along with the inappropriateness of the typical psychodynamic descriptions of the interview, make the need for behavior theory even more urgent.

In the discussion of behavior therapy (classical type), I again brought out the importance of verbal behavior, showing that the verbal conditioning paradigm was an integral part of Wolpe's desensitization procedure. The similarity of the desensitization procedure to an operant shaping procedure was argued. Finally, the idea of combining the operant and respondent types of conditioning in psychotherapy was put forth as a potentially useful procedure.

Programmed psychotherapy, which is the youngest of the three types of therapy and is stimulated by behavior theorists' recent success in the field of programmed instruction, makes use of verbal conditioning in two ways: first, by giving the individual a general knowledge of behavior theory and by training him to follow his own program; second, by conditioning particular kinds of behavior directly by the therapist.

The last part of this chapter reviewed some of the general principles involved in the operant conditioning of verbal behavior and recent developments in behavior theory. The importance of the concept of response class was made evident both in the experimental literature and in the therapy session. Also discussed were the concepts of response unit and awareness (a concept better described in terms of response-produced stimuli than in cognitive language), prompting and fading, and terminal and entering behavior in programmed learning. Their significance, actual and potential, was discussed.

The future of verbal conditioning in psychotherapy depends upon the recognition of its value by the clinician. Psychotherapy has much to gain from the methodical application of the results and techniques of the operant conditioning of verbal behavior.

11

An Appraisal of Teaching Machines and Programmed Instruction with Special Reference to the Modification of Deviant Behavior

EARL C. BROWN
LUCIANO L'ABATE
Georgia State College, Atlanta, Georgia

Introduction

It is the purpose of this chapter to review recent advances in the application of programmed instruction and teaching machines to the process of rehabilitation of deviants or individuals and children who for reasons of physical or psychological disability, or both, cannot be considered normal. Of necessity, the focus of this chapter is embedded within the context of programmed instruction at large, selectively and representatively. No effort has been made to review the whole field of programmed instruction and teaching machines, a task which is beyond the scope of this chapter. The reader will be referred to the pertinent literature whenever it is appropriate.

Like any new field, programmed instruction has engendered a rash of neologisms, many of which are more persuasive than correct. Essentially, a program is a method of instruction and a teaching machine is a device which may or may not be required by the method. The various forms of programmed instruction have these features in common:

1. They engage the attention of a single student and require his attendance to a small amount of information at one time.

2. They require the student to commit himself by making a response to each segment of information before him.

3. The program produces an immediate feedback of results for each response which the student makes.

4. The program permits each student to progress at his own pace.

Some of the advantages of programmed instruction are obvious; for example, the student is relieved of his dependence upon a teacher and a classroom group. In addition, he has an immediate knowledge of the accuracy of his responses; therefore, he does not perpetuate his errors and compound his difficulties in later attempts to learn. Other advantages of programmed instruction are subject to research findings; for example, it is now accepted that programmed instruction is more effective than conventional classroom procedures. This advantage inheres primarily in rate of progress through a given body of information and not in greater mastery of that information. There are other potential advantages of programmed instruction which have yet to be demonstrated, such as the accentuation of individual differences in such attributes as creativity.

Remediation, defined as the removal of specific educational deficiencies, and rehabilitation, defined as education for fuller living, are broadly indicated in our society but narrowly conceived in their execution. Rehabilitation partakes of the general educational process and will benefit from any advances therein. Certainly, the needs of education and rehabilitation for a sounder theory of instruction and for an effective instructional methodology overlap. Rehabilitation does not possess the resources to undertake the development of such a theory and method; thus, rehabilitation is restrained to awaiting "fall-out" from general educational developments.

The central problem in programmed instruction continues to be one of motivation. Given the best program for a particular pupil, his motivation to complete the program remains uncertain. These uncertainties are, of course, compounded in pupils who are the targets of rehabilitation efforts. It would be advantageous if the appreciation of knowledge were widespread. Unfortunately, knowledge per se cannot be assumed to be a significant reinforcer for a large number of people. In certain individuals and contexts, knowledge may be valued for its personally enhancing properties. This personal enhancement holds true only in those social contexts where "being in the know" is prized. For the remainder of the pupil population, it is probable that appeal will have to be made to some ulterior purpose, involving practical applications and consequent benefits. Thus, the instructor must make the connection between the successful completion of the program and some more distant goal. The pupils' attention must then be focused upon the uses of knowledge, personally and interpersonally, educationally and vocationally. This appeal invokes subscription to middle-class ideals, such as delay of immediate gratification for the achievement of later success. Needless to say, subscription to these ideals is frequently lacking in groups which are the targets of rehabilitative enterprises. In sum, the most difficult task of the teacher might be that of establishing the associative bond between the programmed instruction material and the daily life interests and enthusiasms of the pupil.

It is conceivable that the prime benefit of programmed instruction for rehabilitation will be to the instructor rather than to the learner. Careful attention to the demands of the technique may educate the instructor in the nature of the "bits" of information which are appropriate for his population, the number of such bits which can be handled at one time, and the optimal rate of progress through a sequence of bits. Thus far, relatively little attention has been paid to the role of teaching machines and programmed instruction in rehabilitation (Morrill, 1961). Most programming efforts have been directed at the normal, school-age population. It is probable that many of these same programs will apply to rehabilitation populations. Transposition cannot be assumed. Rehabilitation populations, in which intellectual deficit or behavior disorders occur, will at least take a longer time to complete standard programs and may require further refinements of customary steps in the program.

A number of standard works are now available for the newcomer who wishes to familiarize himself with programmed instruction. Deterline (1962) and Taber, Glaser, & Schafer (1965) wrote texts which follow the Skinnerian model. Smith & Moore (1962) compiled a book of readings. Several sets of standards for the evaluation of teaching machines and programmed instruction have been developed (National Education Association, 1964; Jacobs, Maier, & Stolurow, 1966). These criteria of evaluation have been summarized by Lane & Geis (1965). Porter (1967) published a review of the literature dealing with some of the early devices which have been suggested as adjuncts to the teaching process. More recent surveys are to be found in Hansen (1963), Hendershot (1964), Lumsdaine (1961), Lumsdaine & Glazer (1960), Morrill (1961), and Pipe (1966).

Present Status

METHODS

Methodology radiates from the basic technique devised by Skinner (1961) which rests upon the principle of reinforcement. Gilbert (1962) elaborated on the sequence of response "chaining." This method may be described as fixed or extrinsically programmed in a straight-line or linear fashion, with prescribed sequential steps in which the only variable is one of speed or progress through the program. A modification of Skinner's technique has been developed by Crowder (1958) under the name of intrinsic programming or "branching." This procedure has a marked advantage for rehabilitation in that it allows for different sequences, depending upon the individual's response. Thus, while all subjects may start at a common point, the sequence is determined by the responses which a particular subject makes. If a subject makes a deviant response, he is "shunted" to a remedial sequence and then back to the regular sequence. Thus Crowder's program is tailored to the student, with identification of his errors and provision for self-correction. Remediation may be accomplished by retracing steps through that portion of the original program which errors indicate that the student did not learn adequately the first time, or it may include branching into new information not included on the original program. The difference between Skinner and Crowder is more profound than might appear from the foregoing. A discussion of the difference in philosophy of teaching between Skinner and Crowder is to be found in Reigne & Fry (1961). Research has not shown a clear difference in acquisition between the linear and the branching methods.

A second modification of Skinner's method was pioneered by Berlin & Wyckoff (1963) in their development of the General Relationships Improvement Program, which was designed to be used by two people. A third modification, which might better be described as an outgrowth, is to be found in the work of Moore (1965, 1966) with responsive environments and in the work of Coulson (1962; Dick, 1965) with computer-based instruction.

MACHINERY

Perhaps the simplest device used in programmed instruction is a single mimeographed sheet which is "unveiled" by another, blank sheet. Next in complicatedness are programmed workbooks and textbooks. Next are the various items of hardware which contain within them programmed materials mounted on a movable scroll or disc. Next are simple electronic devices, such as Wyckoff's "typewriter," and more elaborate visual display devices, such as the Autotutor manufactured by Rheem-Califone of U. S. Industries. Next are the devices that make provision for both auditory and visual display, such as the foreign language machine which was under development by the Psychological Corporation. Highest on the list are the sort of devices developed by Moore (1965, 1966). No doubt, the ultimate will be found in some classroom or laboratory console, acting as an electronic outpost of a much larger computer facility, containing immediate answers to whatever questions the student is prepared to formulate (Birnbrauer, Bijou, Wolf, & Kidder, 1965).

APPLICATIONS OF PROGRAMMED INSTRUCTION
TO THE MODIFICATION OF NORMAL BEHAVIOR

With the advent of the General Relationships Improvement Program (Human Development Institute, 1963), programmed instruction progressed from the status of an adjunct of behavioral modification to the status of behavioral modification proper. The creators of the Program, Berlin & Wyckoff (1963,

1964), melded the proven efficiency of the operant conditioning method with the necessary conditions for personal growth of client-centered counseling.

The dyadic teaching program involves two people in interaction with the program and with each other. They sit side by side and take turns reading aloud from the program. As instructed by the program, they may answer questions, discuss items, and go through a series of specific interpersonal exercises. The program is arranged in ten sessions requiring about one hour each. Experience has demonstrated an optimal spacing of one week between sessions. Testing during the developmental phases of these programs was conducted with groups from schools, industries, social, and civic organizations. Early results yielded highly optimistic expectations. Several lines of evidence indicated that use of the programs resulted in an increased ability for more meaningful and enhancing relationships. Subsequent studies yielded statistical support, generally confirming the favorable effects for college students, industrial supervisors, and inpatients in a VA hospital.

Brown & Campbell (1966) conducted an evaluation of the Program using matched groups of students, one of which completed the Program while the other completed a psychology of adjustment course. Both groups were administered personality tests on a pre, post, and follow-up schedule extending over a period of four months. This constituted a fairly severe test of the Program, since the students in the psychology of adjustment course received much the same information in the classroom. Intergroup comparisons revealed pretreatment to follow-up changes in the experimental group which were consistent with improved interpersonal relationships. More particularly, there were favorable changes, significant in degree, on five scales of the MMPI, namely, F, Hs, Hy, Sc, and Es. Subjective reports of students completing the Program lent strong positive support to this finding. It appeared that the Program had some effect in producing measurable and durable personality changes which might be expected to generalize to improvements in interpersonal relationships. It is noteworthy that this effect was more marked at follow-up (three months after posttesting) than at posttesting. This finding suggests that some time must be allowed for the effects of the Program to be assimilated before they will become fully manifest.

In a pilot study, Hough (undated) used the Program with preservice teachers. Subjects were 230 students enrolled in ten sections of an introductory course on the teaching-learning process. Seven of these sections were used for the experiment, and three were reserved for control purposes. Rokeach's Dogmatism Scale was administered on pretest, and the Barrett-Leonard Relationship Inventory was used for ratings by partners on pretest and posttest. In 30 to 40 analyses, the groups using the Program made significant positive changes in their human relation skills.

Hough began to state some of the differentiations which will be required before the Program can be prescribed with any degree of confidence. He found that not all of his subjects profited equally. In terms of dogmatism scores, those falling in the middle third seemed to benefit the most while those falling in the highest third, i.e., the most dogmatic, benefited the least.

Granting that the Program augurs well for the inculcation of attitudes and behaviors which make for growth-producing relationships with people, and granting, further, that many rehabilitation populations are in need of such relationships, still the question remains of the applicability of the Program to these populations. There is, of course, the initial requirement which applies to all programmed instruction: the necessity for the subject to be capable of attending, reading, comprehending, and retaining the information. Beyond this requirement is the question of solitary versus joint pursuit of the Program. Conceivably, there are individuals for whom solitary pursuit is to be preferred and others for whom a partnership is to be preferred. Only two applications of the Program to rehabilitation populations are noted in the literature. The first has to do with the Draper Project and the second has to do with a group of inpatients in a VA neuropsychiatry hospital. Campbell compared the completion of the Program with group therapy meetings and a control group in an inpatient setting. Using MMPI blind ratings, the Program group showed higher degrees of improvement when compared with the other groups. Although the results are statistically significant, it should be noted that the sample was small and replication is indicated (cited in Berlin & Wycoff, 1964).

A study was conducted in a public school over a four-month period with 12 junior high school students (McKee, 1963b). These students were selected on the basis of (1) their failing one or more subjects, though of average intelligence, and (2) their exhibiting patterns of deviant behavior which were judged to be stable, capable of modification, and important in the adjustment of the student to school life. Preexperimental and postexperimental ratings and evaluations of students were obtained from teachers; preexperimental and postexperimental academic test measures were obtained; and before and after grades on each student were compared. The experimental condition consisted of a daily fifty-five-minute period in self-instruction for three months, using programmed texts in English, grammar, and math. Results show that 9 of the 12 students were evaluated "improved" on a majority of the "tailored" behaviors selected as criterion measures.

APPLICATIONS OF PROGRAMMED INSTRUCTION
TO THE MODIFICATION OF DEVIANT BEHAVIOR

The best example of a large-scale, long-range evaluation of programmed instruction in a rehabilitative setting is to be found in the Programed Learning Project at Draper Correctional Center, Elmore, Alabama, under the direction of McKee (McKee, 1963a; McKee & Zachert, 1966). This project had the good fortune to have a competent and enterprising director, a variety of able consultants (Gilbert, Slack, and Zachert), a facilitative prison administration, a sharply circumscribed setting in which total control was possible, and a likely target population; namely, inmates who were, on the average, young socio-pathic offenders with a short length of stay. In general, this project sought to discover the best uses of programmed instruction in a self-instructional school in a prison setting. The clearly stated general objective was to reduce the rate of recidivism, which tends to run about 65 percent in this population. An inter-mediate objective was to rehabilitate inmates to enable them to maintain a more succesful adjustment to society. Immediate objectives were to raise the general academic level of the inmates, assist them to obtain vocational skills (as in the electrician's craft), and assist them to develop more functional and socially acceptable attitudes and behaviors. Thus, while the approach was global, the steps were discrete and denotatively realizable.

The procedure began with assessments or "diagnoses." The trend was toward increasing refinement of specification of deficit. From this assessment followed a "prescription," i.e., an assignment of programmed learning. Subse-quent testing was utilized to evaluate progress. Throughout this procedure, the technique of programmed instruction was adapted to the needs of individual inmates.

In the third year of programmed instruction, about 10 percent of an inmate population of 600 was enrolled in the project. A total of 212 inmates had participated in the program as of January, 1964. These participants had an average age of twenty and an average length of participation of 101 days. Over 120 programs, mostly in elementary and secondary education, were avail-able to participants. Over 700 self-instruction courses were completed. Achieve-ment test scores increased an average of 1.7 grades from 8.3 to 10.0. McKee commented that, "Success on parole has been the mark of the program. . . ." Of the 212 participants, 175 have been released from the Center. Of these, only 9 are known to have been recommitted. This constitutes a short-term recidivism rate of 5 percent, a highly significant reduction (McKee & Zachert, 1966). Some indication of the encouragement received by the staff is apparent in its willingness to accept "hard-core learning-problem students" as its next step.

In other areas, programmed instruction has been applied to the voca-tional counseling process (Cahoon & Watson, 1966), to aphasics (Filby & Edwards, 1963; Taylor & Sands, 1966), to senior citizens (Gedye & Wedge-wood, 1966), and to the deaf (Stuckless & Birch, 1964). Palmer (1964) has even developed a program for psychotherapy training.

PROGRAMMED INSTRUCTION AND EXCEPTIONAL CHILDREN

In considering the use of programmed instruction and teaching machines for emotionally disturbed children, the following factors must be considered:

(1) They may relieve the child of interpersonal anxiety and resistance. (2) They qualify instructions step by step, which is a general advantage of any programmed machine regardless of whether it is for normal or deviant children. (3) They benefit some children more than others, but we do not yet know why. We need to break this down in terms of sex, social class, intelligence level, and other more detailed aspects of personality.

A study by McNeill, cited in Schramm's (1964) annotated bibliography, indicated that first-graders evidenced profound sex differences in two different types of learning. Boys learned significantly better than girls under programmed instruction in word recognition. The girls did significantly better than the boys under female teachers in the classroom. Rothkopf, also cited in Schramm, had 12 high school teachers and principals, who had just experienced a summer seminar in programmed instruction, predict the relative effectiveness of four different pretested programs. The rank-order correlation between empirically determined effectiveness and the predictions of the Ss was —.75. This negative correlation suggests that the criteria of selection for programmed instruction cannot be left in the hands of professionally unprepared people. These criteria have been spelled out by Jacobs et al. (1966) in a simple booklet which sets up procedures for selecting a program and for seeing that everyone who uses the program also evaluates it. This booklet has much to recommend it, as does the recent booklet by Pipe (1966) on practical programming in which most of the highly technical problems of construction are worked out in simple language and with fairly clear details.

Eldred and his coworkers at Vermont State Hospital (Chittick et al., 1965) used programmed instruction with disturbed children. Originally, the main purpose of this research was to study the effectiveness of programmed instruction in the academic, therapeutic, and social progress of children and adolescents in a state mental hospital school. Later on, the study was extended to include slow learners and underachievers in a public high school and in a parochial high school, and emotionally disturbed children in a private residential institution. Since this was a pioneer effort, the reactions of the teachers to this kind of instruction were also made part of the study. One of the major initial problems was the selection of special programs of instruction to fit the needs of the individual student. Later on, the authors commented on the difficulty of obtaining test data which would show statistically different results between the control groups, which used conventional teaching materials, and the experimental groups, which used programmed materials. Although the results could not be put in any kind of meaningful group form, seven of the 26 students using programmed instruction in the lower section of the freshman classes in the two high schools showed a year or more improvement in their grade level in basic skills. Of these 26 students, 14 showed a year or more improvement in their grade-level placement on the verbal part of the Lorge-Thorndike Intelligence Test. The most significant part of this study was the enthusiasm of the teachers in the school at Vermont State Hospital. They felt that there was no question that programmed instruction, properly used with the students suited for it, had many advantages. This attitude was shared by the public school teachers as they gained additional experience in using programmed aids for personalized education. Initially, however, the ignorance or the attitudes of the teachers toward using programmed instruction produced a great many problems of selection and control in the evaluation of progress.

On the basis of their experience, the authors felt strongly that there was a need to avoid a steady diet of programmed instruction. This conclusion is especially valid in instances of students becoming bored when programmed instruction was given uninterruptedly and of teachers not providing a break by turning to some other task. In some instances, they learned, unfortunately too late, that the teacher had assumed that variety and flexibility were not permitted. These authors concluded, therefore, that programmed aids may not be the best medium of instruction for all students. It is still necessary to ascertain which students benefit from programmed instruction and which are helped more by more conventional materials. Even though some students in this study made significant improvement by using programmed instruction, other students made equally great improvement by using conventional media of instruction. Although their efforts were directed at finding some method of predicting which method of instruction is best for any given student, they admitted failure in this regard. They felt, however, that it should be possible to predict which students would profit by beginning programmed instruction in the elementary grades and which would be helped more if programmed instruction were postponed until high school. Even though many programmed materials are available, too many of them are not suitable for a state hospital setting.

Another major problem was that the reading disability found in many students made it difficult to find any suitable instructional materials, programmed or not programmed. Chittick, Eldred, & Brooks (1965) became increasingly aware of the number of approaches to the solution of reading difficulties which seem to assume that all or most reading disabilities stem from one cause and can be remedied by the one method advocated by this or that authority. However, an understanding of the multidimensional and multidetermined aspects of reading disability led them to believe that the remedy lies in various combinations of approaches. They concluded that it is possible to develop a body of tasks which would permit the grouping of readers and of nonreaders into a number of subgroups. They cited an example of the problem area which hampered the results obtained even by programmed instruction as being deficiencies of motor and visual perception and auditory discrimination which they find exist unsuspected in many of the students in whom failure was encountered. They felt that personalizing education to the use of programmed instruction or of any other medium of instruction will be distinctly hampered until perceptual difficulties have been recognized, eliminated, or at least decreased by remedial methods available or to be developed. They indicated the necessity of wideband assessment procedures, which should, in the long run, be the most economical step to take before undertaking any kind of rehabilitative effort, including programmed instruction.

Another finding of this study is that not all teachers are suited to use programmed instruction. The teacher who expects programmed instruction to do most of his work for him, to liberate him from lesson plans and the need to cultivate the students' ability to interrelate knowledge and theory, will have poor results from the use of programmed instruction. The teacher who is master of his subject matter and who feels that he must dominate his classroom with his fund of knowledge will also achieve disappointing results from using programmed instruction. The teacher who uses programmed instruction successfully with certain students is the flexible, ingenious, and inquisitive pioneer who likes to experiment. He knows each of his students, and he is cognizantly seeking ways to individualize instruction effectively. He must be a teacher who thinks of programmed instruction as an aid which relieves him of the necessity of being a drillmaster and frees him to be a troubleshooter and a real teacher. Some of these problems have been studied by Ripple, O'Reilly, Wightman, & Dacey (1966).

Malpass, Hardy, Gilmore, & Williams (1964) used programmed instruction with retarded children. The concluded that: (1) Automated instruction procedures seemed effective for helping retarded children acquire word recognition, spelling, and reading skills. (2) Procedures involving the use of multiple-choice, typewriter-keyboard, and completion-type machines seemed more effective than conventional classroom instruction, at least within the limitations imposed by the study. Programmed instruction procedures, however, produce higher levels of retention and word recognition in spelling than did conventional classroom instruction. The significantly higher number of words "retained under automated instructions versus comparable time spent in conventional EMR classroom instruction demands serious consideration of the former over the latter procedures for the purposes described."

The two methods, multiple choice and keyboard, did not seem to be significantly different from each other. Although some individual differences were found among retarded children in terms of who will favor which method, they felt "that control over presentation and response conditions, economy in purchase and maintenance of equipment, and ease in administration of programmed instructional materials are considerations which might lead to preference of one procedure over the other." Kunkel (1961), Blackman & Capobianco (1965), and Price (1963) have also applied programmed instruction to mentally retarded adolescents.

The best and most well-known program of automation for vocational training of mentally retarded and mentally ill adolescents is the one reported by the Devereux Foundation in Devon, Pennsylvania (1964). This program seems akin to the one by McKee (1963a) in Alabama in terms of teaching an adolescent with an IQ range between 60 and 90 very simple skills which will help in his vocational training. This program consists of various steps on the basis of a review and an evaluation of previous functioning in all areas. Step 1 consists of an exploratory program of academic and vocational subjects, therapy, social adjustments, and guidance. Step 2 consists of specialized vocational training, occupational information, vocational evaluation of clinic, and counseling therapy (which is unspecified and presumed to include individual and group therapy). Step 3 consists of specific job training, therapy, vocational counseling, and part-time employment. Step 4 consists of full-time employment in Devereux and maintaining oneself there with proper use of free time. Step 5 consists of employment and self-maintenance in the community, along with intensive vocational counseling, and the final goal is "independent living, productive and satisfying functioning in the home community." A good deal can be said for this kind of program in terms of its clarity of goals and its evaluation procedures.

The autotelic responsive environments designed by Moore (1965, 1966) have received a great deal of attention. Moore described a responsive environment as one which satisfies the following conditions: (1) It permits the learner to explore freely. (2) It informs the learner immediately about the consequences of his actions. (3) It is self-pacing, i.e., events happen within the environment at a rate determined by the learner. (4) It permits the learner to make full use of his capacities for discovering relations of various kinds. (5) Its structure is such that the learner is likely to make a series of interconnected discoveries about the physical, cultural, or social world. *Autotelic,* as defined by Moore, refers to an activity that occurs for its own sake rather than for the sake of obtaining rewards or avoiding punishment that has no inherent connection with the activity itself. Moore's laboratory was designed in accord with objectives that would be conducive to carrying out autotelic activities in young children. Laboratories should be simple, and distinct and separate: simple in the sense that the gameboard or the playing field is devoid of irrelevancies, distinct and separate in the sense that the grandstand has barriers between participants and spectators. The basic component of the laboratory is the booth in which the child is seated in front of a typewriter with colored keys. Behind the keyboard of this typewriter, there is a Lucite housing which permits him to see everything in front of him but which keeps his fingers out of the moving parts of the typewriter. Through the typewriter he controls a computer input and memory device with three distinct systems, an audio-recording system and two visual exhibition systems. All these are integrated by a central electronic control system. The child's behavior in front of the typewriter is divided into different phases to teach him to read and write.

The last part of Moore's report consists of case studies of children in their responsive environments with an example of a journal printed by children in this particular setting. What is most lacking in this kind of study is a base-line evaluation of a child's assets and liabilities, IQ levels, verbal, visuomotor, and other aspects which will be considered in greater detail in Chapter 14.

Fitzhugh (Allied Educational Council, 1966) developed programmed materials in individual booklet form to use for early language and perceptual training with children. The level of this material appears to be usable right after a gross group program of perceptual training developed by Frostig & Horne (1964). Brinkmann (1966) has also produced a technique to improve spatial visualization. Stuckless & Birch (1964) have worked on a programmed instruction written language for the deaf.

Abraham (1966) reviewed the role of programmed instruction with exceptional children. The crucial questions in this regard are: Who are they? How many are there? What do we do about them? Here are included the mentally retarded; the visually, verbally, and auditorily handicapped; the emotionally disturbed; the orthopedic, crippled, and multiply handicapped; and the gifted. To these groups, add the culturally and socially deprived, the borderline impaired, the medical and neurologically sick, and the pseudoretarded. Abraham criticized psychologists, who, with their psychiatric and emotional orientation toward nonschool problems, have attempted to assume leadership positions with a minimal knowledge of and preparation for the needs of children. He warned about "the false assumptions that a program developed for so-called 'typical' children will work for exceptional children, disadvantaged populations, drop-outs, delinquents and others." He suggested that these programs should be developed for and tested on the populations toward which they are aimed. This point is an important one because in years to come we may try to adopt, without adapting, programs for normal individuals for use with the abnormal. As Abraham concluded, "There is a shortage of sound programs and especially for the exceptional." To speak of specialized manpower to administer these programs, however, in the future we envisage the training of specialists in programmed instruction with M.A. and even Ph.D. degrees.

One of the major advantages of programmed instruction for the amelioration of behavior disorders, especially in children, is that programmed instruction and teaching machines may relieve interpersonal anxiety and reinforce the child's self-concept. In dealing with neurotic children, for instance, programmed instruction may have the potential to reduce anxiety attendant upon interpersonal confrontation. In the case of acting-out children, hostile overreactions to teachers as substitute authority figures may also be reduced. The clear step-by-step aspect of programmed instruction would decrease the interfering effects of anxiety or hostility with the introduction of success rather than failure, making for an improvement in the learning process. However, individual differences in children and programs cannot be ignored and we must be ready to expect that some children will learn more than others, and that some children may not even learn because of the inappropriateness of the program.

On the other side of the coin, two major dangers loom in the application of programmed instruction to emotionally disturbed children (and even to adults). First, programmed instruction and teaching machines may increase the withdrawal from interpersonal contact. In other words, a child may learn to respond to a machine, but if he is autistic he may remain autistic. It is clear, therefore, that programmed instruction cannot be conceived of as an universal therapeutic tool. Although reports may reach Sunday supplements (Pines, 1965), more rigorous evidence and less sensationalism will be necessary to assess programmed instruction not only as a propaedeutic but also as a therapeutic tool. The argument that once the behavior is brought under control it can be programmed is an old cliché of programmed instruction as well as of behavioral modifiers. However, behavior modification involves many tailor-made, individualized techniques besides programmed instruction, since programmed instruction by definition is mass-produced for groups and not for individuals (Broudy, 1962). Programming a child for interpersonal contact is easier said than done. Thus far, there is no evidence that a patient's withdrawing tendencies can be improved through programmed instruction. In fact, the real test of programmed instruction in the amelioration of deviant behavior will rest in its use with schizophrenic patients or autistic children.

The second danger of programmed instruction lies in its being misplaced, applying the wrong program to the wrong individual. This issue is especially crucial with children. A child whose major input channel is vision because of functional or organic deafness will not learn by listening to records. If we consider both input and output channels to assess what the child receives and expresses, the problem becomes even more complicated. We need to ask not only about the best input channel, but also about the output channel through which the child can best express himself and communicate what he has acquired. Various combinations of input-output programs may be necessary in order to answer this question. Solution of these problems will require time and a great deal of information that is not presently available.

The Needs of Programmed Instruction

It is obvious that any 100 percent reinforcement schedule is comparable or equivalent to total reinforcement. Such a schedule does not necessarily increase response strength. On the contrary, it may lower response strength, in contrast to irregular or intermittent reinforcement schedules. It follows that programmed instruction cannot be conceived of as a unique and sole form of teaching. A steady diet of programmed instruction may conceivably lower response strength. Satiation may eventually result in complete rejection and refusal to deal with this type of learning. A child who is being consistently reinforced may become tired and bored by the process. Especially very bright or creative children may resent following what appear as mechanical restraints to their inquisitiveness and curious exploration. Increased dependence on this type of program may result even in a denial of dependence and in a proclamation of independence, i.e., refusal to rely on a machine. Consequently, multiple schedules of learning and programmed instruction will be necessary. If reward "feels" or "looks" better in comparison with or in contrast to previous punishment, a variety of programs will or should allow for a combination of successes and failures, frustrations and stresses that will more closely approximate real-life situations. Thus, the 100 percent positive reinforcement schedule implied by programmed instruction is unrealistic. It does not take into consideration variety and diversity in schedules, the importance of nonreinforcement factors, and the differential effects of contrasting schedules of rewards and punishments. A completely programmed course would be rigid. Flexibility in programmed instruction should closely conform to individual differences and external environmental factors. Within this context, there are at least two additional desiderata of programmed instruction that merit consideration.

Programmed instruction should be selective; that is, not all individuals can or do benefit from programmed instruction. Maximal benefit will depend on the types of programs matching various combinations of sense modalities, especially in children. Thus, the problem of who profits by which program and why requires complete preprogram evaluation. Our ignorance of the degree of specificity in this regard is only part of our overall ignorance of problems of rehabilitation in general. If we establish agreed-upon criteria and standards for continuous ongoing evaluation of patient-program matching on a pre-post follow-up longitudinal perspective, our chances of arriving eventually at a successful matching would be enhanced. Only through this matching, we submit, shall we be able to solve specific problems of programmed instruction and general issues within the wider background of rehabilitation.

Programmed instruction should be controlled: the fact that we cannot set up limits to programmed instruction is an indication of limitations in our knowledge. We should be able to set up these control criteria as a basis for reaching a knowledge of limits and specificity of application. Without the controls suggested by the National Society for Programmed Instruction (Jacobs, Maier, & Stolurow, 1966), our chances of accumulating hard, replicable data are minimal and programmed instruction is relegated to the level of magic and professionalism akin to the practice of psychotherapy. The need for intersubjective criteria and standards that can be replicated and checked by various members of the scientific community is paramount in programmed instruction procedures, lest programmed instruction lose its chance of contributing significantly to human welfare.

Critics of programmed instruction (Epperson & Schmuck, 1962; Macchia, 1962; Cohen, 1962; Wholwill, 1962) are concerned with the emphasis on programs to the near exclusion of everything else. This tendency is true in any activity in which somebody becomes overwhelmed by a missionary zeal to propagate his method above all others, as in the early days of psychotherapy. There are motivational factors which programmers have so far not considered to their full extent. The claims of major developers of programmed instruction, those involved in marketing commercial materials, are slanted to represent to the potential buyers that no interpersonal variables are involved in the process of programmed learning worthy of consideration. Silberman (1966) paraphrased them as saying, "Pupils become so absorbed in their step-by-step progression that social variables are irrelevant." Such a generalization can only provoke skepticism, disbelief, and criticism.

Hammock (1964) criticized most of the principles of learning applied to teaching machines and programmed instruction, showing that most of the research in this area was defective in the small number of cases and in the short time span at follow-up. The most important aspect of programmed instruction, as Hammock saw it, is individual pacing. From this viewpoint, a book can do as well as a machine. However, machines allow a more explicit clarification of criteria (testability, reproducibility, and economy) and of variables than books. Machines are more dependable and more reliable. Although the machines can be constant, the program going into it is reproducible and continuously improvable. In conclusion, Hammock also felt that in terms of individual differences, linear programs may be more appropriate for slow learners, while Crowder-type programs may be more appropriate for fast learners.

The Future—Refinements and Evaluations

An approach of relevance to populations which are the target of rehabilitation efforts would be the following: the formation of a team of specialists made up of a subject matter expert, a programming expert, and an expert at teaching the population involved. These three would agree on the content to be programmed. Preparation would be in the hands of the programmer with review by the subject-matter expert and the teacher. Testing would be in the hands of the teacher and revision in the hands of the subject-matter specialist and the programmer. The emphasis in this approach would be upon the evaluation, with close attention to achievement of preformulated criteria.

To prognosticate, the use of teaching machines and programmed instruction in rehabilitation will depend upon the outcome of advances in the much larger realm of education proper. The largest single advance of relevance for rehabilitation lies in the individualization of the instructional process. Programs will have to make greater allowances for individual differences than the linear model, in which speed is the only variable dimension. Those relatively complex and expensive teaching machines which employ electronic computers and cybernetic mechanisms seem to offer the best promise for the attainment of individualized instruction. The day is probably past when a single investigator can make a significant contribution to the technological revolution which is taking place. We are now at a point where a "stable" of specialists, drawn from many disciplines, is required. The support and equipage of such a group now exceeds the resources of any single institution or agency. Advances now rest upon a coalition of behavioral scientists, engineers, and educators, supported by academic institutions, government agencies, and industry. It is likely that a systems development approach, similar to that developed for the U.S. Department of Defense, will bear fruit.

Two barriers loom large: the first is language, since computers do not speak English; the second is cost, since even the simplest computerized devices run into thousands of dollars. Moore (1965, 1966) indicated some ways around the language barrier. Industry has proved itself capable of reducing cost per unit through higher production. Thus, with the combined and vast resources of the universities, government, and industry, it is probable that these barriers will yield to such a massive onslaught. We may yet see the day when a rehabilitation facility contains a central computer with on-line remote consoles and time sharing to permit computer-assisted instruction in a variety of highly individualized settings (Silberman, 1966).

There is general acknowledgment of the need for educational reform. Paradoxically, the professional educators have been most opposed to avenues of reform such as programmed instruction. Nevertheless, it is becoming obvious that programmed instruction is the only precise system known today of proved capability for bringing about educational change. Early experience with teaching machines and programmed instruction leads to a series of conclusions: (1) More effort must be devoted to the elucidation of psychological structures and processes, especially as regards the phenomenon of learning (Hilgard & Bower, 1966; Spence, 1959). (2) Efforts must be made to develop a theory of instruction which has efficient consequences in the learning process (Pressey, 1965). (3) Programmed instruction must extend beyond the primitive linear model and the somewhat more advanced branching model to include much greater student involvement in the instructional process. This extension would involve: (*a*) more sense modalities than vision; (*b*) more interaction with the materials than thinking or writing an answer; (*c*) greater provision for productive inquisitiveness, i.e., the asking of questions and the receiving of answers from an "informational storage bank"; (d) individualization of the instructional process, wherein the program is adaptable to the particular abilities, interests, and progress of the student (Sechrest & Strowig, 1962); (e) greater opportunities for more practice, exercise of skill, and active mastery outside the limits imposed by the machine; (f) greater provision for periodic testing as an integral part of programmed instruction; (g) greater provision for student-keyed programming, based upon an assessment of different kinds of students, different kinds of subject matters, and different kinds of instruction. It is the latter item, of course, which has the greatest relevance for the utilization of teaching machines and programmed instruction with rehabilitation populations.

The general advantages of programmed instruction seem to be well established. Larger organizations have entered the field, reaping the benefits of pioneer work and building now upon a much broader and sounder base of business acumen. The development of programmed instruction has entered the stage of fine-grain inspection and analysis. The question now may be stated as follows: Which programs can be expected to convey what information to whom and under what conditions? With the rapid proliferation of entries into the field, organizations have come into being which have set for themselves the task of promulgating increasingly demanding criteria for the evaluation of new programs. As a consequence, interest seems to be shifting from the technique and the related machinery to the learner.

The immediate prospects of benefit from programmed instruction are primarily in terms of knowledge and secondarily in terms of skills. We are not yet in a position to translate knowledge into behavior modification—witness the issue of insight in psychotherapy. A teaching machine may be a tool, and programmed instruction may be a method for behavior modification, but they seem less potent than direct interpersonal interventions, especially when the question is one of improvement in interpersonal relations.

An ambiguity yet to receive satisfactory consideration is the matter of immediate, positive consequences. Presumably, the consequence of satisfactory response on one item is preparation for the next item: the consequence of satisfactory performance on one lesson is preparation to proceed to the next lesson: the consequence of satisfactory performance on one program is what? Do we say preparedness for the next program? This leaves the pupil moving in a spiral of words. Lindsley (1960) demonstrated that a psychiatric patient in a cubicle will operate a manipulandum to feed a hungry kitten some milk when he will not operate the manipulandum to receive candies and cigarettes for himself. Humanists have long maintained that social reinforcers are the ultimate rewards. Trying to blend in these observations: a pupil's motivation to progress through items, lessons, and programs may be enhanced by a range of personal and social reinforcers, such as: comparison of self now with self in the past; comparison with peers in the present; attentions and rewards from instructor or therapist; application of knowledge or skill in schoolwork for a grade or on a job for a salary—all goals with personal and social implications. This line of reasoning leads to the conclusion that discrimination and generalization must occur from the reinforcements inherent in the program if extinction on the program is to be avoided.

Forebearance of judgment is required. The demonstration of the value of programmed instruction will have to come from latter-day usage by conventional personnel in a customary rehabilitation setting. The Hawthorne Effect is omnipresent, and McKee capitalized on it for motivational purposes. Long-term reliance upon the appeals of novelty and prestige does not seem justified.

An assessment of the current status of teaching machines and programmed instruction from the standpoint of rehabilitation yields the following conclusion: Much more attention will have to be paid to individual differences and educational psychology if the movement is to be of benefit in remediation and rehabilitation. Especially important are those individual differences with respect to the dimensions of intelligence and cognition, drive and habit strength, inhibition and choice, and personality. Further attention must be given to the effects of specific deficits and handicaps upon the nature of individual differences along these dimensions. Recognition must be given to the fact that most of the "laws of learning" have been formulated upon a nomothetic base using "average" subjects. Quite to the contrary, rehabilitation activities have proceded from a clinically informed idiographic base. Much greater attention must be given to the characteristics of the candidate for rehabilitation who stands as a would-be learner in the face of teaching machines and programmed instruction. Jensen (1960) asserted, "The teaching machine, far more effectively than the human teacher, can capitalize on individual differences if they are properly taken into account."

It appears likely that individual differences will receive their due. The "new look" in teaching machines and programmed instruction was heralded by Coulson & Silberman in 1960. These authors described a systems development approach to automated teaching, using a Crowder model and a computer, a projector, and a typewriter. Their procedure provided for the interspersing of instructional items and tests of the student's performance, with allowance for self-evaluation and branching at the student's discretion. The apparatus maintained a record of the student's performance for later analysis.

A distinct benefit for rehabilitation might be found in the development of a large library of fairly discrete programs which are directed to the remediation of specific problems in specific types of persons. Such an arrangement would permit the diagnosis of assets and liabilities and the prescription of a particular program for remediation. The library might well be found in the storage drums of a computer.

In sum, rehabilitation will most likely benefit from a systems approach whereby programming is incorporated into total rehabilitation procedures and utilized only where it proves most useful as a component of all methods available.

Chapter Summary

The initial claims and enthusiasms about the use of teaching machines and programmed instruction in remediation and rehabilitation of defective and deviant behavior have given place to a more temperate appraisal of the limits and limitations of this new way of shaping behavior. Historically, teaching machines were launched by Pressey. They reached their zenith after Skinner had provided a rationale for programmed instruction and refined the devices for its implementation. These early stages are now past and the basic problems are well defined. Further advance requires an amalgamation of the talents and resources of three key groups—education, industry, and government. The heart of the chapter is concerned with the application of programmed instruction and teaching machines to the modification of normal and deviant behavior in adults and exceptional children. Emphasis is given selectively to representative studies, such as McKee's work with inmates at the Draper Correctional Center, Eldred's work with emotionally disturbed children at Vermont State Hospital, and Moore's autotelic responsive environments to teach reading and writing at an early age.

The needs of programmed instruction are summarized in terms of greater flexibility, variety, control, selectivity, and diversification of programs. The major issue of educational remediation and psychological rehabilitation centers about individual differences and the need to adapt programs specifically for rehabilitation populations, rather than about the use of programs for normal populations with deviant ones. Motivation and social reinforcements need to be considered within the context of rehabilitation.

In terms of refinements and evaluations for the future of teaching machines and programmed instruction, various prognostications and suggestions are made, and the main question is: Which programs can be effected to convey information to whom and under what conditions? Answers to this complex question will require a greater knowledge of the laws of learning as applied to the educational enterprise, and a systems approach requiring cooperation not only of vast organizations (universities, industries, and branches of government) but especially of subject-matter experts. This system would consider the need to change and improve behavior through a variety of methods, one of which would be programmed instruction and teaching machines.

PART THREE

Classification, Organizational Scheme, and Training Systems

12

Behavioral Diagnosis*

FREDERICK H. KANFER
GEORGE SASLOW
University of Oregon Medical School, Portland, Oregon

During the past decade criticism of conventional psychiatric diagnosis has been so widespread that many clinicians now use diagnostic labels sparingly and apologetically. In particular, these labels are sometimes useless from the viewpoint of treatment and prognosis. One study investigating the reasons for disagreements among experienced psychiatric diagnosticians (Ward, Beck, Mendelson, Mock, & Erbaugh, 1962) reported that 62.5 percent of the differences were due to inadequacies in the nosological system, the widely used 1952 APA classification. The continued adherence to the nosological terms of this classificatory scheme suggests some utility of the present categorization of behavior disorders, despite its apparently low reliability (Ash, 1949; Rotter, 1954); its limited prognostic value (Freedman, 1958; Windle, 1952); and its multiple feebly related assumptive supports.

The theories of personality underlying the present APA diagnostic classi-

* This chapter is an enlarged and updated version of an earlier paper which appeared in the *Archives of General Psychiatry*, 1965, 12, p. 529–538. Revision of this paper was facilitated by work in conjunction with Research Grant MH 6921–07 from the National Institutes of Mental Health, United States Public Health Service, to Frederick H. Kanfer.

fication system do permit some limited generalizations about a patient's probable behavior under very general conditions. But with the well-documented overlap of symptoms in different groups (e.g., Wittenborn, Holzberg, & Simon, 1953) and poor interjudge reliabilities of categories (Kostlan, 1954; Schmidt & Fonda, 1956) the ubiquity of enduring behavioral characteristics within diagnostic groups is doubtful, at best. However, even if better group separation and improved rater reliability were established, there is still no good basis for assuming even minimal utility of the currently used system for assignment to treatment. Bannister, Salmon, & Leiberman (1964) examined the relationship between diagnosis and treatment in 1,000 psychiatric patients. To test their hypotheses at three levels of diagnostic specificity, all patients were classified three times: (1) as psychotic, neurotic, or organic; (2) according to such commonly used categories as schizophrenics, affectives, hysterics, reactive depressives; and (3) according to the finer differentiation made by the International Classification of Diseases for the World Health Organization in 1948. For each level of classification a matrix was constructed by diagnostic categories and 14 treatment categories. The analyses reveal that the best prediction of treatment for a given diagnosis at level I would result in 18.2 percent correct guesses, for level II in 32.9 percent, and for level III in 30.6 percent in 1,000 cases. The authors conclude that "the findings are not consistent with the notion that each particular diagnosis leads logically (or habitually) to a particular treatment. It suggests that variables other than diagnosis may be as important as, or more important than, diagnosis in predicating choice of treatment" (1964, p. 731).

We propose here to examine some sources of dissatisfaction with the present approach to diagnosis, to describe a framework for a behavioral analysis of individual patients which implies both suggestions for treatment and outcome criteria for the single case, and to indicate the conditions for collecting the data for such an analysis. The most desirable classification system would be one which, from knowledge of only a few salient characteristics of a person, permits highly accurate predictions for many crucial behaviors, including responses to specific treatments, the probability of occurrence of various unacceptable behaviors, and the degree of social effectiveness. While such goals may be unrealistic at the present time, exploration of an empirical and nontraditional approach to diagnosis may contribute new behavioral dimensions for an eventual conceptualization of the behavior disorders nearer to what is desired and clinically useful. The feasibility of handling diagnostic information by data-processing machines has already been demonstrated for some medical diseases (e.g., Brodman, van Woerkom, Erdmann, & Goldstein, 1959; Ledley & Lusted, 1959). The large remaining problem is the provision of meaningful observations and treatment categories to the computer for empirical evaluation of their relationships.

Problems in Current Diagnostic Systems

Numerous criticisms have dealt with the internal consistency, the explicitness, the precision, and the reliability of psychiatric classifications. It seems to us that the more important fault lies in our lack of sufficient knowledge to categorize behavior along those pertinent dimensions which permit prediction of responses to social expectations, social stresses, life crises, or psychiatric treatment. This limitation obviates anything but a crude and tentative approximation to a taxonomy of effective and ineffective behavior. A reasonable expectation of a practical diagnostic schema is that the taxonomic system be closely related to the conceptual and empirical framework of treatment.

Zigler & Phillips, in discussing the requirement for an adequate system of classification, suggest that an etiologically oriented closed system of diagnosis is premature. Instead, they believe that an empirical attack is needed, using "symptoms broadly defined as meaningful and discernible behaviors, as the basis of the classificatory system" (1961, p. 616). But symptoms of a class of responses are defined, after all, only by their nuisance value to the patient's social environment or to himself as a social being. They are also notoriously unreliable in predicting the patient's particular etiological history or his response to treatment. An alternate approach lies in an attempt to identify classes of dependent variables in human behavior which would allow inferences about the particular contemporary controlling factors, the social stimuli, the physiological stimuli, and the reinforcing stimuli, of which they are a function. In the present early stage of the art of psychological prognostication, it appears most reasonable to develop a program of analysis which is closely related to subsequent treatment. A classification scheme which implies a program for behavioral change is the only one which has not only utility but the potential for experimental validation.

The task of assessment and prognosis can be reduced to efforts which answer the following three questions: (1) Which specific behavior patterns require change in their frequency of occurrence, their intensity, their duration or in the conditions under which they occur? (2) What are the conditions under which this behavior was acquired, and what factors are currently maintaining it? (3) What are the best practical means which can produce the desired changes in this individual (manipulation of the environment, the behavior, or the self-attitudes of the patient)? The investigation of the history of the problematic behavior is mainly of academic interest, except as it contributes information about the probable efficacy of a specific treatment method.

EXPECTATIONS OF CURRENT DIAGNOSTIC SYSTEMS

In traditional medicine, a diagnostic statement about a patient has often been viewed as an essential prerequisite to treatment because a diagnosis suggests that the physician has some knowledge of the origin of the difficulty and of the probable future course of the illness. Further, in medicine, diagnosis frequently brings together the accumulated knowledge about the pathological process which leads to the manifestation of the symptoms, and the experiences which others have had in the past in treating patients with such a disease process. Modern medicine recognizes that any particular disease need not have a single cause or even a small number of antecedent conditions. Nevertheless, the diagnostic label attempts to define at least the necessary conditions which are most relevant in considering a treatment program. Some diagnostic classification system is also invaluable as a basis for many social decisions involving entire populations. For example, planning for treatment facilities, research efforts, and educational programs takes into account the distribution frequencies of specified syndromes in the general population.

Ledley & Lusted (1959) give an excellent conception of the traditional model in medicine by their analysis of the reasoning underlying it. The authors differentiate between a disease complex and a symptom complex. While *disease complex* describes known pathological processes and their correlated signs, *symptom complex* represents particular signs present in a particular patient. The bridge between disease and symptom complexes is provided by available medical knowledge, and the final diagnosis is tantamount to labeling the disease complex. However, the current gaps in medical knowledge necessitate the use of probability statements when relating diseases to symptoms, admitting that there is some possibility of error in the diagnosis. Once the diagnosis is established, decisions about treatment still depend on many other factors including social, moral, and economic conditions. Ledley & Lusted (1959) thus separate the clinical diagnosis into a two-step process. A statistical procedure is suggested to facilitate the primary or diagnostic labeling process. However, the choice of treatment depends not only on the diagnosis proper. Treatment decisions are also influenced by the moral, ethical, social, and economic conditions of the individual patient, his family, and the society in which he lives. The proper assignment of the weight to be given to each of these values must in the last analysis be left to the physician's judgment (Ledley & Lusted, 1959).

The Ledley & Lusted model presumes available methods for the observation of relevant behavior (the symptom complex) and some scientific knowledge relating it to known antecedents or correlates (the disease process). But contemporary psychological theory has as yet little scientific knowledge of behavior pathology and therefore no guidelines for the observer to suggest what is to be observed. A patient who presents himself for diagnosis may be examined by five observers with diverse orientations to behavior pathology. One observer might attempt to define the problem in terms of the patient's biological constitution, another in terms of his early life experiences, a third in terms of his interpersonal experiences, a fourth in terms of his unconscious system, and a fifth in terms of faulty communication systems. Each framework influences the observer to elicit data selectively and to accept or reject information as it can be accommodated in his conceptual system. As a result, lack of agreement exists even on what is to be observed as a basis for diagnosis.

In the absence of a unique psychiatric model for psychiatric illness, there tends to be a widespread use of the medical model with demonstrated utility for other types of disorders, even when its relevance may be questionable. In contrast to this solution, Szasz (1960) has expressed the view that the medical model may be totally inadequate because psychiatry should be concerned with problems of living and not with diseases of the brain or other biological organs. Szasz argues that "mental illness is a myth, whose function it is to disguise and thus render more palatable the bitter pill of moral conflict in human relations" (1960, p. 118).

The limitations of the somatic model have been discussed even in some areas of medicine for which the model seems most appropriate. For example, in the nomenclature for diagnosis of disease of the heart and blood vessels, the criteria committee of the New York Heart Association (1953) suggests the use of multiple criteria for cardiovascular diseases, including a statement of the patient's functional capacity. The committee suggests that the functional capacity be "estimated by appraising the patient's ability to perform physical activity" (p. 80) and decided largely by inference from his history. Further, "[it] should not be influenced by the character of the structural lesion or by an opinion as to treatment or prognosis" (p. 81). This approach makes it clear that a comprehensive assessment of a patient, regardless of the physical disease which he suffers, must also take into account the social expectations of his life settings, his social effectiveness, and the ways in which physiological, anatomical, and psychological factors interact to produce a particular behavior pattern in an individual patient. In cardiovascular disease (as, we believe, in psychiatric problems) the patient's functional capacity is evidently not predictable from any single one of a number of highly relevant contributing factors. The importance of the total matrix in which the evaluation is made is indicated by the committee's conclusions that a patient's functional capacity must be observed in its actual manifestations. When medical illness is looked upon in such a comprehensive way, it is possible to find a model which may be common to both medical and psychiatric problems (Guze, Matarazzo, & Saslow, 1953). In terms of such an inclusive model which neglects no dimension relevant to the problem, we can understand that even an acute schizophrenic patient may perform quite adequately in some social interactions or areas of talent, such as musical or literary, while the usual diagnostic label has no value in predicting the total range of his behavioral potentials.

MULTIPLE DIAGNOSIS

A widely used practical solution and circumvention of the difficulty inherent in the application of the medical model to psychiatric diagnosis is offered by Noyes & Kolb (1963). They suggest that the clinician construct a diagnostic formulation consisting of three parts: (1) a genetic diagnosis incorporating the constitutional, somatic, and historical-traumatic factors representing the primary sources or determinants of the mental illness; (2) a dynamic diagnosis which describes the mechanisms and techniques unconsciously used by the individual to manage anxiety and enhance self-esteem, i.e., that traces the psychopathological processes; and (3) a clinical diagnosis which attempts to convey connotations concerning the reaction syndrome, the probable course of the disorder, and the methods of treatment which will most probably prove beneficial. Noyes & Kolb's multiple criteria can be arranged along three simpler dimensions of diagnosis which may have some practical value to the clinician: (1) etiological, (2) behavioral, and (3) predictive diagnosis, or prognosis. The kind of information which is conveyed by each type of diagnostic label is somewhat different and specifically adapted to the purpose for which the diagnosis is used. By this triple-label approach Noyes & Kolb attempt to counter the criticism aimed at use of any single classificatory system. Confusion in a single system of classification as used by other authors is due in part to the fact that a diagnostic formulation intended to describe current behavior, for example, may be found useless in an attempt to predict the response to specific treatment, to "postdict" the patient's past personal history and development, or to permit collection of adequate frequency data on hospital populations.

CLASSIFICATION BY ETIOLOGY

The Kraepelinian system and portions of the 1952 APA classification emphasize etiological factors. They share the assumption that common etiological factors lead to similar symptoms and respond to similar treatment. This dimension of diagnosis is fruitful for immediate treatment when dealing with behavior disorders which are mainly associated with some biological condition or state. When a patient is known to suffer from excessive intake of alcohol, his hallucinatory behavior, lack of motor coordination, poor judgment, and other behavioral evidence of disorganization can often be related directly to some antecedent condition such as the toxic effect of alcohol on the central nervous system, liver, etc. For these cases, classification by etiology also has some implications for prognosis and treatment. Acute hallucinations and other disorganized behavior due to alcohol usually clear up when the alcohol level in the blood stream falls. Similar examples can be drawn from any class of behavior disorders in which a change in behavior is associated primarily or exclusively with a single, *particular* antecedent factor. Under these conditions this factor can be called a pathogen, and the situation closely approximates the condition described by the traditional medical model.

Utilization of this dimension as a basis for psychiatric diagnosis, however, has many problems apart from the rarity with which a specified condition can be shown to have direct "causal" relationship to a pathogen. Among the current areas of ignorance in the fields of psychology and psychiatry, the etiology of most common disturbances probably takes first place. In the present state of knowledge, no specific family environment, no dramatic traumatic experience, no known constitutional abnormality has yet been found which results in the same pattern of disordered behavior. While current research efforts have aimed at investigating family patterns of schizophrenic patients, and several studies suggest a relationship between the mother's behavior and a schizophrenic process in the child (Jackson, 1960), it is not at all clear why the presence of these same factors in other families fails to yield a similar incidence of schizophrenia. Further, patients may exhibit behavior diagnosed as schizophrenic when there is no evidence of the postulated mother-child relationship (Frank, 1965; Freedman, 1958).

CLASSIFICATION BY SYMPTOMS

A clinical diagnosis often is a simple expanded statement about the way in which a person behaves. On the assumption that a variety of behaviors are correlated and consistent in any given individual, it becomes more economical to assign the individual to a class of persons than to list and categorize all his behaviors and to describe his operations in thousands of isolated situations. The utility of such a system rests heavily on the availability of empirical evidence concerning probable correlations among various behaviors (response-response relationships) and the further assumption that the frequency of occurrence of such behaviors is relatively independent of specific stimulus conditions and of specific reinforcement. There are two major limitations to such a system. The first is that diagnosis by symptoms, as we have indicated in an earlier section, is often misleading because it implies common etiological factors.

The second limitation is that the current approach to diagnosis by symptoms tends to center on a group of behaviors which is often irrelevant with regard to the patient's total life pattern. These behaviors may be of interest only for historical reasons, or because they are popularly associated with deviancy and disorder. For example, occasional mild delusions interfere little or not at all in the social interactions or occupational effectiveness of many ambulatory patients. Nevertheless, admission of their occurrence is often sufficient for a diagnosis of psychosis. Refinement of diagnosis by symptoms beyond current usage appears possible, as shown for example by Lorr, Klett, & McNair (1963), but this does not remove the above limitations.

Utilization of a symptom-descriptive approach frequently focuses attention on by-products of larger behavior patterns and results in attempted treatment of behaviors which may be simple consequences of other more important aspects of the patient's life. Much of the emphasis on the patient's subjective experiences, feelings, and moods results in such a syndrome-oriented classification. Subsequent therapeutic efforts are then made to change the feelings, anxieties, and moods (or at least the patient's report about them) rather than to investigate the life conditions, interpersonal reactions, and environmental factors which produce and maintain these habitual response patterns. The questionable value of a treatment approach, founded on the assumption that psychiatric intervention must focus on disordered subjective states, has recently been shown by McPartland & Richart (1966). The authors compiled information from 393 applicants for psychiatric treatment at a public municipally supported center, with regard to (1) clinical features, such as depression, suspicion, and feelings of worthlessness, and (2) problems of living, related to the patient's environment, or plights, such as marital problems, financial problems, and physical or work problems. They found that admissions to some form of treatment (inpatient or nonresidential) were significantly higher for patients who were described as delusional, hallucinating, disorganized and confused, incoherent, suicidal, and hostile. Presence or absence of the remaining eight clinical features (agitated, depressed, fearful-anxious, withdrawn, vague, suspicious, feeling worthless, hypochondriacal) was not significantly selective for admission to treatment. Of the series of presented plights, only one (traumatic event) showed a significant relationship to the decision to treat. The central question of the study addressed itself to the relative persistence of plights and clinical features in a six-month follow-up. A sample of 50 applicants was interviewed in their homes. The sample was matched to the larger base sample, in which approximately three-fourths had undergone treatment. It was found that the eight elements which showed the least relative reduction over the six-month interval were plights (ranging from 45 to 27 percent reduction). The greatest reductions were found in clinical features (e.g., suicidal, hostile, hallucinating, etc.), with a range downward from 95 percent.

McPartland & Richart (1966) conclude that, in their population of disadvantaged people who use public clinics, clearing of the clinical picture is not usually followed by a less problematic way of life. They suggest that the problems of life are unlikely to be the derivatives of disordered thoughts and feelings. It is more plausible to interpret the data as indicating that these disorders are products of life stresses. They comment on the limited role played in clinical decisions by the complex problems of life, and suggest that the current paradigm, treating "inner" symptoms to produce fundamental improvements in the problem areas of patient's lives, may be a poor one.

CLASSIFICATION BY PROGNOSIS

To date, the least effort has been devoted to construction of a classification system which assigns patients to the same category on the basis of their similar response to specific treatments. The proper question raised for such a classification system concerns the manner in which a patient will react to treatments, regardless of his current behavior or past history. The numerous studies attempting to establish prognostic signs from current behaviors by behavioral observations, by projective personality tests, or by somatic tests all represent efforts to categorize the patients on this dimension.

Windle (1952) has called attention to the low degree of predictability afforded by personality (projective) test scores, and has pointed out the difficulties encountered in evaluating research in this area due to the inadequate description of the population sampled and of the improvement criteria. Summaries in the *Annual Review of Psychology* of the yearly crops of outcome research in psychotherapy and of prognostic sign studies attest to the repeated failures to find useful predictors of response to treatment. The lack of reliable relationships between, on the one hand, diagnostic categories, test data, demographic variables, or any other measure of the patient's performance, and on the other hand, duration of illness, response to specific treatment, or degree of recovery precludes the construction of a simple empiric framework for a diagnostic-prognostic classification system based only on an array of symptoms.

None of the currently used dimensions for diagnosis is directly related to methods of possible modification of a patient's behavior. Since the etiological model clearly stresses causative factors, it is much more compatible with a personality theory which strongly emphasizes genetic-developmental factors. Classification by symptoms facilitates social-administrative decisions about patients by providing some basis for judging the degree of deviation from social and ethical norms. Such a classification is compatible with a personality theory founded on the normal curve hypothesis and concerned with characterization by comparison with a fictitious average. The prognostic-predictive approach appears to have the most direct practical applicability. If continued research were to support certain early findings, being able to predict outcome of mental illness from a patient's premorbid social competence score (Zigler and Phillips, 1961), from his score on an ego-strength scale (Barron, 1953), or from many of the other signs and single variables which have been shown to have some predictive powers, it would indeed be comforting. It is unfortunate that these powers are frequently dissipated in cross-validation. As Fulkerson & Barry (1961) have indicated, single predictors have not yet shown much success.

A Functional (Behavioral-Analytic) Approach

The growing literature on behavior modification derived from learning theory (Bandura, 1961; Ferster, 1963; Kanfer, 1961; Krasner, 1962a; Ullmann & Krasner, 1965; Wolpe, 1958; and others) suggests the necessity for a change in effective diagnostic procedures. The learning approach differs in its closer articulation between diagnosis and treatment, with continuing reconsideration of therapeutic efforts on the basis of information obtained during the entire operation. This approach sacrifices the taxonomic features of the usual diagnostic enterprise for greater specificity and heavier contributions of the obtained observations to direct use in the therapeutic intervention. A functional analysis of behavior endeavors to ascertain the explicit environmental and historical variables which control the observed behaviors. In discussing this approach, Ferster (1965) has emphasized that "a functional analysis of behavior has the advantage that it specifies other causes of behavior in the form of explicit environmental events which can be objectively identified and which are potentially manipulable." Such an undertaking makes the assumption that a description of the problematic behavior, its controlling factors, and the means by which it can be changed are the most appropriate "explanations" for the patient's actions. It stresses that the unit of analysis is a relationship between the environment and behavior, with attention not only on antecedent variables but also on the impact of behavioral acts on the patient's environment. The patient is considered to be a member of several social systems, differing in significance to him (e.g., his family, friends, coworkers, clubs), and it is assumed that his behavior contributes to the maintenance or disruption of these systems, just as the group norms of these systems affect his behavior.

Lindsley (1964) has expanded the traditional SR analysis to include the components deemed necessary for a full behavioral analysis. He describes this sequence as: stimulus (S), response (R), contingency (K), consequence (C). This listing suggests separate consideration of each unit in the analysis of operant behaviors. The S component includes antecedent events, the R refers to observed (or reliably reported) behaviors, K describes the schedules or contingency-related conditions, and C refers to events following R, be they environmental or organismic. Our present view expands Lindsley's behavioral view by one additional component, the biological condition of the organism (O), in order to permit inclusion of variables especially relevant to populations with psychological and biological dysfunctions.

Several other characteristics of the type of analysis proposed here need to be listed:

1. Since the patient operates in a complex of systems, not only psychological events but all events, including biologic, economic, and social, must be admitted as potential variables in the analysis, without prior judgment about their order of importance.

2. It is assumed that many of the delicate social interactional patterns are operant responses. Operant responses are maintained by their effect on the environment. Therefore, an account of the consequences of the patient's behaviors on the environment can provide a rough organization of the patient's instrumental acts into classes defined by the outcome of these acts. The verification of specific antecedent stimuli may often be neither feasible nor necessary.

3. The potential range of the behavioral repertoire is limited by the individual's biological, social, and intellectual competence, by his past history of reinforcement for his behaviors, and by the current norms of his membership groups. Consequently, knowledge of the patient's history, of the limits of his capacities, and of the norms of his membership and reference groups is essential for effective therapeutic planning.

4. By emphasis on the importance of individual learning histories, it is reognized that numerous common features appear in the behavior of individuals reared in the same cultural environment and exposed to similar learning experiences. However, the approach stresses the need for individual assessment, and for construction of therapeutic plans which are suited to the unique environmental and behavioral characteristics encountered with each patient. Therefore, no specific limited catalog of treatment techniques is envisioned. Rather, the functional analysis provides a method of analysis and some procedural guidelines. These may need to be combined into unique constellations of operations and priorities in the individual case. The totality of the patient's problems as initially presented does not have to be dealt with immediately, or by the time treatment is terminated. An effective assessment procedure requires only that some hierarchy of problems is established so that priorities can be assigned for treatment of various maladaptive patterns or for specific situational interventions. As some of the patient's problematic behaviors are treated in accordance with the initial decisions about priorities, both priorities and treatment operations are changed by a method of successive approximation. The results of the initial operations determine the choice of appropriate strategies for succeeding problems. It is thus clear that a behavioral analysis is not limited only to formulating an initial strategy but that reanalysis takes place as the treatment plan proceeds.

5. A functional analysis does not inevitably lead to therapeutic interventions in a patient's psychological functioning. In fact, therapeutic interventions may consist solely of modifications of the patient's physical or social environment, or of the behavior of persons other than the patient, or of other variables believed to play a role in the maintenance of the presenting problem.

The present approach shares with many psychological theories the assumption that psychotherapy is not an effort aimed at removal of intrapsychic conflicts, nor at a change in the personality structure by therapeutic interactions of intense nonverbal nature (e.g., transference, self-actualization).

Instead, we adopt the assumption that the job of "psychological" treatment involves the utilization of a variety of methods to devise a program which controls the patient's environment, or enables him to control his behavior and the consequences of his behavior in such a way that the presenting problem is resolved. We hypothesize that the essential ingredients of a psychotherapeutic endeavor with the patient usually involve two separate efforts: (1) to change the patient's approach to perceiving, classifying, and organizing sensory events, including perceptions of himself, and (2) to change the response patterns which he has established in relation to social objects and to himself over the years (Kanfer, 1961).

It is necessary to indicate what the theoretical view here presented does not espouse in order to understand the differences from other procedures. It does not rest upon the assumption that (1) insight is a *sine qua non* of psychotherapy, (2) changes in thoughts or ideas inevitably lead to ultimate changes in actions, (3) verbal therapeutic sessions serve as replications of and equivalents for actual life situations, and (4) a symptom can be removed only by uprooting its cause or origin. In the absence of these assumptions it becomes unnecessary to conceptualize behavior disorder in etiological terms, in psychodynamic terms, or in terms of a specifiable disease process. While psychotherapy by verbal means may be sufficient in some instances, the combination of behavior modification in life situations and in verbal interactions serves to extend the armamentarium of the therapist. Therefore verbal psychotherapy is seen as an adjunct in the implementation of therapeutic behavior changes in the patient's total life pattern, not as an end in itself, nor as the sole vehicle for increasing psychological effectiveness. In embracing this view of behavior modification, there is a further commitment to a constant interplay between assessment and therapeutic strategies. An initial diagnostic formulation seeks to ascertain the major variables which can be directly controlled or modified during treatment. During successive treatment stages additional information is collected about the patient's behavior repertoire, his reinforcement history, the pertinent controlling stimuli in his social and physical environment and the sociological limitations within which both patient and therapist have to operate.

While a behavioral approach stresses the importance of environmental variables, it is not oblivious to the importance of a person's capacity for modifying his environment and his own behaviors in relation to it. Ultimately, most patients leave psychotherapeutic supervision. The changes which can be initiated by a therapist must be maintained by the patient himself. Consequently, proper assessment must include an evaluation of the patient's potentials for self-regulation and for self-initiation, i.e., active participation in the treatment process and in subsequent readjustments to life circumstances. To maximize the probability of successful treatment the clinician's task may necessitate at first direct intervention in the patient's environmental circumstances, and later the modification of the behavior of other people significant in his life, as well as the control of reinforcing stimuli which are available either through self-administration or by contingency upon the behavior of others. These procedures complement the verbal interactions of traditional psychotherapy. They require that the clinician, at the invitation of the patient or his family, participate more fully in planning the total life pattern of the patient outside the clinician's office, until there is reason to believe that either the environmental conditions or the patient's ability to control them have so changed that the therapist's interventions in the patient's environment are no longer necessary. When a behavioral analysis reveals that a patient's problems lie mainly in his dissatisfactions with or uncertainties about his self-attitudes, or a loss of meaning or purpose, there is further a serious question, ably discussed by Schofield (1964), whether such patients should be treated by the traditional professional groups, the psychiatry, psychology, and social work members of the "mental healing" professions. These cases constitute mostly self-referred persons, sensitive to their own plight, psychologically sophisticated, and often functioning effectively in their daily responsibilities. One solution suggested by Schofield lies in recognizing the contributions of "invisible" psychotherapists, i.e., clergymen, teachers, counsellors, work supervisors, even neighbors and friends, who often provide effective help. We agree heartily with Schofield when he says (p. 140):

> Because of the established impossibility of meeting the demand for therapeutic conversation within the present and probably future supply of currently sanctioned psychotherapists, it is essential that careful consideration be given to all possible means of increasing the supply and quality of help from these invisible therapists.

The exploration of such resources early during the behavioral analysis permits the clinician to determine the degree to which clinical intervention can be supplemented by these resources. Such knowledge should also curtail excessive use of the clinician's time and of other psychiatric resources by gradual shifting of therapeutic actions to qualified but nonprofessional (i.e., nonclinical) persons in the patient's natural environment. Again, the underlying stress on the problem not as "internal" but as interactional, not as "pathological" but as related to the patient's life pattern and his physical and social environment, dictates greater concern in diagnosis with matters other than the patient's mental status or emotional-developmental history.

This analysis is consistent with earlier formulations of the principles of comprehensive medicine (Guze, Matarazzo, & Saslow, 1953; Saslow, 1952) which emphasized the joint operation of biological, social, and psychological factors in psychiatric disorders. The language and orientation of the proposed approach are rooted in contemporary learning theory. The conceptual framework is consonant with the view that the course of psychiatric disorders can be modified by systematic application of scientific principles from the fields relevant to the patient's habitual mode of living, e.g., biology, psychology, sociology, clinical medicine. The analysis proposed here is not intended to lead to assignment of the patient to diagnostic categories. It should serve as a basis for making decisions about specific therapeutic interventions, regardless of the presenting problem. The compilation of data under as many of the headings as are relevant should yield a good basis for decisions about the areas in which intervention is needed, the particular targets of the intervention, the treatment methods to be used, and the series of goals at which treatment should aim.

I. *Initial analysis of the problem situation.* A preliminary formulation attempts to sort out the behaviors which are brought to the clinician's attention with regard to their eventual place in the treatment procedures. The patient's repertoire may be conspicuously different from what is required for adequate adjustment to his circumstances because of the unusual frequency with which various acts occur. Further, account is also taken of the extent of the behavioral repertoire which is nonproblematic and the presence of behaviors representing special strengths, qualitatively or quantitatively, which would be available as resources in treatment. Although the classification of behaviors into excesses and deficits is conceptually useful, it is clear that in all but extreme cases humans have a rich and continually changing repertoire, and the interrelationships between the items in the repertoire cannot be ignored. The initial classification may not retain its appropriateness, once changes in the patient's life conditions and his overall activities begin to occur.

Since no objective frequency tables are available for reference, behavior items can be viewed either as excesses or as deficits, depending on the vantage point from which the imbalance is observed. For instance, excessive withdrawal and deficient social initiative, or excessive response to emotional stimulation and deficient self-controlling behavior, may be complementary. However, a decision about the starting point for treatment is necessary, committing the clinician to a set of priorities for treatment which can later be reviewed and changed.

Preference for viewing behavior as excessive or deficient is often determined by cultural valuation of the behavior, based on its consequences to other people. For example, in a child a physical blow in response to a critical remark can be regarded as excessive aggressive behavior, leading to the decision to reduce its occurrence by constraints or punishment. A clearly different consequence results from regarding the same behavior as a deficit in self-control, to be remedied by training the child to substitute acceptable alternative responses. Another choice resulting from the analysis may lie in a dual approach. The therapist may decide to train the child to discriminate among cues which indicate potential acceptance or rejection of the behavior by social members, e.g., the differential reinforcement potentials for physical blows in such sports as boxing, as contrasted to its consequences in conversation. Concurrently, major effort could be spent on remedying the relevant deficits in alternate social behaviors.

A. *Behavioral excess.* A class of related behaviors occurs and is described as problematic by the patient or an informant because of excess in (1) frequency, (2) intensity, (3) duration, or (4) occurrence under conditions when its socially sanctioned frequency approaches zero. Compulsive handwashing, combativeness, prolonged excitement, and sexual exhibitionism are examples of behavioral excesses along one or another of these four dimensions. Less obvious, because they often do not constitute the major presenting complaint and appear only in the course of the behavioral analysis, are examples of socially unacceptable solitary, affectionate, or other private behaviors. For instance, a housewife showing excessive solitary preoccupation can do so by excessive homemaking activities, (1) several hours a day, (2) seven days weekly for most of the waking day, (3) to the extent that phone calls or doorbells are unanswered and family needs are unattended. From this example it is clear that both duration and intensity values of the behavior may jointly determine the characterization of the behavior as excessive.

B. *Behavioral deficit.* A class of responses is described as problematic by someone because it fails to occur (1) with sufficient frequency, (2) with adequate intensity, (3) in appropriate form, or (4) under socially expected conditions. Examples are: reduced social responsiveness (withdrawal), amnesias, fatigue syndromes, and restrictions in sexual or somatic function (e.g., impotence, writer's cramp). Other examples of behavioral deficits can be found in depressed patients who have no appropriate behavior in a new social environment, e.g., after changes from a rural to an urban area, from marital to single status, or from one socioeconomic level to another. "Inadequate" persons often are also found to have large gaps in their social or intellectual repertoires which prevent appropriate actions.

C. *Behavioral asset.* Behavioral assets are nonproblematic behaviors. What does the patient do well? What are his adequate social behaviors? What are his special talents or assets? The content of life experiences which can be used to execute a therapeutic program is unlimited. Any segment of the patient's activities can be used as an arena for building up new behaviors. In fact, his natural work and play activities provide a better starting point for behavior change than can ever be provided in a synthetic activity or relationship. For example, a person with musical talent, skill in a craft, physical skill, or social appeal can be helped to use his strengths as vehicles for changing behavior relationships and for acquiring new behaviors in areas in which some successful outcomes are highly probable. While a therapeutic goal may ultimately be the acquisition of specific social or self-evaluative behaviors, the learning can be programmed with many different tasks and in areas in which the patient has already acquired competence.

II. *Clarification of problem situation.*

A. Assign the classes of problematic responses to group *a* or *b* above, as study of the patient proceeds.

B. Which persons or groups object to these behaviors? Which persons or groups support them? Who persuaded or coerced the patient to come to the clinician?

C. What consequences does the problem have for the patient and for significant others? What consequences would removal of the problem have for the patient or others?

D. Under what conditions do the problematic behaviors occur (biological, symbolic, social, vocational, etc.)?

E. What satisfactions would continue for the patient if his problematic behavior were sustained? What satisfactions would the patient gain if, as a result of psychiatric intervention, his problematic behavior were changed? What positive or aversive effects would occur for significant others if the patient's problematic behavior were changed? How would the patient continue to live if therapy were unsuccessful, i.e., if nothing in his behavior changed?

F. What new problems in living would successful therapy pose for the patient?

G. To what extent is the patient as a sole informant capable of helping in development of a therapy program?

The questions raised here are derived from the assumption that maladjusted behavior requires continued support. It cannot be banished from the patient's life for all future circumstances. Change in it is related closely to the environment in which the person needs to live. Elimination of the problematic behavior is also impossible as long as powerful, and often undefined, reinforcing events operate. The answers to the above questions can help to bring about an early decision about the optimal goals within practical reach of the clinician and within the inevitably fixed boundaries of the patient's life pattern.

III. *Motivational analysis.*[1]

[1] A Reinforcement Survey Schedule, recently prepared by J. R. Cautela & R. Kastenbaum (1967), provides a written instrument which may be of great value in obtaining specific information about some of the reinforcing stimuli elicited by items in this section.

A. How does the patient rank various incentives in their importance to him? Basing judgment on the patient's probable expenditure of time, energy, or physical discomfort, which of the following reinforcing events are relatively most effective in initiating or maintaining his behavior: achievement of recognition, sympathy, friendships, money, good health, sexual satisfaction, intellectual competence, social approval, work satisfaction, control over others, securing dependency, etc.?

B. How frequent and regular have been his successes with these reinforcers? What are his present expectations of success for each? Under what circumstances was reinforcement achieved for each of these incentives?

C. Under what specific conditions do each of these reinforcers arouse goal-directed behavior (biological, symbolic, social, vocational)?

D. Do his actions in relation to these goals correspond with his verbal statements? How does any definable discrepancy affect goals and procedures in therapy?

E. Which persons or groups have the most effective and widespread control over his current behavior?

F. Can the patient relate reinforcement contingencies to his own behavior, or does he assign reinforcement to random uncontrollable factors ("superstitious" behavior, belief in luck, fate, miracles, etc.)?

G. What are the major aversive stimuli for this patient, (1) in immediate day-to-day life, (2) in the future? Are there bodily sensations, conviction of illness, or fears of illness which serve as important aversive stimuli for change? What are his fears, the consequences which he avoids and dreads, the risks which he does not take?

H. Would a treatment program require that the patient give up current satisfactions associated with his problem, e.g., invalid status in the family or on the job; gratifications possibly due to unemployment; life restrictions and special privileges justified by his "nervous" status; illness as justification for failure to fulfill expectations of himself or others?

I. Which events of known reinforcing value can be utilized for learning new interpersonal skills or self-attitudes during treatment? In what areas and by what means can positive consequences be arranged to follow desired behaviors, replacing earlier aversive consequences?

IV. *Developmental analysis.*

A. *Biological changes.*

1. What are the limitations in the patient's biological equipment which may affect his current behavior (e.g., defective vision and hearing; residuals

of illnesses, such as stroke, poliomyelitis, mononucleosis, glandular imbalances)? How do these limitations initiate or maintain undesirable behaviors (e.g., behavioral constrictions due to fatigue, fear of overexertion, avoidance of social exposure of these deficits)? Can the patient's self-limiting expectations of the interfering consequences be changed?

2. When and how did biological deviations or limitations develop? What consequences did they have on his life-pattern and on his self-attitudes? What was done about them, by whom? Has he developed specific consistent response patterns toward some body structure or function?

3. How do these biological conditions limit response to treatment or resolution of his problems?

B. *Sociological changes.*

1. What are the most characteristic features of the patient's present sociocultural milieu (with regard to urban versus rural environment, religious affiliation, socioeconomic status, ethnic affiliation, educational-intellectual affiliation, etc.)? Are his attitudes congruent with this milieu? For instance, how is a college orientation of an adolescent accepted by his peer group in a poor neighborhood? How does the home and neighborhood environment respond to a patient's religious, social, and sexual activities and fantasies?

2. Have there been changes in this milieu which are pertinent to his current behavior? If so, how long ago, how permanently, and under what conditions did such changes occur? What immediate consequences did they have for the behavior of the patient? For example, what impact on a wife did a husband's rapid promotion have? Or a marriage into a different socioeconomic or religious group? Or a move from a rural southern community to an urban northern part of the United States?

3. Does the patient view these changes as brought about by himself, by significant persons, or by fortuitous circumstances? What attitudes does he have about these changes?

4. Are the patient's roles in various social settings congruent with one another? For example, is there role conflict between value systems of the patient's early and adult social environments? Are there behavioral deficits due to the changes (e.g., an inability to cope with new social demands, sexual standards, or affectional requirements, associated with rapid acquisition or loss of wealth, or geographic relocation)? If the roles are incongruent, is incongruence among these roles pertinent to his problem? Does the problematic behavior occur in all or only some of these different settings?

5. How can identified sociological factors in the problematic behavior be brought into relation with a treatment program?

C. *Behavioral changes.*

1. Prior to the time of referral did the patient's behavior show deviations in behavioral patterns compared with developmental and social norms? If so,

what was the nature of changes in social behaviors, in routine self-care behaviors, in verbal statements toward self and others? Under what conditions were these changes first noted?

2. Do identified biological, social, or sociological events in the patient's life seem relevant to these behavior changes?

3. Were these changes characterized by (a) emergence of new behaviors, (b) change in intensity or frequency of established behaviors, or (c) nonoccurrence of previous behaviors?

4. Under what conditions and in which social settings were these behavioral changes first noted? Have they extended to other social settings since the problematic behavior was first noted?

5. Were the behavioral changes associated with the patient's exposure to significant individuals or groups from whom he learned new patterns of reinforcement and the behavior necessary to achieve them? Can the problematic behaviors be traced to a model in the patient's social environment from whom he has learned these responses?

V. *Analysis of self-control.*

A. In what situations can the patient control those behaviors which are problematic? How does he achieve such control, by manipulation of self or others?

B. Have any of the problematic behaviors been followed by aversive consequences by others, e.g., social retribution, jail, ostracism, probation, etc.? Have these consequences reduced the frequency of the problematic behavior or only the conditions under which it occurs? Have these events modified the patient's self-controlling behavior?

C. Has the patient acquired some measure of self-control in avoiding situations which are conducive to the execution of his problematic behavior? Does he do this by avoidance or by substitution of alternate instrumental behaviors leading to similar satisfactions?

D. Is there correspondence between the patient's verbalized degree of self-control and observations by others? Can the patient match his behavior to his intentions?

E. What conditions, persons, or reinforcers tend to change his self-controlling behavior (e.g., a child behaves acceptably at school but not at home, or vice versa)?

F. To what extent can the patient's self-controlling behavior be used in a treatment program? Is constant supervision or drug administration necessary to supplement self-control?

VI. *Analysis of social relationships.*

A. Who are the most significant people in the patient's current environment? To which persons or groups is he most responsive? Who facilitates constructive behaviors? Who provokes antagonistic or problematic behaviors? Can these relationships be categorized according to dimensions which clarify the patient's behavioral patterns (e.g., does a patient respond in a submissive or hostile way to all older men)?

B. In these relationships, by use of what reinforcers do the participants influence each other? For example, analysis may reveal a father who always bails out a delinquent son whose public punishment would be embarrassing to the father. Is the cessation of positive reinforcement or onset of punishment clearly signaled?

C. What does the patient expect of these people in words and in action? On what does he base his verbal expectations?

D. What do these people expect of the patient? Is there consistency between the patient's and others' expectations for him?

E. How can the people who can influence the patient participate in treatment?

VII. *Analysis of the social-cultural-physical environment.*

A. What are the norms in the patient's social milieu for the behaviors about which there is a complaint?

B. Are these norms similar in various environments in which the patient interacts, e.g., home and school, friends and parents, work and social milieu, etc.? If not, what are the major differences in behaviors supported in one but not in other environments?

C. What are the limitations in the patient's environment which reduce his opportunities for continued reinforcement; are social, intellectual, sexual, vocational, economic, religious, moral, or physical restrictions imposed by his environment?

D. In which portion of the environment is the patient's problematic behavior most apparent, most troublesome, or most accepted? Can the congruence of several environments be increased or can the patient be helped by removal from dissonant environments? Does his milieu permit or discourage self-evaluation?

E. Does his milieu regard psychological procedures as appropriate for helping him solve his problems? Is there support in his milieu for the changes in attitudes and values which successful psychotherapy may require?

The preceding outline has as its purpose the definition of a patient's problem in a manner which suggests specific treatment operations and also suggests specific behaviors as targets for modification. It may also lead to the major conclusion that no such operations are possible. Therefore, the formulation is action oriented. It can be used as a guide for the initial collection of information, as a device for organizing available data, or as a design for treatment.

The formulation of a treatment plan follows from this type of analysis because knowledge of the reinforcing conditions suggests the motivational controls at the disposal of the clinician for the modification of the patient's behavior. The analysis of specific problem behaviors also provides a series of goals for psychotherapy or other treatment, and for the evaluation of treatment progress. Knowledge of the patient's biological, social, and cultural conditions should help to determine what resources can be used, and what limitations must be considered in a treatment plan.

The various categories attempt to call attention to important variables affecting the patient's current behavior. Therefore, they aim to elicit descriptions of low-level abstraction. Answers to these specific questions are best phrased by describing classes of events reported by the patient or observed by others, or from critical incidents described by an informant. The analysis does not exclude description of the patient's habitual verbal-symbolic behaviors. However, in using verbal behaviors as the basis for this analysis, one should be cautious not to "explain" verbal processes in terms of postulated internal mechanisms without adequate supportive evidence, nor should inference be made about nonobserved processes or events without corroborative evidence. The analysis includes many items which are not known or not applicable for a given patient. Lack of information on some items does not necessarily indicate incompleteness of the analysis. These lacks must be noted nevertheless because they often contribute to the better understanding of what the patient needs to learn to become an autonomous person. Just as important is an inventory of his existing socially effective behavioral repertoire which can be put in the service of any treatment procedure.

This approach is not a substitute for assignment of the patient to traditional diagnostic categories. Such labeling may be desirable for statistical, administrative or research purposes. But the current analysis is intended to replace other diagnostic formulations purporting to serve as a basis for making decisions about specific therapeutic interventions.

Methods of Data Collection for a Functional Analysis

Traditional diagnostic approaches have utilized as the main sources of information the patient's verbal report, his nonverbal behavior during an interview, and his performance on psychological tests. These observations are sufficient if one regards behavior problems only as a property of the patient's particular pattern of associations or his personality structure. A mental disorder would be expected to reveal itself by stylistic characteristics in the patient's behavior repertoire. However, if one views behavior disorders as sets of response patterns which are learned under particular conditions and maintained by definable environmental and internal stimuli, an assessment of the patient's behavior output by the usual methods is insufficient unless it also describes the conditions under which it occurs. This view requires an expansion of the clinician's sources of observations to include the stimulation fields in which the patient lives, and the variations of patient behavior as a function of exposure to these various stimulational variables. Therefore, the resourceful clinician need not limit himself to test findings, interview observations in the clinician's office, or referral histories alone in the formulation of the specific case. Nor need he regard himself as hopelessly handicapped when the patient has little observational or communicative skill in verbally reconstructing his life experiences for the clinician. Regardless of the patient's communicative skills the data must consist of a description of the patient's behavior in relationship to varying environmental conditions. These comments are not intended to propose that the scope of clinical diagnosis be infinitely expanded. Rather, we suggest that the clinican make a selection from the numerous investigative avenues explicitly opened by the present conceptual model. For instance, a single home visit or telephone call can be far more economical than spending several sessions with one family member in an office. An interview permitting direct observation of the patient in interaction with a significant person in his life may be more fruitful than extended verbal description of this relationship by the patient. A survey of his current sociocultural milieu could yield more valuable clues for a therapy program than prolonged attention to his childhood experiences.

A behavioral analysis excludes no data relating to a patient's past or present experiences as irrelevant. However, the relative merit of any information (e.g., growing up in a broken home or having had homosexual experiences) lies in its relation to the independent variables which can be identified as controlling the current behavior which requires modification. The observation that a patient has hallucinated on occasions may be important only if it has bearing on his present problem. If looked upon in isolation it may be misleading and result in emphasis on classification rather than treatment.

In the psychiatric interview the model here described opposes acceptance of the content of the verbal self-report as equivalent to actual events or experiences. However, verbal reports provide information concerning the patient's verbal construction of his environment and of his person, his recall of past experiences, and his fantasies about them. While these self-descriptions do not represent data about events which actually occur internally, they do represent current behaviors of the patient and indicate the verbal chains and repertoires which the patient has built up. Therefore, the verbal behavior may be useful for description of the way in which a patient construes his world. To make the most of the approach here described, variations on traditional interview procedures may be obtained by such techniques as role playing, discussion, and interpretation of current life events, or controlled free association.

In addition to the use of the clinician's own person as a controlled stimulus object in interview situations, observations of interaction with significant others can be used for the analysis of variations in frequency of various behaviors as a function of the person with whom the patient interacts. For example, prescribed standard roles for nurses and attendants may be used, and members of the patient's family or his friends may be used to obtain data relevant to the patient's habitual interpersonal response pattern. Such observations are especially useful if in a later interview the patient is asked to describe, discuss, and report these observed sessions. Confrontations with sound or video tape recordings for comparisons between the patient's report and the actual session as witnessed by the observer may provide information about the patient's perception of himself and others as well as his habitual behavior toward peers, authority figures, and other significant people in his life.

Except in working with children or family units, insufficient use has been made of material obtained from other informants in interviews about the patient. These reports can aid the observer to recognize behavioral domains in which the patient's report deviates from or agrees with the descriptions provided by others. Such information is also useful for contrasting the patient's reports about his presumptive effects on another person to the stated effects by that person. If a patient's interpersonal problems extend to areas in which social contact is not clearly defined, contributions by informants other than the patient are essential.

It must be noted that verbal reports by other informants may be no more congruent with actual events than the patient's own reports and need also to be related to each informant's own credibility. If such crucial figures as parents, spouses, and employers can be interviewed, the clinician is also provided with some information about those people with whom the patient must interact repeatedly and with whom interpersonal problems may have developed.

Some observation of the patient's daily work behavior represents an excellent source of information, if it can be made available. Observation of the patient by the clinician or his staff may be preferable to descriptions by peers or supervisors. Work observations are especially important for patients whose complaints include difficulties in their daily work activity or who describe work situations as contributing factors to their problem. While freer use of this technique may be hampered by cultural attitudes toward psychiatric treatment in the marginally adjusted, such observations may be freely accessible in hospital situations or in sheltered work situations. With use of behavior-rating scales or other simple measurement devices, brief samples of patient behaviors in work situations can be obtained by minimally trained observers.

The patient himself may be asked to provide samples of his own behavior by making tape recordings of segments of interactions in his family, at work, or in other situations during his everyday life. A television monitoring system for the patient's behavior is an excellent technique from a theoretical viewpoint, but it is extremely cumbersome and expensive. Use of recordings for diagnostic and therapeutic purposes has been reported by some investigators (Bach, in Alexander, 1963; Cameron, Levy, Ban, & Rubenstein, 1964). Playback of the recordings and a recording of the patient's reactions to the playback can further be used in interviews to clarify the patient's behavior toward others and his reaction to himself as a social organism. Such feedback can also be used with video tape recordings. The availability of sophisticated electronic telemetering devices makes possible innovations in observational methods along dimensions barely considered by behavioral scientists until recently (Schwitzgebel, Schwitzgebel, Pahnke, & Hurd, 1964).

Psychological tests represent problems to be solved under specified interactional conditions. Between the highly standardized intelligence tests and the unstructured and ambiguous projective tests lies a dimension of structure along which more and more responsibility for providing appropriate responses falls on the patient. By comparison with interview procedures most psychological tests provide a relatively greater standardization of stimulus conditions. In addition to the specific answers given on intelligence tests or on projective tests, these tests also provide a behavioral sample of the patient's reaction to a problem situation in a relatively stressful interpersonal setting. Therefore, not only can psychological tests provide quantitative test scores but they can also be treated as a miniature life experience, yielding information about the patient's interpersonal behavior and variations in his behavior as a function of the nature of the stimulus conditions.

The advent of conditioning therapies has introduced new techniques for diagnostic analysis. In these methods, the specificity of therapeutic operations requires prior determination of the stimulus conditions and responses which are to be attacked in therapy. Initial explorations in desensitization therapy (Franks, 1964; Rachman, 1963; Wolpe, 1958) complement the usual anamnesis with questions about specific fear-arousing situations, or with questionnaires designed to elicit this information (Wolpe & Lang, 1964), or with observations of the critical behavior in its natural setting (Paul, 1966). The construction of desensitization hierarchies for use as therapeutic implements illustrates well the use of diagnostic procedures with direct relevance for therapeutic intervention and demonstrates the continuing overlap between the diagnostic and treatment portions of the clinical enterprise.

Among these novel techniques are standardized behavioral tests with quantifiable response measures ascertaining the strength of the "problematic" response on presentation of critical stimuli. In treatment of sexual deviations, for example, Freund (1963, 1965), and Solyom & Miller (1965) use pictures of nude males and females as the critical stimuli. The extent of response deviation is assessed by the magnitude of such responses as the galvanic skin response, the volume change of the male genital, or plethysmograph response to pictures of adults or children of either sex. A study by Hess, Seltzer, & Shlien (1965) lends support to the validity of this approach. Clear-cut differences in pupil size changes were found for adult males of known homosexuality and heterosexuality.

Operant conditioning techniques have originated in the animal laboratory. Therefore, it is not surprising that their application to clinical problems has been accompanied by increased utilization of diagnostic methods based directly on long-established laboratory learning procedures. Conceptualization of the therapeutic intervention as a learning process results naturally in procedures which parallel the usual procedures of establishing base lines for a given response prior to learning. Most of the reports of operant conditioning treatments include some description of the pretherapeutic problem behavior, measured under specified conditions. Typically, reports present numerical or graphic records of frequency or intensity of a defined verbal or motoric response class, often obtained in the natural setting in which later behavior modification is attempted. Reports of behavior modification with autistic children in institutions (Ferster & DeMyer, 1962; Lovaas, Berberich, Perloff, & Schaeffer, 1966) or at home (Wolf, Risley, & Mees, 1964), with a hyperactive child in the classroom (Patterson, Jones, Whittier, & Wright, 1965), with a mother-child dyad in the home (Hawkins, Peterson, Schweid, & Bijou, 1966), with adult schizophrenics on a ward (Ayllon & Michael, 1959), with a patient with multiple tics (Barrett, 1962), with juvenile delinquents in a natural setting (Schwitzgebel, 1967), or with numerous other patients, differing in age, complaint, and setting, all are characterized by the use of direct pretherapy and posttherapy measures of the criterion response. Despite problems of statistical control associated with the use of this method in the single case, it represents an approach which may eventually lead to reliable diagnostic devices with the absolutely indispensable pertinence to both assessment and treatment. The outstanding advantage of a behavioral analysis lies in its inherent potential for verification of the effects of treatment by posttherapy reevaluation under the same conditions.

In treatment of groups with similar problematic behaviors, preparation of a treatment program often requires the prior analysis of the setting in which the behavior occurs. An initial step in diagnosis comprises observation of the response reinforcement which the environment provides, definition of the range of undesirable behaviors, and definition of the potential controls available for treatment. This analysis is performed on the group and its environment rather than on individuals. Many recent innovations, combining treatment of individual problems with "social actions," have used this form of diagnosis. The current concern with mental health problems in the poor (e.g., Pearl & Riessman, 1964; Riessman, Cohen, & Pearl, 1964) with delinquency (Slack & Schwitzgebel, 1960), and similar social problems has introduced behavioral analysis methods to the diagnosis of general conditions and to the culturally prevalent contingencies for particular problems. From such analyses the clinician can draw inferences about the conditions maintaining individual problem behaviors, integrating both the societal and individual variables which would require change for therapeutic success.

In this section we have mentioned only some of the numerous life situations, test instruments, and behavioral laboratory analogs which can be evaluated in order to provide information about the patient. Criteria for their use lie in economy, accessibility to the clinician, and relevance to the patient's problem. While gathering data from a patient in the office may be more convenient, acquiring firsthand information about the actual conditions under which the patient lives and works may be far more valuable and economical. Such familiarity may be obtained either by utilization of informants or by the clinician's entry into the home, the job situation, or the social environment in which the patient lives.

The view of psychotherapy as readjustment of the patient's social and physical environment and as learning and unlearning of self-attitudes and behavior patterns suggests full utilization of observational techniques similar to those employed in laboratory and field studies in the behavioral sciences. Wider use of laboratory methods derived from animal and learning experiments is also indicated for assessment of the performance of defined responses. The introduction of new and rigorous methods of behavior assessment and modification may have consequences for the scope and nature of the clinician's activities which are by no means clear at this time. Certainly, the emphasis on behavioral engineering approaches, aimed at changing specific response patterns rather than hypothetical disease processes or personality structures, represents a radical departure from the traditional attacks on behavior disorders and will require continuous reevaluation of all facets of clinical work and training. The present type of approach to behavioral analysis also reveals a similarity of the total clinical strategy to the domain of policy-process models, as described by Bauer (1966) for situations in which no single best solution is available. Clinical strategy seems to be closer to the social process of policy formation, in which constant consideration of the interests of different parties is required and a solution can only be achieved by "negotiation" or compromise between the rationally most desirable and operationally most feasible alternatives, than to a rational process aimed toward restoring a patient to a predefined state of psychological health.

Chapter Summary

Currently used psychiatric classification systems have failed to provide a reliable method for categorization of psychiatric patients, or a schema which permits prediction of response to psychiatric treatment as a result of assignment to diagnostic categories. In this chapter we have examined some of the problems encountered in the use of current diagnostic systems, and the shortcomings associated with them. Even with further technical refinement, important limitations on effective use of current diagnostic categories exist. These are associated with the divergence of complaints presented by psychiatric patients, the current lack of understanding of the genesis of psychiatric disorders, the haphazard selectivity of behavioral observations in arriving at a diagnostic label, and the lack of correlation between diagnostic categories and specific psychiatric treatments.

Recent interest in the direct modification of problematic behaviors by application of learning principles has suggested a new approach to diagnosis, the use of behavioral analysis of individual case data. This procedure sacrifices the taxonomic features of the usual diagnostic enterprise but promises to make greater contributions to the formulation of specific treatment plans in individual cases.

We have described a behavioral analytic approach which presumes that therapeutic intervention can be based on a comprehensive knowledge of two sets of variables which maintain problematic behaviors: those inferred from the patient's history and those in his current situation. We have indicated a set of specific guidelines which help the clinician obtain the type of information from assessment procedures on which subsequent recommendations for therapeutic interventions can be based. The guidelines suggest examination of the following areas in each case:

1. A detailed description of the particular behavioral excesses or deficits which represent the patient's complaints, and of the behavioral assets which may be available for utilization in a treatment program.

2. A clarification of the problem situation in which the variables are sought that maintain the patient's current problem behaviors. Attention is also given to the consequences of psychiatric intervention on the current adjustment balance of the patient in his social environment.

3. A motivational analysis which attempts to survey the various incentives and aversive conditions representing the dominant motivational factors in the patient.

4. A developmental analysis suggests consideration of biological, sociological, and behavioral changes in the patient's history which may have relevance for his present complaint and for a treatment program.

5. An analysis of self-control, which provides assessment of the patient's capacity for participation in a treatment program and of the conditions which may be necessary to control behaviors with untoward social consequences.

6. An analysis of social relationships which provide the basis for assessing social resources in the patient's environment which have affected his current behavior and may play a role in the therapeutic program.

7. An analysis of the social-cultural-physical environment to assess the degree of congruence between the patient's present milieu, his behavioral repertoire, and the type of therapeutic goals which the therapist can establish.

The final section of this chapter indicates the wide variety of assessment techniques, tests, behavioral observations, and laboratory procedures which may be used to provide the data needed for a functional analysis. It is also suggested that therapeutic innovations will probably lead to corresponding expansion of methods for behavioral assessment.

13

A Survey of Current Behavior Therapies and a Proposal for Classification*

FREDERICK H. KANFER
JEANNE S. PHILLIPS
University of Oregon Medical School, Portland, Oregon

Introduction

Current behavior therapies embrace a range of treatment methods which differ in utility for particular patient problems, in utilization of different learning models, and in relative emphasis on the variables associated with the patient's individual history or his social environment at the time of treatment. The main purpose of this chapter is to attempt an organization of these methods in order to identify both their common elements and some areas in which further work is needed to strengthen the relationships between therapeutic strategies and learning principles.

To place these techniques into proper context, it is necessary to note briefly two strong common characteristics apparent in all behavioral approaches. First, the sweeping dominance of Freudian psychology during the first half of the twentieth century in the areas of psychological development,

* This chapter is an expanded and updated version of an earlier paper which appeared in the *Archives of General Psychiatry*, 1966, **15**, 114–128. Revision of this paper was facilitated by Research Grant MH 6921–07 from the National Institutes of Mental Health, United States Public Health Service, to Frederick H. Kanfer.

psychopathology, and psychotherapy has provided a common point of departure from the assumptions in psychoanalysis which behaviorally oriented views cannot accept. Despite this rejection, in substantive and conceptual similarities to earlier psychodynamic systems, behavioral therapies range from efforts to reformulate psychoanalysis in a learning language to nearly complete disregard of Freudian contributions to the understanding of individual behavior (Marks & Gelder, 1966).

The second characteristic common to behavior therapies is their heavy reliance upon learning, perception, motivation, social psychology, and the psychology of verbal behavior as the supporting areas for the development of new methods. Within this common core different directions of interest have developed partly as a result of the choice of learning models, partly as a result of historical accident. For example, Wolpe's early (1958) techniques for the reduction of anxiety responses by reciprocal inhibition resulted in numerous innovations in the treatment of a wide range of neurotic disorders. The early analysis of psychotic behavior by Skinner (1956) and application of operant conditioning to psychotic adults (Lindsley, 1956) and children (Ferster & DeMyer, 1961) has paved the way for innovations in the treatment of schizophrenics and other psychotic patients. Though both of those early developments shared some basic assumptions, their integration has been slow and very recent. While other schools of psychotherapy have shown a splintering in their midst with growing maturity, the proponents of a learning approach have shown differences at the very outset in their preferences for applications of particular learning models to psychotherapy. The rapprochement among behavior therapies may be signaled by several recent efforts to combine the different methods under the generic term of conditioning therapies or behavior therapies. One specific example of a combined program is given in a recent description of a case of agoraphobia by Lazarus (1966a).

Other important factors shaping the development of current practices in behavior therapy were the slow acceptance of conditioning techniques into the mainstream of clinical psychology and psychiatry, and the gradual change in professional attitudes toward acceptance of any radically different approaches to therapy. Although the use of conditioning principles in the treatment of behavior disorders has been advocated with increasing vigor since the advent of Watsonian behaviorism in the mid-twenties, the occasional case reports and theoretical formulations seemed to have contained too few substantive contributions or were of insufficient emotional appeal to influence clinical practice or research in psychotherapy until the early sixties.

The full impact of the decreased prominence of psychoanalytically derived approaches is reflected in Colby's (1964) assessment of the current status of psychotherapy as in a transition period, during which "it is time to halt and question every assumption" (p. 366). Colby sees in the chaotic and transitional state of psychotherapy many of the indicators of imminent revolutionary changes in the field. Following Kuhn (1962), Colby anticipates that the down-fall of old paradigms and the current crisis state will eventually lead to the emergence of new paradigms and new practices.

If Colby's description of the current crisis state applies to the theories of clinicians, their practices and beliefs reflect even deeper inconsistencies and contradictions. At the same time that practitioners and researchers are at-tempting to expand and innovate within their own paradigms, the popular con-ceptions of the origins and treatment of behavior disorders are plagued by even greater discrepancies. While none of the earlier models of psychotherapy have remained unchallenged, none have been completely rejected by the pub-lic. Consequently, there remains a curious hodgepodge of beliefs about mental illness, consisting of a mixture of residues of ancient superstitions, supple-mented by fragments of psychodynamic theories, confounded by the populari-zation of scientific debates, and further muddled by isolated observations about human behavior which fit no framework at all.

It is against this background that a number of theories and techniques found quicker popular acceptance than might have occurred during an era of satisfaction with the prevailing paradigm. Since the work of psychotherapists is directly affected by the power of the public to maintain and reward their practices (and thereby their underlying theories), their success can be as often due to the compatibility of these practices with social directions and mores as to their scientific validity. In competition with other efforts to revise or replace the psychoanalytic paradigm, a group of new techniques, collectively called behavior therapy or behavior modification, rose relatively rapidly to a popular position among schools of psychotherapy. Early reports of the effectiveness of these techniques (e.g., Bandura, 1961; Grossberg, 1964; Rachman, 1963) have accelerated interest in further exploration of the behavioristic model in the field of psychotherapy. The urgency of social demands for new treatment methods and the difficulties posed by the lack of adequate experimental tech-niques for demonstrating effectiveness of methods and validity of assumptions, in a field where a multitude of variables remain uncontrolled, uncontrollable, or even unknown, have added to the danger that faith and complacency will again be substituted for critical examination of the techniques and their under-lying models. At the present, with burgeoning public and professional interest, there is a danger of a premature concentration of efforts on narrow tech-nological problems. Instead of accepting the goal of more refinement of the numerous specific procedures, it may be more useful to strive for their eventual integration into a more comprehensive behavior system. Instead of expecting the discovery of panacea or ubiquitous therapeutic agents, it may be more realistic to anticipate that the clinician of the future will have available a continually expanding storehouse of methods which are only distantly related to those in current use. Thus, the more likely path by which a behaviorally oriented approach might eventually be favored over its competing paradigms is through its ability to organize research and theoretical efforts toward establishing a well-integrated framework from which a practitioner can derive new techniques with clearly stated rationales, with predictable effects, and with well-defined criteria and methods for examining their efficacy.

The first step toward such a framework lies in efforts to find the common elements and the differences among the variety of techniques used. It is recognized that current behavior therapy systems are not able to encompass fully the interelationships within individual clinician-patient pairs as a function of their personal histories and everyday social experiences. For example, questions which relate to variables determining momentary strategy decisions, or observations of subtle relationships between historical variables and symptom behaviors in the patient are not yet accommodated within behavior therapy. The source of many therapeutic maneuvers and diagnostic observations lies in the clinician's familiarity with other theories of personality or therapy, or in his cultural experiences. It is more accurate therefore to view behavior therapies of today as technical tools which can be offered for temporary use in the clinic in combination with skills and knowledge obtained from other sources. Eventually, however, these techniques must be fitted into a broader schema, dealing with the tools (methods), their user (the clinician), their beneficiary (the patient), and the interactions among the three within the same comprehensive system.

The Technology of Psychotherapy

Proponents of various learning approaches have occasionally taken the position that discussion of a conditioning technique is sufficient to characterize the entire clinical process. Actually, the behavior therapy techniques are embedded in a clinical endeavor which includes the diagnostic appraisal of the patient; the exchange of information among the therapist, his patient, and other people who deal with the patient; and the therapeutic program itself. Conditioning therapies cannot be effective if they are foreign bodies grafted onto the total clinical. endeavor but not fully compatible with it. Many behavior therapists have adopted a methodological procedure with great consistency for only part of their total job. They have dealt with the patient in traditional ways in the process of diagnosis, in the accumulation of information about his problems, in regard to analysis of the particular content of his behavioral disorder, and in the acceptance of their own role definitions as therapists (Wolpe & Lazarus, 1966). A consistent behavioristic view requires an understanding of the entire range of psychological principles which can be brought to bear on the problem of an individual patient, from his presentation to his discharge. Such a view cannot disregard the methods by which decisions are made about the utility of a given treatment. It must also be free of any commitment to assess only preselected content areas in the etiology or pathology of the patient. It emphasizes that the presumption of environmental determinants requires the incorporation of techniques for changing such environments as part of therapy.

If the present behavior therapy movement has any long-range merit, it is that the focus on observable events promises to provide a framework for organizing all the clinician's activities. Ultimately, a treatment should not be prescribed just because it is available; rather, it should be selected because factors in the patient's life, history, and environment dictate the choice of a target response (symptom), the use of particular control procedures and reinforcers, and the selection of a given social setting in which treatment should occur.

The main purpose of this chapter is to take a first step toward such a framework by organizing existing behavioral therapies on the basis of the apparent demands of the therapeutic operations with regard to patient capacities, therapist resources, and social context. We will confine ourselves to discussion of techniques related to learning models, and only to that aspect of the total clinical enterprise which concerns therapeutic operations. A detailed presentation of a behavioral approach to diagnosis is given in Kanfer & Saslow, Chapter 12.

Common elements among the many case histories and recently published theoretical and experimental papers led us to propose four treatment paradigms to which most techniques can be assigned on the basis of differences with regard to the following criteria: (1) the relative importance of an intimate doctor-patient relationship as an instrument for behavior modification, (2) the relationship between the critical target behavior ("symptoms")[1] and the particular responses actually presented in the treatment setting, (3) the inclusiveness of the response class for which changes are attempted, and (4) the utilization of various learning parameters in therapy. For expository purposes, these paradigms are described as interactive therapy, instigation therapy, replication therapy, and intervention therapy, respectively. Our attempt to classify these techniques does not imply mutual exclusiveness. There is some overlap among the characteristics defining each paradigm. Further, several methods may be applied across paradigms to the same patient in combination or successively.

Combination of available methods widens the range of application to the endless variety of unique patterns of problems encountered in the clinic (e.g., Cautela, 1966a). Combination also permits exploration with derivatives of more general techniques to suit individuals, and fosters recognition of the need for attending to the particulars of each case.

Lazarus (1965c) calls attention to the need for a synthesis of various methods in a discussion of the treatment of alcoholism. A program of "broad-spectrum behavior therapy" is described in which the usual therapist role is

---

[1] The term "symptom" is used here to refer only to a class of maladaptive behaviors which constitute the complaint. It is used only for expository convenience and none of its surplus meaning related to an etiological model of behavior disorders is implied.

greatly expanded. With us, Lazarus believes that an all-embracing rehabilitation program should include not only conditioning methods but also educative,
environmental-manipulative, chemotherapeutic, socioeconomic, and any other
types of procedures necessary to bring about a change in the patient's disturbing life patterns. Gelder & Marks (1966) demonstrate the restricted improvement obtained when the "classic" target symptom, phobia, is treated by
desensitization while other maladaptive behaviors are ignored. By an overly
narrow restriction of the definition of behavior therapy to desensitization
alone, they illustrate the hazards of single-model adherence which exists when
other behavioral approaches relevant to these socially maladaptive behaviors
are discarded. The separation of techniques into paradigms is desirable mainly
because (1) it permits the clinician to make his choices with some foreknowl-
edge of the requirements of a given paradigm and its characteristic consequences, and (2) it facilitates examination and modifications of the procedures.
Before describing these categories of techniques, it may be helpful to review
a schema of the possible points of intervention which are available.

Different therapists have emphasized intervention at different points in
the behavior sequence constituting a target symptom. Traditional psychoanalysis is primarily concerned with the relationship between R-0 and R-3 (see
Figure 13–1) and only incidentally with the behaviors R-1 and R-5. In relaxation therapy of the Jacobson type (1938), the relationship between R-2 and R-4
is modified, while Skinner (1953) suggests changes of R-4 by extinction, and
between R-5 and the behavioral consequences by operant conditioning. Insight
therapy relates R-0 to R-1 and to R-3, while Wolpe (1958) concentrates mainly
on R-1 and R-4. George Kelly (1955) provides a model for doing psycho-

Figure 13–1. *Locus of treatment.*

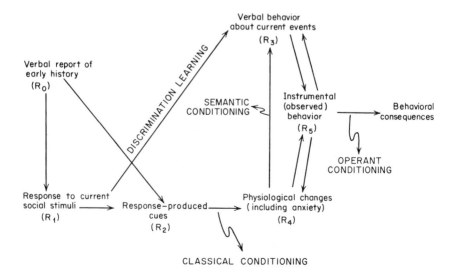

therapy by relating R-3 to R-5. The choice of a point of attack is best based on the particular features of the individual case, rather than on the predilection of the therapist, since decisions about the starting point determine the priorities by which problems are treated. Behavior therapists generally do not attempt to achieve maximal reorganization of the patient's entire behavior repertoire and social environment. The basic task of the practicing clinician is most often to carry out only the minimal intervention necessary to change the patient's behavior repertoire and social environment so that he can return to a satisfactory life in an environment which can support constructive behaviors and which provides opportunity for satisfying his needs. The diagram in Figure 13–1 is highly schematic and does not suggest exclusive concern with any one of the sketched relationships for treatment of an individual. The sketch is intended to suggest that there are different loci of application of learning principles and that each method of treatment may have its own characteristics and requirements. These distinctions should aid the therapist in planning his strategy. They also provide a further basis for our classification scheme.

1. *Interactive therapy* includes those methods which require extended series of personal interviews and utilize the therapist's verbal behavior to catalyze changes in the patient. In this paradigm, the traditional assumption is that anxiety stemming from early unconscious conflicts is the major cause of the patient's problem. The symptom, in turn, has been learned because of its propensity for anxiety reduction. Therefore, the logical target of therapy is the conflict area and the removal of the determinants of the patient's misery and maladaptive behavior. These efforts represent the classical foundations of the merger of psychotherapy and learning theory (Dollard & Miller, 1950; Mowrer, 1950; Rotter, 1954; Shaw, 1948; Shoben, 1949). Attempts to account for social development and behavior pathology within this model did not produce radically new treatment techniques. However, by emphasis on observable behavior the focus of attention was shifted toward increased specificity of cue-response relationships, and research on the dyadic therapy process (Auld & White, 1959; Mowrer, 1953; Murray, 1956) was stimulated. The primary contributions of these early proponents consisted of building a transition between traditional dynamic therapies and current behavior therapies. These writings represent pioneering efforts in the conceptualization of complex human behavior in learning terms. They resulted in the exploration of the relevance for successful treatment of such important variables as the therapist's personality, his nonjudgmental attitudes, his role in anxiety reduction, and the patient's and therapist's expectations for the outcome of treatment. Such insights gained from the interactive therapists have contributed heavily to behavior therapies. However, since the actual procedures and their underlying theory have been discussed extensively over the last two decades, they will not be reviewed again here.

It is noteworthy that the use of conditioning therapy was proposed initially as an alternative to interactive therapy, and the interview as the main instrument of treatment has been minimized in the former approaches. But this vehicle need not be discarded simply because it has carried excess freight in its earlier use (Kanfer, 1966). Most forms of behavior therapy with individuals continue to use interview techniques for diagnosis, treatment, and evaluation of process. Since this form of verbal dyad represents a class of interactions in which patients often demonstrate their problematic responses, the learning of new interpersonal behaviors can sometimes be carried out via this dyadic form. Nevertheless, it is crucial to recognize that changes in verbal and autonomic responding to the therapist are not the main desiderata of effective treatment. Only if generalization to other dyads occurs does the technique appear justifiable.

2. *Instigation therapy* involves the systematic use of specific suggestions and assigned tasks in the patient's daily environment. In this approach the patient's verbal report is accepted by the therapist as a description of outside events. The patient is taught to modify his extratherapeutic environment and to apply learning techniques to his own behavior. This approach is best characterized as one in which the patient learns to become his own therapist. Self-regulating and self-evaluative behaviors are often directly reinforced during psychotherapy, but the actual execution of new behaviors is practiced outside the therapy sessions. Written reports, tape recordings, or other records of outside activities, as well as patient reports, are used in assessment of progress. In instigation therapy, as in replication therapy and interactive therapy, the therapist may also serve as a social model (Bandura & Walters, 1963) but his momentary behavior is not programmed in detail. The natural occurrence of reinforcement consequent to adequate patient behavior in the outside situation is used to enhance the likelihood of a change. Stevenson (1959), Ferster, Nurnberger, & Levitt (1962), Goldiamond (1965b; 1965c), Herzberg (1941), Salter (1949), and others have reported treatment methods of this type.

3. *Replication therapy* encompasses techniques for changing behavior which attempt to replicate some critical segment of the patient's life within the therapy setting. Usually, instructions serve to provide an "as if" set in the patient. The therapist serves both an eliciting and a reinforcing function with regard to the critical responses. He observes and provides reinforcing contingencies for old and new autonomic, skeletal, and verbal responses during the session. The behavior under scrutiny is similar but not identical to the target behavior. It is assumed that the changes in the patient's behavior in this miniature world will generalize to related problem situations outside the therapy sessions. The Human Development Institute (1963); King, Armitage, & Tilton (1960); Lazarus (1966b); Mertens (1964a); Narrol (1964); Sturm (1965); and others have reported use of this approach.

4. *Intervention therapy* entails disruption by the therapist of narrow response classes as they actually appear in the patient's interactions with his natural environment. It does not require an intimate interpersonal relationship.

Since direct intervention includes modification of any of the variables controlling the selected behavior class, treatment can be carried out by arrangement of reinforcing contingencies in a treatment setting or in the patient's daily environment and can be conducted by personnel with relatively few professional skills. When the target behavior is interpersonal, e.g., inappropriate verbal behavior, the treatment may take place in an interactive (dyadic) setting. Although some generalization to other response classes may occur, the particular goal lies in modifying the critical response. Reports by Ayllon & Haughton (1962); Harris, Johnston, Kelley, & Wolf (1964); Rickard, Dignam, & Horner (1960); and others illustrate this approach.

The major distinctions among the last three paradigms lie in the degree of therapist control over the target behaviors, and in the degree of proximity of contingencies between the therapist's actions and the symptomatic responses. In instigation therapy, the therapist has direct contact mainly with the patient's verbal behavior. These verbal responses, in turn, are believed to control other patient responses, and, by mediation, the therapist's actions stimulate socially and personally more acceptable behaviors in the patient's daily life. The new responses, which may be reinforced by the patient's natural environment, also give rise to new verbal descriptive responses upon which the therapist can act directly during treatment sessions. In replication therapy, the therapist selects behavioral units which are similar to the symptomatic behavior and acts upon them by direct reinforcement, by prearranging consequences through participation of others in the session, or by providing a behavior model. The simulated character of the replicated behavior requires that any change generalize to similar behaviors in the patient's daily environment. In intervention therapy, the therapist attempts to use environmental changes and his own behavior for direct control over occurrence of the target response. If the modification is successful, little further generalization is required since the behavior acted upon is, in fact, the symptom.

In the following section, each of the three paradigms will be examined with regard to preconditions necessary for application, advantages and limitations, potential reinforcing stimuli available, extent of stimulus generalization and differentiation, therapist role, and types of problems which appear most accessible to each treatment.

Comparison of Techniques

INSTIGATION THERAPY

The main feature of this technique lies in its use of the therapeutic relationship for joint planning of a program which the patient executes in his daily environment in the absence of the therapist. This technique depends upon verbal communication and upon mediational processes such as those treated by Staats & Staats (1963).

Goldiamond (1965b) differentiates two methods for use of self-control in interview therapy. One is instructing the patient to set up procedures which change the environment and which thereby bring his behavior under different control. This method is the more widely used by therapists of differing orientations. The second method is more specifically rooted in operant conditioning principles and is heavily didactic. It is training the patient in the functional analysis of behavior and having him determine for himself what procedures to apply. This method presumes that knowledge and skill in behavior manipulation can be applied by the patient to his own problems.

Ferster et al. (1962) provide a detailed example of instigation therapy. Obese women learned to control their own eating behavior at home by applying operant learning methods acquired in the clinic. Daily accounts were obtained of the conditions associated with food intake and of the behavior chains culminating in eating. Since actual weight gain is too distant from the act of eating to have any immediate aversive effects, verbal practice was conducted to increase the patient's active verbal repertoire concerning the ultimate aversive consequences of eating. Thus, the verbal stimuli could be used as immediate negative reinforcers. To achieve stimulus control of the symptoms, the therapist prescribed that all eating could occur only in a designated place and at specified times, and that all food-related activities had to be controlled closely.

1. *Treatment focus*—The therapy interaction serves as a vehicle for discussion and control of behaviors not themselves present, even though the latter are the final target of treatment. The essence of this approach is well described by Stevenson (1959, p. 99):

> Mastery by the patient of his relationship with, say his wife, can obviously bring the patient more gratification than achievement of a satisfactory relationship with his physician. Accordingly, perhaps the therapist can best spend his small amount of time with the patient not in studying and improving the patient's relationship with him, but in preparing the patient for improved behavioral responses with others.

Both interactive and instigation therapy rely upon interview methods, but with different goals. In instigation therapy, interview content includes: (a) detailed description of the patient's daily life to provide a basis for a therapeutic program, (b) reports of the patient's execution of assignments, and discussion of their results, and (c) reinforcement of changes in the patient's attitudes and modes of thinking. The patient plays an active role in the planning interview, with emphasis on concrete events rather than feelings.

Instigation methods are not limited to individual treatment. In fact, it is often advantageous to treat a larger natural group as a unit. Individual members of a family can be asked to help with the systematic control of the behavior of other members in the treatment unit (Goldiamond, 1965b). Treatment units may consist of married couples, families, groups of delinquents, or others in residential care. When members of a treatment unit function as surrogate therapists for each other, the techniques used fall within the domain of instigation therapy only if the surrogate therapist himself derives primary benefits and is a target of and participant in behavior change.

2. *Sources of reinforcement*—In instigation therapy three major sources of reinforcement are deliberately used: (*a*) the therapist, (*b*) the patient himself, and (*c*) people, objects, and events in the patient's daily environment.

In considering each source of reinforcement in turn, we find that the therapist most commonly uses only verbal reinforcers, e.g., approval, positive acceptance of the patient, praise, specific approval for compliance with instructions, and selective attention. Unfortunately, generalized verbal reinforcers cannot be standardized for universal application. The therapist needs to adapt his behavior to the history of his patient. As Salter (1949, p. 75) states: "We must talk to people in their private, personally conditioned language . . . with a masochist we must be stern, with a club man type we must be amusing, with a scholarly person we must be as analytic as possible." Even if idiosyncratically appropriate reinforcers were known at the initial interview, their administration would require prior establishment of the therapist as a source of reinforcement by utilization of well-established reinforcing stimuli. The types of reinforcing stimuli which can serve to establish the continuous flow of verbal interchange necessary for instigative therapy may not be different than those used in traditional psychotherapy. For example, Rogerian techniques of offering empathic understanding or unconditional positive regard may enhance patient verbalization in a desired direction, when applied differentially to selected classes of patient responses (Truax, 1966). In expanding from the mere maintenance of verbal interaction during therapy to the initiation of large changes in the patient's daily behavior, the potential effectiveness of the therapist as a reinforcing agent is a major factor in pacing the speed of therapeutic movement.

A second source of reinforcing stimuli is the patient himself. Regardless of their theoretical constructions, most therapists expect the patient to become more realistic in his self-evaluation as a result of treatment. While interactive therapists consider these changes to follow as a result of the therapeutic experience, instigation therapists attempt to modify self-evaluations directly and to use self-reinforcement to mediate execution of new behavior. They may even ask a patient to rehearse overtly self-reinforcing statements which the therapist can reinforce in turn. For example, Ferster, Nurnberger, & Levitt (1962) had their obese patients practice verbal statements regarding the aversive consequences of eating in order to develop an active repertoire of conditioned negative self-reinforcements for utilization during periods of "eating tempation." As Marston (1965) has suggested, the verbalization of self-reinforcing statements may, in fact, become a discriminative stimulus for further activity as well as reinforce the patient when he succeeds in accomplishing an assigned task.

A third source of reinforcement, uniquely stressed in instigation therapy, is the natural consequences of behaviors carried out by the patient in his extratherapy tasks. This goal is consonant with Szasz's viewpoint (1961) that therapy essentially aids the patient in more effective social living and should not be considered treatment of an illness. The strong emphasis on changing the patient's interactions rather than his insights also permits insight to follow therapeutic improvement rather than making it a prerequisite (Cautela, 1965b). Instigation therapists may deliberately program the behavior of other persons in the patient's environment in order to maximize the probability of payoffs (Sulzer, 1962). When it is apparent that a mother serves to maintain her child's undesirable behavior, the mother's behavior becomes the main target of therapy. The mother may be taught to modify her own responses to the child, producing, in turn, changes in her child's deviant behaviors. The observed reduction in the child's symptomatic behavior usually has beneficial consequences in reinforcing the mother's new approach to her child. Wahler, Winkel, Peterson, & Morrison (1965) and Allen & Harris (1966) have reported success in training mothers to apply operant conditioning methods to problem behaviors in their children. These techniques differ from intervention therapy only in that the mother's behavior is the focus of therapeutic attention and the treatment has explicit benefits for the mother as well as the child. Thus, the content of instigation therapy sessions can be the teaching of behavior modification techniques for application to other persons whose behaviors deeply affect the patient.[2]

3. *Extinction and generalization*—There are examples of instigation therapy in which the patient has conducted his own extinction, e.g., Herzberg's (1941) work with phobic patients and Cautela's (1966b) treatment of pervasive anxiety. However, as Ferster et al. (1962) have noted, it is very difficult for the patient to initiate and maintain control over delivery of reinforcers to himself in order to extinguish an undesired response. In the case of many symptoms, the pertinent reinforcers may be entirely under the control of other people, they may be involuntary (e.g., autonomic responses), or the necessary self-control by the patient may be absent (e.g., food consumption). Because of these obstacles, extinction procedures have been of little importance in instigation therapy.

---

[2] When such techniques are taught didactically to persons who are professionally responsible for the modification of the behavior of others (e.g., teachers, child-care workers, clinicians, etc.), the beneficial effects of their increased capacity for effectiveness in human relationships are generally considered to be only a by-product of their increased skill, and these techniques are normally not regarded under the rubric of therapy.

When the treatment unit includes more than one person, e.g., Goldiamond's (1965) marital therapy, extinction can be used more readily because one member of the treatment unit can withhold reinforcers from another.

Instigation therapy reduces the need for generalization since the responses assigned for practice and the stimulus situations in which they are actually practiced are those in which the actual behavior change is desired. This feature, more than any other, supports the expectation of greater efficiency of behavior therapies over interactive or traditional dynamic therapies for some circumscribed behaviors. What generalization is required concerns mostly those verbal behaviors necessary for facilitating execution of the therapeutic program outside the office.

4. *Applications and limitations*—In selecting a behavior for modification, consideration is given to many factors usually inherent in the diagnostic enterprise. Although this topic will not be discussed here, one must recognize that the type of referral as well as the symptom may influence the type of therapy undertaken. For example, instigation therapy requires patient cooperation and participation in therapeutic exercises away from the therapist's presence. Any symptom which is cause for complaint only to the patient's environment and not to the patient himself is not suited for instigation therapy.

One advantage of instigation therapy is that it does not require observation and direct manipulation by the therapist. Consequently, social restrictions on excessive therapist intrusion into a patient's privacy and personal life can be maintained. Furthermore, highly complex behavioral units can be treated. Therefore, this approach seems especially useful for problems which are too "private" (e.g., sexual behavior), too frequent (e.g., eating), too specifically associated with stimuli unavailable to the therapist (e.g., bedtime tantrums), too infrequent (e.g., some phobias), or too broadly defined (e.g., marital conflicts) to be readily simulated in replication therapy or to be brought directly under the therapist's observation and control in intervention therapy. Features of this approach are found in many different therapies. Salter (1949) has applied instigation techniques to a host of neurotic problems ranging from generalized depression to homosexuality and psychopathy. Stevenson (1959) focuses on instigation of practice of new "communicative, assertive, and affiliative responses." Jackson (1960) has used "action suggestions" for altering hostile or dependent behaviors toward a parent or marital partner, and for other specific complaints. Kelly (1955, vol. 2) suggests use of "controlled elaboration" by means of prescribed activities in social, occupational, or recreational areas.

The special features of instigation therapy lead as well to certain disadvantages and restrictions. Its application is limited to those patients who can give reliable verbal reports on the basis of self-observation, who can respond to the therapist as a positive reinforcer, and who are capable of learning some degree of self-control in their role as behavioral engineers. Finally, the patient

must live in an environment which provides the necessary potential reinforcers, suitable stimuli, and places or opportunities for practicing the desired
new behaviors. The treatment is most appropriate for those patients who are
also "ideal" for many other therapeutic approaches, including the traditional
interactive ones (e.g., see Strupp, 1962). The methods are also applicable to
many problems of lesser severity, e.g., poor study habits and smoking addictions, and their use shades into the area of counseling as practiced for problems of limited scope.

The therapist conducting instigation therapy needs expert skills both in
the conduct of interviews as assessment and persuasive devices, and in behavior change technology. Instigation therapy relies upon an intimate interpersonal relationship. In contrast to intervention therapy, its detailed operations are not of a technical and routine variety which can be turned over to
a technician once the general program of therapy has been outlined.

REPLICATION THERAPY

In distinction to other methods, this technique attempts to simulate or replicate significant parts of the patient's extratherapy environment for observation
and manipulation in the therapist's presence. It provides the patient with an
opportunity to evaluate his problematic behaviors and to try out new responses
without fear of traumatic consequences. Contrived role playing by the therapist and others and the use of verbal instructions and other props foster the
replication. In its broadest form, replication therapy may involve construction
of an entire therapeutic community, modeled not after a particular patient's
particular environment but after the general social setting of the community.
Under these conditions, broad classes of social behaviors involved in group
living can be influenced. For example, Narrol (1964) worked with hospitalized
alcoholics in a replicated economy in which points were exchanged for goods
and services in the hospital. A similar token culture for psychotics has been
described by Atthowe & Krasner (1965). Mertens (1964a) describes a form of
psychodrama called "behaviorodrama" in a controlled ward milieu. Regular
meetings were conducted to give alcoholic patients practice in specific behaviors which they could use to improve their daily lives. Similar examples of
replication therapy requiring less complex supporting organization are psychodrama and other group techniques.

The most individualized form of replication therapy is represented by
reciprocal inhibition (Wolpe, 1958), by role-playing episodes or behavior rehearsal (Lazarus, 1963a, 1966b; Wolpe & Lazarus, 1966), and by family therapy, in which the patient's idiosyncratic problems can be scrutinized closely.
Wolpe's approach pioneered application of Hull's learning theory to clinical
problems. The patient is instructed to use mental imagery to replicate traumatic stimuli of varying intensity, while conditioned anxiety responses are

counteracted by relaxation. A recent study explored the interchangeability of imagined and real-life fear stimuli in college students in the desensitization of an "experimental" phobia of laboratory rats (Cooke, 1966). The results indicated greater effectiveness in the imaginal desensitization group only for highly anxious subjects. Covert sensitization, involving imagined aversive as well as pleasurable events, has been successfully used by Cautela (1966a). The available data clearly indicate the need for further exploration of variables which modify the effectiveness of variants of the Wolpian desensitization technique for different populations or conditions. The combined use of imagined and actual elements in the replicated situation may permit more economical use of many aversive conditioning procedures.

In contrast to this use of patient-mediated cues in reciprocal inhibition, other reenactment procedures permit direct therapist observation and prompting. Patterson (1965a) used doll play in a case of school phobia. The child enacted stimuli associated with this phobic response to separation from mother and rehearsed new behaviors for which he received immediate candy reinforcement. Various segments of patient behavior can also be replicated in laboratory analogs. Motor responses similar to those employed in operant learning studies, e.g., bar presses, can be used as a vehicle for promoting social behaviors (Lindsley, 1963a). By this method cooperative behaviors between schizophrenic adults (King, Armitage, & Tilton, 1960) and between children (Hingtgen, Sanders, & DeMyer, 1965) have been established in a laboratory setting.

1. *Treatment focus*—During therapy, response classes closely related and contexts similar to the patient's problems are deliberately constructed. In the less extensive form, where therapeutic controls are minimal, only specific symptoms with unique characteristics are individually treated in the therapist's office. Wolpe's technique of desensitization to imagined stimuli was initially applied most widely to highly specific complaints, e.g., phobias. Recently, Cautela (1966b) has broadened and modified reciprocal inhibition to treat generalized anxiety, and expansion to other problematic behaviors has been reported. Once a particular behavior has been selected for scrutiny by replication, the therapist takes an active role in efforts to modify the patient's actions. In this regard, the technique resembles intervention therapy, except that the behavior content is not spontaneous. Further, the therapist's control is less rigorously programmed, and the obtained benefits must still be generalized to the patient's actual life situation.

The therapist may use individualized reinforcers in a close personal relationship for control over a particular response pattern, or he may set up conditions which virtually guarantee that preselected behaviors evoke predictable beneficial consequences from the environment. While Mertens' behaviorodrama and Wolpe's desensitization techniques illustrate the former, the token culture (Narrol, 1964; Atthowe & Krasner, 1965) represents the latter. In the former, all the variables affecting the traditional patient-doctor relationship may influence the effectiveness of the procedure. In the latter, the relatively impersonal means of control free the patient from direct dependence on a single therapist.

2. *Sources of reinforcement*—The therapist need not rely on fortuitous contingencies provided by the patient's natural environment nor on the patient's self-reinforcements to maintain new behaviors, as he does in instigation therapy. Instead, the therapist, other professional personnel such as nurse's aides, or family members (Lazarus, 1966a) use social or material reinforcers directly. However, if the therapeutic goal is improvement of the patient's self-attitudes, then self-evaluative behaviors must also be practiced in the sessions. Since replication therapy takes advantage of modeling, learning by observation of reward contingencies in others is an important feature of this technique, as illustrated by Hawkins (1964).

3. *Extinction and generalization*—Direct use of extinction is more practical than in instigation therapy because the therapist or other participants in the treatment setting can deliberately withhold reinforcement when necessary. For example, Ayllon & Michael (1959) found that eating problems, bizarre psychotic symptoms, and other target behaviors rapidly dropped in frequency when they were no longer reinforced during structured social interactions. Other replication techniques such as psychodrama and role playing clearly illustrate the use of extinction in participants' failures to respond to maladaptive patient behaviors.

Though therapy may deal with responses which are similar to those in the patient's natural setting, the artificiality of the treatment setting requires that successful new behaviors should ultimately be gained outside the session. These generalizations are not always obtained. Wilson & Walters (1966) successfully modified the speech output of near-mute schizophrenics during training but failed to achieve generalization on the ward. On the other hand, King, Armitage, & Tilton (1960) reported clinical improvement, following use of their operant-interpersonal method, in such extrasession criterion behaviors as interest in occupational therapy, motivation to leave the ward, and level of verbalization. Rachman (1966b) studied the generalization from imaginal desensitization to in vivo avoidance tests in spider-phobic subjects. Fear reductions were noted on the tests almost immediately after treatment sessions. However, these reductions were not always stable on later tests, with relapses on some hierarchial items. Rachman states that these findings and those of Agras (1965) suggest that durability of effects on previously desensitized items be checked at the commencement of each treatment session.

As one proceeds from individually tailored programs to therapeutic community programs, the degree of response generalization required for specific behaviors is likely to increase. In programming contingencies for large groups, it is usually necessary to aim for average situations, so that the resulting contingencies may be only remotely appropriate for any individual patient. However, group programming provides a more economical way to approximate many different responses.

4. *Applications and limitations*—This approach is especially useful for patients who cannot verbalize their problems nor faithfully examine their own behavior nor engineer their environment for change. It permits therapist evaluation of the patient's reaction to confrontation with the impact of his behavior on others. Another advantage lies in the immediacy with which reinforcement can be applied. This permits more careful selection of specific links in a behavioral chain for reinforcement, necessitates only moderate patient capacity for delayed gratification, and allows massed practice of behaviors which usually occur only infrequently. Further, the therapeutic environment can be so structured that initially poorly executed behaviors need not run the risk of aversive consequences. Patterson (1965a) used a graded series of doll-play situations with a phobic child who practiced new behaviors while anxiety was kept at a low level. Wolpe & Lazarus (1966) emphasize the potentiality of behavior rehearsal for gradual refinement and discrimination of a desired response, e.g., assertion.

Replication therapy usually does not require the close dependent relationship on one individual which is characteristic of both interactive and instigation therapy. It is also useful with patients who have a defective repertoire, in particular social behaviors, and who need to be helped in making the initial responses, e.g., in marital or dating situations or other social relationships. Further, many psychotic patients, mental defectives, sociopaths, or young children would be expected to respond more readily to this technique than to interactive therapy or to instigation therapy.

Despite increased stimulus control relative to instigation therapy, there remain serious limitations on the degree of control exercised by the therapist. The extent to which the target behavior can be simulated within therapy represents a difficult issue at times. For instance, with alcoholics, obvious social prohibitions make it impossible to replicate the primary symptoms, i.e., the consumption of alcohol. Narrol (1964, p. 9) comments:

Inclusion of the alcohol in the simulated economy would make it far easier to assess the function of the substance in the behavior of each patient and to evaluate the efficacy of manipulations aimed at terminating or reducing alcohol intake. Certainly our concerns regarding the generalization of new behavior to the normal environment would be considerably allayed if the new behaviors were learned, and shown to be effective, in the presence of alcohol.

Replication techniques are restricted not only by common social values. Further restrictions are imposed on treatment of intimate and personal problems (sexual, aggressive, affectional, etc.) which cannot be directly reconstructed in therapy. Wolpe (1958) avoids this limitation by relying on the patient to visualize his problematic situations. However, the absence of observable stimuli and the lack of responses other than the patient's report in themselves curtail the range of patients with whom this approach is feasible.

INTERVENTION THERAPY

The major defining characteristic of this technique is that the therapist acts directly by attacking a specified observable response (symptom), not by simulation of it or by patient-mediated action on it, but by using the occurrence of the symptomatic response to apply one of several techniques to alter its frequency. It is the application of learning methods par excellence.

The classic example of intervention therapy is Mary Cover Jones' (1924a,b) study of removal of a child's fear. Direct exposure to a series of stimuli provided a hierarchy of furry objects which elicited observable fear responses. Deconditioning, social imitation, positive social reinforcement by peers and others for not responding with fear, and conditioned inhibition were all utilized, with a rabbit as the stimulus. At the end of the treatment, the child was free of fear responses not only to rabbits but also to other furry objects never used in the therapeutic sessions. Other examples of intervention therapy are given in reviews by Grossberg (1964), Rachman (1963), and Ullmann & Krasner (1965).

1. *Treatment focus*—Intervention therapy is the only one among the four categories defined in which a specific symptom is kept under direct consistent attack by the therapist. When a natural environment is partially replicated for therapeutic purposes, the distinction between replication and intervention therapies may become difficult. It may rest not only on the methods used but also on the relationship between the manipulated behavior and the therapeutic objective. The differentiation is illustrated in the case of the chronic hospital patient for whom the institution has become the natural environment. When the treated behavior is of major significance for institutional adjustment, the therapy can be considered to be of the intervention type. Satiation of towel-hoarding behavior or the extinction of patient intrusions in the ward nursing station represent intervention techniques (Ayllon, 1963). On the other hand, Ayllon & Haughton's (1962) efforts to produce increased social cooperation by building behavior chains which included partnership button pushing, and insertion of pennies in a slot to gain admission to the dining room, can be classified as replication therapy since the manipulated behaviors have only an analogous relationship to the therapeutic goal.

A noteworthy feature of this technique lies in the minor and limited role of the patient in defining his problem and his passive role in executing treatment. Intervention methods have often been applied to the more severe and bizarre behaviors of institutionalized chronic patients. The wider range of symptoms in such patients carries a greater freedom for the therapist to select socially rejected behaviors for attack. Society has also shown greater tolerance of imposed controls for extreme behavior deviations. However, some patient cooperation in conducting an initial functional analysis of the problematic behavior may at times be necessary for selecting the problem and suggesting the parameters relevant to the treatment mode.

2. *Sources of reinforcement*—For replication and instigation therapies, there were already existing clinical techniques which could be modified to fit learning-theory models. The newer techniques of intervention therapy, in contrast, are based directly upon traditional methods and variables from the learning laboratory. These variables have two characteristics: (*a*) they are defined by reference to environmental events, and (*b*) they use specified motivational devices such as reward and punishment. In intervention therapy these methods disregard the patient's internal processes and rely on self-reinforcement only adventitiously. This illustrates again the passive role of the patient. When classical conditioning paradigms are used, the therapist retains control of the unconditioned and conditioned stimuli. In operant learning procedures, he controls discriminative stimuli and response contingencies.

The events used as reinforcers are unlimited except that the therapist, much like an experimenter, must be able to keep track of their frequency and intensity of occurrence and to examine their function as reinforcing stimuli. Frequently, deprivation conditions can also be manipulated to increase the effectiveness of the reinforcers. Positive reinforcers have ranged from attention (Ayllon & Haughton, 1964) and social approval (Rickard, Dignam, & Horner, 1960) to money (Slack & Schwitzgebel, 1960); food (Ayllon, 1963); access to visitors, books, and music (Bachrach, Erwin & Mohr, 1965); candy, cigarettes, and gum (e.g., Isaacs, Thomas, & Goldiamond, 1960). While the therapist controls the source of reinforcement, the effects of the reinforcers may be quite independent of any "rapport" between patient and therapist. Only when social reinforcers are used does the therapist's potentiality as a purveyor of reinforcement for the patient become as important as it is in instigation and replication therapy. Nevertheless, the minimal participation in returning for further sessions requires a good relationship as a prior condition for intervention therapy in outpatients. This can become a particularly difficult issue if the treatment involves aversive conditioning.

3. *Extinction and generalization*—The use of extinction procedures in intervention therapy is illustrated by Ayllon's (1963) reduction of patient visits to the nurses' station and Rickard, Dignam, & Horner's (1960) extinction of bizarre verbalizations in a schizophrenic patient. Extinction procedures play a much more prominent role in intervention therapy than in instigation and replication therapy, because the therapist makes the decision on whether or not to reinforce the target response. In instigation therapy, the patient as mediator of treatment controls his own reinforcers to a great extent, and in replica-

tion therapy it may be difficult to avoid reinforcement of symptoms by others. Instigation therapy and replication therapy tend, therefore, to favor those methods in which the development of new behaviors is emphasized rather than the deliberate extinction of undesirable old responses. As Eysenck (1960a) points out, many neurotic complaints can be characterized as surplus conditioned reactions, so that extinction procedures have been prominent in intervention therapy. However, as he also indicates, the distinction between surplus and deficient conditioned reactions may not be as important as it first appears: "It is as easy to look upon conditioning treatment for enuresis as the abolition of a bad habit (bed-wetting), as it is to regard it as the acquisition of a new, 'good' habit" (1960a, p. 375).

The very directness of intervention therapy in attacking the problematic response often reduces the need for detailed attention to setting up conditions facilitating response generalization. However, even though the focus of therapy may be only on one particular symptom, beneficial effects have also been reported in other behaviors. This "snowball effect" (Harris, Johnston, Kelley, & Wolf, 1964; Isaacs, Thomas, & Goldiamond, 1960; Saslow, 1965; and others) can be a powerful ally in treatment and also serves to refute criticisms that this approach is trivial because of its single-response focus.

Conceptually, the broad effects of intervention therapy may be based upon several other mechanisms in addition to generalization. When the target response is a link in a chain of many responses, its change may produce changes in other contingent behaviors. For example, removal of alcohol addiction may result in improvement in contingent physical conditions and bad work record, as reestablishment of walking permits a child to engage in physical play (Harris, Johnston, Kelley, & Wolf, 1964). There may also be partially correlated behaviors which are altered when the target response is manipulated, e.g., improved social relations when stuttering is reduced. There may be generalization among responses which are functionally related because they lead to the same or similar reinforcements, as described by Rotter (1954, p. 184) under the concept of "need potential," e.g., successful social experiences may lead to strengthening of many different behaviors instrumental to social interaction. And, finally, classical response generalization may occur, e.g., with fear responses (Jones, 1924a,b).

When a pervasive symptom is removed, new problems may arise as the patient encounters situations for which he lacks well-learned skills. These new problems are due neither to a failure of response generalization nor to the dynamic concept of symptom substitution (Yates, 1958b). For example, reduction of a phobic response does not automatically make a patient competent in handling social situations previously avoided because of the phobia. His ineptness may require additional treatment. If many unrelated symptoms require treatment, prolonged therapy by successive interventions may be necessary (Ayllon, 1963).

Thus the major concern in intervention therapy is with stimulus generalization. When intervention is vigorously applied only in a circumscribed setting, too sharp a discrimination may be formed and treatment effects may be limited. There are several safeguards to prevent problems due to insufficient stimulus generalization. Among these are the use of varied stimulus components, intermittent schedules of reinforcement, maximization of similarity between treatment stimuli and the wide range of circumstances in which the target response occurs, and elimination of events which may counteract the ongoing therapeutic conditioning.

4. *Applications and limitations*—The passive role of the patient results in several major advantages. The techniques of intervention therapy can be used with relatively uncooperative patients and do not demand the verbal or intellectual skills that are so essential in instigation or any other interview therapy. This extends the possibilities for treatment to such groups as chronic psychotics, sociopaths, defectives, and persons with conditioned autonomic or motor reflex responses as symptoms.

Even with psychotic patients, however, the effectiveness of intervention techniques is increased by appropriate use of the patient's verbal repertoire. For example, Ayllon & Azrin (1964) found that the addition of instructions to patients was necessary to obtain maximal effects of the reinforcement procedure. The verbal control of behavior, either by the patient himself or by the therapist, cannot be ignored, even if large segments of the environment are programmed to yield only response-contingent consequences.

The increased tightness of control and rigor of application also limit the applicability of this method to patients who have already lost a degree of self-determination by social decree (e.g., psychotics, criminals, or children) or who voluntarily submit to such a loss. Also, such extensive intervention in personal liberties is permitted only when the behavior problem is acute or serious. When the patient has some countercontrols over the therapist, e.g., payment by a private patient, unobstructed conduct of the therapy may not be possible.

The requirement of precise definition of target behaviors eliminates handling of such common clinical problems as feelings of worthlessness, marital difficulties, personal inadequacies, and chronic generalized anxiety. To treat these problems at all by intervention, they must be cut down to small, narrowly defined segments. This sacrifice in scope is partially compensated for by the absence of difficulties in response generalization and the opportunity for more objective and valid appraisal of therapeutic progress.

Despite the apparent simplicity of this technique and the limited content of the actual behavior under scrutiny, intervention methods make heavy demands on the therapist's time. Preparation of the environment, rigorous adherence to a programmed procedure, and large numbers of trials are required. Frequently, the treatment spans twenty-four-hour periods, demanding concentrated time expenditure. The burden of such treatment might, in fact, be unbearable were it not for the routine nature of some portions of it which permits use of alternating therapists and of semiprofessional personnel (Ayllon & Michael, 1959; Hart, Allen, Buell, Harris, & Wolf, 1964). There is also the hope that continuing research may provide shortcuts or methods for mass application which would effect further economy.

Critique and Epilogue

Several objections have been voiced, on different grounds, to the assumptions and the claims of behavior therapy. A few of these issues will be briefly summarized here to illustrate the problems which behavior therapists need to face, either by accommodation into a broader framework or by refutation of the logical grounds of the arguments. Franks (1965) has discussed other evidence to counter criticisms, including the misconception of behavior therapy as "simple conditioning," the narrow symptom-removal orientation, and the lack of effectiveness of behavior therapies in removing presenting symptoms.

It has been said that behavior therapy does not meet the needs of the current mental health problems. This argument is encountered as a criticism of the narrow range of cases to which current behavior therapy practices are applicable, as a rejection of the entire approach for its lack of consideration of the broader implications of social control, or as an attack on the emphasis on symptoms rather than causes or preventive measures. The cogency of most of these arguments is maintained because of the frequent failure of a clear differentiation, by attacker and attacked alike, between the professional goals of the clinician who deals with individuals and the social engineer who works toward cultural change. The separation of these goals is probably the more difficult to maintain because of the affinity of members of the "mental healing" professions of all persuasions for initiating social changes. Personality theorists of all eras have aspired toward redesigning their society with their theories as the underlying blueprint for a utopia or, at least, a better world. Many recent leaders in the psychological field (Tolman, 1942; Rogers, 1956; Skinner, 1956; Osgood, 1962; to mention only a few) have shown similar proclivity for cultural prescriptions, carefully deduced from their own theoretical systems. In the case of behavioristic writers, a paradox appears when representatives of a framework which espouses a thorough environmentalism seem to focus only on small bits of behavior (symptoms) without concern for its environmental (or biological) determinants. Although such attacks choose a convenient target for criticism, they fail to distinguish between the context of personal motivations and the context of clinical technology.

The manifestations of the very same dilemma in the physical sciences has been sharply defined by a physicist, A. Weinberg (1966). In a paper entitled "Can Technology Replace Social Engineering?" Weinberg labels the method of the "quick technological fix," which can circumvent complex social problems by reducing them to manageable technological problems. Upon brief reflection, current "fixes" for poverty, war, birth control, or automobile deaths are easily recognized in our society. Weinberg takes the water-resources problem as one example, open to both approaches. To cure the water shortage, the social engineer proposes to educate toward reduced consumption, to overcome prejudice toward reuse of purified water, to discourage people from migrating to water-short areas. The solution of the technologist, however, lies in immediate remedies. He suggests desalting plants, artificial rain, or river diversion. The "fix" is more practical and, in the short term, more efficient.

In dealing with a complex issue, the social engineer focuses on "causes," the technologist on "remedies." But their equally important role is pointed out by Weinberg (1966, pp. 32–33):

> Technology will never *replace* social engineering, even though it may often help make it less futile. Technology has provided and will continue to provide to the social engineer broader options, to make intractable social problems less intractable—to, as Emmanuel G. Mesthene says, change the ground rules of the social games we play and thereby convert hopeless games into winning games. What the social engineers must understand is that we technologists can often buy them the time they need.

Weinberg's distinction applies to the clinician who must decide how much of his patient's behavior needs "fixing" and how soon, as much as to the psychologist who sees the social-environmental contributions to maladjustment, deliquency, or other misery and must decide how large a social unit he can gain as an audience to persuade them toward change, how much change, and how soon. The psychologist who wishes to quell his impatience, or who has to resolve an immediate problem, uses technological "fixes." He cannot, at the same time, satisfy his needs to contribute toward broader, more permanent and more stable changes in his patient, or a family, or a work organization, or the subculture from which the patient came.

The limitations on the social engineering role of the practicing clinician are also implicit in the social limitations imposed on the professions. While the public expects patient changes to suit vague criteria of adjustment or better health, the clinician's armamentarium is generally restricted to verbal interactions in the office, administration of drugs, shock therapy, or patient confinement to institutions built for the purpose of removing the patient from the community as much as for his rehabilitation. Manipulation of social, economic, or geographic environments or even major changes in the patient's social roles are difficult to carry out, even when effective treatment calls for them.

The above considerations do not deny the potential contributions of social scientists and practitioners to social planning in their role as well-informed citizens. It does attempt to separate the job of treating individuals from the clinician's other social responsibilities.

The emphasis on overt behavior, common to all behavior therapies, has been one of the criticisms made by Breger & McGaugh (1965) and by other proponents of dynamic theories. The interesting paradox in this criticism lies in the fact that it was psychoanalysis which originally voiced its suspicion of the patient's verbal reports as unreliable and distorted by the patient's unconscious defenses, leading to the use of the free-association techniques to bypass rationalizations. The solution of psychoanalysis, to circumvent the ego defenses and go directly to hypothesized central processes, has not been accepted by behavior therapists. Nevertheless, the clear recognition by Freud that verbal behaviors, especially self-descriptions, may not match overt behaviors has been maintained also in the emphasis on behavior observations.

The choice of learning approaches to begin by intervention with overt responses does not imply the denial of intervening verbal or autonomic processes which share in the determination of human behavior. The frequent misconceptions that cognitive theorists hold concerning the behavioristic position are well described by Maltzman (1966) in connection with use of the term "awareness." In psychotherapy, as in laboratory research, Maltzman's use of Reichenbach's distinction between the context of discovery and the context of justification can be applied. It is not in their appraisal of a patient nor in development of a plan of treatment that behavior therapists strip off their general knowledge of the content of human experiences (context of discovery). Only in the execution of a therapeutic strategy does the focus shift to observable responses to be learned (context of justification). The behavioristic label is applied most properly not to any clinical approach which is overly restrictive, but to a strategy which deliberately demands that therapeutic operations and the events upon which they act be specifiable in (or reducible to) terms of observable antecedent and consequent conditions, stimuli, and responses. A further demand is made that the observations be described in data language, and that their relationship to known functional variables be noted. It is only with these procedural rules that techniques can be compared and their effectiveness evaluated objectively. Thus the behavioral clinician is not deprived of hypothesis formulation on the basis of his personal experiences, but methodologically, much like any practicing scientist, he is expected to conduct the test of his hypotheses or therapeutic operations in a manner which permits public scrutiny and replicability.

Behavior therapies have been criticized for failing to take into account the "essentially human" aspects of behavior, the self, the value systems, the complex thought processes of men. The early mark of SR psychology as an antimentalistic movement and its predilecton toward the animal laboratory slowed attention to complex human behaviors. With the simple conditioning paradigm as its major offering, the pioneer applications to clinical problems were quite naturally confined to cases which seemed to suit the habit-formation theories best. The earliest application of operant conditioning to chronic psychotics and retardates also seemed to be the most logical starting point. In patients with large behavioral deficits the conditioning paradigm can most easily handle the relative simplicity of the changes necessary to show improvement. The difficulty of the task of expanding learning methods and principles to less accessible behaviors (e.g., neurotic problems, including subjective complaints and subtle interpersonal behaviors) should not be confused with a lack of concern about the role of verbal and other private events as behavior determinants. The recognition of the powerful influence of behaviors which are difficult to observe and cumbersome to attack directly is amply illustrated by research on and utilization of self-regulatory verbal processes. Lovaas' research on verbal control (1961), Lindsley's work on hallucinations (1963b) and on conjugate reinforcement (1962), Ayllon & Azrin's study of the effects of instructions (1964), Cautela's use of covert desensitization (1966a), Kanfer & Marston's research on self-reinforcement (1963), Kanfer & Goldfoot's research on self-control (1966), and Bandura & Walters' (1963) work on personality development are only a few examples of attempts to attack the complexities of human experiences within a behavioristic framework.

Self-regulation in man is largely associated with language. It is the role of language in human experiences which has provided the main stage of contending theories and the currently expanding interest in the study of verbal behavior. Whorf (1956), McLuhan (1965), and writers of science fiction and utopian stories make it clear that modes of action, placements of social values, in fact the entire fabric of a society, are determined by the availability of communicative tools in the culture. A behavioral point of view attempts to free itself from the myths of instinctually recognized causes of human action, from the commonsense beliefs about what is "beneficial" for human development, and from untestable fictions about the true essence of man. The behavior therapy approaches do not inherently carry a solution to questions about man's values and strivings. They merely encompass techniques for changing what appears to be worth changing, as judged on the basis of criteria outside the technology they evolved. But the contribution of a new method can involve the formulation of new questions and the destruction of old myths. The pervasive effectiveness of insight therapies, of institutional confinement, of treatment by love and affection, of emphasis on unconscious motive, all have been questioned with the rise of new approaches to psychiatric treatments.

There is a larger problem raised by the objections to the insufficiency of an SR approach to human behavior. It lies in the question whether any scientific account can "explain" man to the same degree that other natural phenomena are explained. Bronowski (1966, p. 5) succinctly voices one opinion: "It is the language that we use in describing nature that imposes (by its arrangement of definitions and axioms) both the form and the limitations of the laws that we find." And, thinking about thinking implies self-reference, which inevitably leads to ambiguities. Bronowski believes that therein lies the contrast between science and art. The former attempts to resolve ambiguities; in the latter, self-references are used to communicate a view of nature by the very paradoxes and ambiguities which the artist experiences. To Bronowski, the limitations in psychology (and philosophy) are the limits of any system or machine to use logic in examination of its own instructions and to prove them inconsistent.

The issue has been cast also in the oft-quoted attack by Chomsky (1959) on Skinner's *Verbal Behavior*. Bever, Fodor, & Weksel (1965), McNeill (1966), and other linguists have expanded the basic argument that simple associationistic psychology, in principle, cannot ever hope to explain the richness of language. Their research does point to the importance of the speaker's competence and his adoptions of linguistic "rules" which make possible not only rapid learning of grammar but also continuous production of communications that have never before been heard or uttered. The new linguistic movement promises to define the problem more clearly. It does not obviate research findings on the variables controlling verbal behavior, but it poses some difficult questions about the nature of the verbal communication system and man's remarkable adaptiveness for its use. Yet, it must be admitted that the acquisition and facile utilization of speech in myriads of ways has defied adequate explanation by any theoretical system. Although these questions must be resolved for complete coverage of a theory of human behavior, it is possible, from an engineering viewpoint, to deal in the meantime with behavior modification, including the use of verbal behavior, without such complete knowledge. This view implies that resolution can only be postponed and that these problems require continuing attention by research and theoretic formulation. Failure to accommodate these phenomena in a behavioristic theory will ultimately doom the theory to failure.

This chapter was intended to provide an outline for organization of currently practiced behavior therapies, based on similarities of demand characteristics rather than on learning-theory models (Bandura, 1961) or patient problems (Grossberg, 1964). The advantages of such a reorganization lie in increased possibilities of combining assessment techniques with predictable consequences of specific behavior modification methods. For convenience, salient features of each technique are summarized in Table 13–1. The next and more ambitious step needed is to integrate their methods with other phases of the total clinical enterprise. The current organization of techniques provides some possibility of combining assessment techniques with predictable consequences of specific methods. However, it is clear that a precise catalogue of the therapeutic operations or a set of rules correlating diagnostic and therapeutic methods is not feasible at this time. In fact, there are undoubtedly patients whose behavior is not amenable to change by any of the currently

Table 13-1 *Summary of Paradigms of Behavior Theory*

	Instigation	*Replication*	*Intervention*
Vehicle	Interview	Simulated environment	Natural environment
Therapist	Skilled in interpersonal relations	Semiskilled or programmed	Semiskilled or programmed
Target	Broad response patterns	Many observable response classes	Specific, observable response class
Patient requirements	Willing and able to observe and report	Low cooperation; low verbal skills; low social responsiveness	Minimal cooperation; no verbal skills
Reinforcement	Social and self-reinforcement; little therapist control	Moderate therapist control and group influence; wide range of reinforcements	Full control by therapist; wide range of reinforcers
Generalization	Patient-mediated; difficult	Partly provided	Require only stimulus generalization
Learning models	Discrimination; "cognitive"; application of contingencies	Classical; operant; discrimination	Operant

available psychological techniques because the patients lack the necessary behavioral repertoire or because their behavior is not subject to environmental control. Examples include patients whose biological structure severely limits learning, patients who show a total deficit of overt behavior or who are not responsive to available reinforcing stimuli, and patients whose current life situation would be adversely changed by treatment or whose problematic behaviors are maintained by reinforcers which are stronger than those that can be utilized in therapy.

The present schema also points to the wide range of qualifications which may be necessary for the use of different behavior therapy practices. The demands on the therapist's skill are the most strenuous in instigation therapy, and they fit most closely the traditional clinical training model. Ability to relate to others and a high level of skill in face-to-face interaction with patients are essential tools for instigation. In replication therapy, the additional advantage of preprogramming segments of patient behavior imposes less strenuous requirements on the therapist. He may need to have technical skills for modifying individual behavior, and at times he needs specific skills for role playing, reciprocal inhibition, or psychodrama. But he must also have some sensitivity to the essential features of the interactions during replication. In intervention therapy, the skills lie mainly in the planning of a therapeutic strategy. Its execution has already been shown to be within the competence of nonprofessional personnel under the guidance of a skilled clinician (Allen, Hart, Buell, Harris, & Wolf, 1964; Ayllon & Michael, 1959; Saslow, 1965). Preprogramming makes it possible to teach such an approach relatively quickly. However, as Ullmann & Krasner (1965) note, there are two major aspects to the teaching of psychotherapy. The first includes the specifics of current techniques, while the second includes ingenuity in applying the general rules to individual cases. To select desensitization hierarchies, to find effective reinforcers, or to isolate target behaviors requires not only technical skill but the qualities of a *Menschenkenner* who is sensitive to human behavior beyond his academic knowledge.

The most obvious lack in the entire field is that of an underlying theory of human behavior from which a variety of methods could be deduced. The main contribution of behavior therapies has been to methods or process of treatment. Eventually it must be bolstered by a behavior theory on content of behavior. Consequently, the practitioner is often forced to use nonscientific and commonsense conceptualizations when he runs short of well-founded psychological principles. However, until a comprehensive behavior theory is available, it is essential that we keep separate that which is heuristic and utilitarian in the clinical procedure from that which contributes to science or has its origin in science. If we maintain this distinction, it will become clear where our research needs to be done.

It is urgent, if the current rash of behavior therapies is not to become a passing fancy, that practice be supported by stronger research evidence. That this new approach to treatment is not simply an effort to salvage existing therapeutic methods by temporary revisions and novel ritualistic procedures is all too obvious from a survey of its assertions and methods. But to support its claim to greater objectivity, effectiveness, teachability, and scientific rigor, it will need to fulfill the promises implicit in its healthy infancy.

Chapter Summary

The behavior therapies share a strong reliance on the methods and principles of learning psychology, an acceptance of the importance of environmental influences on behavior, and a regard for objective analysis and verifiability of observations. But the choice of particular learning paradigms for behavior segments to which the learning analysis is applied, and of methods for outcome evaluations, has differed among the behavior therapies from the start. To assure greater viability of this approach and an impact beyond passing popularity, the divergences as well as the common features of behavior modification techniques must be consolidated into a comprehensive system for handling behavior problems from their onset to their resolution. An underlying behavioral orientation should eventually permit organization of knowledge into an integrated framework to allow the practitioner to select among sets of techniques according to predictable relationships between treatment methods and variables from the patient's life history, resources, current environment, and available treatment facilities. This organization should also help to clarify the minimal skills required for execution of various treatment operations and help toward a redefinition of the roles and training requirements of "mental health" workers.

   This chapter has attempted to provide a beginning step toward organization of currently practiced behavior therapy methods by analyzing these techniques in terms of their demands on patient capacities, therapist resources, and social context. Only therapeutic operations have been considered here. However, an integral behavioral orientation should eventually encompass all steps in the clinical enterprise. The following four criteria were used to distinguish shared features among reported therapeutic techniques and to separate them into distinct treatment paradigms: (1) the importance of the therapist-patient relationship as an agent of change, (2) the relationship of the behavior manifested in the treatment setting or therapy session to the target symptom, (3) the degree of inclusiveness of the target response class, and (4) the therapeutic utilization of various learning parameters. These criteria yielded the following treatment paradigms, appropriate for distinction among major treatment aspects but showing some overlap in actual practices.

   Interactive therapy represents the classical foundations of the merger of traditional psychotherapy and learning theory. Its rationale and procedures are described post hoc in learning terms, but the operational procedures are the traditional ones. In this paradigm extended personal interviews provide the vehicle for use of verbal and interactional behaviors to catalyze changes in the patient. Interactive therapy methods represent a pioneer bridge between behavioral and dynamic approaches to behavior change, and they initiated important research efforts in dyadic therapeutic interaction and outcome assessment. However, their origin is rooted in psychoanalytic theory and their techniques did not arise from an initially behavioral orientation. Therefore, analysis of the procedures in this paradigm was not included in this chapter.

Instigation therapy involves teaching the patient to become his own therapist. It uses specific suggestions and assigned tasks in the patient's usual daily environment, formulated on the basis of the patient's verbal report of symptomatic behaviors, their context, and their consequences. Interaction within the therapeutic session serves only as a vehicle for discussion and instigation of control of behaviors not themselves present. Self-reinforcement by the patient and the natural occurrence of reinforcement contingent upon adequate patient behavior in his usual environment are used to achieve behavioral control. The need for generalization is reduced because the behaviors assigned for practice and the stimulus situations in which they are practiced are those in which the behavior change is desired. This feature is a major advantage of instigation therapy. Its limitations are determined by its reliance upon patient self-reports and self-observations and upon an environment with adequate opportunities for stimulation and reinforcement of new behaviors.

Replication therapy attempts to simulate or replicate significant parts of the patient's natural environment for observation and change within the therapeutic setting. Rather than relying upon fortuitous contingencies in the patient's natural environment or upon the patient's self-reinforcements, replication therapy permits direct application of social or material reinforcements for responses replicating the target behavior. Modeling or extinction procedures can be used, and broad classes of target behaviors can be attacked within this approach. Since self-reports and self-engineering are not involved and reinforcement can be immediately applied, replication therapy is useful for patients unable to meet the greater demands of instigation therapy. Social restrictions on what may be replicated within the therapeutic session, and practical difficulties in replicating essential elements in the patient's problematic environment impose some limitations on this approach and on its advantages in promoting generalization to the replicated real-life environment.

Intervention therapy requires direct therapist modification of narrow classes of target behaviors as they naturally occur in the patient's behavior. In this approach, therapist control is much greater, while the need for his interpersonal closeness with the patient may be much less than in instigation or replication therapy. Extinction procedures are more readily carried out in intervention therapy. Furthermore, generalization becomes less critical since the target behaviors are treated directly, by changing the consequences of their occurrence in the patient's daily activities and since cooperation by the patient is not essential in this therapeutic paradigm. However, the types of persons and problems to which such extensive environmental controls can be applied is limited by social and ethical considerations.

This organizational schema yields neither rigid boundaries for definition nor unequivocal rules of application, but it can assist in defining and evaluating the formulations and operations proposed by different behavior therapies. By focusing on the prerequisite requirements of the various behavior therapies on the environment and on the patient's resources, the organization of treatment methods offered in this chapter highlights the divergence of roles which the practicing clinician can assume for therapeutic endeavors set by social expectations and role models assigned to mental health workers. In addition to inviting a reconsideration of the proper roles and goals for clinicians, it emphasizes the need for continued study of psychological processes: e.g., the mechanisms of self-control, required for effective instigation therapy; the range of effective reinforcing stimuli for humans, required for intervention therapy; and variables facilitating mediation from verbal to motor behavior, crucial for instigation and replication therapy.

14

The Continuum of Rehabilitation and Laboratory Evaluation:
Behavior Modification and Psychotherapy

LUCIANO L'ABATE

Georgia State College, Atlanta, Georgia

This chapter aims to review briefly the relationship between models and levels of behavior and their preferred therapeutic modes. These modes align themselves along a continuum of psychological rehabilitation—here viewed as the historical context of behavior modification and traditional psychotherapy. The shortcomings of both therapeutic approaches demand detailed base-line, pretherapy and posttherapy evaluations, and follow-up. Finally, the major assumptions and working components of the laboratory method in clinical psychology will be submitted as a possible remedy for the shortcomings of both behavior modification and psychotherapy. Chapter 11 deals with programmed instruction and teaching machines at one extreme of the continuum of rehabilitation. No attempt will be made to deal with the more molar aspects of this continuum, namely, rehabilitation directed toward groups and milieu.

Models of Behavior and Psychological Rehabilitation

Most models of behavior imply their preferred therapeutic approach (Table 14–1). Although this classification may leave much to be desired conceptually, it does furnish an overall scheme that puts each therapeutic approach into a theoretical perspective. From this scheme, one can proceed to a more empirical classification, such as the one contained in Table 14–2, according to levels of behavior. The generalization and oversimplification of both Table 14–1 and Table 14–2 can be broken down and telescoped in greater detail as far as the individual level of rehabilitation is concerned (Table 14–3).

Each model of behavior (Table 14–1) represents a theoretical stance that assumes a major explanatory mechanism for its implied therapeutic approach. These models could be viewed as representing various levels of behavior going from classical conditioning at a molecular level to ecology at a more molar level. The differentiation among these levels, besides its theoretical assumptions, is supposedly based on the size and complexity of the response. The more molar the response, the larger its spatial-temporal complexity. It could be that a complex level subsumes the most immediately simpler level. For instance, a sexual identification, id-ego-superego model (Model 4, Table 14–1) would subsume classical conditioning and instrumental learning. It would be subsumed, however, by an interpersonal model.

When therapeutic modes are grouped according to the size and nature of the response, regardless of their theoretical underpinnings, the sevenfold classification of Table 14–1 can be compressed and viewed according to the empirical operations occurring to modify the response either by acquiring new ones or strengthening old ones. Each of these categories implies different courses of therapeutic action in which rehabilitation is conceived as a multi-treatment approach that assumes complexity and multidimensionality in personality change. Change may not be obtained unless a combination of treatment methods is used, including time (Murray, 1964; Watkins, 1965).

The continuum of rehabilitation from remedial education, behavioral-symptomatic, individual-holistic groups, and ecology can be viewed as a process of one treatment merging into the next form of treatment. Just as behavioral principles may apply to teaching machines, they could also apply to behavior modification, psychotherapy, and group dynamics. This reduction is certainly implicit in the behavior modificators' thinking, but probably will not

Table 14–1 *Models of Behavior and Preferred Therapeutic Modes*

1. Discrimination	Modeling imitation
2. Classical conditioning	Aversion and desensitization
3. Instrumental learning	Reinforcements and rewards
4. Id-ego-superego (identification)	Depth interviews and psychoanalysis
5. Cognition and self-concept	Counseling and psychotherapies
6. Interpersonal	Group therapies
7. Ecological	Milieu and community

Table 14-2 Levels of Behavior and the Continuum of Psychological Rehabilitation from the Molecular to the Molar

Remedial	Symptomatic	Individual	Groups	Milieu
Formal and informal education:	Classical conditioning:	Psychotherapy:	Heterogeneous:	Community:
Teacher-pupil	Inhibition	Analysis	With leader	Preventive propaganda
Classroom	Extinction	Insight	Group-oriented	Clinics and hospitals:
Tutorial	Desensitization	Supportive	Task-activity oriented	Work programs
Programmed instruction:	Hypnosis	Reality	Homogeneous:	Ward management
Teaching machines	Relaxation	Brief	Family and multiple	Day care
Programmed textbooks	Instrumental learning	Interview:	families	Open wards
Audiovisual aids	reinforcement:	Unstructured	Couples	
TV	Institutional groups	Structured	Parents	
Records	Individuals	Counseling:	Children	
Autodydactic methods		Prolonged		
Educational therapy		Brief		

Table 14-3 An Operational Spectrum of the Psychotherapeutic Process in the Continuum of Psychological Rehabilitation

Current nosology (approximate)	Therapeutic modality		Predominant therapeutic characteristic
	Typical	Approximate	
I. Diffuse neurotic problems	Ideal psychoanalysis; resolution with insight and transformation		Exploration
II. Obsessions and compulsions	Intensive insight psychotherapy with some directive intervention; "rational psychotherapy"	Psychoanalysis; "universal thesis" and intellectual insight	Confrontation
III. Depressions	Psychotherapy (more directive); drugs; electrotherapy	Existential therapy; logotherapy	Consolation
IV. Anxiety states; character disorders	Guidance; counseling; drugs; electrotherapy; milieu change	Family therapy; group therapy; child therapy; psychic driving; conditioning	Manipulation
V. Hysteria	Hypnopaedia; Morita (Zen); Christian Science; religious conversion (Lourdes); psychoanalysis without insight; AA	Placebo effect; direct analysis; transference "cures"; autogenic training; Dianetics; yoga conditioning	Persuasion
VI. Schizophrenias	Drugs; psychotherapy; milieu supervision	Direct analysis; supportive care	Supervision
VII. Hypochondriasis; psychopathy	Guidance; milieu control		Containment
VIII. Dilapidated schizophrenia; mental deficiency	Supportive care		Supportive care

SOURCE: Adapted from H. Spiegel & N. Shaines. Operational spectrum of psychotherapeutic process. Archives of General Psychiatry, 1963, 9, 477–488.

be accepted by psychotherapists and group workers (Miller, 1964). The concept of reinforcement has not yet, for instance, been widely applied in the area of group therapy. The meeting point between behavior modification and psychotherapy may be illustrated by Truax (1965). He indicates how, in nondirective psychotherapy, the therapist may be reinforcing certain classes of behavior in an attempt to increase their frequency; and, by virtue of his selective ignoring, other classes tend to be extinguished.

Each mode of treatment contains its peculiar operations which represent a combination of patient-therapist interaction with different mediators. For instance, in remedial education, the nature of these mediators (books, toys, pictures, etc.) is haphazard and strongly dependent on the whim and will of the teacher. In programmed instruction, on the other hand, greater emphasis is given to the nature of the mediator and the student-mediator interaction than to the student-teacher interaction. By the same token, in behavior modification, mediators could be concrete (electric shock apparatus, photographs, etc.) or abstract (words, commands, instructions, verbalized fears, etc.). In psychotherapy, of course, the nature of verbal mediators may become so abstract as to lose direct significance or relevance to the problems of the patient. However, more concrete mediators in general psychiatric practice would be drugs, EST, and allied ancillary practices such as occupational and physical therapies. Thus, a differentiation of various levels of behavior along the continuum of psychological rehabilitation could be obtained even more clearly by looking at the natures of the mediators.

Spiegel & Shainess (1963) suggested an operational spectrum of the psychotherapeutic process which is relevant to the continuum of psychological rehabilitation proposed here. They began by focusing on four dissonant areas in psychiatric therapy, namely: (1) the apparent effectiveness of many and diverse therapeutic approaches, (2) the seeming incompatibility of therapy and research goals, (3) the limitations of classical nosology for patient selection, and (4) the therapeutic specialization which hinders the best selection from a wide range of therapies for a specific patient. To deal with these problems, they proposed a practical operational continuum using special criteria to determine the most appropriate treatment. Aside from an ad hoc theoretical formulation of dubious validity, they came up with eight different nosological groupings, ranging from neuroticism to extreme pathology. Each grouping is matched with the most typical and approximate therapeutic modality as well as with its predominant therapeutic characteristic. The major shortcoming of this otherwise well-thought-out matching lies in its lack of intersubjectivity and the theoretically and empirically weak definitions of the eight different groupings.

Another weakness of the proposal of Spiegel & Shainess is expressed in the question: Who shall implement such a program? If Spiegel & Shainess assume psychiatrists are the therapists of choice, a matter which they consider, they are then restricting the usefulness of their proposal. Yet their spectrum, as well as the continuum of rehabilitation presented here, implies a broad range of therapeutic agents, going all the way from the head of a department to volunteer undergraduates and housewives. Thus, once we select which type of treatment(s) a patient should receive, the next question will be: By whom? Aside from very practical and primary financial considerations (a patient receives the type of treatment he can reasonably afford), our selection of treatment techniques needs to go along with our selection of therapists. This step, therefore, makes mandatory an evaluation of patients, mediators, and therapies, as well as therapists.

Carkhuff & Truax (1965a, 1965b) and Truax & Carkhuff (1964) found that graduate students, lay personnel, attendants, volunteers, and industrial therapists could be trained in group therapy in less than 100 hours. From a certain viewpoint, deflation of the psychotherapeutic market through the use of subprofessional personnel will produce an expectable reaction in the instituted organizations concerned with psychotherapy. Under the threat of diffusion and financial insecurity, they will try to put stronger controls on the practice of psychotherapy. Besides this particular threat, it may put them in the even more defensive position of trying to find out exactly what they are doing. The first aspect of this defensive reaction may be dangerous in terms of inhibiting innovations and research. In the second aspect, the burden of proof may be on therapeutic agencies, private practitioners, psychiatric departments, etc. They will need to prove the usefulness and validity of psychotherapy. Both aspects may eventually have a desirable outcome in terms of controversy and change.

From the viewpoint of the continuum of rehabilitation, one of the major questions that we will be increasingly asking in the future is: What are the qualities and qualifications of the individuals who undertake different types of therapy? Everything else being equal (level of education, age, sex, etc.), what makes an individual select and be successful in remedial techniques, behavior modification, psychotherapy, group work, ward management, and the like? Recent studies show that psychotherapists (Diehm, 1962; Stephens, 1965) tend to fall into at least two different categories of personalities, suggesting the need to differentiate therapists according to which patients and therapies they are best suited for. We need not only to evaluate our students, but, as well, to wait patiently until they have crystallized their interests in different areas as a criterion for our initial evaluation. Through a process of understanding the various therapeutic qualities possessed by different types of rehabilitators, we may understand the process of rehabilitation itself. For instance, we should have people who will be flexible enough to use various forms of treatment. Or, on the other hand, we should have individuals who can only specialize in a single technique. These problems require not only knowledge of occupational choice but also knowledge of the whole profession of clinical psychology. We will need to know ourselves. Although this may indeed be a gratuitous assumption on the writer's part, it makes sense that, if we are to have understanding and control of the variables affecting rehabilitation, we will need to have understanding and control of the variables making for various types of rehabilitators.

The Shortcomings of Behavior Modification and Psychotherapy

Historically, behavior modificators are repeating the same errors perpetrated by conventional psychotherapists. The major errors are at least four: (1) looking at behavior without its context, (2) omnipotence, rigidity, and isolation from other modes of evaluation and treatment, (3) restrictiveness in evaluative practices and procedures, and (4) expense and inefficiency in operations.

1. *Behavior without its context:* With due exceptions (e.g., Feldman, 1966; Meyer, 1966; Paul, 1966; Shafar & Jaffe, 1965), certain behavior modificators (e.g., Ban, 1964; Krasner & Ullmann, 1965; Ullmann & Krasner, 1965; Wolpe, Salter, & Reyna, 1964) proclaim their interest in the specific behavior to be modified and in nothing else. There is the direct implication that once the maladaptive pattern, habit, symptom, or what-have-you has been modified, that is all that matters. Paradoxically, this error is analogous to that of the psychotherapists who have no clear criterion of what needs to be improved. As Kalish (1965, p. 1230) commented in this regard:

> The development of behavior therapy as an explicit set of rules for practice has been exceedingly slow relative to the amount of time that the principles of learning and conditioning have been in existence. Among the important factors contributing to this delay have been the separation between theory and application, reluctance to use the clinic as a laboratory, and *acceptance of the traditional methods as the model for psychotherapy* [italics supplied].

Although it is granted that the concern with context may have reached its extreme in psychoanalytically oriented therapists who emphasize the context of history, traumas, etc., in their zeal to avoid a medical or psychoanalytic model, certain behavior modificators may have gone to the opposite extreme, avoiding the context altogether. A primary corollary of this disdain for context lies in the behavior modificator's disdain for assessment and belittlement of psychodiagnostic procedures. Staats, for instance (in Krasner & Ullmann, 1965, p. 54), is a case in point:

> It might also be suggested that, at first, assessment may not be crucial. It would seem perfectly appropriate at first to apply learning methods solely as methods of treatment. The psychologist who first works out procedures for behavior modification, even without precise means of assessment, will have

performed a service to the science and to the profession. This is especially the case if the procedures can be generally applied.

In the introduction to Bijou's chapter, Krasner & Ullmann (1965, p. 57) are even more specific on their position:

> ...the nature of the treatment determines the focal areas of assessment. This is very different from the current popular views in clinical psychology on the relationship between diagnosis and treatment. In one view diagnostic procedures take on a functional autonomy manifested by long, comprehensive, beautifully written evaluations that are completely irrelevant to subsequent therapeutic endeavors. A reaction to such exercises in futility is the opposite view that diagnosis is unnecessary and even contrary to creating a nonevaluative, accepting, therapeutic atmosphere.

It is evident that the biases of these authors are based on more than rational grounds, at least judging from the degree of derision. Behavior modificators make some gratuitous assumptions about psychological evaluations. In the first place, the above-cited authors seem to be against any form of assessment of anything except the behavior to be modified. It is not clear whether they are against psychiatric or psychological assessment and whether this assessment implies interviewing, testing, or what. In the second place, they confuse assessment and evaluation with psychiatric diagnosis or nosological classification, without considering the position taken by many clinical psychologists that to diagnose means "to understand," not "to pigeonhole." Although it may be granted to Krasner & Ullmann (1965) that psychological reports can be "frustrating exercises in futility" (L'Abate, 1964a), they do not necessarily need to be so. To throw psychodiagnostic reports out on these grounds does not justify throwing out quantitative information.

In the third place, a major assumption made by many behavior modificators is that symptoms which are equivalent at the level of description are essentially homogeneous. Thus, if a patient reports a phobia of snakes and another patient reports a phobia of snakes, apparently both phobias are treated similarly. There is no concern with (1) whether the two phobias are different in intensity, (2) whether they are accompanied by other phobias, and (3) what is the position of the phobia within the overall context of the patient's personality and psychological functioning (Lazarus, 1961; Meyer & Crisp, 1966). This assumption of homogeneity in symptoms and behavior is based on the denial of any underlying causes and on the assumption that only the behavior in itself needs to be treated. Yet some behavior modificators (Blakemore, Thorpe, Barker, Conway, & Lavin, 1963a; Feldman, 1966; Meyer, 1966; Meyer & Crisp 1966; Shafar & Jaffe, 1965) have shown what happens when they disregard comparisons of patients with seemingly similar behavior in terms of group norms or base lines—making it, furthermore, impossible for other psychologists to understand what kind of patients they treat. What are the patients' characteristics? What are their socioeconomic backgrounds? What are their intelligence levels? What peculiar types of people do such behavior modificators treat that may be different from patients who will seek psychotherapy or group therapy? Then, how can we gather this kind of information so that other professionals besides behavior modificators can cooperate? As long as this criticism is ignored, behavior modificators may preclude any kind of rehabilitative cooperation among different types of psychologists. When their case reports (Ullmann & Krasner, 1965) are read, we realize that every case is treated according to its own symptoms, following very loose ad hoc theorizing which may change from one behavior modificator to another. We discover, much to our amazement, that the individual patient elicits the kind of treatment that is necessary. Thus, there is not interpatient comparisons of criteria. This practice is no different in its individualization from the practices of traditional psychotherapists. As long as there are no base-line evaluations in addition to an evaluation of the behavior to be modified, any kind of comparative intersubjective testing of behavior therapy remains impossible. Kennedy's (1965) differentiation of at least two types of school phobias is crucial to the importance of pretreatment evaluation.

2. *Omnipotence, rigidity, and isolation:* The assumption that behavior modifications based on learning theory are the answer to most mental health problems is deeply ingrained in most of the writings of behavioral modificators (Lovibond, 1964a; Wolpe et al., 1964). Staats, perhaps, may be an exception in not sharing the overriding enthusiasm of his colleagues (in Krasner & Ullmann, 1965, p. 53):

> For solving actual problems, however, the simple knowledge of basic learning principles will not provide adequate background. Many learning theorists occupied solely with basic problems will confess quite frankly that they would not have the foggiest notion of how to help solve human problems involving learning, for example, how to train a child to read.

The major by-product of this inferred omnipotence is not that learning theory techniques can, and will, modify just about any behavior, but that this is the *only* way of improving and modifying behavior (Krasner & Ullmann, 1965; Ullmann & Krasner, 1965; Wolpe et al., 1964). This assumption may be as untenable as the early position of many traditional psychotherapists (Hollender, 1964; Spiegel & Shainess, 1963; Wallerstein, 1966) who conceived of individual psychotherapy as the one and only way of helping people. The most practical implication of this way of thinking refers us back to the problem of evaluation by ignoring that maladjustment presents itself in many different forms at various levels (L'Abate, 1964a), and that rehabilitation may require more than one method. The outcome remains that we still do not know by which criteria a patient should receive behavioral modification or by which criteria he should not. Criteria for selection and rejection (if any) appear just as flimsy, arbitrary, and individual as the criteria for selection of patients for psychotherapy (Hollender, 1964; Spiegel & Shainess, 1963).

Ullmann & Krasner (1965, p. 28) insist that "Assessment in behavior modification is directly associated with treatment. A first goal of assessment is to identify the behavior to be modified." Elsewhere (Krasner & Ullmann, 1965, p. 361) they write:

> Assessment and treatment are inseparable. Assessment starts with questions of what behavior is disadvantageous, what reinforcers maintain current behavior, what new reinforcers could replace the disadvantageous behavior, and what reinforcers can be manipulated in order to increase or maintain socially appropriate behavior.

They contrast this type of assessment with assessment based on "internal dynamics" or "sorting of deficient or bizarre behaviors into categories which have little impact on therapeutic strategy." They do admit (1965, p. 28) that psychological tests may be used in work with an individual case to identify critical situations and "may also play a valuable role in determining relevant subject capacities." The assumption that the primary goal of any form of assessment may be the intersubjective, comparative differentiation of patients for various courses of rehabilitation is apparently discarded. This position is not too different from the medical-psychiatric position where there are two courses of action open to a psychiatrist: either medical treatment, EST, drugs, etc., or psychotherapy. Klopfer (1964) indicated the untenability of this position and the necessity for pretherapy assessment, a position which is shared by other psychodiagnosticians (Brown, 1960; L'Abate, 1964a, 1964b; Tallent, 1965).

Was it not Rogers who, in the early beginnings of his method, shunned evaluation as having possibly destructive effects on therapy? Krasner & Ullmann's (1965, p. 57) stance that evaluation is "contrary to creating a non-evaluative, accepting, therapeutic, atmosphere" is not much of an advance considering the fact that no evidence of any kind is presented by these authors to support their position. Rogers took more than twenty years to learn his lesson in small doses, until he finally realized that a warm, accepting, therapeutic atmosphere was not only unnecessary and insufficient but, indeed, detrimental to the treatment of some schizophrenics (Truax & Carkhuff, 1964).

A recent review by Feldman (1966) of the effects of aversion therapy for sexual deviations, suggesting that all is not well with a single-approach treatment, indicates the importance of clinical factors in homosexuality. At least 18 to 20 homosexual patients treated by Feldman & MacCulloch displayed various psychopathological reactions, ranging from psychosis to acute or chronic personality disorders. Feldman states (p. 77):

> It is extremely important, therefore, that there be full psychiatric participation in aversion therapy treatment to enable the diagnosis of coexisting psychopathology, and the treatment of this where necessary and possible. None of the patients in the Feldman and MacCulloch series have received treatment in addition to avoidance learning other than adjuvant drug therapy and supportive psychotherapy of a superficial kind. No patients have received either drug or psychotherapy as the sole or even major portion of their treatment.

To this point, Feldman then added further support for the thesis of this chapter: "A full description of the mental state at the onset of treatment makes it possible to set up predictive relationships between personality factors and the outcome of treatment." He also states, "All too often, the details of follow-up and outcome are extremely scanty." These conclusions are consistent with Meyer's (1966) finding of a relative superiority of psychoanalysis over behavior therapy with male homosexuals.

Since neither psychiatric diagnosis nor interview criteria are the most reliable and intersubjective methods of assessment, we need systematically devised batteries of tests (L'Abate, 1964a, 1964b).

It is clear to me, therefore, that the area of psychological evaluation, insofar as I conceive it, is certainly foreign to the thinking of many behavior modificators. If they cut themselves off from evaluating the individual whose behavior they want to modify, they may be committing the very same error committed by many psychotherapists. In their rush to treat and help, they forget to evaluate, to reevaluate, and to follow up. Consequently, after twenty years of therapy research and practice, we are still unable to tell objectively which patient will benefit by psychotherapy and which will not.

The crucial problem of patient selection is not helped by impressionistic definitions (Hollender, 1964) based on such terms as "capacity to think in psychological terms," "inquisitiveness and reflexiveness," "ability to defer action," "lack of impulsivity and pervasive short-range planning," "tendency to impute feelings and to blame behavior on others," and "submerged aggression." As naïve as Hollender's suggestions may appear, behavior modificators must remember that many of the criteria they use for patient and treatment selection do not have any greater operational status than Hollender's. Even within psychotherapy, with its different techniques, there exist various, still implicit and untested, selective criteria that should make behavior modificators leery of their own shortcomings in this respect.

3. *Restrictiveness:* The sad state of psychotherapy could have been avoided if psychotherapists had used some type of intersubjective pretreat-

ment and posttreatment evaluation and follow-up. This failure is now being replicated by certain behavior modificators (Krasner & Ullmann, 1965; Ullmann & Krasner, 1965; Wolpe et al., 1964), but an outstanding exception is Paul's contribution (1966) which should remain an exemplary standard for psychotherapists and behavior modificators alike. Psychotherapists could be excused on grounds of ignorance, fervor, and other historical, cultural, and clinical considerations; behavior modificators, with their empirical hardheaded rigor, do not have such excuses. Psychotherapists had no history before then; they wrote it and inscribed their errors in it in terms of their failures. Behavior modificators should know this history well and could learn from it.

Behavior modification, despite its claim of inclusiveness, cannot be all-inclusive; as indicated initially, other methods need to be considered. The problems then become: Which patient will profit most by which method or combination of methods by which therapist at what price? Which patient should be treated by which therapist along the continuum of professionals, subprofessionals, volunteer housewives, and undergraduates? We have, therefore, two continua: the continuum of rehabilitation in terms of the types of treatment available to a patient (see Table 14-2) and the continuum of therapists. The failure to acknowledge that, although behavior may change in some still unidentified cases, realistically speaking, behavior modification may only be helpful in 5 to 10 percent—or, most hopefully, 20 percent—of all patients in need of rehabilitation.

Heller (1965), for one, reacted against conditioning therapists "as being unnecessarily narrow and restrictive." They pay attention mostly to either classical conditioning or reinforcement, forgetting other learning principles. He described the overreaction against dynamic therapists as being so strong that many researchers are unwilling to consider learning models that rely heavily on active cognitive abilities. In terms of empirical results from two conditioning studies, Heller concluded that "in some areas (verbal conditioning in particular) simple reinforcement theory is far from adequate." He hoped "that future interview researchers would choose to study experimental variables which are more representative of the cognitive capacities of their human subjects." His most pertinent comments, however, still referred to the therapist's perspective: ". . . if he insists on remaining an expert in only one principal technique which he attempts to apply indiscriminately to all comers, the therapist will find that he will be judged obsolete by a society whose mental health needs are being unmet. He will be considered a too-expensive luxury." Heller concluded his paper with this pertinent note:

> Therefore, it is important to understand that their crucial need at the present time is not to demonstrate that all therapies are in fact the same, all operating by similar principles. While this knowledge might increase the efficiency of already established therapeutic procedures, it would do little toward ex-

panding the scope of treatment possibilities to include those individuals now found not suitable for psychotherapy. Unhampered by parochial affiliations to "schools" of therapy, we need to investigate procedures that facilitate or inhibit behavior change specifying the exact conditions under which they operate. We should insist that our therapy theorists not delude us, or themselves, into thinking that the new treatments they would propose represent the panacea equally appropriate for all disorders. For increased therapeutic effectiveness we need precision rifles, not broad-gauge shotguns.

4. *Expense and inefficiency:* The assumption of psychotherapists that they are uniquely qualified to administer psychotherapy has kept the price for this form of treatment high, and psychotherapy is therefore available mainly to upper-income and upper-middle-income patients. The psychotherapists' restrictiveness has also led to professional practices limited, on the basis of irrelevant academic degrees, to a few individuals regardless of any special personal aptitude, interest, and competence. This restrictiveness is responsible for the failure of psychotherapists to develop a hierarchy of skilled personnel akin to that in any political, industrial, or economic organization. Fortunately, the magical aura of psychotherapy is being gradually dissipated through the increasing use of lay personnel (Carkhuff & Truax, 1965a; Truax and Carkhuff, 1964).

These issues of expense and inefficiency remain unfaced other than through lip service. As Krasner & Ullmann (1965, p. 83) admit: "This issue is related to the training of psychological technicians to administer treatment. While this is still a controversial matter, given the present framework it may be solved through research." Yet no research or recommendation is proposed for resolving this matter. The authors have no trouble attacking traditional forms of psychological assessment and treatment. Why should the issue of technicians be controversial? If behavior modification techniques are as clearly definable as these authors claim, surely they could be just as easily communicated to less trained subprofessionals, especially the techniques that entail routine operations. In practice, this lag is an important failure of behavior modificators. If they cannot communicate their techniques to subprofessional personnel, who will do the actual treatment? What about psychological technicians at the A.B. and M.A. levels? With all their disdain for tradition, surely behavior modificators should have sufficient courage to overcome a conceptual rather than practical controversial matter. Could it be that technicians who do not have the same faith, convictions, and indoctrination as their supervisors (and hence are less prejudiced and biased than their supervisors) may not be able to duplicate the results reported in the literature? Actually, subprofessional personnel may be the best form of control for bias, since they would not be able to make the value judgments and discriminations available to their supervisors. On these grounds, the issue is no longer controversial;

subprofessional personnel could be used to demonstrate a wider usefulness for behavioral techniques than would be possible otherwise.

Evaluation by What Criterion?

Thinking about pretreatment, posttreatment, and follow-up evaluation of patients by behavior modificators has been nonexistent, minimal, or unsophisticated. Although Ullmann & Krasner are aware of these problems (1965, p. 49), their proposed solution leaves much to be desired:

> While methods such as those of own-control study with a chronic case, a comparison of different forms of treatment by different therapists, or contrasting results with a base rate may all generate interest and decrease uncertainty to some degree, eventually, there must be experimental validation. This procedure calls for random assignment of cases to forms of treatment and therapists, the use of an [sic] overt, highly reliable criteria, and the application of the criterion measures by some rater who is either blind as to the treatment the subject was receiving or who cannot alter the subject's response during the criterion measurement.

To ask for ratings in a nonspecific situation, ratings which, in themselves, are highly unreliable methods of observation, is, to say the least, simpleminded—especially when we have highly sophisticated testing instruments which are more objective, specific, and reliable than ratings. Fiske and his coworkers (Cartwright, Kirtner, & Fiske, 1963; Fiske, Cartwright, & Kirtner, 1964; Fiske & Goodman, 1965), based on their extensive and exhaustive research, conclude in essence that: (1) Changes associated with short psychotherapy cannot be adequately represented by a single global rating or by scores for personality traits defined either broadly or narrowly. No single test score and no one rater's rating can be considered adequately representative of the diversity of measured changes accompanying psychotherapy. (2) Changes related to short psychotherapy are so specific to the given method of study that they are difficult or impossible to predict from measures based on independent methods. The authors suggest the isolation of small homogeneous groups of patients with respect to changes observed after therapy. This approach, of course, assumes pretherapy and posttherapy assessment of each patient, a methodological assumption that most behavior modificators have forgotten. (3) On follow-up (eighteen months after termination of therapy), self-reported changes were predictable from several earlier measures at termination of therapy, a finding which strengthens the necessity for follow-up of any patient—a suggestion that should be heeded by behavior modificators.

The various forms of behavioral diagnosis proposed by Kanfer & Phillips (Chapter 13) are inadequate as alternative approaches to the evaluation of behavior modification because of two inherent shortcomings. First, they do not furnish external, independent criteria of the behavior to be evaluated. However, such an evaluation could be found in a standard laboratory psycho-diagnostic battery such as that proposed by L'Abate (1964a, 1964b, manuscript in preparation), which, by its very nature, would provide disparate stimuli from different sources independent from and external to the behavior to be modified or just modified. The analogy of counterreadings would be appropriate for laboratory evaluation but not for behavioral diagnosis. Second, because of its internal nature, behavioral diagnosis is most appropriate and specifically designed for behavior modification and cannot take into account the whole range of behavior to be encompassed by the rehabilitation process as envisaged here. For instance, how can one evaluate the educational achievement or the vocational interests of an individual without a fairly objective assessment of these areas in relation to the individual's intellectual level, visuomotor functioning, and emotional adjustment? Even though behavioral diagnosis may be, or may become, a powerful supplementary observational, and even evaluative, tool, it cannot replace concrete psychodiagnostic norms obtained according to a systematic base line.

In conclusion, Cartwright's (1963, p. 409) comments on this point still bear remembering:

> As of now behavior therapy is less validated than the more traditional forms of psychotherapy but stands a good chance of reaching at least their level of effectiveness.... The state of our present ability to help those burdened with emotional difficulties is such that we should close no doors prematurely because the method differs with our theoretic bias. But neither should we adopt every passing fad and fancy. It is our scientific responsibility to treat each new technique as one to be evaluated systematically and adopted or discarded on the basis of proof.

The Laboratory Method of Evaluation and Rehabilitation

The foregoing considerations suggest that:

1. Behavior modification, or any single method of changing behavior, is based on as limited a view of psychopathology as that assumed by psychotherapy. We must not forget that psychotherapy is based on a psychiatric and psychoanalytic model which concerns itself mostly with neurotic behavior. This model is also based on the proposition that changes occur in the privacy of the interaction between the patient and the therapist. Thus, as Mowrer (1965) noted, the paradox of psychotherapy is essentially that the individual has to keep private behavior that should be acknowledged publicly. On the basis of this viewpoint, one wonders if, indeed, many individuals in "private"

psychotherapy would not be better off in group therapy where there would be a continuous "open" give and take.

2. Clinical psychology needs to liberate itself from the psychiatric model and to develop various models which will transcend and bypass a one-to-one patient-doctor paradigm which is a leftover from the psychiatric and psychoanalytic models.

3. We still have to answer the question: What makes a behavior modificator, a psychotherapist, a group therapist, and a psychoanalyst? Unless we understand the motivations as well as the personality structures of various people interested in the welfare of individuals, it is doubtful that we will understand our patients.

4. Without pretherapy criteria, the choice of the correct rehabilitative technique(s) remains an arbitrary one As long as this arbitrariness persists in our selection of therapies, we shall not be able to compare methods and patients. This lack of comparability is perhaps the most critical shortcoming of psychotherapy and of behavior modification alike.

5. As Bandura & Walters (1963, p. 258ff.) indicate:

> ... nurses, teachers, and parents can serve as effective therapeutic agents under the guidance of well-informed behavioral scientists. Indeed, the primary tasks of the professionally qualified clinician should be to develop effective therapeutic procedures based on social-learning principles, to train available persons in the application of these principles, and set up programs which these persons may implement under his guidance and direction. In this way, more people will receive more help than they do under current professional practices.

This statement should be qualified to include evaluation and reevaluation of patients and of techniques as recommended in the laboratory method.

These conclusions indicate what needs to be done. These needs may be fulfilled by the laboratory method of evaluation and rehabilitation which, for the sake of brevity, can only be outlined:

I. Attempts at rehabilitation should be preceded by base-line evaluations and followed by posttreatment and follow-up evaluations. Reasons for the emphasis on evaluation are:

    A. General:

        1. As context to the specific behavior to be modified

        2. As comparative criteria for patient selection within a setting and among settings

    B. Specific:

        1. To discover which patients would profit by which treatment

        2. To delineate the patient's assets and liabilities

C. Therapeutic:
1. To evaluate change and progress
2. To serve as base lines for subsequent reevaluations
3. To observe any spread of effect from the behavior being modified to other aspects of functioning

II. Increased efficiency to lower costs and reduce waste in clinical psychology can be obtained through:

A. Standard operating procedures to unite service to research:
1. Routine observations of test-taking attitudes
2. Structured interviews
3. Standard test batteries containing at least two tests to assess four major dependent variables:
   a. Intellectual and cognitive functioning
   b. Visuomotor functioning and cerebral dysfunctions
   c. Emotional and psychosexual adjustment
   d. Learning and vocational deficits
4. Automation of these operations

B. Division of labor and hierarchy of skills with subprofessional personnel to perform the technical aspects of these operations:
1. Recording of observations and ratings
2. Conducting structured interviews
3. Administering and scoring standard test batteries
4. Rehabilitative procedures

C. Allocation of a truly professional role to the Ph.D. clinical psychologist through:
1. Systematic construction of structured interviews, ratings, test batteries, and observations
2. Supervision of subprofessional personnel
3. Interpretation and programming of data collected by subprofessional personnel
4. Reporting on results and recommending type of therapy to other professionals
5. Research and theory to improve evaluative and rehabilitative techniques

III. The laboratory method of evaluation and rehabilitation is based on a theoretical viewpoint of multiple operationism that implies:

A. Multiple and simultaneous methods of evaluation (ratings, interviews, test batteries, and observations) in the hands of various, different, and detached raters, interviewers, examiners, and observers

B. Multiple methods of rehabilitation (Tables 14–1 to 14–3) in hands of various and different rehabilitators (including even the Ph.D. psychologist)

Of course, the importance of pretreatment base-line evaluation becomes even more crucial in dealing with children. It is clear that no single treatment approach can be established in dealing with the large variety of deficits in children (L'Abate, 1968a). In order to use differentiated types of treatment, we need to differentiate among at least four different kinds of disabilities, for example: (1) language deficits where speech therapy and language training may be necessary; (2) perceptual motor and visuomotor deficiencies in which perceptual discrimination, eye-hand coordination, form relationships, and conceptual reasoning may be all dealt with through programmed materials; (3) educational deficits such as reading which could well be dealt with through remedial programmed techniques (see Brown & L'Abate, Chapter 11) as well as through the kinds of reinforcements used by Staats (Krasner & Ullmann, 1965); (4) social, emotional, and psychosexual dysfunctions to be dealt with by traditional methods such as play, group, or family therapy; casework with parents; or conditioning-oriented therapies (L'Abate, 1968b).

Chapter Summary

Most models of behavior imply their preferred therapeutic approach. At least seven different models and levels of behavior are available, ranging from discriminative learning to ecology and milieu. From the viewpoint of the nature of the response, another continuum of rehabilitation would range from remedial to behavioral, individual, group, and community levels. A third classification also considered could be obtained on the bases of the degree of pathology and the patients' characteristics.

When behavior modification and psychotherapy are considered from the foregoing assumption of a continuum of rehabilitation, at least four shortcomings become apparent: (1) looking at the behavior without its context, (2) omnipotence, rigidity, and isolation from other models of evaluation and treatment, (3) restrictiveness in evaluative practices and procedures, and (4) expense and inefficiency in operations.

The crucial question still unanswered is: Which patient will profit most by which method or combination of methods by which therapist at what price? On these grounds, the use of subprofessional personnel, even in behavior modification, will become crucial in demonstrating a wider usefulness for behavioral techniques than would be possible otherwise. The problems of rehabilitation consequently became problems of pretherapy, posttherapy, and follow-up evaluation, an area in which the thinking of psychotherapists and behavior modificators alike has been either nonexistent, minimal, or unsophisticated.

These shortcomings suggest also that: (1) Behavior modification or any single method of changing behavior is based on as limited a view of psychopathology as that assumed by psychotherapy. (2) Clinical psychology needs to liberate itself from the psychiatric model and to develop various models which will transcend and bypass a one-to-one patient-doctor paradigm. (3) We still need to answer the question: What makes a behavior modificator, a psychotherapist, a group therapist, and a psychoanalyst? (4) Without pretherapy criteria, the choice of the correct rehabilitation technique(s) remains an arbitrary one. (5) We need to develop ways and means of working through intermediaries within or outside our professions in order to expand our clinical and professional efficiency.

The laboratory method of evaluation and rehabilitation is submitted as one way of remedying some of the foregoing shortcomings. This method attempts to increase efficiency, to lower costs, and to reduce waste in clinical psychology by: (1) adopting standard operating procedures in evaluation through routine observations of test-taking attitudes, structured interviews, and standard test batteries, (2) dividing labors according to a hierarchy of skills and separating sharply between technical skills in the hands of subprofessional personnel and professional responsibilities in the hands of the Ph.D. psychologist. A brief rationale for the method is given.

15

Behavior Therapy as Social Movement

LEONARD P. ULLMANN
University of Illinois, Urbana, Illinois

The medical model has been severely challenged by the reports of the success of behavior therapy and by the failure to find, even under the most rigid searching, any but the most flimsy and infrequent evidence of symptom substitution. The medical model, however, provides an ethical rationale for the treatment of many disorders, since the behavior manifested is presumed to be a deviation from an a priori standard of a "normal" and "natural" state of health. In a psychological model, it is assumed that the behavior to be altered is the result of the individual's history of reinforcement and is in itself not different from normal behavior. The behavior therapies therefore face the problem of altering behavior that is formulated as normal rather than behavior that is by definition abnormal. In short, behavior therapy faces ethical decisions which do not arise under the medical model.

The behavior therapist assumes responsibility for what transpires during therapy (Ullmann & Krasner, 1965). His responses affect his client and he specifically maximizes the strength and direction of his influence. The behavior therapist must accept responsibility for undertaking or refusing therapy and for effects not only on the individual but also on the significant others with whom that individual interacts. Guidelines for such responsibility are currently lacking.

The present chapter will suggest: (1) that abnormal behavior and social movements share similar problems of definition; (2) that the development, effects, and change of target behaviors are similar to joining and defecting from social movements; (3) that the techniques of behavior change involved in social movements are fruitful sources of hypotheses about tactics for behavior therapy; and (4) that the rules guiding the sanctioning of social movements and leadership within them may be applied, as models, for decisions about the limits appropriate to professional behavior modification.

Background

Nearly every textbook of abnormal psychology starts with an attempt to define its subject matter. A recent example (Rosen & Gregory, 1965, p. 11) is instructive:

> No index has so far been proposed that will unfailingly separate normal from abnormal behavior, and it is doubtful that such an index is possible. In case of sufficiently severe disturbance, any of three fundamental criteria is likely to classify the individual as abnormal. The very disturbed individual is statistically different from his fellows, is often (but not always) upset and unhappy and does not conform. *The absence of a universal, foolproof criterion is important only for borderline and questionable cases. For the most part we may explore abnormal behavior untroubled by our inability to define abnormality precisely.* [italics supplied]

For most psychologists, however, the situation is definitely troubling. It is troubling because they are deviating from their role of scholars and scientists when they proceed to deal with a subject they cannot define. It should also trouble them because if abnormality is a variable that is normally rather than bimodally distributed, there should be a great many questionable and borderline cases.[1] Finally, the assumption that there is a psychological state distinguishable as abnormality is likely to lead to a concept of a "separate creation" in which there are different rules and psychologies for abnormality, hypnotism, psychotherapy, and the like.

There has been strong interest recently in the role of learning in the formulation and treatment of abnormal behavior. Over a quarter of a century ago, responding to the questions raised by cultural anthropologists who found many, if not all, so-called abnormal behaviors to be acceptable and even modal in some cultures, Wegrocki (1939) wrote: "The abnormal delusion proper is however, an attempt of the personality to deal with a conflict-producing situa-

---

[1] Scheff (1966, pp. 128–155) presents data indicative of the frequency of this problem and the associated high probability of hospitalization and its attendant stigma.

tion, and the delusion, 'like fever, becomes an attempt by nature at cure.' The patient's delusion is an internal resolution of a problem; it is his way of meeting the intolerable situation. That is why it is abnormal. It represents a spontaneous protective device of the personality, something which is not learned." According to Wegrocki, if the behavior is learned, it is normal; it should be considered inappropriate only if not learned. Unlearned conditions do exist in physical medicine but they have not been demonstrated to exist in the "functional disorders." The result has been twofold. The first is conceptual and has led to a reification, as in the quotation from Wegrocki, of the concept of personality. For example, we find in the *Diagnostic and Statistical Manual of the American Psychiatric Association* (1952) that ". . . a psychoneurotic reaction may be defined as one in which the personality, in its struggle for adjustment to internal and external stresses, utilizes . . . mechanisms . . . to handle the anxiety created. . . ." And in the same reference, it is stated that, " 'Anxiety' in psychoneurotic disorders is a danger signal felt and perceived by the conscious portion of the personality." It is proper to ask what is this thing called personality that *struggles* for adjustment, *utilizes* mechanisms, and *handles* anxiety when it *perceives* such signals in its conscious portion.

A different effect of a formulation such as Wegrocki's is practical. As long as a disease formulation is adhered to, the treatment is likely to be analogous to the practice of physical medicine. Symptoms are ameliorated indirectly through treatment of underlying causes. Because summaries of concepts such as "medical model," "symptom substitution," and "indirect" or "evocative" treatment are available elsewhere (e.g., Ullmann & Krasner, 1965, especially pp. 2–15), this point will not be pursued further than to point out how a theoretical formulation, or—to use Adler's term—a "guiding fiction," may alter the behavior of professional workers. Once "cured," the medical model presumes that the person will return to the natural and normal state without the therapist's further involvement. If the behavior is learned, however, the therapist is involved in making or at least concurring with a value judgment that some other behavior would be preferable. The behavior therapist is responsible not only for the cessation of one set of behaviors but also for the behaviors that replace the previous ones. Incidentally, one probable reason that "symptom substitution" is rarely if ever observed in behavior therapy is that behavior therapists are more likely to select a response (for example, relaxation) to take the place of an undesirable one than they are to extinguish a response without considering the person's subsequent reactions to the previously disruptive stimuli.

Given a concept of disease analogous to the model of physical medicine, the attempt to develop a diagnostic system follows. Just as attempts to develop a definition of abnormality failed (Scott, 1958), so attempts to develop reliable, much less valid, categories of abnormal behavior have failed. The numerous studies of the reliability of psychiatric diagnosis (Ash, 1949; Mehlman, 1952; Pasamanick, Dinitz, & Lefton, 1959; Raines & Rohrer, 1955, 1960; Beck, Ward, Mendelson, Mock, & Erbaugh, 1962; Kreitman, 1961; Kreitman, Sainsbury, Morrissey, Towers, & Scrivener, 1961; Schmidt & Fonda, 1956; Babigian, Gardner, Miles, & Romano, 1965; Sandifer, Pettus, & Quade, 1964; Stoller & Geertsma, 1963) are interesting because: (1) they afford evidence of the practice of societally sanctioned labelers at work and may be contrasted with the material from Rosen & Gregory previously quoted; (2) they present an illustration of how those who wish to believe in a disease model will accept as evidence for their view the very data which those dubious of the disease model take as evidence of unreliability; and (3) they provide an argument against the manner in which diagnoses, once made, are taken as acceptable reasons for further societal action. Once a person has been designated as being of a certain category, all the features of a person belonging to that category are ascribed to him. A person no longer is said to manifest those specific behaviors which led to his being placed in a category, for example, inappropriate affect or anxiety; he is called a schizophrenic or a neurotic and is responded to as such. He is treated as an abstraction rather than an individual. Once diagnosed, the person's complaints may be discounted *ad hominem* and he may be treated (with disdain or with the more scientific procedures of incarceration, shock, lobotomy, drugs, or dynamic interpretation) in terms of his diagnosis rather than his behavior.

There is a pressure of evidence at present to give up the medical model for a behavioral one. The behavioral model rests on the assumption that the behavior is learned and, given the individual's history of reinforcement, is "normal." The behavior therapist is therefore called upon to alter normal behavior, and the crucial issue raised is under what conditions he is justified in so doing.

A behavior is not deviant in itself, but is so defined by an observer. Frequently the observer is a nonprofessional person such as a spouse, parent, employer, law officer, friend, or the subject himself. Something which creates difficulties for the observer is called abnormal. This leads to the enterprising act (see Becker, 1963, pp. 147–163) of bringing the person to the attention of a societally sanctioned labeler such as a psychiatrist who provides a designation which legitimizes the steps taken to alter the behavior. One of the problems involved with the medical model as currently applied is that overt behavior initiates this procedure, while treatment is for a medically defined disease. What behavior will be sufficient to lead to the effort of referral varies with time, place, and person.

In reading about social movements, notably the writings of Cantril (1941), Heberle (1951), Blumer (1951), King (1956), Toch (1965), and Cameron (1966), one finds striking similarities between the conceptualization of psychotherapy and social movements. *That something is a social movement rather than normal behavior is as much a societal judgment as that someone is deviant rather than normal.*

Cantril (1941) presents conceptual material about individuals to explain why they might participate in social movements. Cantril does not define the concept of social movement per se, and while "social context," "social norms," and "social values," appear in his index, "social movement" does not. Operationally, the lynching mob, the Kingdom of Father Divine, the Oxford Group, the Townsend Plan, and the Nazi party are presented as social movements.

Heberle (1951, p. 6) writes: "The main criterion of a social movement, then, is that it aims to bring about fundamental changes in the social order, especially in the basic institutions of property and labor relationships." He also notes (p. 6): "All Western languages use the metaphoric term *movement* or its equivalent for the phenomenon we want to define. . . . The connotation in all these languages is that of a commotion, a stirring among the people, an unrest, a collective attempt to reach a visualized goal, especially a change in certain social institutions." Heberle is not concerned with a hard-and-fast taxonomy, but he rules out short-lived, more or less spontaneous mass actions such as riots, and his definition requires that members of social movements be united through shared sentiments and goals. According to Heberle, a trend, due to the aggregate effect of many individual experiences, is not a social movement; a pressure group, because of its limited goal, is not a social movement; a political party is probably not a social movement, because it has a formal organization. However, the inclusion or exclusion of political parties becomes debatable when, as examples of "The great social movements in the west since the eighteenth century," Heberle (1951, p. 32) cites liberalism, socialism, conservatism, and fascism.

Blumer (1951, p. 199) writes: "Social movements can be viewed as collective enterprises to establish a new order of life. They have their inception in a condition of unrest, and derive their motive power on one hand from dissatisfaction with the current form of life, and on the other hand, from wishes and hopes for a new schema or system of living. The career of a social movement depicts the emergence of a new order of life." Blumer discusses general social movements such as the labor movement, reform and revolutionary movements, and expressive movements such as religious and fashion movements. Among specific leaders mentioned are Hitler, Lenin, Marx, Mary Baker Eddy, and Sun Yat-sen.

King (1956, pp. 25–27) lists three criteria for a social movement: (1) commitment to a goal of change, (2) employment of organization, and (3) geographical scope that transcends the local community. By these criteria the American Automobile Association and the American Association of University Professors are social movements as much as the Grange, Christian Science, the Ku Klux Klan, the Birth Control Movement, and Moral Rearmament which King employs as his major examples.

Toch (1965, p. 5) offers the following definition: *"A social movement represents an effort by a large number of people to solve collectively a problem that they feel they have in common."* Beyond the effects of membership in the movement itself, there is in Toch's work, more overtly than in that of others, an implication that the members of a social movement are different from other people. In Toch's definition, as in King's, many collective activities not usually thought of as social movements would qualify.

One last definition is that presented by Cameron (1966, p. 7): *"A social movement occurs when a fairly large number of people band together in order to alter or supplant some portion of the existing culture or social order."* Cameron proceeds to make the important point that Allport (1933) made for organizations: a social movement is not a material thing but a procession of human behaviors in a given time and place. A social movement "exists" only as an abstraction and a label applied by observers. In this regard, it is similar to the designation "functional mental illness." Cameron's (1966) extended examples of social movements involve the Black Muslims, sometime communists (i.e., defectors), the civil rights movements, and Satyagraha (the non-violent methods of Ghandi). Again, both the definition and the examples deal with people whose behaviors are at variance with those of the larger society.

Considering the three criteria of the disturbed individual proposed by Rosen & Gregory, from the definitions of social movement presented, the participant in a social movement has a good chance of being (1) statistically different along some dimension from his fellows, (2) upset and unhappy, and (3) not conforming to all aspects of the dominant culture. The member of a social movement resembles the person called mentally ill.

If these similarities are sufficient to justify a further discussion, it is possible to ask how a person comes to join a social movement, the consequences of his membership, and the events which lead to his defection. This procedure parallels the sequence of problems of how a person comes to act in a deviant manner, the effect of his deviant behavior, and the methods of modifying that behavior. The tactics of defection or behavior modification are the prime topic of this volume, but formulations of becoming and being a member provide a background which determines much of the resocialization process. Comparing this process in social movements and behavior therapy may be of use to both areas.

Where the Analogy May Break Down

There are two elements which appear to be noticeably different in psychotherapy and social movement. The first is that a social movement implies a collection of people while therapy is usually conducted with a single person.

Second, the goal of a social movement is to alter society, while the goal of therapy is to alter an individual.

Neither of these two variables yields completely clean-cut distinctions. Therapy may well be group therapy, as for example the group desensitization experiments of Lazarus (1961) and Paul & Shannon (1966). The therapeutic procedure may program an entire hospital ward as in the work of Ayllon and his associates (Ayllon, 1963; Ayllon & Michael, 1959; Ayllon & Azrin, 1965) and Atthowe & Krasner (1968), or may program a classroom as in the work of Bijou (1965) or the projects currently under way by Becker and Quay at the University of Illinois.

The second point at which the analogy might break down is that the target of a social movement is society, that of therapy an individual. First, a social movement is an abstraction. Both Blumer and Cantril make this point. To quote Heberle (1951, p. 108): "Groups do not become frustrated; only individuals do. And we may make the further limitation that only individuals who are already frustrated will react to economic or political adversities . . . by joining a radical social movement. . . ." A social movement changes the behavior of its members; if it is successful, the reinforcement contingencies generally available to its members will change. Therapy's aim is to change the behavior of the client and eventually, through the client's altered behavior, that of significant others because his behavior will no longer be aversive to them and they in turn will respond favorably more frequently to his behavior. Again, Sulzer (1965a), Patterson (1965c), Allen, Hart, Buell, Harris, & Wolf (1964), Birnbrauer et al. (1965b), and Harris, Johnston, Kelley, & Wolf (1964) provide examples in which the immediate social environment was changed in order to bring about a change in the individual. Such a change may even be a regular occurrence in groups and not planned with therapeutic intent; for example, Riecken & Homans (1954) point out that when a group consensus has developed, the group members start to concentrate on the person who is deviating. At first there is increased communication with the deviant to alter his behavior. However, over time, the deviant's ranking in the group will decrease and the amount of interaction with him (in the face of lack of change which would reinforce his fellow group members) will also decrease. In short, the analogy need not break down over the variables of number of people or difference in "goal."

Joining, Belonging, and Defecting

Two volumes (Becker, 1963; Blum et al., 1964) provide a model and observations. Becker deals with marijuana users, while Blum deals with users of psychedelic substances, notably LSD. Blum specifically uses the designation "LSD movement." In both, the reader may note the shaping or development of a "career." That is, a person does not become in one step a deviant, an outsider, or a person who cannot be trusted to live by society's rules.

The opposite of deviance is conformity. Deviance should be approached by asking how conformity is learned and maintained. The question is not how a person comes to be paranoid, but how he comes to hold any belief. "Normality" is seen as adherence to group norms; "abnormality" may be viewed as defection from the modal values of a power group such as the white middle class in the United States.

A first step toward defection is failure of reinforcement for socially acceptable behaviors. In the study of social movements this may be called unrest or frustrated motives. This antecedent condition of defection from the dominant group might be called disillusionment, and the emission of overt activities might be called conversion. Some quotations from Toch (1965, p. 128) are germane to this point:

> Usually, the hold of the movement is thus weakened *gradually*: First a few outposts are sacrificed; doubts about minor matters come to the fore; other "weaknesses" are perceived; and eventually, the bonds linking member to movement become sufficiently tenuous to snap under stress. (p. 165).
>
> The convert is a *disillusioned* person, and disillusionment is a slow, surreptitious type of change. It begins with undercover reservations to the effort of remaining loyal. It represents a cumulative record of the costs of adaptation. Whether it dies in its suppressed state or becomes publicized in awareness depends on the number and the import of disillusioning experiences that are encountered.
>
> ... *a person will tend to become disillusioned if he becomes actively involved in life situations for which he has been ill-prepared by socialization.*

Becoming a marijuana user is an example of sequential steps in such a career. In each step, other behaviors become more likely. The key step in a career of deviance is the commission of a deviant act. There are two requirements. The first, as just mentioned, is a breaking of ties, i.e., a reduction of (or lack of) reinforcement for "conventional" or "normal" behavior. The second requirement is the availability of the act. The person who is to become a marijuana user must indulge. He must be shaped into the act. This implies not only that nonusing behavior is extinguished but also that the person is reinforced into the spatial and temporal situation where marijuana is available.

When the person first does use marijuana, he must learn to smoke it properly. If he does not do so, he will not obtain any effect and the likelihood of his again using marijuana will be reduced. Next, the person must learn to identify the effects of marijuana. The person may be noticeably high to observers and yet not "feel different." Next, the person must learn to like the change. Changes in spatial-temporal-kinesthetic phenomena, if they occurred without the proper expectancies or counseling of experienced users would be frightening. The report of different responses to LSD (Blum et al., 1964) and experimental work such as that by Schachter & Singer (1962) attest to the importance of this consideration. Failure either to identify the effects or to enjoy them will reduce the likelihood of repetition of the act. In a different context, it is possible to wonder about the fate of schizophrenic behaviors if they were not differentially responded to by people who identify them as "sick" and cause for concern.[2]

Having learned how to use and enjoy marijuana, the person is in a situation where he may be thought of as a member of a new group and is affected by that group membership. As a group member, he now has a set of rules different from the group whose rules he violated. Being a user is a variable which gains him admission to groups (Blum is particularly clear on this) where he was previously an outsider. He gains attention, support, and other secondary reinforcers. The limitation of a group member's interests is well illustrated by Cameron (1966, pp. 18–20) for the case of the jazz devotee. The new member will increasingly center upon and limit his social contacts to people who will be reinforcing. He will learn the language and customs of his group and hence will be increasingly removed from the mainstream of the larger culture. Becker summarizes these considerations when he writes (1963, p. 31): "The individual *learns,* in short, to participate in a subculture organized around the particular deviant activity."

Finally, if the drug or other activity is illegal and hence likely to be expensive, the person may have to devote increasing effort to ensuring his supplies. This effort may be in terms of either making contacts with suppliers or engaging in activities that will raise money to purchase the supplies.

Another crucial point is reached when the person is caught and publicly labeled or when he labels himself a member of the deviant culture. He is then presumed to have all the undesirable personal and social traits associated with the defining deviant act. This usually leads to a further severing of ties (obtaining positive reinforcement) with the larger culture, as for example, the difficulty of ex-convicts and ex-mental patients in obtaining the employment warranted by their skills and education. There is a self-fulfilling prophecy, because consequences of exposure force the person into further dependence on the subgroup. The person may find that he has no friends other than those who share his deviance. He may develop a set of behaviors, expectancies, and

[2] Scheff (1966, pp. 47–50) documents the point that relative to the rate of treated (labeled) mental illness, the rate of unrecorded "residual rule-breaking" is extremely high. In short, only a minority of the people emitting behavior that might draw the label of deviant are so categorized. This implies special conditions for the activity of providing and accepting the categorization of deviant. Scheff (1966, pp. 84–87) outlines some of the conditions and rewards which lead to acceptance and maintenance of the deviant label.

daily routines based on adjustment within the subgroup. Finally, and this is perhaps best seen in the LSD movement, with its articulate and intelligent spokesmen, the person may reduce cognitive dissonance (Festinger, 1957) by developing a rationale for his behavior which emphasizes its superiority to the perspectives of the larger culture. He possesses knowledge that others do not have. He is free of certain rules that are meaningless, and he can enjoy stimuli which the outsiders do not understand or may not even know exist. In short, he is an "insider" and they are "outsiders" and "squares." Studies that compare deviants with normals in order to determine personality characteristics of the deviant which are in turn presumed to be causal or predisposing are likely to be ineffective and misleading. The vast majority of differences measured by personality and opinion tests are probably the result of the deviance rather than the cause of it. Many of the supposed regularities observed in hospitalized schizophrenics may be the result of the treatment rather than the "disease."

A Sociopsychological Model of Schizophrenia

Both the unreliability of psychiatric diagnosis and the social nature of referral to the sanctioned labeler have already been touched on in this paper. Given the relatively greater amount of work dealing with neuroses from a behavioral viewpoint (e.g., Eysenck & Rachman, 1965), the following will focus on schizophrenia.

If there is one defining trait of schizophrenia, it is disorganization of thinking. There is, however, a base rate of schizophrenic ideation among normals that may be shaped. Adult, logical behavior is an achievement (e.g., Werner, 1948). Under conditions in which there is an absence of reinforcement for previous patterns of behavior, whether called stress, incongruous percepts (McReynolds, 1960), or "strong emotion" (Bridger, 1964), first-signal-system behavior may be observed. The key is to define stress, emotional state, or incongruous percepts in behavioral terms. If this can be done, then the experimental work and deductions of these excellent authors may be of great use to behavioral psychologists. The concept of stress to be proposed has been touched on previously: it is an absence of behaviors that are positively reinforced. In depression, transient situational maladjustments, and many forms of brain syndrome, there is a loss of sources of positive reinforcement. This may be loss of loved ones, home, or job. The person is faced with his prior behaviors being inappropriate to changed circumstances (and hence extinction of previously reinforced behaviors) and a task of learning new social roles and skills. The proper behaviors must be emitted, which involves learning not only an act per se but the conditions (discriminative stimuli) under which the act is appropriate. The person is likely to make errors due to generalization from previously successful modes of adjustment as well as errors common to any complicated new learning. Under these conditions he is likely to find much of the environment aversive, and he is likely to have to redevelop his premises. Until he does so, he may appear to be generalizing on physical-functional (concretistic, primitive) dimensions, rather than logical, abstract, second-signal-system levels. In addition, as modern societies become more complex, the individual is subject to an increasing number of frames of reference, and the complexity of the situation may lead to a decreased frequency of reinforced behavior. King (1956) makes a particular point of this in his discussion of social movements.

Not everyone, and probably only a small fraction of the people who emit schizophreniclike behavior, is taken to a psychiatrist. Reasoning by assertion of the predicate (Von Domarus principle) is a frequent occurrence, especially in discussions of politics and love. Sidman (1960) notes the large role played by affirming the consequent in research.

Poor judgment and other psychiatric symptoms involve essentially a cultural evaluation (e.g., Maher, 1966, p. 170): ". . . the practical criterion by which anxiety is judged to be inappropriate or pathological is based upon what appears to be 'normal' anxieties in the general population." Cameron & Magaret (1951, p. 316) provide an additional example: "We reserve the diagnosis of *depressive disorder* for behavior that resembles the grief-stricken person, but in which the excitants are not identified, or seem not to deserve so intense a reaction. . . ." A person may also act in a frame of reference different from that of his immediate observers. For example, the college boy who heeds his mother's precepts while parked in a car with a coed is likely to be judged socially inept. It is a cultural judgment whether a person should be declared incompetent if he buys a stock with a price-to-earnings ratio of 65:1, gives his money to esoteric charities, gambles on the weather in terms of soybean futures, or tries to fill inside straights.

Only a fraction of the people who manifest any particular deviant behavior are brought to the attention of the authorities. Before they are so referred, there must be recognition on the part of the observers that the behavior is meaningful. The act of referral to a psychiatrist must be learned in the same manner as other behaviors. In this regard, Frank (1961, pp. 6–7) has noted that mental health workers comprise the only profession that creates the disease it cures.

With schizophrenia, the psychiatrist's decision is typically a social one, to hospitalize or not to hospitalize, which he then justifies on the basis of a medical decision, the presence or absence of an acknowledged diagnosis. Two realistic considerations are rarely mentioned: first, the number of beds available may make an enormous difference in decisions about admission and release. In a study of 30 psychiatric hospitals Ullmann (1967, p. 101, Table 13), found that even with size, staffing ratio, and percentage of psychiatric patients taken into account, the number of new applications per bed correlated .45 with relatively rapid release of schizophrenic patients and −.54 with the number of patients who had remained in the hospital two or more years. In short, pressure for bed usage was significantly correlated with the hospitals' relative effectiveness. Anecdotal material abounds (e.g., Kennard, 1957; Glasscote, Cumming, Hammersley, Ozarin, & Smith, 1966, pp. 83–84) on the effects of administrative considerations on the admission and release of psychiatric patients. Second, the psychiatrist may base his decision on whether admission to the hospital would be beneficial to the patient. This may be in terms of removing him from an unfortunate situation such as one in which he is rejected by his wife or children, or it may be one in which he thinks treatment will be helpful. This decision must then be sanctioned by a label.

As noted by Lehrman (1961) the psychiatrist's behavior may reinforce and shape the patient to emit diagnosable verbalizations. The work on verbal operant conditioning provides ample evidence that the schizophrenic symptoms may be manipulated by selective reinforcements (Ayllon & Haughton, 1964; Ullmann et al., 1965). The person who does not respond to the psychiatrist's little jokes may well be considered withdrawn, unresponsive, and inappropriate, and suffer for it. The process is one in which a behavior is elicited, interpreted as belonging to a larger class, and that class is in turn an example of the still larger class of illness.

Once the patient is in the hospital, there are strong influences to alter his behavior toward the pattern of schizophrenia observed in our institutions.

Barton (1959) and Sommer & Osmond (1961) have listed the symptoms of institutional care. The individual is placed in an environment whose large size, inadequate staffing, conservative adherence to rules found in public institutions, and inappropriate application of the bureaucratic model (see Ullmann, 1967) lead to the reinforcement of behavior on the part of both staff and patients which is different from, if not antithetical to, the return of the patient to the larger extramural community. Historically (e.g., Bockoven, 1963) the coming of the medical model, the increased number of patients, reduced expenditures, and the development of the aide culture, fostered the conditions currently observed. The thrust in a large public mental hospital is towards a clean, quiet, untroublesome patient. Belknap (1956), Dunham & Weinberg (1960), and Goffman (1961) are among authors who have detailed the procedures by which response-contingent reinforcement is used for the comfort of the attendant rather than the ultimate reintegration of the patient into the extrahospital community. Two quotations may make clear the general tenor of this literature. Bloom (1963, p. 191) writes: "He is taught first of all, how to behave in his new role as a hospital patient." Dunham & Weinberg (1960,

p. 66) quote a patient: " 'Everything here is definite,' said one patient. 'You soon learn what you should do and mainly what you should not do.' " Empirical illustration of this process at an attitude level is provided by McReynolds & Guevara (1967) and at a behavioral level by McInnis & Ullmann (1967).

The hospital situation is one in which there is monotony of activity and food as well as reinforcement for nonassertive, withdrawn behavior. Within this context it is possible to ask what would occur if response-contingent reinforcement were provided counter to the general institutional drift. This question has been answered in two ways. The first is the series of studies with specific cases by Ayllon and his coworkers (Ayllon, 1963; Ayllon & Azrin, 1965; Ayllon & Haughton, 1962, 1964; Ayllon & Michael, 1959). The second method has been the more traditional method of experimentation using very modest reinforcing stimuli on subjects assigned to "one-shot" experiments in which a major symptom of schizophrenia was the key dependent variable. Emotional expressiveness (Salzinger & Pisoni, 1958; Weiss, Ullmann, & Krasner, 1963), social interactions (King, Armitage, & Tilton, 1960; Ullmann, Krasner, & Collins, 1961), sick talk (Ullmann, Forsman, Kenny, McInnis, Unikel, & Zeisset, 1965), and disorganized thinking (Ullmann, Krasner, & Edinger, 1964; True, 1966; Meichenbaum, 1966a) have all been significantly altered by response-contingent reinforcement.

Beyond these considerations is the finding that schizophrenics are very responsive to changed environments. Perrow (1965, p. 934) notes: "Too many of the structural changes announced in the literature have produced no lasting results; too many of the results appear to be due to the 'Hawthorne' effect, whereby merely to show some interest in patients and to increase interaction has a beneficial effect—although it may disappear as soon as the research team or change agents leave the scene." In a later section, Perrow (p. 941) writes: "There is a persistent theme in the literature that almost anything can have its effect where conditions are bad. Kamman and his associates reported on a survey of 90 articles on psychotherapy with schizophrenics. They found a wide variation in technique, theory, and qualifications of the therapists and concluded that 'almost anything that has at one time or another been tried has been of benefit in the treatment of schizophrenia.' (Kamman, et al., 1954.)" Two articles appearing in the *New York Times* make the point eloquently. On March 31, 1966, a front-page story related how a physician reported that nicotinamide adenine dinucleotide (NAD) had led to striking improvement in 13 of 17 cases of schizophrenia after three to five days of treatment. On June 25, 1966 a follow-up article began with the sentence: "A drug initially said to erase the symptoms of schizophrenia in a matter of days has been found to be no more effective than a sugar pill. . . ." The article relates failure to obtain significant differences between patients receiving NAD and matched patients receiving a sugar pill prepared to resemble the drug. This is the entire point: the changes observed in the first study reported on March 31, 1966, were real and no issue is raised with the honesty of purpose or accuracy of observation of the researcher. Rather than a specific chemical effect called for by a theory of a specific physiological etiology, the effects observed were associated with the interest, attention, expectation, and encouragement of new behavior which was reinforcing to the research worker. Psychologists are not free from such blind spots. An example of such a blind spot is provided by Buss (1966, pp. 265–270) in his discussion and less than favorable evaluation of what he calls theories of schizophrenia which posit a lack of motivation. Buss presumes that schizophrenics, when reinforcing stimuli are made available, should not only improve but improve to a significantly greater extent than normals. Such experimental results do exist, especially when the reinforcement involves avoidance of noxious stimuli. The key point, however, is the significant responsiveness of schizophrenics to the relatively slight, brief presentations of stimuli that the research worker presumes to be positively reinforcing (although frequently such secondary reinforcing stimuli may well have been extinguished in the hospital setting).

To summarize the main points, schizophrenia may be viewed as a multistage process, a career, in which the person, once labeled (by a social process with far from perfect reliability) is treated in terms of that label rather than overt behavior. The person is placed in social and institutional situations in which patterns of withdrawal and avoidance of punishment are reinforced. Many of the regularities observed in the behavior of the hospitalized people called schizophrenics may be the result rather than the cause of their treatment. Throughout the various stages of a schizophrenic career there may be the failure to reinforce (through absence in the environment, changes of reinforcing contingencies, or reinforcement of alternative behaviors) "normal" behaviors. Through responses by the public to the label "schizophrenia," the person is extinguished for responses to people as secondary reinforcers. He may not respond appropriately, that is, like other people, because he has not had or has not been maintained in responses like other people. Social withdrawal, inappropriate behavior, poverty of affect, and apathy may well follow. Stimuli which are presumed to be meaningful have been extinguished, and the result is a failure to attend. "One who readily engages in a given activity is not showing an interest, he is showing the effect of reinforcement" (Skinner, 1953, p. 72). In addition to changes in environmental contingencies calling for new and complicated learning, reinforcement for institutional behavior may lead to lack of "interest" and hence to the inappropriate responses observers classify as disorganization of thinking. Researches by Ullmann, Krasner, & Edinger (1964), True (1966), and Meichenbaum (1966b) indicate that under reinforcing contingencies "schizophrenics' " disorganization of thinking may be reversed. In Skinner's words (1953, p. 112): "To ask whether someone *can* turn a handspring is merely to ask whether there are circumstances under which he will do so."[3]

Behavior Therapist as Leader

The next two sections will pursue the analogy between social movement and behavior therapy in terms of tactics. It will be argued that abnormal behavior involves designation to a group and the therapist acts as a leader who encourages membership in some groups and defection from others. The following quotation from Toch (1965, p. 83) may well summarize what follows:

> When a self-change movement claims to be effective, this claim comprises *three separate assumptions*. The first of these is that *a social movement* can solve the person's problems, although he may not be able to solve them himself. The second claim is that the *movement in question* can solve the problem. The third proposition is that *the specific techniques of the movement are the best or the only techniques which can accomplish the job.*...
> By spelling out the undesirable consequences of the member's condition, the movement defines his problem. The result is to *reinforce the member's conviction that he must take action.*

Parenthetically, there is a great similarity between a patient's "insight" and the concept of identification with the aggressor (see especially Schein, Schneier, & Barker, 1961, on brainwashing and Frank, 1961, on training analysts). The therapist plays a crucial and responsible role in behavior ther-

---

[3] The review of definitions of social movements and the discussion of joining and defecting may combine with this section to indicate an alternative interpretation of the title of this chapter. The sociopsychological model could (and if valid, should) be applicable to all social behaviors, including presumably valuable ones such as the perpetration of behavior therapy. Behavior therapy has its revered forerunners, its leaders, its core writings, its favored journals, its factions, and even a formal organization for its advancement. Behavior therapy is different enough for a recent article about it (Hartman, 1966) to be entitled "Unconventional Psychotherapy" and to include the question to Joseph Wolpe: "Do you really think American psychiatrists are going to take this kind of therapy seriously?" The background of many behavior therapists involves defection from the evocative procedures that currently comprise the norm of American psychotherapy and conversion to behavior therapy. If the ideas presented in this chapter are correct, the practice and practitioners of behavior therapy do indeed represent a social movement. In this context, however, the designation of social movement is anything but pejorative and merely indicates an approach to what is formulated as normal behavior (e.g., extinction of some therapeutic maneuvers and reinforcement of different ones in terms of effectiveness) but is evaluated by a dominant social group as deviant (e.g., "unconventional psychotherapy").

apy, yet there is a very small amount of empirical work on the qualities of the effective therapist. It is reasonable to turn to the literature on leadership, therefore, where there are more data using behavioral criteria.

Like the therapist in behavior modification (e.g., Ullmann & Krasner, 1965, pp. 39–44), ". . . the leader is the chief agent of control" (Riecken & Homans, 1954, p. 816). What I noted about mental health professionals in regard to schizophrenia is similar to what Riecken & Homans (1954, p. 818) point out: ". . . the leader's behavior, just as much as other members', will illustrate the laws of social structure and social control." The leader and his power or authority may be defined by the probability that his orders will be obeyed (i.e., that he has influence) and this, in turn, ". . . will depend ultimately on the interests of the persons ordered, as they see these interests."

The traits of leadership should be referred to a particular situation and may be further defined as ". . . any or all of those personality traits which, *in any particular situation*, enable an individual to (i) contribute significantly to group locomotion in the direction of a recognized goal, and (ii) be perceived as doing so by fellow group members" (Gibb, 1954, p. 889). Following Gibb (pp. 889–890), among behaviors which are thought of as germane to the leadership role are performing technical or professional acts, knowing subordinates, keeping communication channels open, accepting responsibility, setting an example, initiating and directing action, training members as a team, and making decisions. Leaders categorize the situation and give information for action to be taken. In all these matters there is a direct parallel with the behavior therapist. A crucial point, which has already been made, bears repetition: "Leadership is always relative to the situation" (Gibb, 1954, p. 901). The person who has provided the most information on the matching of leadership characteristics to effectiveness in particular situations is Fiedler (1965). He reports on a long series of studies of the effectiveness of leaders. He makes use of three variables: (1) leader-member relations, (2) task structure, and (3) position power. Through this model, Fiedler reconciles a number of previously inconsistent empirical findings. Of major importance to clinicians is that there is not one pattern of effective leadership behavior, but a number which depend upon the group task situation. In therapy the situations change. Extrapolating from Fiedler, one might hypothesize that democratic and permissive traits such as establishing rapport and devising a hierarchy would be most useful in the early stages of treatment, while relatively managing, controlling, autocratic leadership would be more effective during the procedure of desensitization per se.

The analogy between leadership in a social movement and by a therapist may be carried one bit further to illustrate the development of hypotheses on optimum therapist behaviors. Blumer (1951, pp. 203ff.) proposes four stages in the cycle of a social movement. In the first of these, there is unrest and the people are susceptible to appeals. In this stage, the major function of the leader is agitation to gain new recruits by awakening them to new ideas, loosening their standards, and breaking down their previous ways of thinking and acting. The agitator must gain attention, arouse feelings, and offer some program to ameliorate these feelings. There is an understandable but unfortunate professional reticence on the subject of recruiting patients for psychotherapy, and what literature exists deals usually with the age, sex, social class status, or personality of people who remain or terminate treatment. A frequent problem in hospital and clinic settings is how to "motivate" the patient or "how to get him into therapy." The problem of the private practitioner, "how to get patients at all," is ignored. The analogy would suggest that a key aspect of the first step in psychotherapy is gaining an audience and directing attention to behavior which the therapist then labels as (1) bad, but (2) treatable.

A second stage is called popular excitement by Blumer. It seems to be a transition between the previous stage and the subsequent one. There is a sharpening of objectives, an agreement on the causes of difficulties and the methods of altering them. Much of this work and the development of rapport (*esprit de corps* and morale) is accomplished in the first interviews. In this stage the therapist has the role of prophet of good tidings and reformer without office. Having convinced the patient that something is wrong and should be altered by the therapist's plan, the therapist can focus on outcome rather than current difficulty. This not only builds his halo or "placebo," it also leads naturally into the specific indoctrination and formalization of the treatment with its attendant clearer organization of procedures, rules, tactics, and discipline. In this third stage the leader takes on the role of statesman as he integrates the patient with the procedure. Examples are the training of the person in the elements of the therapy, such as free association or relaxation. In the final institutional stage, the purposes of the movement or treatment are carried out. Here the leader may be considered an administrator following well-formulated procedures. While schematic, the point is that during therapy, both the client and the therapist change, and to be most effective the same therapist must fulfill different functions at different stages. To be an agitator when the administrator's role is called for would be as wasteful as to be an administrator during the first stage.

Tactics

While using a generally cognitive approach, authors writing on social movements describe both the career of movements and the members in ways which are directly translatable into behavioristic terms. For instance, movements may be said to illustrate both extinction and satiation: ". . . some movements cease to exist essentially because they can no longer change the culture, or themselves, and . . . other movements change conditions around themselves so that they become no longer feasible or necessary" (Cameron, 1966, p. 8). The effect of positive reinforcement is stated as follows: ". . . we must recognize that a movement succeeds and continues when it offers something that people want, and it ceases to exist when people no longer want what it offers or when they can get it more satisfactorily by other means" (p. 29). The proper scheduling of reinforcement is stated in descriptions of social movements in a manner which many therapists may recognize: "It is up to the leader to judge how far out to dangle the rabbit. Too close, and the dogs slow down. Too far, and they quit. Just far enough, and they run as hard as they can. And, the farther out the leader holds the rabbit, the bigger the rabbit must be" (p. 81).

Both the therapist and the leader of a social movement obtain their best results when they place new behaviors in tension-reducing contexts: "Its [the Oxford Movement's] effectiveness came in part from letting people who thought they were sophisticated do something naive and still feel very sophisticated in the process. The Townsend Plan, on the other hand, appealing largely to older people, reassured them that its revolutionary ideas were quite respectable and sound because the form of meeting the clubs held was patterned after old-fashioned church meetings" (Cameron, 1966, p. 90).

The role of interpretation in expressive therapy is to obtain material; an analog in behavior modification is the need to obtain behavior that can be shaped (p. 108).

> If the leader can constantly irritate his people, even with "smoke-screen" accusations which do not bear up under scrutiny, he can arouse emotions. Part of this annoyance may even be directed initially at him, but if he can make himself appear invulnerable to attacks, the populace will vent its spleen elsewhere. . . .
>
> There need be *no* truth whatsover to the original charges, although a slight factual support does no harm. If the smoke-screen is dense enough, people will convince themselves there is a fire behind it—if only to excuse their own fears.

An emphasis on a behavioral goal may provide a measure of both progress and point of termination. However, even for behavior therapists there may be some point to the following citation: "Finally, goals and ends often masquerade as means; this is to say that peculiar procedures carried on by the movement and explained by them as expeditious responses to social exigencies may instead be the genuine *raison d'être* of the movement for some of the members" (Cameron, 1966, p. 159). Certainly, the finding of new objectives after success is something that will occur in behavior therapy. Success with a minor problem may be the demonstration required for the subject to continue to more extensive difficulties. It may, however, also be an unwarranted "functional autonomy of psychotherapy" (Astin, 1961). "The end point in the confusion of means and ends is seen when a movement has clearly worked itself out of a job, but persists nonetheless and perhaps even searches for new jobs to do so it can keep going" (Cameron, 1966, p. 162).

Autonomous Therapy

The problem raised by considering "mental illness" a myth is highlighted by a recent book, *Ethics of Psychoanalysis* by Thomas Szasz (1965b). Having brought together logical and historical arguments against the medical model (Szasz, 1961) and having demonstrated its dangers in sociolegal procedures (Szasz, 1963, 1965a), Szasz approaches the difficult task of what the psychoanalyst may do in his practice. Szasz takes liberalism as a starting point and as given. "The aim of psychoanalytic treatment is . . . comparable to the aim of liberal political reform. . . . The purpose of psychoanalysis is to give patients constrained by their habitual patterns of action greater freedom in their personal conduct" (Szasz, 1965b, p. 18). Many of his assumptions are not unlike those of Adler (Ansbacher & Ansbacher, 1956). Two assumptions seem crucial: the individual is capable of making a rational choice for which he should be held responsible, and while the therapist may present evidence and serve as an expert in the analysis of problems in living with other people, he may not influence, guide, coerce, or, for his own integrity and that of the therapy process, assume more than very limited and circumscribed responsibility. Szasz sees the analytic therapy situation as a game. Games have the following characteristics (Szasz, 1965b, p. 65): play is a free and voluntary activity; playing a game is unproductive; play is governed by rules applicable only to the specific game and differing from the rules of other games and of real life; play is make-believe and the player is aware of a second reality (that of real-life experiences).

Specific to therapy, Szasz writes as follows: "Psychoanalysis is an activity separate from real life only for the patient, not for the analyst" (Szasz, 1965b, p. 66). "The analytic situation has a make-believe quality only for the patient. As mentioned above, this is because the patient 'plays' whereas the analyst 'works' " (p. 67). "It is the autonomous psychotherapist's responsibility to keep an impenetrable wall between the therapeutic situation and the patient's real life" (p. 67).

The first difference in point of view is that behavior therapy deals with real-life behavior. Work in the home, classroom, ward, and the like facilitates generalization and fosters the changes in behavior which are the target of behavior therapy. Parents, spouses, friends, nurses, attendants, teachers, and peers have all been "programmed" to extinguish maladaptive behaviors and reinforce new responses. Ullmann (1967) suggests that administrators might do well to systematically reinforce staff behaviors likely to benefit hospitalized patients, and to encourage research on new treatment techniques (and even poor research designs) in order to heighten aspects of the placebo situation such as involvement, interest, and reinforcement for movement toward social responsibility (operationally, discharge from the hospital).

A second point of difference is the matter of ability to make choices. Because there is only heredity and environment, one must accept the position that any given act, if all antecedents were known, would be determined and completely predictable. All the forces are potentially measurable. In this regard, the individual has no "choice." The more that is known about a situation, the less likely will be the use of either the concept of choice or the concept of personality. In this sense, choice is a cover for ignorance. The concept of choice also poses a logical problem, that of an endless regress. If a person makes a "free choice," what chooses the choice, and what chose that which chooses? However, three factors, (1) the complexity of the forces, (2) the variety of possible responses, each of which has a probability, and (3) the very nature of measurement, which must have an effect, make behavior as theoretically impossible to predict completely as it is theoretically determined. Behavior is not completely predictable or determined from the viewpoint of the observer whether that observer is the psychologist or the person himself. The degree of determinism, then, is a function of the theoretical level, and to a lesser extent, the observer's knowledge. It is paradoxical that the very unpredictability of his behavior may lead the patient to presume that it is determined. From the standpoint of the person observing his own behavior, behaviors which are "foolish," "irresistible," "unpredictable," or, in latter-day parlance, "sick," are evidences of his lack of power to make rational choices, i.e., they are determined. There may be real comfort in being powerless and not responsible.

In terms of responsibility the paradigm of developing a conditioned response seems little different from taking a tranquilizer. Short of injection while being held down by nursing personnel, the patient does have the choice of whether or not to take the pill and swallow it. In a similar manner, the person being trained in behavior therapy has a "choice." He may decide not to follow the rules, and one could conceivably say that if he does follow the rules, he is responsible.

The skill of the therapist is directed toward having the patient make the "right" choice. The therapist brings to bear his experience and technology in introducing the series of acts involved in the therapeutic regimen. He may use modeling as he demonstrates the procedures. He may use response-contingent reinforcement as he praises the person for a good performance (and may even build up a deficit, such as hunger, and use a primary reinforcement, such as food for a good performance). He may place the subject who refuses to cooperate in a conflict situation: "You say you want to get better but you won't play my game. If you don't do this simple thing, you obviously don't want to get better and are a liar." The very skills of the therapist are involved in decreasing the likelihood that the subject will not cooperate, and while it is indeed possible for the subject not to cooperate, the cards are so stacked against him that words such as "choice" and "personal responsibility" seem less than accurate.

This situation may be illustrated by treatment of hysterical aphonia (Bangs & Freidinger, 1949; Walton & Black, 1959) in which the first step in treatment was the selection of a behavior that the person could and would emit. The person could not refuse the request without denying that she was "ill and wanted to be helped." Once she complied, each subsequent step followed. It is part of the psychologist's professional skill to be able to select an appropriate starting point and shape the person. The person apparently has a choice of emitting the first response, but if the psychologist has selected his behavior carefully and presented it skillfully, the probabilities of compliance with the request are much greater than a rejection which would imply many unfavorable things about the subject. Blau & Scott (1962, p. 29) summarize the point: "The compliance of subordinates in authority relations is voluntary but not independent of social constraints. It is as voluntary as is our custom of wearing shoes on the street." The subject, however, may think of himself as "deciding" and indeed may control the therapist by his response, as is illustrated by King's (1965, p. 116) story of an American Indian tribe's manifesto to religious missionaries: "No more blanket, no more hallelujah!"

The behavior therapist's task is to make more likely different reactions to situations which have previously been difficult for the patient and in which he acted in a manner that either he or others considered ineffective, inappropriate, upsetting, or the like. This may be done by many different methods (desensitization, behavior rehearsal, modeling, selective reinforcement, etc.). In all, the therapist programs himself and the environment to obtain greatest effect on the patient. Skill lies in being effective: the very context of therapy as well as the specific actions must be in terms of what the patient will respond to. The context of the procedure is as important as the procedure itself. It must be presented in such a manner that the patient will accept it and give it a fair try. In American society, the concepts of independence and freedom are deeply positive, the concepts of coercion and manipulation deeply aversive. There is a distinction (based on a discriminative stimulus) between behavior which is spontaneously the patient's own ("really himself") and behavior he emits for someone else in response to suggestion or compulsion. Just as the therapist must talk to the patient in the language he understands, so the therapist must work within the framework of his fictions. If a placebo will achieve the desired result, it is the result of psychological rather than physical-chemical variables. For the present discussion, the person giving the placebo performs an act which is "real" in the context of the patient's fictions and one which is "false" in the context of his own scientific background. But he also performs a procedure which he believes will help. Therefore, he is telling the truth rather than lying, and as Henderson (1935) long ago pointed out, truth and falsity are blended.

The therapist makes responses and once he does so, things are never again the same, because the decision alters the therapy. If a particular decision works well, it increases in likelihood of emission the next time a similar situation arises. The therapist never knows whether another response or decision would have been better: on the one hand, what works is repeated, and on the other hand, there may be avoidance of consequences that have been erroneously presumed aversive. An example of such a situation, at the level of nearly an entire profession, was the belief in symptom substitution following direct treatment of maladaptive behaviors. Without the corrective of controlled research, the therapist is likely to be as much under the control of fictions and short-term benefits as the patient. At best, the therapist can retrieve only a limited segment of his experience within the very short time allotted to him to respond to the patient. If, to an external observer, the therapist's behavior seems unpredictable under these circumstances, this does not mean that it is "free." The dynamics and principles of behavior are reflected in both the therapist and the patient.

Social Movements and the Limits of Behavior Modification

What is called abnormal behavior is distinguished from normal behavior not by any act or characteristic of the individual, but by a societal designation. If this is so, it becomes necessary to study the historical development of the rules for the designation of a behavior as abnormal and the sociology of those people culturally designated as labelers. Further, it is not legitimate to alter a behavior simply because it is called "sick." Having given up the concepts of "sick" and "healthy," behavior therapy faces an ethical problem and probably a legal one. The injustices perpetrated in the name of mental healing have been well documented by Szasz (1963, 1965a) and Sulzer (1965b). The situation of the psychiatrist in our present culture is not unlike that of the Court of King's Bench. Hart (1966) in his *Law, Liberty and Morality* reviews the Shaw case, a situation in which a man published a detailed listing of the propensities of certain ladies of liberal sexual behavior. This *Ladies' Directory* was considered a conspiracy to corrupt public morals and the judges in the House of Lords said that the Court of the King's Bench was *custos morum* of the people and had the superintendency of offenses *contra bonos mores*, that is, the court had the residual power, where no statute had yet intervened, to supersede the common law and superintend those offenses that were prejudicial to the public welfare. The point, which is reflected in the custody and treatment of people called mentally ill, is highlighted by Hart (1966, p. 12): "The particular value which they sacrificed is the principle of legality which requires criminal offenses to be as precisely defined as possible, so that it can be known with reasonable certainty beforehand what acts are criminal and what are not." A person designated as mentally ill does not have this safeguard, and the mental health professional determines socially appropriate behavior. The power that the opinion of a mental health professional may have is illustrated by the Iowa Supreme Court case (*Time*, Feb. 25, 1966, pp. 45–48) in which a child was withheld from his father because his grandparents would provide him a more stable, dependable, conventional, middle-class home than his father who had no concern for formal religious training and read works on Zen Buddhism.

The most widely accepted concepts of the reciprocal roles of individual and government in English-speaking countries are those called liberalism. Heberle (1951), who discusses the social movements of liberalism and conservatism, calls attention to the recent and relative nature of these thoughts now taken as nearly axiomatic. Heberle (1951, p. 38) quotes G. de Ruggiero's defining article on liberalism in *The Encyclopedia of Social Sciences* as follows: "It follows therefore . . . that any attempt on the part of constituted authorities to exert artificial pressure or regulation on the individual . . . is an unjustified interference, a stultification of his personality and initiative. Against such coercive interference, whether in the moral, the religious, the intellectual, the economic, or the political spheres, liberalism has constantly arrayed its forces."

By this definition, altering an individual's behavior should be undertaken only with extreme reluctance. There is a genuine survival value for a society in tolerating and even encouraging innovations in social behavior. Heberle (1951, p. 456) and Toch (1965, p. 247) make this point in terms of social movements. Changes in values, norms, and social organizations are necessary for the continued survival of the society. If the dominant minority in the society does not make necessary adjustments, then social movements, even if they are at first repressed and particularly if they are in harmony with the broader values of the society, may well be the saviors of the society. In similar manner, individuals may introduce or be the focus of innovations in behavior; while by chance the vast majority of individual nonconformities will be trivial, by the very nature of their great number, some of the innovations will be of social value, perhaps even of a critical nature.

In democracies a social movement is tolerated until it has broken a specifically promulgated rule. Such clear, before-the-fact rules are not available in the mental health setting.

Next, the individual's freedom should not encroach upon the rights of other individuals. This is crucial for behavior modification, since abnormality is defined in terms of evaluation by some observer (including the person himself). In the absence of law, as proposed in the paragraph above, the psychiatrist determines when one person has infringed upon the rights of or made unreasonable demands on another. Until the person has broken a rule, trespassed severely on another's rights, or specifically requested help in changing membership, no change in membership may be encouraged by representatives of society such as policemen or therapists. If anything, in his professional role the therapist should be more circumscribed than in his private role of citizen or friend.

A person joining a social movement or a person emitting behavior of low probability in his society has the rights and responsibilities of a consumer making contracts. Even though the behavior may appear unwise, it must be respected unless it violates explicit rules or rights of others. On the other hand, the person must be prepared to accept the consequences of his action. One of the consequences of enacting the sick role is treatment. Treatment, in essence, is training in following rules. "If the law is viewed as a system of rules governing the game of social living, then enforcing the law is the same as penalizing cheating in a game" (Szasz, 1963, pp. 117–118). "Reward and punishment have always been the basic principles of society. To inflict punishment is a responsibility that society cannot shirk" (p. 144). "By treating offenders as responsible human beings, we offer them the only chance, as I see it, to remain human" (p. 137). Clear delineation of the reinforcing contingencies (expectations, if one wishes) and response-contingent reinforcement are the crux of the institutional application of behavior therapy. The patient's behavior has meaningful consequences. In situations in which he is considered "sick," all behavior may be equally accepted or equally ignored. In the present frame of reference, the application of learning concepts enhances rather than deprives the individual of his liberty and dignity.

Are there certain areas where the therapist may not alter behavior? Pepinsky (1966) claims that if a therapist alters the behavior of person A for the sake of person B, he is in an ethically improper position. This is indeed what is done in much of child therapy, work with retardates, correctional procedures with criminals, and hospitalized schizophrenics. In the last two instances, the therapeutic procedures may be coercive in terms of deprived liberties. In the behavior modification literature there are reports of experiments involving depriving both children and adult psychotics of food. There are instances of the use of electric shock in a response-contingent manner with children. Though an explicit value judgment is involved, it would seem a strange person who would permit a child to do permanent damage to himself rather than use a response-contingent electric shock which imparted information definitely related to his long-term survival (Lovaas, Schaeffer, & Simmons, 1965). It would also seem strange to permit a child to lose his eyesight rather than deprive him of food for a period of time long enough to develop an effective reinforcing stimulus (Wolf, Risley, & Mees, 1964).

It is possible to add to Pepinsky's point that whenever a change in the person receiving therapy will have an effect on another person, the therapist is on ethically difficult grounds. If a college student who is afraid of girls is treated so that he becomes "normal," the therapist bears an ethical burden. Normality in the college culture has a high probability of carrying with it behavior that parents, ministers, and deans of students disavow, at least in their official roles. The therapist is faced with more than one standard of culturally acceptable behavior and he may well aid a person to a statistical normality which is contradictory to some other standard of approved behavior.

If the therapist believed in freedom of choice, he could solve this problem. The point of the previous section is that he cannot believe in freedom of choice and his very competence as a therapist increases his responsibility. The therapist cannot say that he is making it possible for the student to choose between chastity and its loss: to the extent that he has shaped the student toward geographical proximity, interpersonal interaction, and other expected social behaviors, he is responsible for the increased probability of the student's deviation from one concept of virtue. The therapist bears some responsibility to the people involved: in this case, to the girls, as well as to his successfully treated patient. Similarly, if the therapist aids a person to talk back to his wife or boss, the therapist is altering not only his client's life, but the life of the wife or boss. For this reason, it seems wrong to say that anything a client requests is ethically acceptable. In short, when therapist A deals with patient B, he must think of the consequences for person C.

The ethical problem may be pushed to the limit by considering the research situation. By definition, researchers exploit (make use of for their own advantage) people included in the control group. Placebo groups which are hypothesized not to benefit the subjects but which incorporate hope-giving elements and are administered as treatment, and experimental conditions under which manifestly valuable environmental contingencies are reversed to demonstrate their crucial nature, pose grave ethical problems. Where Schreiber (1961) used placebo therapy for the good of his patient, in research these procedures are not intended to benefit the patient, even though they may do so (Paul, 1966).

The very nature of a good control condition is one which is as similar as possible to the experimental procedure. The "therapist's" contract is entered into falsely. The goal is the benefit of some party other than the subject (in Pepinsky's terms, A treats B for the benefit of C). The realities of careers in science are such that the person likely to reap the greatest gains is A himself, especially if the person, B, in the control group, does not improve. Given work such as Rosenthal's (1963), there may be subtle bias against improvement, although this need not be the case, as evidenced by the effectiveness of Paul's placebo condition. The ethical point is that the experimenter tells the subject that he will receive treatment, when the experimenter intends to supply something he considers inferior if not valueless. If the experimenter controls for the patient's expectancies (Goldstein, 1962), then he cannot tell the subject he is a "control."

There is no easy solution to this problem. Control groups must be employed, for only in this way can psychologists discard erroneous methods. Only in this way will therapists be able to enter a therapeutic contract with evidence that goes beyond a belief that they are giving the client value for his money.

Utilization of control groups in research and manipulation of environmental conditions to influence people without their consent imply that one group of people knows better than another what is good for it. By implication there are conditions in which people may be exploited and influenced without prior consent. These people have not broken any explicit legislated rule and their behavior is not formulated as sick. If such dispensation is granted to people doing research on abnormal behavior, there is nothing to stop the increase of such categories, the range of behaviors so categorized, or the development (already under way) of a society in which dissent and conflict are considered prima-facie signs of "illness" suitable for treatment. Mental health practitioners have been given power to diagnose, incarcerate, and alter behavior which is not explicitly in violation of the legal code. Szasz has shown the alarming number of cases (1965a, pp. 50–54) and the degree of violation of the Bill of Rights (1963, pp. 182–190) that may take place.

Social movements, as noted above, are analogous in membership and objectives to recipients of therapy; the leaders of social movements bear analogies to therapists in terms of tactics. Other than where paternalism is justified, as with children and the severely retarded, the limits set on leadership may prove a guide. Explicitly, if the tactics of either the social movement vis-à-vis society or its leadership vis-à-vis its members break the written laws of the society, society's sanctions against rule breaking should be enforced. Beyond this, the similarity in tactics, for example, adequate rate of reinforcement to forestall disaffection on the one hand and to promote group membership on the other, would not unduly cramp the behavior therapist. This is not a perfect solution to the dilemma raised by abandonment of the medical model and the continuing need to accommodate to individuals emitting low-probability and disruptive (but not illegal) behavior. However, the therapeutic act must be placed in the same sociopsychological framework as the abnormal act. The model of social movement does this and also provides some guidelines which may serve the behavior therapist until better ones, so badly needed, are devised.

The movement in which the behavior therapist is a leader is preponderantly that of the society as it is. While therapy can aid the person in changing his environment and the responses of others to him, the basic choice of the behavior therapist involves the propriety (or likelihood of reinforcement) of alternative behaviors for specific people in given times and places. The behavior therapist is not necessarily the unquestioning servant of society, but he is the servant of reality. As such, the situation as it is does necessarily limit his choices. The behavior therapist is also the servant of the person he works with, and his effect is to provide stimuli which will increase the range of behaviors in the individual's repertoire or, if the behaviors are already in the repertoire, the range of situations in which such behaviors will be appropriately emitted. Just as the behavior therapist makes alternative behaviors more probable, the behaviors he encourages in general are those probable in the treated individual's age, sex, and social class group. The techniques of the behavior therapist are those of providing information (experiences) that lead to defection from current behavioral categories and joining or gaining membership in different groups.

The tactics which are legitimate for encouraging joining and defecting behavior are many: the leader's behavior is prosecuted only if he breaks a major law (does not play fair with his followers, for example, by embezzling) or breaks the rules which make possible the society itself (for example, advocates the forceful overthrow of the government). The member of a social movement, unless incarcerated or physically coerced, is held responsible for his own actions in a manner that seems desirable for those categorized as mentally ill (Szasz, 1963).

It was pointed out that social movements may lead to necessary and desirable social innovations. As a leader, the behavior therapist certainly need not aim for adjustment to the status quo or automaton conformity. But the limits are present: adherence to the broad rules which make social living itself possible.

Just as the parent does not hesitate to punish his child in order to provide information about the realities of social living, and the teacher does not hesitate to place students in the stress-producing ritual of examinations, so the therapist as an expert on interpersonal relations assumes the responsibility of reflecting reality. The latitude with which this is carried out with regard to both technique and direction is limited but slightly by reference to behaviors that are legitimate for the leader of a social movement. If anything, the range of potential techniques and directions remains uncomfortably great for the person who would wish to have his method and goal prescribed by authority. By following the analogy to the social movement, the ethical limits of behavior therapy may be charted. By reference to the corpus of theoretical, judicial, and social experience developed for social movements, the behavior therapist's enterprise may be legitimized without recourse to a medical model.

Chapter Summary

This chapter started with a problem faced by behavior therapists: in abandoning the medical model a source of legitimacy of psychotherapeutic activities was lost. In a "background" section, two points were advanced. The first was a recapitulation of some of the conceptual and clinical problems of defining mental illness and hence work within a medical model. What is called abnormal behavior involves a social judgment and is properly as much a study of the labeler as of the labeled. The second topic dealt with the similarities, at least at a definitional level, between the labeling of behaviors emitted by individuals as indicating the presence of abnormality and the behaviors indicating the presence of a social movement. Again, this involves the judgment of the labeler as much as the behavior of the labeled. After briefly discussing two areas which might lead to the breakdown of the proposed analogy, a formulation of functional behavioral difficulties was advanced. This formulation drew heavily on theory and examples from sociology and social reinforcement theory and was designated a sociopsychological model. In the present work, more attention was devoted to antisocial and schizophrenic behavior than to neurotic behavior since I thought neurotic behavior had received excellent coverage in previous work on the topic. In all acts of labeling or of emitting behavior labeled deviant, the person who acts is reinforced. The behavior in and of itself is not different in either kind or degree from behaviors labeled normal, whether the label applied is that of a diagnostic category or of a social movement.

Given these considerations, the chapter returned to behavior therapy. The role of the therapist was approached from the view of social movements. The therapist was equated with the leader of a social movement and his manipulations of the environment with actions taken within a social movement. The following section was devoted to the concept that the therapist cannot escape the burden of leadership and influence. In this regard, an alternative, the autonomous therapy of Thomas Szasz, was discussed. If Szasz's solution were viable, the problem would be solved; the thrust of this part of the chapter, which included a discussion of determinism in terms of levels of observation and purposes of the observer, was that autonomous psychotherapy is not theoretically feasible. Autonomous psychotherapy casts the situation as a game for the patient. Behavior therapy, in order to enhance the chances of generalization, strives to make the therapy situation as real and as similar to the extratherapy situation as possible.

The similarity between behavior therapy and social movement was next investigated for purposes of solving the ethical dilemma of responsibility for changing behavior that is conceptualized as not different in itself from what is judged normal. Where the medical model not only has been accepted by our society during the past century but is currently being extended in judicial application, there are no legitimizing (and limiting) guidelines for behavioral or sociopsychological models. The limitations placed on social movements and their leaders have been far more clearly defined both in theory and in judicial practice.

Investigation of sanctioned leadership behaviors in social movements indicated that the behavior therapist would not necessarily be restricted in technique or goal. The limitations imposed on the behavior therapist are essentially the limitations imposed on the citizen in general: not to violate the rules that make social living possible.

A second problem was approached: if the behavior therapist is a leader, where shall he lead? Within the limits presented, the behavior therapist evaluates and represents the realities of the social environment. As an expert he provides the experiences which give the client feedback. The behavior therapist does not "change" people but rather programs situations (including his own behavior) that differentially reinforce people and alter the probability of emission of various behaviors. It is these experiences and not the therapist that "change" the patient. The behavior therapist as a leader encourages defection from some movements and subscription to others. The range of behavior encouraged by social movements and the social utility of such movements argues against the notion that the present formulation must lead to automaton conformity. Further, the individual in behavior therapy is often encouraged to alter his behavior in a manner that will alter his environment. The model of social movements permits the behavior therapist to serve both the individual and society without violating his trust to either, and without seeking his source of legitimacy from a medical model or by denying his responsibility.

16

The Rationale, Practice, and Future of Behavior Therapy:
A Biomedical Perspective

SANFORD I. COHEN
Louisiana State University Medical School,
New Orleans, Louisiana

Introduction

This book is a testimony to the fact that many research investigators and clinicians are attempting to reevaluate the constructs and practices related to the therapy of the so-called mental disorders. In this reevaluation, concepts concerning the etiology of symptoms, the rationale of treatment practices, and the very notion of mental disease have been carefully scrutinized. At times, however, the search for truth seems to degenerate into a struggle among supporters of various theoretical schools and among various professional disciplines. At such times, the desire to improve clinical practice tends to deteriorate into a battle of dogmas filled with clichés, accusations, and derogations. One problem is: Who is qualified to do therapy? Such problems have become so important that they occasionally overshadow some of the major scientific questions with which biobehavioral research is confronted.

Some of the ideas to be discussed are so self-evident that a formal presentation of them seems absurd. The fact is, however, that these seemingly simple guidelines and constructs are not always observed either in clinical practice or in experimental studies. It is the present contention that such failures can block the development of a perspective broad enough to allow the full utilization of information currently available about CNS activity in its relation to behavior therapy (see also Franks, Susskind, & Violet Franks, 1969, pp. 359–366).

Some Nonbiological Issues Related to Clinical Research and to the Practice of Behavior Therapy

PROBLEMS OF TECHNIQUES, GOALS, AND EVALUATIONS

Many problems confront the laboratory and clinical scientists who are engaged in research related to clinical psychopathology. Perhaps the most basic is the necessity for developing a more rational diagnostic nomenclature based on integrative neurobiological mechanisms. This type of framework is essential to the development of more precise techniques for choosing the most appropriate therapeutic modality. A related problem is the need for developing carefully defined criteria for symptoms and alterations in symptoms which would lead to more meaningful studies of prognostic criteria and therapeutic results.

In order to treat individuals with nervous system, personality, neurotic, or behavioral problems (whatever term one finds most acceptable), it seems that we need to come to grips with issues such as: What is treatment? Who needs treatment? What should be treated? What specific goals can be formulated for people with specific dysfunctions or maladaptations? How can these goals be attained, or how can one implement a program of treatment, management, counseling, guidance, or manipulation? What kind of training is necessary for a "therapist" to make "valid and reliable" observations of symptoms or signs in order to treat these difficulties and to employ meaningful methods for evaluating the results of treatment? Perhaps the effectiveness of therapy depends more upon the talents of the therapist than upon the degree he holds. A belief in, or an opposition to, some person, cause, religion, or theory should not determine the criteria for judging a person's adequacy to conduct therapy.

Regardless of their professional training or persuasion, individuals interested in the treatment process and its results should all agree on the necessity for applying the scientific method in clinical and laboratory investigations. Unfortunately, even if all clinical and laboratory workers were able to suppress their commitments to theoretical orientation and professional identity, it would not be easy to determine which are the most appropriate areas for investigation or to determine the specific experimental questions that will be most pertinent to the problems confronting the people engaged in the diagnosis and treatment of psychiatric cases.

The following facts should be self-evident, but often are not: The work of clinicians and the work of laboratory scientists concerned with human behavior and higher nervous system functions are complementary and not mutually exclusive. It is unfortunate that so many clinicians feel that laboratory research is sterile, constricted, and contrived, and hence cannot be extrapolated to human behavioral problems or utilized in handling human dysfunction. Laboratory scientists, on the other hand, need to know the kinds of variables that are involved in human psychopathological research. Even the "detached" and "disinterested" laboratory worker should be comfortable with these variables so that he will be better able to make contributions toward developing the strategy, tactics, and techniques needed to undertake the very difficult problems of clinical research.

The value of clinical descriptive data is increased immeasurably when it is obtained without a positive bias (seeing more than is actually present) or a negative bias (seeing less than is actually present). Personal bias can affect the methods by which we examine patients, report observations, and make interpretations.

Subjectivity is a source of error which makes organized scientific observation extremely difficult, but does not, in and of itself, keep it from being scientific. Failure to recognize and compensate for subjective error is what may make an approach nonscientific. Many researchers in the behavioral areas may secretly envy physicists, who deal with what appear to be precise and objective instruments. But it is a common observation in both physics and chemistry that the data obtained from the reading of a calibrated scale are influenced by previous readings; hence the careful investigator in the natural sciences makes sure that knowledge of previous readings is obliterated. More subtle subjective bias seems to be introduced by conscious (or perhaps unconscious) selection interposed between the taking and the reporting of an observation.

There is an impelling need to make more explicit the techniques of treatment employed in psychiatry and the goals at which these are directed. Although therapists of all persuasions are agreed on the necessity for setting specific goals, it is surprisingly difficult to establish appropriate goals for patients with various symptom patterns. Truly eclectic, noncommitted research, it would seem, should establish preset criteria for determining the success of a therapeutic effort, not some vague or diffuse category such as "social adjustment" or "overall clinical impression" (which is so dependent on expectation, motivational factors, and environmental demands). The criteria of success might be more profitably based on some predetermined goal such as the modification of a specific preoccupation, value, or attitude which has led the patient to see too much or too little in his environment, to feel too much or too little, or to behave in too exaggerated or too inhibited a fashion. Further, any judgment concerning the results of therapy should include a determination of whether the goals set are feasible and logical.

It has been said that the analyst's explanation of symptom substitution based on unconscious determinants is illogical. But are the constructs really illogical or is it the framework in which they are expressed that causes them to be rejected? Just because some of the psychoanalytic explanations about how certain relationships develop appear illogical, should the observations themselves be rejected? Razran (1961) has described a number of Russian studies in which a dog is trained to lift her leg defensively when a bell is rung and air is blown into a Fallopian tube. Eventually the activity of the Fallopian tube comes to be associated with the bell as well as with the motor activity. These inter-exteroceptive conditioning experiments raise a number of questions and certainly require replication. I mention them not to suggest that these results be accepted uncritically, but to make the point that some persons who are committed to behavior therapy nevertheless give careful consideration to the methods and data reported in such studies, even though it is not "logical" for the bell to activate the Fallopian tube. Yet, if a psychoanalyst reported a case in which certain words or thoughts or images produced changes in a female patient's Fallopian tube, these same persons would probably consider the report ridiculous and smacking of quackery or mysticism. The techniques employed by psychoanalysts may not be unscientific if the objective of the technique is stated and if the goal of therapy is associated with what the technique is designed to accomplish. Further, if the criteria for change in specific functions were clearer, perhaps there would be less controversy about the area.

As long as behavioral therapists are concerned primarily with the treatment of symptoms involving motor behaviors or acute emotional reactions, then the theoretical backgrounds and the therapeutic techniques of behavior therapies and psychotherapies may stand in rather sharp contrast. However, unless behavior therapy becomes a "movement" enabling some individuals to dissociate themselves from any type of treatment involving the second-signal system or cognitive activity, it seems that persons engaged in behavior therapy will tend to become more concerned with the treatment of persistent attitudes, values, ways of perceiving, and the like which may be strongly influenced by words and symbolic signals. At this point they will have to become more concerned with verbal reinforcement and verbal conditioning techniques, and will find that the behavior of the therapist may be of considerable importance and the environmental setting for the therapy of great significance. Techniques might be employed which are intended to reinforce attitudes by influencing the patient to focus on a specific area and positively reinforcing it with a word or gesture.

Before it is possible to determine the type of intervention that will help a particular patient, there must be a careful delineation of (1) the dimensions of nervous system functioning, (2) the environmental conditions which may require modification, and (3) the manner in which nervous system activity or environmental conditions can and should be altered and the results anticipated if the "desirable" changes are brought about. The definition of "helping" a patient could be in terms of what the patient experiences or what the therapist observes. This implies that, in the development of a systematic and scientific approach to the treatment of disorders of the nervous system, one must avoid both rigid commitment to the rationale of any particular kind of therapy and an overly vigorous and biased defense of its results.

There is a danger that certain psychologists and other nonmedical therapists might commit themselves to behavior therapy largely because it is a therapeutic technique that can be undertaken without the necessity for medical supervision. The type of training advisable for an individual treating disorders of the higher nervous system will be discussed in more detail later in this chapter. Suffice to say, at this point, that the academic degree a person possesses is insufficient evidence that he has the qualifications necessary to undertake therapy. Many nonmedical persons are far more competent psychotherapists and behavior therapists than their medical "supervisors." It is hoped that the inequities in our present system regulating decisions about who can undertake therapy, and under what conditions, can be solved without segmenting the specific approaches into those which can and cannot be employed without medical supervision. Such segmentation would be a disservice to all persons involved, since it would limit the development of a body of information relevant to biobehavioral sciences concerned with treatment techniques and their evaluation. The most serious consequence might be the disadvantage to those seeking treatment.

If behavior therapy is used as a device to achieve freedom from medical control by the nonmedical therapist, then the danger exists that behavior therapy may become separated from the mainstream of biological investigation into nervous system functioning (see Cohen, Chapter 19). Furthermore, if a therapist's professional identity becomes dependent on the type of therapy he employs, similarities in the different approaches to treatment might become obscured and the presentation of data and techniques which increase these similarities might be resisted. Furthermore, it is perfectly conceivable that, during the course of behavior therapy, pharmacological agents might be useful in facilitating or inhibiting various nervous system activities. In this instance the patient could be transferred from a behavior therapist to somebody doing drug therapy, but it would be better if the therapist were a person trained to handle both conditioning and pharmacological techniques and, in addition, able to undertake any physiological measurements necessary to evaluate specific aspects of nervous system functioning.

My purpose is not to suggest any specific solution to the training problem, but to emphasize the need for training therapists able first to determine what type of treatment is best suited for an individual patient and then to carry out this treatment. Training should be determined by identifying the talents and knowledge necessary to carry out this role. This is not as simple as it sounds. There are a number of issues which impede an easy solution, not the least of which is the fact that, at the present time, there are large numbers of trained people already committed to various points of view and theories. To carry this further, there are some people whose positions would be jeopardized if some new professional governing body set up standards for which they could not qualify. Yet, in spite of this, it is probable that the vast majority of persons interested in the clinical problems of CNS function and dysfunction recognize that their major task is to enhance and not impede the increasing utilization of scientific method in order to provide relief for the suffering of the patient.

A number of so-called basic concepts which have long been accepted require definition. For example, what is psychopathology? What is maladaptive? What is dysfunction? What is mental illness? What is sick? What is normal? If we use statistical definitions, what should we look at? What specific phenomena should we compare in a population? A statistical definition must rely heavily on a cultural definition of what is normal. Unfortunately, we do not have adequate actuarial information about the frequency of behavioral patterns and the kinds of variations that can be noted in large samples of different populations. It is for this reason that the late John Benjamin (1959) suggested actuarial studies as one of the most essential investigations needed in the clinical behavioral sciences. Without this type of information, we really do not know how greatly an individual's behavior differs from that of the rest of the population. Further, we cannot really be sure a particular behavior is more prominent in an individual because the behavior has increased, but it may be related to the reduction of other behaviors which makes the behavior in question more prominent.

In trying to define the normality of certain behaviors, should we look merely at the frequency of certain events within a population, or should we outline as pathological those behaviors or thoughts which are associated with discomfort, suffering, unhappiness, inefficiency? If we use the latter definition, the whole population could, on occasion, be said to display pathological behavior. There are many other possible approaches to the definitions of normality and abnormality, but the point I wish to make is that we should avoid the misconception that there is a specific entity which, under all conditions at any time in any person, could be considered maladaptive, sick, or pathological.

The attempt to appraise the present position and role of behavioral therapy in the mental health movement leads one to consider methods of handling the problem of scientific uncertainty. Rene Fox (1959) has suggested that a major aspect of the training of a clinician is preparation for managing uncertainty. True eclecticism implies a greater tolerance for uncertainty but may lead to certain difficulties, reflected in the fact that therapists with a broad eclectic approach often report more failures (or are less certain of success) than those who seem more committed to one approach to treatment. Critics of these eclectic therapists often blame their failures with a particular technique on its improper use or application. However, the continued attempt to rational-ize failures in this way is particularly disconcerting when it comes from the behavior therapists—a group which has been openly, and often justifiably, critical of therapists from other persuasions for their excessive attempts to explain away or justify failures. This kind of "explaining away" of all failures implies, "We know the truth and the way to apply it, hence, failure can only come from the improper use of techniques or from inadequate knowledge." Such devotion to a belief and such commitment to a technique usually suggest some uncertainty about one's theories, methods, or techniques, and, more specifically, some discomfort with that uncertainty. It makes one wonder whether the evaluations of some behavior therapists are as objective as the basic philosophy upon which behavior therapy is founded.

Another question that is raised is whether some behavior therapists are following the specific principles of treatment and techniques as closely as their publications imply. Any therapist—psychoanalyst as well as behavior therapist—is justified in introducing changes in the therapeutic procedure in the service of a patient's needs (e.g., a psychoanalyst may modify his treat-ment procedure by utilizing certain kinds of verbal reinforcement as a reward or punishment). However, if modifications are made, and if the therapist is aware of them, then they should be presented for appraisal and critical review. Unfortunately, it is difficult at times to tell whether a therapist's behavior is motivated by a desire to help the patient or by the need to support a theory. If both motivations are present (as may usually be the case), modifications in treatment that are introduced for the patient's benefit may be rationalized in such a way that any favorable changes in the patient's symptoms are attributed to theoretical considerations to which the therapist is committed. The work of Marks & Gelder (1965, 1966) illustrates well the point that a broad eclectic approach may be quite useful in the treatment of psychopathology.

Considerations for Training and Clinical Practice

CONSIDERATIONS IN THE TRAINING OF NEUROBEHAVIORAL CLINICIANS

In the training of clinicians concerned with problems of higher nervous system functions (associated with difficulties in adapting to one's current environment regardless of whether stressful current life situations, developmental traumas, or altered brain functions are the major determinants), there are a number of areas where attempts to study brain functions, or human thought and behavior associated with clinical disorders, could go astray. If the learning of the sub-ject matter concerned is undertaken purely in terms of abstract principles, even though derived from laboratory experiments, without any real consideration being given to the actual events occurring in people's lives, then the view becomes shortsighted and the perspective narrow. The events and life responses which should be of particular interest are those related to functions or dysfunctions of behavior and thinking which can be identified as adaptive or maladaptive in response to stressful life situations, or those related to behavior which has been described as efficient or inefficient.

To avoid difficulties engendered by clinical constructs which develop mainly from theoretical or laboratory-derived considerations, it would seem advisable that an individual interested in the treatment of higher nervous system disorders develop a broad familiarity with a wide range of clinical case material. Also, it would be valuable for him to have a broad knowledge of major and minor life stresses in diverse cultures and the adaptive and maladaptive patterns utilized by individuals within such cultures. This would considerably expand the scope of observational data available, particularly if the information were examined from an eclectic point of view, and would facilitate the development of a more meaningful framework. We hope that such an approach would become not an exercise in theory replacement or refutation but an attempt to utilize clinical and life observations and experimental data in the development of a body of meaningful knowledge about behavior which is maximally independent of the theoretical orientations of the persons reviewing or collecting the data.

Familiarity with various theories (even if one is not in complete agreement with these theories) does more than just help one understand why certain kinds of observations are usually made by persons of different disciplines. Familiarity would imply some knowledge of the history of these theories, including the observations which led to their development and an understanding of why, at some moment in time, a grouping of facts and observations was involved in a particular theoretical framework.

Familiarity with clinical symptoms should include not only so-called psychiatric diseases or stress syndromes but also neurological and neurosurgical syndromes, in addition to classical psychopathology. These types of data are a valuable source of information about the effects of integrative nervous system functions or structural and toxic alterations of the CNS. Further, they provide a source of information about the effects of neurobiological factors on recently and remotely learned CNS capacities. The observation of patients with nervous system diseases might also provide suggestive leads about the relationship of integrative neurophysiological functions with environmental events, current interpersonal relations, environmental pressures, demands and expectations: in other words, how does an alteration in the excitatory and inhibitory capacities of various brain areas due to brain disease change the ability of a person to adapt to the complex conditions of his environment?

Knowledge of clinical neurophysiological disorders should be accompanied by a knowledge of neurobiological research and the multiple molecular and biophysical determinants of neurochemical and neurophysiological activity, as well as the relationship of various areas of the CNS with the patterns of behavior, cognition, and emotional expression which emerge in response to environmental signals or altered internal states. Active training or participation in areas such as electrophysiology and neuropharmacology would force individuals to utilize criteria which are more rigorous than the criteria utilized in clinical approaches at the present time. A discipline of data analysis may be a very meaningful facet in the training of clinical, as well as experimental, behavioral and neurobiological scientists, and it might provide an antidote to the deadly scholastisim of more fixed programs.

For members of some disciplines dealing with the treatment of CNS disturbances, a major weakness in training is centered around the lack of cognizance of, or the failure to utilize, proper scientific methodology. Resistance to the application of scientific method in the study of complex human behavior seems to stem from the feeling that to do so must be at the cost of sacrificing humanitarian values or, at least, of losing human feelings in approaching or dealing with these problems. However, the point would seem to be that there is a need to resolve behavior into operationally analyzable and definable components to allow for the carrying out of more effective studies, and that this in no way negates the importance of subjective or experiential factors as dimensions of human responsivity requiring both consideration and investigation. (Of course, the basic assumption is retained that all psychological activities, no matter how "subjective," are properties of biological processes which cannot function outside the laws of physics and chemistry).

In addition to the introduction of better controls and better methods in clinical research and in the evaluation of diagnostic and treatment methods, there is a need for the therapist to have a broad familiarity with experimental studies of personality, perception, behavioral analysis, and cognition, and to have also a particularly intimate knowledge of research involving modification of these functions by any means whatsoever. The methods, as well as the results, of learning and conditioning studies should be understood rather than used merely to develop techniques for the collection of information to support one's theoretical notions. This kind of training is necessary if the therapist, regardless of orientation, is to be capable of evaluating the available information and asking questions which will allow him to broaden his store of information about the phenomena in which he is interested rather than the theory to which he is devoted.

In addition to being familiar with the clinical aspects of behavioral and nervous system dysfunction, a familiarity with human responses in a variety of different types of laboratory situations should be part of the training of the clinician. It is often said that the contrived and unreal characteristics of laboratory studies of complex CNS functions gives them a limited applicability in explaining abnormal behavior or thought in life situations. But we would argue that the repertoire of man is not so extensive that his laboratory responses are qualitatively or quantitatively vastly different from those observable in analogous life situations. There are many reasons to believe that careful laboratory studies may help delineate the components of the complex responses which are observed in the clinic and in life situations. As Skinner (1966b) points out, "no land mammal is now living in the environment which selected its principle genetic features, behavioral or otherwise. Current environments, certainly for man, are almost as unnatural from a biological point of view, as a laboratory. What an organism does is a fact about that organism regardless of the conditions under which it does it."

Franks (1966a) correctly suggests that events occurring later in an individual's life may change and modify the impact of an earlier stimulus, but that this is in accordance with the laws governing the behavior and the functioning of the nervous system. Further, he suggests that a scientific study of behavior must begin on the basis that the behavior which is being sought is not a nebulous concept of the mind, but is one which can be found in the physiological and neurological events occurring in the CNS. The question then arises whether the focus should be on the abstract laws which have been developed from stimulus-response-type experiments or observations of output following modification of input, or whether the goal should be to establish the principles of nervous system functioning, e.g., the ways it can be altered by internal and external stimuli that occur at various moments in time. Training in integrative neurobiology should provide the basis for establishing principles by which one can understand and possibly predict the influences of (1) sequential maturational changes, (2) neurochemical and physiological activity associated with drive or motivational factors, and (3) external situational, interpersonal, and cultural events on altering or fixing the pattern of nervous system characteristics.

A PLAN FOR FUTURE CLINICAL FACILITIES

In this concluding section, a plan is developed for a future clinical facility concerned with the diagnosis and treatment of higher nervous system disorders. It is intended to represent only one possible direction that could be followed if the research, clinical, and training problems reviewed in this chapter were pursued. The specific focus, limited to the planning of inpatient facilities and emphasizing the use of physiological measures, reflects my own interests, but it is hoped that the philosophy is sufficiently broad to have some applicability to a wide variety of clinical problems, including the particular interests of behavior therapists.

The problem of integrating behavioral and biological sciences is one that must be resolved in the development of medical and bio-psychological graduate curricula. It has been said that the study of behavior is in all respects the paradigm of the study of developmental and adaptational biology of the organism and that the study of behavior should not represent a separate substantive area. This is not to imply that transcultural, social, and family phenomena are not important influences in the shaping of behavior or the development of psychopathology, but that these influences are also part of a total biological framework.

A growing area of concern in the training of therapists is the need to undo not only the segregation of biological from cultural and social phenomena, but also the segregation of experimental sciences from clinical diagnostic and therapeutic activities. There is an immediate and long-range need to develop clinicians, as well as laboratory investigators, who are knowledgeable about neurobiology and/or are skilled in biological research. To implement such goals, future clinical facilities should be planned so that studies can be conducted with clinical populations in an environment where precise controls can be established in order to maintain the quality and quantity of external inputs to which the patient is exposed. In addition, it would be important to develop the capability to monitor the patient's responses behaviorally and neurophysiologically during these controlled environmental conditions.

Facilities should be available in which temperature, sensory input, and interpersonal stimuli could be controlled, and in which the patient's responses from a psychological, physiological, and neurophysiological standpoint could be continuously monitored. This type of clinical facility should be equipped with centralized control centers in which bioelectrical and television monitoring devices, as well as signal generators, programmers, and data computers, are located. Control centers would permit a maximum number of studies to be carried out with a minimal amount of interference with clinical activity. Satellite monitoring stations, for example nurses' stations, should be provided with information after the analoged physiologic data had been processed in an analog-to-digital conversion system and an "on-line" data-logging facility, providing a digital readout for routine physiologic measures.

The immediate aim of the observations would be to determine whether the specific relationships gleaned from anecdotal reports could be identified in terms of psychological traits, situational factors, neurophysiological activity, physio-endocrine-metabolic function and the like. I hope that such information would provide data for better-integrated treatment programs in which the rationale for specific therapeutic modalities would be based less on empirically derived concepts and more on systematically established observations.

The treatment modalities would include: (1) modification of the patterns of interpersonal interactions, (2) modification of the perceptual field or problem-solving abilities through verbal psychotherapeutic techniques, (3) change in the patient's internal state through the use of pharmacologic agents, (4) modification of repetitive maladaptive response patterns through behavioral therapies and other conditional reflex techniques. This, indeed, may be what Lazarus's (1966b) broad-spectrum behavior therapy really entails (see Franks, 1966b). Treatment would be based less on purely empirical criteria and more on the results of predictive pretherapy test procedures.

The need for more precise diagnostic and therapeutic approaches which utilize objective techniques does not at all imply that valuable historical, developmental, or subjective experiential data will be minimized. Rather, there is a vital need to develop approaches tailored to the idiosyncratic nature of the individual patient's biography and reactions, although the tests would be based on general principles of integrative CNS function.

In the future development of such treatment centers, a regrouping of basic science and clinical disciplines may well need to be considered. This would not only involve the development of a central facility for experimental neural and behavioral or brain sciences, but might also include clinical diagnostic and patient-care functions which currently are the responsibility of a number of disciplines—for example, clinical research and patient-care facilities might be localized in one area concerned with: (1) psychopathology and neurobehavioral dysfunctions; (2) clinical neurology, neurosurgery, stroke centers, etc.; (3) neuropathology; (4) psychosomatic and psychophysiological functions (e.g., psychoneurocardiology); (5) clinical psychopharmacology. Related basic research areas might also be included in the same facility, and those basic research areas having specific and direct relationships to particular clinical areas might be advantageously placed in close physical proximity to each other (e.g., clinical psychopharmacology unit and laboratories for neuropharmacology).

The concept of centralization of clinical and experimental neurosciences is something which would have to be very carefully considered in the future development of a medical center because it might possess disadvantages which would outweigh any benefits. On the other hand, there are certain advantages which should at least be considered: (1) Centralization could have considerable value for research, particularly as a result of the increased communication between investigators in related fields. (2) A grouping of clinical and experimental neurosciences could have clinical and research training significance in providing a much more comprehensive and efficient program. (3) This kind of centralization might lend itself to the standardization of techniques which would be of value to clinical and experimental activities in the neural and behavioral science areas. Further, the more efficient use of computer analog-digital conversion facilities, TV, and bioelectrical and neurochemical measures might be envisioned if they were all placed at some central location in this futuristic "neurobehavioral research and treatment center."

One of the obvious disadvantages of this type of future development in medical centers is that the geographic separation of neural and behavioral scientists from their so-called parent departments may present a rather cumbersome administrative situation. Also, the possibility of dual allegiances might be an inhibiting factor not only in recruiting personnel but in the efficient functioning of any unit. However, it is always difficult to write of the future without bringing into the discussion some of our own present. In other words, far too often, projections into the future are unfortunately merely extensions of the present; they seldom represent really novel and creative departures from current thinking.

Chapter Summary

From a biomedical point of view, behavior therapy should be firmly rooted in an integrative neurobiological framework. Unfortunately, there are a number of nonbiological, even nonscientific, issues which are impeding the assimilation of the findings of current neurobiological research into clinical diagnostic and treatment activities. Of equal importance is the difficulty encountered when an effort is made to define the requirements for training therapists.

Perhaps the most basic need is for a more rational and objective diagnostic nomenclature and the development of carefully defined criteria for "symptoms" and symptom change. Improvement in definition is essential to the development of more precise behavioral, verbal, and physiological techniques. It might then be possible to choose the most appropriate therapeutic modality, establish more meaningful prognostic criteria and conduct more valid studies of therapeutic results.

Another major problem seems to be associated with the differences encountered between various disciplines or "schools" in the formulation, comparison, and evaluation of techniques, goals, and treatment results. Semantic differences are involved, but it is suggested that biases associated with professional problems are impeding effective communication and distorting the use of "objective" scientific methods in assessing the results of other workers.

The development of a broader, more scientific sociobiologically oriented program of training of therapists and of treatment should incorporate: (1) scientific methods of studying higher nervous system functions; (2) information gathering and integrating techniques which provide data of clinical value; (3) measurement techniques which assess biological functions and minimize the need for metapsychological, metaphysiological, or pseudoneurological constructs. Such a program is perhaps what is really encompassed by broadspectrum behavior therapy.

17

Behavior Modification—Values and Training:

*The Perspective of a Psychologist**

LEONARD KRASNER

State University of New York at Stony Brook

Why should there be a chapter on values and training in a book which focuses on reviewing the field of behavior modification? This chapter will justify the view that the issues raised by the interrelationship between values and training are central to the social utilization of behavior modification and must be explicitly faced in all research and applications in this field. Ullmann (Chapter 15) emphasizes that "behavior therapy faces ethical decisions which do not arise under the medical model." We contend that these ethical decisions are part of all social influence situations, including traditional psychotherapy, but it is the behavior modifier, because of his theoretical model, who must bring these issues out clearly and resolve them in order to justify his role in society.

I will start with definitions of the terms used in this chapter—ethics, value, training, behavior influence, behavior modification, and behavior therapy. *Ethics* is defined as the "discipline dealing with what is moral duty and obligations" (*Webster*, 1963, p. 289) and "the rules of conduct recognized in certain limited departments of human life" (*Oxford Universal*, 1955, p. 637). *Value* is "that which is worthy of esteem for its own sake; that which has

* The research reported in this chapter was supported, in part, by Grant No. 11938, National Institute of Mental Health, United States Public Health Service.

intrinsic worth" (*Oxford Universal,* 1955, p. 2332). Although the dictionary definitions limit the area of discussion to some extent, I will use the terms values and ethics interchangeably to refer to the verbal behavior elicitable from a given individual in response to the question: What general type of behaviors or rules of conduct do you as a human being consider to be good (desirable, esteemable, worthy) or bad (undesirable, unworthy) in yourself and in others and under what circumstances? If we can obtain a description of critical incidents of good and bad behaviors, we will h̃ave elicited the individual's ethical or value system.

The potentially verbalizable value system is related to specific behavior of the individual, but not in a clear-cut causal manner. People do not always behave in accordance with the logical consequences of their value system. Value systems may change to some extent during life, depending upon circumstances under which they are elicited, but it is generally assumed, since there is no experimental evidence to the contrary, that there is a consistency in statable values during different periods of an individual's life. It is clear that we do not conceive of a value system as comprising a metaphysical series of entities within the individual but rather as observable and measurable behavior which is a function of eliciting environmental stimuli.

To train is "to form by instruction, discipline or drill; to teach so as to be fitted, qualified, or proficient" (*Webster,* 1963, p. 939). Hence, I would use the term as synonomous with *to teach.* To train, or teach, another person is to demonstrate the contingencies influencing his behavior, to help him have available in a given situation enough alternative behaviors so that he can control the situation, and to help him be able to verbalize correctly the consequences of his own behavior and that of key people in his environment. The individual who is trained has available enough information on the principles of behavior in general, and on the principles governing his own behavior specifically, to carry out adequately and with satisfaction the behaviors required in his various social roles. We will use the term *training* to cover three kinds of human interactions: between a behavior modifier and his client; between a behavior modifier and significant figures in the client's life; and between a behavior modifier and individuals in a student role being trained to become behavior modifiers. This trichotomy emphasizes that basic training principles are the same in these different situations, although the specific techniques of training may differ as appropriate to the goal of the specific situation. The goals of training, who is to be trained, and the consequent social role of the trained person are determined by the values of the individuals doing the training. The values of the trainer insofar as they concern both professional and social roles are expressed by the kinds of behavior modeled for and expected of the student in the training program itself.

Values can be approached as any other behavior; they are expressable via verbalization, they are learned, they are modifiable, they are complex, they are uniquely human behavior. The approach to values, from both a research and an applied point of view, as in other behavior modification procedures, is to first specify the behaviors involved. In this instance the behavior is verbal, and individuals can and, often subtly, do indicate the value rating they attach to their own behavior and that of others. An individual can rate his overt behavior in terms of "goodness" or "badness." Thus, if values are definable in terms of verbal behavior, we can have available a measure of the difference in worthiness between values and overt behavior. This could give us an index of consistency between values and behavior, and offers interesting research possibilities.

Values and Behavior Modification

A clear delineation between the terms behavior influence and behavior modification should further clarify the relation between values and the other topics of this book. I find useful a hierarchy of terms: behavior influence, behavior modification, and behavior therapy.

Behavior influence, the broadest term, is defined as any situation in which deliberate control or influence is exerted on human behavior. Formal schoolroom education falls into this category, as do psychological studies involving opinion change, techniques of learning, obedience, perception, or sensory deprivation. In some instances the behavior change effected may well be socialy undesirable, such as the decrease in intellectual or perceptual acuity which may result from sensory deprivation experiments (Solomon, 1961). The focus in behavior influence studies is upon the process and lawfulness of change itself, and not upon an evaluation of the goodness or badness of the behavior being changed.

Behavior modification involves the application of principles derived from the psychological laboratory to the changing of undesirable human behaviors. It involves a decision on the part of someone who evaluates the social desirability of a particular behavior in a given context. Behavior modification includes such techniques as enhancing patient expectancies (Goldstein, 1962), the application of institutional controls such as token economies (Ayllon & Azrin, 1965; Atthowe & Krasner, 1968), operant conditioning of undesirable behaviors of autistic or retarded children (Ferster, 1961; Bijou, 1965), and the use of desensitization conditioning to change levels of anxiety (Paul, 1966).

The term *behavior therapy* will be used as synonymous with behavior modification. The only reason to do so is the historical artifact of the term's originally being applied by Eysenck to Wolpe's (1958) procedures (Eysenck, 1959). The term "therapy" is appropriate to a disease model of abnormal behavior, not to a behavioral model, but for the purposes of this chapter I will continue to use "behavior therapy" in its recent historical context to denote procedures designed to alter directly human behavior labeled as deviant.

I contend that the training of behavior modifiers must take place in the context of training psychologists as behavior influencers, the most generic of the three categories. The behavior modifier is the individual working with behaviors societally labeled as deviant (clearly, value judgments on the part of the social labelers). This individual, the behavior modifier, used to be called a clinical psychologist. We are faced with a difficult choice in training: Shall we retain the label of clinical psychologist or shall we train individuals under a new label such as behavior modifier? One argument against the label clinical psychologist is that it connotes an individual working within a medical model, doing therapy in a clinic setting. Further, in most academic circles, the aura of the clinical person, deserved or not, is of a nonobjective, inadequate, weak, professionally oriented, second-class citizen, slightly above the social worker, a shade below the psychiatrist.

Yet people involved in training graduate students should not give up on clinical psychology, which has a short but honorable history. Rather, the emphasis should be on changing the image and functions of the clinical psychologist so that they are equivalent to the functions and goals of the behavior modifier discussed in this chapter. When I talk about the behavior modifier and his values and training, I am describing the clinical psychologist as he eventually will be and as many clinical psychologists already are.

If we view values as verbal behavior, then what is the relationship between values and the actual behavior of the therapist? Is there any correlation between the kinds of behavior he reinforces and expects in others (clients or students) and his own values? There have been relatively few studies which have demonstrated that the values of the therapist are related to the kinds of behavioral change he brings about, although this seems to be a very reasonable hypothesis.

One such study is by Holzman (1961). She tested the hypothesis that there is a positive relationship between improvement in a patient's social adaptation and an increased similarity of his value judgments to those of the therapist regarding behaviors relevant to the patient's life experience. She used two samples of patients receiving intensive traditional psychotherapy from first- and second-year psychiatric residents. One group of patients was hospitalized, primarily psychotics, while the second group comprised outpatients labeled as neurotic or as having character disorders. The measurement of values was based upon a 33-item value inventory given to all patients and therapists at the beginning of the study and after seven months of psychotherapy. The two patient samples were further divided into a group similar in life situation to the therapist group and one dissimilar to it. The variables used to assess similarity of life situation were age, education, occupation, intelligence, religion, and race. The results indicated that for the outpatient sample with individuals similar in life situation to their therapist, improvement in social adaptation was significantly associated with increased similarity of the patient's value judgment to those of his therapist. Patients similar in life situations but unimproved did not show increased similarity of value judgments. Neither outpatients dissimilar in life situations nor either inpatient group showed a relationship between improved social behavior and similarity in value judgments.

Holzman's results tend to confirm those of an earlier study by Rosenthal (1955) which also found that there was a significant correlation between improvement in behavior and change in "moral" values on the part of the patient in the direction of those of the therapist. The Holzman study points up the subtler relationship between these kinds of changes and similarity in socioeconomic variables. Combined with the Hollingshead & Redlich (1958) findings about who gets psychotherapy and who profits from it, it seems that traditional psychotherapy can be interpreted as involving individuals of middle-class background (the therapists) who persuade other individuals of similar background to adopt their way of looking at life. To the extent that this persuasion or influence is successful, the patient will be considered improved.

There is even further evidence, certainly fragmentary and inconclusive, but provocative, that the influencing process of the therapist includes not only values but other kinds of therapist behavior usually identified as "personality." For example, Sheehan (1953) and Graham (1960) both report studies in which key Rorschach categories of successful patients changed significantly in the direction of those of the therapist. We would also briefly refer to the verbal conditioning studies insofar as they may relate to the transmission of therapist values. Krasner (1965, 1966a) has argued that the verbal conditioning studies demonstrate one way in which the therapist may control the verbal behavior of the patient by his reinforcement (verbal and motoric cues) of "appropriate" verbalization. The therapist may not deliberately set out to control patient verbalization. However, the evidence seems to be that the therapist, even when he is "nondirective," is as controlling of verbal behavior as if he were doing it "purposely" (Truax, 1966). Further, these changes can be brought about without the patient's awareness of the contingencies of his behavior (Krasner, 1967). Whitehorn (1959) summarizes these points by arguing that successful psychotherapy involves leadership "toward preferred values, toward the therapist's conception of what constitutes value in life."

Values and the Societal Role of the Behavior Modifier

If it is true that the therapist or modifier of behavior can bring about specified changes in behavior in an individual, on whose behalf is he acting? For whom is the new behavior "good" or desirable, or valuable—for the client, for the therapist, or for society? Ideally, it should be "good" for both the individual and society, but there are many instances of individual behavior, which may involve sex or politics or social radicalism, on the desirability of which the individual and society may be at sharp odds. In such instance, whose agent is the therapist, that of the individual or that of society?

We cannot avoid this dilemma by saying that it would depend upon the context or the setting; e.g., working in an institution would put the therapist in the role of society's agent, but in a private office he would be the individual's agent. Even in a clinic or private office, there is an implicit institutional situation; even in the hospital, the patient has his individual rights. In whatever setting he may be, the behavior modifier arrives at choice points in his procedures. These involve a decision on what behaviors to shape, modify, or reinforce. The modifier must consider who will benefit from the consequences of this particular change in behavior, the individual or society. In most instances, both will equally benefit and this can be expressed by saying that the individual is able to maximize the reinforcement possibilities from his environment (society). However, there are instances in which there is clear conflict. For example, if a patient seeks help in his desire to adjust to a homosexual relationship, and the therapist has available techniques to help the individual, should he? From the point of view of society, homosexual behavior is undesirable (a value judgment). It is certainly not conducive to the perpetuation of the species, it offends the mores and beliefs of our society, and it decreases the reinforcement potential for the individual. If, as the behavior modifier contends, the therapist can literally help the client to shape his behavior in either direction, toward adjustment to deviancy or toward normality, what should he do? I could weasel out of this dilemma by some kind of compromise; I could say that I have drawn the issue too sharply, that life is rarely clear-cut, and that the decision is up to the patient. Yet I will not try to avoid this issue and will take a stand that the therapist is always society's agent. Szasz (1963) takes an apparently opposite point of view in arguing that an individual should have absolute choice over his own behavior, including self-destruction if he so desires.

Does this mean that I am developing a picture of a behavior modifier defending the social status quo, an archconservative who will "reinforce" only those behaviors consistent with the views of the dominant "middle-class bourgeoisie" or the "Protestant ethic"? Not at all; in fact, I refer to the view of the therapist himself as an instrument of social change, a modifier of social institutions. We thus have a picture of a therapist who is modifying an individual behavior in a socially desirable direction, but using his own values as the determinant of what is most socially desirable. In effect the therapist, society's agent, helps change individual behavior and also social institutions themselves.

The behavior modifier, if he so desires, can step into the relatively untried role of changing social institutions, but to do so, he must be trained appropriately, and that is why there is a close linkage between this type of professional role and training programs. Unfortunately, many traditional therapists see their role only as helping the individual adjust to society and to reality, and hence they are towering forces of social conservatism, a charge Lindner (1956) has cogently made.

When we view the therapist as the agent of society we are making a value decision. Society, in this instance, is other people. The major focus, then, is the impact of an individual's behavior upon other people; the kinds of consequences which his behavior elicits from others. Society is others; the basis of self-reinforcement (Kanfer, 1965a) is the behavior of others as they either reinforce us or serve as a model for desirable behavior.

I contend that the decision of the therapist in any given instance has been previously determined by the nature of the training which he has received even before encountering his first patient. The ethical and value issues are inexorably bound into the training procedure, by the very nature of where the training is taking place, the theoretical models of the trainers, and the implicit selection of behaviors labeled abnormal and hence modifiable.

In part this ethical decision-making process follows from the nature of the role model for which the therapist is trained. For example, therapist role models may be seen as analogous in our society to the roles of physician, teacher, minister, and friend. If the therapist is trained with the standard values of most traditional psychoanalytically oriented therapies, his approach to the person seeking help is similar to that of the physician who seeks to restore health. The patient is presumed to be not responsible for his behavior (motivated by hidden and mysterious drives) and hence incapable of making his own decisions. Literally, he does not know what is best for him. The issues of the individual versus society are clearly resolvable in favor of a society which must protect itself from the dangers of the irresponsible individual. Papa, society, and the physician know best. A sick individual can and should be helped and pitied but cannot really be respected.

It may look as if behavior modifiers are inconsistent in their view of the relation between society and the individual; in one instance they are agents of society, in the other they denounce society for its rejection of the individual. But these views complement each other. As the agent of society, the behavior modifier must view the patient as being a responsible individual who must become free of the debilitating behaviors which have prevented him from achieving the most freedom possible to him, a wider repertoire of behaviors from which to chose. It is in this sense that society benefits; society cannot afford to reject anyone for "abnormal" behavior when it is the society which has given the "bad" label to the behavior. The therapist represents society, but it is a society which is not punitive but rather seeks ways to supply maximum positive social reinforcement to the individual.

On the other hand, training the therapist in the role of an educator has far different value implications. The educator in our society is, or at least should be, a leader in molding of opinion on basic issues of our society. However, he is also primarily a technician trained to utilize the best available techniques to facilitate learning in a given individual. The evidence seems to be that learning is most effective when the individual is himself most directly involved. A behavior modifier respects the learning capacity of the individual and utilizes the best available techniques to facilitate change. Society may take precedence, as we have indicated above, but in a different context than in the medical role. The individual is seen as capable of coping with society, as a responsible individual whose greatest source of satisfaction (in the long run) will come from being a productive and socially reinforcing individual himself. The good society is one in which all people are positive social reinforcers. The important value is to behave so as to please others and to contribute (as assessed by others) to the general welfare of all men—society.

Are we destroying individuality by this humanistic viewpoint? Only in one sense, the individualism of the person who is unresponsive to external social reinforcement, whose own "needs" come first, who uses the excuse of individualism (or free will or free enterprise) to justify aggrandizement of others. Individuality as unusual, creative, exciting, even unpredictable behaviors elicits positive reinforcement in others, if the behaviors have a social utility, if they are "good" behaviors.

How can the question of values be conceptualized so that they can be specifically carried into the training situation? There are at least three ways of approaching this problem. The first is to deny the relevance of the question of values for behavior modification. The second is to affirm it as a given fact of life and let it go at that. The third is to accept the responsibility of value decision and to attempt to measure and control it. I am, of course, presenting arguments for the third of these views. However, some behavior modifiers, like most traditional therapists, may prefer to deny the relevance of the question.

Wolpe (1958, 1964a), for example, tends to view the problem along the denial dimension. If a patient comes to him with a complaint or a particular problem, then he, as the therapist, sees his task as one of helping the patient to change the behavior involved irrespective of what this may mean in value terms. For example, if a patient's major problem were impotence in an extramarital relationship, then Wolpe would devise techniques to enable the patient to cope with the impotence. Wolpe argues that this is a situation in which his own values as a therapist do not intrude; he is not making a value decision. He would argue that whereas personally he may or may not approve of extramarital relationships his own views do not intrude into the therapeutic procedures. But this is not the case because the patient's judgment that the behavior involved is an acceptable one socially is actually a decision involving the value structure of the therapist. The therapist may be saying, "This is a behavior which I myself would not indulge in, but I am not permitting my values to intrude and, if this is what the patient wants, I will encourage it." Yet this statement is in itself a value judgment that, in our society, the behavior is an acceptable one for the patient. To push the point further, I would ask the behavior therapist how he would handle a situation in which a patient's primary complaint was that an arm paralysis prevented him from making an attempt to strangle a friend. I doubt that the therapist would say that the problem was to help rid the patient of the maladaptive behavior.

The alternative view is to accept the inevitability of the value decisions of the therapist and to train him to accept this social responsibility. However, we must be aware of the danger that the patient's behavior would be manipulated by the therapist in order to arrive at behaviors only because they were consistent with the therapist's own values and not because they would be maximally reinforcing for the patient. Such an occurrence would represent a confirmation of the severest criticism of the behavior modifier. The therapist must continually examine the consequences and value implications of behavior changes, both for the individual and for the society. It is this avowed recognition of the value decisions attendant upon the consequences of change in behavior which should be the trademark of the behavior modifier.

I have thus argued that behavior modification, in both its therapeutic and its training manifestations, is not and cannot be value-free. But the behavior modifier is also a behavioral scientist. In fact, I contend that two aspects of the same complex social role are molded together in the behavior modifier: basic scientist and professional applier of science. There is considerable controversy about whether science is or should be value-free. These views are similar to those expressed by Gouldner (1962) who argues that "it is a myth . . . that social science should and could be value free." He points out that sociology is not a value-free discipline and that it is impossible for sociologists to exclude their values and their beliefs from their scientific work. Gouldner argues that it is more desirable for a sociologist as a teacher or researcher to express his values "overtly and deliberately." He argues further that the sociologists have used this myth of a value-free sociology "as an excuse for pursuing their private impulses to the neglect of their public responsibility" and have as a consequence become "morally insensitive." The end product is a situation in which the value-free myth has been used "to justify the role of selling one's talents to the highest bidder and is, far from new, a contemporary version of the most ancient sophistry."

Similar views have been applied to the role of the psychologists by London (1964) and Krasner (1966a), among others. Krasner has argued that the belief in the value-free nature of psychotherapy is one of the myths behind which psychotherapists find it convenient "to hide." Szasz (1965a) extends this viewpoint further, to the value implications inherent in the role of the psychiatric labeler as it affects the behavior of criminals and the "mentally ill."

The problem of the value implications of the control of behavior may occur in its sharpest form in the field of genetics. If, as seems likely, genetic structures can be determined and controlled, the implication is that determining the physical, intellectual, and probably emotional characteristics of future generations is almost within the grasp of man. Who will make the decisions on such matters, and how shall they be derived? Such decisions are analogous and complementary to similar decisions regarding change in human behavior which has been discussed in this chapter.

Until fairly recently the ethical problems inherent in the application of scientific discovery were limited to the hard core sciences of physics, biology, and chemistry. In recent years it has been psychology's turn. As Kanfer (1965a) expresses it, "perhaps the sudden widespread concern with test makers, public opinion surveyors and adjustment manipulators simply indicates that psychology finally may have something to offer which has applicability in every day life." It is not the purpose of this book to discuss the implication of the test makers and public opinion swayers which are covered extensively elsewhere (e.g., *American Psychologist*, 1966), but certainly the full impact of this book would indicate that behavior modification does indeed have something to offer. The newness does not lie in behavior influence or behavior control itself, for it has been going on since man came out of the caves. Attempts at control of behavior have been made throughout history, usually with coercion, force, and political manipulation. What is new is the emphasis on a scientific and objective investigation of the process involved in influencing behavior, and the opportunity to apply the process in helping unhappy individuals and in changing aversive social institutions. The effect of the Skinnerian revolution is to emphasize the positive and eliminate the negative in societal and individual controls.

One aspect of the problem, inherent in all fields of scientific endeavor, is: What are the social consequences of a scientific achievement? The most obvious has been in the field of physics with a scientific breakthrough in the utilization of energy resulting in the atomic and hydrogen bombs, consequent destruction of the Japanese cities, and the threat of total destruction hanging over the world. A perusal of newspapers, magazines, and professional journals (e.g., *Bulletin of the Atomic Scientists*) of the period of the late 1940s and the 1950s shows that many physicists were greatly concerned about the social implications of their scientific behavior. The behavior of these scientists varied from withdrawal of further scientific work in the field to intensive efforts to seek test bans and peaceful coexistence. But in many instances it is difficult to predict the social consequences of a scientific breakthrough.

A popular humorist (Tom Lehrer) captured the spirit of the extreme example of the noninvolved scientist in a satiric song. A prominent rocket scientist is portrayed as saying that it is his job to see to it that rockets go up —where they come down is not his department. I would expect that no scientist would, should, or could maintain this "detachment."

The relationship between science and values is summarized by the geneticist Glass (1965, p. 69) with the view that:

> It has been said that science has no ethical basis, that it is no more than a cold, impersonal way of arriving at the objective truth about natural phenomena. This view I wish to challenge, since it is my belief that by examining critically the nature, origins, and methods of science we may logically arrive at a conclusion that science is ineluctably involved in questions of values, is inescapably committed to standards of right and wrong, and unavoidably moves in the large toward social aims.

Values and the Model of Man

The conceptual model (or hypothesis explaining behavior) of man which the therapist holds determines to a large extent his behavior vis-à-vis the patient and society. Behavior modification starts with different premises and models from traditional psychotherapy with consequent differences in value and training issues. If the purpose of your role is to restore health by taking away from an individual something that does not naturally belong to him, such as "conflict," or "anxiety," then the values (of the therapist or patient) need not be considered because the question is one of reconstructing a previous condition of health. The acceptance or denial of value involvement follows from differences in theoretical models.

There are many subtle consequences in behavior which derive from the differences in models. For example, the traditional psychotherapist conceives of his relationship with the patient as unique, whereas the behavior modifier views the process of change as prototypical of the more general process of behavior influence. If treatment involves a unique social relationship, then it is less necessary to look beyond it to the real world outside. The traditional therapist is of course concerned about consequent changes in the patient's life outside the therapy hour, but he is viewing the outside world from an unusual and encapsulated situation with a unique behavioral pattern. It is not surprising that traditional psychotherapy often evolves a life of its own and becomes "functionally autonomous" (Astin, 1961), nor that traditional psychotherapists become absorbed with process to the almost complete neglect of outcome (Rubenstein & Parloff, 1959).

On the other hand, a procedure which is prototypical of real-life influence must stay in direct contact with the real world. The social environment of the individual is the laboratory of the behavior modifier. In fact, one critique of the behavior modifier is that he has not sufficiently followed through on the consequences of the differences in conceptualization from traditional psychotherapy and has not yet moved clearly enough in the direction of social movement. Scheff (1966, p. 20), in advancing this critique, argues that behavior modification in practice "tends to be used as an individual system model of mental disorder." Scheff points out that, although conceptually this is not necessarily so, in practice the emphasis is on techniques for changing the patient's psychological system rather than the interpersonal or social system of which he is a member. This points up the fact that the full implications of a behavior modification approach as a social movement have yet to be manifested. The potentialities of this viewpoint will be discussed in a later section of this chapter.

One way of conceptualizing the relation of values to models of behavior involves the broader view of the "nature of man" which the therapist believes in implicitly or explicitly. It is thus important to determine what kind of conceptual model the behavior modifier might be willing to accept. In discussing this, at least two models must be dealt with. First is a model acceptable to the behaviorist, and second is the model attributed to him by those who disparage his viewpoint. We must refer to both because of the strong and violent reactions the behaviorist frequently elicits from his professional colleagues.

The usual critique of the behaviorist involves the attribution to them of a model of man as a robot or as an "impotent reactor." In perhaps the most bitter (value negative) attack on what he considers the robot view of the behaviorists, Chein (1962, p. 3) contends that:

> The contrasting and, among psychologists whose careers are devoted to the advancement of the science, the prevailing image of Man is that of an impotent reactor, with its responses determined by two distinct and separate, albeit interacting, sets of factors: (1) the forces impinging on it and (2) its constitution (including in the latter term, for present purposes, momentary physiological states). Response is at all times and at every moment an automatic consequence of the interaction of body and environment. He is implicitly viewed as a robot—a complicatedly constructed and programmed robot, perhaps, but a robot nevertheless.

In his counterargument to the attributed behavioral viewpoint Chein contends that an organism "is an active agent in the universe. It is not merely a passive medium for the interplay of constitution and environment; its own activities affect that interplay" (p. 13).

Carney (1964), in defending the behaviorist position, argues that Chein has created a straw man and that no serious theoretician recently considers any living thing as an "impotent reactor." Chein rebuts this point by saying that whether anyone takes an image seriously is beside the point. It is "not what psychologists believe, but the properties of the model they use" which is important. I disagree with this and argue that it is indeed what the modifiers believe and expect of the human individual which determines their behavior, and not the inherent properties of a group of words put together and labeled a model.

What does a behavioristic position on man imply about the nature of man? First and foremost is the belief, backed by a considerable amount of laboratory data, that man's behavior is a function of, is elicited by, and is controlled by environmental stimuli. If the behavior modifier is a scientist interested in man, he has no choice but to deal with the functional relationship between man's behavior and his environment. Man does not have a basic predetermined nature; his behavior is characterized by learning and change. From the individual's point of view, the key question is how much control he has over the events which determine change in his life.

There is no discussion in science as old and hackneyed as that of free will and determinism, and we do not propose to raise this issue from its richly deserved death. Everything worth saying about this topic has almost certainly been said by somebody somewhere. If human behavior is lawful, predictable, and controllable, is it also, therefore, completely determined and mechanical? Do we have a picture of man as a puppet, dancing to the tune of whatever stray stimuli may entice him, without a will of his own; or is man able to direct his own destiny? The metaphors used by Urban & Ford (1961, p. 3) which describe man in terms of a robot or a pilot are particularly vivid and useful:

> Man is often conceived to be an apparatus, although an extremely intricate one, who behaves after the fashion of a programmed machine. In this approach he is conceived as having a behavioral repertoire, built-in as a consequence of his innate equipment on the one hand, and subsequent events of his training on the other.
>
> He is represented as entering the world with a basic behaviorial program, equipped with reflex circuits of a motoric and physiological nature which will operate automatically whenever the appropriate antecedents occur to trigger them off.... From this point of view all behavior, no matter how intricate, is situation-determined in the final analysis. By inference, therefore, control of behavior is accomplished by situational control. If the experimenter can accomplish controlled manipulation of the external stimuli and their pattern of presentation, he can operate the person as if he were a machine. Clearly in this view, man is the product of the situational events to which he has been exposed and those which come to be imposed upon him. The work of Pavlov, Watson, Hull, and Skinner exemplify this viewpoint.

On the other hand, Urban & Ford's conceptualization of man as a pilot views him in terms of inner self-direction. Man's consciousness is his most crucial characteristic. "This view sees man himself as exercising control over his responses and the situations which he encounters. He influences situations as much as they influence him." By the use of higher mental processes, "man seems to be able to seat himself at a point far distant in time and space from a specific situation, conceptually rehearse different alternatives, predict their respective consequents, and select a preferred outcome. . . . The individual, in short, is being viewed as steering his own behavioral course." To accomplish this the individual must be alert and aware; the substance for such operations must be accessible to his symbolic manipulation, and thus it is a hallmark of such a view that additional emphasis is placed upon attention and awareness. Emphasis is given, not only to awareness of situational events, but also to awareness of himself and his own behavior. Urban & Ford find this view in the systems of Adler, Jung, Rank, Sullivan, Horney, and Rogers.

To state the problem in these simple terms, is man a robot or a pilot? The commonsense view, based on observing human beings, would be that man is both. Urban & Ford conclude that the two views really complement each other in that each accounts for a different set of behaviors and each neglects behaviors the other accounts for. This is the easy, logical way out. Others such as Chein conclude that only the "man as pilot" view can be acceptable to psychologists, which is clearly a value judgment on their part. The behavior modifier would conceive of man clearly in the robot end of the continuum. His behavior can be completely determined by outside stimuli. That is, man's behavior may be determined in many circumstances by hypothesized internal mediating events such as awareness, thinking, anxiety, and guilt (concepts which we are all reluctant to give up because they verify the existence of our soul, of our real self, of "me"). However, the behaviors which follow such "internal" events can also be manipulated by outside events; in fact, these "internal" events themselves can be controlled by outside stimuli. Hence we can conclude that behavior may clearly be externally controlled without denying the obvious fact that man "thinks."

However, there are several important points which may save the day, for even the most behaviorally oriented investigators would really like to put man in the driver's seat as the pilot. The kind of control which makes man fully a robot does not exist; it is only theoretical. Society is not set up to manipulate man's behavior systematically in a given direction, fortunately. Most external controls cancel each other out. It is also unlikely in the near future that out of the laboratory will come the kinds of experimental results which will tell us all that has to be known about the tremendous complexities of human behavior, so that complete social control will be possible. Thus, man can and should behave *as if* he were the pilot. He still is free to the extent that there is no systematic manipulation of his behavior and to the extent that he acts as if he were free. Further, even in dealing with a robot, what is often neglected is the point that the robot's behavior is determined by human beings. Man may be a robot, but man also programs or controls the input into the machines. To the extent that a human being has alternative behaviors available to him, to that extent he is "free" and not a passive reacting robot.

In fact, the individual who believes that his behavior is determined by unconscious forces within him is trapped by forces beyond his control and is in no sense "free." To investigate how human behavior works, to determine the laws of behavior, is not to robotize man but to humanize him.

A recent paper by Truax (1966) illustrates how fixed are some attitudes about the attribution to the behaviorists of mechanization and robotism even in the face of clear-cut contradictory evidence. Truax, himself dedicated to the nondirective school, did a series of detailed analyses of a successful psychotherapeutic case seen by Carl Rogers. Truax felt that his data analysis could be decisive in determining whether Skinner or Rogers was right about the directiveness of psychotherapy. Truax's (1966, p. 7) experimental evidence enabled him to conclude that, insofar as he could determine, Skinner seemed to be right about psychotherapy.

> The present findings point to the presence of significant differential reinforcement effects imbedded in the translations of client-centered psychotherapy. Since differential reinforcement is one of the procedures used in operant research to alter (or control) behavior, the findings suggest that the therapist, in this case Rogers, implicity alters (or controls) the patient's behavior in the therapeutic setting. To this extent, then, the evidence weighs in favor of the view proposed by Skinner rather than that of Rogers. The present findings are not consistent with Rogers' view that relatively uniform conditions which are globally "facilitative of personal growth and integration," are offered to patients in a manner not contingent upon the patient's behavior.

However, despite his own evidence Truax could not refrain from concluding his article with an attack on the view that the therapist is a "social reinforcement machine," since he felt that implied in such a model would be a therapist who could not communicate, even contingently, warmth and empathy (1966, p. 8):

> As the communication of any "reinforcing machine" qualities would by definition mean a low level of empathy and warmth, the present viewpoint is in full agreement with Schonbar's (1964) statement that "as a therapist I am no more a 'reinforcing machine' than my patient is a 'talking pigeon.'"

"Social reinforcement machine" (Krasner, 1962a) is a phrase which is useful in describing the role of the therapist in a behavioral model, for it carries with it the implication of a well-trained human being who is making use of social reinforcement principles in such a way as to affect human behavior systematically. "Machine," of course, has many different definitions; included among these is "a device, often complex, for doing work beyond human physical or mental limitations or faster than human hand or mind" (*Oxford Universal*, 1955). In other words, the behavior modifier, by virtue of his training and by virtue of the model of man implicit in such training, reacts quickly, and in many instances reacts automatically, in terms of the kinds of stimuli to which he has been trained to react. In this respect, all successful psychotherapists are social reinforcement machines, but the implications of this view are usually denied or deliberately avoided because they apparently threaten the view of man (thrapist and patient) as the pilot.

Training and Social Change

If, as Ullmann (Chapter 15) so cogently emphasizes, behavior modification is related to social movement, then what are the implications for our discussion of values and training? Social movements (and psychotherapeutic procedures) have relatively brief prominence in the history of human behavior unless some efforts are made to train newer, younger, and more eager people in the techniques, ideas, and framework of the innovators and current leaders of the movement. Bockoven (1963) points out that moral treatment, the approach to modifying behavior which in the early 1800s was so effective in helping individuals with problems in living, literally disappeared from mental institutions with the death of its originators. "Of the many factors which contributed to the decline and the eventual discard of moral treatment, lack of inspired leadership after the death of its innovators was probably the most important. The founders of moral treatment were shortsighted in not providing for their own successors in numbers adequate to meet the needs of the future" (Bockoven, 1963, p. 20).

If the behavior modification "movement" is to have an eventual social impact, a major effort must be made to train younger people, with the likelihood that improved techniques, more carefully controlled research, and newer fields of application will emerge from their fresher and less blinded efforts. However, it must be clear to the trainer and the trainee what "brand" of help is to be offered to "suffering" individuals.

Krasner (1966c) offered the prediction that eventually at least three clearly delineated types of psychotherapeutic procedures will evolve. First, there will be procedures in which people will pay for friendship, companionship, love, affection, and general attention to their affairs. Kanfer (1966a) refers to this as "friendship therapy," and Schofield (1964) refers to "the purchase of friendship." It might be argued that all human beings have the inalienable right to have other human beings interested in them. Traditional psychotherapy should not be denigrated. The subjective reports of many therapists and patients indicate that both feel there is value in these procedures. Paul (1966) demonstrated that traditional insight psychotherapy was at least as effective as placebo procedures in changing "anxiety." Therapists and patients will continue to carry out psychoanalytic types of psychotherapy for many years to come. The procedures are far too satisfying to both participants for them to be drastically curtailed. One has but to listen to a psychotherapist describe the latest juicy foibles of his patient to a rapt social gathering to realize how reinforcing the psychotherapeutic hour is to the therapist. We see no harm in this procedure provided it is clearly labeled and the therapist explicitly indicates to the patient the nature of the relationship between them. If the therapist were to advertise his wares, discretely and circumspectly of course, as involving friendship for sale, he would probably obtain even more patients than he now has. Many individuals, lonely and despairing yet justifiably afraid of being labeled "sick," would now be eagerly willing to participate in "psychotherapy."

The second type of helping procedure will be behavior modification in which individuals would seek specific ways of changing behavior which may be disturbing to themselves and others. In this category the individual is taken seriously in his verbalizations about the nature of his problem. If he reports a variety of disturbing behaviors, such as stuttering, fears, anxiety, excessive drinking, and aggressive or withdrawn behavior, these will be the behaviors the behavior modifier will work with. He will not be concerned with a reconstruction of the individual's personality, but will expect that as behavior changes, other people will respond differently to the individual and elicit different behaviors, resulting in a "different" person. It is to the description of this kind of procedure that most of this book is devoted.

The third type of psychotherapeutic procedure will explicitly involve social engineering, the changing of social institutions to affect the behavior of groups of individuals. The social institutions involved may range from mental hospitals to "pockets of poverty," and the procedures may range from "token economies" to poverty programs. Thus far, very little in the way of research on the role of the behavior modifier as social engineer has appeared, although social engineering may eventually emerge as the most important aspect of his role.

Training, then, involves preparing individuals for participating in one, two, or even all three of these social roles. In a later section in this chapter a specific training program will be presented for preparing students for two of these social roles, the individual behavior modifier and the social engineer.

The studies on token economies (Ayllon & Azrin, 1965; Atthowe & Krasner, 1968; Burchard, 1966; O'Leary & Becker, 1967) represent a major linkage between the psychological laboratory and broader social institutions. Tokens, in and of themselves, will not be the salvation of many social ills. However, the approach which involves a functional analysis of the reinforcing events in an institution which maintain current behavior (Ferster & Skinner, 1957) will be the first and major step in any changes in social institutions

The same procedures which are used in an institutional setting such as a mental institution or a schoolroom can also be applied to broader units of society.

The Token Economy as an Instrument of Social Change

The experimental work in this area, particularly that of Ayllon, has already demonstrated that the behavior of large groups of individuals can be brought under the control of a behavioral engineer (Ayllon & Michael, 1959). Ayllon & Azrin (1965) and Atthowe & Krasner (1968) have reported investigations of application of token economics in a psychiatric hospital setting. What are the implications and consequences of such studies for values and training, our concern in this chapter? The most important is that in the token economy we have an approach which combines not only the usual three functions of the clinical psychologist—training, research, and service—but also an avowed incorporation of the value system of the behavior modifier as social engineer. The token economy is the prototype of the procedures and techniques of long-range and large-scale modification of social institutions.

The first step in examining the variables of a token-economy program is to designate the behavior to be changed. We start with an assessment of the situation, which includes an observation of the patient behavior and its current consequences. Let us start with the patients on a selected ward. We may observe certain characteristics of their behavior, such as apathy, withdrawal, and nonresponsiveness. The observer may quickly make a value decision and label these as undesirable behaviors and hence changeable. He may also note that the aides and nurses are maintaining certain of the withdrawn types of behaviors by which patients make the aides' and nurses' life easier, such as sitting peacefully. But it is insufficient to merely select one behavior such as sitting and its consequent maintaining social approval and then to say we will modify this behavior by altering its consequences. There are many pressures on the aide that differentially reinforce and shape his behavior toward the patient. The pressures are directly expressed by the aides' immediate supervisor, but one can work up through the power hierarchy in the institution to determine where the ultimate value decisions are made, the consequences of which emanate throughout the institution down to the lowliest aide. We could even become too broad and contend that the power structure of the particular institution is responsible to the values of a larger society outside the institution. However, within broad limits, most social institutions such as mental hospitals, prisons, state departments, and nations have considerable autonomy of their own and are amenable to social engineering from within.

If this is so, then the value decision to be made by the behavior modifier on the target behaviors of the individual patient to be shaped as desirable must include the consequences of changed behavior for all levels of institutional functioning. Let us take one behavior as an illustration. As we observe the patients on the ward and on the hospital grounds, the patients' dress is quite distinctive. You can easily differentiate a patient from a nonpatient by the clothes each wears. The clothes are discriminative stimuli which, for patients, elicit from others the appropriate and expected "reaction to patients" role. An assessment of the situation would indicate that the consequences of changing appearance via clothing might have ramifications at many different levels. If it is impossible to tell by appearance whether the person you are talking to is a patient or a staff member, you are likely to respond to him as if he were "normal," until it is proved that he is not. This principle extends beyond the reactions of an individual aide to the key figures in the institution's power structure. The sight of a well-dressed patient is impressive to visitors and gives favorable feedback to the hospital administration. The expectancies of the power figures of the hospital about the potentialities of patient behavior should change. Patients can be considered responsible human beings with problems in living, who are temporarily utilizing hospital facilities. This change in behavior, then, wearing ordinary neat clothing, could have consequences in helping to change the value system of the hospital power structure. If such a change were one of the goals of the social engineer, as it should reasonably be, then there would be strong reason for selecting dress as a key target behavior to modify and shape.

A study by O'Leary & Becker (1967) that extended the token economy into the classroom further illustrates how a behavior modification program can begin to affect values of key societal figures such as teachers, and can have consequent effect on a major social institution, the schoolroom. The subjects were 17 nine-year-old children described as "emotionally disturbed." Although the token reinforcement system was in effect for the whole class, observation was focused on the eight most disruptive children. A base period of observation was established to obtain the frequency of deviant behavior under usual classroom procedures. When the token reinforcement period began, the experimenter placed the following instructions on the blackboard: "in seat, face front, raise hand, working, pay attention, and desk clear." The teacher ranked each child from 1 to 10 on the extent to which he followed the instructions. These ratings or points could be exchanged for a variety of back-up reinforcers such as candy, comics, perfume, and kites. The ratings were done by the teacher in a very brief period of time, enabled the teacher to give individual attention and feedback to each child, and enabled her to shape each child's behavior. The teacher also ignored deviant behavior and reinforced appropriate behavior. The results clearly indicated that the token reinforcement program produced a dramatic and abrupt reduction in deviant behavior. The teacher's behavior was particularly affected in that she was able to devote more time to working with each child and in that she found her job more pleasant. It was clear that the teacher's expectancies about the potentiality of her students' performance had enormously changed.

With these and similar imaginative procedures, the behavior modifier is in a position to affect the value system of the teacher (at least insofar as the behavior of the children in her class is concerned) and even that of the school administrator analogous to the description of the effects on the power structure in a mental hospital.

Because of the development of the kinds of behavior modification procedures which lend themselves to usage in a multiplicity of social institutions, we can foresee a development in the coming years which will have profound effects on many social institutions. Universities, where behavior modifiers are trained, will increasingly utilize schools, hospitals, clinics, courts, and industrial organizations in programs that combine training, service, and research. Behavior modification clearly becomes social movement when the university has administrative control of a community's elementary school, a mental hospital, or a local industrial corporation. The training function of the behavior modifier then clearly comes into primary focus.

The Identification of "Bad" Social Behavior (Value Judgments)

If we are going to train students to view their professional role as involving the modification of social institutions, we have to identify the institutions and particularly the behaviors and values associated with each of them that should be changed. The social institutions may be real installations, such as mental hospitals, universities, prisons, courts, corporations, churches, television companies, and publishing houses, or they may be accepted ways of behavior of specific groups of people, such as aggression, war, poverty, discrimination, homosexuality, or "making the scene." Eventually, professional behavior modifiers will develop procedures for assessing the usefulness of both kinds of social institutions to groups of individuals in the society, and will also develop techniques of changing the institutions so that they are more consistent with the values of the individual. At first a statement of such goals sounds like utter arrogance on the part of the behavior modifier. Change social institutions to suit the individual, what individual? The behavior modifier? The vision of a Platonic society with its rigid caste of a ruling, wise decision-making elite is not what I am suggesting. Rather, I envision and "believe it possible" that people trained to use "scientific techniques," as tempered by their learned value systems, can determine the behaviors which will lead to maximum reinforcement for most people.

I will illustrate how this might occur with one specific behavior: aggresson, unprovoked behavior that is aversive and highly undesirable to other people. This may refer to behavior of one individual toward another, or one group of individuals (gang, church, state, nation) toward another group. Aggression is a major socially bad behavior (a value judgment), and the efforts of the behavior modifier can be used to change the social institutions which maintain aggression. Human beings are not innately aggressive, but they learn how to be aggressive, as they learn to whom one can display aggression and under what circumstances. There are many social factors which enhance the learning and maintenance of aggression. First and foremost in maintaining aggressive behaviors is the belief or expectancy derived from many "depth" theories of personality which have led people to accept the view that man is inherently an aggressively, warlike creature. Second, children and adults learn much about behavior from the models of violence mediated via television, newspapers, and movies. Third, aggressive behavior is reinforced in our society, if it is not too far out and antisocial, by peer and parental approval, and often by success in the business world. Fourth, we have an inbuilt method of exculpating responsibility for extreme forms of violence in which physical harm is done to others. This is the notion of nonresponsibility because of mental illness. For example, the belief is prevalent in our society that murder may be considered an expression of individual pathology and sickness.

The role of being mentally ill is still an attractive one despite many undesirable aspects. It is a clear social role with certain specified behavioral concomitants. It relieves anxiety, resolves conflicts and crises, elicits attention and interest, creates a meaningful place in life, and offers an excuse for failure. The alternative role of a responsible human being is much harder and more reality-oriented, and allows little escape from the problems of life.

Goldiamond (1965a) points out that "if behavioral psychology does not allow the criminal the out of escaping the consequences of his act by referring to the events which were beyond his control, neither does it allow the teacher to escape the consequences of his sloppy training procedures by blaming the inabilities of the students." This is a statement of the twofold responsibilities involved in behavior modification. An individual who has problems is responsible for his own behavior and cannot blame illness, nor can the therapist attribute his lack of success to the patient's lack of readiness to be helped.

In every social act of violence, evil, or destructive behavior, the first question that is asked is: Was this person mentally ill? Can we attribute his behavior to the evil demons which have possessed him? If only he can be "labeled," then we can offer an explanation, expiate any feelings of involvement or guilt, and proceed to punish him by ostracizing him from society. It was far easier to attribute the violent behavior of the boy who killed 16 people from the University of Texas tower to a lump in his brain or to a psychosis than to his early learning experiences about violence, as evidenced by the pride in his father's voice as he described how he brought his son up to love guns and shoot them frequently.

Bandura & Walters (1959) and Bandura (1965a) have amply demonstrated the role of modeling in the learning, shaping, and maintenance of aggressive human behavior. Wertham (1949, 1966) has argued that the consequence of the dissemination and acceptance of the psychoanalytic model of man has been to justify violence and sadism (via books, movies, and TV) on the basis that it is a manifestation of the true inner nature of man.

Everything which occurs in our society is explainable in so-called psychological terms: the inner devils which abound and which explain violence. The assassin of the president, the killer of eight Chicago nurses, the University of Texas tower killer, were all "sick" people; the locus of violence was the disease within them, negating responsibility on their part. A widely accepted view about the German mass horrors at Auschwitz, as expressed in the form of a "drama," *The Investigation* by Peter Weiss, is that they were a result of something inherently evil within the nature of man, which, by dint of circumstances, could have occurred in any society, and may even be occurring today again (with possible reference to Vietnam). It may be fashionable to beat one's breast and say we are all responsible for the German war crimes, since man is such an evil creature driven to violence by uncontrollable hidden inner forces. But in condemning all, we are exonerating those whose behavior was murder, persecution, sadism, brutality, and rape—bad behaviors all.

We are currently witnessing a societal glorification or reinforcement of murder and violence. Truman Capote's *In Cold Blood* (1965), and the almost uncritical acceptance and acclaim it received, illustrates how a skillful author can take a "bad," "cruel," vicious behavior—the murder of innocent human beings—and build it into meaningful, existential, romantic behavior. While not necessarily overtly justifying this romantic behavior, Capote builds up a sympathetic understanding for these two obviously "sick" and "rejected" youths; he offers the usual psychiatric jargon and psychoanalytic explanations, which explain nothing but seem to justify everything. If murder as a social institution represents a quick and easy path to glory, then, is it any wonder that a youth in Phoenix, Arizona, sought a way of "making a name for myself," as he explained it, and calmly walked into a beauty parlor and shot five women to death. If he (or his lawyer) follow the usual prescribed procedure, he will in due course receive a psychiatric examination, be declared insane (it is really "sick" to kill people), and be put in an asylum (for the criminally insane) where he can join other "sick" killers (such as, presumably, the "Boston Strangler").

Many aspects of our social environment are programmed for acceptance of violence and agression. It starts with childhood and toys. One need only go into a toy store or watch TV commercials around Christmas time to see the plethora of war toys with which a child may "play war" or "kill": toy guns, tanks, bazookas, games of violence and war. A Christmas, 1966, super special was a genuine replica of the medieval torture rack which was guaranteed to be so strong that it would break the back of any doll put on it. Wertham (1966,

p. 67) declares that after years of studying this situation and advocating toy disarmament, he has learned what the obstacles are:

> . . . they are not the destructive instincts in children or the lack of good sense on the part of parents. The major obstacle is the high pressure advertising of the manufacturers. Another is the rationalizations supplied by the psychologists, psychiatrists, and child experts. In Freud's *Peaceful Vienna*, a dream about a gun may have been a harmless sex symbol, but in our civilization it is more likely to be a crystallized intention to kill, in play or in earnest. Again and again it has been stated that guns are good for building a boy's character. One psychiatrist has observed that 'as small boys shoot each other without mercy, their faces glow with excitement.' He upholds the notion that this kind of excitement is all right because 'the boys are working through their ancestral past,' 'they are as innocent as the kittens pouncing on each other's tail.' Such opinions, propounded in the name of psychiatry, are part of the intellectual decadence, and violence-mindedness of our time.

We live surrounded by movies, TV, books, newspapers filled with gory reports of crimes, rapes, murders. Guns are obtainable from any "sports" shop and many mail-order catalogs. A recent TV documentary, based on Bakal's (1966) book on the "right" to bear arms, describes an experiment in which a reporter went into a gun shop in Dallas, purchased a gun similar to the one that killed former President Kennedy, and proceeded to walk through the streets of Dallas for several hours carrying the gun openly, without anyone stopping him or even paying any attention to him.

The major effect of violence on human behavior is not necessarily that violence will be repeated but that violence will become accepted as a way of life. We live with violence, tolerate it, and really object only when we are the victims. Children are not reinforced for behavior showing respect for life but, rather, become conditioned to accept violence and war as ways of life.

Enormous reinforcement is given to violence directly, and vicariously via rewarded models for violence, by the social sanction of the communication media such as TV shows, novels, and films, and of the general support of the war in Vietnam, with its destruction of civilians including children. Writing books or dramas of violence is a well-reinforced financial operation. There is no comparable payoff for writings emphasizing goodness, altruism, and love of mankind. In fact, society uses a range of aversive reinforcers, from censure to imprisonment, in its attempt to control undesirable (and unpredictable) non-aggressive behavior. The aversive consequences of refusing to be inducted into the armed forces or refusing to bear arms in the armed forces are quite clear. A recent incident in New York City emphasizes the threat felt by society to any attempt to modify the independence of an aggressive social system. A group of 14 children aged four to twelve picketed the Ideal Toy Company for selling war toys. Their inflammatory signs included slogans such as "Ban toy bombs" and "War toys kill people." The official societal reaction was the arrest of the children by the police and the confiscation of their signs. Subsequently the children were released after their ages had been recorded in the police records. The incident perfectly captures the spirit of the point that our officially sanctioned models of behavior are aggressive ones and any deviations from this model are reacted to as bad (value decision) and "abnormal." To go against the approved value system of society (even on reluctantly accepted behaviors such as aggression) is to indicate psychopathy, disease, and unacceptable behavior.

Another illustration of how a theoretical model of man's nature interacts with a value system comes from a report by Bettelheim (1966) on his observations of the behavior of a group of American psychiatrists, psychoanalysts, and psychologists visiting a kibbutz in Israel. A number of the Americans were disturbed by the lack of emphasis on private property among the children in the kibbutz. The value which was reinforced in the life of the kibbutz was that group needs take precedence over those of the individual. Bettelheim points out that the Americans did not even comprehend the value system involved, being blinded by their own theoretical model. This is evidenced by their suggestions on child-rearing practices, which they felt the kibbutz should adopt, including: "Children should not only have their own individual toys; they should also have facilities for safeguarding these as their own, as something one does not have to share with anybody else" and "every child should be encouraged to have some personal possession or possessions in his corner; that each child's bed should look different from the other bed in his room just so he will know it's *his*." The kibbutz managers and the American professionals could not communicate with each other, nor understand each others' basic value systems. It was clear, in fact, from Bettelheim's description that neither even saw the problem in value terms but rather in terms of the other's failure to comprehend the true nature of man. We have cited this report because it illustrates the point that the model of man which a professional group, or a society, holds can be reduced to a value system which one has learned. The model does not represent the true nature of man but, rather, is a set of hypotheses which, although sometimes testable, are seldom questioned once they are acquired, even by people who label themselves "scientists."

Even at the level of interpreting the most extreme form of human aggressive behavior, namely, wars, the tendency has been, in some quarters, to consider war a psychiatric problem. Wars are represented as a mental disease or an aberration of society. The roots of war, contends the psychoanalyst, lie in the feelings of inferiority and guilt which dominate the human unconscious. However, the disease model cannot continue to be used as an excuse for evading responsibility. The origins of war lie in social, economic, and historical forces and in the specific reinforcement that war brings to key individuals in power positions in a society. The origin of wars, like the origin of any other socially undesirable behavior, does not lie within the individual's psyche. "The image of man that we start from is most important. If we say that the human being is and always will be violent . . . we are giving in to civil and military violence. If atomic scientists are guilty of participating in the misuse of their discoveries, we psychiatrists are equally guilty, if not more so, when we use our theories to explain away the true nature of war and to furnish evasive generalizations for it" (Wertham, 1966, p. 133).

Training for the Role of Modifier of Social Institutions

Once we have isolated the objectives of our training program—for example, the substitution of less aggressive behaviors for the kinds of violence we have been maintaining in the past—then the specifics of our training programs can become clearer. The hypothetical internship year described below illustrates one aspect of a program to train modifiers of social institutions.

What might be the content of such an internship year? First let us dispose of two aspects of training to which "tradition" now gives top priority in the internship year: diagnosis and therapy. In the internship year these should be relegated to minor importance. The trainee should be exposed to this aspect of the psychologist's role, but with a view that professional competence in these areas will have to wait for the postdoctoral year of training. At present, both traditional psychotherapy and psychodiagnosis essentially consist of a series of "at best" questionable techniques, which all too often are presented to the trainee as a gospel with which he must arm himself. The emphasis must be on the social context within which these two procedures take place, and particularly on the purposes and goals of assessment and of treatment.

A feasible program could be made during a year's internship which would place particular emphasis on training the student for his dual role as the behavior controller and as the research investigator into behavior control. He could be particularly exposed to a variety of situations which would help him to understand and be in a position to further investigate five major variables, the interactions among them, and the value systems of each. The five major variables are: the patient, the institution, the community, the behavior controllers, and the student himself.

I will hypothesize the installation as a neuropsychiatric hospital, since doing so allows more opportunities for the approach I am describing. A similar program can be set up at other types of internship installations The timing of this internship in the trainee's overall program would be in the third year of graduate school. Two years of course work should be sufficient to give him the background for the kind of internship described and should allow sufficient time, an additional year at the university, after its completion. The internship should be paid for by the university or through public health funds, to lessen the pressure of service needs at the installation on the trainee.

The trainee would be welcomed by the chief of the psychology service, assigned to a staff or faculty supervisor, and on his first day admitted to the hospital as a patient. He would go through the same procedure as any patient would go through. There would be no attempt to hide his identity, no attempt to treat him in a special manner. He would spend two weeks in the hospital, and his discharge would be a function of having completed this time period and not necessarily a function of being "cured." Throughout the rest of the year, he would spend time in a variety of activities, described below. During each of these activities, he would maintain close contact with his supervisor, meeting with him at least one hour a week to help integrate his experiences into a meaningful pattern. One afternoon a week would be spent in a continuing seminar, or series of seminars, which would consist of speakers, discussions, research reports, and other activities aimed (1) at helping to expose the trainee to the potentialities inherent in the psychologist's role and (2) at helping him to integrate his experiences. The university liaison person and other university consultants should be heavily involved in these seminars with the aim of helping to incorporate the trainee's experiences into the science of psychology as taught at the University. The trainee would be given assignments related to four areas of investigation: the patient, the installation, the community, and the psychologist.

The "patient" assignment would include spending various periods of time in the following activities: serving as a nursing assistant on a ward other than the one to which he was admitted; visiting and spending time in homes of parents or relatives of hospitalized patients; returning to the community with one or more patients as they leave the hospital and observing them in their experiences.

The "institution" assignment would consist of spending various periods of time in the following activities: being assigned to the offices of the Manager and the Director of Professional Services, to participate in all conferences, meetings, and contacts in which they are involved; assignment to various professional people with whom the trainee comes into contact, to observe behavior systematically.

In the "community" assignments would be included: contacts in the community with employers, labor, and industrial groups, with emphasis on determining their attitudes and feelings about "mental illness," adjustment, and life in general; assignment to the local police department to become aware of problems of crime, delinquency, suicide, and alcoholism; assignment to the local school system to have contacts with teachers, counselors, psychologists, principals, school board members, and PTA groups.

As part of the "psychologist" assignment the trainee would: spend periods of time with various psychologists as a member of a ward team participating in the ward decision-making process; observe his supervisor to analyze his role and function as a psychologist; be in the office of the chief of the psychological service, participating in all meetings and contacts in which the service is involved; study the various research programs; interview faculty members and sit in on faculty meetings of the psychology department of the local university if one is near the installation (not in the role of a student, but rather in the role of the observer and investigator of an important professional and social phenomenon); and observe the psychology staff of the installation in a similar manner.

At the beginning of the year, the trainee would be given a series of assignments which he would be expected to complete and present to the seminar for discussion, at least several weeks prior to the completion of his year. These would include the following:

1. What is the role of mental health professionals in the community? What are the value systems of these professionals? How do the professionals' value systems differ from those of patients and the general community? This assignment would encompass an analysis of the attitudes, values, and goals of psychologists, social workers, and psychiatrists, based on the trainee's observations of them at meetings, discussions, and interviews; the analysis would include members of the psychology and psychiatry departments at local universities or medical schools, if there were any in the community. What are the sources of reinforcement which are maintaining the current values and behavior of the professionals vis-à-vis patients and students?

2. What are the major research needs of the institution and how would you go about investigating them?

3. An analysis of the communication system, formal and informal, within the hospital structure.

4. An analysis of informational media in the community relative to mental health. What messages are communicated by newspapers, radios, etc., about mental illness?

5. What behaviors are labeled mental illness in this community?

6. For what purposes would you use assessment procedures? What procedures would you use for what specific purposes?

7. Devise and carry out one project involving the modification of human behavior. Demonstrate how the modification is related to assessment procedures.

8. How would you conceive of your own role as a psychologist in the hospital and in the community? What would be your goals and purposes?

9. Write your conception of a "utopian" society.

During the year there would be several reports on the trainee's progress by his supervisor and by the liaison person. There would also be self-evaluative reports by the trainee, and he would prepare a critique of the program.

There would also be a series of interviews and assessment procedures, given to him at the beginning of the year and at the end, to measure changes in his behavior, attitudes, and values.

At the end of this year, the student could return to the university, finish his courses and dissertation, and take a postdoctoral internship. The purpose of this internship would be to become skilled with evaluation, modification, and other techniques, which, by this time, should have a useful meaning for him and which he should pick up readily. Further, he should be able to bring to his professional role a clear conception of his role, new conceptions and techniques of research, and an awareness of the relationship between his role and his value system and that of society.

The overall purpose of such an internship would be to help the trainee to develop goals, social perspectives, and an awareness and appreciation of the role of value systems in the professional community. These goals will not arise spontaneously in the trainees, but must be guided by the staff supervisor and the university consultant. Unfortunately, the major defect in this program may be that most psychologists, academic and clinical, are not yet ready to face this problem for themselves, let alone for the new trainee.

That what I am proposing is well within the current *Zeitgeist* is indicated by the Ulrich & Kent (1966) description of "new tactics" in educating psychologists. They point out cogently that in education, as in all other human behaviors involving change, the first step in planning, or programming, is to delineate our goals and specify what behavior we desire. One way to do this is to select behaviors of respected scientists as models to follow in establishing behavioral goals. This might include specific technical skills; methodology; application of psychological principles; ability to read, write, and speak to students and colleagues; ability to administer, teach, and train others; and ability to be creative. "We should approach the problem of education from the point of view that the teacher, as the behavioral engineer, is primarily responsible for what the student learns." To meet these goal requirements, Ulrich & Kent recommend a Ph.D. "apprenticeship program in which the individual to be trained comes to the university not as a student but as a staff member and colleague. Status, salary, and duties would then be commensurate with an apprentice level, not a student's." Such a program is clearly learning by doing based on model behavior. One way of making apprenticeship training more realistic in applied research is to tie the university operations more closely to those of existing institutions such as state mental hospitals, public schools, and Job Corps. This is involved in the university's "running" certain social institutions, as described above.

Although the Ulrich & Kent program based on learning via model behavior offers many exciting possibilities, there is one inherent drawback which manifests itself in all programs based on education via models. It does not take into consideration the major goals in training or behavior modification, namely, training for changed roles. We do not want to perpetuate the failures, incompetences, and stupidities of the past. We cannot present an alternative model and say, "This is it." Rather, the goal of training in behavior modification must become that of training people for social roles which do not yet exist but which must develop out of the kind of training to be given to future generations of students. What we can do at this point is specify the general behaviors we may expect or desire of future behavior modifiers and then, as best we can, develop the techniques to achieve these goals.

Walden Two, Where Are You?

In line with the view that eventually behavior modification will extend to social institutions, it is of interest to determine the latest developments in thought or action about the possibilities of the "Walden Two" era.

Mertens (1967) reports that in December, 1966, St. Cloud State College and the Johnson (Wax) Foundation cooperated in holding a conference called "On the Experimental Community." This conference, attended by Skinner, represents the most concrete steps yet taken to plan and implement an actual experimental community. One of the most interesting and important elements in the planning for a social organization based on behavior principles is the interest in the relation between architecture and behavior. Mertens (1967) has organized a directory of people such as architects and city planners who are interested in behaviorally engineered cultures.

We have repeatedly emphasized that training for the role of clinical psychologist must prepare him to function as a social planner. In the long run the clinical psychologist will make his greatest contribution to the welfare of individuals by the programming of social communities. It is to these goals that the training of the behavior modifier must place its major emphasis.

Chapter Summary

This chapter discusses the implications of the growth and expansion of behavior modification procedures for training of future behavior modifiers. Because of its explicit delineation of the variables involved in the psychotherapeutic situation, behavior modifiers raise the issue of the value implications involved in helping another individual change his behavior. Training and values are directly interrelated with one another. There is considerable evidence that all psychotherapeutic interactions involve implicitly and explicitly the control of the subject's behavior, including his value system. The therapist is in a position to impose his own value system. He cannot avoid the issue by denying it. The behavior modifier must accept the responsibility inherent in the therapeutic role. It is only by recognizing and acknowledging this aspect of the therapeutic role that the rights of the individual patient can be protected. The behavior modifier as an educator helps the individual with whom he is working to be able to be in a position to have a choice in his life, to be a freer individual.

The behavior modifier has a clear philosophical position insofar as his role relates to representing society or the individual when they are in conflict. Since the major source of reinforcement for the individual is considered to be the attention, interest, and love of other people, the therapist is then functioning as the agent of others, as the agent of society. The goal is to maximize the possibility of social reinforcement for the individual, and, in this sense, there is no real conflict, since individual goals are primarily social in nature.

The model of man held by the therapist has important consequences for what he actually does in psychotherapy. The behavior modifier views the locus of change in human behavior as being determined primarily by environmental events. With such a view the therapist is more likely to be interested in the changing of social institutions to effect individual change. The programming of an entire environmental unit such as involved in a token economy represents a major step in the direction of modifying a social institution. The same approach which is involved in setting up a token economy on a psychiatric ward can be used in approaching other social institutions such as aggression or war.

Specific suggestions for implementing changes via training are offered. It is the next generation of behavior modifiers, trained in a highly complex scientific and professional role, who may bring about social changes which will have lasting and positive effects on human behavior.

PART FOUR

Commentaries and General Critique

Verbal Conditioning, Behavior Therapy, and Behavior Change:

Some Problems in Extrapolation*

KENNETH HELLER

Indiana University, Bloomington, Indiana

G. ALAN MARLATT

University of British Columbia, Vancouver, British Columbia

Behavior therapy is at the forefront of a growing revolution in psychotherapy. The characterstics of this revolution are not difficult to discern. To begin with, impatience with the inadequacies of traditional dynamic psychology has led many to rebel against what seems to be an unwillingness to deal directly with the real behavioral complaints of patients. While self-understanding is also a desirable goal, behavior therapists are among those unwilling to settle for the latter without changes in the former, and would take the position that in many cases increased behavioral effectiveness results in increased understanding (see also Hobbs, 1962, for amplification of this point).

The behavior therapists are also among those who stress the importance of strengthening adaptive behaviors rather than concentrating on "sick" maladaptive behaviors. They suggest that it is often a mistake to allow exces-

* Preparation of this manuscript was facilitated by Grant MH-10225 from the National Institute of Mental Health, United States Public Health Service. Research conducted by Heller was partially supported by this grant and by Grant MH-07679, National Institute of Mental Health. Research by Marlatt was also partially supported by a National Institute of Mental Health predoctoral research fellowship (MH-31,637).

sive attention and practice to be focused on erroneous or undesirable responses which could thereby be strengthened. Goldstein, Heller, & Sechrest (1966, p. 236) agree that the probability of positive transfer of pro-social responses from therapy to real life is increased "if very strong emphasis is placed in therapy on emitting responses considered desirable in other circumstances."

The traditional view of patient psychopathology assumes a benign environment into which the patient projects inappropriate behaviors learned under past aversive conditions. It is usually further assumed that adaptive behaviors are already part of the patient's repertoire, so that the function of psychotherapy is to free the patient to use the abilities he already possesses. However, there is a growing recognition that in many cases of psychopathology, the patient may not have adaptive pro-social responses as part of his behavioral repertoire, his maladaptive behaviors may be sustained by environmental contingencies which encourage and reward deviance, or he may be operating in a completely malevolent environment. Thus, in many cases a functional analysis of the patient's capabilities and the environmental contingencies sustaining his behavior is in order. While the traditional therapists have often ignored these problems, the behavior therapists have been among those insisting on a systematic and detailed analysis of the patient's presenting problem and the conditions sustaining that behavior. Their view has been that, regardless of the conditions under which maladaptive behaviors were originally learned, changing the current environmental contingencies sustaining that behavior should do much to alter the deviant behavior itself.

Revolutions bring changes which often represent an overall gain to society. This is particularly true in the intellectual realm, where the revolutionary gains are advances in knowledge. In the field of psychotherapy, the end product of the current intellectual ferment has considerable pragmatic import since advances in knowledge can be directly transferable to increased efficiencies in treatment. Unfortunately, revolutionary movements themselves are not known for being conducive to dispassionate inquiry and the objective advancement of knowledge. Often, established procedures and older ideas are denounced with bitterness, and it is only after the fury of charges and counter-charges has abated that an impartial assessment of evidence is possible. During the initial stages of a revolutionary movement, the combatants usually see themselves as underdogs fighting a numerically superior and more powerful enemy. They are more easily recognized by what they are against than by what they advocate, for divergent opinions are tolerated only as long as all swear allegiance against the common enemy. A most important characteristic of revolutionary movements is the tendency to deny the possibility that the existing establishment possesses positive traits; loyalty to the cause is considered in danger of erosion if the enemy's point of view can be accepted as even partially reasonable or plausible.

At times, the publications of some behavior therapists convey the spirit of a small band of revolutionaries fighting against a more powerful and hostile adversary. For example, consider the following statement by Rachman & Eysenck (1966, p. 168):

> In half a dozen years a relatively small number of behavior therapists, with little official support and often against the most hostile opposition, have succeeded in carrying out more controlled (and better controlled) studies than have hundreds of psychiatrists and psychoanalysts in 60 years, with all the financial resources and the prestige so readily available to them.

Another example of the extent to which some leaders of the behavior therapy movement picture the enemy as representing an all-powerful establishment, belligerent and repressive of new ideas, is given by Eysenck (1965b, pp. 328–329):

> In the United States at least, and to a somewhat lesser degree in many other countries as well, psychoanalysis and psychoanalytically oriented psychotherapy have achieved a position of unrivaled dominance ... alternate approaches and methods are not even mentioned in textbooks, these alternate approaches are not taught to trainee psychiatrists, and criticisms of the existing orthodoxy are suppressed and withheld from students and practitioners alike. The effects of such a policy are of course very clear. Professional advancement, the obtaining of research grants, and the very earning of a livelihood are to a large extent dependent on the young psychiatrist's acceptance of this premature crystallization of spurious orthodoxy. All experimentation which takes inspiration from sources other than Freud, or which uses methods other than psychotherapy, is made as difficult as possible or preferably aborted on the grounds that as the truth is already known no experimentation is needed to establish it, and no alternative methods can possibly bring any enlightenment or improvement.

It is unfortunate that the published views of some behavior therapists have often obscured the real contributions of their movement. For example, they have insisted that their procedures are more scientific, when in fact they rely as heavily on uncontrolled case studies as have other therapeutic schools. They proclaim that their methods represent the only therapeutic procedures that consistently utilize learning principles, when in fact they ignore a good deal of the relevant literature on human learning apart from classical and instrumental conditioning. In addition, procedures unrelated to learning theory (carbon monoxide inhalation, drugs, and hypnosis) are accepted as long as they demonstrate an effectiveness for changing behavior (see Ullmann & Krasner, 1965, p. 32). Finally, they have been unwilling to recognize that the other points of view which they chastise so readily have also been experiencing similar forces of change.

While one might find fault with the chauvinism, proselytizing, and condescending attitude of some behavior therapists, we should not permit the more basic contribution of this movement to be hidden by the excesses of revolutionary zeal. The behavior therapists have accurately spotlighted some of the weaknesses in theory and inefficiences in technique that have become associated with psychotherapy. It is clear that the behavior therapists are an important part of a new movement in psychotherapy the primary goals of which are to help patients become more effective in their daily lives. This important change in the orientation of psychotherapy comes closer to the values of society (and of patients themselves) than does the exclusive emphasis on self-understanding and inner contentment found in the more traditional psychotherapies (Ford & Urban, 1967).

The Extrapolation of Laboratory Research to Behavior Change in Psychotherapy

Psychologists working in such diverse areas as learning, propaganda and persuasion, opinion and attitude change, group conformity pressures, and psychotherapy are all concerned with the same basic problem, namely specifying the conditions which mediate behavior change. More than any other group, the behavior therapists have recognized the desirability of deriving their clinical procedures from a more basic psychology of behavior change (Krasner, 1962c). That the behavior therapists have largely restricted themselves to the literature on conditioning techniques is unfortunate, but may simply represent a first step in attempting to integrate behavior change phenomena from such diverse settings as the learning laboratory and the clinical consulting room.

The extrapolation of research findings from one research domain to another is not without difficulties. In drawing conclusions from his research, any investigator must be concerned with the "external validity" (Campbell & Stanley, 1963) of his findings, that is, the degree to which the conclusions he draws will apply to any groups or situations other than the ones with which his research was mainly concerned. A perfectly good experiment from the standpoint of design and execution may have little if any external validity, since questions of research design, by and large, involve those issues that make it possible to have confidence in the conclusions drawn from the experiment, but have little to do with the application of those conclusions to new situations. The validity of applying experimental findings to new situations, new groups of persons, and new procedures depends on the degree to which the original experiment was representative of the new situations. In general, the greater the differences between the original research setting and any other subsequent application, the more cautious must be the extrapolation attempt. However, not all differences are equally relevant. Any generalizations we make may be quite erroneous if subtle changes occur in relevant variables and yet may hold well under seemingly drastic changes in other more extraneous variables. For example, in attempting to generalize a particular research finding in the field of psychotherapy, one might find that the results hold for patients and therapists of different sexes and ages and yet fail to hold if a therapist has an accent suggestive of a particular national origin. (See Goldstein, Heller, & Sechrest, 1966, pp. 32–39, for a fuller discussion of the problems of external validity as applied to psychotherapy research.)

Problems of external validity become even more serious when one attempts to extrapolate a research finding to areas of application quite different from the original experimental setting. Still, an extrapolation strategy has much to recommend it when the possibilities for rigorous research in the primary area of interest are quite limited. For example, it is doubtful that research will ever be done in which school children are subjected to severe punishment in order to discover the effects of punishment on learning ability, but laboratory research and even animal research on punishment is often generalized to the school and other applied learning situations. In the field of psychotherapy, the generalization of findings from diverse areas of research has much to recommend it because of the pragmatic complexities involved in doing research on the therapeutic enterprise itself. This is not to say that good outcome studies are impossible, but even the best outcome study, especially one testing new and unconventional methods of treatment, could benefit from prior evidence from the laboratory or other controlled research situations that would help determine the conditions under which the new procedures might prove applicable.

Similarly, with already established therapeutic techniques it is extremely difficult for an outcome study to isolate the exact factors in the global therapeutic technique that are responsible for the changes seen in patients. This point can be illustrated by considering the therapeutic procedures proposed by Wolpe (1958). If Wolpean techniques prove effective, which aspects of his method are most crucial? Are the effective therapeutic ingredients to be found in the relaxation procedures; the use of imagery instead of the overt confrontation of fear-eliciting stimuli; the approach to feared objects in hierarchical order; the extinction of fears; the counterconditioning of relaxation or other adaptive responses to replace fears; the neurological inhibition of fear; the therapist's explicit theoretical explanation of how symptoms are learned and how they can be removed; faith in the therapist; friendship and love provided through the therapeutic relationship; or some combination of the above? It is difficult to imagine how a proper test of the exact factors responsible for change in Wolpean psychotherapy could be made except in a controlled laboratory situation. (Two carefully controlled recent attempts are those of Davison, 1968a, and Lang, Lazovik, & Reyonlds, 1965.)

Even those already committed to the application of the findings of laboratory research to real-life situations often do not recognize the complexities involved. Most often lacking in extrapolation attempts is some form of "bridging" research (Goldstein & Dean, 1966) which tests the conditions under which a particular laboratory finding might apply. This point has been made most explicitly by Hilgard & Bower (1966) who describe six types of research which should be undertaken before principles of learning developed in the experimental laboratory can be adopted in school classrooms. Similarly, in social psychology, Hovland (1959) has indicated the variables that must be considered before the contradictions in the findings of laboratory and field studies of social influence can be resolved. McGuire (1968) also notes that mediating variables play a large part in determining the nature of the results obtained in studies of persuasibility, since individual difference variables (such as intelligence, anxiety level, and self-esteem) interact differentially with attention, comprehension, or yielding to persuasive messages.

The translation of basic principles of behavior change into psychotherapeutic practice is described by Ford & Urban (1967) as requiring at least a three-step process. Principles of behavior change are first distilled in a series of experimental studies. A second stage involves clinical research in which the focus is on the interaction of individual difference variables and experimental variables. The third stage involves a series of clinical trials in which general principles are tried out with real patients under more usual clinical conditions. One should not expect to move directly from experimental research to clinical trials without prior information concerning the interaction of mediating variables such as personality, task, and setting. This seems to be more clearly understood by social psychologists (Hovland, 1959; McGuire, 1968) than by their more clinical brethren, for among the latter the expectation that there should be an exact correspondence between experimental research and clinical trials is still quite common. That this expectation has generated some disappointing attempts to apply the principles of behavior change derived in the laboratory to the practice of psychotherapy can be illustrated by research on verbal and conversational "conditioning."

The "Conditioning" of Verbal Behavior and Psychotherapy

Early workers in the field that has now come to be known as "verbal conditioning," saw as their goal the extension of Skinnerian principles of operant conditioning derived from animal research to human verbal behavior (Krasner, 1958a; Kanfer, 1968). The most widely cited of these studies (Greenspoon, 1951) investigated the effects of introducing a brief verbal response by the experimenter ("mmm-hmm" or "huh-uh") on the emission of plural nouns during a task which required saying individual unrelated words. Other contingent stimuli were also tested in other groups which received a visual stimulus (a red light flash) or an auditory stimulus (a 190-cycle tone) as the conditioning stimulus. Greenspoon found that the verbal stimulus "mmm-hmm," the visual stimulus, and the auditory stimulus all resulted in significant increases in the number of plural noun responses emitted by subjects, when compared to a control group which received no such stimuli during the task. It was the results of experiments such as these (see reviews by Krasner, 1958a; Greenspoon, 1962; Williams, 1964; and Kanfer, 1968), most of which have demonstrated significant experimental effects, that led some researchers (i.e., Greenspoon, 1962, p. 511) to hope that:

> ... it should be possible to work with verbal behavior in much the same way as experimenters have worked with the behavior of rats, pigeons, etc. It should also be possible to investigate the same kinds of variables that have been investigated with the non-verbal behavior of humans and infrahumans.

The clinical implications of this work seemed immediately apparent (e.g., Taffel, 1955), and at various times, clinicians have looked toward the verbal conditioning experiment as an analog to psychotherapy, as a treatment procedure in and of itself, as a method for studying the situational variables in projective testing, as a method for studying interviewer bias, and as a procedure by which hypotheses about psychopathological processes could be tested (Kanfer, 1968). But perhaps the most challenging and controversial implication of verbal conditioning studies has been the claim that all forms of psychotherapy derive their effectiveness from the reinforcing power of the therapist and that the inefficiencies in psychotherapy derive from therapists' lack of recognition of their own reinforcing properties.

Despite the enthusiasm generated, principles of conditioning worked out "with the behavior of rats, pigeons, etc." (Greenspoon, 1962) were not sufficient to explain the results reported in a number of studies. A case in point involves simple approval and disapproval, which were regarded by the Skinnerians as functioning as generalized positive and negative conditioned reinforcers (Krasner, 1958a). This position was derived from the following definition by Skinner (1957, pp. 53–54):

> Any event which characteristically precedes many different reinforcers can be used as a reinforcer to bring behavior under the control of all appropriate conditions of deprivation and aversive stimulation. A response which is characteristically followed by such a generalized conditioned reinforcer has dynamic properties similar to those which it would have acquired if it had been severally followed by all the specific reinforcers at issue.
>
> A common generalized conditioned reinforcer is approval: it is often difficult to specify its physical dimensions. It may be little more than a nod or smile on the part of someone who characteristically supplies a variety of reinforcements. Sometimes ... it has a verbal form: *Right!* or *Good!* Because these

signs of approval frequently precede specific reinforcements appropriate to many states of deprivation, the behavior they reinforce is likely to be in strength much of the time.

Problems with this conceptualization arose almost immediately. To begin with, there is some difficulty in construing verbal responses as analogous to motor responses in conditioning experiments. A bar press can be conditioned easily through operant procedures, with the result that frequency of bar presses increases over time. Conceiving of a word as a single response akin to the bar press seems to be an overly simple analogy. If the analogy held without restriction, then application of a verbal reinforcer to the plural noun "horses" should lead to an increase in this word alone. How, then, can one explain the generalization to other plural nouns, such as "cats," "birds," or "houses"? This can only be done by bringing in the concept of stimulus class. Here it is concluded that the class of plural nouns has been "conditioned." All items within the class are said to have increased probability of occurrence following reinforcement.

When one speaks of class instead of individual response items, one begins to tread on cognitive ground. The argument for the operation of cognitive strategies in verbal conditioning experiments has been made elsewhere (Dulany, 1961; Spielberger, 1965). It is our own view that verbal "reinforcers" are best characterized as discriminative stimuli which provide information as to the appropriate or desired response class for the subject; this is similar to what occurs in a concept-formation task, where the experimenter provides the subject with knowledge of the "correctness" of his choices.

Other more practical difficulties also became apparent because some so-called "generalized reinforcers" did not control behavior in a consistent and predictable manner. In the Greenspoon experiment mentioned above, it was found that the effects of the verbal stimulus "huh-uh" varied as a function of the response class made contingent with it. When "huh-uh" followed plural nouns, there was a tendency for the frequency of that response class to decline. However, when the same stimulus was introduced following nonplural nouns, the opposite result was obtained. A similar inconsistent finding was reported in another study conducted as a follow-up to the Greenspoon experiment. Ball (1952) found that "huh-uh" had two opposite effects on speech. For some subjects, it was associated with a decrease in the frequency of the response on which conditioning was attempted (animal words), while for other subjects it was associated with an increase in the frequency of animal words.

The inconsistent results produced by the early studies using the stimulus "huh-uh" were duplicated by other studies of verbal disapproval. Azrin, Holz, Ulrich, & Goldiamond (1961) found that experimenter disagreement raised or lowered the reported level of opinion statements emitted by subjects depending upon expectancies induced in the experimenters. When experimenters were led to believe that disagreement blocked the catharsis of emotion, their subjects produced increases in opinion statements following experimenter disagreement. However, when experimenters were instructed that disagreement produced an extinction effect, the number of opinion statements emitted by subjects following experimenter disagreement was reduced. Azrin et al. did not speculate about the possible mechanisms that might mediate this experimenter bias effect,[1] but concluded from this and three other attempts at conversational conditioning that "the results of studies in verbal conditioning may be more of a reflection of the experimenter's expectation and theories than of the subject's behavior" (p. 30).

In the context of a personal interview in which subjects were requested to speak about themselves, Heller, Brahlek, & Morris (described by Heller, 1968) found that interviewer comments presented as one-word verbalizations ("no," "uh-uh") decreased the frequency of the response on which conditioning was attempted (past verbs), but that more active and longer disagreements, in which the interviewer stated the exact subject remark with which he disagreed, produced an increase in the frequency of past verbs. A second study, by Heller, Marlatt, & Bailey (described by Heller, 1968), replicated the finding that subjects would persist in talking on those topics marked by interviewer disagreement. In this experiment, subjects, whose instructions were to talk about themselves, were required to press a key in front of them in order to hear from an interviewer who was hidden from view behind a wooden screen. Subjects persisted in requesting responses from interviewers who disagreed with them. When confronted with interviewer agreement, subjects requested the interviewer to speak much less often and changed topics more frequently following an interviewer remark. In both of the above experiments, subjects indicated on a postinterview questionnaire that they felt more comfortable with and liked the positive, agreeing interviewers. Yet despite this preference, subjects persisted in discussing those topics which met with interviewer disagreement or disapproval. The authors interpret their results as indicating that when the interviewer controls the conversation by producing few orienting cues by which the subject can monitor his own responding, the subject is forced to follow the only cues available as best he can. But when the subject is provided with enough information so that he himself can judge the adequacy of his own response and postulate possible reasons for the interviewer's disagreement, he feels much more free to persist in the same topic, argue with the interviewer, and attempt to convert him. In this case, rather than remaining the passive recipient of influence, the subject attempts to exert counter-influence.

The claim that verbal conditioning effects are robust and operate in

---

[1] See Rosenthal, Kohn, Greenfield, & Carota (1966) for a more detailed description of the operation of experimenter bias in a verbal conditioning experiment.

diverse settings including psychotherapy requires the demonstration of significant experimental effects in a variety of situations in which diverse subject response classes are modified by various verbal reinforcers. While the general trend of the results has been positive, not all verbal statements of approval or disapproval have been found to be equally effective as reinforcers (Hildum & Brown, 1956; Mandler & Kaplan, 1956; Merbaum & Southwell, 1965) and not all classes of subject verbalization have been found to be equally modifiable (Koenig, 1966; Lanyon, 1967; Matarazzo, Saslow, & Pareis, 1960). Furthermore, while it would be expected that reinforced verbal behavior would be as amenable to generalization as any other form of learned behavior, research on the generalization of reinforced verbal responses has not been encouraging (Greenspoon, 1962). On the positive side, Insko (1965) presents evidence that reinforcement of an attitude during a telephone conversation can carry over to an attitude questionnaire administered one week later. On the other hand, while Lovaas (1964b) did find an increase in the consumption of food following the verbal reinforcement of the corresponding food word, the generalization effect dissipated on successive conditioning days. Similarly, success in verbal "conditioning" but failure in generalization was obtained when the experimenter was no longer present in the experimental room (Singer, 1961); when generalization was tested by a different experimenter (Moos, 1963); and when generalization was measured by tasks such as dynamometer (Krasner, Knowles, & Ullmann, 1965) or personality test performance (Stollak, 1966; Wimsatt & Vestre, 1963).

While the inconsistencies reported in some of the research reports cited above raise questions concerning the generality of the verbal conditioning phenomenon, there is an even greater handicap in the extrapolation of the results of verbal conditioning experiments to social interchange in general and to psychotherapy in particular. Verbal conditioning effects have been demonstrated only when the experimenter (or interviewer) remains minimally responsive. In the typical verbal conditioning experiment, such as the Taffel or the Greenspoon procedures, the experimenter remains silent except when uttering the "reinforcing" stimulus. (Some experiments also allow a few simple verbal prods such as "Go on" if the subject stops talking.) Only two attempts at "conversational conditioning" report success in conditioning opinion statements during naturally occurring conversations (Verplanck, 1955; Centers, 1963), but in both studies the interviewer was either silent or minimally responsive during the operant and extinction phases of the experiment. In these experiments interviewer silence was used to determine operant levels, probably with the assumption that silence is neutral and is equivalent to "no treatment." However, the results of an experiment by Heller, Davis, & Myers (1966) suggest that, in an interview, silence on the part of one participant fails to represent a neutral condition against which the natural state of the other person can be measured. Heller and his coworkers found that silence was most verbally inhibiting in the sense of producing least subject talk time when compared with four conditions of interviewer responsiveness. Thus, in verbal conditioning experiments, response increases during conditioning over that obtained at the operant level with interviewer silence may represent a spurious change. Furthermore, if the interviewer is silent except when emitting the reinforcing stimulus, the cue value of that stimulus is excessively enhanced. A better test of conversational conditioning would involve embedding the reinforcing stimulus in a larger, more naturally occurring verbal stimulus and determining operant levels by using a schedule of interviewer responding that is non-contingent with the class of subject response to be subsequently reinforced, such as fixed-interval responding (also see Dean & Hiesinger, 1964). Attempts at conversational conditioning without the above modifications should be interpreted with caution.

At present we can conclude only that the generality and applicability of verbal conditioning findings are quite limited. To be sure, the large body of research demonstrating "conditioning" phenomena would ordinarily be quite impressive. The problem is that almost all these studies demonstrate positive results only under conditions of minimal experimenter responsiveness which serves to enhance the cuing properties of the reinforcing stimuli. Those few attempts to demonstrate a verbal conditioning phenomenon in more active and mutually responsive social interactions have proved disappointing. What relevance do these results then have for the psychotherapeutic interaction? It would seem that, in general, the less responsive the therapist and the more ambiguous the stimulus field in which the patient must operate, the more likely will the patient be to follow the few orienting cues that the therapist provides. Under these conditions, the patient will probably monitor his responses so as to present what he thinks the therapist requires of him. This problem is quite relevant for some therapy systems, namely those which urge the therapist to minimize his responsiveness. For example, in the traditional Freudian model the entire therapy situation is designed to minimize the intrusion of the therapist into the field of consciousness of the patient. The therapist sits behind his patient so that his personal reactions to the patient's remarks are hidden, he says little, and the instruction to the patient, "Tell me whatever comes to your mind," gives no direction to the course the patient is to follow. These procedures are justified as necessary for free association and the development of transference reactions in the patient. However, it is precisely this kind of ambiguous situation that is most susceptible to the subtle interpersonal influence described in verbal "conditioning" experiments.

Thus we see that the transposition of laboratory research to applied settings is not an automatic process; mediating variables need to be given careful consideration. In the case of verbal conditioning, positive effects are more likely to appear as the task demands of the experimental situation become more ambiguous and the interviewer restricts his general response level. While the verbal conditioning literature is quite voluminous, few attempts have been made to vary the responsivity of the experimenter. In all probability, the requirement that the experimental interaction be devoid of all stimuli except those actually utilized for purposes of reinforcement is related to the attempt by experimenters to approximate the control and precision of the animal laboratory, or in the words of Krasner, Knowles, & Ullmann (1965, p. 408), to make the verbalization "mm-hmm" "analogous to a food pellet." However, until positive experimental effects can be demonstrated in more interactive conversations, the generality and usefulness of the verbal conditioning phenomenon will remain limited.

Beyond Conditioning

The behavior therapists have championed the position that psychotherapeutic procedures should be based on the laws of "modern learning theory" (Eysenck, 1965a). Yet, as a group, these therapists have thus far ignored much of the literature concerned with more complex human learning, for the most part staying within a conceptual framework developed through animal experimentation. Thus, terms which have clearly definable properties in the animal laboratory (e.g., stimulus, response, reinforcement) were adopted for use with patients. On the other hand, concepts which referred to cognitions (e.g., thinking, understanding, planning) were looked upon as untestable, unnecessary, and suspiciously reminiscent of the foggy dynamic insight therapies which clearly were to be avoided.

That conditioning techniques developed in the animal laboratory were seized upon so eagerly is not difficult to understand from a historical perspective. The post-World War II period saw a growth of clinical psychology in which services were provided to persons previously untouched by the mental health professions. But along with and perhaps as a result of extensive application, the limitations of traditional personality theory, dynamic assessment procedures, and standard forms of psychotherapy became quickly apparent. This same time period also saw the development of theories of learning based upon experimentation with simple organisms, whose originators hoped would eventually provide general "laws of learning" applicable across species to the behavior of humans in fairly complex situations. It is no small wonder that many clinical psychologists, disillusioned with the excesses of dynamic psychiatry and psychology, turned toward the new more vigorous field of learning with high expectations. Conditioning research flourished, and with it a technology was developed that in time would influence traditional classroom instruction, textbook writing, language laboratories, the education of the mentally retarded, and the treatment of behavior disorders.

Developments in human learning proceeded at a slower pace, and for a number of years represented a simple extension of conditioning research from animal to human subjects. Furthermore, only in recent years have interested psychologists been able to apply the precise quantification and experimentation usually associated with animal research to the study of the more integrative and cognitive aspects of human learning. Thus for some time there was little empirical work, aside from conditioning research, for the behaviorally oriented clinican to consider in building treatment procedures based on learning principles. This state of affairs is no longer true today. We have now accumulated a fair amount of knowledge about human learning from rather diverse experimental settings and it behooves those truly interested in building a comprehensive technology for the treatment of the behavior disorders to welcome and try out these new ideas without excessive theoretical biases.

Therapy as a Problem for Discrimination Training

It is our belief that a conditioning model as a framework on which to base therapeutic practice is appropriate only in certain clearly restricted cases. In some instances, the therapist is concerned with building patient response repertoires in situations where previously there had been none, as might be required, for example, in the socialization of a psychotic child. Or it is possible that some disorders acquired in an automatic reflexive manner would respond best to a counterconditioning procedure, as might be true, for example, in some cases of enuresis (Lovibond, 1964a). However, even in these cases there is no evidence that disorders acquired through simple classical conditioning are removed most efficaciously by conditioning therapies. In most cases the task of the therapist is even more difficult. Rarely does he face a naïve organism with simple unidimensional response repertoires. Most often the patient has already developed a varied though inadequate pattern of responding to which feelings and attitudes become attached and which lead to and perpetuate further misperceptions and faulty responding in a circular, self-defeating pattern. The task of the therapist then becomes one of helping the patient sort out his experiences and his reactions to them. That is, the patient must learn to differentiate aspects of the environment that are aversive from those that are not, and must further differentiate both of these from environmental events which were aversive at one time but are now no longer so (Dollard & Miller, 1950). He must learn to recognize and must practice more adaptive responses in situations where maladaptive responses had previously been prepotent. However, it is our impression that like the psychoanalyst who believes that changes in behavior will occur automatically with the removal of a crucial repression, some behavior therapists seem to feel that changes in cognition, feelings, and other more overt behaviors will occur automatically with the removal of some crucial fear. While this certainly does occur in some instances, it would be a mistake to perpetuate the belief that this is all that is needed in the majority of cases.

What changes in the practice of behavior therapy would result from the adoption of a discrimination learning framework?

STIMULUS DIFFERENTIATION

A persistent problem for all forms of psychotherapy is the difficulty of determining the environmental stimuli to which the patient is responding. The patient himself may not know and if pressed may give faulty information. This problem can become manifest in systematic desensitization therapy, for example, when both patient and therapist misjudge the relevant ingredients in an anxiety-producing situation, or when particular anxiety stimuli are simply unreported because they are not perceived by the patient (Hain, Butcher, & Stevenson, 1966). In these cases, the initial discrimination of stimulus cues controlling the patient's behavior may be faulty. In order for progress to be made, the therapist will need to train the patient to differentiate aspects of stimulus patterns which he does not yet perceive.

Even after specific fears have been lifted, the patient may still be unable to perceive his situation accurately due to faulty prior learning. As long as the patient's fears keep him from normal social interaction, accurate perceptions of the real world probably do not develop. Nuances of relationships remain unperceived because the patient lacks the training required to discriminate their characteristics. Encouraging contact with others after the removal of fears has been achieved may be of some help and in some cases may be all that is necessary. But further work with patients in discrimination training in order to correct perceptual distortions may also be necessary.

THE CODING AND INTEGRATION OF STIMULUS EVENTS

Although the patient may recognize fear-inducing stimuli and may be capable of reporting them accurately, both patient and therapist may be uncertain about which aspect of the stimulus is most aversive. Further complicating the picture is the possibility that the patient may not be reacting to the physical properties of the stimulus per se, but to the meaning he has attached to it. In other words, stimuli may become aversive because they have been physically associated with aversive consequences, or they may be judged aversive because such an interpretation has been placed upon them by the patient as a result of chronic mislabeling and inappropriate classification. One cannot assume that classification or coding systems are isomorphic with and completely determined by physical events. Factors determining the selection of a coding system may be quite independent of the factors determining the presence or absence of the event to be coded (Lawrence, 1963). Thus, there are times when the behavior therapist might want to attend to the coding operations of the patient with the view in mind of helping the patient achieve a more meaningful and adaptive system.

Taken together, poor stimulus differentiation and inadequate or inappropriate coding operations make for poor ability to discriminate between aversive and nonaversive components of stimulus events, and can lead to frustration on the part of a behavior therapist whose procedures do not allow for the analysis and integration of stimuli in terms of their meaning for the patient.

BUILDING RESPONSE REPERTOIRES

The emphasis in behavior therapy is on learning and performing new responses. The behavior therapist works toward the identification of adequate, integrative responses which the patient can then practice, first in therapy and then in real life. But what if the patient is unable to perform these new responses? In general, the behavior therapist proposes two solutions. If anxiety prevents the performance of pro-social responses, then anxiety must first be inhibited or extinguished, as for example through a systematic desensitization procedure. If the patient is unable to perform the new response because the skills necessary for its execution are missing from his repertoire, the behavior therapist recommends a shaping procedure to build in slowly the necessary response components. But to the extent that behavior therapists accept reinforcement principles, they are united in the assumption that new responses cannot be adopted until they are performed by the patient and subsequently reinforced. This requirement is consistent with the general assumption implicit in reinforcement theories, that in order for learning to occur, the subject must perform a response which then leads him to experience prompt response-contingent reinforcing consequences. The above conceptualization as a basis for helping patients develop more adequate response repertoires suffers from several inadequacies both as a general theory of behavior change and as a model for therapeutic practice. It assumes that learning can occur only where there are direct consequences to the subject; and it provides no basis for explaining the acquisition of response components which are so unique and infrequent that the subject would be unable to perform even remote approximations spontaneously. These criticisms have been extensively amplified by Bandura (1965a) and need not be further elaborated here. However, they become particularly cogent when applied to therapeutic practice. Therapists are not often in a position to manipulate response consequences directly in the day-to-day life of the patient. Furthermore, patients must often act in situations where mistakes can have extremely deleterious consequences. Encouraging action without providing the patient with a guide to when his acts may not be appropriate, simply invites setbacks triggered by punishment from environmental agents. For example, it is not sufficient to shape assertive responses in an otherwise inhibited patient if he then behaves in an indiscriminately assertive manner even in situations which are certain to invite punishment. The therapist is then faced with a double problem. How can he demonstrate that new behaviors will not have aversive consequences, before they are performed by the patient? And how can the patient be taught to discriminate circumstances which would lead to positive reinforcement from those which would lead to punishment, before he receives direct consequences for his acts?

One answer provided by Bandura (1965a) is that the acquisition of new responses occurs most effectively through the observation of the behavior of others. While direct reinforcement techniques may be effective in strengthening and maintaining responses that already exist in an individual's behavioral repertoire, they are relatively laborious and inefficient for the development of novel responses. On the other hand, observational learning, quite common in the socialization of children, is particularly indispensable in situations where errors are extremely dangerous or costly. Yet, it is interesting to note that, for the most part, modeling procedures have not found a place in the practice of behavior therapy. The behavior therapist provides as little opportunity for modeling to occur as his more traditional, insight-oriented colleague. By perpetuating the one-to-one mode of office treatment, by providing little opportunity for the patient to see the therapist in action with others, and by providing the patient with few opportunities to observe others similar to himself emitting desirable behaviors, the behavior therapist minimizes the opportunities for imitation learning to occur.

Research on modeling effects to which the behavior therapist might refer, although of recent origin, is not wanting. The program of research by Bandura and his associates has been summarized on several occasions (Bandura, 1962, 1965a; Bandura & Walters, 1963). More recently, research demonstrating the usefulness of a model in a group therapy setting has been reported by Schwartz & Hawkins (1965), Goldstein et al. (1967), and Truax, Wargo, Carkhuff, Kodman, & Moles (1966). Several studies conducted at Indiana University have explored the effects of modeling procedures in personal interviews. It has been found that subjects with prior exposure to a problem-admitting model exhibited similar behavior in their own personal interviews when consequences to the model were either passive acceptance or active encouragement; both model conditions elicited significantly greater problem admission than when the model was discouraged or when there was no model (Marlatt, Jacobson, Johnson, & Morrice, 1966). The model may be presented in person or on tape, or the subject may simply read the model's responses in a written script without apparent loss of effectiveness (Duke, Frankel, Sipes, & Stewart, 1965). As in verbal conditioning, modeling effects have been found to be most powerful when the subject is presented with an unstructured task. With increased task uncertainty, the model appears to function as a "signifier" pointing out relevant alternatives which can be utilized by the uncertain interviewee (Marlatt, 1968a).

Most relevant to our present discussion is a study which found that the presentation of a model elicited and maintained greater problem admission over two interviews than direct reinforcement to the subject. In this experiment (Marlatt, 1968b) direct reinforcement to the subject for problem admission did not maintain that behavior to a significant extent after exposure to a problem-admitting model. Positive reinforcement to subjects for problem admission after hearing a tape in which the model received similar consequences for the same behavior, served to depress problem admission compared with subjects exposed to the same model consequences (positive) but who themselves received neutral feedback from their interviewers. Marlatt interprets this last finding as indicating that the subject receives the necessary information to function appropriately in his interview after exposure to an encouraged model and that further reinforcement by the subject's own interviewer may actually serve as a distraction in his task.

Modeling procedures can be useful in therapy in teaching new responses and in encouraging the reemergence of previously learned but inhibited responses. However, modeling procedures represent only one of several possible approaches a therapist might take in order to provide the patient with an opportunity to anticipate response consequences before they are directly experienced. Role playing, fixed role therapy, emotional sensitivity training, and group therapy participation are all capable of demonstrating nonaversive consequences for previously inhibited behaviors. And finally, not to be overlooked is the possibility of encouraging the anticipation of events through direct instruction. Evidence is beginning to accumulate which suggests that in some situations direct instruction may be more efficacious than observational learning (Jacobson, 1968), but we do not yet know enough to determine when each is most applicable. However, it does seem that simply telling patients what may be the most likely consequences for responses in specific circumstances can go a long way in helping them learn how to plan and control their own behavior.

THE GENERALIZATION OF THERAPEUTIC EFFECTS

From the perspective of some of the classical learning theories, the wonder of psychotherapy is that any patients improve in their functioning at all, since the conditions necessary for the generalization of behavioral changes specified by these theories are typically absent in psychotherapy. To begin with, the therapist is rarely fortunate enough to control the reinforcement contingencies in the patient's environment. Regardless of how much practice in correct responding the patient receives in psychotherapy, a punishing environment can undo much of this work. In addition, the therapy situation is usually so different from what the patient encounters in his own world, that little transfer between the two should be expected to occur. As a matter of fact, much of the therapist's behavior is oriented toward enhancing the differences between therapy and real life with the view in mind of thus encouraging the patient to talk freely (Goldstein, Heller, & Sechrest, 1966, p. 226). With few possibilities for manipulating the reinforcement consequences for new behavior as it is performed extratherapy, and with little similarity between therapy and the patient's normal environment, how can the generalization of therapeutic effects possibly occur?

For the most part, the theorists of the various schools of therapy have paid little attention to this problem. For example, Freud, Rogers, Dollard, & Miller, and to some extent Wolpe assume that changes in extratherapy behaviors occur automatically with changes in intrapsychic functioning. The implicit assumption is that while the patient's environment may have been aversive at one time, it is now no longer so. Thus, if new behaviors emerge, they are bound to be reinforced if they are displayed outside of therapy. It is quite likely that success in psychotherapy to a large extent has depended on the beneficence of the environment, and this may be one reason that greater overall effectiveness has not been demonstrated. A therapist should be able to do more to free patients trapped by circumstances imposed by others, and indeed the current interest in milieu and family therapies documents the general recognition of the problem of encouraging extratherapy change. Among the behavior therapists there are those who have developed ingenious techniques for increasing the probability that new responses exhibited by the patient will be positively reinforced. This is possible when the therapist can control the total milieu of the patient (Cohen, 1968) or when he can instruct crucial socialization agents in the delivery of reinforcement, as for example in the training of teachers (Baer, 1968) or parents (Patterson, 1965a). However, without environmental control, the therapist must rely on his own efforts with the patient.

Once new responses have been developed in therapy and their transfer to extratherapy situations has become desirable, several possibilities are open to the therapist to enhance this process (Goldstein, Heller, & Sechrest, 1966, pp. 212–259). Generalization can be maximized by increasing the similarity between stimulus events. Thus, the therapist might find it desirable to decrease the distinctiveness of therapy by bringing its positive features closer to important stimuli in the patient's environment. Significant others can be included in the therapy process either in person or through symbolic representation (e.g., pictures of the patient's wife, boss, or friends, etc.), thus giving the patient an opportunity to relate to them or their stimulus characteristics under the benign supervision of the therapist. The patient and therapist might leave the confines of the office, and some interviews might be carried out in the patient's home or place of employment, or perhaps even in the local bar. The most appropriate place for an interview should be determined by its relevance to the topic under discussion. Thus, if therapy is at the point of dealing with attitudes toward authority figures, it may be helpful to hold sessions in places where authority figures are actually visible, perhaps in the presence of a policeman in the park, in the patient's place of employment, or in other situations in which authority cues are very strong (Goldstein, Heller, & Sechrest, 1966, p. 227).

As reasonable as the above suggestion might seem, there is a finite limit in the amount of similarity the therapist can induce between therapy and extratherapy events. For example, having the patient practice telling off his boss as a therapeutic exercise, even in the boss's presence and with his passive consent, is of limited value if the patient does not learn some important principle from this exercise which he can use to monitor his own behavior in subsequent encounters without the necessity of the therapist's constant presence. The therapist can increase his effectiveness by working toward the establishment of such principles.

Chapter Summary

The derivation of research hypotheses directly from clinical practice has been the traditional approach to problems of research in psychotherapy. Recently an alternative research strategy has been receiving considerable attention. Sensing commonalities between psychotherapy and other forms of behavior change, some investigators have turned to these other areas for the generation of research hypotheses to be applied to psychotherapy. However this strategy, while providing the advantage of opening new possibilities for treatment, also introduces the danger of premature extrapolation across research domains.

The attempt to apply the findings of verbal conditioning research to the practice of psychotherapy can be viewed as an example of premature extrapolation. It was hoped by some that various forms of psychotherapy could be shown to derive their effectiveness from the often unrecognized reinforcing power of the therapist. However, accumulating research did not support this expectation. For example, it soon became apparent that generalized reinforcers did not always show consistent effects. Similarly, research on the generalization of reinforced verbal behavior proved disappointing, and positive conditioning effects were demonstrable only under conditions of minimal experimenter responsiveness. Thus the relevance of this body of research for therapy must be considered limited at this time. It would seem that the type of interpersonal influence described in verbal conditioning experiments becomes important in therapy only in those systems in which the responsivity of the therapist is minimal and the stimulus field in which the patient must operate is marked by excessive ambiguity.

The behavior therapists have been most aware of the possibility of deriving clinical procedures from basic laboratory behavior change research, but they have generally concentrated on the conditioning literature to the exclusion of research concerned with more complex human learning. This emphasis is unfortunate since a conditioning model provides too limited a framework on which to base therapeutic practice. Greater attention should be focused on studies of discrimination training, the integration of stimulus events, observational learning, direct instruction, stimulus and response generalization, and the development of cognitive plans and strategies. Appropriate bridging research between laboratory and clinical application is needed before consistent results in applied settings should be expected.

Psychotherapy, both past and present, has been in a constant state of flux. At the present time, more efficient and briefer techniques are being called for, and therapists are being urged to avoid consuming their professional energies in exceedingly long, drawn-out commitments to relatively few individuals. The growing discontent has stimulated even those of more traditional theoretical background (e.g., Bellak & Small, 1965). Behavior therapists recognized the need for change earlier than many others and have been leaders in the reactivation of older techniques and in the development of new approaches for making treatment briefer and more effective. Their demonstrations of improvement in specific cases unresponsive to long-term verbal psychotherapy has sparked the imagination of many looking for new guidelines around which to orient their therapeutic activities. But will behavior therapy fulfill the high expectations held for it or will it become encapsulated into a frozen technology championed only by dogmatic disciples?

We believe that behavior therapy can fulfill its promise of becoming a consistent set of treatment procedures based on a psychology of learning. But in order to do so, greater emphasis is needed on research oriented toward understanding the role of anticipation and planning in behavior change. One cannot long neglect these human abilities and expect to produce a comprehensive treatment approach. To those who believe that such an emphasis would rob behavior therapy of its essential characteristics as practiced today, we can only suggest that such may in fact happen if what is meant by behavior therapy is a commitment to specific techniques regardless of how limited they may prove to be.

Neurobiological Considerations for Behavior Therapy

SANFORD I. COHEN

Louisiana State University Medical School,
New Orleans, Louisiana

Introduction

The title of this chapter reflects my concern about the increasing gap between neurobiological studies of brain mechanisms and efforts to establish a more scientific basis for the diagnosis and treatment of disturbances in cognition, behavior, and interpersonal relations. There is a need for psychopathological studies to move closer to the stream of biological research concerned with nervous system functioning. It is this research which should constantly replenish or support the diagnostic and therapeutic practices, as well as the research efforts, of the clinician.

It is not my intent to attempt the development of an "organic" or constitutional explanation of mental diseases or maladaptive behavior which will exclude the influence of social, cultural, developmental, and situational factors. Rather, I will attempt to analyze and integrate research concerned with molecular, cellular, and physiological factors affecting nervous system function, recognizing that these factors, in turn, are related to the way the nervous system responds to a variety of external conditions or environmental contingencies. This chapter will look at characteristics of the input, some of the details of the machinery of the nervous system, and some of the observable characteristics of the output. Changes in neural transmission, brain pathology, chemical factors, and memory will be considered, together with the development and maturation of CNS structures. Whether they act as anticipatory or preparatory signals or as reinforcers, external stimuli seem to exert either a facilitating or an inhibiting influence on the maturation, emergence, and expression of complex CNS functions.

Although the emphasis in this chapter will be on genetically determined neurobiological characteristics, there is no intention of minimizing the need for experimental analyses of behavior and the contributions already made by such analyses. A recent article by Skinner (1966b) suggests that phylogenetic and ontogenetic influences may act at different times and may shape and maintain behavior in different ways. For this reason, it is dangerous to try to arrange their products on a single continuum or to describe them with a single set of terms. He points out that "no reputable student of animal behavior has ever taken the position that the animal comes into the laboratory as a tabula rasa, that species differences are insignificant and that all responses are equally conditionable." He does not question the importance of genetic influences in shaping CNS response characteristics, but he emphasizes the need for sharper distinction between the features or dimensions of behavior that are bound more to the biological characteristics of the nervous system and those more related to the contingencies of reinforcement. He also suggests that the important data that have emerged from the experimental analysis of behavior are related to the "probability of response" rather than to the fact that an organism does behave in a given way or to a description of the behavior. Skinner feels that probability of response is an important dimension in examining the "inheritance, not only of specific forms of behavior, but of behavioral processes and characteristics often called traits." He reasons that the entire repertoire of an individual or species must exist prior to ontogenetic or phylogenetic influences shaping complex forms of behavior from relatively undifferentiated material.

Environmental contingencies which influence behavior include a number of simple and complex stimuli among which sensory signals with symbolic or "second-signal" significance require particular attention. These can be viewed as signals which, because they have become "associated" with some sort of patterning or coding, convey more information than is contained merely in their characteristics as sensory stimuli. The importance of early life events and later life situations cannot be neglected in examining the influence of environmental and neurobiological factors, since memory patterns, engrams, neuronal models, or programmed expectancies may influence later perception and behavioral responses. Furthermore, life events which are "traumatic" may lead to adaptive changes, physiological, endocrinological, and/or behavioral, which, if sufficiently intense, could influence other neural functions. Therefore, a focus on biological considerations of CNS functions might initially suggest consideration of molecular, cellular, enzymatic, endocrine, and physiological factors; but it is apparent that these biological factors cannot be meaningfully studied apart from the stimulus field which determines how they are expressed.

Physiologists and biochemists are able to convey a great deal of information about the functioning of the components of the nervous system, but they have no generally accepted way of talking about how the learning process takes place. On the other hand, valuable observations on complex mental functioning and behavior have been made by clinicians, who have attempted to describe them in metaphysiological or metapsychological abstractions that they have developed. Such descriptions fail to relate the observed operations to the nervous system cells in which they originate.

Much has been written about utilizing an integrative nervous system approach to the understanding of maladaptive behavior and mental disease. Unfortunately, these seemingly self-evident psychobiological constructs have not had very much impact on either diagnostic nomenclature, criteria and procedures used for classification of clinical cases, prognostic indices and therapeutic methods, or techniques for evaluating therapy. Work in the laboratory, utilizing increasingly sophisticated techniques and tools, has continued, as it should, to be concerned with highly specific questions. Work in the clinic still reflects loyalties and antagonisms to a number of "schools," and the constructs of the schools gain support from increasingly detailed systems of logic (with or without supporting data).

This chapter does not contain suggestions for specific changes that should be made in laboratory research or clinical practice, nor does it even suggest specific techniques that can be usefully employed. What it does attempt is to describe a limited number of areas in which experimental studies suggest possibilities for developing clinical methods which at least consider the impact of external and internal variables on CNS functioning. A small number of constructs will be presented which may have some value in restructuring the data from which clinical inferences are made.

Some Current Neurobiological Concepts of Conditioning and Implications For Behavior Therapy

The feeling is often expressed that theories based on metapsychology, metaphysiology, or biological abstractions no longer will be (or no longer are) meaningful or helpful models as the story of the intracellular, molecular, and enzymatic processes within the nervous system unfolds. This discussion will be briefly focused on the consideration of the future role of theoretical constructs of learning and conditioning as experimentally developed operational concepts which stand outside the nervous system and are, at best, abstractions of biological phenomena. This reevaluation is necessitated by both the current neurobiological information explosion and our need to determine whether "older" theories formulated prior to current neurobiological understanding are obscuring the interpretation of new data by forcing it into "old molds" or whether these older notions do indeed provide a flexible, but more important and more meaningful, creative framework by which new data can be interpreted and from which cogent new hypotheses can be generated.

Part of the disappointment with some of the past efforts to integrate biological and psychological data may be associated with the fact that this integration was attempted with data and observations collected under different circumstances, with different population samples and in different periods of time. Further, at the present time, there are many highly specialized techniques for the study of isolated neurobiological phenomena but few experimental strategies and physiological approaches for the investigation of neurophysiological events in relation to complex human psychological activity. The work of Pavlov (1927) seems to represent a valuable method of integrating clinical and cultural information and neurobiological observations, since Pavlov's concepts are concerned with intervening variables by which clinical observations or observations of overt behavior can be related to more recent ideas about integrative CNS functions and possibly correlated with specific electrophysiological indices of nervous system activity.

Pavlov's contribution was not merely developing a scientific method for the objective evaluation of nervous system functions in the laboratory. In many ways, his careful attention to the details of an animal's daily behavior and the innumerable events which influenced it remain a model for clinician and experimenter alike. As Liddell (1958) pointed out, modern neurophysiologists and psychologists, in abandoning the laborious and time-consuming methods used by Pavlov in favor of studies of short-term behavior and the acute experiment, are prone to develop blind spots. This emphasis is, in part, a result of the formidable armamentarium of exquisitively precise surgical, electrical, and chemical techniques which are now available. This embarrassment of riches inclines the enthusiastic young investigator to brief spurts of focused zeal in his observations of behavior. Moreover, the automatic registration of the performance of numerous animals at the same time creates an anonymity of the experimental animal, just as the study of large groups of human subjects provides the same kind of anonymity. This anonymity is impossible with Pavlov's tedious but rewarding method of the conditional reflex in which, after months and even years of training, the animal emerges an individual. With slight rephrasing, Liddell's admonition to laboratory scientists is quite applicable to clinical behavioral scientists looking for a quick solution or panacea to the problems of therapy (see also Franks, 1967a).

The advantage of the laboratory approach is that precise laws and relationships can be delineated. However, without the data which come from careful study of clinical patients, careful evaluation of the personal biographies and response patterns of individual subjects, even the highly skilled neurobiological investigator will stand poised with his precise and accurate techniques waiting for questions to come along so that he can use his techniques to answer them.

Although the behavior therapies are based only indirectly on Pavlov's work, his ideas and methods are considered an acceptable model of CNS function by many behavior therapists, and his work has influenced the notions of Hull (1943), Guthrie (1952), Thorndike (1944), and Skinner (1966a), all of whose work represents the bases for those learning theories upon which behavior therapy leans so heavily. Eysenck (1960a, 1966), in pointing out that the methods of reciprocal inhibition are derived from the work of Pavlov (although some would credit Guthrie), further suggests that many learning theorists explicitly translate Pavlov's concepts into modern learning theory.

More recently, as increased efforts have been made to integrate current biological nervous system research into a systematic body of knowledge of brain-behavior relationships, Pavlov's physiological theories of CNS reactivity have had a renaissance. However, it is important to recognize that the terms excitation and inhibition, which play an important role in Pavlov's concepts of the nervous system, do not refer directly to the specific neurochemical and neurophysiological processes used by contemporary neurobiologists. Pavlov's concepts, best regarded as abstractions about CNS functions, are extremely valuable if it is kept in mind that the words he used are descriptions of two complex processes rather than of activities in specific physiological units. In fact, they may have little to do either with excitation or inhibition as measured by the electrophysiologists. Pavlov described as excitation any change in the general level of central activity which showed itself as a measurable increase in conditional reflex activity, and as inhibition any change which manifested itself in decreasing conditional reflex activity. In a number of areas, an increase in activity is often a function of increasing inhibition of inhibitory areas so that, in effect, there is an increase of excitation in the areas which were originally inhibited. Pavlov's original concepts are now being carefully scrutinized and modified by such East European workers as Anokhin (1961, 1966a, 1966b), Sokolov (1960, 1963), and Konorski (1948). These modifications are largely a function of an increasing number of studies of the neurophysiology of conditional reflexes, studies of physiology of specific organ systems, and studies of the neurochemistry and biophysics of synapses and the transmitter substances, etc. These investigations are concerned with extending previous notions of the afferent, efferent, and integrative functions of the nervous system. Hence, theoretical constructs and technical practices which are in any way derived from conditional reflex concepts or techniques may require modification as a more definitive biobehavioral model emerges.

With the increasing use of drugs, either as independent treatment modalities or in conjunction with psychotherapies and/or behavior therapies, it becomes increasingly imperative to consider the neurophysiological and neurochemical factors involved in the development, perpetuation, and release of behavior. Certain behavior therapies focus virtually exclusively on repetitive patterns of behavior, or on repetitive perceptual or affective responses when an individual is confronted with certain stimulus patterns. Schedules of reinforcement and extinction are utilized without active consideration of internal motivational factors, the point being made that such influences do not necessarily have to be dealt with as part of the evaluation or treatment of the patient. It is often emphatically noted that the patient does not have to develop an awareness of these instinctual forces. In contrast, many psychotherapists emphasize the importance of identifying these internal motivations and the need in treatment to delineate how these drives or instincts express themselves or are defended against.

Since the choice of treatment technique is, in part, determined by which view one accepts, there is some need to reappraise the positions taken by the various "types" of therapists and hence to reconsider some constructs concerned with drive, instinct, or internal biological motivations which have been discussed by learning and psychoanalytic theoreticians. Some of the work of Anokhin in the U.S.S.R., and the concepts he has developed about biologically positive and negative reflexes, illustrate specific points which it might be helpful to consider.

Anokhin (1961) states that the basic law governing the formation of conditional activity is the law of formation of a temporary bond between a given stimulus and any inborn activity of the organism—alimentary, defensive, sexual, or orienting. From the point of view of this basic law, the whole life of a higher animal (especially man) consists of a continuous formation of ever-new conditional bonds on the basis of unconditional stimuli of different biologic quality. The selfsame cell of the cerebral cortex, having innervation relations to a certain muscle, may take part biologically in the most diverse functional systems: "It may pull the trigger of a gun, write a love letter or turn on a motor."

He describes experiments which suggest the antagonistic character of biologically positive reactions (such as alimentary reactions) and biologically negative reactions (such as the defensive reactions). Alimentary and defensive activities not only may have an opposite biological quality but also may have different cortical representations and represent different functional systems. According to Anokhin, it is possible, by means of drugs, to block a particular biologic reaction so that, freed from the inhibiting effect of this reaction, the reactions of the opposite biological quality can be expressed; e.g., chlorpromazine blocks the activating affect of the reticular system for conditional defensive reactions and yet retains the activating effect for conditional alimentary reactions in the rabbit. The blocking of defensive activation of cortical electrical activity by chlorpromazine fails to eliminate the animal's waking state. Hence, a number of influences act on the cerebral cortex, and each may be blocked individually because of the different channel specificities of the neural substrates on which each of these biologically different reactions occur. If this is so, then the formation and extinction of various reflex-determined behaviors and physiological activities could be inhibited or facilitated by agents acting in internal states, as well as by environmental contingencies associated with the emergence or repression of various behaviors.

Anokhin's comments are, of course, highly speculative. However, his formulations are of interest in that, starting from a physiological and conditional reflex base, he develops theoretical constructs which strongly emphasize the influence of the "past" on current behaviors. He does not exclude the importance of current environmental contingencies or the demands associated with a person's current state in influencing choice of behavior. However, his biologically based formulations may have value in cautioning persons who might too easily repudiate internal determinants of behavior.

Anokhin's neurophysiological studies and theoretical formulations of the neural bases of conditional reflexes raise a number of questions about the specific neural pathways of "drive states." If this work is replicated and these concepts incorporated into the body of knowledge guiding behavior therapists, then there are implications with respect to the type of reinforcement or extinction procedures employed, and with respect to the use of drugs in altering behavior which is, in part, dependent on drive states or internal motivational factors.

Anokhin and his associates (1966a, b) have more recently suggested that different biological "states" excite different complexes of neural elements and that, in turn, each of the specific states of reticular formation activity mobilizes in the cerebral cortex neural elements which have historically become associated with a given inborn activity. The historical associations would be mediated by certain memory mechanisms. The influence of "memory" on behavioral acts and conditional responses is described as being exerted through the molecular fixation of past experience.

Anokhin attempts to introduce the findings from current biological research into a model by which complex higher nervous functions such as memory can be conceptualized. Recent neurochemical studies are used as a basis for constructing a working hypothesis on the convergent linking of a conditional reflex. The core of his hypothesis is the processes of the subsynaptic membrane by which fixed elements of past life are extracted from the molecules of the nervous cell. This concept of molecular fixation of past experience involves chains of chemical reactions developing on the subsynaptic membranes which are continued in the exoplasma where they possess "very strong fermentative specificity." Anokhin's working hypothesis is that, beginning with the fermentative chain from the subsynaptic membrane, past impressions may be "aligned" in strict accordance with the afferent synthesis at any moment. Afferent synthesis, according to Anokhin, is the key mechanism shaping behavioral acts, or the most significant moment in CNS integration concerned with deciding the "what, how and when" parameters of any behavioral act. Afferent synthesis refers to the neurobiological processes which are concerned with processing, collating, and synthesizing all the information that the organism needs to perform an adaptive act which corresponds to a given condition. Hence, Anokhin attempts to integrate current neurochemical data into a cybernetic model for integrative nervous system functions.

Another series of studies which have broadened conditional reflex formulations relevant to behavior therapy has been conducted by Luria (1966). Luria's work with patients having frontal lobe lesions suggests that therapies derived from learning and conditioning theories need to be reassessed and placed in an integrative neurobiological framework. He feels that it is impossible to form a comprehensive or meaningful concept of frontal lobe functions within the framework of the reflex arc alone and that the concept of self-regulating reflex cycles must be added.

Luria's studies over the past twenty years have suggested the importance of the frontal lobes in regulating motor actions and in developing complex behavioral programs. This work has been especially concerned with the verbal regulation of motor actions and behavior. Disturbances in this regulation have been noted when the program of motor reactions comes into conflict with the immediate influence of stimuli. It has been noted that patients with severe frontal lobe lesions are unable to regulate their actions via complex verbal programs. These patients show a marked dissociation of verbal analyses and constructive activity which results in severe disturbance of problem-solving behavior.

Luria concludes that the functions of the frontal lobes are necessary for a complex selective organization of the orienting activity of a person and that the normal functions of this portion of the CNS make it possible to construct preliminary dynamic schemes of behavior and to evaluate the results of focused behavior with reference to prior plans. Lesions of this area result in disturbances of complex forms of selective controlled behavior, especially noted in the loss of the controlling function of speech and in disturbances in the verbal regulation of behavior.

Such work highlights the need for more systematic studies to develop programs of psychological and behavioral management of patients with neuropathological lesions of the CNS or persons with CNS functional characteristics which may lead to psychopathology if they are exposed to certain demands from their environment. Luria's work further suggests the need in treatment for more clearly defining and utilizing the role of verbal symbolic factors in the alteration of perception of the world and the self, and in the modification of the range, type, and appropriateness of available adaptive behaviors.

The next section will consider a few selected trends in current neurobiological research which may further extend the considerations necessary for the development of a scientific biobehavioral therapy.

Survey of Some Current Neurobiological Research and Possible Applications to Clinical Neurobehavioral Problems

GENERAL RESEARCH TRENDS

One of the most active trends in current nervous system research is concerned with man's search for the physical bases or substrates of mental processes. Current work involves a number of disparate neural sciences, and there are attempts to achieve a new synthesis, to identify basic concepts, and to develop new approaches. Many of the attempts are concerned with efforts to apply the science of electronic computers to the understanding of brain function. Another is coming to be called molecular neurology. This has been encouraged by the success of the subdiscipline of molecular biology in elucidating mechanisms whereby organisms store, read, and transfer genetic and immunologic information. It is essential, of course, that the contributions of the molecular approach be continuously integrated with experimental behavioral data *and* with clinical, neurologic, and psychopathologic data. Some investigators have suggested that there is a similarity between the biological mechanisms for immunologic and psychic memory, if one considers the acquisition, storage, and the use of information. Immunologic models have been developed for memory dysfunctions of an organic or functional nature. The major importance of these models is not that it actually allows us to develop a testable or tenable theory, but that this type of speculating has forced behavioral scientists to define phenomena more carefully if they hope to examine any possible correlations between biological and psychological data, or if they wish to consider the possible mediating mechanisms involved in functions such as memory. Many laboratory studies of neurobiologic phenomena provide information about conduction in nerves, transmission of impulses, action at synapses, biochemical reactions occurring within the cells, impulses coming into the nervous system, the discharge of centers within the nervous system, and outgoing impulses from a vast number of CNS centers. More complex models for input and output have been developed for biological reflex activity involving conditional reflexes in which environmental stimuli are considered triggering or initiating signals leading to behaviors of biological significance. However, the plasticity and variability of the nervous system as a functioning entity may not be adequately accounted for by a model that may be perfectly satisfactory when applied to an impulse.

Sherrington (1906) has perhaps contributed as much as anyone to enlightenment in matters of the integrative action of the nervous system, showing that not all input necessarily has the effect of creating impulse-carrying excitation in the cells, for some input fibers may have the opposite effect of quietening cells down or inhibiting them. (This concept has been confirmed and identified more recently by Eccles, 1957). Hence, each cell would seem to be influenced by both excitatory and inhibitory states and whether it actually sends an impulse through a muscle depends on which influence predominates. To develop a complete picture of the nervous system from an integrative point of view, the simultaneous functioning of a number of cells from different areas of the brain would have to be envisioned; that is, techniques for pattern analysis of brain cell activity will have to be worked out. This is not to minimize the absolute necessity for single-cell studies in order to understand basic cellular functions. It is of considerable importance to demonstrate the influences that come into play between input and output at any moment in time and through time.

One can assume that the rapid accumulation of knowledge in this area will fill in many of the gaps of information which are now present. However, this does not reduce the complexity of brain function and does not minimize the need to view complex psychologic functions as not only dependent upon molecular and intracellular events (and hence, in one sense, cell-bound or molecule-bound) but also stimulus-bound and time-bound. Further, it is assumed that there is a constant interaction between events in the outside world at any moment in time and the state of the cells within the organism at that moment.

Kety (1961) suggests "that even if one merely casually reviews the research of the past decade there is some cause for optimism in the neurobiological sciences." The electron microscope has begun to outline the synapse, a structure which heretofore has been an operational concept, and to establish precise localization of certain neurosecretory elements within the cell (De Robertis, 1961; Whittaker, 1961). Embryologists and immunochemists have focused on the development of growth-promoting substances with specific actions in the nervous system and the ability to inhibit the growth of certain other tissues (Levi-Montalcini & Angeletti, 1961). Anatomists, physiologists, psychologists, and sociologists have contributed to knowledge of the functional organization of the brain and its relationship to individual and social behavior. Advances have been recorded in mapping the human cerebral cortex in relationship to cortical physiology as it relates to subjective states and memory (Penfield, 1950). Energy metabolism in the brain has been studied, particularly as it correlates with mental and emotional states. The physiological substrates of emotions and sex behavior have been studied in relation to specific brain areas such as the limbic system. Highly specific chemical receptors in portions of the brain such as the hypothalamus have been investigated and appear capable of triggering sexual behavior in response to sex hormones (Michael, 1961). Studies of noradrenaline, serotonin, and other biogenic amines have suggested that they are differentially distributed in various portions of the brain and may be involved in behavior, motor activity, and cognitive functions associated with different brain areas. Further, the selective distribution of these substances may be concerned with the action of the various drugs. Some studies have suggested that differential development may be associated with the differential distribution of substances in the chemical map of the nervous system (Kety, 1961; Elkes, 1961). New concepts related to the control and modulation of sensory input have been suggested by investigations of the reticular system (Livingston, 1959) and the more recently described sensory feedback systems. A number of studies have been devoted to the synthesizing and degrading of various neurohormones. Substances which are chemical mediators, especially those associated with some aspects of the metabolism, have been thought by some to show abnormal functioning on levels in disorders such as schizophrenia (La Brosse, 1961). Interesting hypotheses have recently been developed about the role of protein substances, their structure and metabolism, in memory and learning (Dingman & Sporn, 1961).

More specific questions are now being raised about the relationship of systemic, biochemical changes to events within the nervous system and the accuracy with which peripheral biochemical indicators actually reflect what may be local intracerebral events (Elkes, 1958). Data in these areas are more readily obtainable from animal experiments, but studies have been initiated in man with the aid of radioactive tracer techniques. It may be possible to carry out studies of the effects of a few selected drugs on endocrine and biochemical responses in the individual patient over a long period of time. This may contribute to a definition of prognostic indicators in the choice of individual drugs for particular syndromes. Recent studies which appear to be a step in this direction attempt to predict the effects of a drug over a long period of time by investigating the responses to it in a number of biochemical, physiological, and psychological parameters over a short period of time within an individual. This is in contrast to much of the research now being conducted in which attempts are made to predict the response of a drug over time by assessing parameters which may be entirely unrelated to the action of the drug within a specific individual. It is equally possible, according to Elkes, "that drugs discriminantly used may lead to the recognition of pharmacological and biochemical cleavage planes between syndromes bearing superficial clinical resemblance and this could contribute to a clear and more rigorous classification of the phenomena of mental disorders."

Progress is also being recorded in "basic" biobehavioral studies. For example, studies of the imprinting process by ethologists are concerned with the bases upon which young animals are believed to acquire crucial behavioral patterns from early experience on a genetically prepared substrate. This type of study has done a good deal to broaden our concept of instinctive behavior (Tinbergen, 1951). Appetitive and aversive centers within the brain seem to have significance in studying the physiology of motivation and affect (Olds, 1958). Increasing use of an animal model for neurosis and psychosomatic illness have been recently described, and paradigms for maternal protection and deprivation in monkeys seem to provide fruitful hypotheses for studying complex phenomena in man. Hilgard (1952), Mirsky (1959), Kubie (1960), and Kety (1961) have reviewed the evidence from basic research in animals and man which is related to some assumptions made from clinical observations.

Elkes (1957) feels that perhaps the ultimate in the study of CNS functions may be the introduction of a model that is concerned with developing an ability to recognize relationships, particularly in time, in terms of essential mathematical functions. The essentially random nature of the assembly of units which make up information carrying systems or systems capable of adaptation in the face of change seems to be receiving steadily increasing recognition. Wiring theories of the past seem to be giving way to less rigid and more statistically valid models. Information theory, which has really only tenuously interacted with genetics and immunochemistry wherever the implications were obvious, may now be more meaningfully used in the strategy and design of specific projects. It has already proved of value in study of the CNS with respect to understanding the coding process along sensory pathways, and it is to be anticipated that the theoretical framework will be expanded to accept and manipulate data in other areas such as the process of recognition of universals in language, the process of abstraction, or the study of second-signal systems. The concept of the nervous system as a chemically mediated organ of information might, in this way, be made a little more real because "unless we understand the code and cipher in which the brain constructs and stores, quietly and with amazing speeds, its models of reality and the distortion of this coding, by controlled chemical means, we will, whatever language is chosen and whatever chemical aspect is followed, be standing outside the phenomena in which we are interested. Language would remain descriptive and do justice merely to some properties of the process rather than the process itself" (Elkes, 1957).

In terms of man, the importance of extending this topic is geared to the fact that man relates to man by means of communciation and that, when this relatedness is interrupted, pathology may develop. Signals coded in words can influence not only the listener's behavior, but his health as well. Further, by tracing a signal through the sense organs in the CNS, back through the muscles and into the outside world, behavioral scientists have found in the study of messages a method which enables them to bridge various scientific universes. As a signal passes from person to person, the system of codification seems to change, but the information remains the same except for the distortions, additions, or subtractions that occur at points of transformation. According to Reusch (1961), the study of transformations and mediating mechanisms that convert visual and auditory signals into nervous and hormonal impulses, and in turn into contractions of the smooth and stripped muscles, presents a very real challenge to investigators interested in information transmission between and in humans.

SPECIFIC NEUROBIOLOGICAL INVESTIGATIONS

The previous sections merely touched upon a number of areas of current interest in nervous system research. The present section is designed to present, in a little more detail, information about the relationship of certain specific neurochemical substances to complex CNS activities relevant to conditional reflexes. The intent is to suggest a few of the many details that might be considered if an actual effort were planned to utilize biological data in clinical as well as experimental studies of higher CNS functions. All too often, clichés are employed to describe mind-body relations, or oversimplified notions are developed which are unfortunately translated into poorly conceptualized diagnostic and treatment approaches. Certainly, if behavior therapy is to be integrated into the broad biological framework of which it claims to be part, approaches such as the following will have to be considered. It is in this spirit that the ensuing material is offered, rather than with any intent to provide definitive answers.

There is evidence to suggest that conditional behavior is sensitive to internal changes associated with endocrine factors or associated with the changes brought about by the introduction of pharmacological agents. Hence, any type of therapy or diagnostic procedures concerned with shaping, molding, modifying, altering, or changing complex nervous system functioning, whether or not it is based on learning theory or psychodynamic principles (which may not be mutually exclusive of each other), should be consistent and integrated with current neurobiological data. The immediate need for integrating biological and behavioral data in clinical practice is suggested by studies in which operant behavior has been altered by physiological, metabolic, or endocrine variables. This point needs to be emphasized, since operant conditioning studies represent one of the "scientific" psychological bases from which behavior therapy has been developed.

It is not possible here to review all the many studies of the effects ·of biochemical substances on CNS functions. Hence, a limited number of studies in a circumscribed area have been selected to illustrate the kinds of data which may be pertinent to an integrative neurobiological perspective. The area selected pertains to studies of sympathetic-adrenal activity and adrenaline and noradrenaline. This choice is, in part, determined by the fact that studies in this area have been undertaken specifically in relation to emotions and behavior. Further, the activity of the sympathetic nervous system and the adrenal medulla has been related to anxiety.

A number of drugs have been studied in regard to their effect on animal operant behavior, and those involving adrenergic mechanisms and behavior have been summarized by Marley (1966). In one investigation, Wurtman et al. (1959) administered adrenaline and noradrenaline to pigeons who were on a multiple fixed-ratio, fixed-interval schedule. Both adrenaline and noradrenaline suppressed the output of learned behavior, but adrenaline was three times more potent. The catechol amines are substances which are endogenously released within the organism (adrenaline from the adrenal medulla and noradrenaline from sympathetic adrenergic endings), although it is not known whether their effects on behavior when they are released naturally are similar to the effects when they are administered. Sharpless (1963), using chronically implanted cortical recording electrodes and a cannula implanted in the external jugular vein in cats during a period of time when the performance of an instrumental hunger-motivated response was carried out, found that both adrenaline and noradrenaline depressed performance. The depression was unlikely to be due to a rise in blood pressure (according to Marley) since continued infusion or secretion of the substances was associated with the blood pressure's returning gradually to its normal level. Such experiments are important because they emphasize the central depressant effect of the catechol amines and, in addition, provide data for assessing whether soporific effects can be caused by secretion of adrenal medullary amines.

In experiments with human subjects, differences in sympathetic adrenal responsivity have been noted in young and aged persons—more specifically, an apparent lack of adrenal medullary responsivity in the aged has been noted in a number of experiments (Bergsman, 1959; Cohen & Shmavonian, 1967). The findings, at least as noted in the urine, did not suggest that the excretion levels (or secretion levels) were lower. Rather, the evidence suggested that, in aged subjects, exposure to a variety of conditions associated with central stimulations, such as the administration of pharmacologic agents or external environmental situations leading to CNS activation, was not accompanied or associated with increases in adrenaline levels as in the younger subjects. The release of adrenaline from the adrenal medulla is usually associated with generalized metabolic, vascular, and neural actions which tend to prepare the organism for activities to remove itself from danger once it has been alerted or made vigilant by something in the environment. Classically, one thinks of adrenaline as a hormonal substance which prepares the organism to make adaptive changes. In spite of this, one also sees frequent reference to the action of adrenaline in the CNS as leading to EEG activation patterns (that is, predominant beta rhythms). However, it has never been clearly established what dose of exogenous adrenaline or what endogenous levels are associated with various brain rhythms.

Adrenaline has a variety of effects on the CNS (Rothballer, 1959), in that it can facilitate or inhibit neural activity.[1] Peripheral autonomic inhibitory effects have been reported, and other reports describe adrenaline as stimulating different brain mechanisms, the end effects of which may be mutually opposed. To identify the effect of adrenaline on the CNS, one would need to specify the area of the brain, its state of activity, and the dose level of adrenaline.

---

[1] Bonvallet, Dell, & Hueglin (1954) showed that injected adrenaline may facilitate or inhibit evoked monosynaptic response measured at the sectioned ventral root. Facilitation seems to require the integrity of the posterior hypothalamus and anterior mesencephalic reticular areas, whereas inhibitory effects seem to be mediated more caudally in the brain stem.

Gelhorn (1953) describes an upward, or hypothalamic-cortical, and a downward, or hypothalamic, discharge to autonomic effectors. Although he feels these often parallel each other, they appear to be independent since autonomic blockage, cervical sympathectomy, and bilateral adrenal vein ligation do not interfere with upward discharge. In his opinion, increased sympathetic discharge is an indicator of a simultaneous hypothalamically induced increase in autonomic and cortical activity. Work by Bonvallet, Dell, & Hueglin described by Lacey & Lacey (1958) indicated that the upward and downward discharge set off initially by neural impulses is maintained by adrenaline.

Lacey & Lacey (1958) feel not only that autonomic and cortical activity parallel each other but that some autonomically induced visceral activity can, by feedback, maintain cortical activation. This neurally induced activation is often maintained by a slower humoral phase following the neural activity. On the other hand, cardiovascular hemodynamic changes associated with an increase in carotid sinus pressure may lead to predominantly inhibitory cortical effects. Adrenaline produces a tachycardia which is associated with an increase in carotid sinus pressure if peripheral resistance does not drop. Hence, endogenously released adrenaline can decrease cortical excitation if its release is associated with an increase in carotid sinus pressure.

The excitatory effects of adrenaline and noradrenaline are said to result from the direct action on the reticular formation and the hypothalamus, while the inhibitory action of adrenaline may be, in part, related to the effect of increased arterial pressure on sinoaortic-baroreceptor reflexes (there is evidence that there is a reduction in sensitivity of these reflexes in the aged).

Another factor which needs to be considered in studying the effect of catechol amines on the CNS is the level of central excitability at the time of administration. For example, cortical strychninization increases hypothalamic excitability; adrenaline given in this condition excited the hypothalamus, though it had reduced it before strychnine had been given. This may be related to the finding that high adrenaline levels are associated with cortical excitation in the aged (Gellhorn, 1964, 1967).

The relationship of adrenaline to complex CNS behavior has been studied. DeJong (1943) described small doses of adrenaline as increasing conditional reflex activity while larger doses caused a depression of conditional reflex activity and very large doses led to stupor. In cats, one may see EEG activation with the cat lying prostrate which is similar to the EGG–behavioral dissociation phenomenon reported to occur with atropine.

The acquisition of conditioned avoidance responses has been reviewed by Latane & Schachter (1962), who showed that the administration of adrenaline, up to a certain dose, improved the learning of avoidance behavior, but larger dose levels either had little effect or led to the animal's learning more poorly. Rats whose pituitaries were removed had greater difficulty in establishing avoidance responses but not in establishing escape responses (Applezweig

& Moeller, 1959). The same finding was noted in sympathectomized dogs and in reserpine-treated cats. This work suggested a relationship between behavior and neuroendocrine responses, with the anticipatory avoidance respone appearing to be more readily interrupted by certain procedures than the direct response to a noxious stimulus.

It has been reported that cholinergic drugs are associated with sustained theta rhythm from the hippocampus, and that they also lead to an inability to avoid shock. In animals who have already been trained, the administration of cholinergic drugs, inducing a theta rhythm, results in the return of orienting responses to a CS similar to those which had occurred at the onset of training.

It has been theorized by some (e.g., Grastyan, 1959) that when the CS becomes a "significant" stimulus to the animal, dissociation of neocortical and hippocampal rhythms appears. When an indifferent stimulus is first presented, desynchrony occurs in the hippocampus and the cortex; however, the presence of an orienting response to a stimulus is associated with a "synchronous" theta rhythm from the hippocampus and desynchrony in the cortex. Reduction of hippocampal theta and return of desynchronized response is associated with an inhibition of the orienting pattern and the initiation of discrete CRs. The effects of cholinergic drugs on behavior appears similar to the results reported in the experiments in which sympathetic blockade has been associated with the impairment of avoidance learning without affecting the performance or maintenance of escape behavior.

The learning of motor avoidance behavior has been noted to be accompanied by evidence of sympathetic neurogenic activity in response to anticipatory signals. This may reflect the activation of brain areas concerned with motor activity which also leads to cardiovascular changes necessary to supply muscular areas activated by the motor efferents. On the other hand, the interoceptive cues associated with sympathetic discharges or alterations in brain functions associated with adrenergic stimulation may be changes which are necessary for avoidance learning to occur. This might involve excitation of brain areas concerned with a motivational state appropriate for defensive avoidance reactions and a level of responsiveness to external cues in which discrimination is enhanced and appropriate motor activity is facilitated.

The ability to adapt physiologically and psychologically to arousing situations, particularly if integrative sensorimotor functioning is necessary, may require a certain level of neurochemical or endocrinological substances, or some optimal balance among central excitation, peripheral sensory and motor functioning, peripheral autonomic activity, and the central and peripheral affects of hormonal substances. An imbalance of endocrinologic and CNS activity may contribute to a disturbance in integrative neurophysiological functioning and lead to inability to utilize complex psychological adaptive techniques.

External sensory inputs related to survival of the organism—for example, those which lead to fight, flight, pain, and pleasure—may lead to the liberation of biogenic amines from localized areas in the brain. It is assumed by many that discrimination in learned perception generally has an underlying emotional base. Accordingly, Hecktor & Halkerston (1964) assume that all sensory inputs which are significant involve activation of certain neurons which contain stores of biogenic amines. There are innumerable endocrine substances, as well as transmitter substances, which may directly affect areas concerned with excitation or inhibition of other central areas or peripheral physiological or skeletal motor areas. The levels of these substances may vary with behavior and/or may be altered by behavior. Perception of situations that call for problem solving, that arouse fear, or that stimulate approach or avoidance behavior may lead to changes in the CNS as well as in some of these substances. For these and many other reasons, it seems difficult to ignore the need to study the relationship of neurochemical and neurophysiological processes in higher nervous system functions, particularly those involved with complex coordinative problem solving and sensorimotor patterns.

Chapter Summary

In the development of behavior therapy programs for the treatment of "disorders" of higher nervous system functions, there is a need to consider current neurobiological research related to motivation, behavior, and memory. Further, theoretical formulations, such as learning and conditional reflex theories, which are often the rationale for various treatment approaches, may require modification as new information on CNS functioning is acquired, since the operational concepts are, at best, abstractions of biological phenomena. It is especially important to consider modifications of conditioning concepts emerging from studies of the neurophysiology of conditional reflexes; the neurochemistry and biophysics of synapses and transmitter substances; and the biology of information coding, storage, and retrieval. With the increasing availability of pharmacological agents with specific actions in the CNS, the use of these agents either as independent treatment modalities or in conjunction with behavior therapy will depend largely on a better understanding of the neurophysiological and neurochemical factors involved in the development, perpetuation, and release of various behaviors, feelings, thoughts, or motivations. The development of a scientific biobehavioral therapy also requires the expansion of a theoretical model upon which therapy is based to include consideration of the programmed patterns of perception and behavior stored in the CNS and the manner in which "internally" programmed patterns regulate the behavior and communication of an individual. The regulations described may be dependent on complex verbal programs; hence, a clearer understanding of the role of verbal symbolic factors seems indicated in attempts to modify the range and type of adaptive behaviors.

Central nervous system arousal and its related orienting, scanning, and vigilance concomitants; the processing of sensory input and its registration; the integration of current and past inputs from multiple sensory modalities into complex programs of response; the regulation of efferent discharge; and the sensitivity of end organ responsiveness (visceral, muscular, or sensory receptors) may all be due to the influence of hormonal substances such as adrenaline. Further, changes in any of the functions just mentioned can alter the acquisition, retention, or expression of conditioned behavior. Hence, it would seem logical to conclude that predictable modifications of CNS functions in the laboratory or clinic can be more precisely formulated when controlled environmental contingencies are employed in conjunction with chemical, sensory, or electrical methods to regulate the activity of various brain areas concerned with input and output processes and with stored programs and codes.

20

Some Comments on the Foundations of Behavior Therapy

ALEXANDER M. BUCHWALD
RICHARD D. YOUNG
Indiana University, Bloomington, Indiana

This chapter will concentrate on the empirical and theoretical foundations of behavior therapy. It should be made clear at the outset that a discussion of this type is not an evaluation of the effectiveness of therapeutic techniques. Evaluation of technique is primarily an empirical matter which is best considered separately. Charges that therapeutic procedures are superficial, naïve, or overly simple are mere propaganda unless substantiated by data indicating that patients are not benefited by the procedures. What will be evaluated are the theoretical formulations that some behavior therapists have offered concerning the nature of behavior disorders, and their ontogeny in individuals. We will discuss some of the problems which seem to have been overlooked in the attempt to present the definition, the origin, the maintenance, and the treatment of behavior disorders, in terms of learning theory.

Conceptualization of Disorder

Behavior therapy tends to be identified with the slogan "The symptom is the neurosis." Despite some dissenting voices (e.g., Costello, 1963; Lovibond,

1964b) the core of the behavior therapists' conceptualization of behavior disorders is that the disorder consists of nothing more than learned behaviors which are maladaptive or unadaptive. For purposes of exposition we shall discuss three sets of issues: (1) those involved in the definition and identification of maladaptive behavior; (2) those involved in the assertion that disorders are merely behavior; (3) those involved in the assertion that disorders are learned.

THE DEFINITION AND IDENTIFICATION OF MALADAPTIVE BEHAVIOR

If behavior disorders consist of responses acquired and maintained in exactly the same manner as all other behaviors, they must somehow be distinguished from normal, ordinary behavior. Behavior therapists commonly suggest the maladaptive nature of the behavior as a defining criterion. The idea that behavior disorders typically involve maladaptive behavior is not unique to behavior therapy. Most therapists, of almost any persuasion, would probably agree with this statement. But making maladaptiveness the defining characteristic raises certain problems to crucial importance. How can "maladaptive" be defined so that it encompasses all the phenomena that it is desired to include, and none other? How can we decide whether a person's behavior is more maladaptive than adaptive, or is sufficiently maladaptive so that we should attempt to alter it?

The concept of adaptation was originally a biological one relating to factors which promote survival of the individual or of the species. Wolpe (1958, pp. 32–33) defines "adaptiveness" primarily in biological terms: response consequences which lead toward "satisfaction of a need" or away from "possible danger or deprivation" are contrasted with "the expenditure of energy or the occurrence of damage or deprivation." A strictly biological view of adaptiveness as the sole criterion for behavior disorder is not tenable since vast portions of socially dictated behavior have no biological advantages. An alternative is to define "adaptiveness" at least partly in social terms. Ullmann & Krasner (1965) characterize maladaptive behavior as being "considered inappropriate by those key people in a person's life who control reinforcers," and as leading to a reduction in the amount of positive reinforcement given to the individual.

The first part of this statement cannot be taken literally. Anyone who has worked in a children's clinic has seen instances in which a child whose behavior is normal and commonplace is brought for treatment by parents who believe his behavior is inappropriate. The child's behavior is not "maladaptive" in the usual sense of the word, nor does it make sense to consider that such a child is displaying a behavior disorder. On the other hand, there are those who display behavior which would be considered inappropriate by most people, but which is not considered inappropriate by their parents, spouses, or families. Of course, standards of acceptable behavior vary from society to society, and among subgroups within a society. But some spouses, families, or associates are more tolerant of "inappropriate" behavior than others. It seems peculiar to have the issue of maladaptiveness of behavior rest solely upon the reactions of others to it.

The second part of the Ullmann–Krasner statement asserts that maladaptive behavior results in a diminution in the amount of positive reinforcement. On the face of it this seems like an objective criterion, and it is objective in certain limited situations. The rat that stops pressing the bar for food when a tone which has been paired with shock is presented is clearly exhibiting maladaptive behavior. But we can know this only because we know the history of the animal and what the positively reinforcing consequences available in this situation are. When we deal with the free-ranging person we cannot specify exactly what will be reinforcing to him, and to what extent. Different people have different goals, aims, interests, incentives, and reinforcement values. What is strongly positively reinforcing to one person may actually be aversive to another. The available data show not only that what is reinforcing to one subject may not be reinforcing to another (Premack, 1965) but also that a given consequence can be switched from positive to negative in its response-strengthening effects (Buchwald, 1959a, 1959b, 1960). In the absence of knowledge of what are the reinforcement values of various consequences for a given individual, how can we use a "reduction in the amount of positive reinforcement" as the criterion for the maladaptiveness of behavior?

One possible solution to the problem posed by the difficulty in identifying individual reinforcement values is to concentrate on forms of reinforcement that are typical within a society (Ullmann & Krasner, 1965). This solution has two flaws. Not only does it ignore the facts of diversity of goals in a complex society but it may hide an important distinction within the realm of the disordered. There are those who seek the typical rewards of the society but are unable to achieve them. There are others who seek rewards which are sufficiently atypical for them to be considered disordered even though they achieve them. Both could well show maladaptive behavior in the sense of failing to maximize the extent to which they receive typical forms of reinforcement.

ARE DISORDERS MERELY BEHAVIOR?

Some behavior therapists emphasize differences in response between normal and abnormal persons, rather than differences in motivation, incentives, goals, or reinforcement values. This leads to the three issues to be discussed in this section: (1) the nature of symptoms, (2) the organization of behavior, (3) symptom substitution.

The Nature of Symptoms. The idea that a disorder consists merely of behaviors, symptoms, or simple habits is deceptively simple. It suggests that what is being talked about are discrete, easily identified overt responses, of the kind traditionally studied in the learning laboratory. While there are numerous instances in which such responses are manipulated (Ullmann & Krasner, 1965), many symptoms are not responses in this sense of the word.

Consider phenomena as diverse as tics and anxiety. A tic is a discrete episodic movement, often easily discernible to an observer, and frequently relatively easy to specify, or at least to point to.[1] We look at a person with a facial tic and can easily discern whether or not he is "ticking" at a given moment, the rate at which tics occur, and so on. The term "anxiety," on the other hand, does not refer to any specific movement or class of movements. Definitions such as Wolpe's (1958, p. 34) ("the autonomic response pattern or patterns that are characteristically part of the organism's response to noxious stimulation") should not blind us to the fact that anxiety is not the same kind of phenomenon as a tic. Wolpe's definition is of a hypothetical "response," and this must be clearly recognized. We do not know what the organism's characteristic autonomic response pattern to noxious stimulation is. We cannot guarantee that any given organism shows the same autonomic response pattern to all noxious stimulation and to no other stimuli, let alone that there is a pattern which is common to different individuals. Further, we do not decide whether a person is anxious or not by examining his autonomic response pattern, but on the basis of motor and verbal responses which are at least several steps removed from his autonomic responses. In short, the term "anxiety" refers to an inferred state and not to an overt, specifiable response. Similar remarks apply to such common symptoms as depression, feelings of insecurity, obsessive thinking, phobias, hallucinations, and delusions, all of which must be inferred by the therapist from the patient's behavior.

An additional difficulty exists with certain terms, such as "anxiety," which are used in two rather different senses, descriptive and explanatory, which are sometimes confused. On the one hand, "anxiety" refers to a rather low-level concept. The patient complains of a feeling of dread, terror, or fear, and of various somatic upsets. He appears tense, strained, and tremulous; sweats profusely; and exhibits a considerable amount of restless movement. The anxiety he displays is a phenomenon to be explained; it does not itself explain anything. On the other hand, the term is also used to refer to a theoretical concept. When a symptom is said to be established or maintained because it reduces or prevents anxiety, "anxiety" is being used in this explanatory manner. We no longer describe the patient as "anxious" on the basis of signs such as those described above. Indeed, he shows no anxiety in the descriptive sense.

The confusion between these two concepts stems from Freud, who tried to explain the occurrence of the phenomenon of anxiety in terms of the

---

[1] While it is easy to point to a particular tic, it is extremely difficult to give an adequate verbal specification of the generic class "tic."

damming up of libido (1894), and who later introduced anxiety as a theoretical concept which was the basis of various defensive maneuvers (1926). Freud thought of "anxiety" in the second sense as being identical with "anxiety" in the first sense—an identification which most psychologists continue to make.

The practice of extending the use of a term in this manner is not necessarily harmful, just so long as we are aware of what we are doing. But when we talk about "anxiety" in this second sense, or about "underlying fears" or "primary conditioned responses," we are talking about theoretical concepts and not about observed behaviors or symptoms, and it is necessary to recognize this. Lazarus (1964b, p. 319), for example, argues that while behavior therapists deny the validity of "putative, repressed complexes, they certainly do not overlook primary conditioned responses which frequently underlie the higher-order maladaptive responses of which their patients complain." The "primary conditioned responses" referred to are just as much theoretical concepts as are "repressed complexes." The fact that the term "conditioned responses" is also used to refer to such an observable event as an eyeblink made to a change in illumination, whereas there are no observable repressed complexes, should not be allowed to hide this important point.

This error is not peculiar to Lazarus. A little reflection may convince all of us who have attempted to describe psychopathology in stimulus-response terms (including ourselves, we must admit) that we have been guilty of a similar offense. We have typically used terms such as "habit" and "response" as rather indiscriminate class terms to cover all manner of psychological events and processes.

The Organization of Behavior. Traditional conceptions of mental disorder tend to consider all of an individual's behavior as being integrated or interrelated. Different symptoms are seen as stemming from the same sources. In the most extreme form of this doctrine every bit of behavior is viewed as being "significant" in just this way, i.e., in reflecting the central core of the personality.

Traditional conceptions of behavior stemming from the learning laboratory, in contrast, tend to portray separate behaviors as independent of each other. The basis for this view is not difficult to see; it parallels laboratory practice. In the classical experiment we select one particular bit of behavior and proceed to study it. We do not ask what effect reinforcing or extinguishing one response has upon some entirely different kind of behavior. But is the idea of independence of behaviors a law of nature, or is it merely a function of the particular apparatus that has been used and the particular experiments that have been performed?

Questions about the interrelationships among various behaviors are important in connection with the formulation of all cases of behavior disorder. One basis for the conceptualization of symptoms as representing underlying pathological processes is the belief that various behaviors are not independent.

But the questions are particularly important in connection with patients with multiple symptoms. How are the various symptoms related to each other?

Behavior therapists tend to suggest two answers to this question. Either each symptom is viewed as having arisen independently and having remained independent, or one symptom is viewed as primary and the others as responses to it. The commonest example of the latter view is the conceptualization of some symptoms as being derived from and maintained by their anxiety-reducing effects.

These two conceptions do not exhaust the plausible possibilities, even within the framework of learning theory. Not only may the acquisition of symptoms differ from both of these patterns, but whatever their origin, symptoms may become fused or interrelated, or become separated from their initiating circumstances.

Very little is known about the organization of behavior or about the extent to which different behaviors are interrelated or are independent of each other. Some of the work of the behavior therapists provides a few clues to the answer. The studies of Ayllon and his colleagues (Ayllon, 1963; 1965; Ayllon & Michael, 1959; Haughton & Ayllon, 1965) strongly suggest that at least some behaviors are independent of others. They were able to eliminate, or to reduce the frequency of, various problem-causing actions of psychotic patients by manipulation of environmental contingencies. The fact that particular behaviors could be directly influenced without simultaneously affecting other aspects of the patient's behavior is important. It clearly indicates that even in the most serious cases of behavior disorder there are some "symptoms" which are either independent of, or separable from, any psychotic processes which may exist. On the other hand, clinical reports indicate some general improvement going beyond the specific symptoms tackled (see, for example, Lovibond, 1964a; Hain, Butcher, & Stevenson, 1966). To the extent that therapeutic efforts were directed solely to single symptoms, this would suggest some degree of interrelatedness of symptoms.

Some behavior therapists, notably Costello (1963) and Lovibond (1964b), have suggested that in some cases the disorder may consist only of the symptoms of which the patient complains, while in other cases there may be underlying disturbances giving rise to the symptoms. The results of an outcome study by Marks & Gelder (1965) seem to fit with this suggestion. They found that graded desensitization was more effective than psychiatric management with patients with relatively unusual phobias, but not with those who manifested agoraphobia. Patients in the former group were more apt to have symptoms restricted to the phobia. Patients in the latter group tended to be severely handicapped with a long history of fluctuating disturbances including generalized anxiety, depression, and sex difficulties, as well as fears of going out in public places.

One possible explanation of the results is that there may be two distinctly different groups of people with phobias. One group may consist of otherwise normal individuals who have undergone a painful or frightening experience, and who are anxious when confronted with the situation in which that experience occurred. The feared object or situation in cases of this type should be quite idiosyncratic. A prime example of such a case is that of the woman who developed a phobia of riding in cars after having twice been involved in severe auto accidents (Wolpe, 1962). In a case such as this, the explanation that anxiety has become conditioned to being in a car seems to cover the facts adequately. For such people it would be literally true that the symptom (phobia) is the disorder, and that there is no other disturbance. The other group may consist of individuals whose symptoms arise as manifestations of an underlying disturbance of some sort. For such people the disorder would be broader than any single symptom, and multiple fluctuating symptoms might well be manifest. There is no reason why symptoms that appear to be similar cannot arise in more than one way. In this connection it should be noted that some early workers in aversion therapy with alcoholics (Franks, 1966) suggested that the treatment was more effective for patients who were normal except for their drinking problem than for those who were not.

Symptom Substitution. The issue of symptom substitution is a major impetus for the view that the symptom is the disorder. Behavior therapists wish to justify a direct attack upon the complaints which bring the patient to seek help. However, over the years the belief that to do so is likely to result in the appearance of new, substitute symptoms, has become widespread.[2] One important source of this belief has been the psychoanalytic formulation that symptoms function to permit some gratification of repressed impulses while at the same time serving to keep them repressed. Crudely put, the notion is that the repressed impulses are striving for gratification and that if gratification is not obtained by one symptom it will be by another. The danger of new symptoms appearing, the near inevitability of it, is frequently emphasized in various undergraduate abnormal psychology texts. However, some practicing psychoanalysts seem less impressed with the inevitability of symptom substitution. Fenichel (1945, pp. 554–567) is at pains to explain in psychoanalytic terms why nonpsychoanalytic treatments, including direct attack on symptoms, can sometimes be successful. Alexander & French (1946) also advocate a direct attack on symptoms as helpful for some cases.

The issue of symptom substitution involves two separate kinds of questions. This has not been easy to see because the term itself suggests both an

[2] Although Ullmann & Krasner (1965) identify the idea of symptom substitution with "the medical model," symptomatic treatment is accepted medical practice— for example, the use of aspirin to relieve fever. There is nothing in medical theory to suggest that symptomatic treatment will result in new symptoms.

empirical phenonmenon and a theoretical explanation of that phenomenon. For the sake of clarity, empirical and theoretical issues should be treated separately.

At the empirical level we must determine what happens when a direct attack on some symptom succeeds in eliminating it. How frequently will novel symptoms appear? (The term *novel symptoms* may be used for both new symptoms and the exacerbation of symptoms other than the target symptom.) To answer this question we must specify what will count as a novel symptom and then determine the frequency with which novel symptoms appear in samples of treated patients drawn from various representative patient populations. The frequency may vary from group to group, and may also depend upon the target symptom (Costello, 1963; Eysenck, 1960b) and the treatment procedures used (Ullmann & Krasner, 1965; Franks, 1966a).

It is important to distinguish between "symptom substitution" in this empirical sense and "symptom substitution" as an explanation of the appearance of a novel symptom. The distinction has not always been made. For example, Ullmann & Krasner (1965) describe a case in which a child exhibits a series of new undesirable behaviors as old ones are extinguished. They say that this is "not symptom substitution" because these various behaviors already existed in the subject's hierarchy of responses. This is an alternative theoretical explanation of the appearance of the novel symptoms rather than a denial that they appeared.

It is amply clear from the recent work in behavior therapy that novel symptoms do not always appear when a symptom is successfully removed. The best available systematic data, based primarily on the treatment of enuresis and phobias, suggest that novel symptoms do not appear very frequently when these are successfully removed (Lovibond, 1964a; Marks & Gelder, 1965; Hain, Butcher, & Stevenson, 1966). In fact, the original symptoms seem to return more frequently than new ones appear, according to these data.

Suppose it turns out, more generally, that novel symptoms rarely appear: What implications does this have for conceptualizations of disorder? Unless a theory clearly demands that novel symptoms frequently or always appear, the answer is "none." It is unclear whether psychoanalytic theory demands this or not.

Aside from psychoanalytic theory there are many possible formulations which would not predict the appearance of novel symptoms, even though complaints are considered to be symptomatic of an underlying state of affairs. For example, any conceptualization which portrays a disorder as consisting basically of a disposition to develop symptoms under certain conditions would not require novel symptoms to appear very frequently. The "neurotic" might be free of distress that would lead him to seek aid until the occurrence of events which initiate (precipitate) symptoms. Once initiated, the symptoms may persist, perhaps indefinitely, unless treated. Treatment directed primarily at the symptom may result in its disappearance, returning the individual to his former symptomatically silent state. Yates (1958b) has described the distinction between "neuroticism" and "neurosis" in this way, arguing that the disposition is neuroticism and the symptoms are the neurosis. But the basis for this choice of terminology is unclear. We may equally well conceive of the disorder as being the underlying state of affairs. The idea that the neurosis exists only when symptoms appear makes a neurosis analogous to an acute physical illness such as pneumonia, tuberculosis, or measles. Perhaps a better analogy might be made with chronic illnesses, such as asthma, in which the individual is symptom-free except when attacks have been precipitated, and in which medical treatment is directed toward relief of symptoms.

THE ONTOGENY OF DISORDERED BEHAVIOR

The idea that behavior disorders are learned reactions, acquired in the same way as any other behaviors, has several implications. For one, it implies that disorders are acquired through experience rather than being due to pathology of the body tissues.[3] More importantly, it is intended to mean that the acquisition of the problem behavior takes place according to certain known processes.

The assertion that neurotic reactions are learned is to be understood as meaning that they are acquired in accordance with the theoretical principles espoused by men such as Guthrie, Hull, Pavlov, and Skinner, together with a few emendations and additions to these principles. However, these principles do not lead to any single account of the acquisition of disordered behavior. In part this is due to disagreements about the basic theoretical principles governing learning. In larger part it is due to the fact that these principles are very general and that rules for their application to specific instances of behavior are largely nonexistent. It is the fact that learning theory is so open that allows Eysenck (1960b) to suggest that classical conditioning is the paradigm for symptom formation, while Ullmann & Krasner (1965) emphasize operant conditioning, and Dollard & Miller (1950) couch their discussion in terms of conflict, repression, anxiety, and defense, all within the framework of learning theory.

Behavior therapists tend to minimize the importance of these differences in the analyses of behavior disorders (and of learning, generally). They have noted the points of agreement between theorists, and have emphasized the empirical laws of learning. The argument, in essence, is that neurotic reactions, like other acquired behaviors, must obey the laws of learning, laws which are known from laboratory experimentation (Eysenck, 1960b; Rachman, 1963).

Careful analysis of this argument indicates that it is not as straightforward as it first appears. If "learning" is taken as synonymous with "the

---

[3] Space limitations preclude a discussion of the possible role of tissue pathology in producing behavior disorders.

acquisition of behavior," any supposed law of learning must either accurately describe behavior in general, or be a law of limited scope or not a law at all. But it seems doubtful that there is any large body of relationships, known on the basis of laboratory investigations, that are sufficiently general in scope to apply to the acquisition, maintenance, and change of any behavior whatsoever.

Many of the established generalizations about behavioral change have been established using particular types of subjects, restricted types of behaviors, and limited varieties of experimental arrangements. Experiments with animals and with college sophomores, done under rigidly restricted environmental conditions, and using relatively simple behaviors, can be immensely useful in the acquisition of knowledge. The strategy of proceeding from the investigation of simple situations to more complex ones has much to recommend it. But the proper application of this strategy is to proceed step by step experimentally, rather than to extrapolate from that which has been investigated to that which has not. This will be elaborated upon in a later section. At this point it suffices to present two examples of well-established empirical generalizations which do not hold in certain situations.

Extinction.   At a strictly empirical level, the principle of extinction relates the cessation of responding to the repeated absence of any external event describable as a "reinforcement" following the occurrence of the response. The observations leading to the establishment of this law consist of phenomena such as the cessation of salivation to a conditioned stimulus when it is repeatedly presented without being accompanied by the unconditioned stimulus, or the decline in the rate of bar pressing after the magazine has ceased to deliver food pellets to the rat. But extinction does not always take place. Buchwald (1959a) had subjects learn to choose the correct member of each of several pairs of nonsense syllables under various "verbal reinforcement combinations." Under extinction conditions most of the subjects failed to show any signs of extinction, but instead continued to select the correct responses.

It may be that these findings can be explained in terms of Hullian or Skinnerian theory, and that the *theoretical* law of extinction can be maintained. That is not the point. The point is that a simple empirical generalization (responses become less probable when they are followed by an absence of environmental consequences) failed to hold in this situation.[4]

---

[4] Any proposed explanation should deal with the fact that human subjects react differently when a machine stops providing reinforcement than when another person stops providing reinforcement. Buchwald's subjects continued to respond when the experimenter ceased saying "right" or "wrong." Greeno (personal communication) found that subjects engaged in guessing which of two lights on a machine would be lit stopped pressing when a series of blank trials was introduced. They complained that the machine was broken. We know of no psychological theory that can explain this discrepancy except in an ad hoc manner.

Delay of Reinforcement. The literature on animal learning and on classical conditioning leads to the empirical generalization that a time delay between the occurrence of a response and the external reinforcing event, or between the CS and the UCS, retards response acquisition. This principle holds both for rewards and for punishment. (The fact that punishment generally is found to be effective in suppressing a response only when it occurs immediately after the response has been noted by Kushner & Sandler, 1966, in connection with aversion therapy.) However, recent experiments (e.g., Brackbill, 1964; Buchwald, 1967; Kintsch & McCoy, 1964) show that in some situations human subjects exposed to lengthy delays of reinforcement learn as well as, or even better than, those given immediate reinforcement.

These findings do not imply that a typical delay-of-reinforcement effect never occurs in human learning. They do imply that the principle that immediate reinforcement leads to faster, stronger, or better learning than delayed reinforcement, is of limited generality; that it holds in some situations but not in others. Determining under what circumstances it holds and under what circumstances it does not hold is a difficult, challenging, and important task for psychology.

There may be those who will wish to reject the relevance of these experiments as counterexamples to the established principle on the grounds that some inferred or hypothetical aspect of the subjects' own reactions to his behavior constituted a source of immediate reinforcement. Whether a theoretical explanation of this type will or will not be successful in accounting for the data simply cannot be judged until it is put forth. But two things should be realized about such explanations: (1) They do not alter the fact that the empirical principle is of limited generality so far as observable external reinforcing stimuli are concerned. (2) They involve the expansion of the term "reinforcing stimulus event" to cover hypothetical events quite different in kind from those originally subsumed under this term. (See Chomsky, 1959, for additional discussion of this point.) Such expansion may be a quite dangerous procedure. Unless used cautiously it can result in a meaningless version of the immediacy-of-reinforcement principle which could never be found wrong because of our insistence that there must be hidden immediate reinforcing events whether they can be identified independently of their effects or not.

Skinner (1953) has described a "functional analysis of behavior" as consisting of determining the external variables of which behavior is a function. Psychologists committed to his program should bear this in mind. He also pointed out that in instances in which the behavior does not correspond to demonstrated principles, "other variables may have to be taken into account" (p. 33). We agree, and we believe that it is high time to investigate in a serious way the possibility that other variables have to be taken into account.

It is sometimes suggested that the successes of behavior therapy confirm the idea that disorders are learned. However, the implication of successful treatment for etiological theories is not necessarily simple. The demonstration that behavior can be changed by some particular procedure does not guarantee that the behavior was originally produced by a similar procedure. For example, a number of studies (Ullmann & Krasner, 1965) indicate that the behavior of psychotic adults can be altered through making reinforcement contingent on particular behaviors. Such studies serve as adequate demonstration that the empirical law of effect—future behavior will be affected by the consequences of past behavior—holds for psychotics. To conclude from this that the behavior was originally produced by reinforcement is clearly not warranted. Peterson & London (1965, p. 290) have forcefully pointed out that while learning can take place without it, "cognition, can significantly facilitate the acquisition of adaptive skills." Perhaps the same is true of maladaptive behavior.

In passing, mention might be made of Haughton & Ayllon's (1965) production of "symptomatic" behavior. They trained a psychotic woman to hold a broom by supplying her with cigarettes if she was holding the broom, and not otherwise. Two psychiatrists who were allowed to watch her from behind a one-way mirror were duped into making some silly assertions about why she held the broom. Haughton & Ayllon note that the "apparent uselessness and irrelevance of the patient's behavior" resembles compulsive or psychotic behavior. Yet, it may differ from such behavior in a very important respect. It is quite possible that if asked why she held the broom the patient might have explained that she was given cigarettes for doing it. Neither psychotic nor compulsive patients are ordinarily able to give a similar rational and veridical account of their symptoms. We submit that it is this inability to account for the behavior plausibly, and not the action per se, which is the "hallmark of behavior often clinically described as 'compulsive' or 'psychotic.' "

Other studies have shown that we can reduce people's fears by systematic desensitization and that in some instances we can eliminate certain behaviors by shocking the patient. This tells us nothing about the way in which the fears or behaviors were acquired. It is important to remember that behavior is a final common pathway, that it is susceptible to a large number of influences. The way in which responses are changed need not parallel the way in which they were originally acquired. The asymmetry between the source of a behavioral disorder and the method of treatment may be illustrated by the case of aphasic patients. They have lost the ability to speak as a result of a vascular accident or other brain lesion, but they can sometimes be taught to speak again. The behavioral loss is due to a physiological insult, but there is no known physiological or medical technique for overcoming this handicap. That the only known successful treatment is a behavioral one implies nothing about the origin of the deficit. Similarly, if a mute schizophrenic can be taught to speak again by shaping and reinforcement (and such efforts have had some limited success), there is no implication that his speech was lost due to the operation of reinforcing factors in his social environment.

There is no doubt that procedures such as conditioning, desensitization, and the judicious use of reward and punishment can affect the behavior of neurotic and psychotic individuals. Any attempt at a theoretical formulation of behavior disorders must deal with these facts. While the use of these procedures has been suggested by learning-theory formulations, the results cannot be said to confirm them to any large extent. This is because the details and the results of many of the procedures cannot be deduced from any set of basic principles, or even explained by them without a large amount of ad hoc modification or supplementation. Consider the following examples.

Reciprocal Inhibition. The behavior therapy technique which has been most widely investigated and most generally accepted is Wolpe's reciprocal inhibition procedure. The term "reciprocal inhibition" was borrowed from physiology, where it refers to the condition in which one set of muscles or nerves acts antagonistically to another set so that both activities cannot occur simultaneously. Wolpe has somewhat metaphorically applied this term to his procedure for the treatment of anxiety-based disorders. Wolpe believes there are a number of responses (e.g., relaxation, sex, assertion) which are inherently antagonistic to anxiety.[5] In Wolpe's procedure the patient attempts an antagonistic response while imagining the stimuli which he had previously reported to elicit anxiety. The purpose of the procedure is to inhibit the occurrence of the anxiety and thus weaken the stimulus-response association so that it will no longer occur. Wolpe does not suggest that the inhibitory response in itself will become attached to the conditioned stimulus. Theoretically the inhibitory response appears to be catalytic in action, facilitating, but not itself involved in, what is essentially an extinction process. This is an interesting idea but one which has not been explored in the conditioning laboratory.

Despite Wolpe's assertion that all anxiety is of a kind and that in principle any inherently inhibiting response can be used, in many cases the selected inhibitory response appears to be particularly relevant to the source of the anxiety. Frequently in such cases therapy appears to be specifically directed toward encouraging the patient to do what he has been afraid of doing. The inhibitory responses, sexual behavior or assertive behavior, are themselves appropriate in the circumstances in which avoidance behavior was previously elicited. The therapist acts to reinforce such responses, and it is likely that the natural environment does so as well. Thus the probability of these responses will be increased and they should ultimately replace the original responses. The learning paradigm is simple counterconditioning.

However, counterconditioning is not a sufficient explanation for all cases of reciprocal inhibition. This can easily be seen in the research on snake phobias, where the cured cases do not report feelings of relaxation when they see a snake. They simply report no longer feeling anxious. As pointed out by

[5] At present there is little, if any, evidence to indicate that relaxation of striate muscles, for example, influences autonomic nervous functioning. In view of Wolpe's definition of anxiety, this is of crucial importance.

Lomont (1965) this suggests that the behavioral changes following reciprocal inhibition may be due primarily to extinction. Eysenck & Rachman (1965) assume that extinction processes are largely responsible for spontaneous remission. However, both they and Wolpe (1958) dismiss extinction as an explanation of the results of the reciprocal inhibition technique.

The role of relaxation responses in reciprocal inhibition therapy has been experimentally investigated. In a recent review of systematic desensitization, Rachman (1967, pp. 98–99) concluded: "At the very least, these three studies now justify the conclusion that reciprocal inhibition produced by relaxation is superior to extinction as a method for reducing fear." One of the studies reviewed was Rachman's (1965c, p. 246), where part of the experimental procedure was described in the following words: "In the normal therapeutic procedure, one does not present the next item on the hierarchy until the patient reports little or no disturbance from the item under consideration. For the purposes of the present experiment, however, this precaution was disregarded." It seems particularly odd to test the influence of relaxation versus extinction under conditions where there is minimal concern for the "relaxed" state of the subject. Apparently clinical application is more vigorous at times than experimental testing.

The second report cited by Rachman is an animal study by Gale, Sturmfels, & Gale (1966) which compared the effects of simple desensitization (extinction), desensitization combined with feeding response (reciprocal inhibition), and no treatment. The only significant difference between extinction and reciprocal inhibition occurred on treatment trials. The fact that there were no differences between extinction and reciprocal inhibition groups when tested on the original conditioned stimulus indicates that there are at least two ways to produce the same effect.

The third study (Lomont & Edwards, 1967) was an attempt to evaluate the efficacy of relaxation in reciprocal inhibition therapy. The "desensitization" procedure was not Wolpian, in that the subject maintained a mild degree of muscular tension during each stimulus visualization and relaxed after imagining. How this procedure would provide any data revelant to reciprocal inhibition, or for that matter relevant to any theory of the extinction process, is difficult to determine. None of the pretreatment-posttreatment comparisons were significant for either treatment, indicating that neither procedure was particularly effective.

Other recent studies provide data which bear upon the question of reciprocal inhibition versus extinction. Bandura, Grusec, & Menlove (1967) examined the effects of two forms of vicarious extinction of fear of dogs in children three to five years of age. Children who observed that a model was not harmed by the dog showed a reduced fear of dogs. The context in which the modeling occurred, either with or without a party, had no apparent effect upon the children's fear.

Finally Nelson (1966) found that, while the effect of eating was to facilitate the elimination of a conditioned fear, this effect could not be attributed to reciprocal inhibition. Rather, eating seemed to increase the amount of time that the subject was exposed to fear-producing cues and thus to facilitate extinction.

In view of these various findings the question remains open: How does the reciprocal inhibition procedure work?

Aversion Therapy. A different problem is illustrated by the recent use of aversive stimulation in behavior therapy. Successful treatment of homosexuality has been reported, using electric shock as the unconditioned stimulus within both classical conditioning and escape-avoidance training procedures. On the assumption (Feldman, p. 66, 1966) that homosexual behaviors are "initiated by the visual response of looking at an attractive sexual object," both learning procedures have utilized photographs of males as the conditioned stimulus. A great deal of attention has been paid to the specifics of the procedures, e.g., distributed versus massed trials, delay of reinforcement, and shock intensity. However there has been a failure to deal seriously with the question, how does pairing electric shock with a photograph of a male, or pushing a button to avoid shock while observing a photograph of a male, result in the cessation of particular sexual practices?

The experimental research cited as the foundation of aversion therapy has dealt exclusively with the application of an unconditioned stimulus to the specific response to be eliminated. The application of the unconditioned stimulus to the "looking-at" response in order to eliminate overt homosexual behavior is not the same sort of thing. Using either escape or avoidance learning as a paradigm, two possible explanations of the reported efficacy of the treatment are suggested. One is that there is an established response chain which is initiated by the "looking-at" response, and which culminates in some form of overt homosexual behavior. Punishment of the initial response is supposed to lead to an inhibition of the remaining responses in the chain. Although this idea seems plausible, there is no experimental evidence on the effects of punishment on heterogeneous behavioral chains, and there have been only three animal studies on the influence of aversive stimulation applied to particular sections of a homogeneous response chain (Azrin & Holz, 1966). Further, (1) the chain in question is hypothetical, and (2) details concerning its components have not been suggested. The second explanation involves the idea that "looking at" is a member of a general class of homosexual responses, and that punishment of it should reduce the frequency of other members of the response class. This idea also has some plausibility. However, it requires both an explicit set of rules for judging membership in a response class and evidence that the effects of punishment will generalize in the manner suggested. In the absence of relevant detail and of corroborative data, these proposed explanations are at best plausible speculation.

Let us ask what a learning-theoretic stimulus-response formulation of disordered behavior requires. This is nothing more, nor less, than a general account of how certain persons become the people they are. A mere statement that this follows the "laws of learning" will not suffice. A particularistic account of the ontogeny of each disordered case is not required, but some general statements are. We need to have some general rules regarding the formation of stimulus classes and response classes, the individual's acquisition of reinforcement values, drive states, and so on. We require some general evidence that particular events, or series of events, or classes of events, antedated the occurrence of particular behavioral disturbances. We need both an explicit body of laws or assumptions that explain the relationship between these antecedent events and disordered behavior, and adequate empirical tests of these assumptions and explanations. What are the learning principles by which we explain, or even predict, why one person is benefitted somewhat by massed practice on his tics (Yates, 1958a) while another's condition is worsened (Feldman & Werry, 1966)? How do we account for the remarkable cure of a case of eyebrow plucking (Taylor, 1963) when the woman says to herself, "No, stay where you are" as she begins to raise her hand? How can learning theory account for the fact that electric shocks administered to a patient while he was fondling his favorite fetish lead to his reporting that his masochistic interests had ceased and that intercourse with his wife was now satisfactory (Marks, Rachman, & Gelder, 1965)? Questions such as these ought to nag at us until we arrive at a solution. They should not be glossed over.

Basic Research and Applied Research

Research on the treatment of behavior disorders has two aims: If treatment is to be made more effective, we need to develop an applied science or technology of treatment. If treatment is to be on a rational basis, rather than an empirical one, we need to develop explicit formulations of the relationships between specific therapeutic procedures and specific behavioral changes. The distinction between the two has not always been recognized. Indeed some behavior therapists have seemed to suggest that traditional psychotherapy must be ineffective because it is not based upon knowledge that has been accumulated by experimentation in the psychological laboratory. Such a position is untenable since it ignores not only the distinction between technology and basic science, but also the fact that laboratory experimentation is merely one of the ways in which scientific knowledge is gained.

In their zeal to apply principles gained from laboratory research, behavior therapists have at times attempted to move too quickly from the laboratory to the clinic. Behavior therapy might profit from the experience of those experimental psychologists who have attempted to apply laboratory-based learning principles to the technology of teaching and instruction. The potential pitfalls of direct and simple extrapolation have been forcefully discussed by

Gagné (1962). Gagné does not suggest that simple learning principles are invalid but rather that they are inadequate to handle the training job. He suggests that overconcern with the elicitation and reinforcement of responses can lead the psychologist away from what is required to have the task learned efficiently. Somewhat similarly, Glaser (1964), after reviewing the experimental literature on teaching and instruction, concludes that until researchers spend much more time carefully analyzing the component tasks involved in the behavior sequence under study (task analysis) and in delineating the pertinent determining variables, we cannot hope to know how, or when, to apply the principles of learning established in the laboratory. What we need is a clearer conception of the relationship between research in basic science and research in technology and a greater appreciation of the procedures appropriate to each. Hilgard & Bower (1966) have proposed that we identify six steps encompassing basic research on learning and the technology of instruction. When modified, this analysis may be useful to the continued development of behavior therapy.

BASIC PSYCHOLOGICAL RESEARCH

The first three steps are characterized by investigations which are directed toward establishing quantitative laws which relate the behavior of the organism to its determining conditions. There is no direct concern with the relevance of the research to practical problems of psychopathology or psychotherapy.

In step 1 the research is concerned with basic phenomena with no necessary relevance or similarity to the therapy situation, e.g., transfer of learning in animal mazes, physiological and biochemical correlates of learning, eyelid conditioning. In step 2 subjects or procedures are used which appear somewhat relevant to therapy, e.g., the use of human subjects, or the study of memory, concept formation, or extinction of the conditioned GSR. In step 3 the subjects or the procedures are similar to those found in therapy, although no attention is paid to the possibility of adapting the processes studied to an applied setting, e.g., studies of verbal reinforcement with schizophrenics, fear stimulus generalization among neurotics, or anxiety in the sociopathic personality.

TECHNOLOGICAL RESEARCH AND DEVELOPMENT

A sharp dividing line between basic research and technological research does not exist, but a definite shift in emphasis begins to become evident. Beginning with step 4, the research is characterized by questions primarily concerned with establishing the effectiveness and utility of therapeutic techniques applied under various conditions.

In step 4 research is conducted in highly controlled laboratory situations usually with experimental "therapists" and frequently using behaviors not considered to be severe pathologies, e.g., analog desensitization studies such as that of Lang & Lazovik (1963). In step 5 procedures previously used in experimental research are investigated using professional therapists in a clinical setting, e.g., Paul's (1966) study of insight versus desensitization in psychotherapy. In step 6 the procedures which have been found to be effective in steps 4 and 5 are given practical clinical evaluation in what has been called "outcome studies," e.g., the retrospective and prospective studies of Marks & Gelder (1965, 1966).

No one of the research steps is scientifically more pure than any other, and no one has a priority on scientific ingenuity and innovation. It is obvious that research at each of the various steps stimulates work at other levels, and that similar ideas and problems can be encountered at several steps. Although it is not necessary to pigeonhole each research report, it is important to recognize that there are various levels in research and that the levels exist for a reason. The remarks made by Hilgard & Bower (1966, pp. 577–578) in connection with educational research hold true for behavior therapy: "it would be fair to say that too much of the research has rested at Steps 1 and 2 to be educationally relevant; . . . [psychologists] have tended to work at this end of the spectrum and then to jump, by inference, to Step 6, without being sufficiently patient about Steps 4 and 5." Confusion occurs when studies (e.g., Isaacs, Thomas, & Goldiamond, 1960; Sherman, 1965) on step 3 are mistaken by some behavior therapists for research on step 5.

Closely related to the distinction between basic and applied research is one particular element of research design which produces particularly significant problems for behavior therapies. That element is the concern for validity. Campbell & Stanley (1963) have pointed out that all research is concerned with internal validity: Did the experimental manipulations produce the observed changes? They also discuss external validity: To what populations, environments, treatment, and measurement variables can the experimental effects be generalized? While basic research may temporarily ignore external validity for the sake of maximizing internal validity, it is obvious that the raison d'être of applied research is external validity. One might view the successive steps presented above as increasing the emphasis upon the external validity of the investigations. Internal validity is no substitute for external validity in applied research.

Chapter Summary

This chapter has focused on some of the problems and difficulties which confront behavior therapy. We believe that failure to deal with these issues will retard the development of behavior therapy and its associated explanatory systems. Many of the critics of behavior therapy seem to suggest that neither the procedures nor the theoretical approach can conceivably be useful. We do not share this pessimism; we are interested in the improvement of this movement, not in its destruction.

References

Abelson, R. P., & Lesser, G. S. Personality correlates of measurement of persuasibility in children. In I. Janis, C. Hovland, P. Field, H. Linton, E. Graham, A. Cohen, D. Ruge, R. P. Abelson, G. S. Lesser, & S. King, (Eds.), *Personality and persuasibility*. New Haven, Conn.: Yale University Press, 1959. Pp. 141–146.

Abraham, W. Programmed learning and the exceptional child. *Journal of the National Society of Programmed Instruction*, 1966, **5**, 5–7.

Adams, H. B., Carerra, R. N., Cooper, G. D., Gibby, R. G., & Tobey, H. R. Personality and intellectual changes in psychiatric patients following brief sensory deprivation. *American Psychologist*, 1960, **15**, 448.

Agras, W. S. An investigation of the decrement of anxiety responses during systematic desensitization therapy. *Behaviour Research and Therapy*, 1965, **2**, 267–270.

Albee, G. The dark at the top of the agenda. *Clinical Psychologist*, 1967, **20**, 7–9.

Alexander, F., & French, T. M. *Psychoanalytic therapy*. New York: Ronald Press, 1946.

Alexander, L. *Objective approaches to treatment in psychiatry*. Springfield, Ill.: Charles C Thomas, 1958.

———— Differential diagnosis between psychogenic and physical pain. *Journal of the American Medical Association*, 1962, **181,** 855–861.

Allen, K. E., & Harris, F. Elimination of a child's excessive scratching by training the mother in reinforcement procedures. *Behaviour Research and Therapy*, 1966, **4,** 79–84.

Allen, K. E., Hart, B. M., Buell, J. S., Harris, F. R., & Wolf, M. M. Effects of social reinforcement on isolate behavior of a nursery school child. *Child Development*, 1964, **35,** 511–518.

Allied Education Council. *The Fitzhugh plus program materials.* Distribution Center, P.O. Box 78, Galien, Mich. 49113, 1966.

Allport, F. *Institutional behavior.* Chapel Hill, N.C.: University of North Carolina Press, 1933.

American Psychiatric Association. *Diagnostic and statistical manual of mental disorders.* Washington, D.C.: APA, 1952.

+ *American Psychologist*, **21,** May, 1966. (Special Issue.)

Anant, S. S. The treatment of alcoholics by verbal aversion techniques: a case report. *Manas*, 1966, **13,** 79–86.

———— A note on the treatment of alcoholics by the verbal aversion technique. *Canadian Psychologist*, 1967, **8a,** 19–22.

Anderson, D. Application of a behavior modification technique to the control of a hyperactive child. Unpublished M.A. thesis, University of Oregon, 1964.

Andrews, J. D. W. Psychotherapy of phobias. *Psychological Bulletin*, 1966, **66,** 455–480.

Anokhin, P. K., Electroencephalographic analysis of cortico-subcortical relations in positive and negative conditioned reflexes, *Annals of the Academy of Science*, 1961, **2,** 799–938.

———— Cybernetics and integrative brain activity. *Proceedings of the XVIII International Congress of Psychology. Symposium 2.* 1966, 3–45. (a)

———— Special features of the afferent apparatus of the conditioned reflex and their importance to psychology. In A. Leontiev, A. Luvia, & A. Smirnov (Eds.), *Psychological Research in the U.S.S.R.* Moscow: Progress Publishers, 1966. Pp. 67–98. (b)

Ansbacher, H. L., & Ansbacher, R. R. (Eds.) *The individual psychology of Alfred Adler.* New York: Basic Books, 1956.

Antonov, N. P. Specific nature of the individual consciousness of man as the highest degree of mental development. *Voprosy Psikhologii*, 1958, **4,** 79–87. English translation in *The central nervous system and behavior*, Washington D.C., USPHS, 1959, 1–12.

Applezweig, M., & Moeller, G. The pituitary-adrenal system and anxiety in avoidance training. *Proceedings of the 15th International Congress of Psychology*, Amsterdam: North Holland Publ. Co., 1959. Pp. 602–603.

Asch, S. E. The doctrine of suggestion, prestige, and imitation in social psychology. *Psychological Review*, 1948, **55,** 250–276.

——— *Social psychology.* Englewood Cliffs, N.J.: Prentice-Hall, 1952.

Ash, P. The reliability of psychiatric diagnoses. *Journal of Abnormal and Social Psychology,* 1949, **44,** 272–277.

Ashem, B. The treatment of a disaster phobia by systematic desensitization. *Behaviour Research and Therapy,* 1963, **1,** 81–84.

Asratyan, E. A. *I. P. Pavlov: His life and work.* Moscow: Foreign Languages Publishing House, 1953.

——— The functional architecture of instrumental conditioning. *Conditional Reflex,* 1967, **2,** 258–272.

Astin, A. W. The functional autonomy of psychotherapy. *American Psychologist,* 1961, **16,** 75–78.

Astrup, C. *Schizophrenia: Conditional reflex studies.* Springfield, Ill.: Charles C Thomas, 1962.

——— *Pavlovian psychiatry: A new synthesis.* Springfield Ill.: Charles C Thomas, 1965.

Atkinson, R. L., & Robinson, N. M. Paired-associate learning by schizophrenic and normal subjects under conditions of personal and impersonal reward and punishment. *Journal of Abnormal and Social Psychology,* 1961, **62,** 322–326.

Atthowe, J. M. Jr., & Krasner, L. The systematic application of contingent reinforcement procedures (token economy) in a large social setting: A psychiatric ward. Paper presented at the Annual Meeting of the American Psychological Association, Chicago, 1965.

——— A preliminary report on the application of contingent reinforcement procedures (token economy) on a "chronic" psychiatric ward. *Journal of Abnormal Psychology,* 1968, **73,** 37–43.

Auld, F., Jr., & White, A. Sequential dependencies in psychotherapy. *Journal of Abnormal and Social Psychology,* 1959, **58,** 100–104.

Ax, A. F. The physiological differentiation between fear and anger. *Psychosomatic Medicine,* 1953, **15,** 433–442.

Ayllon, T. Intensive treatment of psychotic behavior by stimulus satiation and food reinforcement. *Behaviour Research and Therapy,* 1963, **1,** 53–61.

——— Some behavioral problems associated with eating in chronic schizophrenic patients. In L. P. Ullmann & L. Krasner (Eds.), *Case studies in behavior modification.* New York: Holt, Rinehart and Winston, 1965. Pp. 73–77.

Ayllon, T., & Azrin, N. H. Reinforcement and instructions with mental patients. *Journal of the Experimental Analysis of Behavior,* 1964, **7,** 327–331.

——— The measurement and reinforcement of behavior of psychotics. *Journal of the Experimental Analysis of Behavior,* 1965, **8,** 357–383.

Ayllon, T., & Haughton, E. Control of the behavior of schizophrenic patients by food. *Journal of the Experimental Analysis of Behavior,* 1962, **5,** 343–352.

————— Modification of symptomatic verbal behavior of mental patients. *Behaviour Research and Therapy*, 1964, **2**, 87–97.

Ayllon, T., Haughton, E., & Hughes, H. B. Interpretation of symptoms: Fact or fiction? *Behaviour Research and Therapy*, 1965, **3**, 1–8.

Ayllon, T., & Michael, J. The psychiatric nurse as a behavioral engineer. *Journal of the Experimental Analysis of Behavior*, 1959, **2**, 323–334.

Azrin, N. H. Effects of two intermittent schedules of immediate and non-immediate punishment. *Journal of Psychology*, 1956, **42**, 3–21.

Azrin, N. H., & Holz, W. C. Punishment. In W. K. Honig (Ed.), *Operant behavior: Areas of research and application*. New York: Appleton-Century-Croft, 1966. Pp. 38–447.

Azrin, N. H., Holz, W., Ulrich, R., & Goldiamond, I. The control of the content of conversation through reinforcement. *Journal of the Experimental Analysis of Behavior*, 1961, **4**, 25–30.

Azrin, N. H., & Lindsley, O. R. The reinforcement of coöperation between children. *Journal of Abnormal and Social Psychology*, 1956, **52**, 100–102.

Babigian, H. M., Gardner, E. A., Miles, H. C., & Romano, J. Diagnostic consistency and change in a follow-up on 1215 patients. *American Journal of Psychiatry*, 1965, **121**, 895–901.

Babkin, B. P. *Pavlov, a biography*. Chicago: Chicago University Press, 1949.

Bach, G. In Alexander, S.: Fight promoter for battle of sexes. *Life*, May 17, 1963, **54**, 102–108.

Bachrach, A. J. Some applications of operant conditioning to behavior therapy. In J. Wolpe, A. Salter, and L. J. Reyna (Eds.), *The conditioning therapies*. New York: Holt, Rinehart and Winston, 1964. Pp. 62–75.

Bachrach, A. J., Erwin, W. J., & Mohr, J. P. The control of eating behavior in an anorexic by operant conditioning techniques. In L. P. Ullmann & L. Krasner (Eds.), *Case studies in behavior modification*. New York: Holt, Rinehart and Winston, 1965. Pp. 153–163.

Baer, D. M. Laboratory control of thumbsucking by withdrawal and re-presentation of reinforcement. *Journal of the Experimental Analysis of Behavior*, 1962, **5**, 525–528.

————— Some remedial uses of the reinforcement contingency. In J. M. Shlien (Ed.), *Research in psychotherapy*. Vol. III. Washington, D.C.: American Psychological Association, 1968. Pp. 3–20.

Baer, D. M., Peterson, R. F., & Sherman, J. A. The development of imitation by reinforcing behavioral similarity to a model. *Journal of the Experimental Analysis of Behavior*, 1967, **10**, 405–416.

Baer, D. M., & Sherman, J. A. Reinforcement control of generalized imitation in young children. *Journal of Experimental Child Psychology*, 1964, **1**, 37–49.

Baer, D. M., & Wolf, M. M. The reinforcement contingency in preschool and remedial education. In R. D. Hess & R. M. Bear (Eds.), *Early education: Current theory, research, and action*. Chicago: Aldine, 1968. Pp. 119–129.

———— Some recent examples of behavior modification in preschool settings. In C. Neuringer & J. L. Michael (Eds.), *Behavior modification in clinical psychology*. New York: Appleton-Century-Crofts, in press.

Bakal, C. *The right to bear arms*. New York: McGraw-Hill, 1966.

Ball, R. S. Reinforcement conditioning of verbal behavior by verbal and nonverbal stimuli in a situation resembling a clinical interview. Unpublished doctoral dissertation, Indiana Universty, 1952.

Ban, T. A. *Conditioning and psychiatry*. Chicago: Aldine, 1964.

Ban, T. A., & Levy, L. Physiological patterns: A diagnostic test procedure based on the conditioned reflex method. *Journal of Neuropsychiatry*, 1961, **2**, 228–231.

Bancroft, J. Aversion therapy. Unpublished Diploma in Psychological Medicine dissertation, University of London, 1966.

Bandura, A. Psychotherapy as a learning process. *Psychological Bulletin*, 1961, **58**, 143–159.

———— Social learning through imitation. In M. R. Jones (Ed.), *Nebraska symposium on motivation*. Lincoln, Nebr.: University of Nebraska Press, 1962. Pp. 211–269.

———— Behavioral modification through modeling procedures. In L. Krasner & L. P. Ullmann (Eds.), *Research in behavior modification*. New York: Holt, Rinehart and Winston, 1965. Pp. 310–340. (a)

———— Influence of models' reinforcement contingencies on the acquisition of imitative responses. *Journal of Personality and Social Psychology*, 1965, **1**, 589–595. (b)

———— Social-learning theory of identificatory processes. In D. A. Goslin Glass (Ed.), *Handbook of socialization theory and research*. Chicago: Rand McNally, 1969. Pp. 213–262.

Bandura, A., Grusec, J. E., & Menlove, F. L. Vicarious extinction of avoidance behavior. *Journal of Personality and Social Psychology*, 1967, **5**, 16–23.

Bandura, A., & Huston, A. C. Identification as a process of incidental learning. *Journal of Abnormal and Social Psychology*, 1961, **63**, 311–318.

Bandura, A., & Kupers, C. J. The transmission of patterns of self reinforcement through modeling. *Journal of Abnormal and Social Psychology*, 1964, **69**, 1–9.

Bandura, A., & Rosenthal, T. L. Vicarious classical conditioning as a function of arousal level. *Journal of Personality and Social Psychology*, 1966, **3**, 54–62.

Bandura, A., & Walters, R. H. *Adolescent aggression*. New York: Ronald Press, 1959.

———— *Social learning and personality development*. New York: Holt, Rinehart and Winston, 1963.

Bangs, J. L., & Freidinger, A. Diagnosis and treatment of a case of hysterical aphonia in a thirteen year old girl. *Journal of Speech and Hearing Disease*, 1949, **14**, 312–317.

Bannister, D., Salmon, P., & Leiberman, D. M. Diagnosis-treatment relationships in psychiatry: A statistical analysis. *British Journal of Psychiatry*, 1964, **110**, 726–732.

Barber, T. X. Experimental analysis of "hypnotic" behavior: A review of recent empirical findings. *Journal of Abnormal Psychology*, 1965, **70**, 132–154.

Barber, T. X., & Hahn, K. W. Hypnotic induction and "relaxation." *Archives of General Psychiatry*, 1963, **8**, 295–300.

Barlow, D. H., Leitenberg, H., & Agras, S. W. Preliminary report on the experimental control of sexual deviation by manipulation of the US in covert sensitization. Paper presented at the Annual Meeting of the Eastern Psychological Association, Washington, D.C., April, 1968.

Barrett, B. H. Reduction in rate of multiple tics by free operant conditioning methods. *Journal of Nervous and Mental Disease*, 1962, **135**, 187–195.

Barron, F. Ego-strength scale which predicts response to psychotherapy. *Journal of Consulting Psychology*, 1953, **17**, 235–241.

Barry, H., Etheredge, E. E., & Miller, N. E. Counterconditioning and extinction fail to transfer from amobarbital to nondrug state. *Psychopharmacologia*, 1965, **8**, 150–156.

Barton, R. *Institutional neurosis*. Bristol, England: Wright, 1959.

Baruch, D. *How to discipline your children*. New York: Public Affairs Committee, 1945.

Battle, C. C., Imber, S. D., Hoehn-Saric, R., Stone, A. R., Nash, E. R., & Frank, J. D. Target complaints as criteria of improvement. *American Journal of Psychotherapy*, 1966, **1**, 184–192.

+ Bauer, R. A. The obstinate audience. *American Psychologist*, 1964, **19**, 319–328.

+ ⸺ Social psychology and the study of policy formation. *American Psychologist*, 1966, **21**, 933–942.

Beck, A. T., Ward, C. H., Mendelson, M., Mock, J. E., & Erbaugh, J. K. Reliability of psychiatric diagnoses: 2. A study of consistency of clinical judgments and ratings. *American Journal of Psychiatry*, 1962, **119**, 351–357.

⸺ Becker, H. S. *Outsiders: Studies in the sociology of deviance*. New York: Free Press, 1963.

Beech, H. R. The symptomatic treatment of writer's cramp. In H. J. Eysenck (Ed.), *Behaviour therapy and the neuroses*. London: Pergamon, 1960. Pp. 349–372.

⸺ Some theoretical and technical difficulties in the application of behaviour therapy. *Bulletin of the British Psychological Society*, 1963, **16**, 1–9.

Bekhterev, V. K. *General principles of human reflexology*. New York: International Publishers, 1932.

Belknap, I. *Human problems of a state mental hospital*. New York: McGraw-Hill, 1956.

Bellak, L., & Small, L. *Emergency psychotherapy and brief psychotherapy.* New York: Grune & Stratton, 1965.

Benjamin, J. Prediction and psychopathologic theory. In L. Jessner & E. Pavenstedt (Eds.), *Dynamic psychopathology in childhood,* New York: Grune & Stratton, 1959. Pp. 6–77.

Bentler, P. M. An infant's phobia treated with reciprocal inhibition therapy. *Journal of Child Psychology and Psychiatry,* 1962, **3,** 185–189.

Berenda, R. W. *The influence of the group on the judgements of children.* New York: Columbia University, Kings Crown Press, 1950.

Berger, S. M. Conditioning through vicarious instigation. *Psychological Review,* 1962, **69,** 450–466.

Bergin, A. E. Some implications of psychotherapy research for therapeutic practice. In G. E. Stollack, B. G. Guerney, and M. Rothberg (Eds.), *Psychotherapy research.* Chicago: Rand McNally, 1966. Pp. 118–129.

Bergsman, A. The urinary excretion of adrenaline and noradrenaline in some mental disorders. *ACTA Psychiatric et Neurologica Scandinova, Supplement, 133,* 1959, **34,** 1–82.

Beritoff, J. S. *Neural mechanisms of higher vertebrate behavior.* Boston: Little, Brown, 1965.

Berlin, J. I., & Wyckoff, B. The teaching of improved interpersonal relations through programmed instruction for two people working together. In E. C. Brown (Chmn.), Application of behavior analysis and programmed instruction to classification and change in complex social behavior patterns. Symposium presented at the Annual Meeting of the American Psychological Association, Philadelphia, 1963.

―――― Human relations training through dyadic programed instruction. Paper presented at the Annual Meeting of the American Personnel and Guidance Association Convention, Chicago, 1964.

Bettleheim, B. Children without parents. *New York Review of Books,* 1966, **7** (5), 12–15.

Betz, B. Experiences in research in psychotherapy with schizophrenic patients. In H. H. Strupp & L. Luborsky (Eds.), *Research in psychotherapy.* Vol. II. Washington, D.C.: American Psychological Association, 1962. Pp. 41–60.

Bevan, J. R. Learning theory applied to the treatment of a patient with obsessional ruminations. In H. J. Eysenck (Ed.), *Behaviour therapy and the neuroses.* New York: Pergamon Press, 1960. Pp. 165–169.

Bever, T. G., Fodor, J. A., & Weksel, W. Is linguistics empirical? *Psychological Review,* 1965, **72,** 493–500.

Beyme, F. Hyperesthesia of taste and touch treated by reciprocal inhibition. *Behaviour Research and Therapy,* 1964, **2,** 7–14.

Bijou, S. W. Experimental studies of child behavior, normal and deviant. In L. Krasner & L. P. Ullmann (Eds.), *Research in behavior modification.* New York: Holt, Rinehart and Winston, 1965. Pp. 59–81.

Bijou, S. W., & Baer, D. Child development I. New York: Appleton-Century-Crofts, 1961.

Birnbrauer, J. S., Bijou, S. W., Wolf, M. M., & Kidder, J. D. Programed instruction in the classroom. In L. P. Ullmann & L. Krasner (Eds.), Case studies in behavior modification. New York: Holt, Rinehart and Winston, 1965. Pp. 358–363. (a)

Birnbrauer, J. S., Wolf, M. M., Kidder, J. D., & Tague, C. E. Classroom behavior of retarded pupils with token reinforcement. Journal of Experimental Child Psychology, 1965, 2, 219–235. (b)

Birren, J. E., Cardon, P. V., Jr., & Phillips, S. L. Reaction time as a function of the cardiac cycle in young adults. Science, 1963, 140, 195–196.

Black, A. H. Cardiac conditioning in curarised dogs: The relationship between heart rate and skeletal behaviour. In W. F. Prokasy (Ed.), Classical conditioning: A symposium. New York: Appleton-Century-Crofts, 1965. Pp. 20–47.

Blackman, L. S., & Capobianco, R. J. An evaluation of programed instruction with the mentally retarded utilizing teaching machines. American Journal of Mental Deficiency, 1965, 70, 262–269.

Blake, B. G. The application of behaviour therapy to the treatment of alcoholism. Behaviour Research and Therapy, 1965, 3, 78–85.

———— A follow-up of alcoholics treated by behaviour therapy. Behaviour Research and Therapy, 1967, 5, 89–94.

Blakemore, C. B., Thorpe, J. G., Barker, J. C., Conway, C. G., & Lavin, N. I. The application of faradic aversion conditioning in a case of transvestism. Behaviour Research and Therapy, 1963, 1, 29–34. (a)

———— Follow-up note to: The application of faradic aversion conditioning in a case of transvestism. Behaviour Research and Therapy, 1963, 1, 191. (b)

Blau, P. M., & Scott, W. R. Formal organizations. San Francisco: Chandler, 1962.

Bloom, S. W. The doctor and his patient. New York: Russell Sage Foundation, 1963.

Blum, R., et al. Utopiates: The uses and abuses of L S D—25. New York: Atherton Press, 1964.

Blumer, H. Collective behavior. In A. M. Lee (Ed.), Principles of sociology. New York: Barnes & Noble, 1951. Pp. 165–222.

Bockoven, J. S. Moral treatment in American psychiatry. New York: Springer, 1963.

Bolgar, H. The case study method. In B. B. Wolman (Ed.), Handbook of clinical psychology. New York: McGraw-Hill, 1965. Pp. 28–39.

Bond, I. K., & Hutchison, H. C. Application of reciprocal inhibition therapy to exhibitionism. Canadian Medical Association Journal, 1960, 83, 23–25.

Bonvallet, M., Dell, P., & Hugelin, A. Influence de l'adrénaline sur le contrôle réticulaire des activités corticales et spinales, *Journal de Physiologie (Paris)*, 1954, **46**, 262–265. (a)

Bonvallet, M., Dell, P., & Hugelin, A. Tonus sympathique et activité electrique corticale. *EEG and Clinical Neurophysiology*, 1954, **6**, 119–144. (b)

Bordin, E. S. Simplification as a strategy for research in psychotherapy. *Journal of Consulting Psychology*, 1965, **29**, 493–503.

——— Curiosity, compassion, and doubt: The dilemma of the psychologist. *American Psychologist*, 1966, **21**, 116–121.

Bower, G. H. Application of a model to paired-associate learning. *Psychometrika*, 1961, **26**, 255–280.

Bowman, W. C., & Zaimis, E. The effects of adrenaline, noradrenaline and isoprenaline on skeletal muscle contractions in the cat, *Journal of Physiology (London)*, 1958, **144**, 92–107.

Brackbill, Y. The impairment of learning under immediate reinforcement. *Journal of Experimental Child Psychology*, 1964, **1**, 199–207.

Brackbill, Y. & O'Hara, J. The relative effectiveness of reward and punishment for discrimination learning in children. *Journal of Comparative and Physiological Psychology*, 1958, **51**, 747–751.

Brady, J. P. Brevital-relaxation treatment of frigidity. *Behaviour Research and Therapy*, 1966, **4**, 71–77.

Brady, J. P., & Lind, D. L. Experimental analysis of hysterical blindness. *Archives of General Psychiatry*, 1961, **4**, 331–339.

Breger, L., & McGaugh, J. L. Critique and reformulation of "learning theory" approaches to psychotherapy and neurosis. *Psychological Bulletin*, 1965, **63**, 338–358.

——— Learning theory and behavior therapy: A reply to Rachman and Eysenck. *Psychological Bulletin*, 1966, **65**, 170–173.

Brethower, D. M., & Reynolds, G. S. A facilitative effect of punishment on unpunished behaviour. *Journal of the Experimental Analysis of Behavior*, 1962, **5**, 191–199.

Bricker, W. H. Speech training with autistic and mentally retarded children. Paper presented at the Annual Convention of the Society for Research in Child Development, Minneapolis, Minn., 1965.

Bridger, W. H. Pavlovian concepts and human behavior. In W. H. Gantt (Ed.), *Physiological bases of psychiatry*. Springfield Ill.: Charles C Thomas, 1958. Pp. 96–111.

——— Contributions of conditioning principles to psychiatry. In *Pavlovian conditioning and American psychiatry*. (GAP Symposium No. 9.) New York: Group for the Advancement of Psychiatry. 1964. Pp. 181–198.

Bridger, W. H., & Mandel, I. A comparison of GSR fear response produced by threat and electric shock. *Journal of Psychiatric Research*, 1964, **2**, 31–40.

——— Abolition of the PRE by instructions in GSR conditioning. *Journal of Experimental Psychology*, 1965, **69**, 476–482.

Brill, A. A. Selected papers on hysteria and other psychoneuroses; Sigmund Freud. *Nervous and Mental Disease Monograph Series,* 1909, No. 4.

Brinkmann, E. H. Programed instruction as a technique for improving spatial visualization. *Journal of Applied Psychology,* 1966, **50,** 179–184.

Broadhurst, P. L. Abnormal animal behaviour. In H. J. Eysenck (Ed.), *Handbook of abnormal psychology.* London: Pitman Medical Publishers, 1960. Pp. 726–763.

Brodman, K., Van Woerkom, A. J., Erdmann, A. J., & Goldstein, L. S. Interpretation of symptoms with a data-processing machine. *Archives of Internal Medicine,* 1959, **103,** 776–782.

Bromberg, W. *The mind of man: A history of psychotherapy and psychoanalysis.* New York: Harper & Row, 1959.

Bronowski, J. The logic of the mind. *American Scientist,* 1966, **54,** 1–14.

Broudy, H. S. Teaching machines: Threats and promise. *Educational Theory,* 1962, **12,** 151–156.

Brough, D. I., Yorkston, N., & Stafford-Clark, D. A case of wasp phobia treated by systematic desensitization under light hypnosis. *Guy's Hospital Reports,* 1965, **114,** 319–324.

Brown, E. C., & Campbell, R. L. Programed interpersonal relationships improvement: Objective benefits to college students. *Journal of Programed Instruction,* 1966, **3,** 1–6.

Brown, F. Contributions of the psychodiagnostician to problems of therapy. *American Journal of Orthopsychiatry,* 1960, **30,** 811–818.

Brown, T. Characteristics of models and subjects that elicit a negative set in children. Unpublished M.S. thesis, University of Oregon, 1966.

Brozek, J. Recent developments in Soviet psychology. *Annual Review of Psychology,* 1964, **15,** 493–594.

———— Contemporary Soviet psychology. In Neil O'Connor (Ed.), *Present-day Russian psychology.* London: Pergamon Press, 1966. Pp. 178–198.

Buchwald, A. M. Extinction after acquisition under different verbal reinforcement combinations. *Journal of Experimental Psychology,* 1959, **57,** 43–48. (a)

———— Experimental alterations in the effectiveness of verbal reinforcement combinations. *Journal of Experimental Psychology,* 1959, **57,** 351–361. (b)

———— Supplementary report: alteration in the reinforcement value of a positive reinforcer. *Journal of Experimental Psychology,* 1960, **60,** 416–417.

———— The effects of immediate vs. delayed outcomes. *Journal of Verbal Learning and Verbal Behavior,* 1967, **6,** 317–320.

Buckley, N. Programed learning: Return to reality. *Dun's Review and Modern Industry,* 1964, **83,** 46, 123–129.

Buehler, R. E., Patterson, G. R., & Furniss, J. The reinforcement of behavior in institutional settings. *Behaviour Research and Therapy,* 1966, **4,** 157–167.

Burchard, J. D. A residential program of behavior modification. Paper presented at the Annual Meeting of the American Psychological Association, New York, September, 1966.

Burnett, A., & Ryan, E. Conditioning techniques in psychotherapy. *Canadian Psychiatric Association Journal*, 1964, **9**, 140–146.

Burnham, W. H. *The normal mind.* New York: Appleton, 1924.

Buss, A. H. *Psychopathology.* New York: Wiley, 1966.

Buss, A. H., & Lang, P. J. Psychological deficit in schizophrenia: I. Affect, reinforcement, and concept attainment. *Journal of Abnormal Psychology*, 1965, **70**, 2–24.

Bykov, K. M. *The cerebral cortex and the internal organs* (translated by W. H. Gantt). New York: Chemical Publishing, 1957.

Cahoon, D. D. Symptom substitution and the behavior therapies. *Psychological Bulletin*, 1968, **69**, 149–156.

Cahoon, D. D., & Watson, C. G. An experimental programed introduction to the vocational counseling process. *Journal of Clinical Psychology*, 1966, **22**, 354–356.

Cairns, R. B. Antecedents of social reinforcer effectiveness. USPHS Project Report M-4373, 1962.

——— Attachment behavior of mammals. *Psychological Review*, 1966, **73**, 409–426.

Calloway, E. Response speed, the EEG alpha cycle, and the autonomic cardiovascular cycle. In A. T. Welford & J. E. Birren (Eds.), *Behavior, aging and the nervous system.* Springfield Ill.: Charles C Thomas, 1965. Pp. 217–234.

Cameron, D. E., Levy, L., Ban, T., & Rubenstein, L. Automation of psychotherapy. *Comprehensive Psychiatry*, 1964, **5**, 1–14.

Cameron, N. Paranoid conditions and paranoia. In S. Arieti (Ed.), *American handbook of psychiatry.* Vol. 1, New York: Basic Books, 1959. Pp. 508–539.

Cameron, N., & Magaret, A. *Behavior pathology.* New York: Houghton Mifflin, 1951.

Cameron, W. B. *Modern social movements: A sociological outline.* New York: Random House, 1966.

Campbell, D., Sanderson, R. E., & Laverty, S. G. Characteristics of a conditioned response in human subjects during extinction trials following a single traumatic conditioning trial. *Journal of Abnormal and Social Psychology*, 1964, **68**, 627–639.

Campbell, D. T., & Stanley, J. C. Experimental and quasi-experimental designs for research on teaching. In N. L. Gage (Ed.), *Handbook of research on teaching.* Chicago: Rand McNally, 1963. Pp. 171–246.

——— *Experimental and quasi-experimental designs for research.* Chicago: Rand McNally, 1966.

Cantril, H. *The psychology of social movements.* New York: Wiley, 1941.

Capote, T. *In cold blood.* New York: Random House, 1965.

Caprio, F. S. *Female homosexuality.* New York: Citadel Press, 1954.

Carkhuff, R. R., & Truax, C. B. Lay mental health counseling: the effects of lay group counseling. *Journal of Consulting Psychology,* 1965, **29,** 426–431. (a)

────── Training in counseling and psychotherapy: An evaluation of an integrated didactic and experimental approach. *Journal of Consulting Psychology,* 1965, **29,** 333–336. (b)

Cartwright, D. S., Kirtner, W. L., & Fiske, D. W. Method factors in changes associated with psychotherapy. *Journal of Abnormal and Social Psychology,* 1963, **66,** 164–175.

Cartwright, R. D. Review of H. J. Eysenck (Ed.), Behavior therapy and the neuroses. *Contemporary Psychology,* 1963, **8,** 408–409.

Cautela, J. R. The application of learning theory "as a last resort" in the treatment of a case of anxiety neurosis. *Journal of Clinical Psychology,* 1965, **21,** 448–452. (a)

────── Desensitization and insight. *Behaviour Research and Therapy,* 1965, **3,** 59–64. (b)

────── Desensitization factors in the hypnotic treatment of phobias. *Journal of Psychology,* 1966, **64,** 277–288. (a)

────── A behavior therapy treatment of pervasive anxiety. *Behaviour Research and Therapy,* 1966, **4,** 99–109. (b)

────── Treatment of compulsive behavior by covert sensitization. *Psychological Record,* 1966, **16,** 33–41. (c)

────── Covert sensitization. *Psychological Record,* 1967, **20,** 459–468.

Cautela, J. R., & Kastenbaum, R. A reinforcement survey schedule for use in therapy, training and research. *Psychological Reports,* 1967, **20,** 1115–1130.

Centers, R. A laboratory adaptation of the conversational procedure for the conditioning of verbal operants. *Journal of Abnormal and Social Psychology,* 1963, **67,** 334–339.

Chapman, L. J. Illusory correlation in observational report. *Journal of Verbal Learning and Verbal Behavior,* 1967, **6,** 151–155.

Chapman, L. J., Chapman, J. P., & Miller, G. A. A theory of verbal behavior in schizophrenia. In B. A. Maher (Ed.), *Progress in experimental personality research.* Vol. I. New York: Academic Press, 1964. Pp. 49–77.

Charlesworth, R., & Hartup, W. W. Positive social reinforcement in the nursery school peer group. *Child Development,* 1967, **38,** 993–1002.

Chatterjee, B., & Eriksen, C. Cognitive factors in heart rate conditioning. *Journal of Experimental Psychology,* 1962, **64,** 272–279.

Chein, I. The image of man. *Journal of Social Issues,* 1962, **18,** 1–35.

Chittick, R. A., Eldred, D. M., & Brooks, G. W. The use of programed instruction with disturbed students. Waterbury, Vt.: Vermont State Hospital, June, 1964–May, 1965.

Chomsky, N. A review of B. F. Skinner's *Verbal behavior. Language*, 1959, **35**, 26–58.

Church, R. The varied effects of punishment. *Psychological Review*, 1963, **70**, 369–402.

Clark, D. F. The treatment of monosymptomatic phobia by systematic desensitization. *Behaviour Research and Therapy*, 1963, **1**, 63–68. (a)

—— The treatment of hysterical spasm and agoraphobia by behaviour therapy. *Behaviour Research and Therapy*, 1963, **1**, 245–250. (b)

Cohen, H. L. Educational therapy: The design of learning environments. In J. M. Shlien (Ed.), *Research in psychotherapy*. Vol. III. Washington, D.C.: American Psychological Association, 1968. Pp. 21–53.

Cohen, I. S. Programed learning and the Socratic dialogue. *American Psychologist*, 1962, **17**, 772–775.

Cohen, S., & Shmavonian, B. Catechol amines, vasomotor conditioning and aging. In L. Gitman (Ed.), *Endocrines and aging*, Baltimore: Williams and Wilkins, 1967. Pp. 102–141.

Colby, K. M. Psychotherapeutic processes. *Annual Review of Psychology*, 1964, **15**, 347–370.

Conger, J. J. Reinforcement theory and the dynamics of alcoholism. *Quarterly Journal of Studies on Alcohol.* 1956, **17**, 296–305.

Cook, S. W., & Harris, R. E. The verbal conditioning of the GSR. *Journal of Experimental Psychology*, 1937, **21**, 202–210.

Cooke, G. The efficacy of two desensitization procedures: An analogue study. *Behaviour Research and Therapy*, 1966, **4**, 17–24. (a)

—— *Identification of the efficacious components of reciprocal inhibition therapy.* Unpublished doctoral dissertation, University of Iowa, 1966. (b)

Cooper, A. J. A case of bronchial asthma treated by behaviour therapy. *Behaviour Research and Therapy*, 1964, **1**, 351–356.

Cooper, J. E. A study of behaviour therapy in thirty psychiatric patients. *Lancet*, 1963, **1**, 411–415.

Cooper, J. E., Gelder, M. G., & Marks, I. M. Results of behaviour therapy in 77 psychiatric patients. *British Medical Journal*, 1965, **1**, 1222–1225.

Coquery, J. M., & Lacey, J. I. The effect of foreperiod duration on the components of the cardiac response during the foreperiod of a reaction-time experiment. Paper presented at the Annual Meeting of the Society for Psychophysiological Research, Denver, Colo., October, 1966.

Costello, C. G. Behaviour therapy: Criticisms and confusions. *Behaviour Research and Therapy*, 1963, **1**, 159–161.

—— Lysergic acid diethylamide (LSD25) and behaviour therapy. *Behaviour Research and Therapy*, 1964, **2**, 117–129.

Coulson, J. E. (Ed.) *Programed learning and computer based instruction.* New York: Wiley, 1962.

Coulson, J. E., & Silberman, H. F. Effects of three variables in a teaching machine. *Journal of Educational Psychology,* 1960, **51,** 135–143.

Cowden, R. C., & Ford, L. I. Systematic desensitization with phobic schizophrenics. *American Journal of Psychiatry,* 1962, **119,** 241–245.

Crider, D., Shapiro, D., & Tursky, B. Reinforcement of spontaneous electrodermal activity. *Journal of Comparative and Physiological Psychology,* 1966, **61,** 20–27.

Cronbach, L. J. *Essentials of psychological testing,* (2d ed.) New York: Harper & Row, 1960.

Crowder, N. A. Intrinsically programed material for teaching complex skills and concepts. Paper presented at the Annual Meeting of the American Psychological Association, Washington, D.C., August, 1958.

Crutchfield, R. S., & Edwards, W. The effect of a fixated figure on autokinetic movement. *Journal of Experimental Psychology,* 1949, **39,** 561–578.

Cushing, M. C. Components of the response class as a factor in verbal conditioning. Unpublished doctoral dissertation, University of Nebraska, 1957.

Das, J. P. Conditioning and hypnosis. *Journal of Experimental Psychology,* 1958, **56,** 110–113. (a)

——— The Pavlovian theory of hypnosis: An evaluation. *Journal of Mental Science,* 1958, **104,** 82–90. (b)

Davidson, H. A. Discussion. In H. J. Eysenck (Ed.), *The effects of psychotherapy.* New York: International Science Press, 1966. Pp. 73–75.

Davison, G. C. A social learning therapy programme with an autistic child. *Behaviour Research and Therapy,* 1964, **2,** 149–159.

——— The influence of systematic desensitization, relaxation, and graded exposure to imaginal aversive stimuli on the modification of phobic behavior. Unpublished doctoral dissertation, Stanford University, 1965. (a)

——— Relative contributions of differential relaxation and graded exposure to in vivo desensitization of a neurotic fear. *Proceedings of the 73rd Annual Convention of the American Psychological Association,* 1965, **1,** 209–210. (b)

——— An intensive, long-term social-learning treatment program with an accurately diagnosed autistic child. *Proceedings of the 73rd Annual Convention of the American Psychological Association,* 1965, **1,** 203–204. (c)

——— The training of undergraduates as social reinforcers for autistic children. In L. P. Ullmann & L. Krasner (Eds.), *Case Studies in Behavior Modification.* New York: Holt, Rinehart and Winston, 1965. Pp. 146–148. (d)

——— Anxiety under total curarization: Implications for the role of muscular relaxation in the desensitization of neurotic fears. *Journal of Nervous and Mental Disease,* 1966, **143,** 443–448. (a)

―――― Differential relaxation and cognitive restructuring in therapy with a "paranoid schizophrenic" or "paranoid state." *Proceedings of the 74th Annual Convention of the American Psychological Association,* 1966,**2,** 177–178. (b)

―――― Elimination of a sadistic fantasy by a client-controlled counterconditioning technique: A case study. *Journal of Abnormal and Social Psychology,* 1968, **73,** 84–90. (a)

―――― Systematic desensitization as a counterconditioning process. *Journal of Abnormal Psychology,* 1968, 73, 91–99. (b)

Davison, G. C., & Krasner, L. Behavior therapy with an autistic child. 1964. 16mm film, Public Health Service Audiovisual Facility, Atlanta, Georgia. #MIS-895.

Dean, S. J. Implications of recent research on "classical" conditioning for the management of behavior. Paper presented at the meeting of the American Psychological Association, New York, 1966.

Dean, S. J., & Hiesinger, L. Operant level, awareness and the Greenspoon effect. *Psychological Reports,* 1964, **15,** 931–938.

Dejong, H. *Experimental catatonia,* Baltimore: Williams & Wilkins, 1943.

De Robertis, E. Morphological basis of synaptic processes and neuro secretion. In S. Kety & J. Elkes (Eds.), *Regional neuro chemistry,* London, Pergamon Press, 1961. Pp. 248–258.

Deterline, W. A. *An introduction to programed education.* Englewood Cliffs, N.J.: Prentice-Hall, 1962.

Deutsch, M., & Gerard, H. E. A study of normative and informational social influences upon individual judgment. *Journal of Abnormal and Social Psychology,* 1955, **51,** 629–636.

Devereux Foundation. Automation in vocational training of mentally retarded and/or mentally ill adolescents. In *Information Bulletin.* Devon, Pa.: Institute for Research and Training, 1964.

Diamond, S., Balvin, R. S., & Diamond, S. R. *Inhibition and choice.* New York: Harper & Row, 1963.

Dick, W. The development and current status of computer-based instruction. *American Educational Research Journal,* 1965, **2,** 41–53.

Diehm, D. F. A factor analytic study of psychotherapists. *Dissertation Abstracts,* 1962, **23,** 320–321.

Dingman, W., & Sporn, M. The incorporation of 8 azoguanine into rat brain RNA and its effects on maze learning by the rat, *Journal of Psychiatric Research,* 1961, **1,** 1–11.

Dinoff, M., Horner, R. F., Kurpiewski, B. S., & Timmons, E. O. Conditioning verbal behavior of schizophrenics in a group therapy-like situation. *Journal of Clinical Psychology,* 1960, **16,** 367–370.

Dinoff, M., Horner, R. F., Kurpiewski, B. S., Rickard, H. C., & Timmons, E. O.

Conditioning verbal behavior of a psychiatric population in a group therapy-like situation. *Journal of Clinical Psychology*, 1960, **16**, 371–372.

Dinsmoor, J. A. A discrimination based on punishment. *Quarterly Journal of Experimental Psychology*, 1952, **4**, 27–45.

——— Punishment: I. The avoidance hypothesis. *Psychological Review*, 1954, **61**, 34–46.

Dixon, P. W., & Oakes, W. F. Effect of intertrial activity on the relationship between awareness and verbal operant conditioning. *Journal of Experimental Psychology*, 1965, **69**, 152–157.

Dollard, J., & Miller, N. E. *Personality and psychotherapy.* New York: McGraw-Hill, 1950.

Dreikurs, R. The interpersonal relationship in hypnosis: Some fallacies in current thinking about hypnosis. *Psychiatry*, 1962, **25**, 219–226.

Drennen, W. T. Transfer of the effects of verbal conditioning. *Journal of Abnormal and Social Psychology*, 1963, **66**, 619–622.

Duffy, Elizabeth. *Activation and behavior.* New York: Wiley, 1962.

Duke, M. P., Frankel, A. S., Sipes, M., & Stewart, R. W. The effects of different kinds of models on interview behavior and feelings about an interview situation. Unpublished research, Indiana University, 1965.

Dulany, D. E., Jr. Hypotheses and habits in verbal "operant conditioning." *Journal of Abnormal and Social Psychology*, 1961, **63**, 251–263.

Duncker, K. Experimental modifications of children's food preferences through social suggestion. *Journal of Abnormal and Social Psychology*, 1938, **33**, 489–507.

Dunham, H. W., & Weinberg, S. K. *The culture of the state mental hospital.* Detroit: Wayne State University Press, 1960.

Dunlap, K. *Habits: Their making and unmaking.* New York: Liveright, 1932.

Ebner, M. An investigation of the role of the social environment in the generalization and persistence of the effect of a behavior modification program. Unpublished doctoral dissertation, University of Oregon, 1967.

Eccles, J. *The physiology of nerve cells,* Baltimore, Johns Hopkins Press, 1957.

Edwards, A. L. *Experimental design in psychological research.* (Rev. ed.) New York: Holt, 1960.

Edwards, A. L., & Cronbach, L. J. Experimental design for research in psychotherapy. *Journal of Clinical Psychology*, 1952, **8**, 51–59.

Ekman, P., & Friesen, W. V. The conditioning of hostile responses to photographs of peers. Paper presented at the Annual Meeting of the Eastern Psychological Association, 1960.

Elkes, J. Effects of psychosomimetic agents in animals and man. In H. A. Abramson (Ed.), *Neuropharmacology, Transactions of 3rd Conference.* New York: Josiah Macy Foundation, 1957. Pp. 205–295.

——— Drug effects in relation to receptor specificity within the brain. In G. E. W. Wolstonholme & C. M. O'Connor (Eds.), *Neurological basis of behavior. Ciba Foundation Symposia,* New York: 1958, pp. 303–332.

—————— Drugs influencing affect and behavior. Possible neural correlates in relation to mode of action. In A. Simon (Ed.), *The physiology of emotions*, Springfield, Ill.: Charles C Thomas, 1961. Pp. 95–149.

Emery, J. R., & Krumboltz, J. D. Standard versus individualized hierarchies in desensitization to reduce test anxiety. *Journal of Counseling Psychology*, 1967,**14**, 204–209.

Engel, B. T., & Hanson, S. P. Operant conditioning of heart rate slowing. *Psychophysiology*, 1966, **3**, 176–187.

Epperson, D. C., & Schmuck, R. A. An experimentalist critique of programed instruction. *Educational Theory*, 1962, **12**, 247–254.

Erickson, M. T. Effects of social deprivation and satiation on verbal conditioning in children. *Journal of Comparative and Physiological Psychology*, 1962, **55**, 953–957.

Eriksen, C. W. (Ed.) *Behavior and awareness*. Durham, N.C.: Duke University Press, 1962.

Estes, K. W. Some effects of reinforcement upon verbal behavior of children. Unpublished doctoral dissertation, University of Minnesota, 1945.

Estes, W. K. An experimental study of punishment. *Psychological Monographs*, 1944, 47 (Whole No. 263).

Estes, W. K., & Skinner, B. F. Some quantitative properties of anxiety. *Journal of Experimental Psychology*, 1941, **29**, 390–400.

Ewing, T. N. Changes during counseling appropriate to the client's initial problem. *Journal of Counseling Psychology*, 1964, **11**, 146–150.

Eysenck, H. J. The effects of psychotherapy: An evaluation. *Journal of Consulting Psychology*, 1952, **16**, 319–324.

—————— Learning theory and behaviour therapy. *Journal of Mental Science*, 1959, **105**, 61–75.

—————— (Ed.) *Behaviour therapy and the neuroses*. London: Pergamon Press, 1960. (a)

—————— Learning theory and behavior therapy. In H. J. Eysenck (Ed.), *Behaviour therapy and the neuroses*. London: Pergamon Press, 1960. (b)

—————— The effects of psychotherapy. In H. J. Eysenck (Ed.), *Handbook of abnormal psychology*. London: Pitman Medical Publishers, 1960. Pp. 697-725. (c)

—————— Conditioning and personality. *British Journal of Psychology*, 1962, **53**, 299–305.

—————— (Ed.) *Experiments with drugs*. Oxford: Pergamon Press, 1963.

—————— (Ed.) *Experiments in behaviour therapy*. New York: Macmillan, 1964.

—————— The effects of psychotherapy. *International Journal of Psychiatry*, 1965, **1**, 99–142. (a)

—————— The effects of psychotherapy: A reply. *International Journal of Psychiatry*, 1965, **1**, 328–335. (b)

———— Extraversion and the acquisition of eyeblink and GSR conditioned responses. *Psychological Bulletin*, 1965, **63**, 258–270. (c)

———— *Experiments in behaviour therapy.* London: Pergamon Press, 1965. (d)

———— *The effects of psychotherapy.* New York: International Science Press, 1966.

Eysenck, H. J., & Rachman, S. *The causes and cures of neurosis.* London: Routledge and Kegan Paul, 1965.

Fairweather, G. W. (Ed.) *Social psychology in treating mental illness.* New York: Wiley, 1964.

Farina, A., Arenberg, D., & Guskin, S. A scale for measuring minimal social behavior. *Journal of Consulting Psychology*, 1957, **21**, 265–268.

Farnsworth, K. E. Application of scaling techniques to the evaluation of counseling outcomes. *Psychological Bulletin*, 1966, **66**, 81–93.

Feldman, M. P. Aversion therapy for sexual deviations: A critical review. *Psychological Bulletin*, 1966, **65**, 65–79.

Feldman, M. P., & MacCulloch, M. J. The application of anticipatory avoidance learning to the treatment of homosexuality. I Theory, technique and preliminary results, *Behaviour Research and Therapy*, 1965, **2**, 165–183.

———— Personal communication, 1967.

Feldman, R. B., & Werry, J. S. An unsuccessful attempt to treat a tiqueur by massed practice. *Behaviour Research and Therapy*, 1966, **4**, 111–118.

Fenichel, O. *The psychoanalytic theory of neurosis.* New York: Norton, 1945.

Ferster, C. B. Positive reinforcement and behavioral deficits in autistic children. *Child Development*, 1961, **32**, 437–456.

———— Essentials of a science of behavior. In J. I. Nurnberger, C. B. Ferster, & J. P. Brady (Eds.), *An introduction to the science of human behavior.* New York: Appleton-Century-Crofts, 1963. Pp. 197–345.

———— Classification of behavioral pathology. In L. Krasner & L. P. Ullmann (Eds.), *Research in behavior modification.* New York: Holt, Rinehart and Winston, 1965. Pp. 6–26.

Ferster, C. B., & DeMyer, M. K. The development of performances in autistic children in an automatically controlled environment. *Journal of Chronic Diseases*, 1961, **13**, 312–345.

———— A method for the experimental analysis of the behavior of autistic children. *American Journal of Orthopsychiatry*, 1962, **32**, 89–98.

Ferster, C. B., Nurnberger, J. I., & Levitt, E. B. The control of eating. *Journal of Mathetics*, 1962, **1**, 87–110.

Ferster, C. B., & Skinner, B. F. *Schedules of reinforcement.* New York: Appleton-Century-Crofts, 1957.

Festinger, L. Laboratory experiments. In L. Festinger & D. Katz (Eds.), *Research methods in the behavioral sciences.* New York: Dryden Press, 1953. Pp. 136–172.

———— A theory of cognitive dissonance. Stanford: Stanford University Press, 1957.

Fiedler, F. E. The contingency model: A theory of leadership effectiveness. In H. Proshansky & B. Seidenberg (Eds.), *Basic studies in social psychology*. New York: Holt, Rinehart and Winson, 1965, 538–551.

Filby, Y., & Edwards, A. E. An application of automated teaching methods to test and teach form discrimination to aphasics. *Journal of Programed Instruction*, 1963, **2**, 25–33.

Finney, B. C. A scale to measure interpersonal relationships in group therapy. *Group Psychotherapy*, 1954, **7**, 52–66.

Fiske, D. W., Cartwright, D. S., & Kirtner, W. L. Are psychotherapeutic changes predictable? *Journal of Abnormal and Social Psychology*, 1964, **69**, 418–426.

Fiske, D. W., & Goodman, G. The posttherapy period. *Journal of Abnormal Psychology*, 1965, **70**, 169–179.

Flanagan, B., Goldiamond, I., & Azrin, N. Operant stuttering: The control of stuttering behavior through response-contingent consequences. *Journal of the Experimental Analysis of Behavior*, 1958, **1**, 173–177.

Folkins, C. H., Lawson, K. D., Opton, E. M., Jr., & Lazarus, R. S. Desensitization and the experimental reduction of threat. *Journal of Abnormal Psychology*, 1968, **73**, 100–113.

Ford, C. S. & Beach, F. A. *Patterns of sexual behaviour*. London: Eyre & Spottiswoode, 1952.

Ford, D. H. Research approaches to psychotherapy. *Journal of Counseling Psychology*, 1959, **6**, 55–60.

Ford, D. H., & Urban, H. B. Psychotherapy. In P. R. Farnsworth (Ed.), *Annual Review of Psychology*, 1967, **18**, 333–372.

Fox, L. Effecting the use of efficient study habits. *Journal of Mathetics*, 1962, **1**, 75–86.

Fox, R. Training for uncertainty. In R. K. Merton, G. S. Reader, & P. L. Kendall (Eds.), *The student-physician*. Cambridge, Mass: Harvard University Press, 1959. Pp. 207–241.

Frank, G. *The Boston strangler*. New York: New American Library, 1966.

Frank, G. H. The role of the family in the development of psychopathology. *Psychological Bulletin*, 1965, **64**, 191–205.

Frank, J. D. *Persuasion and healing*. Baltimore: Johns Hopkins Press, 1961.

———— Problems of controls in psychotherapy as exemplified by the psychotherapy research project of the Phipps Psychiatric Clinic. In E. A. Rubinstein & M. B. Parloff (Eds.), *Research in Psychotherapy*, Vol. I. Washington, D.C.: American Psychological Association, 1959. Pp. 10–26.

Frankl, V. E. Paradoxical intention: A logotherapeutic technique. *American Journal of Psychotherapy*, 1960, **14**, 520–535.

Franks, C. M. Alcohol, alcoholism and conditioning: A review of the literature and some theoretical considerations. *Journal of Mental Science,* 1958, **104,** 18–33.

——— Conditioning and abnormal behaviour. In H. J. Eysenck (Ed.), *Handbook of abnormal psychology.* New York Basic Books, 1960. Pp. 457–487.

——— Personality and eyeblink conditioning seven years later. *Acta Psychologica,* 1963, **21,** 295–312. (a)

——— Behavior therapy, the principles of conditioning and the treatment of the alcoholic. *Quarterly Journal of Studies on Alcohol,* 1963, 24, 511–529. (b)

——— (Ed.) *Conditioning techniques in clinical practice and research.* New York: Springer, 1964.

——— Behavior therapy, psychology and the psychiatrist: Contributions, evaluation and overview. *American Journal of Orthopsychiatry,* 1965, **35,** 145–151.

——— Clinical applications of conditioning and other behavioral techniques. *Conditional reflex,* 1966, **1,** 36–50. (a)

——— Conditioning and conditioned aversion therapies in the treatment of the alcoholic. *International Journal of the Addictions,* 1966, 1, 61–98. (b)

——— A longitudinal conditional eyeblink reflex study of four adult men. *Australian Journal of Psychology,* 1967, 19, 125–132. (a)

——— Reflections upon the treatment of sexual disorders by the behavioral clinician: an historical comparison with the treatment of the alcoholic. *Journal of Sex Research,* 1967, **3,** 212–222. (b)

——— The use of alcohol in the investigation of drug-personality postulates. In Ruth Fox (Ed.), *Alcoholism—Behavioral research, therapeutic approaches.* New York: Springer, 1967. Pp. 55–79. (c)

Franks, C. M. & Susskind, D. J. Behavior modification with children: rationale and technique. *Journal of School Psychology,* 1968, **6,** 75–88.

Franks, C. M., Susskind, D. J., & Franks, Violet. Behavior modification and the school psychologist. In M. G. Gottsegen & G. B. Gottsegen (Eds.), *Professional School Psychology.* Vol. III. New York: Grune & Stratton, 1969. Pp. 359–396.

Freedman, D. A. Various etiologies of the schizophrenic syndrome. *Diseases of the Nervous System,* 1958, **19,** 1–6.

Freeman, H. L., & Kendrick, D. C. A case of cat phobia (treatment by a method derived from experimental psychology). In: H. J. Eysenck (Ed.), *Experiments in behaviour therapy.* New York: Pergamon, 1964. Pp. 51–61.

Freeman, T. A psychoanalytic critique of behaviour therapy. *British Journal of Medical Psychology,* 1968, **41,** 53–59.

Freud, S. The justification for detaching from neurasthenia a particular syndrome: The anxiety neurosis [1894]. In S. Freud, *Collected papers volume 1*. London: Hogarth Press, 1924. Pp. 76–106.

—— The problem of anxiety [1926]. New York, Norton, 1936.

Freund, K. A laboratory method for diagnosing predominance of homo- or hetero-erotic interest in the male. *Behaviour Research and Therapy*, 1963, **1**, 85–93.

—— Diagnosing heterosexual pedophilia by means of a test for sexual interest. *Behaviour Research and Therapy*, 1965, **3**, 229–234.

Friedman, D. E. A new technique for the systematic desensitization of phobic symptoms. *Behaviour Research and Therapy*, 1966, **4**, 139–140. (a)

—— Treatment of a case of dog phobia in a deaf mute by behaviour therapy. *Behaviour Research and Therapy*, 1966, **4**, 141. (b)

Frolov, Y. P. *Pavlov and his school* (translated by C. P. Dutt). Fair Lawn, N.J.: Oxford University Press, 1937.

Frostig, M., & Horne, D. *The Frostig program for the development of visual perception*. Chicago: Fowlett Publishing Co., 1964.

Fulkerson, S. E., & Barry, J. R. Methodology and research on prognostic use of psychological tests. *Psychological Bulletin*, 1961, **58**, 177–204.

Fuller, P. R. Operant conditioning of a vegetative human organism. *American Journal of Psychology*, 1949, **62**, 587–590.

Gagné, R. M. Military training and principles of learning. *American Psychologist*, 1962, **17**, 83–91.

Gale, D. S., Sturmfels, G., & Gale, E. N. A comparison of reciprocal inhibition and experimental extinction in the therapeutic process. *Behaviour Research and Therapy*, 1966, **4**, 149–156.

Gantt, W. H. Psychosexuality in animals. *Psychosexual development in health and disease*. New York: Grune & Stratton, 1949.

—— The conditional reflex function as an aid in the study of the psychiatric patient. In P. H. Hoch & J. Zubin (Eds.), *Relation of psychological tests to psychiarty*, New York: Grune & Stratton, 1950. Pp. 165–188.

—— *Physiological bases of psychiatry*. Springfield, Ill.: Charles C Thomas, 1958.

—— Ivan Petrovich Pavlov. In Joseph Wortis (Ed.), *Recent advances in biological psychiatry*. Vol. IV. New York: Plenum Press, 1962. Pp. 3–12.

—— Autonomic conditioning. In J. Wolpe, A. Salter, & L. J. Reyna, (Eds.), *The conditioning therapies*. New York: Holt, 1964. Pp. 115–126.

—— Conditional or conditioned, reflex or response? *Conditional Reflex*, 1966, **1**, 69–73.

—— Pavlovian, classical conditional reflex—a classical error? *Conditional Reflex*, 1967, **2**, 255–257.

Garvey, W. P., & Hegrenes, J. R. Desensitization techniques in the treatment of school phobia. *American Journal of Orthopsychiatry*, 1966, **36**, 147–152.

Gedye, J. L. & Wedgewood, Y. Experience in the use of a teaching machine for the assessment of senile mental changes. Paper presented at the Seventh International Congress of Gerontology, Vienna, 1966.

Geer, J. H. Phobia treated by reciprocal inhibition. *Journal of Abnormal and Social Psychology,* 1964, **69,** 642–645.

Geer, J. H., & Katkin, E. S. Treatment of insomnia using a variant of systematic desensitization: A case report. *Journal of Abnormal Psychology,* 1966, **71,** 161–164.

Geer, J. H., & Silverman, I. The treatment of a recurrent nightmare by behavior modification procedures: A case study. *Journal of Abnormal Psychology,* 1967, **72,** 188–190.

Geer, J. H., & Turteltaub, A. Fear reduction following observation of a model. *Journal of Personal and Social Psychology,* 1967, **6,** 327–331.

Gelber, H., & Meyer, V. Behaviour therapy and encopresis: The complexities involved in treatment. *Behaviour Research and Therapy,* 1965, **2,** 227–231.

Gelder, M. G. Assessment of behaviour therapy. *Proceedings of the Royal Society of Medicine,* 1965, **58,** 525–529.

———— Desensitization and psychotherapy research. *British Journal of Medical Psychology,* 1968, **41,** 39–46.

Gelder, M. G., & Marks, I. M. Severe agoraphobia: a controlled prospective trial of behaviour therapy. *British Journal of Psychiatry,* 1966, **112,** 309–319.

Gelder, M. G., Marks, I. M., Sakinofsky, I., & Wolff, H. H. Behaviour therapy and psychotherapy for phobic disorders, alternative or complementary procedures? Paper presented at the Sixth International Congress of Psychotherapy, London, August, 1964.

Gelder, M. G., Marks, I. M., & Wolff, H. H. Desensitization and psychotherapy in the treatment of phobic states: A controlled inquiry. *British Journal of Psychiatry,* 1967, **113,** 53–73.

Gelfand, D. M., & Hartmann, D. P. Behavior therapy with children: a review and evaluation of research methodology. *Psychological Bulletin,* 1968, **69,** 204–215.

Gellhorn, E. *Physiologic foundations of neurology and psychiatry.* Minneapolis, University of Minnesota Press, 1953.

———— Motion and emotion: the role of proprioception in the physiology and pathology of the emotions. *Psychological Review,* 1964, **71,** 457–472.

———— *Autonomic-somatic integration.* Minneapolis: University of Minnesota Press, 1967.

Gellhorn, E., Ballin, H. M., & Kawakami, M. Studies on experimental convulsions with emphasis on the role of the hypothalamus and the reticular formation, *Epilepsia,* 1960, **1,** 233–254.

Gericke, O. L. Practical use of operant conditioning procedures in a mental hospital. *Psychiatric Studies and Projects,* 1965, **3,** 2–10.

Gewirtz, J. L., & Baer, D. M. Deprivation and satiation of social reinforcers as drive conditions. *Journal of Abnormal and Social Psychology*, 1958, **57,** 165–172.

Gewirtz, J. L., & Gewirtz, H. B. Stimulus conditions, infant behaviors and social learning in four Israeli child rearing environments: a preliminary report illustrating differences in environment and behavior between the "only" and the "youngest" child. In B. M. Foss, (Ed.), *Determinants of infant behavior.* Vol. III. London: Methuen, 1965. Pp. 161–186.

Gibb, C. A. Leadership. In G. Lindzey (Ed.), *Handbook of social psychology.* Vol. II. Cambridge, Mass.: Addison-Wesley, 1954. Pp. 877–920.

Gilbert, T. F. Mathetics: The technology of education. *Journal of Mathetics,* 1962, **1,** 7–73.

Giles, D. K., & Wolf, M. M. Toilet training institutionalized, severe retardates: An application of operant behavior modification techniques. *American Journal of Mental Deficiency,* 1966, **70,** 766–780.

Glaser, R. Implications of training research for education. In E. R. Hilgard (Ed.), *Theories of learning and instruction.* Chicago: University of Chicago Press, 1964. Pp. 153–181.

Glass, B. *Science and ethical values.* Chapel Hill, N.C.: University of North Carolina Press, 1965.

Glasscote, R. M., Cumming, E., Hammersley, D. W., Ozarin, L. D., & Smith, L. H. *The psychiatric emergency.* Washington, D.C.: Joint Information Service, 1966.

Glasser, W. *Reality therapy, a new approach to psychiatry.* New York, Harper & Row, 1965.

Glick, B. S. Conditioning therapy by an analytic therapist. *Archives of General Psychiatry,* 1967, **17,** 577–583.

Glover, E., Fenichel, O., Strachey, J., Bergler, E., Nunberg, N., & Bibring, E. Symposium on the theory of the therapeutic results of psychoanalysis. *International Journal of Psychoanalysis,* 1937, 18, 125–189.

Goffman, E. *Asylums.* New York: Doubleday, 1961.

Gold, S., & Neufeld, I. A learning theory approach to the treatment of homosexuality. *Behaviour Research and Therapy,* 1965, 2, 201–204.

Goldfried, M. R., & Pomeranz, D. Role of assessment in behavior modification. *Psychological Reports,* 1968, **23,** 75–87.

Goldiamond, I. Perception. In A. J. Bachrach (Ed.), *Experimental foundations of clinical psychology.* New York: Basic Books, 1962. Pp. 280–340.

—— Justified and unjustified alarm over behavioral control. In Ohmer Milton (Ed.), *Behavior disorders: Perspectives and trends,* Philadelphia: Lippincott, 1965, Pp. 237–261. (a)

—— Self control procedures in personal behavior problems. *Psychological Reports,* 1965, **17,** 851–868. (b)

—— Stuttering and fluency as manipulatable operant response classes. In

L. Krasner & L. P. Ullmann (Eds.), *Research in behavior modification.* New York: Holt, Rinehart and Winston, 1965. Pp. 106–156. (c)

Goldiamond, I., Dyrud, J. E., & Miller, M. D. Practice as research in professional psychology. *Canadian Psychologist,* 1965, **6a,** 110–128.

Goldiamond, I., & Hawkins, W. F. Vexierversuch: The log relationship between word-frequency and recognition obtained in the absence of stimulus words. *Journal of Experimental Psychology,* 1958, **56,** 457–463.

Goldstein, A. P. *Therapist-patient expectancies in psychotherapy.* New York: Pergamon Press, 1962.

——— Psychotherapy research by extrapolation from social psychology. In Goldstein, A. P., & Dean, S. J. *The investigation of psychotherapy.* New York: Wiley, 1966. Pp. 36–42.

Goldstein, A. P., & Dean, S. J. *The investigation of psychotherapy: Commentaries and readings.* New York: Wiley, 1966.

Goldstein, A. P., Gassner, S., Greenberg, R., Gustin, A., Land, J., Liberman, B., & Streiner, D. The use of planted patients in group psychotherapy. *American Journal of Psychotherapy,* 1967, **21,** 767–773.

Goldstein, A. P., Heller, K., & Sechrest, L. B. *Psychotherapy and the psychology of behavior change.* New York: Wiley, 1966.

Gordon, M. (Ed.) *Psychopharmacological agents.* Vol. I. New York: Academic Press, 1964.

Gottschalk, L. A., & Auerbach, A. H. (Eds.) *Methods of research in psychotherapy.* New York: Appleton-Century-Crofts, 1966.

Gouldner, A. Anti-minotaur: The myth of a value-free sociology. *Social Problems,* 1962, **9,** 199–213.

Graham, D. T., Kabler, J. D., & Graham, F. K. Physiological response to the suggestion of attitudes specific for hives and hypertension. *Psychosomatic Medicine,* 1962, **24,** 159–169.

Graham, S. R. The influence of therapist character structure upon Rorschach changes in the course of psychotherapy. *American Psychologist,* 1960, **15,** 415 (Abstract).

Grastyan, E. The hippocampus and higher nervous activity. In Molly Brazier (Ed.), *Second Conference on the central nervous system and behavior.* New York: Josiah Macy Foundation, 1959. Pp. 119–205.

Gray, B. B., England, G., & Mohoney, J. L. Treatment of benign vocal nodules by reciprocal inhibition. *Behaviour Research and Therapy,* 1965, **3,** 187–193.

Gray, J. A. (Ed.) *Pavlov's typology: recent theoretical and experimental developments from the laboratory of B. M. Teplov.* London: Pergamon Press, 1964.

——— Attention, consciousness and voluntary control of behaviour in Soviet psychology: Philosophical roots and research branches. In N. O'Connor (Ed.), *Present-day Russian psychology.* London: Pergamon Press, 1966. Pp. 1–38.

——— Strength of the nervous system, introversion-extraversion, condition-ability and arousal. *Behaviour Research and Therapy,* 1967, **5**, 151–169.

Graziano, A. M., & Kean, J. E. Programmed relaxation and reciprocal inhibition with psychotic children. *Proceedings of the 75th Annual Meeting of the American Psychological Association, Washington, D.C.,* 1967, **3**, 253–254.

Greenhouse, S. W. Principles in the evaluation of therapies for mental disorders. In P. H. Hoch, & J. Zubin (Eds.), *The evaluation of psychiatric treatment.* New York: Grune & Stratton, 1964. Pp. 94–106.

Greenspoon, J. The effect of verbal and non-verbal stimuli on the frequency of members of two verbal response classes. Unpublished doctoral dissertation, Indiana University, 1951.

——— The effect of two nonverbal stimuli on the frequency of members of two verbal response classes. *American Psychologist,* 1954, **9**, 384.

——— The reinforcing effect of two spoken sounds on the frequency of two responses. *American Journal of Psychology,* 1955, **68**, 409–416.

——— Verbal conditioning and clinical psychology. In A. J. Bachrach (Ed.), *Experimental foundations of clinical psychology.* New York: Basic Books, 1962. Pp. 510–553.

Greenwald, H. *The call girl.* New York: Ballantine Books, 1958.

Grindee, K. T. Operant conditioning of "attending behaviors" in the classroom for two hyperactive Negro children. Unpublished manuscript, Reed College, 1964.

——— Operant conditioning of attending behavior in the classroom: A case study. Unpublished B.A. thesis, Reed College, 1965.

Grings, W. Verbal-perceptual factors in the conditioning of autonomic responses. In W. Prokasy (Ed.), *Classical conditioning.* New York: Appleton-Century-Crofts, 1965. Pp. 71–89.

Grings, W., & Lockhart, R. Effects of "anxiety-lessening" instructions and differential set development on the extinction of GSR. *Journal of Experimental Psychology,* 1963, **66**, 292–299.

Grossberg, J. M. Behavior therapy: A review. *Psychological Bulletin,* 1964, **62**, 73–88.

——— Successful behavior therapy in a case of speech phobia ("stage fright"). *Journal of Speech and Hearing Disorders,* 1965, **30**, 285–288.

——— The physiological effectiveness of brief training in differential muscle relaxation. Technical Report No. IX, Western Behavioral Sciences Institute, Inc., La Jolla, Calif., 1965.

Grosz, H. J., & Zimmerman, J. Experimental analysis of hysterical blindness. *Archives of General Psychiatry,* 1965, 13, 255–260.

Group for the Advancement of Psychiatry (GAP). *Pavlovian conditioning and American psychiatry.* New York: Symposium No. 9, 1964.

Guthrie, E. R. *The psychology of learning.* (Rev. ed.) New York: Harper, 1952.

——— *The psychology of human conflict.* Boston: Beacon Press, 1962.

Guze, S. B., Matarazzo, J. D., & Saslow, G. Formulation of principles of comprehensive medicine with special reference to learning theory. *Journal of Clinical Psychology*, 1953, **9**, 127–136.

Hagen, J. M. The conditioning of vebal affect responses in two hospitalized schizophrenic diagnostic groups during the clinical interview. Unpublished doctoral dissertation, University of Washington, 1959.

Hain, J. D., Butcher, R. H. G., & Stevenson, I. Systematic desensitization therapy: an analysis of results in twenty-seven patients. *British Journal of Psychiatry*, 1966, **112**, 295–307.

Haley, J. *Strategies of psychotherapy*. New York: Grune & Stratton, 1963.

Hallsten, E. E. Adolescent anorexia nervosa treated by desensitization. *Behaviour Research and Therapy*, 1965, **3**, 87–91.

Hammersley, D. W. Conditioned reflex therapy. In R. S. Wallerstein (Ed.), *Hospital treatment of alcoholism. Menninger Clinic Monographs*, 1957, **11**, 11–18.

Hammock, J. C. Programing principles at work. Paper presented at the Fall Conference and Workshop, Atlanta Chapter of National Society for Programed Instruction, Dec. 5, 1964.

Hansen, L. F. (Ed.) *Programs, 1963: A guide to programed instruction materials available to educators*. Washington, D.C. U.S. Government Printing Office, 1963.

Harlow, H. F. *The development of patterns of affection*. Salmon Lectures, 1960, Springfield, Ill.: Charles C Thomas, 1961.

———— Basic social capacity of primates. In C. H. Southwick (Ed.), *Primate social behavior*. New York: Van Nostrand, 1963. Pp. 153–160.

Harris, A. M. Differences between severely retarded children and normal children in the frequencies of peer interaction, adult interaction and nonsocial behavior. Unpublished M.S. thesis, University of Oregon, 1966.

Harris, C. W. (Ed.), *Problems in measuring change*. Madison, Wis.: University of Wisconsin Press, 1963.

Harris, F. R., Johnston, M. K., Kelley, C. S., & Wolf, M. M. Effects of positive social reinforcement on regressed crawling of a nursery school child. *Journal of Educational Psychology*, 1964, **55**, 35–41.

Hart, B. M., Allen, K. E., Buell, J. S., Harris, F. R., & Wolf, M. M. Effects of social reinforcement on operant crying. *Journal of Experimental Child Psychology*, 1964, **1**, 145–153.

Hart, H. L. A. *Law, liberty, and morality*. New York: Random House, Vintage Books, 1966.

Hart, J. D. Fear reduction as a function of the assumption and success of a therapeutic role. Unpublished master's thesis, University of Wisconsin, 1966.

Hartman, K. B. Unconventional psychotherapy: Treatment by reciprocal inhibition. *S K & F Psychiatric Reporter*, 1966, **27** (July–August), 13–16.

Haslam, M. T. The treatment of psychogenic dyspareunia by reciprocal inhibition. *British Journal of Psychiatry,* 1965, **111,** 280–282.

Hastorf, A. H. The "reinforcement" of individual actions in a group situation. In L. Krasner & L. P. Ullmann (Eds.), *Research in behavior modification.* New York: Holt, Rinehart and Winston, 1965. Pp. 268–284.

Haughton, E., & Ayllon, T. Production and elimination of symptomatic behavior. In L. P. Ullmann & L. Krasner (Eds.), *Case studies in behavior modification.* New York: Holt, Rinehart and Winston, 1965. Pp. 94–98.

Hawkins, H. L. Imitative learning in therapy groups comprised of chronic schizophrenic patients. Unpublished M.A. thesis, University of Oregon, March, 1964.

Hawkins, R. P., Peterson, R. F., Schweid, E. J., & Bijou, S. W. Behavior therapy in the home: Amelioration of problem parent-child relations with the parent in a therapeutic role. *Journal of Experimental Child Psychology,* 1966, **4,** 99–107.

Hebb, D. O. Spontaneous neurosis in chimpanzees: Theoretical relations with clinical and experimental phenomena. *Psychosomatic Medicine,* 1947, **4,** 3–16.

———— *Organization of behavior.* New York: Wiley, 1949.

———— Heredity and environment in behavior. *British Journal of Animal Behaviour,* 1953, **1,** 43–47.

Heberle, R. *Social movements.* New York: Appleton-Century-Crofts, 1951.

Hecktor, O., & Halkerston, I. On the nature of macromolecular coding in neuronal memory. *Perspectives in Biology and Medicine,* 1904, **VII,** 183–198.

Hefferline, R. F. Learning theory and clinical psychology—an eventual symbiosis? In A. J. Bachrach (Ed.), *Experimental foundations of clinical psychology.* New York: Basic Books, 1962. Pp. 97–138.

Heller, K. A broader perspective for interview therapy. Paper presented at the Annual Meeting of the Midwestern Psychological Association, Chicago, 1965.

———— Ambiguity in the interview interaction. In J. M. Shlien (Ed.) *Research in psychotherapy.* Vol. III. Washington: American Psychological Association, 1968. Pp. 242–259.

Heller, K., Davis, J. D., & Myers, R. A. The effects of interviewer style in a standardized interview. *Journal of Consulting Psychology,* 1966, **30,** 501–508.

Heller, K., Myers, R. A., & Kline, L. V. Interviewer behavior as a function of standardized client roles. *Journal of Consulting Psychology,* 1963, **27,** 117–122.

Hendershot, C. H. *Programed learning: A bibliography of programed and presentation devices,* (3d ed.) Cleveland, Miss.: Delta College, 1964.

Henderson, L. J. Physician and patient as a social system. *New England Journal of Medicine,* 1935, **212,** 819–823.

Henker, B. A. The effect of adult model relationships on children's play and task imitation. *Dissertation Abstracts*, 1964, **24**, 47–49.

Herman, R. C., & Azrin, N. H. Punishment by noise in an alternative response situation. *Journal of the Experimental Analysis of Behavior*, 1964, **7**, 185–188.

Herzberg, A. Short treatment of neuroses by graduated tasks. *British Journal of Medical Psychology*, 1941, **19**, 36–51.

Hess, E. H., Seltzer, A. L., & Shlien, J. M. Pupil response of hetero and homosexual males to pictures of men and women: A pilot study. *Journal of Abnormal Psychology*, 1965, **70**, 165–169.

Hewett, F. M. Teaching speech to an autistic child through operant conditioning. *American Journal of Orthopsychiatry*, 1965, **35**, 927–936.

Hildum, D. C., & Brown, R. W. Verbal reinforcement and interviewer bias. *Journal of Abnormal Psychology*, 1956, **53**, 108–111.

Hilgard, E. R. Experimental approaches to psychoanalysis. In E. Pumpian-Mindlin (Ed.), *Psychoanalysis as science*, Stanford, Calif., Stanford University Press, 1952. Pp. 3–45.

———— *Theories of learning*. New York: Appleton-Century-Crofts, 1956.

———— *Hypnotic susceptibility*. New York: Harcourt, Brace & World, 1965.

Hilgard, E. R., & Bower, G. H. *Theories of learning*. New York: Appleton-Century-Crofts, 1966. Pp. 541–584.

Hingtgen, J. N., Sanders, B. J., & De Myer, M. K. Shaping cooperative responses in early childhood schizophrenics. In L. P. Ullmann & L. Krasner (Eds.), *Case studies in behavior modification*. New York: Holt, Rinehart and Winston, 1965. Pp. 130–138.

Hnatiow, M., & Lang, P. J. Learned stabilization of cardiac rate. *Psychophysiology*, 1965, **1**, 330–336.

Hobbs, N. Sources of gain in psychotherapy. *American Psychologist*, 1962, **17**, 741–747.

Hoch, P. H. Methods of evaluating various types of psychiatric treatments: Discussion. In P. H. Hoch & J. Zubin (Eds.), *The evaluation of psychiatric treatment*. New York: Grune & Stratton, 1964. Pp. 52–57.

Hoch, P. H., & Zubin, J. (Eds.) *Anxiety*. New York: Grune & Stratton, 1950.

———— (Eds.), *The evaluation of psychiatric treatment*. New York: Grune & Stratton, 1964.

Hogan, R. A. Implosive therapy in the short-term treatment of psychotics. *Psychotherapy: Theory, Research, and Practice*, 1966, **3**, 25–32.

Hohman, G. W. Some effects of spinal cord lesions on experienced emotional feelings. *Psychophysiology*, 1966, **3**, 143–156.

Holland, J. G. Human vigilance. *Science*, 1958, **128**, 61–67.

Holland, J. G., & Skinner, B. F. *The analysis of behavior*. New York: McGraw-Hill, 1961.

Hollender, M. H. Selection of patients for definitive forms of psychotherapy. *Archives of General Psychiatry*, 1964, **10**, 361–369.

Hollingshead, A. R., & Redlich, F. C. *Social class and mental illness: A community study.* New York: Wiley, 1958.

Holly, D. *Principles of behavior.* New York: Appleton-Century-Crofts, 1943.

Holt, R. R. Experimental methods in clinical psychology. In B. B. Wolman, (Ed.), *Handbook of clinical psychology.* New York: McGraw-Hill, 1965. Pp. 40–77.

Holz, W. C., & Azrin, N. H. Conditioning human verbal behavior. In W. K. Honig (Ed.), *Operant behavior: Areas of research and application.* New York: Appleton-Century-Crofts, 1966. Pp. 790–826.

Holz, W. C., Azrin, N. H., & Ayllon, T. Elimination of behavior of mental patients by response-produced extinction. *Journal of the Experimental Analysis of Behavior,* 1963, **6,** 407–412.

Holzman, M. The significance of the value systems of patient and therapist for the outcome of psychotherapy. Unpublished doctoral dissertation, University of Washington, 1961.

Homme, L. E. Perspectives in psychology—XXIV: Control of coverants, the operants of the mind. *Psychological Record,* 1965, **15,** 501–511.

Honig, W. K. (Ed.) *Operant behavior: Areas of research and application.* New York: Appleton-Century-Crofts, 1966.

Hoppock, R. What is the "real" problem? *American Psychologist,* 1953, **8,** 124.

Hotchkiss, J. The modification of maladaptive behavior of a class of educationally handicapped children by operant conditioning techniques. Unpublished doctoral dissertation, University of Southern California, 1966.

Hough, J. B. A study of the use of Human Development Institute programs for improving the human relations skills of pre-service teachers: A pilot study. (Mimeographed.) Columbus, Ohio: Author, undated.

Hovland, C. I. Reconciling conflicting results derived from experimental and survey studies of attitude change. *American Psychologist,* 1959. **14,** 8–17.

Hsu, J. Electroconditioning therapy of alcoholics: A preliminary report. *Quarterly Journal of Studies on Alcohol.* 1965, **26,** 449–459.

Hugo, F. G. Conforming behavior in two groups of adolescent children and its relation to certain parental attitudes and personality characteristics. Unpublished doctoral dissertation, Cornell University, 1956.

Hull, C. L. *Principles of behavior.* New York: Appleton-Century-Crofts, 1943.

Human Development Institute: General Relationship Improvement Program. (3d ed.) Atlanta: Human Development Institute, 1963.

Hunt, H. F. Problems in the interpretation of "experimental neurosis." *Psychological Reports,* 1964, **15,** 27–35.

Hunt, H. F., & Brady, J. V. Some effects of punishment and intercurrent anxiety on a simple operant. *Journal of Comparative Physiological Psychology,* 1955, **48,** 305–310.

Hunt, H. F., & Dyrud, J. E. Commentary: Perspective in behavior therapy. In J. M. Shlien (Ed.), *Research in psychotherapy, Volume III.* Washington, D.C.: *American Psychological Association,* 1968. Pp. 140–152.

Hunt, J. McV. Toward an integrated program of research on psychotherapy. *Journal of Consulting Psychology*, 1952, **16**, 237–246.

Hussain, A. Behavior therapy using hypnosis. In J. Wolpe, A. Salter, & L. J. Reyna (Eds.), *The conditioning therapies*. New York: Holt, Rinehart and Winston, 1964. Pp. 54–61.

Hutchinson, R. R., & Azrin, N. H. Conditioning of mental-hospital patients to fixed-ratio schedules of reinforcement. *Journal of the Experimental Analysis of Behavior*, 1961, **4**, 87–95.

Hyman, R., & Berger, L. Discussion. In H. J. Eysenck (Ed.), *The effects of psychotherapy*. New York: International Science Press, 1966. Pp. 81–86.

Insko, C. A. Verbal reinforcement of attitude. *Journal of Personality and Social Psychology*, 1965, **2**, 621–623.

Isaacs, W., Thomas, J., & Goldiamond, I. Application of operant conditioning to reinstate verbal behavior in psychotics. *Journal of Speech and Hearing Disorders*, 1960, **25**, 8–12.

Ivanov-Smolensky, A. G. On the methods of examining the conditioned food reflexes in children and in mental disorders. *Brain*, 1927, **50**, 138–141.

Jackson, D. D. *Etiology of schizophrenia*, New York: Basic Books, 1960.

Jacobs, P. I., Maier, M. H., & Stolurow, L. M. *A guide to evaluating self-instructional programs*. New York: Holt, 1966.

Jacobson, E. *Progressive relaxation*. Chicago: University of Chicago Press, 1938.

Jacobson, E. A. The influence of instructional set and model characteristics on the interview behavior of high and low dependent subjects. Unpublished doctoral dissertation, Indiana University, 1968.

Jakubczak, L. F., & Walters, R. H. Suggestibility as dependency behavior. *Journal of Abnormal and Social Psychology*, 1959, **59**, 102–107.

James, C. E. Operant conditioning in the management and behavior of hyperactive children: Five case studies. Unpublished paper, Orange State College, 1965.

Janis, I., Hovland, C., Field, P., Linton, H., Graham, E., Cohen, A., Ruge, D., Abelson, R., Lesser, G. S., & King, S. *Personality and persuasibility*. New Haven, Conn.: Yale University Press, 1959.

Jensen, R. R. Teaching machines and individual differences. *Automated Teaching Bulletin*, 1960, **1**, 12–17.

Jessor, S. G. The effects of reinforcement and the distribution of practice on psychological satiation. Unpublished doctoral dissertation, Ohio State University, 1951.

Johnson, S. M. The effects of desensitization and relaxation in the treatment of test anxiety. Unpublished master's thesis, Northwestern University, 1966.

Johnston, M. K., Kelley, C. S., Harris, F. R., & Wolf, M. M. An application of reinforcement principles to development of motor skills of a young child. *Child Development,* 1966, **37,** 379–387.

Jones, E. The psycho-analytic method of treatment. *Journal of Nervous and Mental Disease,* 1910, **37,** 285–295.

Jones, H. G. The behavioural treatment of enuresis nocturna. In H. J. Eysenck (Ed.), *Behaviour therapy and the neuroses.* London: Pergamon Press, 1960. Pp. 377–403.

Jones, M. C. A laboratory study of fear: The case of Peter. *Pedagogical Seminary,* 1924, **31,** 308–315. (a)

———— The elimination of children's fears. *Journal of Experimental Psychology,* 1924, **7,** 382–390. (b)

Jones, N., Kahn, M., & Wolcott, O. Wearing of street clothing by mental hospital personnel. *International Journal of Social Psychiatry,* 1964, **10,** 216–222.

Jones, R. B. Parent-child interaction in two cases of early infantile autism. Unpublished Master's thesis, University of Oregon, 1965.

Jourard, S. M. *The transparent self.* Princeton, N.J.: Van Nostrand, 1964.

Kahn, M., & Quinlan, P. Desensitization with varying degrees of therapist contact. Paper presented at the Annual Meeting of the Association for the Advancement of Behavior Therapy, Washington, D.C., Sept. 3, 1967.

Kalish, H. I. Behavior therapy. In B. B. Wolman (Ed.), *Handbook of clinical psychology.* New York: McGraw-Hill, 1965. Pp. 1230–1253.

Kamiya, J. Personal communication, October, 1966.

Kamman, G. F., Lucero, R. J., Meyer, B. T., & Rechtschaffen, A. Critical evaluation of a total push program for regressed schizophrenics in a state hospital. *Psychiatric Quarterly,* 1954, **28,** 650–667.

Kanfer, F. H. Comments on learning in psychotherapy. *Psychological Reports,* 1961, **9,** 681–699.

———— Issues and ethics in behavior manipulation. *Psychological Reports,* 1965, **16,** 187–196. (a)

———— Vicarious human reinforcements: A glimpse into the black box. In L. Krasner & L. P. Ullmann (Eds.), *Research in behavior modification.* New York: Holt, Rinehart and Winston, 1965. Pp. 244–267. (b)

———— Implications of conditioning techniques for interview therapy. *Journal of Counseling Psychology,* 1966, **13,** 171–177. (a)

———— The influence of age and incentive conditions on children's self-rewards. *Psychological Reports,* 1966, **19,** 263–274. (b)

———— Verbal conditioning: A review of its current status. In T. R. Dixon & D. L. Horton (Eds.) *Verbal behavior and general S-R theory.* Englewood Cliffs, N.J.: Prentice-Hall, 1968. Pp. 254–290.

Kanfer, F. H., & Goldfoot, D. A. Self control and tolerance of noxious stimulation. *Psychological Reports,* 1966, **18,** 79–85.

Kanfer, F. H., & Marston, A. R. Conditioning of self-reinforcement responses: An analogue to self-confidence training. *Psychological Reports,* 1963, **13,** 63–70. (a)

———— Determinants of self-reinforcement in human learning. *Journal of Experimental Psychology,* 1963, **66,** 245–254. (b)

———— Human reinforcement: Vicarious and direct. *Journal of Experimental Psychology,* 1963, **65,** 292–296. (c)

Kanner, L. Early infantile autism. *Journal of Pediatrics,* 1944, **25,** 211–217.

Kantor, J. R. Behaviorism in the history of psychology. *Psychological Record,* 1968, **18,** 151–166.

Kaplan, M. (Ed.) *Essential works of Pavlov.* New York: Bantam Books, 1966.

† Katahn, M., & Koplin, J. H. Paradigm clash: Comment on "Some recent criticisms of behaviorism and learning theory with special reference to Breger and McGaugh and to Chomsky." *Psychological Bulletin,* 1968, **69,** 147–148.

Katahn, M., Strenger, S., & Cherry, N. Group counseling and behaviour therapy with test anxious college students. *Journal of Consulting Psychology,* 1966, **30,** 544–549.

Keehn, J. D. Consciousness and behaviourism. *British Journal of Psychology,* 1964, **1,** 89–91.

Keller, F. S., & Schoenfeld, W. N. *Principles of psychology.* New York: Appleton-Century-Crofts, 1950.

Kelly, G. A. *The psychology of personal constructs.* New York: Norton, 1955. 2 vols.

Kennard, E. A. Psychiatry, administrative psychiatry, administration: A study of a veterans hospital. In M. Greenblatt, D. J. Levinson, & R. H. Williams (Eds.), *The patient and the mental hospital.* New York: Free Press, 1957. Pp. 36–45.

Kennedy, T. Treatment of chronic schizophrenia by behavior therapy: Case reports. *Behaviour Research and Therapy,* 1964, **2,** 1–6.

Kennedy, W. H. School phobia: Rapid treatment. *Journal of Abnormal Psychology,* 1965, **70,** 285–289.

Kepner, Elaine. Application of learning theory to the aetiology and treatment of alcoholism. *Quarterly Journal of Studies on Alcoholism,* 1964, **25,** 279–291.

Kerr, N., Meyerson, L., & Michael, J. A procedure for shaping vocalizations in a mute child. In L. P. Ullmann & L. Krasner (Eds.), *Case studies in behavior modification.* New York: Holt, Rinehart and Winston, 1965. Pp. 360–370.

Kety, S. The heuristic aspects of psychiatry, *American Journal of Psychiatry,* 1961, **118,** 385–397.

Kety, S., & Elkes, J. (Eds.) *Regional neurochemistry.* London: Pergamon Press, 1961.

Kiesler, D. J. Some myths of psychotherapy research and the search for a paradigm. *Psychological Bulletin*, 1966, **65**, 110–136.

Kiev, A. (Ed.) *Psychiatry in the communist world*, New York: Science House, 1968.

Kimble, G. A. *Hilgard and Marquis' conditioning and learning*. New York: Appleton-Century-Crofts, 1961.

—— *Conditioning and learning*. London: Methuen, 1964.

—— The basic tenet of behaviorism. In G. A. Kimble (Ed.), *Foundations of conditioning and learning*. New York: Appleton-Century-Crofts, 1967. Pp. 73–81.

King, C. W. *Social movements in the United States*. New York: Random House, 1956.

King, G. F., Armitage, S. G., & Tilton, J. R. A therapeutic approach to schizophrenics of extreme pathology: An operant-interpersonal method. *Journal of Abnormal and Social Psychology*, 1960, **61**, 276–286.

Kintsch, W., & McCoy, D. F. Delay of informative feedback in paired-associate learning. *Journal of Experimental Psychology*, 1964, **68**, 372–375.

Kirchner, J. H., & Hogan, R. A. The therapist variable in the implosion of phobias. *Psychotherapy: Theory, research and practice*, 1966, **3**, 102–104.

Klopfer, W. G. The blind leading the blind: Psychotherapy without assessment. *Journal of Projective Techniques and Personality Assessment*, 1964, **28**, 387–392.

Knight, R. P. Evaluation of the results of psychoanalytic therapy. *American Journal of Psychiatry*, 1941, **98**, 434–446.

Koenig, K. P. Verbal behavior and personality change. *Journal of Personality and Social Psychology*, 1966, **3**, 223–227.

Koenig, K. P., & Masters, J. Experimental treatment of habitual smoking. *Behaviour Research and Therapy*, 1965, **3**, 235–243.

Kolvin, I. Aversive imagery treatment in adolescents. *Behavioural Research and Therapy*, 1967, **5**, 245–248.

Konorski, J. *Conditioned reflexes and neuron organization*. London: Cambridge University Press, 1948.

Koshtoyants, K. S. *Essays on the history of physiology in Russia* (translated by D. P. Hoder, K. Hanes, & N. O'Brien). Washington, D.C.: American Institute of Biological Sciences, 1964.

—— I. M. Sechenov (1829–1965). In I. M. Sechenov, *Reflexes of the brain: An attempt to establish the physiological basis of psychological processes* (translated by S. Belsky). Cambridge, Mass.: M.I.T., 1965. Pp. 119–139.

Kostlan, A. A method for the empirical study of psychodiagnosis. *Journal of Consulting Psychology*, 1954, **18**, 83–88.

Kraft, T., & Al-Issa, I. The application of learning theory to the treatment of traffic phobia. *British Journal of Psychiatry*, 1965, **111**, 277–279. (a)

———— Behaviour therapy and the recall of traumatic experience—a case study. *Behaviour Research and Therapy*, 1965, **3**, 55–58. (b)

Krasner, L. Studies of the conditioning of verbal behavior. *Psychological Bulletin*, 1958, **55**, 148–170. (a)

———— A technique for investigating the relationship between the behavior cues of the examiner and the verbal behavior of the patient. *Journal of Consulting Psychology*, 1958, **22**, 364–366. (b)

———— The therapist as a social reinforcement machine. In H. H. Strupp & L. Luborsky (Eds.), *Research in psychotherapy*. Vol. II. Washington, D.C.: American Psychological Association, 1962. Pp. 61–94. (a)

———— Behavior control and social responsibility. *American Psychologist*, 1962, **17**, 199–204. (b)

———— Therapist's contribution. In H. H. Strupp & L. Luborsky (Eds.), *Research in psychotherapy*. Vol. II. Washington, D.C.: American Psychological Association, 1962. Pp. 263–268 and 102–104. (c)

———— Verbal conditioning and psychotherapy. In L. Krasner & L. P. Ullmann (Eds.), *Research in behavior modification*. New York: Holt, Rinehart and Winston, 1965. Pp. 211–228.

———— The behavioral scientist and social responsibility: No place to hide. *Journal of Social Issues*, 1966, **21**, 9–30. (a)

———— Behavior modification research and the role of the therapist. In L. A. Gottschalk (Ed.), *Methods of research in psychotherapy*. New York: Harper & Row, 1966. Pp. 292–311. (b)

———— The translation of operant conditioning procedures from the experimental laboratory to the psychotherapeutic interaction. Paper presented at the Annual Meeting of the American Psychological Association, New York, September, 1966. (c)

———— Verbal operant conditioning and awareness. In K. Salzinger and S. Salzinger (Eds.), *Research in verbal behavior and some neurophysiological implications*. New York: Academic Press, 1967. Pp. 57–76.

Krasner, L., Knowles, J. B., & Ullmann, L. P. Effect of verbal conditioning of attitudes on subsequent motor performance. *Journal of Personality and Social Psychology*, 1965, **1**, 407–412.

Krasner, L., & Ullmann, L. P. *Research in behavior modification: New developments and implications*. New York: Holt, Rinehart and Winston, 1965.

Krasner, L., Weiss, R., & Ullmann, L. P. Responsivity to verbal conditioning as a function of awareness. *Psychological Reports*, 1961, **8**, 523–538.

Krasnogorski, N. I. The conditioned reflexes and the children's neuroses. *American Journal of Diseases of Children*, 1925, **30**, 753–768.

Kreitman, N. The reliability of psychiatric diagnosis. *Journal of Mental Science*, 1961, **107**, 876–886.

Kreitman, N., Sainsbury, P., Morrissey, J., Towers, J., & Scrivener, J. The reliability of psychiatric assessment: An analysis. *Journal of Mental Science*, 1961, **107**, 887–908.

Krueger, J. R. An early instance of conditioning from the Chinese dynastic histories. *Psychological Reports,* 1961, **9,** 117.

Kubie, L. Psychoanalysis and the scientific method. *Journal of Nervous and Mental Disease,* 1960, **131,** 495–512.

Kuhn, T. S. *The structure of scientific revolutions.* Chicago: University of Chicago Press, 1962.

Kunkel, J. L. An experiment with teaching machines in classrooms for the educable mentally retarded. Unpublished doctoral dissertation, University of Nebraska, Teachers College, 1961.

Kushner, M. Desensitization of a post-traumatic phobia. In L. P. Ullmann & L. Krasner (Eds.), *Case studies in behavior modification.* New York: Holt, Rinehart and Winston, 1965. Pp. 193–196.

—— The reduction of a long-standing fetish by means of aversive conditioning. In L. P. Ullmann & L. Krasner (Eds.), *Case studies in behavior modification.* New York: Holt, Rinehart and Winston, 1965. Pp. 239–247.

—— Faradic aversive controls in clinical practice. In C. Neuringer & J. L. Michael (Eds.), *Behavior modification in clinical psychology.* New York: Appleton-Century-Crofts, 1968.

Kushner, M., & Sandler, J. Aversion therapy and the concept of punishment. *Behavior Research and Therapy,* 1966, **4,** 179–186.

L'Abate, L. *Principles of clinical psychology.* New York: Grune & Stratton, 1964. (a)

—— Specialized training and innovation in psychodiagnosis. In L. Blank & H. P. David (Eds.), *Sourcebook for training in clinical psychology.* New York: Springer, 1964. Pp. 157–174. (b)

—— *The laboratory method in clinical psychology. The Clinical Psychologist,* 1968, **21,** 182–183. (a)

—— An input-output approach to psychodiagnosis of children. 46th Annual International CEC Convention Papers, Washington, D.C., NEA, 1968, 271–279. (b)

La Brosse, E., Mann, J. D., & Kety, S. The physiological and psychological effects of intravenously administered epinephrine and its metabolism in normal and schizophrenic men, *Journal of Psychiatric Research,* 1961, **1,** 50–57.

Lacy, J. I. Psychophysiological approaches to the evaluation of psychotherapeutic process and outcome. In E. A. Rubinstein and M. B. Parloff (Eds.), *Research in Psychotherapy.* Vol 1. Washington, D. C.: National Publishing Co., 1959. Pp. 160–208.

Lacey, J. I., & Lacey, B. C. The relationship of resting autonomic activity to motor impulsivity. In H. C. Solomon, S. Cobb, & W. Penfield (Eds.), *The brain and human behavior,* Proceedings of the Association for Research in Nervous and Mental Disease. Baltimore: Williams & Wilkins, 1958. Pp. 144–209.

Landau, R., & Gewirtz, J. L. Differential satiation for a social reinforcing stimulus as a determinant of its efficacy in conditioning. *Journal of Experimental Child Psychology*, 1967, **5**, 391–405.

Lane, H. L., & Geis, G. L. A program for reviews and a review of a program. *Contemporary Psychology*, 1965, **10**, 441–445.

Lang, P. J. Experimental studies of desensitization psychotherapy. In J. Wolpe, A. Salter, & L. J. Reyna (Eds.), *The conditioning therapies.* New York: Holt, Rinehart and Winson, 1964. Pp. 38–53.

——— Behavior therapy with a case of nervous anorexia. In: L. P. Ullmann & L. Krasner (Eds.) *Case studies in behavior modification.* New York: Holt, Rinehart and Winston, 1965. Pp. 217–221. (a)

——— Psychotherapy, pseudotherapy, and behavior therapy. Paper presented at the Annual Meeting of the Midwestern Psychological Association, Chicago, May, 1965. (b)

——— Fear reduction and fear behavior: Problems in treating a construct. In J. M. Schlien (Ed.), *Research in Psychotherapy.* Vol. III. Washington, D.C.: A.P.A., 1968, 90–102.

Lang, P. J., & Lazovik, A. D. Personality and hypnotic susceptibility. *Journal of Consulting Psychology*, 1962, **26**, 317–322.

——— Experimental desensitization of a phobia. *Journal of Abnormal and Social Psychology*, 1963, **66**, 519–525.

Lang, P. J., Lazovik, A. D., & Reynolds, D. J. Desensitization, suggestibility, and pseudotherapy. *Journal of Abnormal Psychology*, 1965, **70**, 395–402.

Lang, P. J., Sroufe, L. A., & Hastings, J. E. Effects of feedback and instructional set on the control of cardiac rate variability. *Journal of Experimental Psychology*, 1967, **75**, 425–431.

Lanyon, R. I. Verbal conditioning: Transfer of training in a therapylike situation. *Journal of Abnormal Psychology*, 1967, **72**, 30–34.

Larsen, S. Strategies for reducing phobic behavior. *Dissertation Abstracts*, 1966, **26**, 6850.

Latane, B., & Schachter, S. Adrenaline and avoidance learning. *Journal of Comparative and Physiological Psychology*, 1962, **55**, 369–372.

LaVerne, A. A. Rapid coma technique of carbon dioxide inhalation therapy. *Diseases of the Nervous System*, 1953, **14**, 141–146.

Lawrence, D. H. The nature of a stimulus: Some relationships between learning and perception. In S. Koch (Ed.), *Psychology: A study of a science.* Vol. 5. New York: McGraw-Hill, 1963. Pp. 179–212.

Lazarus, A. A. New methods in psychotherapy: A case study. *South African Medical Journal*, 1958, **33**, 660.

——— The elimination of children's phobias by deconditioning. In H. J. Eysenck (Ed.), *Behaviour therapy and the neuroses.* London: Pergamon Press, 1960. Pp. 114–122.

——— Group therapy of phobic disorders by systematic desensitization. *Journal of Abnormal and Social Psychology*, 1961, **63**, 504–510.

———— The treatment of chronic frigidity by systematic desensitization. *Journal of Nervous and Mental Disease*, 1963, **136**, 272–278. (a)

———— The results of behaviour therapy in 126 cases of severe neurosis. *Behaviour Research and Therapy*, 1963, **1**, 69–79. (b)

———— Objective psychotherapy in the treatment of dysphemia. In H. J. Eysenck (Ed.), *Experiments in behaviour therapy*. New York: Pergamon Press, 1964. Pp. 401–406. (a)

———— Behaviour therapy with identical twins. *Behaviour Research and Therapy*, 1964, **1**, 313–319. (b)

———— Crucial procedural factors in desensitization therapy. *Behaviour Research and Therapy*, 1964, **2**, 65–70. (c)

———— The treatment of a sexually inadequate man. In L. P. Ullmann & L. Krasner (Eds.), *Case studies in behavior modification*. New York: Holt, Rinehart and Winston, 1965. Pp. 243–245. (a)

———— Behavior therapy, incomplete treatment, and symptom substitution. *Journal of Nervous and Mental Disease*, 1965, **140**, 80–86. (b)

———— Towards the understanding and effective treatment of alcoholism. *South African Medical Journal*, 1965, **39**, 736–741. (c)

———— Broad-spectrum behaviour therapy and the treatment of agoraphobia. *Behaviour Research and Therapy*, 1966, **4**, 95–97. (a)

———— Behaviour rehearsal vs. non-directive therapy vs. advice in effecting behavior change. *Behaviour Research and Therapy*, 1966, **4**, 209–212. (b)

———— In support of technical eclecticism. *Psychological Reports*, 1967, **21**, 415–416. (a)

———— Personal communication, 1967. (b)

———— Behavior therapy in groups. In G. M. Gazda (Ed.), *Basic approaches to group psychotherapy and counseling*. Springfield, Ill.: Charles C Thomas, 1968. Pp. 149–175.

Lazarus, A. A., & Abramovitz, A. *Learn to relax—A recorded course in muscular relaxation*. Troubadour Records, Wolhunter, Johannesburg, 1962. (a)

———— The use of "emotive imagery" in the treatment of children's phobias. *Journal of Mental Science*, 1962, **108**, 191–195. (b)

Lazarus, A. A., & Davison, G. C. The reciprocal inhibition concept and desensitization therapy. In R. M. Jurjevich (Ed.), *Handbook of direct and behavior psychotherapies*, in press.

Lazarus, A. A., Davison, G. C., & Polefka, D. A. Classical and operant factors in the treatment of a school phobia. *Journal of Abnormal and Social Psychology*, 1965, **70**, 225–229.

Lazarus, A. A., & Rachman, S. The use of systematic desensitization in psychotherapy. *South African Medical Journal*, 1957, **31**, 934–937.

Lazarus, A. A., & Serber, M. Is systematic desensitization being misapplied? *Psychological Reports*, 1968, **23**, 215–218.

Lazarus, R. S. *Psychological stress and the coping process.* New York: McGraw-Hill, 1966.

Lazarus, R. S., & Alfert, E. The short-circuiting of threat by experimentally altering cognitive appraisal. *Journal of Abnormal and Social Psychology,* 1964, **69,** 195–205.

Lazarus, R. S., Speisman, J. C., Mordkoff, A. M., & Davison, L. A. A laboratory study of psychological stress produced by a motion picture film. *Psychological Monographs,* 1962, **76** (Whole No. 556).

Lazovik, A. D., & Lang, P. J. A laboratory demonstration of systematic desensitization psychotherapy. *Journal of Psychological Studies,* 1960, **11,** 238–247.

Ledley, R. S., & Lusted, L. B. Reasoning foundations of medical diagnosis. *Science,* 1959, **130,** 9–21.

Lefkowitz, M. M., Blake, R. R., & Mouton, J. S. Status factors in pedestrian violation of traffic signals. *Journal of Abnormal and Social Psychology,* 1955, **51,** 704–706.

Lehmann, H. E. The placebo response and the double-blind study. In Hoch, P. H., & Zubin, J. *The evaluation of psychiatric treatment.* New York: Grune & Stratton, 1964. Pp. 75–93.

Lehrman, N. S. Do our hospitals help make acute schizophrenia chronic? *Diseases of the Nervous System,* 1961, **22,** 489–493.

Lemere, F., & Voegtlin, W. An evaluation of the aversion treatment of alcoholism. *Quarterly Journal of Studies on Alcohol,* 1950, **11,** 199–204.

Lesse, S. Introduction, *American Journal of Psychotherapy, Supplement 1,* 1964, **18,** 1–2.

―――― Evaluation and process—the road to the future. *American Journal of Psychotherapy,* 1966, **20,** 1–2.

Leventhal, A. M. Use of a behavioral approach within a traditional psychotherapeutic context: A case study. *Journal of Abnormal Psychology,* 1968, **73,** 178–182.

Levi-Montalcini, R., & Angeletti, P. Biological properties of a nerve growth promoting protein and its antiserum. In S. S. Kety & J. Elkes (Eds.), *Regional neuro chemistry,* London: Pergamon Press, 1961. Pp. 362–377.

Levin, G. R., & Simmons, J. J. Response to praise by emotionally disturbed boys. *Psychological Report,* 1962, **11,** 10. (a)

―――― Response to food and praise by emotionally disturbed boys. *Psychological Reports,* 1962, **11,** 539–546. (b)

Levis, D. J. Implosive therapy: The theory, the subhuman analogue, the strategy, and the technique. Part II: The subhuman analogue, the strategy, and the technique. In S. G. Armitage (Ed.), *Behavior modification techniques in the treatment of emotional disorders.* Battle Creek, Mich. VA Publication, 1967. Pp. 22–37.

Levison, D. J. The psychotherapist's contribution to the patient's treatment career. In H. H. Strupp & Luborsky, L. (Eds.), *Research in psycho-*

therapy. Vol. II. Washington, D.C.: American Psychological Association, 1962. Pp. 13–24.

Levitt, E. E. Results of psychotherapy with children: An evaluation. *Journal of Consulting Psychology,* 1957, **21,** 189–196.

————— Psychotherapy with children: a further evaluation. *Behaviour Research and Therapy,* 1963, **1,** 45–51.

Lichtenstein, F. E. Studies in anxiety: I. The production of a feeding inhibition in dogs. *Journal of Comparative and Physiological Psychology,* 1950, **43,** 16–29.

Liddell, H. S. A biological basis for psychopathology. In P. H. Hoch & J. Zubin (Eds.), *Problems of addiction and habituation.* New York: Grune & Stratton, 1958. Pp. 183–196.

Lindner, R. M. *Must you conform.* New York: Holt, 1956.

Lindsley, O. R. Operant conditioning methods applied to research in chronic schizophrenia. *Psychiatric Research Reports,* 1956, **5,** 118–139.

————— Characteristics of the behavior of chronic psychotics as revealed by free-operant conditioning methods. *Diseases of the Nervous System, Monograph Supplement,* 1960, **21,** 66–78.

————— Direct behavioral analysis of psychotherapy sessions by conjugately programmed closed-circuit television. Paper presented at the Symposium of the American Psychological Association, St. Louis, Mo., September, 1962.

————— Free operant conditioning and psychotherapy. In J. H. Masserman, (Ed.), *Current psychiatric therapies.* Vol. 3. New York: Grune & Stratton, 1963. Pp. 47–56. (a)

————— Direct measurement and functional definition of vocal hallucinatory symptoms. *Journal of Nervous and Mental Disease,* 1963, **136,** 293–297. (b)

————— Direct measurement and prosthesis of retarded behavior. *Journal of Education,* 1964, **147,** 62–81.

————— Training teachers to change environment. Presentation at University of Oregon Colloquium on Behavior Modification, sponsored by School of Education, Eugene, Oreg., May, 1966.

Lindsley, O. R., & Skinner, B. F. A method for the experimental analysis of the behavior of psychotic patients. *American Psychologist,* 1954, **9,** 419–420.

Lippitt, R., Polansky, N., & Rosen, S. The dynamics of power: A field study of social influence in groups of children. *Human Relations,* 1952, **5,** 37–64.

Liversedge, L. A., & Sylvester, J. D. Conditioning techniques in treatment of writer's cramp. *Lancet,* 1955, **1,** 1147–1149.

Livingston, R. B. Central control of receptors and sensory transmission systems. In J. Fields, H. Magoun, & V. Hall (Eds.) *Handbook of physiology, Section I. Neurophysiology,* Washington, D.C.: American Physiological Society, 1959. Pp. 741–760.

Loevinger, J. Measurement in clinical research. In B. B. Wolman (Ed.), *Handbook of clinical psychology*, New York: McGraw-Hill, 1965. Pp. 78–94.

Lomont, J. F. The ethics of behavior therapy. *Psychological Reports*, 1964, **14**, 519–531.

———— Reciprocal inhibition or extinction? *Behaviour Research and Therapy*, 1965, **3**, 209–219.

Lomont, J. F., & Edwards, J. E. The role of relaxation in systematic desensitization. *Behaviour Research and Therapy*, 1967, **5**, 11–25.

London, P. *The modes and morals of psychotherapy*. New York: Holt, Rinehart and Winston, 1964.

Lorr, M., Klett, C. J., & McNair, D. M. *Syndromes of psychosis*, New York: Macmillan, 1963.

Lott, A. J., & Lott, B. E. Group cohesiveness as inter-personal attraction: A review of relationships with antecedent and consequent variables. *Psychological Bulletin*, 1965, **64**, 259–309.

Loucks, R. B. An appraisal of Pavlov's systematization of behavior from the experimental standpoint. *Journal of Comparative Psychology*, 1933, **15**, 1–47.

Lovaas, O. I. Interaction between verbal and non-verbal behavior. *Child Development*, 1961, **32**, 329–336.

———— Cue properties of words: The control of operant responding by rate and content of verbal operants. *Child Development*, 1964, **35**, 245–256. (a)

———— Control of food intake in children by reinforcement of relevant verbal behavior. *Journal of Abnormal and Social Psychology*, 1964, **68**, 672–678. (b)

Lovaas, O. I., Berberich, J. P., Perloff, B. F., & Schaeffer, B. Acquisition of imitative speech by schizophrenic children. *Science*, 1966, **151**, 705–706.

Lovaas, O. I., Freitag, G., Kinder, M., Rubenstein, B., Schaeffer, B., & Simmons, J. Experimental studies in childhood schizophrenia: Establishment of social reinforcers. Paper presented at the Annual Meeting of the Western Psychological Association, Portland, Oregon, 1964.

Lovaas, O. I., Freitas, L., Nelson, K., & Whalen, C. The establishment of imitation and its use for the development of complex behavior in schizophrenic children. *Behaviour Research and Therapy*, 1967, **5**, 171–181.

Lovaas, O. I., Schaeffer, B., & Simmons, J. Experimental studies in childhood schizophrenia: Building social behaviors using electric shock. Paper presented at the Annual Meeting of the American Psychological Association, 1964.

———— Building social behavior in autistic children by use of electric shock. *Journal of Experimental Research in Personality*, 1965, **1**, 99–109.

Lovibond, S. H. Intermittent reinforcement in behaviour therapy. *Behaviour Research and Therapy*, 1963, **1**, 127–132. (a)

———— The mechanism of conditioning treatment of enuresis. *Behaviour Research and Therapy*, 1963, **1**, 17–21. (b)

———— Conditioning and enuresis. London: Pergamon Press, 1964. (a)

———— Personality and conditioning. In B. A. Maher (Ed.), *Progress in experimental personality research*. Vol. 1. New York: Academic Press, 1964. (b). Pp. 115–168.

———— The current status of behavior therapy. *Canadian Psychologist*, 1966, **7a**, 93–101.

Luborsky, L., & Strupp, H. H. Research problems in psychotherapy: A three-year follow-up. In H. H. Strupp & L. Luborsky (Eds.), *Research in psychotherapy*, Vol. II. Washington, D.C.: American Psychological Association, 1962. Pp. 308–329.

Lucero, J., Vail, D. J., & Scherber, J. Regulating operant conditioning programs. *Hospital and Community Psychiatry*, 1968, **19**, 53–54.

Lumsdaine, A. A. (Ed.) *Student response in programed instruction: A symposium on experimental studies of cue and response factors in group and individual learning from instructional media*. Washington, D.C.: National Academy of Sciences–National Research Council, 1961.

Lumsdaine, A. A., & Glaser, R. (Eds.) *Teaching machines and programed learning: A source book*. Washington, D.C.: National Education Association, 1960.

Lundin, R. W. *Personality: An experimental approach*. New York: Macmillan, 1961.

Luria, A. R. *The role of speech in the regulation of normal and abnormal behavior*. New York: Liveright, 1961.

———— Higher cortical functions in man. New York: Basic Books, 1966.

Lynn, R. Russian theory and research on schizophrenia. *Psychological Bulletin*, 1963, **60**, 486–498.

———— Abnormal psychology in the USSR. In N. O'Connor (Ed.), *Present-day Russian psychology*. London: Pergamon Press, 1966. Pp. 92–108. (a)

———— Attention, arousal and the orientation reaction. London: Pergamon Press, 1966. (b)

Lynn, R., & Eysenck, H. J. Tolerance for pain, extraversion aand neuroticism. *Perceptual and Motor Skills*, 1961, **12**, 161–162.

Maccia, E. S. Epistemological considerations in relation to the use of teaching machines. *Educational Theory*, 1962, **12**, 234–240, 246.

MacCulloch, M. J., Feldman, M. P., Orford, J. F., & MacCulloch, M. L. Anticipatory avoidance learning in the treatment of alcoholism: a record of therapeutic failure. *Behaviour Research and Therapy*, 1966, **4**, 187–196.

MacCulloch, M. J., Feldman, M. P., & Pinschof, J. M. The application of anticipatory avoidance learning to the treatment of homosexuality. II. Avoidance response latencies and pulse rate charges. *Behaviour Research and Therapy*, 1965, **3**, 21–44.

MacMillan, M. Pavlov's typology. *Journal of Nervous and Mental Diseases,* 1963, **137,** 447–454.

Madsen, C. H., & Hoffman, M. Behavior therapy and self-control. Manuscript in preparation, 1967.

Madsen, C. H., & Ullmann, L. P. Innovations in the desensitization of frigidity. *Behaviour Research and Therapy,* 1967, **5,** 67–68.

Maher, B. A. *Principles of psychopathology: An experimental approach.* New York: McGraw-Hill, 1966.

Makarov, P. O. Ivan Petrovich Pavlov. *Conditional Reflex,* 1966, **1,** 288–292.

Malleson, N. Panic and phobia: A possible method of treatment. *The Lancet,* 1959, **1,** 225–227.

Malmo, R. B. Measurement of drive: An unsolved problem in psychology. In M. R. Jones (Ed.), *Nebraska symposium on motivation.* Lincoln, Nebr.: University of Nebraska Press, 1958. Pp. 229–265.

Malpass, L. F., Hardy, M. W., Gilmore, M. A., & Williams, C. F. Automated instruction for retarded children. *American Journal of Mental Deficiency,* 1964, **69,** 405–412.

Maltzman, I. Awareness, cognitive psychology vs. behaviorism. *Journal of Experimental Research in Personality,* 1966, **1,** 161–165.

Mandler, G., & Kaplan, W. K. Subjective evaluation and reinforcing effect of a verbal stimulus. *Science,* 1956, **124,** 582–583.

Mandler, G., Mandler, J. M., & Uviller, E. T. Autonomic feedback: The perception of autonomic activity. *Journal of Abnormal and Social Psychology,* 1958, **56,** 367–373.

Mangan, G. L. Studies of the relationship between neo-Pavlovian properties of higher nervous activity and Western pesonality dimensions: II. The relation of mobility to perceptual flexibility. *Journal of Experimental Research in Personality,* 1967, **2,** 107–116. (a)

——— Studies of the relationship between neo-Pavlovian properties of higher nervous activity and Western personality dimensions: III. The relation of transformation mobility to thinking flexibility. *Journal of Experimental Research in Personality,* 1967, **2,** 117–123. (b)

——— Studies of the relationship between neo-Pavlovian properties of higher nervous activity and Western personality dimensions: IV. A factor analytic study of extraversion and flexibility, and the sensitivity and mobility of the nervous system. *Journal of Experimental Research in Personality,* 1967, **2,** 124–127. (c)

Mangan, G. L., & Farmer, R. G. Studies of the relationship between Neo-Pavlovian properties of higher nervous activity and Western personality dimensions: I. The relationship of nervous strength and sensitivity to extraversion. *Journal of Experimental Research in Personality,* 1967, **2,** 101–106.

Marinho, H. Social influences in the formation of enduring preferences. *Journal of Abnormal and Social Psychology,* 1942, **37,** 448–468.

Marks, I. M., & Gelder, M. G. A controlled retrospective study of behaviour therapy in phobic patients. *British Journal of Psychiatry*, 1965, **111**, 561–573.

—— Common ground between behavior therapy and psychodynamic methods, *British Journal of Medical Psychology*, 1966, **39**, 11–23.

—— Severe agoraphobia. A controlled prospective trial of behaviour therapy. *British Journal of Psychiatry*, 1966, **112**, 309–320.

—— Transvestism and fetishism: Clinical and psychological changes during faradic aversion. *British Journal of Psychiatry*, 1967, **119**, 711–730.

Marks, I. M., Rachman, S., & Gelder, M. G. Methods for assessment of aversion treatment in fetishism with masochism. *Behaviour Research and Therapy*, 1965, **3**, 253–258.

Marlatt, G. A. Exposure to a model and task ambiguity as determinants of verbal behavior in an interview. Paper presented at the Annual Meeting of the Western Psychological Association, San Diego, 1968. (a)

—— Vicarious and direct reinforcement control of verbal behavior in an interview setting. Unpublished doctoral dissertation, Indiana University, 1968. (b)

Marlatt, G. A., Jacobson, E. A., Johnson, D. L., & Morrice, D. J. Effects of exposure to a model receiving varied informational feedback upon consequent behavior in an interview. Paper presented at a meeting of the Midwestern Psychological Association, Chicago, 1966.

Marley, E. Behavioral and electrophysiological effects of catecholamines, *Pharmacological Reviews*, 1966, **18**, (Part 1), 753–748.

Marley, E., & Key, B. J. Maturation of the electrocorticogram and behavior in the kitten and guinea pig and the effect of some sympathomimetic amines. *EEG and Clinical Neurophysiology*, 1963, **15**, 620–636.

Marston, A. R. Self reinforcement: The relevance of a concept in analogue research to psychotherapy. *Psychotherapy Research, and Practice*, 1965, **2**, 1–5.

Martin, B. Reward and punishment associated with the same goal response: a factor in the learning of motives. *Psychological Bulletin*, 1963, **60**, 441–451.

Masserman, J. M. *Behavior and neurosis.* Chicago: University of Chicago Press, 1943.

Masters, W., & Johnson, V. *Human sexual response.* London: Churchill, 1966.

Matarazzo, J. D., Saslow, G., & Pareis, E. N. Verbal conditioning of two response classes: Some methodological considerations, *Journal of Abnormal and Social Psychology*, 1960, **61**, 190–196.

Max, L. W. Breaking up a homosexual fixation by the conditioned reaction technique. A case study. *Psychological Bulletin*, 1935, **32**, 734.

May, R. Discussion on existentialism and current trends in psychology, Conference at Sonoma State College, 1962. Cited by L. Krasner, 1966. (a)

May, P. R. A., Tuma, A. H., & Kraude, W. Community follow-up of treatment of schizophrenia—issues and problems. *American Journal of Orthopsychiatry*, 1965, **35**, 754–763.

McConaghy, N. A year's experience with non-verbal psychotherapy. *Medical Journal of Australia*, 1964, **1**, 831–837.

McConnell, J. Learning theory. In *If—worlds of science fiction*, 1957. Republished: In R. A. Baker (Ed.), *Psychology in the wry*. Princeton, N.J.: Van Nostrand, 1963. Pp. 66–81.

McGuire, R. J., Carlisle, J. M., & Young, B. G. Sexual deviations as conditioned behaviour: A hypothesis. *Behaviour Research and Therapy*, 1965, **2**, 185–190.

McGuire, R. J., & Vallance, M. Aversion therapy by electric shock, a simple technique. *British Medical Journal*, 1964, **1**, 151–152.

McGuire, W. J. Personality and susceptibility to social influence. In E. F. Borgatta & W. W. Lambert (Eds.), *Handbook of personality theory and research*. Chicago, Ill.: Rand McNally, 1968. Pp. 789–1187.

McInnis, T. L., Jr., & Ullmann, L. P. Positive and negative reinforcement with short- and long-term hospitalized schizophrenics in a probability learning situation. *Journal of Abnormal Psychology*, 1967, **72**, 157–162.

McKeachie, W. J. The case for multiple models. *Clinical Psychologist*, 1967, **20**, 108–110.

McKee, J. M. The Draper experiment: A programed learning project. Paper presented at the First Annual Convention of the National Society for Programed Instruction, San Antonio, Tex., January, 1963. (a)

—— Programed instruction as a therapeutic tool. Paper presented at the Symposium on Techniques for Resocialization of the Delinquent, American Psychological Association, Philadelphia, September, 1963. (b)

McKee, J. M., & Zachert, V. The programed learning project at Draper correctional center: Year two. *Journal of the National Society of Programed Instruction*, 1966, **5**, 3–5, 15.

McLuhan, M. *Gutenberg galaxy*. Toronto, Canada: University of Toronto Press, 1965.

McNeill, D. Developmental psycholinguistics. In F. Smith & G. A. Miller (Eds.), *The genesis of language: A psycholinguistic approach*. Cambridge, Mass.: M.I.T. Press, 1966. Pp. 15–84.

McPartland, T. S., & Richart, R. H. Social and clinical outcomes of psychiatric treatment. *Archives of General Psychiatry*, 1966, **14**, 179–184.

McReynolds, P. Anxiety, perception, and schizophrenia. In D. D. Jackson (Ed.), *The etiology of schizophrenia*. New York: Basic Books, 1960. Pp. 248–292.

McReynolds, P., & Guevara, C. Attitudes of schizophrenics and normals toward success and failure. *Journal of Abnormal Psychology*, 1967, **72**, 303–310.

Meehl, P. E. On the circularity of the law of effect. *Psychological Bulletin*, 1950, **47**, 52–75.

———— Psychotherapy. *Annual Review of Psychology*, 1955, **6**, 357–378.

Mehlman, B. The reliability of psychiatric diagnosis. *Journal of Abnormal and Social Psychology*, 1952, **47**, 577–578.

Meichenbaum, D. H. The effects of social reinforcement on the level of abstraction in schizophrenics. *Journal of Abnormal Psychology*, 1966, **71**, 354–362. (a)

———— The effects of instructions and reinforcement on thinking and language behaviors of schizophrenics. Unpublished doctoral dissertation, University of Illinois, 1966. (b)

———— Sequential strategies in two cases of hysteria. *Behaviour Research and Therapy*, 1966, **4**, 89–94. (c)

Menaker, T. Anxiety about drinking in alcoholics. *Journal of Abnormal and Social Psychology*, 1967, **72**, 43–49.

Merbaum, M., & Southwell, E. A. Conditioning of affective self-references as a function of the discriminative characteristics of experimenter intervention. *Journal of Abnormal Psychology*, 1965, **70**, 180–187.

Mertens, G. C. *The manual for the alcoholic.* Willmar, Minn.: Willmar State Hospital, 1964. (a)

———— *The therapist's manual—A manual for assisting an alcoholic in his development of self-control.* Willmar, Minn.: Willmar State Hospital, 1964. (b)

———— Behavioral planning. Unpublished manuscript, St. Cloud State College, 1967.

Mertens, G. C., & Fuller, G. B. Conditioning of molar behavior in "regressed" psychotics. *Journal of Clinical Psychology*, 1963, **19**, 333–337.

Metz, J. R. Imitation in autistic children. *American Psychologist*, 1964, **19**, 478.

———— Conditioning generalized imitation in autistic children. *Journal of Experimental Child Psychology*, 1965, **2**, 389–399.

Meyer, A. E. Psychoanalytic versus behavior therapy of male homosexuals: A statistical evaluation of clinical outcome. *Comprehensive Psychiatry*, 1966, **7**, 110–117.

Meyer, V. The treatment of two phobic patients on the basis of learning principles. *Journal of Abnormal and Social Psychology*, 1957 **55**, 261–266.

———— Modification of expectations in cases with obsessional rituals. *Behaviour Research and Therapy*, 1966, **4**, 273–280.

Meyer, V., & Crisp, A. H. Some problems in behaviour therapy. *British Journal of Psychiatry*, 1966, **112**, 367–381.

Meyer, V., & Gelder, M. G. Behaviour therapy and phobic disorders. *British Journal of Psychiatry*, 1963, **109**, 19–28.

Meyer, W. J., & Seidman, S. B. Relative effectiveness of different reinforcement combinations on concept learning of children at two developmental levels. *Child Development*, 1961, **32**, 117–127.

Michael, R. An investigation of the sensitivity of circumscribed neurological areas to hormonal stimulation. In S. Kety & J. Elkes (Eds.), *Regional Neurochemistry*, London: Pergamon Press, 1961. Pp. 465–480.

Migler, B., & Wolpe, J. Automated self-desensitization: A case report. *Behaviour Research and Therapy*, 1967, **5**, 133–135.

Millenson, J. R. *Principles of behavioral analysis*. New York: Macmillan, 1967.

Miller, E., Dvorak, B., & Turner, D. A method of creating aversion to alcohol by reflex conditioning in a group setting. In C. M. Franks (Ed.), *Conditioning techniques in clinical practice and research*. New York: Springer, 1964. Pp. 157–164.

Miller, J. G. Objective methods of evaluating process and outcome in psychotherapy. *American Journal of Psychiatry*, 1951, **108**, 258–263.

Miller, N. E. Liberalization of basic S-R concepts: Extensions to conflict behavior, motivation, and social learning. In S. Koch (Ed.), *Psychology: A study of a science*. Vol. 2. New York: McGraw-Hill, 1959. Pp. 191–292.

———— Learning resistance to fear and pain. *Journal of Experimental Psychology*, 1960, **60**, 137–142.

———— Some implications of modern behavior theory for personality change and psychotherapy. In P. Worchel & D. Byrne (Eds.), *Personality change*. New York: Wiley, 1964. Pp. 73–99.

Miller, N. E., & DiCara, L. Instrumental learning of heart rate changes in curarized rats: Shaping, and specificity to discriminative stimulus. *Journal of Comparative and Physiological Psychology*, 1967, **63**, 12–19.

Miller, N. E., & Dollard, J. *Social learning and imitation*. New Haven, Conn.: Yale University Press, 1941.

Minz, A. I. P. Pavlov and Soviet psychology. *I.C.R.S. Medical Reports*, 1964, **6**, 2–5.

Miron, N. B. Issues and implications of operant conditioning. The primary ethical consideration. *Hospital and Community Psychiatry*, 1968, **19**, 226–228.

Mirsky, A. I. Psychoanalysis and human behavior, experimental approaches. In A. D. Boss (Ed.), *Evolution of nervous control*, Washington, D.C.: American Association for the Advancement of Science, 1959. Pp. 195–226.

Mischel, W. Theory and research on the antecedents of self-imposed delay of reward. In B. A. Maher (Ed.), *Progress in experimental personality research*. Vol. 3. New York: Academic Press, 1966. Pp. 85–132.

———— *Personality and assessment*. New York: Wiley, 1968.

Moore, N. Behaviour therapy in bronchial asthma: A controlled study. *Journal of Psychosomatic Research*, 1965, **9**, 257–276.

Moore, O. K. The responsive environments project and the deaf. *American Annals of the Deaf*, 1965, **110**, 604–614.

———— Autotelic responsive environments and exceptional children. In O. J. Harvey (Ed.), *Experience, structure, and adaptability*. New York: Springer, 1966. Pp. 169–216.

Moore, R., & Goldiamond, I. Errorless establishment of visual discrimination using fading procedures. *Journal of the Experimental Analysis of Behavior*, 1964, **7**, 269–272.

Moos, R. H. The retention and generalization of operant conditioning effects in an interview situation. *Journal of Abnormal and Social Psychology*, 1963, **66**, 52–58.

Morgenstern, F., Pearce, J., & Davies, B. The application of aversion therapy to transvestism. Paper presented at the Annual Meeting of The British Psychological Society, Reading, England, 1963.

Morgenstern, F., Pearce, J. F., & Rees, W. L. Predicting the outcome of behaviour therapy by psychological tests. *Behaviour Research and Therapy*, 1965, **2**, 191–200.

Morrill, C. S. Teaching machines: A review. *Psychological Bulletin*, 1961, **58**, 363–375.

Moss, T., & Edwards, A. E. Conflict vs. conditioning: Effects upon peripheral vascular activity. *Psychosomatic Medicine*, 1964, **26**, 267–273.

Mowrer, O. H. Apparatus for the study and treatment of enuresis. *American Journal of Psychology*, 1938, **51**, 163–166. (a)

———— Preparatory set (expectancy)—A determinant in motivation and learning. *Psychological Review*, 1938, **45**, 61–91. (b)

———— On the dual nature of learning—A reinterpretation of "conditioning" and "problem solving." *Harvard Educational Review*, 1947, **17**, 102–148.

———— *Learning theory and personality dynamics*. New York: Ronald Press, 1950.

———— (Ed.), *Psychotherapy: Theory and research*. New York: Ronald Press, 1953.

———— *Learning theory and behavior*. New York: Wiley, 1960. (a)

———— *Learning theory and the symbolic processes*. New York: Wiley, 1960. (b)

———— Learning theory and behavior therapy. In B. B. Wolman (Ed.), *Handbook of clinical psychology*. New York: McGraw-Hill, 1965. Pp. 242–273.

Mowrer, O. H., & Mowrer, W. M. Enuresis: A method for its study and treatment. *America and Journal of Orthopsychiatry*, 1938, **8**, 436–459.

Mullen, F. G. Unpublished research on the effect of covert sensitization on smoking, 1967.

Murray, E. J. A content-analysis method for studying psychotherapy. *Psychological Monographs*, 1956, **70**, 1–32.

———— Learning theory and psychotherapy: Biotropic versus sociotropic approaches. *Journal of Counseling Psychology*, 1963, **10**, 250–255.

———— Sociotropic-learning approach to psychotherapy. In P. Worchel & D. Byrne (Eds.), *Personality change*. New York: Wiley, 1964. Pp. 249–288.

Murphy, I. C. Extinction of an incapacitating fear of earthworms. *Journal of Clinical Psychology*, 1964, **60**, 396–398.

Narrol, H. *A learning therapy for alcoholics: Upon what behavior should re-training focus?* Paper presented at the Annual Meeting of the American Psychological Association, Los Angeles, September, 1964.

National Education Association, Division of Audio-visual Instructional Service. *Selection and use of programed materials.* Washington, D.C.: Author, 1964.

Neale, D. H. Behaviour therapy and encopresis in children. *Behaviour Research and Therapy,* 1963, **1**, 139–149.

Nelson, F. Effects of two counterconditioning procedures on the extinction of fear. *Journal of Comparative and Physiological Psychology,* 1966, **62**, 208–213.

Newcomb, T. M. The prediction of interpersonal attraction. *American Psychologist,* 1956, **11**, 575–586.

New York Heart Association. *Nomenclature and criteria for diagnosis of diseases of the heart and blood vessels.* New York: Author, 1953.

Nixon, S. B. Ways by which overly active students can be taught to concentrate on study activity. Cooperation Research Project No. S-379, Office of Education, U.S. Department of Health, Education and Welfare, 1966.

Noyes, A. P., & Kolb, L. C. *Modern clinical psychiatry.* Philadelphia: Saunders, 1963.

Oakes, W. F. Reinforcement of Bales' categories in group discussion. *Psychological Reports,* 1962, **11**, 427–435.

Oakes, W. F., Droge, A. E., & August, B. Reinforcement effects on participation in group discussion. *Psychological Reports,* 1960, **7**, 503–514.

Oerton, R. T. Critical notice: Review of H. J. Eysenck, "Crime and personality." *British Journal of Medical Psychology,* 1965, **39**, 67.

Olds, J. Self-stimulation of the brain. *Science,* 1958, **127**, 315–324.

O'Leary, K. D. & Becker, W. C. Behavior modification of an adjustment class: A token reinforcement program. *Exceptional Children,* 1967, **33**, 637–642.

O'Leary, K. D., O'Leary, Susan, & Becker, W. C. Modification of a deviant sibling interaction pattern in the home. *Behaviour Research and Therapy,* 1967, **5**, 113–120.

Olson, H. *Sumner Purvess: A pioneer in northern Minnesota.* Tower, Minn.: Tower-Soudan Historical Society, 1966.

Orne, M. On the social psychology of the psychological experiment: With particular reference to demand characteristics and their implications. *American Psychologist,* 1962, **17**, 776–783.

Osgood, C. E. *Method and theory in experimental psychology.* New York, Oxford, 1953.

———— *An alternative to war or surrender.* Urbana: University of Illinois Press, 1962.

Osgood, C. E., Suci, G. J., & Tannenbaum, P. H. *Measurement of meaning.* Urbana: University of Illinois Press, 1957.

Otis, L. S. Discussion of Working Group 3: Psychology and experimental psychopathology. In D. Bente & P. B. Bradley (Eds.), *Neuro-psychoparmacology.* Vol. 4. Proceedings of the Fourth Meeting of the Collegium Internationale Neuro-Psychopharmacologicum, Birmingham, England, September, 1964. New York: Elsevier Publishing Co., 1965. Pp. 91–114.

Oxford universal dictionary. (3rd ed.) London: Oxford University Press, 1955.

Palmer, B. E. A programed instruction method for psychotherapy training. *Dissertation Abstracts,* 1964, **23,** 4413.

Parloff, M. B., & Rubinstein, E. A. Research problems in psychotherapy. In E. A. Rubinstein & M. B. Parloff (Eds.), *Research in psychotherapy,* Vol. I. Washington, D.C.: American Psychological Association, 1959. Pp. 276–293.

Pasamanick, B., Dinitz, S., & Lefton, M. Psychiatric orientation and its relation to diagnosis and treatment in a mental hospital. *American Journal of Psychiatry,* 1959, **116, 127**–132.

Pascal, G. R. *Behavioral change in the clinic: A systematic approach.* New York: Grune & Stratton, 1959.

Patrick, H. T., & Bassoe, P. *Nervous and mental diseases.* Chicago: Year Book Publishers, 1910.

Patterson, G. R. A learning theory approach to the treatment of the school phobic child. In L. P. Ullmann & L. Krasner (Eds.), *Case studies in behavior modification.* New York: Holt, Rinehart and Winston, 1965. Pp. 279–284 (a)

——— Responsiveness to social stimuli. In L. Krasner & L. P. Ullmann (Eds.), *Research in behavior modification.* New York: Holt, Rinehart and Winston, 1965. Pp. 157–178 (b)

——— An application of conditioning techniques to the control of a hyperactive child. In L. P. Ullmann & L. Krasner (Eds.), *Case studies in behavior modification.* New York: Holt, Rinehart and Winston, 1965. Pp. 370–375. (c)

Patterson, G. R., & Anderson, D. Peers as social reinforcers. *Child Development,* 1964, **35, 951**–960.

Patterson, G. R. & Brodsky, G. D. A behavior modification programme for a child with multiple problem behaviors. *Journal of Child Psychology and Psychiatry,* 1966, **7, 277**–295.

Patterson, G. R., & Fagot, B. Selective responsiveness to social reinforcers and deviant behavior in children. *Psychological Record,* 1967, **17,** 369–378.

Patterson, G. R., Hawkins, N. McNeal, S. & Phelps, R. Reprograming the social environment. *Journal of Child Psychology and Psychiatry,* 1967, **8,** 181–195.

Patterson, G. R., & Hinsey, W. C. Investigations of some assumptions and characteristics of a procedure for instrumental conditioning in children. *Journal of Experimental Child Psychology,* 1964, **1,** 111–122.

Patterson, G. R., Jones, R., Whittier, J., & Wright, M. A behavior modification technique for the hyperactive child. *Behaviour Research and Therapy,* 1965, **2,** 217–226.

Patterson, G. R., & Littman, R. Social reinforcers and social behavior. Progress Report, U.S. Public Health Service 88009–02, 1965.

Patterson, G. R., Littman, R., & Bricker, W. Assertive behavior in children: A step toward a theory of aggressive behavior. *Monographs of the Society for Research in Child Development,* 1967, **32,** 1–38.

Patterson, G. R., Littman, R., & Hinsey, W. C. Parental effectiveness as reinforcers in the laboratory and its relation to child rearing practices and child adjustment in the classroom. *Journal of Personality,* 1964, **32,** 180–199.

Patterson, G. R., Littman, I., & Brown, T. R. Negative set and social learning. *Journal of Personality and Social Psychology,* 1968, **8,** 109–116.

Paul, G. L. Modifications of systematic desensitization based on case study. Paper presented at the Annual Meeting of the Western Psychological Association, Portland, Oreg., April, 1964.

———— *Insight vs. desensitization in psychotherapy: An experiment in anxiety reduction.* Stanford, Calif.: Stanford University Press, 1966.

———— Insight vs. desensitization in psychotherapy two years after termination. *Journal of Consulting Psychology,* 1967, **31,** 333–348.

———— A two year follow-up of systematic desensitization in therapy groups. *Journal of Abnormal Psychology,* 1968, **73,** 119–130.

Paul, G. L., & Eriksen, C. W. Effects of test anxiety on "real-life" examinations. *Journal of Personality,* 1964, **32,** 480–494.

Paul, G. L., & Shannon, D. T. Treatment of anxiety through systematic desensitization in therapy groups. *Journal of Abnormal Psychology,* 1966, **71,** 124–135.

Pavlov, I. P. Conditioned reflexes: An investigation of the physiological activity of the cerebral cortex (translated by G. V. Anrep). London: Oxford University Press, 1927.

———— *Lectures on conditioned reflexes, Vol. 1* (translated by W. H. Gantt). London: Lawrence and Wishart, 1928.

———— *Conditioned reflexes and psychiatry* (translated by W. H. Gantt). New York: International Publishers, 1941.

———— Autobiography. In I. P. Pavlov, *Selected works: Psychopathology and psychiatry* (translated by S. Belsky). Moscow: Foreign Languages Publishing House, 1955. Pp. 41–46.

———— *Psychopathology and psychiatry. Selected works* (translated by D. A. Myshne & S. Belsky). Moscow: Foreign Languages Publishing House, 1960.

Pearl, A., & Riessman, F. *New careers for the poor; The non-professional in human service.* New York: Free Press, 1965.

Penfield, W. *The cerebral cortex of man,* New York: Macmillan, 1950.

Pepinsky, H. B. Help-giving in search of a criterion. In E. Landy & A. M. Kroll (Eds.), *Guidance in American education.* Vol. III. Cambridge, Mass.: Harvard University Press, 1966. Pp. 197–223.

Perrow, C. Hospitals: Technology, structure, and goals. In J. G. March (Ed.), *Handbook of organizations.* Chicago: Rand McNally, 1965. Pp. 910–971.

Peters, H. N., & Jenkins, R. L. Improvement of chronic schizophrenic patients with guided problem-solving motivated by hunger. *Psychiatric Quarterly Supplement,* 1954, **28,** 84–101.

Peterson, D. R., & London, P. Neobehavioristic psychotherapy: Quasihypnotic suggestion and multiple reinforcement in the treatment of a case of post-infantile dyscopresis. *Psychological Record,* 1964, **14,** 469–474.

——— A role for cognition in the behavioral treatment of a child's eliminative disturbance. In L. P. Ullmann & L. Krasner (Eds.), *Case studies in behavior modification.* New York: Holt, Rinehart and Winston, 1965. Pp. 289–295.

Peterson, R. F. The organization of experimentally generated imitative behaviors in the retardate. Unpublished doctoral dissertation, University of Washington, 1965.

Pines, M. What the talking typewriter says. *New York Times Magazine,* May, 1965, **23,** 74–76, 78–80.

Pipe, P. *Practical programing.* New York: Holt, 1966.

Platonov, K. *The word as a physiological and therapeutic factor: The theory and practice of psychotherapy according to I. P. Pavlov* (translated by D. A. Myshne). Moscow: Foreign Languages Publishing House, 1959.

Popper, K. R. On the sources of knowledge and of ignorance. *Encounter,* 1962, **19,** 42–57.

Porter, D. A critical review of a portion of the literature on teaching devices. *Harvard Educational Review,* 1957, **27,** 126–147.

Portnoy, S., Portnoy, M., & Salzinger, K. Perception as a function of association value with response bias controlled. *Journal of Experimental Psychology,* 1964, **68,** 316–320.

Portnoy, S., & Salzinger, K. The conditionability of different verbal response classes: Positive, negative and nonaffect statements. *Journal of General Psychology,* 1964, **70,** 311–323.

Poser, E. G. Training behavior therapists. *Behaviour Research and Therapy,* 1967, **5,** 37–41.

Poser, E. G., & Ashem, B. Establishing a behaviour therapy teaching unit. *Newsletter of the Association for Advancement of Behavior Therapy,* 1968, **3,** 5–7.

Postman, L. Perception and learning. In S. Koch (Ed.), *Psychology: A study of a science.* Vol. 5. New York: McGraw-Hill, 1963. Pp. 30–113.

Premack, D. Toward empirical behavior laws: I. Positive reinforcement. *Psychological Review,* 1959, **66,** 219–233.

———— Reinforcement theory. In D. Levine (Ed), *Nebraska symposium on motivation: 1965.* Lincoln, Nebr.: University of Nebraska Press, 1965. Pp. 123–180.

Pressey, S. L. Two basic neglected psychoeducational problems. *American Psychologist,* 1965, **20,** 391–395.

Price, J. E. Automated teaching programs with mentally retarded students. *American Journal of Mental Deficiency,* 1963, **68,** 69–72.

Prince, A. I. Relative prestige and the verbal conditioning of children. *American Psychologist,* 1962, **17,** 378 (abstract).

Pyke, S., Agnew, N. M., & Kopperud, J. Modification of an overlearned maladaptive response through a relearning program: A pilot study on smoking. *Behaviour Research and Therapy,* 1966, **4,** 197–203.

Rachman, S. The treatment of anxiety and phobic reactions by systematic desensitization psychotherapy. *Journal of Abnormal and Social Psychology,* 1959, **58,** 259–263.

———— Sexual disorders and behaviour therapy. *American Journal of Psychiatry,* 1961, **118,** 235–240.

———— Introduction to behavior therapy. *Behaviour Research and Therapy,* 1963, **1,** 3–15.

———— Aversion therapy: Chemical or electrical? *Behaviour Research and Therapy,* 1965, **2,** 289–300. (a)

———— Pain-elicited aggression and behaviour therapy. *Psychological Record,* 1965, **15,** 465–467. (b)

———— Studies in desensitization–I: The separate effects of relaxation and desensitization. *Behaviour Research and Therapy,* 1965, **3,** 245–252. (c)

———— Studies in desensitization—II: Flooding. *Behaviour Research and Therapy,* 1966, **4,** 1–6. (a)

———— Studies in desensitization—III: Speed of generalization. *Behaviour Research and Therapy,* 1966, **4,** 7–15. (b)

———— Systematic desensitization. *Psychological Bulletin,* 1967, **67,** 93–103.

Rachman, S., & Eysenck, H. J. Reply to a "critique and reformulation" of behavior therapy. *Psychological Bulletin,* 1966, 65, 165–169.

Rachman, S., Turner, R. K., & Young, G. The effects of conditioning treatment of nocturnal enuresis. Paper presented at the British Psychological Society Annual Conference, Belfast, 1967.

Raimy, V. C. (Ed.) *Training in clinical psychology.* Englewood Cliffs, N.J.: Prentice-Hall, 1950.

Raines, G. N., & Rohrer, J. H. The operational matrix of psychiatric practice: I. Consistency and variability in interview impressions of different psychiatrists. *American Journal of Psychiatry,* 1955, **111,** 721–733.

———— The operational matrix of psychiatric practice: II. Variability in psychiatric impressions and the projection hypothesis. *American Journal of Psychiatry,* 1960, **117,** 133–139.

Ramsay, R. W., Barends, J., Breuker, J., & Kruseman, A. Massed versus spaced desensitization of fear. *Behaviour Research and Therapy*, 1966, **4**, 205–207.

Ratliff, F., Hartline, H. K., & Miller, W. H. Spatial and temporal aspects of retinal inhibitory interaction. *Journal of the Optical Society of America*, 1963, **53**, 110–120.

Ray, R. The training of mothers of atypical children in the use of behavior modification techniques. Unpublished M.S. thesis, University of Oregon, 1965.

Raymond, M. Case of fetishism treated by aversion therapy. *British Medical Journal*, 1956, **2**, 854–857.

——— The treatment of addiction by aversion conditioning with apomorphine. *Behaviour Research and Therapy*, 1964, **1**, 287–291.

Razran, G. The observable unconscious and the inferable conscious in current Soviet psychophysiology: Interoceptive conditioning, semantic conditioning, and the orienting reflex. *Psychological Review*, 1961, **68**, 81–147.

——— Russian physiologists' psychology and American experimental psychology: A historical and a systematic collation and a look into the future. *Psychological Bulletin*, 1965, **63**, 42–64.

Reed, J. L. Comments on the use of methohexitone sodium as a means of inducing relaxation. *Behaviour Research and Therapy*, 1966, **4**, 323.

Reed, J. L., & Cohen, S. I. The treatment of conditioned autonomic disorders by desensitization. Paper presented at the Fourth World Conference of Psychiatry, Madrid, 1966.

Reigne, J. W., & Fry, E. B. A survey and analysis of current teaching-machine programs and programing. *ONR technical report*. No. 31. Washington: Office of Naval Research, 1961.

Reusch, J. Psychosomatic medicine and the behavioral sciences, *Psychosomatic Medicine*, 1961, **23**, 277–285.

Rickard, H. C. Tailored criteria of change in psychotherapy. *Journal of General Psychology*, 1965, **72**, 63–68.

Rickard, H. C., & Brown, E. C. Evaluation of a psychotherapy case in terms of change in a relevant behavior. *Journal of Clinical Psychology*, 1960, **16**, 93.

Rickard, H. C., Dignam, P. J., & Horner, R. F. Verbal manipulation in a psychotherapeutic relationship. *Journal of Clinical Psychology*, 1960, **16**, 364–367.

Rickard, H. C., & Dinoff, M. A follow-up note on "Verbal manipulation in a psychotherapeutic relationship." *Psychological Reports*, 1962, **11**, 506.

Rickard, H. C., & Mundy, M. B. Direct manipulation of stuttering behavior: An experimental-clinical approach. In L. P. Ullmann & L. Krasner (Eds.), *Case studies in behavior modification*. New York: Holt, Rinehart and Winston, 1965. Pp. 268–274.

Riecken, H. W., & Homans, G. C. Psychological aspects of social structure. In G. Lindzey (Ed.), *Handbook of social psychology.* Vol. II. Cambridge, Mass.: Addison-Wesley, 1954. Pp. 786–832.

Riessman, F., Cohen, J., & Pearl, A. *Mental health of the poor: New treatment approaches for low income people,* New York: Free Press, 1964.

Rimland, B. *Infantile autism.* New York: Appleton-Century-Crofts, 1964.

――― Breakthrough in the treatment of mentally ill children. Address presented at the Annual Meeting of the National Society for Autistic Children, New York, 1965.

Ripple, R. E., O'Reilly, R. P., Wightman, L., & Dacey, J. Programed instruction and learner characteristics: A brief review of an ongoing three-year research project and preliminary results from the first year of research. *Child Study Center Bulletin,* 1966, **2,** 19–26.

Risley, T., & Wolf, M. M. Establishing functional speech in echolalic children. *Behaviour Research and Therapy,* 1967, **5,** 73–88.

Rogers, C. R. Implications of recent advances in prediction and control of behavior. *Teachers College Record,* 1956, **57,** 316–322.

――― *On becoming a person.* Boston: Houghton Mifflin, 1961.

Rosen, E., & Gregory, I. *Abnormal psychology.* Philadelphia: Saunders, 1965.

Rosenthal, D. Changes in some moral values following psychotherapy. *Journal of Consulting Psychology,* 1955, **19,** 431–436.

Rosenthal, R. On the social psychology of the psychological experiment: The experimenter's hypothesis as unintended determinant of experimental results. *American Scientist,* 1963, **51,** 268–282.

Rosenthal, R., Kohn, P., Greenfield, P. M., & Carota, N. Data desirability, experimenter expectancy, and the results of psychological research. *Journal of Personality and Social Psychology,* 1966, **3,** 20–27.

Rosenzweig, M. R. Salivary conditioning before Pavlov. *American Journal of Psychology,* 1959, **72,** 628–633.

Ross, L. E., & Hartman, T. F. Human-eyelid conditioning: The recent experimental literature. *Genetic Psychology Monographs,* 1965, **71,** 177–220.

Rothaus, P., & Hanson, P. G. The path of inquiry in mental illness and problem-centered self-description. *Community Mental Health Journal,* 1965, **1,** 29–36.

Rothaus, P., Hanson, P. G., Cleveland, S. E., & Johnson, D. L. Describing psychiatric hospitalization: A dilemma. *American Psychologist,* 1963, **18,** 85–89.

Rothaus, P. Morton, R. B., Johnson, D. L., Cleveland, S. E., & Lyle, F. A. Human relations training for psychiatric patients. *Archives of General Psychiatry,* 1963, **8,** 572–581.

Rothballer, A. The effects of catechol amines on the central nervous system. In *Symposium on catechol amines.* Baltimore: Williams & Wilkins, 1959.

Rotter, J. B. *Social learning and clinical psychology.* Englewood Cliffs, N.J.: Prentice-Hall, 1954.

—— Psychotherapy. *Annual Review of Psychology,* 1960, **11,** 381–414.

Rowley, V. N., & Stone, B. F. Changes in children's verbal behavior as a function of social approval, experimenter differences, and child personality. *Child Development,* 1964, **35,** 669–676.

Rubinstein, E. A., & Parloff, M. B. (Eds.), *Research in psychotherapy.* Vol. I. Washington, D.C.: American Psychological Association, 1959.

Salter, A. *Conditioned reflex therapy.* New York: Farrar, Strauss, 1949. Republished: New York: Capricorn Books, Putnam, 1961, paperback.

Salzinger, K. The experimental approach to the interview. In J. Zubin (Ed.), *Experimental abnormal psychology.* New York: Columbia University Library, 1959 (Mimeo). Pp. 1–48. (a)

—— Experimental manipulation of verbal behavior: A review. *Journal of General Psychology,* 1959, **61,** 65–94. (b)

—— Some problems of response measurement in verbal behavior: The response unit and intraresponse relations. Paper presented at the Conference on Methods of Measurement of Change in Human Behavior, Montreal, Canada, 1962.

—— On the operant conditioning of complex behavior. In J. M. Shlien & H. F. Hunt (Eds.), *Research in Psychotherapy,* Vol. III, American Psychological Association, Washington, D.C., 1968. Pp. 122–129.

—— The problem of response class in verbal behavior. In K. Salzinger & S. Salzinger (Eds.), *Research in verbal behavior and some neurophysiological implications.* New York: Academic Press, 1967. Pp. 35–54.

Salzinger, K., Feldman, R. S., Cowan, J. E., & Salzinger, S. Operant conditioning of verbal behavior of two young speech-deficient boys. In L. Krasner & L. P. Ullmann (Eds.), *Research in behavior modification.* New York: Holt, Rinehart and Winston, 1965. Pp. 82–105.

Salzinger, K., Feldman, R. S., & Portnoy, S. The effects of reinforcement on verbal and nonverbal responses. *Journal of General Psychology,* 1964, **70,** 225–234.

Salzinger, K., & Pisoni, S. Reinforcement of affect responses of schizophrenics during the clinical interview. *Journal of Abnormal and Social Psychology,* 1958, **57,** 84–90.

—— Reinforcement of verbal affect responses of normal subjects during the interview. *Journal of Abnormal and Social Psychology,* 1960, **60,** 127–130.

—— Some parameters of the conditioning of verbal affect responses in schizophrenic subjects. *Journal of Abnormal and Social Psychology,* 1961, **63,** 511–516.

Salzinger, K., & Portnoy, S. Verbal conditioning in interviews: Application to chronic schizophrenics and relationship to prognosis for acute schizophrenics. *Journal of Psychiatric Research,* 1964, **2,** 1–9.

Salzinger, K., Portnoy, S., & Feldman, R. S. Experimental manipulation of continuous speech in schizophrenic patients. *Journal of Abnormal and Social Psychology*, 1964, **68**, 508–516.

Salzinger, K., Portnoy, S., Zlotogura, P., & Keisner, R. The effect of reinforcement on continuous speech and on plural nouns in grammatical context. *Journal of Verbal Learning and Verbal Behavior*, 1963, **1**, 477–485.

Salzinger, K., & Salzinger, S. (Eds.) *Research in verbal behavior and some neurophysiological implications.* New York: Academic Press, 1967.

Salzinger, S., Salzinger, K., Portnoy, S., Eckman, J., Bacon, P. M., Deutsch, M., & Zubin, J. Operant conditioning of continuous speech in young children. *Child Development*, 1962, **33**, 683–695.

Salzman, L. Paranoid state—theory and therapy. *Archives of General Psychiatry*, 1960, **2**, 679–693.

Sanderson, R. Campbell, D., & Laverty S. Traumatically conditioned responses acquire during respiratory paralysis. *Nature*, 1963, **196**, 1235–1236.

———— An investigation of a new aversive conditioning technique for alcoholism. In C. M. Franks (Ed.), *Conditioning techniques in clinical practice and research.* New York: Springer, 1964. Pp. 165–177.

Sandifer, M. G., Jr., Pettus, C., & Quade, D. A study of psychiatric diagnosis. *Journal of Nervous and Mental Disease*, 1964, **139**, 350–356.

Sandler, J. Masochism: An empirical analysis. Psychological Bulletin, 1964, **62**, 197–204.

Sarason, I. G. The human reinforcer in verbal behavior research. In L. Krasner, and L. P. Ullmann (Eds.), *Research in behavior modification.* New York: Holt, Rinehart and Winston, 1965. Pp. 229–243.

Sarbin, T. R., & Hardyck, C. D. Conformance in role perception as a personality variable. *Journal of Consulting Psychology*, 1955, **19**, 109–111.

Sargant, W. *Battle for the mind.* Baltimore, Md.: Penguin Books, 1961.

Saslow, G. On the concept of comprehensive medicine. *Bulletin of the Menninger Clinic*, 1952, **16**, 57–65.

Saslow, G. A case study of attempted behavior manipulation in a psychiatric ward. In L. Krasner & L. P. Ullmann (Eds.), *Research in behavior modification.* New York: Holt, Rinehart and Winston, 1965. Pp. 285–304.

Saslow, G., & Matarazzo, J. D. A psychiatric service in a general hospital: A setting for social learning. *International Journal of Social Psychiatry*, 1962, **8**, 5–18.

Schachter, J. Pain, fear, and anger in hypertensives and normotensives. *Psychosomatic Medicine*, 1957, **19**, 17–28.

Schachter, S., & Singer, J. E. Cognitive, social, and physiological determinants of emotional state. *Psychological Review*, 1962, **69**, 379–399.

Schaefer, H. R., & Emerson, P. E. The development of social attachments in infancy. *Monographs of the Society for Research in Child Development*, 1964, **29**, 1–77 (Whole Number).

Scheff, T. J. *Being mentally ill: A sociological theory.* Chicago: Aldine, 1966.

Schein, E. H., Schneier, I., & Barker, C. H. *Coercive persuasion.* New York: Norton, 1961.

Schmidt, E. A comparative evaluation of verbal conditioning and behavior training in an individual case. *Behaviour Research and Therapy,* 1964, **2,** 19–26.

Schmidt, E., Castell, D., & Brown, P. A retrospective study of 42 cases of behaviour therapy. *Behaviour Research and Therapy,* 1965, **3,** 9–19.

Schmidt, H. O., & Fonda, C. P. The reliability of psychiatric diagnosis: A new look. *Journal of Abnormal and Social Psychology,* 1956, **52,** 262–267.

Schofield, W. *Psychotherapy: The purchase of friendship.* Englewood Cliffs, N.J.: Prentice-Hall, 1964.

Schonbar, R. A. A practitioner's critique of psychotherapy research. Paper presented at the Annual Meeting of the American Psychological Association, Los Angeles, September, 1964.

Schramm, W. *The research on programed instruction: An annotated bibliography.* No. 35. Washington, D.C.: United States Office of Education, 1964.

Schreiber, Y. L. The method of indirect suggestion as used in hysteria. In R. B. Winn (Ed.), *Psychotherapy in the Soviet Union.* New York: Philosophical Library, 1961. Pp. 85–88.

Schubot, E. D. The influence of hypnotic and muscular relaxation in systematic desensitization of phobias. Unpublished doctoral dissertation, Stanford University, 1966.

Schultz, J. H., & Luthe, W. *Autogenic training.* New York: Grune & Stratton, 1959.

Schwartz, A. N., & Hawkins, H. L. Patient models and affect statements in group therapy. *Proceedings of the 73rd Annual Convention of the American Psychological Association.* 1965, 265–266.

Schwartz, D. A. A review of the "paranoid" concept. *Archives of General Psychiatry,* 1963, **8,** 349–361.

Schwartz, N. An experimental study of imitation. The effects of age and reward. Unpublished senior honors thesis, Radcliffe College, 1953.

Schwitzgebel, R. L. Short-term operant conditioning of adolescent offenders on socially relevant variables. *Journal of Abnormal Psychology,* 1967, **72,** 134–142.

Schwitzgebel, R. K., Schwitzgebel, R. L., Pahnke, W. N., & Hurd, W. S. A program on research in behavioral electronics. *Behavioral Science,* 1964, **9,** 223–238.

Scott, W. A. Research definitions of mental health and mental illness. *Psychological Bulletin,* 1958, **55,** 29–45.

Sechenov, I. M. *Reflexes of the brain: An attempt to establish the physiological basis of psychological processes* (trans. by S. Belsky). Cambridge, Mass.: M.I.T., 1965. (a)

———— *Autobiographical notes* (trans. by K. Hanes). Washington, D.C.:

American Institute of Biological Sciences, 1965. (Published in Russian by the Academy of Medical Sciences of the U.S.S.R., 1952). (b)

Sechrest, L., & Strowig, R. W. Teaching machines and the individual learner. *Educational Theory*, 1962, **12**, 157–169.

Secord, P. F., & Backman, C. W. *Social psychology*. New York: McGraw-Hill, 1964.

Seeman, J. Psychotherapy. *Annual Review of Psychology*, 1961, **12**, 157–194.

Shafar, S., & Jaffe, J. R. Systematic desensitization therapy in the treatment of psychoneuroses: Some observations and report of two cases. *Journal of Nervous and Mental Disease*, 1965, **141**, 463–467.

Shaffer, L. F. The problem of psychotherapy. *The American Psychologist*, 1947, **2**, 459–467.

Shallenberger, P., & Zigler, E. Rigidity, negative reaction tendencies and co-satiation effects in normal and feebleminded children. *Journal of Abnormal and Social Psychology*, 1961, **63**, 20–26.

Shannon, D. T., & Wolff, M. E. The effects of modeling in reduction of snake phobia by systematic desensitization. Urbana, Ill.: University of Illinois, 1967.

Shapiro, M. B. The single case in fundamental clinical psychological research. *British Journal of Medical Psychology*, 1961, **34**, 255–262.

Sharpless, S. The effects of intravenous epinephrine and norepinephrine on a conditioned response in the cat. *Psychopharmacologica*, 1963, **4**, 418–423.

Shaw, F. J. Some postulates concerning psychotherapy. *Journal of Consulting Psychology*, 1948, **12**, 426–431.

Sheehan, J. G. Rorschach changes during psychotherapy in relation to personality of the therapist. *American Psychologist*, 1953, **8**, 434 (abstract).

Sherif, M. A study of some social factors in perception. *Archives of Psychology*, 1935, **27**, (187), Whole Number.

Sherman, J. A. Reinstatement of verbal behavior in a psychotic by reinforcement methods. *Journal of Speech and Hearing Disorders*, 1963, **28**, 398–401.

—— Modification of nonverbal behavior through reinforcement of related verbal behavior. *Child Development*, 1964, **35**, 717–723.

—— Use of reinforcement and imitation to reinstate verbal behavior in mute psychotics. *Journal of Abnormal Psychology*, 1965, **70**, 155–164.

Sherrington, C. S. *The integrative action of the nervous system*. New Haven, Conn.: Yale University Press, 1906.

Shlien, J. M. Cross-theoretical criteria for the evaluation of psychotherapy. *American Journal of Psychotherapy*, 1966, **1**, 125–134.

Shoben, E. J. Psychotherapy as a problem in learning theory. *Psychological Bulletin*, 1949, **46**, 366–392.

Sidman, M. *Tactics of scientific research.* New York: Basic Books, 1960.

—— Operant techniques. In A. Bachrach (Ed.), *Experimental foundations of clinical psychology.* New York: Basic Books, 1962. Pp. 170–210.

Silberman, C. E. Technology is knocking at the school house door. *Fortune,* 1966, **74,** 120–125, 198, 203–205.

Silverman, A. J., & Cohen, S. I. Affect and vascular correlates to catechol amines. In L. J. West & M. Greenblatt (Eds.), *Explorations in the Physiology of emotions.* Psychiatric Research Reports. No. 12. Washington, D.C.: American Psychological Association, January, 1960. Pp. 16–30.

Silverman, J. The problem of attention in research and theory in schizophrenia. *Psychological Review,* 1964, **71,** 352–379.

Simkins, L. D. Effects of examiner attitudes and type of reinforcement on the conditioning of hostile verbs. *Journal of Personality,* 1961, **29,** 380–395.

Simkins, L. D. Behavior modification: Research or engineering. Paper presented at the meeting of the Southwestern Psychological Association, Arlington, Tex. 1966.

Singer, R. D. Verbal conditioning and generalization of prodemocratic responses. *Journal of Abnormal and Social Psychology,* 1961, **63,** 43–46.

Skinner, B. F. *The behavior of organisms.* New York: Appleton-Century-Crofts, 1938.

—— The operational analysis of psychological terms. *Psychological Review.* 1945, **52,** 270–278.

—— "Superstition" in the pigeon. *Journal of Experimental Psychology,* 1948, **38,** 168–172. (a)

—— *Verbal behavior.* Cambridge, Mass.: Harvard University Press, 1948. *William James lectures* (b)

—— *Science and human behavior.* New York: Macmillan, 1953.

—— What is psychotic behavior? In *Theory and treatment of the psychoses.* Washington University studies. Committee on publications. St. Louis, Mo.: Washington University, 1956.

—— *Verbal behavior.* New York: Appleton-Century-Crofts, 1957.

—— Teaching machines. *Scientific American,* 1961, **205,** 90–107.

—— *Cumulative record.* New York: Appleton-Century-Crofts, 1966. (a)

—— The phylogeny and ontogeny of behavior. *Science,* 1966, **153,** 1205–1213. (b)

Slack, C. S., & Schwitzgebel, R. *Reducing adolescent crime in your community: A handbook.* Cambridge, Mass.: July 4, 1960.

Slater, L., & Leavy, A. The effects of inhaling a 35 per cent CO_2–65 per cent O_2 mixture upon anxiety level in neurotic patients. *Behaviour Research and Therapy,* 1966, **4,** 309–316.

Smith, W. I., & Moore, J. W. *Programed learning: Theory and research.* Princeton, N.J.: Van Nostrand, 1962.

Snider, J. G., & Oetting, E. R. Autogenic training and the treatment of examination anxiety in students. *Journal of Clinical Psychology*, 1966, **22**, 111–114.

Sokolov, E. Neuronal models and the orienting reflex. In Molly Brazier (Ed.), *Central nervous system and behavior, Transactions of the 3d Conference*. New York: Josiah Macy Foundation, 1960. Pp. 187–276.

Sokolov, Y. N. *Perception and the conditioned reflex*. New York: Macmillan, 1963.

Solomon, P. (Ed.) *Sensory deprivation*. Cambridge, Mass.: Harvard University Press, 1961.

Solomon. R. L. Punishment. *American Psychologist*, 1964, **19**, 239–253.

Solomon., R. L., & Brush, E. S. Experimentally derived conceptions of anxiety and aversion. In M. R. Jones (Ed), *Nebraska symposium on motivation*. Lincoln, Nebr.: University of Nebraska Press, 1956. Pp. 212–305.

Solomon, R. L., & Turner, L. H. Discriminative classical conditioning in dogs paralyzed by curare can later control discriminative avoidance responses in the normal state. *Psychological Review*, 1962, **69**, 202–219.

Solomon, R. L. & Wynne, L. C. Traumatic avoidance learning: The outcome of several extinction procedures with dogs. *Journal of Abnormal and Social Psychology*, 1953, **48**, 291–302.

——— Traumatic avoidance learning: The principles of anxiety conservative and partial irreversability. *Psychological Review*, 1954, **61**, 353–385.

Solyom, L. & Miller, S. A differential conditioning procedure as the initial phase of the behavior therapy of homosexuality. *Behaviour Research and Therapy*, 1965, **3**, 147–160.

Sommer, R., & Osmond, H. Symptoms of institutional care. *Social Problems*, 1961, **8**, 254–263.

Sommer, R., Witney, G. & Osmond, H. Teaching common associations to schizophrenics. *Journal of Abnormal and Social Psychology*, 1962, **65**, 58–61.

Spence, K. W. The relation of learning theory to the technology of education. *Harvard Educational Review*, 1959, **29**, 84–95.

——— Anxiety (drive) level and performance in eyelid conditioning. *Psychological Bulletin*, 1964, **61**, 129–139.

——— Cognitive factors in the extinction of the conditioned eyelid response in humans. *Science*, 1965, **140**, 1224–1225.

Spence, K. W., & Goldstein, H. Eyelid conditioning performance as a function of emotion-producing instructions. *Journal of Experimental Psychology*, 1961, **62**, 291–294.

Spence, K. W., and Taylor, J. A. Anxiety and strength of the UCS as determiners of the amount of eyelid conditioning. *Journal of Experimental Psychology*, 1951, **42**, 183–188.

Spiegel, H. Is symptom removal dangerous? *American Journal of Psychiatry,* 1967, **10,** 1279–1282.

Spiegel, H., & Shainess, N. Operational spectrum of psychotherapeutic process. *Archives of General Psychiatry,* 1963, **9,** 477–488.

Spielberger, C. D. The role of awareness in verbal conditioning. In C. W. Eriksen (Ed.), *Behavior and awareness.* Durham, N.C.: Duke University Press, 1962. Pp. 73–201.

———— Theoretical and epistemological issues in verbal conditioning. In S. Rosenberg (Ed.), *Directions in psycholinguistics.* New York: Macmillan, 1965. Pp. 149–200.

———— (Ed.) *Anxiety and behavior.* New York: Academic Press, 1966. (a)

———— Theory and research on anxiety. In C. D. Spielberger, (Ed.), *Anxiety and behavior.* New York: Academic Press, 1966. Pp. 3–20. (b)

Spielberger, C. D., & DeNike, L. D. Descriptive behaviorism versus cognitive theory in verbal operant conditioning. *Psychological Review,* 1966, **73,** 306–326.

Spielberger, C. D., & Katzenmeyer, W. G. Manifest anxiety, intelligence, and college grades. *Journal of Consulting Psychology,* 1959, **23,** 278.

Staats, A. W. (Ed.) *Human learning.* New York: Holt, Rinehart and Winston, 1964.

———— Emotions and images in language: A learning analysis of their acquisition and function. In K. Salzinger & S. Salzinger (Eds.), *Research in verbal behavior and some neurophysiological implications.* New York: Academic Press, 1967. Pp. 123–145.

Staats, A. W., & Staats, C. K. *Complex human behavior: A systematic extension of learning principles.* New York: Holt, Rinehart and Winston, 1963.

Stafford, K. R., & Combs, C. F. Radical reductionism: A possible source of inadequacy in auto-instructional techniques. *American Psychologist,* 1967, **22,** 667–669.

Stampfl, T. G. Implosive therapy: A learning theory derived from psychodynamic therapeutic technique. Paper presented at the University of Illinois, Urbana, Ill., 1961.

———— Implosive therapy: The theory, the subhuman analogue, the strategy, and the technique. Part I: The theory. In S. G. Armitage (Ed.), *Behavior modification techniques in the treatment of emotional disorders.* Battle Creek, Mich. VA Publication, 1967. Pp. 22–37.

Starr, R., & Patterson, G. R. Use of criticism and praise in operant conditioning of a simple motor response. Unpublished mimeographed paper, National Science Foundation undergraduate report, 1961.

Steffy, R. A., Hart, J., Craw, M., Torney, D., Marlett, N., & Fenz, W. D. A report of a token-economy project directed toward the behavior modification of deviant meal and bedtime behaviors with a ward of severely regressed psychotic patients. Personal communication, 1966.

Stephens, J. H. Treatment outcome in "process" and "nonprocess" schizophrenics treated by "A" and "B" types of therapists. *Journal of Nervous and Mental Diseases*, 1965,**140**, 449–456.

Sternbach, R. A. The effects of instructional sets on autonomic responsivity. *Psychophysiology*, 1964, **1**, 67–72.

—— *Principles of psychophysiology.* New York: Academic Press, 1966.

Stevenson, H. W. Social reinforcement with children as a function of CA, sex of E, and sex of S. *Journal of Abnormal and Social Psychology*, 1961, **63**, 147–154.

—— Social reinforcement of children's behavior. In L. P. Lipsitt & C. C. Spiker (Eds.), *Advances in child development and behavior.* Vol. II. New York: Academic Press, 1965. Pp. 98–125.

Stevenson, H. W., & Knights, R. M. Social reinforcement with normal and retarded children as a function of pretraining, sex of E, and sex of S. *American Journal of Mental Deficiency*, 1962, **66**, 866–871.

Stevenson, I. Direct instigation of behavioral changes in psychotherapy. *Archives of General Psychiatry*, 1959, **1**, 99–107.

Stewart, M. A. Psychotherapy by reciprocal inhibition. *American Journal of Psychiatry*, 1961, **118**, 175–177.

Stollak, G. E. Conditioning and transfer effects of verbally reinforcing choices of personality statements. *Psychological Reports*, 1966, **19**, 427–437.

Stollak, G. E., Guerney, B. G., & Rothberg, M. (Eds.) *Psychotherapy research.* Chicago: Rand McNally, 1966.

Stoller, R. J., & Geertsma, R. H. The consistency of psychiatrists' clinical judgments. *Journal of Nervous and Mental Disease*, 1963, **137**, 58–66.

Stone, A. R., Frank, J. D., Nash, E. H., & Imber, S. D. An intensive five-year follow-up study of treated psychiatric outpatients. *Journal of Nervous and Mental Disease*, 1961, **133**, 410–422.

Straughan, J. H. Treatment with child and mother in the playroom. *Behaviour Research and Therapy*, 1964, **2**, 37–41.

—— Conditioning technique with elective mutism and autism. Paper presented at the annual convention of the Society for Research in Child Development, Minneapolis, Minn., 1965.

Strupp, H. H. *Psychotherapists in action.* New York: Grune & Stratton, 1960.

—— Some comments on the future of research in psychotherapy. *Behavioral Science*, 1960, **5**, 60–71.

—— Psychotherapy. *Annual Review of Psychology*, 1962, **13**, 445–478. (a)

—— Patient-doctor relationships: The psychotherapist in the therapeutic process. In A. J. Bachrach (Ed.), *Experimental foundations of clinical psychology.* New York: Basic Books, 1962. Pp. 576–615. (b)

—— What is psychotherapy? *Contemporary Psychology*, 1967, **12**, 41–42.

Strupp, H. H., & Luborsky, L. (Eds.) *Research in psychotherapy.* Vol. II. Washington, D.C.: American Psychological Association, 1962.

Stuart, R. B. Behavioral control of overeating. *Behaviour Research and Therapy,* 1967, **5**, 357–365.

Stuckless, E. R., & Birch, J. W. Programed instruction in written language for the deaf. *Exceptional Children,* 1964, **30**, 296–303.

Sturm, I. E. The behavioristic aspect of psychodrama. *Group Psychotherapy,* 1965, **18**, 50–64.

Sulzer, E. S. Reinforcement and the therapeutic contract. *Journal of Counseling Psychology* 1962, **9**, 271–276.

―――― Behavior modification in adult psychiatric patients. In L. P. Ullmann & L. Krasner (Eds.), *Case studies in behavior modification.* New York: Holt, Rinehart and Winston, 1965. Pp. 196–200. (a)

―――― Individual freedom, law, and social welfare. Paper presented at the 92nd Annual Forum of the National Conference on Social Welfare, Atlantic City, N.J., May, 1965. (b)

Sutherland, E. H. (Ed.) *The professional thief, by a professional thief.* Chicago: University of Chicago Press, 1937.

Sylvester, J. D., & Liversedge, L. A. Conditioning and the occupational cramps. In H. J. Eysenck (Ed.), *Behaviour therapy and the neuroses.* London: Pergamon Press, 1960. Pp. 334–348.

Szasz, T. S. The myth of mental illness. *American Psychologist,* 1960, **15**, 113–118.

―――― *The myth of mental illness:* Foundations of a theory of personal conduct. New York: Hueber-Harper, 1961.

―――― *Law, liberty, and psychiatry.* New York: Macmillan, 1963.

―――― *Psychiatric justice.* New York: Macmillan, 1965. (a)

―――― *The ethics of psychoanalysis: The theory and method of autonomous psychotherapy.* New York: Basic Books, 1965. (b)

Taber, J. I., Glaser, R., & Schafer, H. H. *Learning and programed instruction.* Reading, Mass.: Addison-Wesley, 1965.

Taffel, C. Anxiety and the conditioning of verbal behavior. *Journal of Abnormal and Social Psychology,* 1955, **51**, 496–501.

Tagiuri, R. Relational analysis: An extension of sociometric methods with emphasis upon social perception. *Sociometry,* 1952, **15**, 91–104.

Tallent, N. Clinical psychological testing: A review of premises, practices, and promises. *Journal of Projective Techniques and Personality Assessment,* 1965, **29**, 418–435.

Taylor, J. G. A behavioural intepretation of obsessive-compulsive neurosis. *Behaviour Research and Therapy,* 1963, **1**, 237–244.

Taylor, M. L., & Sands, E. Application of programmed instruction to the language training of severely impaired aphasic patients. *Journal of the National Society of Programed Instruction,* 1966, **5**, 10–11.

Teplov, B. M. Typological properties of the nervous system and their psychological manifestations. In Neil O'Connor (Ed.), *Recent Soviet psychology.* London: Pergamon Press, 1961. Pp. 21–51.

Teplov, B. M., & Nebylitzyn, V. D. The study of the basic properties of the nervous system and their significance for the psychology of individual differences. *Soviet Psychology and Psychiatry*, 1966, **4,** 80–85. (Translated from *Voprosy Psikhologii*, 1963, **9,** 38–46.)

Terrace, H. S. Discrimination learning with and without "errors." *Journal of the Experimental Analysis of Behavior*, 1963, **6,** 1–27. (a)

—— Errorless transfer of a discrimination across two continua. *Journal of the Experimental Analysis of Behavior*, 1963, **6,** 223–232. (b)

—— Stimulus control. In W. K. Honig (Ed.), *Operant behavior: Areas of research and application.* New York: Appleton-Century-Crofts, 1966. Pp. 271–346.

Thorndike, E. *The fundamentals of learning,* New York: Columbia University, Teachers College, 1944.

Thorne, F. C. Rules of evidence in the evaluation of the effects of psychotherapy. *Journal of Clinical Psychology*, 1952, **8,** 38–41.

Tinbergen, N. *The study of instincts,* London: Oxford University Press, 1951.

Toch, H. *The social psychology of social movements.* Indianapolis: Bobbs-Merrill, 1965.

Tolman, E. C. *Drives toward war.* New York: Appleton-Century-Crofts, 1942.

Tolman, E. C., & Honzik, C. H. Introduction and removal of reward, and maze performance in rats. *University of California Publications in Psychology*, 1930, **4,** 257–275.

Tooley, J. T. The state of human behavior. Address presented at the Kansas State Nurses' Association Annual Convention, Wichita, Oct. 13, 1966.

Trowill, J. A. Instrumental conditioning of the heart rate in the curarized rat. *Journal of Comparative and Physiological Psychology*, 1967, **63,** 7–11.

Truax, C. B. Behavior therapy and psychotherapy: Toward a constructive encounter. Paper presented at the Annual Meeting of the Midwestern Psychological Association, Chicago, 1965.

—— Reinforcement and non-reinforcement in Rogerian psychotherapy. *Journal of Abnormal Psychology*, 1966, **71,** 1–9.

Truax, C. B. & Carkhuff, R. R. Significant developments in psychotherapy research. In L. E. Abt & B. F. Riess (Eds.), *Progress in clinical psychology.* Vol. VI. New York: Grune & Stratton, 1964. Pp. 124–155.

Truax, C. B., Wargo, D. G., Carkhuff, R. R., Kodman, F., Jr., & Moles, E. A. Changes in self-concepts during group psychotherapy as a function of alternate sessions and vicarious therapy pretraining in institutionalized mental patients and juvenile delinquents. *Journal of Consulting Psychology*, 1966, **30,** 309–314.

True, J. E. Learning of abstract responses by process and reactive schizophrenic patients. *Psychological Reports*, 1966, **18**, 51–55.

Turner, L. H., & Solomon, R. L. Human traumatic avoidance learning: Theory and experiments on the operant-respondent distinction and failures to learn. *Psychological Monographs*, 1962, **76**, (Whole No. 559).

Turner, R. K., & Young, G. C. CNS stimulant drugs and conditioning treatment of nocturnal enuresis: A long term follow-up study. *Behaviour Research and Therapy*, 1966, **4**, 225–228.

Ullman, A. D. The experimental production and analysis of a compulsive eating syndrome. *Journal of Comparative and Physiological Psychology*, 1951, **44**, 575–581.

Ullmann, L. P. *Institution and outcome: A comparative study of psychiatric hospitals.* New York: Pergamon Press, 1967.

Ullmann, L. P., Forsman, R. G., Kenny, J. W., McInnis, T. L., Jr., Unikel, I. P., & Zeisset, R. M. Selective reinforcement of schizophrenics' interview responses. *Behaviour Research and Therapy*, 1965, **2**, 205–212.

Ullmann, L. P., & Krasner, L. (Eds.), *Case studies in behavior modification.* New York: Holt, Rinehart and Winston, 1965.

——— *A psychological approach to abnormal behavior.* Englewood Cliffs, N.J.: Prentice-Hall, 1969.

Ullmann, L. P., Krasner, L., & Collins, B. J. Modification of behavior through verbal conditioning.: Effects in group therapy. *Journal of Abnormal and Social Psychology*, 1961, **62**, 128–132.

Ullmann, L. P., Krasner, L., & Edinger, R. L. Verbal conditioning of common associations in long-term schizophrenic patients. *Behaviour Research and Therapy*, 1964, **2**, 15–18.

Ullmann, L. P., Krasner, L., & Ekman, P. Verbal conditioning of emotional word: Effects on behavior in group therapy. *Research Reports of VA Palo Alto*, No. 15, 1961.

Ullmann, L. P., Krasner, L., & Gelfand, D. M. Changed content within a reinforced response class. *Psychological Reports*, 1963, **12**, 819–829.

Ullmann, L. P., Krasner, L., & Sherman, M. The verbal conditioning of pleasant and unpleasant emotional words: Further investigation of an effect of social reinforcement. Progress report. National Institute of Mental Health, Grant M-6191. September, 1963.

Ullmann, L. P., Weiss, R. L. & Krasner, L. The effect of verbal conditioning of emotional words on recognition of threatening stimuli. *Journal of Clinical Psychology*, 1963, **19**, 182–183.

Ulrich, R. Behavior control and public concern. *Psychological Record*, 1967, **17**, 229–234.

Ulrich, R., Hutchinson, R., & Azrin, N. Pain-elicited aggression. *Psychological Record*, 1965, **15**, 511–520.

Ulrich, R., & Kent, N. D. New tactics for the education of psychologists. Paper presented at the Annual Meeting of the American Psychological Association, New York, September, 1966.

Ulrich, R., Stachnik, T., & Mabry, J. (Eds.), *Control of human behavior*. Chicago: Scott, Foresman, 1966.

Underwood, B. J. *Psychological research*. New York: Appleton-Century-Crofts, 1957.

Urban, H., & Ford, D. Man: A robot or pilot. Paper presented at the Annual Meeting of the American Psychological Association, New York, September, 1961.

Van Proosdij, C. *Smoking: Its influence on the individual and its role in social medicine*. New York: Elsevier, 1960.

Verhave, T. (Ed.) *The experimental analysis of behavior*. New York: Appleton-Century-Crofts, 1966.

Verplanck, W. S. The control of the content of conversation: reinforcement of statements of opinion. *Journal of Abnormal aand Social Psychology*, 1955, **51,** 668–676.

Voegtlin, W., & Lemere, F. The treatment of alcohol addiction. *Quarterly Journal of Studies on Alcohol*, 1942, **2,** 717–803.

Voronin, L. G., Leontiev, A. N., Luria, A. R., Sokolov, E. N. & Vinogradova, O. S. *Orienting reflex and exploratory behavior* (translated by V. Shmelev and K. Hanes). Washington, D.C.: American Institute of Biological Sciences, 1965.

Wahler, R. G., Winkel, G. H., Peterson, R. F., & Morrison, D. C. Mothers as behavior therapists for their own children. *Behaviour Research and Therapy*, 1965, **3,** 113–124.

Wallerstein, R. S. The current state of psychotherapy: Theory, practice, research. *Journal of the American Psychoanalytic Association*, 1966, **14,** 183–225.

Walters, R. H., & Ray, E. Anxiety, social isolation, and reinforcer effectiveness. *Journal of Personality*, 1960, **28,** 358–367.

Walton, D. The relevance of learning theory to the treatment of an obsessive-compulsive state. In H. J. Eysenck (Ed.), *Behaviour therapy and the Neuroses*. New York: Pergamon Press, 1960. Pp. 153–166. (a)

——— Strengthening of incompatible reactions and the treatment of a phobic state in a schizophrenic patient. In H. J. Eysenck (Ed.), *Behaviour therapy and the neuroses*. London: Pergamon Press, 1960. Pp. 170–180. (b)

——— The application of learning theory to the treatment of a case of neurodermatitis In H. J. Eysenck (Ed.), *Behaviour therapy and the neuroses*. London: Pergamon Press, 1960. Pp. 272–277. (c)

Walton, D., & Black, D. A. The application of learning theory to the treatment of stammering. *Journal of Psychosomatic Research*, 1958, **3,** 170–179.

—— The application of modern learning theory to the treatment of chronic hysterical aphonia. *Journal of Psychosomatic Research*, 1959, **3**, 303–311.

Walton, D., & Mather, M. D. The relevance of generalization techniques to the treatment of stammering and phobic symptoms. *Behaviour Research and Therapy*, 1963, **1**, 121–125.

—— The application of learning principles to the treatment of obsessive-compulsive states in the acute and chronic phases of illness. In H. J. Eysenck (Ed.), *Experiments in behaviour therapy*. London: Pergamon Press, 1964. Pp. 117–151.

Ward, C. H., Beck, A. T., Mendelson, M., Mock, J. E., & Erbaugh, J. K. The psychiatric nomenclature, reasons for diagnostic disagreement. *Archives of General Psychiatry*, 1962, **7**, 198–205.

Watkins, J. G. Psychotherapeutic methods. In B. B. Wolman (Ed.), *Handbook of clinical psychology*. New York: McGraw-Hill, 1965. Pp. 1143–1167.

Watson, J. B., & Rayner, R. Conditioned emotional reactions. *Journal of Experimental Psychology*, 1920, **3**, 1–14.

Watson, R. I. Research design and methodology in evaluating the results of psychotherapy. *Journal of Clinical Psychology*, 1952, **8**, 29–33.

—— The great psychologists: From Aristotle to Freud. Philadelphia: Lippincott, 1963.

Webster's Seventh New Collegiate Dictionary. Springfield, Mass.: Merriam, 1963.

Wegrocki, H. J. A critique of cultural and statistical concepts of abnormality. *Journal of Abnormal and Social Psychology*, 1939, **34**, 166–178.

Weil-Mahlerbe, H. The passage of catechol amines through the blood brain barrier. In G. E. W. Wolstenholme & C. M. O'Connor (Eds.), *Adrenergic mechanisms*. Ciba Foundation Symposium. Boston: Little, Brown, 1960. Pp. 107–149.

Weinberg, A. Can technology replace social engineering? *Scientific Research*, 1966, **1**, 32–34.

Weinburg, N. H., & Zaslove, M. "Resistance" to systematic desensitization of phobias. *Journal of Clinical Psychology*, 1963, **19**, 179–181.

Weiner, H. Some effects of response cost upon human operant behavior. *Journal of the Experimental Analysis of Behavior*, 1962, **5**, 201–208.

Weinreb, S. L. The effects of inhaling aromatic spirit of ammonia upon anxiety level in neurotic patients. Unpublished manuscript, Temple University Medical School, 1966.

Weiss, R. L. Studies in emitted reinforcing behavior. Paper presented at the meeting of the Western Psychological Association, Honolulu, Hawaii, 1965.

—— Some determinants of emitted reinforcing behavior: Listener reinforcement and birth order. *Journal of Personality and Social Psychology*, 1966, **3**, 489–492.

Weiss, R. L., Krasner, L., & Ullmann, L. P. Responsivity to verbal conditioning as a function of emotional atmosphere and pattern of reinforcement. *Psychological Reports,* 1960, **6,** 415–426.

———— Responsivity of psychiatric patients to verbal conditioning: "Success" and "failure" conditions and pattern of reinforced trials. *Psychological Reports,* 1963, **12,** 423–426.

Weiss, R. L., Ullmann, L. P. & Krasner, L. On the relationship between hypnotizability and response to verbal operant conditioning. *Psychological Reports,* 1960, **6,** 59–60.

Weitzman, B. Behavior therapy and psychotherapy. *Psychological Review,* 1967, **74,** 300–317.

Wells, H. K. *Pavlov and Freud. I. Ivan P. Pavlov. Toward a scientific psychology and psychiatry.* London: Lawrence and Wishart, 1956.

Werner, H. *Comparative psychology of mental development.* (Rev. ed.) Chicago: Follett, 1948.

Wertham, F. *The show of violence.* Garden City, N.Y.: Doubleday, 1949.

———— *Sign of Cain.* New York: Macmillan, 1966.

Wesley, F. Was Raehlmann the first behaviorist? *Journal of the History of the Behavioral Sciences,* 1968, **4,** 161–162.

Wetzel, R. Use of behavioral techniques in a case of compulsive stealing. *Journal of Consulting Psychology,* 1966, **30,** 367–374.

White R. W. *The abnormal personality.* New York: Ronald Press, 1956.

Whitehorn, J. C. Goals of psychotherapy. In E. A. Rubinstein and M. B. Parloff (Eds.), *Research in psychotherapy.* Vol. I. Washington, D.C.: American Psychological Association, 1959. Pp. 1–9.

Whittaker, V. P. The binding of neurohormones by subcellular particles of brain tissue. In S. Kety & J. Elkes (Eds.), *Regional neurochemistry,* London: Pergamon Press, 1961. Pp. 259–263.

Wholwill, J. F. The teaching machine: Psychology's new hobby-horse. *Teachers College Record,* 1962, **64,** 139–146.

Whorf, B. L. *Language, thought and reality.* Cambridge, Mass.: Technology Press, 1956.

Wickens, D., Allen, C., & Hill, F. Effect of instructions and UCS strength on extinction of the conditioned GSR. *Journal of Experimental Psychology,* 1963, **66,** 235–240.

Wiest, W. M. Some recent criticisms of behaviorism and learning theory with special reference to Breger and McGaugh and to Chomsky. *Psychological Bulletin,* 1967, **67,** 214–225.

Wike, E. L. (Ed.) *Secondary reinforcement.* New York: Harper & Row, 1966.

Wilder, S. N. The effect of verbal reinforcement and verbal modeling on the frequency of emission of self referred affect statements. Unpublished doctoral dissertation, Columbia University, Teachers College, 1967.

Williams, C. D. The elimination of tantrum behaviors by extinction procedures. *Journal of Abnormal and Social Psychology,* 1959, **59,** 269.

Williams, J. H. Conditioning of verbalization: A review. *Psychological Bulletin,* 1964, **62,** 383–393.

Willoughby, R. R. Norms for the Clark-Thurstone Inventory. *Journal of Social Psychology,* 1934, **5,** 91–97.

Wilson, F. S., & Walters, R. H. Modification of speech output of near mute schizophrenics through social learning procedures. *Behaviour Research and Therapy,* 1966, **4,** 59–67.

Wilson, G. T. & Evans, W. I. M. Behavior therapy and not the behavior "therapies." *Newsletter of the Association for Advancement of Behavior Therapy,* 1967, **2,** 5–7.

Wilson, W. C., & Verplanck, W. S. Some observations on the reinforcement of verbal operants. *American Journal of Psychology,* 1956, **69,** 448–451.

Wimsatt, W. R., & Vestre, N. D. Extraexperimental effects in verbal conditioning. *Journal of Consulting Psychology,* 1963, **27,** 400–404.

Winder, C. L. Psychotherapy. *Annual Review of Psychology,* 1957, **8,** 309–330.

Windle, C. Psychological tests in psychopathological prognosis. *Psychological Bulletin,* 1952, **49,** 451–482.

Winn, R. B. (Ed.) *Psychotherapy in the Soviet Union.* New York Philosophical Library, 1961.

Wirt, R. D., & Wirt, A. L. Psychotherapeutic processes. *Annual Review of Psychology,* 1963, **14,** 365–390.

Wittenborn, J., Holzberg, J., & Simon, B. Symptom correlates for descriptive diagnosis. *Genetic Psychology Monographs,* 1953, **47,** 237–301.

Wolberg, L. R. *The technique of psychotherapy.* New York: Grune & Stratton, 1954.

Wolf, M. M., Birnbrauer, J. S., Williams, T., & Lawler, J. A note on apparent extinction of the vomiting behavior of a retarded child. In L. P. Ullmann & L. Krasner (Eds.), *Case studies in behavior modification.* New York: Holt, Rinehart and Winston, 1965. Pp. 364–366.

Wolf, M. M., Giles, D. K., & Hall, V. R. Experiments with token reinforcement in a remedial classroom. *Behaviour Research and Therapy,* 1968, **6,** 55–64.

Wolf, M. M., Risley, T., Johnston, M., Harris, F., & Allen, E. Application of operant conditioning procedures to the behavior problems of an autistic child: A follow-up and extension. Paper presented at the meeting of the Western Psychological Association, Portland, Oreg., 1964.

—— Application of operant conditioning procedures to the behavior problems of an autistic child: A follow-up and extension. *Behaviour Research and Therapy,* 1967, **5,** 103–111.

Wolf, M. M., Mees, H., & Risley, T. Application of operant conditioning procedures to the behaviour problems of an autistic child. *Behaviour Research and Therapy,* 1964, **1,** 305–312.

Wolpe, J. Experimental neurosis as learned behaviour. *British Journal of Psychology*, 1952, **43**, 243–268. (a)

———— Objective psychotherapy of the neuroses. *South African Medical Journal*, 1952, **26**, 825–829. (b)

———— Reciprocal inhibition as the main basis of psychotherapeutic effects. *Archives of Neurology and Psychiatry*, 1954, **72**, 205–226.

———— *Psychotherapy by reciprocal inhibition.* Stanford, Calif.: Stanford University Press, 1958.

———— Psychotherapy based on the principle of reciprocal inhibition. In A. Burton (Ed.), *Case studies of counseling and psychotherapy.* Englewood Cliffs, N.J.: Prentice-Hall, 1959. Pp. 353–381.

———— The systematic desensitization treatment of neuroses. *Journal of Nervous and Mental Disease*, 1961, **132**, 189–203.

———— Isolation of a conditioning procedure as the crucial therapeutic factor: A case study. *Journal of Nervous and Mental Disease*, 1962, **134**, 316–329.

———— Psychotherapy: The nonscientific heritage and the new science. *Behaviour Research and Therapy*, 1963, **1**, 23–28.

———— Behaviour therapy in complex neurotic states. *British Journal of Psychiatry*, 1964, **110**, 28–34. (a)

———— The comparative clinical status of conditioning therapies and psychoanalysis. In J. Wolpe, A. Salter, & L. J. Reyna (Eds.), *The conditioning therapies.* New York: Holt, Rinehart and Winston, 1964. Pp. 5–20. (b)

———— Moral issues in psychotherapeutic practice and training: A behavioristic view. Paper presented at the First International Congress on Social Psychiatry, London, August, 1964. (c)

———— Conditioned inhibition of craving in drug addiction: A pilot experiment. *Behaviour Research and Therapy*, 1965, **2**, 285–288.

———— Presidential message. *Newsletter of the Association for Advancement of Behavior Therapy*, 1968, **3**, 1–2.

Wolpe, J., & Lang, P. J. A fear survey schedule for use in behavior therapy, *Behaviour Research and Therapy*, 1964, **2**, 27–30.

Wolpe, J., & Lazarus, A. A. *Behavior therapy techniques: A guide to the treatment of neuroses.* London: Pergamon Press, 1966.

Wolpe, J., Salter, A., & Reyna, L. J. (Eds.) *The conditioning therapies.* New York: Holt, Rinehart and Winston, 1964.

Wolpin, M., & Pearsall, L. Rapid deconditioning of a fear of snakes. *Behaviour Research and Therapy*, 1965, **3**, 107–111.

Wolpin, M., & Raines, J. Visual imagery, expected roles and extinction as possible factors in reducing fear and avoidance behavior. *Behaviour Research and Therapy*, 1966, **4**, 25–37.

Wortis, J. Pavlovianism and clinical psychiatry. In J. Wortis (Ed.), *Recent advances in biological psychiatry.* Vol. IV. New York: Plenum Press, 1962. Pp. 13–23.

Wurtman, R. J., Frank, M. M., Morse, W. H., & Dews, P. B. Studies on behavior. V. Actions of I-epinephrine and related compounds. *Journal of Pharmacology*, 1959, **127**, 281–287.

Yadoff, B. An attempt to change word meaning and a personality test score through semantic generalization. Unpublished doctoral dissertation, University of Pittsburgh, 1958.

Yates, A. J. The application of learning theory to the treatment of tics. *Journal of Abnormal and Social Psychology*, 1958, **56**, 175–182. (a)

—— Symptoms and symptom substitution. *Psychological Review*, 1958, **65**, 371–374. (b)

Yealland, L. R. *Hysterical disorders of warfare*. London: Macmillan, 1918.

Zax, M., & Klein, A. Measurement of personality and behavior changes following psychotherapy. *Psychological Bulletin*, 1960, **57**, 435–448.

Zeisset, R. M. Desensitization and relaxation in the modification of psychiatric patients' interview behavior. *Journal of Abnormal Psychology*, 1968, **73**, 18–24.

Zigler, E., & Phillips, L. Psychiatric diagnosis: A critique. *Journal of Abnormal and Social Psychology*, 1961, **63**, 607–618.

Zilboorg, G., & Henry, G. W. *A history of medical psychology*. New York: Norton, 1941.

Zimmerman, E. H., & Zimmerman, J. The alteration of behavior in a special classroom situation. *Journal of the Experimental Analysis of Behavior*, 1962, **5**, 59–60.

Zimmerman, J., & Grosz, H. J. "Visual" performance of a functionally blind person. *Behaviour Research and Therapy*, 1966, **4**, 119–134.

Zubin, J. Evaluation of therapeutic outcome in mental disorders. *Journal of Nervous and Mental Disease*, 1953, **117**, 95–111.

—— Technical issues: Discussion. In P. H. Hoch & J. Zubin (Eds.), *The evaluation of psychiatric treatment*. New York: Grune & Stratton, 1964. Pp. 122–128.

Name Index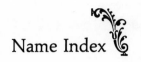

Name Index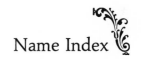

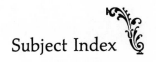

Subject Index

Subject Index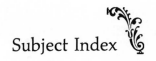

This book was set in Palatino by Monotype Composition Company, Inc., and printed on permanent paper and bound by The Maple Press Company. The designer was J. E. O'Connor; the drawings were done by J. & R. Technical Services, Inc. The editors were Walter Maytham and David Dunham. Stuart Levine supervised the production.